WORLD CHAMPIONS

The Story of South African Rugby

by

Jonty Winch

Published by BestRed, an imprint of HSRC Press
Private Bag X9182, Cape Town, 8000, South Africa
www.bestred.co.za

First published 2022

ISBN (soft cover) 978-1-928246-43-5

Copy-edited by Louis Botes
Proofread by Alison Lockhart
Typeset by Firelight Studio
Cover design by Firelight Studio
Top image: Several unsuccessful attempts were made to arrange an international tour before the British
arrived in 1891. This rugby scene is from the third 'Test' played that year at Newlands. Photo from SA
Rugby Football Board (now SA Rugby Union).
Left: The earliest recorded football match to have been staged in South Africa was played between
'colonial-born' and 'home-born' on 23 May 1862 in Port Elizabeth. Photo from Cape Archives.
Right: William Webb Ellis statue. Photo by Jonty Winch.
Center: South Africa's Siya Kolisi lifts the Webb Ellis cup after South After win the 2019 Rugby World
Cup FInal match at Yokohama Stadium. Photo by David Davies, supplied by Alamy.

Printed by Print on Demand (Pty) Ltd

Distributed in Africa by Blue Weaver
Tel: +27 (021) 701 4477; Fax Local: (021) 701 7302
www.blueweaver.co.za

Distributed in Europe and the United Kingdom by Eurospan Distribution Services (EDS)
Tel: +44 (0) 17 6760 4972; Fax: +44 (0) 17 6760 1640
www.eurospanbookstore.com

Distributed in The US and its possessions, Canada, and Asia with the exception of China
Tel: +1 303 444 6684 | Fax: +001 303 444 0824 | Email: questions@rienner.com

Suggested citation: Winch J (2022) *World Champions: The story of South African rugby*. Cape Town:
BestRed

To

Rob Jarvis
A product of Manicaland where Bubbles Koch, Salty du Rand and Ryk van
Schoor were once farmers and rugby heroes, Rob became a rugby legend in
Kadoma where former Springbok captain Piet Greyling had once led the local
Jameson High School under 14 team.

and

Mark Venner
In a distinguished rugby career, Mark represented Pearson High School First XV;
Port Elizabeth Schools, Weston Super Mare 175 times; Somerset as captain in a
county final; Richmond; Henley in 154 games; the Barbarians on five occasions
and England Legends.

Comments on *World Champions: The story of South African rugby*

Jonty Winch has written the definitive book on the history of rugby in South Africa. From the very first match to the World Cup triumph in Tokyo, Winch explores the story of the game using deep research and passionate narrative. He uncovers the lost history of black and coloured rugby, reassesses the controversies of the past, and examines why rugby is so important to South Africans of all backgrounds. For anyone interested in rugby and its place in South African life, this is essential reading.

Tony Collins
Emeritus Professor of History, De Montfort University
Research Fellow at the Institute of Sports Humanities
Author of *A Social History of English Rugby Union* **and** *The Oval World: A Global History of Rugby*

South Africa has developed a reputation as a sports-mad country, but till recently historians have lagged behind in coming to academic grips with its multi-faceted sporting past. Increasingly, however, books and articles have appeared which looked beyond the scoreboard and sought to unravel the often complicated linkages between sport and society.

In this book Jonty Winch has admirably demonstrated his mastery of the relevant literature to provide a wide-ranging, balanced, informed and eminently readable overview of South African rugby. In taking a long view of the game, Winch succeeds in providing new perspectives of apartheid as well as anti-apartheid politics and sport.

Albert Grundlingh
Emeritus Professor, Department of History, Stellenbosch University
His publications include *Potent Pastimes: Sport and Leisure in Modern Afrikaner History* **and (co-authored)** *Beyond the Tryline: Rugby and South African Society*

Jonty Winch has already made an enormous contribution to South African sports history and this definitive volume will only enhance his reputation as a meticulous scholar and a masterly story-teller. His awareness of the wider social and political context adds depth and significance to his account of what has happened on and off the field of play. We are left in no doubt that, for South Africans, rugby has always been much more than a game.

Dilwyn Porter
Emeritus Professor of Sports History and Culture
International Centre of Sports History and Culture, De Montfort University

Jonty Winch is a historian who does not get tired. Having just finished four co-authored books of high value on early South African sport, he has done it again. South African rugby needs to interrogate its origins more closely. It has a history tied closely to the oppressive power and networks of British colonialism, and its close relative, apartheid, that needs to be talked about. The rugby context that the author provides is invaluable for us to understand the long journey that preceded Siya Kolisi's triumphant embrace of the William Webb Ellis Trophy at Yokohama in 2019.

André Odendaal
Honorary Professor in History and Heritage Studies, University of the Western Cape
Founding Director of the Robben Island Museum, the first official heritage institution of democratic South Africa

Until now, South African rugby literature has been lacking an in-depth, inclusive and balanced chronicle of its history. Jonty Winch's *World Champions: The Story of South African Rugby* admirably fills this void. It consists of 24 carefully chosen topics, all contributing to a chequered and chronological tale of triumph over adversity. It contains plenty of original research and copy, which is quite an achievement, given the plethora of annual outpourings on rugby.

Winch is a formally trained and experienced researcher and historian and it shows in the large number of primary and secondary sources that he consulted in carefully drafting a most readable and authentic text. Neither apologising nor accusing, *World Champions* is a benchmark in modern South African rugby literature.

WG (Heinrich) Schulze
Professor in Banking Law, University of South Africa
Sports book reviewer: SABC Radio (RSG)

About the author

Jonty Winch received a Master of Arts degree with distinction from De Montfort University's International Centre for Sports History and Culture and was then awarded his PhD from Stellenbosch University. He has balanced his career interests in photography, journalism and education with involvement in more than a dozen books on sporting history in southern Africa. His research has also led to articles on the game for accredited international academic publications, and his winning the British Society of Sports History's 'Best Article in *Sport in History*' in 2008. In recent years, Jonty has played a prominent role in the task of recording a full history of South African cricket and placing the development of the game in a political context. He co-authored *Cricket & Conquest: The History of South African Cricket Retold 1795–1914* (2016); *Cricket & Society in South Africa 1910–1971: From Union to Isolation* (2018); and *Too Black to Wear Whites: The Remarkable Story of Krom Hendricks, a Cricket Hero Who Was Rejected by Cecil John Rhodes's Empire* (2020). The last-named publication was a 'highly commended runner-up' in the 2021 Cricket Writers' Club book awards on the occasion of their 75th anniversary at The Oval.

Contents

Foreword

The history of rugby, especially its undeniable role in colonisation, segregation and apartheid up to today was a neglected and under-researched part of South African history. Beyond the fact that it actively contributed to the foregrounding of white excellence, it turned the history of black players and whole communities into an 'unmapped historical landscape' in which its players, personalities, venues, competitions, legacy and playing communities continued to be treated as marginal to the main discourse. Furthermore, the propensity of the bulk of the existing body of knowledge to skirt these issues, especially its intersections with issues such as race, gender, religion and amateurism, continue to subalternise and silence an important part of the game's constituency at a time that more rather than less is needed. Decolonising theorists viewed the portrayal of those at the bottom of the power hierarchy as strange subjects and exotic curiosities with no recognizable history, as acts of 'epistemic violence' and a demonstration of the subalternising, agency-stripping and silencing effect of the workings of the 'coloniality of power'

This well-researched book, firstly, succeeded in foregrounding the role of rugby in colonisation and secondly, thoroughly revealed its complicity in exclusionary and racial practices. Particularly impressive is its comprehensive utilisation of the best of the latest published scientific and peer-reviewed research in the field. Its additional strength lies in the fact that the author was able to tap into previously-restricted archival material and was able to reveal rugby's intersection with the shaping influences such as racial politics. Through this narrative, which straddles the late nineteenth and full 20th century and a significant part of the first decades of the democratic Republic, the reader is provided with the first integrated and comprehensive record of the sport in South Africa in which the black contribution and legacy is not 'ghetto-ised' and presented as a mere footnote of history. By providing a fully-contextualised and inclusive general history of one of South Africa's major sports, one in which the black contribution to South Africa's sports identity is finally and substantially recognised, the foundation has been laid for the further decolonisation of the history of rugby. Indeed, this book sets the standard against which all others will be measured as historians continue to research and rewrite South Africa's sport history in order to comprehensively deal with the unfinished business of the past and its meaning for nation today.

Hendrik Snyders, PhD (History), University of Stellenbosch
Head of Department of History at the National Museum, Bloemfontein
Author of *BlitzBoks – Rugby Sevens in South Africa: A History, 1904–2019* and co-author of *Tries and Conversions: South Africans in Rugby League*

Acknowledgements

This book has its origins in an M-Net-sponsored research project on the 'reconciliation of sport in South Africa'. Minisha Patel and I worked together to collect material during the latter part of the 1990s. Various sports were covered, but rugby was prominent as its administrators had been front runners in the formation of the National Sports Congress. We interviewed leading personalities in South African sport, particularly those who had been involved in the unification process.

The document we produced – *Playing the Game: The Unification of South African Sport* – presented a significant base upon which several chapters could be built for this publication. Thanks should, therefore, be extended to Minisha for her invaluable assistance, as well as to Luke Alfred who created the opportunity for us to become involved in the research, Imtiaz Patel who represented the sponsors, and Graham Abrahams who arranged interviews in various parts of the country. In addition, David Williams and Helene Perold provided editorial support.

In the years that followed, I became involved in research projects that had a cricket focus but proved extremely useful when it came to writing this book. The same influential Western Province clique that dominated cricket during the late nineteenth and early twentieth century also controlled rugby at provincial and national levels.

In 1998, the United Cricket Board of South Africa (now Cricket South Africa) committed itself to 'recording the full history of South African cricket', and appointed Professor André Odendaal as chairman of its Transformation Monitoring Committee. André invited me to assist him with *Cricket & Conquest: The History of South African Cricket Retold 1795–1914* (2016). This was a welcome opportunity in my developing a better understanding of the structure of South African sport during the nineteenth century.

I also joined Bernard Hall, Geoff Levett, Richard Parry and Dale Slater in a London-based steering group that met regularly. We linked with historians, Professor Bruce Murray at Wits and Professor Goolam Vahed at KwaZulu-Natal, in publishing *Empire & Cricket: The South African Experience 1884–1914* (2009) and *Cricket & Society in South Africa 1910–1971: From Union to Isolation* (2018). Richard Parry and I then co-authored *Too Black to Wear Whites: The Remarkable Story of Krom Hendricks, a Cricket Hero Who Was Rejected by Cecil John Rhodes's Empire* (2020).

As with cricket, the traditional historiography of South African rugby was largely confined to whites, with blacks and politics left out. Ivor Difford's *History of South African Rugby Football 1875–1932* (1933) was written without a single reference to 'non-European' rugby in its 735 pages. Nearly sixty years later, Paul Dobson, in *Rugby in South Africa 1861–1988* (1989), made the first real attempt to produce a history that included blacks. It was written for and published by Danie Craven's SA Rugby Board but was unable to obtain 'help or information' from SARU, the most powerful black rugby body.

Important academic works followed unity. Albert Grundlingh, André Odendaal and Burridge Spies produced *Beyond the Tryline* (1995), a groundbreaking publication. It served admirably as an introduction to a revised history of South African rugby, despite *The Citizen* complaining that the authors had gone 'too far beyond the tryline' and spent 'far too much time in archives digging up "evidence"'.[1] Three years later, David Black and John Nauright published *Rugby and the South African Nation: Sport, Cultures, Politics and Power in the Old and New South Africa* (1998).

The thrust of the new, emerging historiography of South African sport was essentially to recapture black achievements and place them in a political context. The SA Rugby Football Union sponsored *112 Years of Springbok Rugby Tests and Heroes 1891–2003*, a detailed reference book that covers 'matches and the men who played them ... [an attempt] to record every Test match ...'. In 2006, the union sponsored *The Badge*, an attractively presented and informative book about the centenary of the springbok as a rugby emblem.

In the course of these publications, Vuyisa Qunta, Harold Wilson and Anthony Mackaiser made notable contributions to the history of black rugby in South Africa. Manie Booley's self-published *Forgotten Heroes: History of Black Rugby 1882–1992* was another well-received publication, and I was also helped by the work of Jeff Peires, '*Facta non Verba*: Towards a History of Black Rugby' (1981); Michael Morapeli, 'The Rock: The History of Orlando High School 1939–1984' (1984), and Hendrik Snyders' research in 'Rugby, National Pride and the Struggle of the Black South Africans for Recognition, 1897–1992'.

Paul Dobson, the most prolific of rugby writers, continued to be at the forefront of a growing rugby literature in the country. There have been outstanding publications covering the modern era. I gained illumination from books such as those by Ted Partridge, *A Life in Rugby* (1991); John Carlin, *Playing the Enemy: Nelson Mandela and the Game that Made a Nation* (2008), and Dan Retief, *The Springboks and the Holy Grail: Behind the Scenes at the Rugby World Cup 1995–2007* (2011). In addition, many players and coaches have called upon professional journalists to assist them in their autobiographies/ biographies. Collectively, they have produced an impressive historical record of South African rugby over the past forty years.

Fascinating theses and research projects – some unpublished – present vital insights into rugby during different periods. These include Grant Christison, 'African Jerusalem: The Vision of Robert Grendon' (2007); Thomas Weir, 'James Peters: The Man They Wouldn't Play: England's First Black International and the 1906 Springboks' (2015); Gert Kotzé, 'Sportrevolusie en die Beesblaasbond (Sport Revolution and the Cattle Blowing Alliance)' (2012); and Mike Buckley, '"A Colour Line Affair": Race, Imperialism and Rugby Football Contacts between New Zealand and South Africa to 1950' (1996).

My research has allowed me to enjoy the privilege of working in impressive libraries and archives. The bulk of the research was undertaken at the National Library of South Africa (Cape Town); the British Newspaper Library (at Colindale and, latterly, St Pancras); the Rugby Football Union Library at Twickenham; the Johannesburg Public Library, and the William Cullen Library at the University of the Witwatersrand, Johannesburg. A debt of gratitude is extended to the staff of these institutes. Special mention must be made of Margaret Atsango, senior librarian in the African collections at the William Cullen Library. She and her staff members, Mary Mabote and Bethuel Lekganyane, were of considerable assistance in obtaining information. David Khukhele at the Johannesburg Public Library was also very helpful.

Selected minutes from the South African Rugby Football Board files were a key resource. I travelled to De Aar where Professor Piet van der Schyff kindly provided copies of relevant sections. When the files were later transferred to Stellenbosch, Professor Albert Grundlingh allowed me to make use of them. The Board's records begin in 1889 but I was able to collect detailed newspaper reports of meetings prior to that date.

William Milton has been frequently noted as having persuaded the Cape to play rugby. An early task in my research was to ascertain the extent of his involvement in rugby and Cape politics. I visited the Bodleian Library of Commonwealth and African Studies at Rhodes House, Oxford. The archivist, Lucy McCann, kindly arranged for me to see the papers of Cecil John Rhodes, which include references to Milton. I also made use of deposits located at the National Archives, Zimbabwe, and am most grateful to Ian Johnstone for his expert advice over several years.

The Marlborough College records were of importance in establishing an understanding of Milton's early enthusiasm for sport and the influence of the formidable Dean Farrar. The College archivist, Dr Terry Rogers, assisted me in locating material. The chairman of the Trollope Society, Michael G. Williamson, kindly let me have details of links between the Milton family and the famous Trollopes. At Bedford School, Guy Fletcher provided various cuttings and copies of documents related to the achievements of Freddie Brooks. In addition, Jane Reid-Rowland forwarded further information from Harare on Brooks.

My initial findings led to an article, 'Unlocking the Cape Code: Establishing British Football in South Africa' (2010), which prompted a welcome exchange of ideas with Professor Floris van der Merwe. He had also commented on the period in the course of his research.

My interest in pursuing aspects of South Africa's rugby history was greatly assisted through postgraduate studies. At De Montfort University's International Centre for Sports History and Culture, I worked under leading rugby historian, Professor Tony Collins, and Professor Dilwyn Porter. At Stellenbosch University, my supervisors were two of South Africa's most eminent historians, Professor Albert Grundlingh and Professor Bill Nasson. Their guidance in pointing me in the right direction was always appreciated.

Jill Wolvaardt proofread selected chapters before I forwarded the manuscript to the Human Sciences Research Council (HSRC). I was also assisted by my son Matthew who helped prepare the illustrations.

Finally, I greatly appreciate the patient and professional cooperation I have received from the HSRC. I am grateful to Jeremy Wightman, the publishing director, for his interest and encouragement; Mmakwena Chipu, the commissioning editor who set up the project; and Samantha Hoaeane, the editorial project manager who guided me through the various stages of production. In addition, I benefited from the expertise of Louis Botes who completed the copy-editing process.

I thank them and everyone else in the production and promotion of this book.

Note
1   *The Citizen*, 11 July 1995.

Abbreviations and acronyms

ANC	African National Congress
ANOCA	African National Olympic Committees Association
ANS	Afrikaanse Nasionale Studentebond
Anti-CAD	Anti-Coloured Affairs Department
APO	African Political/People's Organisation
CAD	Coloured Affairs Department
CARE	Citizens' Association for Racial Equality
CC	Cricket Club
COSATU	Congress of South African Trade Unions
ERPM	East Rand Propietary Mines
FA	Football Association
HART	Halt All Racist Tours
HNP	Herstigte Nasionale Party
ICU	Industrial and Commercial Union
IDASA	Institute for Democratic Alternatives in South Africa
IOC	International Olympic Committee
IRB	International Rugby Football Board/Island Rugby Board
MCC	Marylebone Cricket Club
MDM	Mass Democratic Movement
MWU	Mineworkers' Union
NOCSA	National Olympic Committee of South Africa
NOSC	National Olympic and Sports Congress
NRC	Native Recruiting Corporation
NSC	National Sports Congress/Council
NUSAS	National Union of South African Students
OAU	Organisation of African Unity
PAC	Pan Africanist Congress
RFC	Rugby Football Club
RFU	Rugby Football Union
SACBOC	South African Cricket Board of Control
SACOS	South African Council on Sports
SACS	South African College School
SANOC	South Africa National Olympic Committee
SANROC	South African Non-Racial Olympic Committee
SANZAR	South African, New Zealand, Australian Rugby
SARFU	SA Rugby Football Union
SARU	SA Rugby Union

SCSA	Supreme Council of Sport in Africa
SRC	Student Representative Council
STST	Stop the Seventy Tour Committee
UDF	United Democratic Front
WRC	World Rugby Corporation

Author Disclaimer: A central theme of this publication is the subjective and transitory nature of racial categorisation, based primarily on culture and economic position. The quoted material reflects terminology and associated ideologies held by those quoted during the period covered by the work. On occasion, contemporary expressions are used that might be considered racist, offensive and demeaning. They have been retained in the interests of historical accuracy and because they serve as clear evidence of the attitudes often contained in language. To lessen their effectiveness might create opportunities for the continuation of the historical denial that this work seeks to oppose.

Introduction

Poor old South Africa is pretty much like a good, tough
old football in many a 'scrummage'. Fortunately, she seems
made of good leather and a good goal will no doubt be one
day kicked in due course of time, when its inhabitants all
round must, like forward football players do, take a good
many thumps and kicks in the process of moulding.

– Frederick York St Leger, *Cape Times*, 20 September 1884

A tour of Rugby School usually begins in front of a plaque which commemorates
the legendary exploits of William Webb Ellis who 'with a fine disregard for the
rules of football as played in his time first took the ball in his arms and ran with
it thus originating the distinctive feature of the Rugby game AD 1823'. When
he caught the ball in his arms – which was permitted – 'he ought to have retired
back as far as he pleased without parting with the ball'. He chose not to and
rushed forward with the ball in his hands.[1]

The William Webb Ellis story only surfaced after 1895 when the Old Rugbeian
Society decided to look into the origins of their game. A subcommittee concluded
their investigation by stating that 'in all probability' Ellis had introduced the
concept of running with the ball, and a plaque was erected at the school in 1900.
Later, his story became firmly entrenched in rugby's folklore when the Webb Ellis
Cup – the trophy presented to the winning team in the men's Rugby World Cup –
was named after him.[2]

In 1857, Thomas Hughes's novel, *Tom Brown's Schooldays*, brought Rugby
School's variant of the game of football to public attention. It told of a starry-
eyed, young boy leaving home in Berkshire to attend Rugby School, where he
was transformed into a robust, manly student. The much-revered headmaster
Thomas Arnold was depicted as considering sport to be important to the boys'

all-round development; but in reality the world of *Tom Brown's Schooldays* was very different to Arnold's 'high-minded idealism'.[3] It was members of staff at Rugby who supported the athletic movement, and they continued their interest in games when they moved to other schools.

Marlborough College was 'the first of the great schools to imbibe the traditions of the Rugby of Arnold'.[4] In 1852, George Cotton – the young master referred to in *Tom Brown's Schooldays* – became Master of Marlborough in the wake of a schoolboy rebellion. He quickly identified a lack of recreational provision as being a major cause of the problems that existed amongst school pupils. His answer to the indiscipline was to ensure the boys were profitably occupied. He appointed to his staff new assistant masters from Rugby who successfully reformed the games, particularly football.

William 'Joey' Milton, who was to have an enormous impact on South African sport, began his school career at Marlborough as a thirteen-year-old in 1868. To his immense delight, school authorities were in the process of giving sport due consideration by improving facilities, hiring professional coaches and employing teachers who were also sportsmen steeped in the traditions of fair play. Milton was a competitive player in the annual cricket match between Marlborough and Rugby at Lord's, and impressive in rugby football – he was described as 'a most brilliant and dashing half-back'.[5]

Milton's later sense of 'fair play' – or lack of it – was shaped by prevailing assumptions of the moral and physical superiority of the English race. He came under the influence of the new Master of Marlborough, Frederic William 'Dean' Farrar, whose work *Aptitude of Races* in 1867 gave further clear expression to Semitic and Aryan superiority over the Mongoloid and, lower still, the Negroid.[6] Such views on race have since been dismissed as representing 'crassly insensitive, ethnocentric nonsense'.[7] But at the time they were believed, and would have been of interest to pupils at a school that contributed enthusiastically to the staffing of administrations in distant outposts of empire.

Milton was groomed to fit the mould of colonial recruit. He joined an active movement of young men who disseminated the imperial games across the world. His old school mate Hugh Hamilton became a vice-president of the New South Wales Rugby Union in the years prior to the formation of a national governing body. Another Marlburian of similar vintage, former England rugby captain Alfred Hamersley, was an eminent rugby missionary in both New Zealand and Canada. Like the others, Milton possessed the valuable qualification of being a rugby international, and became more influential than anyone else in the diffusion of the imperial ball games to southern Africa.

When Milton arrived at the Cape in 1877, he was called upon to fight rugby's cause at a time when rivalry between codes was attracting attention. The *Cape Times* recognised Milton's value as a standard-bearer for both 'Englishness' and sport; his achievements on and off the field catching the public eye. Within a short time, he had persuaded the Cape to play rugby. A growing reputation also brought him into contact with the leading politicians, Cecil John Rhodes and J.H. 'Onze Jan' Hofmeyr. Under their watch and at the height of imperial expansion, the old 'Cape liberal' notion of individual advancement gave way to a system of segregation.

In this critical formative period, Milton surrounded himself with like-minded men who followed the direction that he provided on behalf of the Cape government. By the time he left for Rhodesia in 1896, Milton's legacy had fixed the colour bar, leaving Cape sport well set along the segregation route.[8]

The major administrative developments in South African rugby during the nineteenth century were the establishment of the white SA Rugby Football Board (1889), which became the SA Rugby Football Board in 1893, and the non-racial SA Coloured Rugby Football Board (1897). They were the two main pillars around which the South African game was built and administered for almost the entire twentieth century. While the pillars were ever-present, they were at times affected by splits, changing identities and motivations that were at play in the different rugby constituencies at different times. To understand South African rugby, it is important to trace and analyse these parallel histories, as well as that of the unified governing body – the SA Football Union – established in 1992.

This book explores the drama, complexities and contradictions that have accompanied the growth of rugby in southern Africa for more than 150 years. Histories of the game played by the different population groups are revisited, with new insights emerging as entrenched narratives are questioned and sometimes replaced. The extensive research should engage the academic reader, while the chapters are structured in a way to interest the average rugby follower. Each tells its own story, recording the sport's development chronologically from the early 1860s to World Cup successes in the truly global game of recent years.

Sport in the late nineteenth century was woven into the fabric of imperial power, but the Afrikaner developed a special affinity for games, and rugby became an important part of his culture. According to Ivor Difford's *History of South African Rugby Football 1875–1932*, rugby in the 1880s 'spread like wildfire into all farming districts of the country ... the result is that the young South African Dutchman or Afrikaner, as he is now styled, has become probably the greatest natural exponent of the rugby game there is'.[9]

Rugby brought together the two white races – the Afrikaner and the Englishman. John Honey commented in his publication, *Tom Brown in South Africa*:

In England, rugby football is socially divisive: it is the game identified with the middle and upper classes, and, apart from a few special cases, the social pretensions are classifiable by whether they play rugger or soccer. In South Africa, on the other hand, this kind of classification has never caught on ... the function of rugby football has been, rather, to unite the white nation, to bridge the differences between Afrikaner and English in a common religion, with common rituals and a common language.'[10]

Yet, rugby was played just as enthusiastically by the black communities. From the late nineteenth century, the game had great significance both for Muslim descendants of slaves and ethnically mixed communities in the western Cape, as well as the emergent black middle class, educated at mission stations in the eastern Cape. André Odendaal opened up an almost forgotten world of early black sport in his seminal paper, 'South Africa's Black Victorians'. He wrote of sport as an integral part of a 'process of assimilation and mobilisation ... It enabled the new black elite to demonstrate their ability to adopt and assimilate European culture and behave like gentlemen – and by extension to show their fitness to be accepted as full citizens of Cape society.'[11]

Rugby was the first sport at the Cape to become segregated, with separate white and coloured provincial governing bodies being formed in the Western Province in 1883 and 1886, respectively. This development attracted relatively little press coverage and was virtually, but not entirely, unchallenged. One of Milton's disciples, Billy Simkins, not only engineered this division but as president of the Western Province Rugby Football Union (1889–1906) and SA Rugby Football Board (1890–1913) ensured the Cape government's discriminatory practices were maintained.

Arguably the single most significant decision in South African sporting history occurred when Rhodes blocked Krom Hendricks's selection for the South African cricket tour to England in 1894. Milton, who was head of Rhodes's prime minister's department and chaired the selection committee, accepted responsibility for a decision that had widespread repercussions as Hendricks became the central figure in the evolution of sports segregation in South Africa.

Two years later in 1896, Rhodes's involvement in the infamous Jameson Raid caused a breakdown in relations between the Afrikaners and the English. A worsening situation, driven by the mining industry and Sir Alfred Milner, effectively culminated in the second Anglo-Boer War (1899–1902). The largest

British army sent overseas – 450 000 – beat the Boers in the end, 'only by ruthless and laborious methods of attrition, burning their farms, herding their women and children into detention camps, and criss-crossing the entire countryside with interconnecting blockhouses'.[12]

Imperial rhetoric that the war had been fought to bring equal rights was a lie. Promises made by the British leaders were broken and there was bitter disappointment for coloureds and Africans who suffered huge casualties and were betrayed by a 'white man's' peace.

Sport brought white people together and improved relationships. Rugby's leaders directed their efforts towards establishing a South African national identity involving distinctive team colours, a springbok emblem and criteria that determined who was eligible to represent South Africa. All but one of the first rugby tour party in 1906/07 were South African born. They were highly successful: Hofmeyr claimed that they 'had made the Dutch and English almost one and had taken a great step in the direction of racial unity'.[13]

In the formation of Union in 1910, the British supported the Boer leader General Louis Botha as the best man to lead the government and promote a policy of reconciliation and cooperation between Briton and Boer. They also brought together the previously separate colonies – Cape, Natal, Transvaal and Orange Free State – into a self-governing dominion within the empire.

The Springboks were the first side to be invited to Britain for a second tour. Billy Millar's team achieved the first 'grand slam' of victories over the home unions in 1912/13. Links with New Zealand followed when their services team toured South Africa in 1919. The SA Rugby Football Board voted by a narrow margin to request the exclusion of Maori players. It began a process whereby South Africa dictated to other nations who could be selected in their touring teams.

The SA Coloured Rugby Football Board held the Rhodes Cup competition on seven occasions between 1903 and 1914. This was a notable achievement as there were only five white Currie Cup tournaments during the same period. Rugby had succeeded amongst communities of diverse traditions and cultures who lived in disadvantaged communities and built their lives under the ever-present framework of colonial power.

A time of great upheaval after the war resulted in the Rhodes Cup tournament not being played between 1914 and 1928. Despite a successful revival of the competition, the first major rugby split occurred in 1935 when African players broke away and established their own governing body. The eastern Cape led the movement with the aim of achieving greater exposure for African rugby as numerous good players had migrated from the eastern Cape to the mines in Kimberley and Johannesburg.

The Springboks became unofficial world champions when they defeated the All Blacks in New Zealand in 1937. The coloured population filed through turnstiles at Newlands and other grounds to watch whites play rugby. Their support was unwavering yet taken for granted. During a period when coloured people gave much to rugby at the Cape but received little in return, the Springbok captain Bennie Osler set a rare example in the divided society. His brother Stanley, also a Springbok and later headmaster of Kearsney College, wrote of Bennie:

> He knew and loved the all too human coloured folk of the Cape and was, in turn, loved and respected by the Malays ... Indeed so loved was Bennie that it was truly said that he alone in Cape Town could have walked safely in the notorious District Six, the den of slum-created crime ... He scorned snobbery, the 'Cliveden Set' of Constantia and the society of the Cape who believed they had built Table Mountain. Bennie's penchant was rather for the Malay fisherman ... the world where there were no posers, no Charlatans, no hypocrites.[14]

The home in which Bennie Osler grew up was one remembered vividly by his brother: 'a religious home with daily prayers which all our coloured servants and the chauffeur attended, sitting respectfully on the kitchen chairs they brought in with them'. Jimmy Allen, a prominent Cape and suburban rugby administrator, recalled, 'Bennie would meet the non-white sportsmen as just fellow human beings.' George Manuel added: He used to coach players on our old Caledonian field at Mowbray and I remember how delighted he used to be on a Saturday if he saw that his coaching was bearing fruit.'[15]

After the Second World War, Dr. D.F. Malan's Herenigde Nasionale Party (Reunited National Party) came to power, and began to shape South Africa in the way they had promised. The segregationist strategy was solidified through the implementation of apartheid (separatism). They aimed to divide South Africans into four main racial groups, the Population Registration Act of 1950 categorising people as white, coloured, Indian and African. The Group Areas Act of 1950 and the Separate Amenities Act of 1953 provided the legislative basis to implement the historical racial platform.

By the 1950s, 'social segregation in South Africa was as much a matter of custom as of law – it was part of what were called the "mores" of the country'.[16] The government simply confirmed the notion that whites and blacks should organise their sports separately as mixed sport was formally prohibited within

South Africa. No mixed teams could compete abroad and any international sides competing in South Africa would have to be all-white, though black sportsmen from overseas would be allowed to compete against South African blacks. Who could play with or against whom, and where, were enshrined in law as well as practice.[17]

As the government implemented its apartheid policies, the Springboks confirmed their world supremacy. They beat New Zealand 4–0 in 1949 and achieved an impressive third 'grand slam' during their 1951/52 overseas tour, with Afrikaners playing a huge part in the success. The first faltering steps for Danie Craven and his Springbok team did not come until 1955 when the British Lions drew a thrilling series 2–2. The All Blacks defeated the Springboks in New Zealand in 1956 and the French beat them at home in 1958.

Rugby league sensed the time was right to encroach upon rugby union territory in South Africa. Over a relatively short time, numerous white and black South Africans defected to rugby league clubs in Britain and Australia. Martin Pelser, one of rugby's finest loose forwards, commented: 'I cannot recount the many days of unpaid leave I had to make for the sake of amateur rugby ... Amateur rugby, and especially Springbok rugby, is a game for rich men's sons. I, and others like me, could no longer afford it.'[18]

Coloured and African Springboks were engaged in internal Tests from 1950. Their matches coincided with resistance movements focusing international attention on South Africa's apartheid policy. The Cape leader of the African National Congress (ANC), Professor Z.K. Matthews, called for a Congress of the People where demands were made for change. A Freedom Charter was adopted, which called, inter alia, for equal rights for all ethnic groups, and put forward the claim that South Africa belonged to all its inhabitants.

The early months of 1960 were eventful. Harold Macmillan, the British prime minister, made his famous 'wind of change' speech in February; a police station at Sharpeville was surrounded and shots were fired at demonstrators in March, leaving 69 dead and 180 wounded; and, in April, the government responded with the Unlawful Organisations Act, declaring the ANC and the Pan-Africanist Congress prohibited organisations.

Protests followed but rugby was generally unaffected. The All Blacks were defeated in 1960 prior to Avril Malan's Springboks achieving a remarkable fourth successive 'grand slam'. When the country became a republic in May 1961 and departed from the Commonwealth, the International Rugby Board was supportive, stating that 'the change would not make any difference whatever in regard to South Africa's position in rugby'.[19]

The anti-apartheid movements had different ideas during the 1960s. The SA Non-Racial Olympic Committee coordinated a boycott at international level and there were worldwide protests against links with the apartheid regime.

The SA Coloured Rugby Football Board dropped the racial designation it had carried since its foundation in 1897. Its name changed to the SA Rugby Union (SARU) in 1966 and, three years later, it rejected the political legacy of Rhodes by ending the Rhodes Cup competition.

The SA Rugby Football Board was badly affected by the decision to call off the 1967 All Black tour. Then prime minister John Vorster was forced to concede that his government could no longer dictate to traditional rivals whom they may or may not include in their teams. But he then refused to allow Basil D'Oliveira, the South African-born coloured cricketer, to tour South Africa with the Marylebone Cricket Club (MCC) team in 1968/69. His blunder had severe repercussions for South African sport with demonstrations wrecking Springbok rugby tours to Britain and Ireland in 1969/70 and Australia in 1971.

SARU withdrew from the ethnic Tests in 1970 and committed themselves to non-racial rugby. In 1973, they became a founder member of the South African Council on Sport (SACOS), which was recognised as the domestic sports wing of the anti-apartheid movement. The sporting boycott gathered in strength and the Springboks struggled to find opponents in the late 1970s. Their 1981 tour of New Zealand went ahead amid massive demonstrations. The third Test was disrupted by an aeroplane repeatedly swooping low over the ground and dropping flour bombs on the players.

With apartheid crumbling, SA Rugby Board president Danie Craven made some of the first moves seen in official circles towards reconciliation with the ANC. By the late 1980s, the ANC-backed National Sports Congress had become the most powerful non-racial movement, replacing SACOS whose rigid non-collaborative approach was viewed as adversely affecting progress in non-racial sport. 'The sole objective of the international community's boycott was to integrate South African sport,' wrote sports historian, Douglas Booth, but 'SACOS turned the boycott into a strategy against apartheid *per se*'.[20]

Unity was achieved in 1992 and South Africa was readmitted to world rugby and given the opportunity to host the World Cup in 1995. Initial right-wing resistance to change was countered by the ANC warning: 'They can make rugby a reconciler of people, or they can use it as a ritual that celebrates conquest and domination of black people.'[21]

The new president, Nelson Mandela, believed that sport, and in particular rugby, could play an important role in the post-apartheid reconciliation process. At the 1995 Rugby World Cup final, he wore his Springbok cap and a replica no. 6 jersey.

It was probably the most symbolically unifying event in South Africa's post-apartheid history, a moment of reconciliation for the country and its sports culture. Rugby had the ability to break down barriers and the Springboks had the capacity to contribute significantly to the country's unity.

The images of Mandela celebrating victory were matched by fleeting ecstasy for the 'rainbow nation'. Rugby chiefs were already brokering a transition to professionalism and World Cup euphoria evaporated rapidly.

Transformation towards racial representativity presented a political minefield for South African sports. The policy was difficult and awkward to implement at first, but conscious efforts were made to achieve desired changes in the make-up of South African rugby. ESPN's Tom Hamilton commented on 'real, merit-based integration resulting from professional development initiatives in academies and the allotment of coaching and training resources to the black and coloured rugby community'.[22]

Jake White led the Springboks to World Cup success in 2007 but was not reappointed. The Rugby Board replaced him with Peter de Villiers who was introduced as 'an affirmative-action appointment'.[23] The latter's task was never going to be easy, but he did inherit an outstanding group of players. By 2009, the Springbok trophy cabinet included the Webb Ellis Cup, the Tri-Nations trophy, the IRB 'Team of the Year' and the Unity Cup (British Lions series).

The All Blacks learnt from South Africa's success and did not look back, winning the World Cup in 2011 and 2015, before inflicting record defeats on the Springboks. The South African side reflected the challenges they faced. Oregan Hoskins, who was president of the SA Rugby Union for ten-and-a-half years up to 2016, asserted 'our sport is massively transformed from where it was in 1992', but conceded:

> [It] is very difficult in 21 years or so to undo a historical legacy that led to a massive class divide, a massive racial divide. To undo it in just over two decades is asking too much … transforming rugby means transforming the socio-economic landscape of South Africa, and that can't be done overnight.[24]

Coaches struggled to field competitive international teams, not least because of the mounting list of 'exiles'. The exodus came to a head in 2016 when the depleted Springboks lost eight Tests out of twelve. Close to 400 South Africans were playing in Europe, largely for financial reasons because their home currency was weak compared to the euro or pound. Playing overseas enables South Africans to gain invaluable experience in different conditions. A negative aspect from a Springbok perspective is that French, English, Irish and Scottish teams, amongst others, strengthen their sides through the acquisition of South African players.

The modern professional era has brought many changes. One of the most exciting is the greater emphasis on 'sevens' rugby. Here the South African Blitzbokke have not only excelled but more than met transformation requirements. In the course of an outstanding decade up to 2017/18, they won three World Series titles, gold medals at the World Games (2013) and Commonwealth Games (2014), and bronze at the summer Olympic Games in 2016.

Women's rugby in South Africa is in its infancy but is set to become an important part of the country's rugby reputation. The South African women's team has been playing since 2004 and has participated in three World Cups. Marijke Nel, granddaughter of the 1937 Springbok captain, Philip Nel, was a key member of the 2005/06 teams. The Eastern Cape has produced three impressive Springbok captains in 'Noms' Tsotsobe, Nolusindiso Booi and Lusanda Dumke. In early 2020, Babalwa Latsha became the first player from the women's team to sign an overseas professional contract.

South Africa's growing rugby family has made wonderful progress. Yet the fascinating story of the South African game could not have been adequately written until the Rugby World Cup of 2019. It was on the glittering Yokohama stage that Makazole Mapimpi and Cheslin Kolbe scored their country's first-ever tries in a final; Duane Vermeulen was 'man of the match', and Siya Kolisi held aloft the Webb Ellis Cup. This massively memorable triumph illuminated a genuine appreciation of the skills that have always existed across the racial spectrum.

The national governing bodies

1889   SA Football Board

1893   SA Rugby Football Board

1897   SA Coloured Rugby Football Board

1935   SA Bantu Rugby Board (breaks away from the SA Coloured Rugby Football Board)

1952   Non-European Rugby Football Federation (an umbrella body encompassing the SA Coloured Rugby Football Board and SA Bantu Rugby Board)

1958   SA African Rugby Board (formerly the SA Bantu Rugby Board)

1959   SA Rugby Football Federation (breaks away from the SA Coloured Rugby Football Board)

1966   SA Rugby Union – SARU (formerly the SA Coloured Rugby Board)

1977   SA Rugby Board – consisting of the SA Rugby Football Board, SA
        Rugby Association (formerly the SA African Rugby Board) and SA
        Rugby Football Federation
1992   SA Rugby Football Union – SARFU (unified SA Rugby Board and SA
        Rugby Union)
2001   SA Rugby (SA Rugby Football Union approved the creation of a
        commercial arm)
2005   SA Rugby Union (formerly the SA Rugby Football Union)

Notes

1   D. Ray, *From Webb Ellis to World Cup* (Rugby: Rugby School, 2015), 3.
2   Ellis went up to Oxford, won a cricket blue, became an Anglican clergyman and died in southern France in 1872.
3   J. Honey, *Tom Brown in South Africa* (Grahamstown: Rhodes University, 1972), 5.
4   A. Bradley, A. Champneys and J. Baines, *A History of Marlborough College during Fifty Years from its Foundation to the Present Time* (London: John Murray, 1893), 55.
5   Report in Charles Alcock's *Football Annual* referred to in *The Marlburian*, March 1873.
6   In 1866, Charles Darwin successfully nominated Farrar for the Fellowship of the Royal Society.
7   J. Mangan, *The Games Ethic and Imperialism* (Harmondsworth: Viking, 1985), 113.
8   Milton never regretted the decisions he made. In 1930, he commented in Ivor Difford's *History of South African Rugby Football* that 'the result has been even more magnificent than any of us could have anticipated'.
9   I. Difford (ed.), *The History of South African Rugby Football 1875–1932* (Wynberg: Speciality Press, 1933), 15.
10   Honey, *Tom Brown in South Africa*, 15.
11   A. Odendaal, 'South Africa's Black Victorians: Sport, Race and Class in South Africa before Union' in *Africa Perspective*, 1, 7 & 8, 1989, 75, 78.
12   J. Morris, *Farewell the Trumpets: An Imperial Retreat* (Harmondsworth: Penguin, 1982), 71–72.
13   F. Piggott, *The Springboks: History of the Tour 1906/07* (Cape Town: Dawson & Sons, 1907), 105.
14   C. Greyvenstein, *The Bennie Osler Story* (Cape Town: Howard Timmins, 1970), 136, 141.
15   Greyvenstein, *The Bennie Osler Story*, 139, 62.
16   B. Murray, *Wits: The Open Years – A History of the University of the Witwatersrand, Johannesburg 1939–1959* (Johannesburg: Witwatersrand University Press, 1997), 47–48.
17   The Minister of the Interior, Dr T.E. Donges, announced the government's policy on sport in June 1956.
18   *The Sportsman*, March 1966, 12.
19   T. Collins, *The Oval World: A Global History of Rugby* (London: Bloomsbury, 2015), 396.
20   D. Booth, 'The South African Council on Sport and the Political Antinomies of the Sports Boycott' in *Journal of Southern African Studies*, 23, 1, March 1997.
21   *Business Day*, 20 August 1992.
22   T. Hamilton, ESPN, 17 September 2015.
23   P. de Villiers with G. Rich, *Politically Incorrect: The Autobiography* (Cape Town: Zebra Press, 2012), 9.
24   T. Hamilton, ESPN, 17 September 2015.

1

'Mission Accomplished'

They told US we couldn't, but WE did. Any country was
probably better off to win it. SOUTH AFRICA is still going
through a tough time, but this one moment, this victory brought
the most unbelievable 'gees' and unity to our nation. It didn't
fix South Africa, but it brought a massive shift. And that is
a story of Hope. A story to everyone that no matter what, it
CAN be done. EVEN with ALL our differences, with all our
backgrounds, with all our setbacks, it was done through unity!![1]

– Cheslin Kolbe

Yokohama, 2 November 2019 ... South Africa had established an 18–12 lead
by the 65th minute of the Rugby World Cup final. England were battered and
struggling, but still in the game. Their scrum-half, Ben Youngs, put up a high kick
which South Africa's full-back Willie Le Roux collected just inside the England
half of the field. He was tackled and the English players charged into the ruck,
eager to secure the turnover. South Africa recycled the ball quickly.

Faf de Klerk attacked on the left flank where four of his players were waiting.
The ball moved quickly through the hands. De Klerk linked with Lukhanyo Am.
An off-load followed to Malcolm Marx who rifled a pass to Makazole Mapimpi.
The powerfully built wing had space in which to move.

Billy Vunipola covered for England but Mapimpi chipped over his head and
slightly infield. The perfectly weighted kick was chased by Am. Outpacing his
pursuers, the centre gathered the ball on the bounce. He might easily have scored,
but instinctively slipped an incisive pass to Mapimpi who cruised across the line
unopposed.

South Africa had recorded their first try in a World Cup final. Am laughed
as Mapimpi drifted past him in an apparent trance, absorbed by the magical

moment. Handré Pollard converted the try and South Africa had built a 25–12 lead. The tide was heading in one direction.

Eight minutes later, Malcolm Marx launched a massive hit on Henry Slade, the England centre. The ball was dislodged and Am pounced on it, unleashing another counter-attack. Pieter-Steph du Toit drew his man before passing to Cheslin Kolbe on the England 10-metre line. The little wing seemed boxed in as five English players swarmed towards him in cover defence.

He hopped, then accelerated, leaving the ponderous Dan Cole and Joe Marler in his wake. Owen Farrell had him covered. Vunipola was corner-flagging. In a flash, Kolbe side-stepped to his left and away from the touchline. He straightened and exploded through the Farrell barrier. The England captain was left spread-eagled on the ground. Vunipola gave up hope of catching the flying wing. A spectacular try had resulted from nothing.

Pollard, Franco Mostert and 'R.G.' Snyman embraced Kolbe in a triumphant salute to the appreciative 75 000 Yokohama crowd. 'When Chessie beat Farrell on the inside,' said Pollard, 'we knew we had won it.'[2] A few minutes still remained as images of the trophy being engraved appeared on the giant screen.

'The noise and fury of global triumph on the final whistle,' observed Stephen Jones in the English *Sunday Times*, 'came from the spectators in green.'[3] A record-equalling third World Cup victory: South Africa 32, England 12. Pollard kicked 22 points.

'It was as close to a perfect performance in a final as there could possibly be,' wrote former England fly-half, Toby Flood, in *The Mail on Sunday*.[4]

'We played rugby the way only the Springboks can,' commented Schalk Burger, a 2007 World Cup winner.[5]

Joyous images of the iconic trophy presentation were beamed around the world. Siya Kolisi hoisted the Webb Ellis Cup skywards as his team cheered in celebration behind him. 'We can achieve anything if we work together,' proclaimed the Springbok captain on a glorious night for South Africans in the stadium and around the world.[6]

The Springboks were the first team to win the Rugby Championship and the World Cup in the same year. They also won World Rugby's trifecta of team, coach (Rassie Erasmus) and player of the year (Pieter-Steph du Toit) at the annual awards the following day.

The 2007 World Cup-winning captain, John Smit, had wondered if it was too much of a fairy tale to see Siya win the trophy, adding it could not have happened at a better time. Much was said about the Springboks being empowered by a higher purpose, playing for people back home. They dedicated their success to the strife-torn nation in the grip of an economic crisis, with widespread poverty, record unemployment, power cuts and water shortages. Problems were momentarily forgotten as millions became transfixed by the drama and, for a brief few days, they had something to celebrate.

President Cyril Ramaphosa lauded the feel-good atmosphere created by the national team. 'At a time when South Africa is experiencing profound challenges, we have rallied around the victory in Japan,' he said. 'The outpouring of support for the Springboks on the road to the final once again showed the immense potential of sport to unite us as a people.'[7]

Two years earlier, South African rugby had been in decline. Pessimistic reports were predicting the possible demise of the Springboks as an international power. Defeats by record margins had been recorded in 2016 and 2017, a period in which just 11 Tests were won out of 25. The country had slipped to sixth place in the world rankings.

Then, with just 18 months to the World Cup in Japan, significant developments occurred. An incredible transformation began.

The reasons behind this dramatic upsurge in fortune have been widely documented. The appointment in February 2018 of Rassie Erasmus as head coach was crucial. Players on overseas contracts were key to potential success, while the internal search was relentless in assembling the best possible side. Opportunities were created, with Erasmus capping 19 new Springboks in his first year in charge. The exercise highlighted the wealth of raw talent that existed in a land where a passion for the game encompassed all races, colours and creeds.

In May 2018, Erasmus took the far-reaching decision to appoint Siya Kolisi as Springbok captain. The flanker had grown up in impoverished circumstances in the township of Zwide outside Port Elizabeth. Born to teenage parents, he was looked after by his grandmother, who cleaned kitchens to make ends meet. He sometimes wondered where his next meal was coming from, but he loved rugby. His ability in the game was noticed and he was offered a full scholarship to Grey High School in Port Elizabeth, a semi-private institute with a rugby tradition.

As Springbok captain, Kolisi hoped to go beyond simply inspiring black children: 'When I'm on the field and I look into the crowd, I see people of all races and social classes.'[8]

Success did not come easily for the Springboks in 2018. There was a period when they came close to losing Erasmus. Reports state that he was prepared to resign his position if his side lost a third straight game following defeats to Argentina and Australia. The crucial match was a daunting clash against the All Blacks in Wellington. Erasmus's future was in his players' hands, but they did not let him down. Intense pressure placed on All Black Damian McKenzie resulted in a dropped pass in the very last play. It enabled the Springboks to seal a thrilling 36–34 win.

Victory marked the beginning of a Springbok resurgence. In the return encounter in Pretoria, they led the All Blacks 30–13 after an hour's play. They comprehensively outplayed their opponents but then the wheels came off in a disastrous last 20 minutes. The Springboks gave the game away, but there was sufficient evidence in the first hour to confirm they could become world champions.

For Erasmus, it made sense to resurrect the traditional South African game plan. One that was driven by a dominant pack, backed by a solid defence and a strong kicking game. They had little time to waste. 'We wouldn't call it sacrifice,' he explained, 'but we needed to be 20 weeks together to have a chance as we were so far behind the other teams.'[9]

Kolisi said the players from different backgrounds bought into the coach's message from the very first meeting. Erasmus had told them: 'There are so many good things in South Africa but always in the past, we seem to look at all the bad things. We just decided, "Listen, let's stand together and work really hard and play well on the field and then from that all the other things will come out later." And that's what we did.'[10]

In 2019, a 16–16 draw against the All Blacks in Wellington followed victories over Argentina and Australia. It resulted in South Africa's first Tri Nations/ Rugby Championship title since 2009. The reigning world champions, the All Blacks, were restricted to one try in their 16 points by a fast-moving defence that prevented the ball from being shifted wide. In the estimation of rugby analyst Ben Smith, the Springboks had perfected and mastered a high-risk, high-energy defensive system.[11]

Playing New Zealand in the opening group stage of the World Cup was nevertheless a formidable challenge. Erasmus accepted responsibility for the team's failure. 'We were tense that week,' he confessed, 'and it was a terrible build-up.' But lessons were learnt that would aid the South Africans in later matches, notably the quarter-final and semi-final.[12]

Of all the concepts and details covered in his 20 months of meticulous planning, Erasmus regarded 'context' as being of great importance for his Springboks. He did not want pressure placed on Kolisi or any of the Springbok team. 'In South Africa,' he cautioned, 'pressure is not having a job, having a close relative who is murdered. Rugby shouldn't be something that creates pressure. It brings hope.' As he saw it, rugby players were privileged, and the game should not be burdened by any form of duress.[13]

New Zealand, Wales, England and the surprise team, Japan, made the early running. They won their respective groups, with South Africa finishing second to the All Blacks in their section. The Springboks were subsequently pleased to defeat Japan in the quarter-final and overcome Wales 18–14 in a difficult semi-final encounter.

England accounted for Australia in their quarter-final and the All Blacks in the semi-final. An ecstatic English press were keen to drive home the psychological advantage. Stephen Jones asked: 'When did New Zealand suffer the most crushing defeat in their history? No, you don't need the record books. It was yesterday ... they have surely never had so little of a big game, have never been played to a standstill and then to something approximating a rabble.'[14]

It did not take long before Lynn McConnell responded: 'Forgetting all the journalistic hyperbole, and the never-ending desire to get a rise out of New Zealand fans, the simple fact is that it wasn't the most crushing defeat.' He pointed out that:

> The most crushing New Zealand defeat must remain the third Test 17–6 loss to the Springboks in 1937. This was a game in which New Zealand, in the series decider, were so comprehensively out-played, and out-thought, that South Africa scored five tries to nil. And if Gerry Brand had had his goal-kicking boots on it would have been even worse. Based on modern scoring the score would have been 27–6. It was relentless. And if New Zealand looked bereft in the face of England's challenge in Yokohama, they at least continued to play and to try and get some momentum throughout the 80 minutes. But the men of 1937 were stuffed from the first time the Springboks called for a scrum.[15]

McConnell's message to Jones provided an ominous warning, at least as far as the scrum was concerned. In 1937, the legendary former South African captain Paul Roos had sent a pre-match telegram to the Springboks, which stated simply: 'Skrum, skrum, skrum'.[16] History repeated itself in 2019, with Erasmus reverting to an emphasis on the set-piece. He did it openly, naming two full front rows in his squad – one for each half – but the England coach Eddie Jones remained oblivious of the tactic.

On the surface, it appears England supporters badly underestimated the strength of South African rugby. They paid no attention to the fact that their opponents were not only the southern hemisphere champions but had also beaten Wales, the northern hemisphere champions. Former Welsh centre, Jamie Roberts, sensed 'an air of "we have already won the World Cup", not from within the England camp but certainly from outside it. The Springboks probably fed off that. There is no doubt that would have motivated them.' In contrast, Roberts added, 'South Africa were fairly quiet in the week, kept their heads down, as they have done throughout the tournament.'[17]

In one of very few Springbok utterings, Tendai 'The Beast' Mtawarira had special words for his captain, Siya Kolisi:

> What Siya has achieved has been remarkable. For a young kid from Zwide township in Port Elizabeth to rise above his circumstances and become Springbok captain, and lead the way he has, it's been inspirational to all South Africans – from all walks of life. We are all proud of him, and we ultimately want to make it very special for him on Saturday.[18]

With the English media installing their team as firm favourites, former international players jumped on the bandwagon. They provided comments that the English public wanted to hear. Matt Dawson claimed a combined 15 would not feature a single Springbok; Stuart Barnes argued that their captain Siya Kolisi should be benched, and David Flatman offered the view, 'I just do not see how South Africa can win this final. Just don't think there's a way.'[19] Nick Easter told *Daily Mail* readers:

> I am expecting revenge for 2007 … This England team at the moment have the best pack in the world. If you break it down – we have the best front-row in the world, the best second-row and the best back-row. At this point, we have the best of each row in the pack.[20]

And when the BBC conducted a poll – 'Who will win the Rugby World Cup?' – the votes were recorded as follows:

England by seven points or fewer – 41%
England by plenty – 46%
South Africa by seven points or fewer – 9%
South Africa by plenty – 2%
England after extra-time – 2%
South Africa after extra-time – 0%.[21]

Millions believed that by mid-morning, United Kingdom time, on 2 November, captain Owen Farrell would be lifting the cup. They crowded into pubs and clubhouses, suitably attired in their white shirts and happily assured of a day of celebration. At the Cabbage Patch, 'a pub in the shadow of the spiritual home of English rugby at Twickenham, staff pulled an astonishing 2900 pints in three hours … everyone was caught up in the anticipation, the hype, the expectation, the excitement: convinced that England would win'.[22]

Sir Clive Woodward was virtually on his own in expressing some concern about England's chances. The manager of their only World Cup-winning team expressed the view that the South African team knew the English players better than almost any other team in the world. In his match previews, he mentioned that many of South Africa's top players were key men for premiership teams, while others in France played top English clubs in Europe. It bothered him that they knew England's strengths and weaknesses and could take advantage of such intelligence in their game plan.

Coach Eddie Jones was unperturbed, warning the South Africans that the World Cup final was the game he had been planning for since he took control of the team in January 2016. He attempted to conjure up an aura of invincibility. 'We've had four years to prepare for this game,' he divulged. 'That's why the players can be relaxed because we know we've done the work.' He had no doubt that South Africa would deliver the traditional power game and that England had to meet their physicality, 'but we are looking forward to that and being able to impose our game on them.'[23]

The game did not pan out the way England thought it might. They were initially out-muscled, then out-run and ultimately out-classed by an outstanding South African team. The former British Lions' player and later coach, Sir Ian McGeechan, acknowledged the 'tactical masterclass from Rassie Erasmus who completely out-thought Eddie Jones'. England were dismantled by an approach that 'was a mix of flawless planning and execution, where those massive first-up tackles worked alongside a defensive system that functioned perfectly'.[24]

'South Africa made a fast start,' stressed former England flank, Lawrence Dallaglio, 'there was an energy and resolve to everything they did from the first minute.' The English weren't allowed to settle, resulting in errors made under sustained pressure. 'England were taken to the cleaners at the set-piece' with the game played in the areas and at the tempo that South Africa wanted it to be. 'The Springbok back row were magnificent.'[25]

Flanker Pieter-Steph du Toit was amazed that England should early on run the ball from behind their own tryline: 'I just thought, "Are you guys crazy? This is a World Cup final, you don't play like this."' He recalled in an interview with BBC's Mike Henson: 'We were quite physical in that game and they were quite afraid of us. That was what the plan was.'[26]

The psychological advantage of the first half resulted from South Africa's total control of their own scrum ball. 'You play to your strengths,' opined Jamie Roberts. 'South Africa have gone back to doing that and it has won them the World Cup.' He emphasised the point that teams don't succeed at international level without an outstanding set-piece: 'They squeezed the life out of England and stopped them playing.'[27]

When reporters pressed Eddie Jones for an explanation, he admitted that he was not really sure what went wrong. 'Sometimes you never know, mate ... You can have the most investigative debrief of your game, and you still don't know what was wrong. It just happens sometimes.' He did accept that England struggled in the scrum, particularly in the first half: 'We made some personnel changes ... and got back into it but again South Africa were too strong'.[28] The beleaguered coach appeared to indicate that there wasn't much more that could have been done: 'We're now going to be kicking stones for four years.'

Stephen Jones lambasted both Eddie Jones's lame excuse and his team selection. 'Was there really nothing that England could have done?' he asked. 'The lie to that theory is given by the sight of South Africa, a known power team embarrassing England by destroying them in the scrum.' The *Sunday Times* rugby writer lamented the power, the range, the size, and the effectiveness of the Springbok props in their winning squad. In contrast, England had a player like Cole who 'was poor in the previous World Cup; Jones should have been searching avidly four years ago and brought three tight-heads'.[29]

England had fielded Kyle Sinckler as a prop at the start of the game, but he left the field with a concussion after three minutes. It will never be known whether Sinckler would have coped against Mtawarira. Stephen Jones believed it likely that he would have struggled to hold on.[30] Tom Cary provided further opinion on the subject, stating that while Sinckler was a far better player in the loose than Leicester tighthead Dan Cole, he was not a significantly better scrummager. And in a scrum that 'did not so much creak as get blown off its hinges ... it is unlikely Sinckler would have made much difference.'[31]

Woodward thought it difficult to think that England did not respect the physicality of South Africa. 'You know what's coming when you play South Africa. When the pressure is on, they revert to what's in their DNA and their fans love it, the whole place loves it. England knew what was coming but still were powerless'.[32] Toby Flood echoed the Woodward viewpoint: 'South Africa won every single physical battle. England knew they were going to bring their physicality, but it is one thing knowing it's coming and another being able to stop it.'[33]

Dan Cole was subjected to a brutal ordeal against Mtawarira, just as Phil Vickery had experienced when playing for the British Lions against South Africa at Durban in 2009. 'Back then,' asserted Chris Foy, 'the Lions were destroyed in the set-piece battle, setting the tone for a series defeat. This time, England's demise came about in much the same way.'[34] Mtawarira was on the field at Yokohama for 44 minutes but his contribution was decisive.

Woodward praised South Africa's 'bomb-squad': 'The starting props Tendai Mtawarira and Frans Malherbe were immense and when Steven Kitshoff and Vincent Koch arrived early in the second half, the Boks kept their foot on the throttle.' Woodward believed the six forwards that the South Africans used off the bench during the tournament were essentially Test starters; some people would have Malcolm Marx and Franco Mostert in their current World XV. Add to those names, François Louw, so influential against Wales in the semi-final, and it was clear the 'bomb-squad' was of great importance: 'South Africa's pack lose nothing when they come on – in fact, they often go up a notch. England just couldn't combat that.'[35]

There was of course a great deal more to the game. According to David Walsh, it wasn't just the scrum that made the difference. 'South Africa were the more composed team, they handled the ball better, created more openings, outplayed England in the air and on the ground. Most of all, they were far better dealing with the pressure that comes when trying to perform on the ultimate stage.'[36] McGeechan was impressed with the way South Africa dictated the position and pace of the breakdowns and slowed England's recycling: 'They were also clever in committing just one or two forwards to each breakdown, while England had to commit three or four.'[37]

The writers marvelled at South Africa's defence. Its structure, contended Ben Smith, appeared vulnerable but it was able to withstand immense pressure. The aggressive teamwork and organisation in defence were significant features in the unravelling of England.[38] They were also a reflection on the outstanding contribution of the Springboks' defence coach Jacques Nienaber who had worked with Erasmus for some years at the Cheetahs, the Stormers and at Munster in Ireland.

McGeechan maintained the sheer weight of tackling from the Springboks was the key to this victory. He commented on the way the South Africans – with Duane Vermeulen and Pieter-Steph du Toit particularly prominent – smashed England's ball-carriers on the gain line. This, he intimated, prevented England from building any front-foot momentum.[39]

It was all about winning wrote Roberts: 'The Springboks were disciplined, ferocious in the contact area, won the advantage line.' He compared England's performance with the previous week's semi-final where they had capitalised on the space that the All Blacks left in the wider channels. In the final, every time England tried to move the ball wide against the Springboks, 'there was nothing out there and they could not find a solution'.[40]

Scrum-half Faf de Klerk was an essential cog in the defensive pattern as he could handle any winger one-on-one. His ability to read the game gave him a distinct advantage over opponents, enabling him to make crucial split-second decisions. Ben Smith rated him highly, noting his uncanny ability to shut down overlaps even when outnumbered. 'He knows when to shoot up and take space, when to commit to the tackle and when to hold off. He rarely comes off second best and consistently wins from disadvantaged positions.'[41]

Pieter-Steph du Toit's alignment with the England fly-half, George Ford was influential. It placed additional pressure on the Englishman who was hunted and haunted mercilessly. In his analysis, Ben Smith said Du Toit had a directive to follow Ford around all night, and it seemed to play on the latter's mind and affect his confidence. Every time Ford looked up, he had Du Toit coming. As a result, he 'often shied away after the pass ... Ford looked panicked and shaken and after 49-minutes he was pulled from the field.'[42]

It did not all go South Africa's way. There was a sustained period of pressure midway through the first half when England mounted a 25-phase attack on the South African line. The Springboks were fully extended but defended superbly. They knew when to give up the penalty and, when they did, it was a defining moment in the game. England had failed to cross their line despite throwing everything into the onslaught. It served as a huge boost to South Africa's confidence. They knew then that England did not have the firepower to break down their defence.

Stephen Jones made the revealing comment that 'everything we thought we knew about England came into question'. To their credit, the English writers and indeed the nation's large rugby following, generally acknowledged that South Africa had some fine players. 'Tendai Mtawarira and company up front were ferociously good, and the two backrowers alongside Kolisi – Duane Vermeulen and Pieter-Steph du Toit – were brilliant. Willie le Roux and his wings were glorious, and Damian de Allende simply went steaming at England's midfield ... It was no contest.'[43]

There was certainly something special about De Klerk to keep a player as good as Herschel Jantjies on the bench. Another world-class performer was the athletic Eben Etzebeth, a towering figure in the line-outs and colossal in defending the advantage line. Lood de Jager and starting hooker Bongi Mbonambi were injured early on in the final but the team's strength in depth enabled them to press on seamlessly. South Africa could include six forwards in a bench strength of eight because François Steyn, the sole Springbok to have played in the World Cup win in 2007, could play virtually anywhere behind the pack. His selection was an astute move by Erasmus.

Duane Vermeulen was man of the match at the Yokohama stadium – his remorseless driving power, work in contact, presence on the ball and ability to control the back of the scrum proved invaluable. He was central to the moment when the Springboks produced possibly their most audacious rugby. 'Oh, for the purist and the analyst,' enthused Mark Keohane, 'the Springboks' midfield maul on 60 minutes was poetry.' He pointed out that 'it is hard enough to defend a lineout maul, but to defend an unstructured midfield lineout maul is impossible. It resulted in a penalty that took South Africa out to a nine-point lead.'[44]

South Africa's triumphant players were not only world champions but also top of the World Rugby rankings for the first time since 16 November 2009. The victory over England in the World Cup final saw them awarded 3.48 rating points to go from third to first. Their victory lifted their total to 94.19 points – their highest ever and 6.85 points more than when their campaign began with the side in fourth place in the rankings. New Zealand stayed second, but with an improved rating of 92.11 points. England ended the period in third place with Wales fourth.[45]

Players filtered home over several flights to be warmly welcomed and thousands greeted South Africa's Rugby World Cup-winning players when they arrived at Johannesburg's O.R. Tambo airport. Cheslin Kolbe recorded the scenes on his cellphone. Damian de Allende, with his gold medal draped round his neck, pumped his arms in the air, and Duane Vermeulen dished out high-fives to fans.[46] When Mapimpi emerged into view, he held his hands up and clasped them together as the crowd roared. His six tries at the World Cup were the second highest. 'It means a lot to me,' he revealed, 'because I'm coming from a long way.' He grew up in Tsholomnqa in the rural eastern Cape where his early years were marked by a succession of family tragedies that saw him lose his mother, his sister and his brother.[47]

Kolisi's men fully deserved their period of celebration. Jamie Roberts applauded them in the *Sunday Telegraph*:

> To lose their first game of the World Cup against the defending champions in New Zealand and then regroup and regather speaks volumes about South Africa's composure. I am so impressed by their humility, their approach to the game. On the field, they might be ruthless, brutal. But they are exceptional people.[48]

'The mythology of South Africa and the Springbok,' Mick Cleary, chief rugby writer of *The Telegraph* was moved to write, 'is an elemental experience, triggering something deep within each and every one of them.'[49]

A series of parades around the country saw thousands of supporters come together to celebrate the World Cup triumph. From Thursday to Monday, open-top bus tours took the rugby heroes through Johannesburg, Pretoria, Soweto,

Durban, East London, Port Elizabeth and Cape Town. Green and gold caps and jerseys prevailed as people lined the streets in each city to honour the conquering heroes. Lonwabo Melhwana from Khayelitsha was not surprised by their success: 'I feel like every time we have a good president, the Springboks win the world cup.' Laeticia Gamiet from Eerste River was delighted:

> What an awesome game they played … my favourite part was when Cheslin scored a try, it was amazing – as short as he is, he went through two very huge guys. I'm very proud of the Springboks and proud to be a South African. It's just great what the Bokke does for the country.[50]

Eric Songwiqi, who was Kolisi's headmaster and mentor at Emsengeni Primary and the African Bombers Rugby Club, could barely contain his pride. He summed up South Africa's emphatic Rugby World Cup victory as 'mission accomplished. I'm so ecstatic about the Bok win', adding 'by the [way] it's something I expected.'[51]

No one, however, could have imagined that the Springboks would not play again for 20 months. The Covid pandemic precluded South Africa's involvement in international rugby in 2020. Their first match was a 40–9 win over Georgia in late July 2021, but a second fixture against the tourists was cancelled because of an outbreak of infections in both camps.

The long-awaited tour by the British and Irish Lions began at the same time, with South Africa struggling on and off the field. The pandemic affected training plans and forced organisers to rearrange Test venues. There was no traditional highveld advantage for the Springboks as the matches scheduled to be played at altitude were moved to the Cape Town Stadium. Moreover, coronavirus restrictions prevented spectators from attending the games.

The Lions were better prepared after their six-nations tournament, a Test against Japan and early tour matches. It was anticipated that their superior fitness and conditioning would play a part in the tour outcome. South Africa could rely on some players who had been involved in overseas rugby but injuries prevented World Cup heroes Duane Vermeulen and R.G. Snyman from making an appearance.

A Test-strength South Africa 'A' team defeated the Lions 17–13 before the Test series began. They scored no second-half points, but their achievement was encouraging. In the first Test, the Springboks led 12–3 at half-time but went down 17–22. The contest was unpleasant and controversial, prompting Rassie Erasmus to produce an hour-long video that highlighted 26 incidents. He laid bare weaknesses in the officiating and requested 'fair treatment'.

That the Springboks should win back-to-back Tests and take the series 2–1 was a remarkable achievement and underlined the team's champion qualities.

In the second Test, they scored 21 unanswered points in a dominant second-half display to complete a 27–9 victory. The downside was that injuries prevented Pieter-Steph du Toit and Faf de Klerk from playing in the decisive third Test.

Not unexpectedly, a tense battle unfolded in a gripping finale during which the Springboks managed to grind out a victory founded on dogged resilience. Surprisingly, it had a 'fairy tale' ending. Morné Steyn returned to the side at 37 years old and landed a last-minute penalty goal that not only sealed a 19–16 victory but won the series 2–1. It was a repeat of the second Test of 2009 when he kicked the penalty that gave South Africa an unassailable 2–0 lead over Paul O'Connell's Lions.

The Springbok success was a magnificent triumph over adversity. New coach Jacques Nienaber and his assistants had lost the better part of two seasons, a period in which they were unable to develop players or implement new strategies. It was a case of relying on tried and trusted methods. Their defensive prowess – where big men such as Eben Etzebeth, Franco Mostert and Lood de Jager continued to amaze – was allied to an uncanny ability to launch scything counter-attacks.

The Springboks were criticised by the overseas media for their lack of enterprise. Yet their four tries scored by backs – Faf de Klerk, Makazole Mapimpi, Lukhanyo Am and Cheslin Kolbe – were spectacular moments. The Lions managed just two tries over the three Tests, both from driving mauls. Factor in the South Africa 'A' match and it was six tries by the hosts' backs against three by the Lions' front–row.

Jeremy Gruscott, a 1997 Lion, conceded that 'over the three matches the Springboks were very consistent, they were the better team in the end. The Lions can be generally proud but it wasn't quite good enough.'[52]

Siya Kolisi's Springboks were holders of Rugby's World Cup, the Rugby Championship and the newly awarded trophy for the Castle Lager Lions series. 'This is a special group,' commented John Smit. 'It's a Springbok team that continues to give hope to South Africa.'[53]

By the end of 2021, the Springboks had retained their world number 1 ranking, while the Blitzbokke – the 2020/21 winners of the World Rugby Sevens Series – were heading the field in the 2021/22 championship.

Notes

1   C. Kolbe, Instagram, 3 November 2020.
2   *Sport 24* (SA Rugby Podcast), 'Kolbe and Pollard lift the lid on RWC final try', 18 May 2020.
3   S. Jones, 'England bashed by jolly green giants', *Sunday Times*, 3 November 2019.
4   T. Flood, 'It's agonising', *The Mail on Sunday*, 3 November 2019.
5   *The Citizen*, 'Bok win so much bigger than rugby, says legendary Habana', 2 November 2019.

6   G. Thornley, 'Siya Kolisi: We can achieve anything if we work together', *The Irish Times*, 2 November 2019.

7   C. Ramaphosa, 'From the Desk of the President', 4 November 2019.

8   C. Ray, 'Siya Kolisi: We represent something much bigger than we can imagine', *The Guardian*, 6 June 2018.

9   *The Asahi Shimbun*, 'No burden, no pressure as Erasmus steers Boks to victory', 3 November 2019.

10   J. Linden, 'Brutal Boks destroy Eddie's World Cup dreams', *The Chronicle* (Toowoomba), 2 November 2019.

11   B. Smith, 'The players the Springboks simply cannot be without for the British and Irish Lions tour', *Rugby Pass*, 12 April 2020.

12   *The Asahi Shimbun*, 'No burden, no pressure as Erasmus steers Boks to victory', 3 November 2019.

13   J. Pye, 'Springboks' coach Rassie Erasmus says pressure is "having a relative murdered"', *Stuff* 3 November 2019.

14   S. Jones, 'Majestic England crush All Blacks to reach World Cup final', *Sunday Times*, 27 October 2019.

15   L. McConnell, 'World Cup loss wasn't the worst', 27 October 2019.

16   P. Dobson, *Doc: The Life of Danie Craven* (Cape Town: Human & Rousseau, 1994), 68.

17   J. Roberts, 'Scintillating Springboks should have the whole of rugby smacking their lips for the Lions tour', *Sunday Telegraph*, 3 November 2019.

18   N. Squires, 'South Africa boss Rassie Erasmus hails Siya Kolisi ahead of Rugby World Cup final', *Daily Express*, 2 November 2019; *The Herald* (Zimbabwe), 31 October 2019.

19   *BBC Sport*, 31 October 2019; A. Spink, 'Rugby World Cup final: England dream dies in 32-12 battering by South Africa', *Daily Mirror*, 3 November 2019.

20   *Daily Mail*, 29 October 2019.

21   *BBC Sport*, 'Who will win the Rugby World Cup?', 1 November 2019.

22   B. Starling, 'It wasn't supposed to be like this: Red rose wilts in the glare of the final spotlight', *Sunday Telegraph*, 3 November 2019.

23   E. Jones, *BBC Sport*, 1 November 2019.

24   I. McGeechan, 'Tactical masterclass from Erasmus keeps rivals guessing', *Sunday Telegraph*, 3 November 2019.

25   L. Dallaglio, 'No need to panic', *Sunday Times*, 3 November 2019.

26   M. Henson, 'Pieter-Steph du Toit: South African questions England's Rugby World Cup final tactics', *BBC Sport*, 2 October 2020.

27   J. Roberts, 'Scintillating Springboks should have the whole of rugby smacking their lips for the Lions tour', *Sunday Telegraph*, 3 November 2019.

28   D. Walsh, 'Crushed', *Sunday Times*, 3 November 2019; T. Morgan, 'Jones future uncertain after he admits: "I don't know why we lost"', *Sunday Telegraph*, 3 November 2019; W. Kelleher, 'We will live with this pain for four years, says Jones', *The Mail on Sunday*, 3 November 2019.

29   S. Jones, 'Inspirational, yes, but some of Eddie's decision-making was just plain wrong', *Sunday Times*, 3 November 2019.

30   S. Jones, 'Cole has been a warrior but he collapsed under the pressure', *Sunday Times*, 3 November 2019.

31   T. Cary, 'Erasmus and Kolisi conjure a day of hope for a troubled land', *Sunday Telegraph*, 3 November 2019.

32   C. Woodward, 'England got the basics wrong. It's that simple', *The Mail on Sunday*, 3 November 2019.

33   T. Flood, 'It's agonising', *The Mail on Sunday*, 3 November 2019.

34   C. Foy, 'The Beast has worked all his career for this: now Tendai can go out on a high', *The Mail on Sunday*, 3 November 2019.

35   C. Woodward, 'England got the basics wrong. It's that simple', *The Mail on Sunday*, 3 November 2019.

36   D. Walsh, 'Crushed', *Sunday Times*, 3 November 2019.

37   I. McGeechan, 'Tactical masterclass from Erasmus keeps rivals guessing', *Sunday Telegraph*, 3 November 2019.

38   See B. Smith, 'The players the Springboks simply cannot be without for the British and Irish Lions tour', *Rugby Pass*, 12 April 2020; B. Smith, Analysis: What the Springboks did to dismantle England's attack', *Rugby Pass*, 6 November 2019.

39   I. McGeechan, 'Tactical masterclass from Erasmus keeps rivals guessing', *Sunday Telegraph*, 3 November 2019.

40   J. Roberts, 'Scintillating Springboks should have the whole of rugby smacking their lips for the Lions tour', *Sunday Telegraph*, 3 November 2019.

41   B. Smith, 'The players the Springboks simply cannot be without for the British and Irish Lions tour', *Rugby Pass*, 12 April 2020; B. Smith, Analysis: What the Springboks did to dismantle England's attack', *Rugby Pass*, 6 November 2019.

42   B. Smith, Analysis: What the Springboks did to dismantle England's attack', *Rugby Pass*, 6 November 2019.

43   S. Jones, 'England bashed by jolly green giants', *Sunday Times*, 3 November 2019.

44   M. Keohane and M. Greenaway, 'Our magical Springbok moments from the Rugby World Cup 2019 final', *IOL News*, 4 November 2019.

45   *RWC 2019 News*, 'Springboks on Top of the World', 4 November 2019.

46   *Times of India*, 'Springboks come home to rapturous welcome', 6 November 2019.

47   *Sowetan*, 'Record try-scorer Mapimpi's come a long way', 4 November 2019.

48   J. Roberts, 'Scintillating Springboks should have the whole of rugby smacking their lips for the Lions tour', *Sunday Telegraph*, 3 November 2019.

49   M. Cleary, 'Shell-shocked England are battered by power of Springboks', *Sunday Telegraph*, 3 November 2019.

50   N. Daniels, 'Capetonians overwhelmed with pride after Springboks win Rugby World Cup', *Cape Times*, 4 November 2019.

51   *News 24*, 'From Zwide to World Cup champion: The Siya Kolisi story', 5 November 2019.

52   *Sport 24*, 'Colossal effort took Kolisi's Springboks to triumph, says 2009 skipper Smit', 8 August 2021.

53   Ibid.

2

The Origins of Rugby at the Cape

> Such ostentatious pursuit of leisure during
> 'working hours' was a mark of social standing, a
> token of the newly desirable masculinity.[1]

> – N. Worden, E. van Heyningen and V. Bickford-Smith

The earliest recorded football match to have been staged in South Africa was played in front of the original site of Siya Kolisi's alma mater in Port Elizabeth. An announcement was made on Friday, 23 May 1862, in the 'Local and General' column of the *Eastern Province Herald*:

> Foot Ball – The old game of Foot Ball is again to be revived here. We are informed that the first game of the season will be played on Saturday afternoon next, in front of the Grey Institute at three o'clock. Saturday is a capital day for such sports and the pleasure to be derived from witnessing this game will doubtless induce many of our townsfolk to be present.[2]

The wording 'again to be revived here' suggests previous matches had been played and this fixture was merely 'the first game of the season'.

Little is known about the match which was played between 'colonial-born' and 'home-born'. Photographs that were taken of the two teams indicate an 18-a-side encounter, but there is no record of the score. A further report appeared in the *Eastern Province Herald* on Tuesday, 10 June, but did little more than confirm that the match had taken place 'on the Hill in front of the Grey Institute'.[3]

Three months later, on Saturday 23 August 1862, the first recorded football match to take place in Cape Town was played. It was some years before the establishment of formal football clubs. The *Cape Argus* stated:

Foot-ball – We are happy to find that this fine old English school game has been introduced among us. On Saturday next sides consisting of fifteen officers of the army and a like number of gentlemen in the civil service will open the Ball with a game on the race-course at Green Point. Of course, this example will be speedily followed, and we shall have foot-ball treading closely on the kibes [blistered heels] of cricket and our other imported manly games.[4]

The newspaper later announced that 'this is the first time within our recollection that so large a party of gentlemen have made a public appearance at Cape Town in this manly English school-game'.[5] The writer would almost certainly have taken into account that the Diocesan College had started its own game the previous year and that the military might have kicked a ball in the area at some stage.

Links with the 'Mother Country' feature prominently in the *Cape Argus* report of the match at Green Point. His Excellency the Governor, Sir Philip Wodehouse, and the Colonial Secretary, Lieutenant-Colonel Jenner, were in attendance, and it is recalled the game involved 'Eton, Rugby, Winchester, Marlborough and other schools'. Radley might be added to the list: John X. Merriman – a member of the Civil Service team and future prime minister of the Cape – had 'played an early version of football' at the Oxfordshire school.[6] Adriaan van der Byl, the most prominent sportsman amongst the local footballers, had initially attended Marlborough College, a rugby-playing school, before transferring to Merchiston Castle in Scotland. He captained his new school against Edinburgh's Royal High in the first inter-school rugby match in 1858, an historic occasion when not all the boys were able to 'fully understand all [Rugby's] rather complex rules'.[7]

The products of public schools who gathered at Green Point would have brought with them different interpretations of football. It did not adversely affect their game, the match report doing much to reflect a happy occasion. They played for an hour and 45 minutes in front of a large crowd, before deciding to stop play and to continue another day. Those participating in the keenly contested but goalless draw probably drew inspiration from the football chapter in *Tom Brown's Schooldays*, a remarkably successful book that first appeared in 1857. The *Cape Argus* report echoed the writing of Thomas Hughes in recalling 'over and over again did the combatants roll in their brave charges; over and over again did the unerring drop kick of the goalkeepers save the game as those terrible rushing outsiders swept past ... We have never seen so thoroughly plucky a game.'[8]

To commemorate the match, a poem – 'The Ballad of Mauliana' – was published. It was based on Tennyson's 'Ballad of Oriana' and from the opening lines we gather the Civilian team wore long white flannel trousers and magenta-coloured shirts:

> My belt was braced, my heart was light,
> Mauliana!
> Ere I 'sailed-in' to the fight-
> Mauliana!
> With flannel bags my legs were dight,
> My shirt's hue was magenta bright-
> Mauliana!
> In short, I was a glorious sight,
> Mauliana!
> Van der Byl started the foot-ball,
> Mauliana!
> His crest shone first among us all ...[9]

The *Cape Argus* reporter hoped to see a 'display of strength and science worthy of *Tom Brown's Schooldays*' when the civil service and military met in a return match at Green Point on Friday, 5 September. The game was umpired by the colonial secretary and 'watched by a large party of ladies and gentlemen in carriages and on horseback'. It was easier to follow play as the goals were 'placed 100 yards asunder, instead of the 150, as in the former contest'. The report recalled the officers winning by two goals after three-quarters of an hour and then embarking on a 'third struggle [which] ended at sunset uncompleted.'[10]

It is quite possible that these early matches at the Cape made use of Rugby's rules. Van der Byl, who was described as 'the very best man' in the second match, would almost certainly have put his case forward. Participants in the match would also have been aware of *Tom Brown's Schooldays* and the opportunity to play under similar rules might well have had some appeal, an assertion that is supported by press reports.

In Cape Town, the success of the first football at Green Point encouraged further encounters, with one report marvelling at the playing of games on various days during the week and 'at any time of the year'. It claimed that 'such ostentatious pursuit of leisure during "working hours" was a mark of social standing, a token of the newly desirable masculinity'.[11] It was a time when rules were settled shortly before kick-off and depended to a great extent on the backgrounds of men who comprised teams such as Town and Country, Officers and Civilians, the Civil Service and All-comers, and the Diocesan College and 11th Regiment. Some ambiguity was inevitable, with one interpretation going so far as to state that 'the earliest forms of the game in South Africa resembled both the chaotic, rowdy football of nineteenth-century English public schools and universities and the pre-industrial "folk" game of artisans, apprentices, and rural workers'.[12]

The different football codes in Britain were also struggling to reach a consensus. Although the Football Association (FA) was formed in 1863, it was not until April 1877 that one set of laws was finally achieved.[13] The new body struggled to make an impact and 'was not a very powerful organisation in the 1860s and 1870s. The young men who had set it up were not sure what they wanted or what the eventual outcome would be.'[14] FA rules still allowed handling the ball, which demonstrated 'not only the fluid state of the various rules of football at this time but also how little difference the FA's formation made to the game'.[15]

Rugby had comparatively fewer difficulties in establishing a coherent structure in Britain and, by the time its ruling body was formed in 1871, it was the dominant football code. In standardising its rules, the Rugby Football Union (RFU) removed some of the more violent aspects of the Rugby School game, notably 'hacking'.

At far-away Diocesan College in Cape Town, another game developed when the headmaster, Canon George Ogilvie, introduced a mixture of Winchester and Bradfield rules in 1861. Ogilvie had been a pupil at Winchester, where the field was narrow and dribbling was 'unpermissible'. On his appointment as a second master at the newly founded Bradfield College in the early 1850s, he was almost certainly required to address the question of dribbling. It 'was the chief feature of the Bradfield game', but Ogilvie probably discouraged it for the two-and-a-half years he was there.[16]

The Bradfield College archivist, Lucy Norman, commented on Ogilvie's stint at Bradfield:

> After his departure, the school began to play the early FA rules against teams from Oxford University and other schools; handling of the ball gradually fell out of favour. The version of the game that went to South Africa with Ogilvie included handling and this feature was retained as football there developed along different lines.[17]

Ogilvie preferred Winchester's rule not to permit dribbling and he did not wish it to become part of a form of football that the Cape boys called 'Gog's game or Gogball' – names relating to the only legible letters of his signature.[18]

Canon H.E. Morris, who knew Ogilvie well, said that there were no written rules of the Winchester game in Cape Town and 'as the rules had been so much altered that no one would have recognised them, there were frequent disputes'.[19] This was evidently the case in a match between the Garrison and Bishops on 9 June 1869. The schoolboys won in an hour by three goals to nil. The military were unhappy about the result and Captain Sandford forwarded 11 rules to the *Cape Argus* so that players could be assisted in future matches.[20]

Ogilvie has been compared to Marlborough's George Cotton who believed organised games would 'instil a common endeavour which would strengthen school feeling and, at the same time, encourage good behaviour and discipline'.[21] It was no different at the Diocesan College, where Ogilvie was confronted by 'pupils who had the run of a wild estate and were themselves wild'.[22] He soon joined their cricket (which had been introduced earlier) and then challenged the boys at football. According to Paul Dobson, there were no written rules for 'Gog's game', 'but as the inventor was also a player that problem was probably overcome, probably amicably, as the good Canon believed in sportsmanship'.[23]

Jack Heyneman, president of the SA Rugby Football Board during 1913–27, recalled playing 'Old Gog's Game' and thought it 'was really a glorified hallelujah of kicking shins'.[24] John Reid, who went to Bishops in 1868, disagreed, claiming 'it may be considered heresy to say so, but the old game was more scientific than, and far superior to either rugby union or association, combining as it did most of the best points of each game, though possibly it may have been more dangerous'.[25]

John James Graham, who was from Grahamstown – the town named after his grandfather – wrote an article 'Evolution of Rugby at the Cape'. He was not a student under 'Gog' but said he was often involved in both cricket and football against Bishops, and also played under the headmaster's leadership in cricket matches against naval and military teams. In the *Cape Times* of 5 April 1927, he wrote:

> In the early days, the rules of football were in a state of flux. At St Andrew's College where I learnt the game under the Reverend George Cotterill, a Cambridge blue in both cricket and football, we played a modified form of what were known as the Shrewsbury rules; dribbling was an important feature in that code, especially as handling or running with the ball was not permitted except after a fair catch ... When I came to Cape Town in 1870, I found to my disgust that the rules played under Canon Ogilvie's influence barred dribbling ... Hacking, or as Mr Heyneman calls it, 'kicking shins', was allowed at that time at the Diocesan College as it was at St Andrew's, Grahamstown generally, but somehow or other we managed to win through without serious mishaps in that practice ... Football was also played at Green Point, generally on what was part of its old racetrack ... We were faced with great disadvantages there: the

ground was full of holes and in winter the field was flanked by pools of water. Recalling those days, I have often wondered how we carried on peacefully, for we played without referee or umpire of any sort.[26]

A crucial development occurred in 1873 when John Graham advocated the need to establish a uniform code of laws for playing football in Cape Town and its suburbs. He was a respected 26-year-old who had been appointed as assistant registrar in the Supreme Court of the Colony. He was also from a distinguished background: a descendant of the old Scottish kings, he became the 15th Graham of Fintry on his father's death. And on his grandmother's side, he was a descendant of Jacob Klute, the first permanent settler at the Cape who, it is said, landed in 1652 with Jan van Riebeeck.

Graham chaired a committee formed to establish a set of uniform football laws. It met on 27 May 1873, with delegates from Civilians (William Harwell), Civil Service (Clarke Thwaites/John Graham), the Diocesan College (William Hopley) and the South African College (Johan Gie). Graham had been exposed to various codes of football, but at least one committee member, 19-year-old Hopley – later a judge and father of an England rugby international – would have known of Ogilvie's creation.

The game decided upon and referred to simply as 'foot-ball' was based on no more than the 15 rules that were published in the *Standard and Mail*. It borrowed from existing codes but reflected local influence and preference. Much that existed in Gog's game would have been considered and utilised in establishing the rules, although Winchester's narrow pitch was not in evidence as dimensions of up to 200 yards by 100 yards were allowed. Goals were won when the ball was kicked 'between the goal posts at any height'; the ball could be handled in certain circumstances, such as after a fair catch, with dribbling, marks, free kicks, tackling, and scrimmages or 'hots' playing their part.[27] Hacking and tripping were no longer allowed.[28]

The decision by the Cape to establish its own form of football was a practical necessity and not a case of players liberating themselves in the light of the Cape Parliament's acceptance of responsible government in 1872. It largely resembled an earlier situation in Australia where ten not dissimilar rules had been instituted by the Melbourne Football Club in 1859. The founders of football in Melbourne, explained Tony Collins, 'saw themselves as being no less British than those living in Britain. They were merely engaging in the same discussions about how football should be played that were taking place among British footballers at the same time.'[29]

At the Cape, the new rules were implemented immediately, and subsequently used by clubs when they were first established in 1875. Institutionalising the game ensured greater control in a programme that involved matches being played virtually every Saturday during the winter months. The first inter-club season featured teams from the two colleges (which offered university courses and therefore attracted older students), Hamilton's, Green Point, Gardens and the Country Club (later Western Province Club), as well as the traditional Civil Service versus All-comers and Town versus Country. Late in the season, a new side from Stellenbosch was praised by the *Daily News and General Advertiser* for 'their pluck, by challenging, in their infancy, a club of so long-standing as the Civil Service Club'.[30]

With added entertainment often provided by the band of the 24th Regiment, the football field was a place to be on Saturday afternoons.

The first two seasons of the newly instituted game were problem-free but, when Graham left for Grahamstown in 1876, members of the Western Province Club challenged the Cape rules. They declared an interest in playing Rugby's rules, thereby forcing a split within the club. A group led by Howard Jones remained loyal to Graham's game and a meeting was called to form the breakaway Villager Football Club.

Rugby had a strong following in Britain and was expected to attract interest at the Cape. 'The adherents of Rugby rules,' wrote Collins, 'had both the certainty of Arnoldian self-belief and the public profile generated by the success of *Tom Brown's Schooldays* … The class identification of Rugby School football and Muscular Christianity also gave the code a resonance beyond the British Isles.'[31] Western Province Club players such as Louis Péringuey (an entomologist who became director of the South African Museum), Eustace Pillans (a noted horticulturalist and contributor to the Natural History Museum) and William Finlay (an astronomer at the Royal Observatory who discovered Comet Finlay in the solar system) enjoyed their rugby but underestimated the opposition to changing football codes at the Cape.

On 15 July 1876, the Western Province Club hosted Villager's at Rondebosch. The *Cape Times* described the match as 'not by any means a successful performance. Rugby union rules were adopted for the afternoon (and we hope for the last time).' The newspaper emphasised the unhappy circumstances of a clash in which 'even those who professed to propound the rules seemed to possess very hazy notions indeed of their first principles'. It added, somewhat disconcertingly for the future of rugby: 'It is not at all surprising under the circumstances that many of the players at the conclusion of the game should have openly declared their intention never to use this code again.'[32]

The *Daily News* reinforced this assessment. It claimed 'the old players did not appear to enjoy the spectacle nor to approve of the changes introduced. We fancy the new game will hardly be a very popular one at the Cape.'[33]

Frederick York St Leger, editor of the *Cape Times*, empathised with localised football and its contribution towards fostering feelings of community identity. He stated that the Cape had developed its own 'well-known game, which has grown up in the colony, has its own peculiarities, and has been called football; its principles are generally understood by young South Africa'. His report concluded: 'It certainly seems to be a mistake to introduce a new game in place of the old one, unless some particular advantage can be shown in the proposed code.'[34]

A lively debate ensued, with letters reflecting views on issues such as rules, a preference for the dribbling over handling code and the dangers of playing Rugby's rules. One writer pointed out that the simple structuring of Cape rules made more sense than the 'fifty-nine' compiled to play rugby. Another conceded 'the union rules are a degree less harassing than those used at Rugby School' but then claimed, 'they labour under the great objection that the ball is more often carried than kicked'.

Concern was expressed that the Western Province Club had allowed hacking and 'a few gentlemen suffered from "shinners"'. Perhaps it was a desire to prove a point against opponents who had defected from the club less than two weeks earlier, or the chance to demonstrate a sense of masculinity that other codes lacked. There was certainly truth in the assessment that the rules of Rugby as applied in the match at Rondebosch were 'a little too severe for those who have neither seen nor played them before'.

'Old Rugbeian' referred to Charles Alcock's *Football Annual* in arguing that his game should prevail at the Cape because in Britain more clubs 'use the [Rugby] union rules than all the others put together'. 'Floreat Rugby Union' forwarded lists of clubs, universities and schools that played rugby and, when 'JB' challenged the veracity of his claims, a threat was issued that the matter would be taken to the query column of *Bell's Life*.[35]

The ever-present 'Home' factor could not be discounted in a society where 'deference in all cultural matters, including sport, went to Britain and British institutions and authorities'.[36] And, amidst the raging debate, 'Old Rugbeian' identified the crucial weakness in the Cape game when he stated it was 'difficult to say' under what rules the game was played – they did not comply with any known English brand.[37]

St Leger, who gained a reputation as 'the mouthpiece for imperialism', pondered the significance of 'Old Rugbeian's' argument.[38] The *Cape Times* was aware of sport's place in the cultural exchange developing within the empire. They published details of Australia's achievements in their cricket matches against English teams at home and abroad during 1877/78, and there was generous coverage of other British sports, such as the boat race, intervarsities and rugby 'Test' matches. St Leger also realised there was no reason why South Africa could not forge highly visible links with the Mother Country and become part of an imperial sporting network.

The administrative support that St Leger gave to games was complemented by a growing belief in their value as a force for the 'Englishness' he advanced. 'The new English-language journals of the 1870s,' says Vivian Bickford-Smith, 'were, unlike the [Cape] Argus, unashamedly jingoistic'. St Leger and the editors of the Lantern became the prime mobilisers of a 'more assertive Englishness in the Colony', a development attributable to 'imperial intervention in southern Africa and opposition to that intervention'.[39] Initiatives aimed at bringing about a confederated South Africa under the British flag saw the Transvaal Republic annexed in 1877 and the Africans defeated in Natal and the eastern Cape.

Although rugby was the preferred English code, its support base was in disarray. The game needed a champion and, miraculously, he arrived in late 1877. William Milton was a product of Marlborough College during a glorious period in its rugby history when an impressive number of England internationals were produced. He played at a time when the drop-kick was one of the leading features of the game and, it was argued, formed 'a prettier incident in the play than the latter-day system of passing'. In a history of the college, Milton was singled out as one of three 'safe-footed kickers [who] would sometimes with their sweeping drops keep the ball flying to and fro over the forwards for some five or six turns, till a short kick or a plucky charge brought it once more into general play'.[40]

Two years after leaving school, the nineteen-year-old Milton was selected for England in the twenty-a-side matches against Scotland and Ireland in 1874/75. His involvement in the game since he began playing at Marlborough spanned periods before and after the establishment of the RFU and, it is stated in an Australian publication, that he and the Scottish international Hugh Hamilton were instrumental in initiating the 'passing game'.[41] They had played together at school and for one of England's leading clubs, Marlborough Nomads.

Tall and well built, Milton cut an imposing figure and had clearly been a very good player. Arthur Budd, an England international who became president of the RFU in 1888/89, commented on the leading players of the 1871–84 period: Harold Freeman, a great goal-dropper and a powerful runner, was the most celebrated three-quarter of his time. The most distinguished halves were

Stephen Finney and W.H. Milton. The most famous forwards were Frederick Stokes, C.W. Crosse and F.H. Lee.[42]

Milton arrived in Cape Town at the height of the boom during 1875–82. The discovery of diamonds had quickened the growth of the Cape's economy and also encouraged people to move to the city from the agricultural hinterland. Cape Town's municipal population rose from 33 000 to 40 000 between 1875 and 1880, making it the largest city in southern Africa.[43]

There was much in Milton's favour. If products of the public schools did not make the empire, they 'at least maintained and administered it through their members'.[44] Moreover, a reputation as 'a punishing bat' and the honour of being an England rugby international served as useful qualifications in a distant outpost of empire.[45] Milton was also fortunate that his father's cousin and famous Victorian novelist, Anthony Trollope, was visiting South Africa in order to write a book. Admittance to the more influential Cape society was made possible through Trollope, who was regarded as a celebrity and attracted considerable press coverage. Sir Henry Barkly, the late governor of the Cape Colony, provided 'with great minuteness a sketch of [Trollope's journey] as, in his opinion, it ought to be made'. Trollope was also able to acknowledge 'the great courtesy' he received from Sir Bartle Frere, the high commissioner for southern Africa.[46] Such links made a visit to the country a great deal more comfortable than it might have been, but it was Trollope's close association with the permanent under-colonial secretary, Captain Charles Mills, that would pave the way for Milton to obtain a position in the Cape civil service.

For a young white man such as Milton, the accepted meeting place in an alien land was the sports club, which served to integrate new arrivals into Cape Town society. Within months of his arrival at the Cape, he was prominent in the development of rugby and cricket – games that would play a crucial role in the evolution of southern African society. He gained a foothold in the administration of cricket, having been elected secretary/treasurer of Cape Town's premier Western Province Cricket Club. Then, in the ensuing winter, he joined the Villager Football Club. Sport and club committees helped him build a social network that he would use to advantage in achieving his goals.

Milton was keen to emulate what was happening at 'home'. This appealed to St Leger who appreciated the young man's value as a player of international status and his capacity for hard work. Milton's efforts to develop Wynberg as a cricket venue attracted favourable publicity in the *Cape Times*, and when football started, he received support because he was regarded as a voice of authority.

He was possibly aware that a fellow Marlburian, J.J. Sewell, was the prime mover in the first recorded 'rugby' match in Natal. It was a drawn encounter between J.J. Sewell's XV and C.A. Hall's XV at Alexandra Park in June 1877. Sewell adopted a formation of 'ten forwards, three half-backs and two backs' against Hall's 'nine forwards, one full-back, two half-backs, two quarter-backs and a three-quarter back'. The strange arrangement was compounded by there being 'no umpires for the game and disputes lasted quite some time as everybody, not just the captain, had his say'.[47]

Persuading the Cape to play rugby was no easy task. It was well known that the Western Province Club had failed in its attempt to introduce the game, culminating in its football section folding in early 1877. Furthermore, the Villager's committee did not wish to instigate trouble and initially demonstrated a reluctance to even consider the question of rugby. There was enjoyment in playing the Cape's version of football and the youth of the city were content to continue a game they had learnt at school.

Milton liked to have his way and discovered some interest in rugby at Hamilton's. Clubs were administered by young men, and 23-year-old Milton was able to enlist the support of 21-year-old Billy Simkins who was born in London 'within the sound of Bow Bells', and had become the key figure at Hamilton's. They worked together in the civil service and shared a passion for sport, fitting the mould of youthful officialdom that was commonplace in British rugby. Huw Richards wrote of two consequences: 'long careers' and 'to give substance to rhetoric about the game being run for players. In time, this became tired and irksome – not least to the alleged beneficiaries – but in the early days it was based in reality.'[48]

Towards the end of July 1878, Milton and Simkins were responsible for organising a match under Rugby's rules. Hamilton's hosted Villager's at Green Point in a game in which opponents of the code, such as Howard Jones and his brother, Walter, did not participate. It was a one-off arrangement as Villager's played under Cape rules in their remaining fixtures. A point was nevertheless made, and Milton sought to reaffirm his intentions by opting not to play the local version of football. In August he received strong backing for his stand when the *Cape Times* announced: 'At a meeting recently held in connection with the Hamilton Football Club to decide whether the old rules as heretofore played or the rugby union should be the standing rules of the club, we were glad to find that the new rules were unanimously adopted.'[49]

Momentum had switched dramatically in favour of rugby. In late September, the *Cape Times* reported that the last match of the season would see Milton's United Services play Hamilton's at rugby.[50] A public relations exercise, it gave rugby the last word before the long South African summer.

The situation concerning the conflicting winter codes needed to be addressed. In 1878, John Graham returned from his stint in the eastern Cape to become chief clerk to the attorney-general in the capital and clerk of the peace for the city. He was also called upon to determine the direction that football would follow in the Western Province.

Graham and Milton met on several occasions before the new rugby season began. They played cricket together during the summer, notably for the Civil Service against All-comers at Wynberg on Boxing Day. Also in attendance was Advocate Shepstone Giddy, a pro-rugby member of Villager's who had learnt the game at Christ's College, Finchley, and was keen to promote its cause in South Africa. The leading figures at Villager's formulated their plan of action in good time. Howard Jones agreed to hold the annual general meeting at his home in Stanmore (which later became part of the Diocesan College Preparatory School) and St Leger provided a front-page advertisement in the *Cape Times*.[51]

Symbolically, the meeting in May 1879 marked the end of Cape rules. Milton wrote: 'John Graham moved, and I seconded a resolution that the Villager's should play under rugby union rules. That was unanimously agreed to: and was the real beginning of the rugby union game in the Cape.'[52]

Graham recalled Milton later and reminded him that

> a meeting was held in a small schoolroom in Rondebosch (called I think the Oak Hall) to consider the adoption of a definite code of rules and that he proposed, and I seconded that Rugby should be accepted ... Mr Heyneman is quite right in giving credit to Sir William for the successful introduction of the new rules, for he pushed them in his masterly fashion, and they were soon followed generally.[53]

It did not really matter whether Milton or Graham proposed the resolution that they play rugby as they had planned the meeting together. The former's impact and meticulous preparation, however, was such that opponents to the change – notably Ogilvie at Bishops – would soon give way. 'The game,' according to Heyneman, 'was really introduced into South Africa by Joey Milton ... I remember him saying to me: "Jack, it's a good game but you must get your colleges and schools to take it up."'[54]

Milton and Graham – both knighted in later years – were sufficiently influential to carry the players with them, the latter setting an example by participating in the game even after he was appointed as secretary of law.[55] The period of transition was also assisted by unprecedented coverage in the *Cape Times* during the 1879 season. The report of 18 June 1879 on the opening fixtures began:

If anyone had entertained any doubt whether the good old English game of football had taken root on African soil, a visit to the Camp-ground at Rondebosch last Saturday would speedily have dispelled it. No less than ten fifteens of various ages and sizes had come out in jerseys and flannels ready and equipped to wipe out old scores or win fresh laurels ...

The newspaper did not mention that the junior teams were not as yet playing to Rugby's rules.[56] The Diocesan College opposed the switch to the new game in 1879 but thereafter struggled to find opponents. Headmaster Ogilvie first refused and then gave grudging permission for his school to play rugby, stating, 'Well, if you boys want to kill yourselves, do so!'[57] The irony is that 'Steele and two others [at the College] had legs broken in 1879' whilst engaged in a non-rugby code.[58]

Notes

1   N. Worden, E. van Heyningen and V. Bickford-Smith, *Cape Town: The Making of a City* (Cape Town: David Philip, 1998), 197.
2   *Eastern Province Herald*, 23 May 1862.
3   Ibid., 10 June 1862. The Hill overlooks Algoa Bay where the 1820 settlers landed and is now part of the area known as the Donkin Reserve, named after an early acting governor, Sir Rufane Shaw Donkin.
4   *Cape Argus*, 21 August 1862.
5   Ibid., 26 August 1862.
6   P. Lewsen, *John X. Merriman: Paradoxical South African Statesman* (New Haven: Yale University Press, 1982), 11.
7   'Rugby Notes', in *Merchiston Castle School Register, 1833–1903*.
8   *Cape Argus*, 25 August 1862.
9   *Cape Times*, 10 April 1937.
10   *Cape Argus*, 8 September 1862.
11   Worden, Van Heyningen and Bickford-Smith, *Cape Town*, 197.
12   P. Alegi, *Laduma! Soccer, Politics and Society in South Africa* (Scottsville: University of KwaZulu-Natal Press, 2004), 16.
13   T. Mason, *Association Football and English Society 1863–1915* (Brighton: Harvester Press, 1980), 15.
14   C. Eisenberg, P. Lanfanchi, T. Mason and A. Wahl (eds), *100 Years of Football : The FIFA Centennial Book* (London: Weidenfeld & Nicolson, 2004), 18.
15   T. Collins, *A Social History of English Rugby Union* (Abingdon: Routledge, 2009), 15.
16   J. Blackie, *Bradfield 1850–1975* (Bradfield: Bradfield College, 1976), 42; L. Norman, 'Bradfield', in M. Tozer (ed.), *Puddings, Bullies & Squashes: Early Public School Football Codes* (Truro: Sunnyrest Books, 2020), 26.
17   Norman, 'Bradfield', 36.
18   P. Dobson, *Bishops Rugby: A History* (Cape Town: Don Nelson, 1990), 12, 19.
19   I. Difford (ed.), *The History of South African Rugby Football 1875–1932* (Wynberg: Speciality Press, 1933), 700.
20   *Cape Argus*, 12 June 1869.
21   G. Lenehan, 'Marlborough', in M. Tozer (ed.), *Puddings, Bullies & Squashes: Early Public School Football Codes* (Truro: Sunnyrest Books, 2020), 263.
22   Dobson, *Bishops*, 21.
23   P. Dobson, *Rugby in South Africa: A History 1861–1988* (Cape Town: SARB, 1989), 19.
24   *Cape Times*, 30 March 1927.
25   Dobson, *Rugby in South Africa*, 17.
26   *Cape Times*, 5 April 1927.

27 The term 'hots' was used to describe a melee at both Winchester and Bradfield.

28 *Standard and Mail*, 7 June 1873.

29 Collins, *A Social History of English Rugby*, 16.

30 *Daily News and General Advertiser*, 21 August 1875, referred to in F. van der Merwe's 'The First Football in the Cape and the Emergence of the Stellenbosch Rugby Football Club'.

31 Collins, *A Social History of English Rugby*, 16.

32 *Cape Times*, 18 July 1876.

33 *Daily News*, 18 July 1876.

34 *Cape Times*, 18 July 1876.

35 Ibid., 20 July–4 August 1876.

36 D. Black and J. Nauright, *Rugby and the South African Nation: Sport, Cultures, Politics and Power in the Old and New South Africa* (Manchester: Manchester University Press, 1998), 25.

37 *Cape Times*, 4 August 1876.

38 Worden, Van Heyningen and Bickford-Smith, *Cape Town*, 218.

39 V. Bickford-Smith, *Ethnic Pride and Racial Prejudice in Victorian Cape Town: Group Identity and Social Practice 1875–1902* (Cambridge: Cambridge University Press, 1995), 40, 50.

40 A. Bradley, A. Champneys and J. Baines, *A History of Marlborough College during Fifty Years from its Foundation to the Present Time* (London: John Murray, 1893), 269.

41 *Sydney Morning Herald*, 12 August 1930; H. Holt, *Australian Dictionary of Biography*, Volume 9, (Melbourne: Australian National University Press, 1983), 175–176.

42 S. Jones and N. Cain, *Behind the Rose: Playing Rugby for England* (Edinburgh: Birlinn, 2014), 5.

43 Bickford-Smith, *Ethnic Pride and Racial Prejudice*, 11.

44 J. Mangan, *The Games Ethic and Imperialism* (Harmondsworth: Viking, 1985), 21.

45 *Cricket: A Weekly Record*, 12 May 1892.

46 A. Trollope, *South Africa (Volume I)* reprint (Stroud: Nonsuch Publishing, 2005), 12.

47 *Natal Witness*, 26 June 1877.

48 H. Richards, *A Game for Hooligans: The History of Rugby Union* (Edinburgh: Mainstream Publishing, 2006), 42.

49 *Cape Times*, 21 August 1878.

50 Ibid., 21 September 1878.

51 Ibid., 10 May 1879.

52 Difford, *The History of South African Rugby Football*, 457.

53 *Cape Times*, 5 April 1927.

54 Ibid., 30 March 1927.

55 *South African Law Journal*, 4 January 1906, pp.361–364. Graham received the CMG in 1899 and was knighted six years later.

56 *Cape Times*, 18 June 1879.

57 Dobson, *Rugby in South Africa*, 20.

58 *Cape Times*, 9 July 1883.

3

Rugby, Soccer and Segregation at the Cape during the Nineteenth Century

Affiliation to the Union shall be open only to such clubs as shall consist entirely of European players.[1]

– Western Province Rugby Football Union

A feature of society during the late nineteenth century was the significance and fluidity of the main individuals involved in sport and politics. William Milton and Billy Simkins built on the niche they had carved for themselves in rugby history. Milton's sporting focus, however, switched to cricket and the Western Province Cricket Club (CC) where he became the dominant personality. The club operated in a fashion after London's Marylebone Cricket Club (MCC) and served as a retreat where the English could escape an alien culture and celebrate an imperial lifestyle with fellow expatriates. Milton captained the South African side, arranged the first tours to the country, controlled the administration of the game at provincial and national levels, and shouldered responsibility for the establishment of Newlands. His growing reputation brought him into contact with Cecil John Rhodes, an alliance that shaped the direction that South African sport would take.

Simkins, who served Milton loyally in both rugby and cricket, was heartened by his own early accession of status and became an ambitious sports administrator. He not only headed Western Province's rugby and cricket for varying periods but was president of the SA Rugby Football Board for 23 years until 1913. A quintessential Englishman who was passionate about rowing at the Alfred Club on Table Bay, he established a stockbroking business in the early 1880s. He also came under the influence of J.H. 'Onze Jan' Hofmeyr, the Afrikaner Bond leader whose political stance encouraged the recruitment of Englishmen as a testament to the Bond's success. Progress was reflected through securing equality between the two white races: 'If we shall follow this path we shall become one volk.'[2]

With the advent of organised Afrikaner politics from the late 1870s, they were 'well poised to take advantage of their numerical superiority and to make their mark on the colonial state'.[3] Hofmeyr worked towards Afrikaner solidarity but created a party with moderate views that became the most powerful single force in Parliament. Rhodes acknowledged the English to be hopelessly divided in the Cape Assembly and sought the support of the Bond. Between the parliamentary sessions of 1885 and 1886, Rhodes 'more or less, completed his strategic volte-face, becoming converted more clearly to Cape sub-imperialism'. It was a 'conscious, concerted effort to win over Hofmeyr', a move that would 'bewilder and frustrate his friends from the opposition ... who could not figure out where exactly he stood politically'.[4] In time, Milton would work closely with Rhodes and understand the arrangement with the Bond, but in the eighties, he would likely have been as puzzled as politicians on all sides.

Hofmeyr's position was no less complex. He was prepared to remain a British subject 'in the sense of subjection to law and authority and attachment to the cause of order' but he was not prepared to become an Englishman.[5] Politically, Hofmeyr wanted to eliminate the imperial factor in South Africa, 'that is the power of the British government to interfere in South African affairs to the embarrassment of a self-governing colony'.[6] It did not, however, affect the attraction he developed for the imperial sports as he appreciated the virtues acquired in playing games and wanted his people to play them. He formed the Cape Town CC and actively supported rugby. Yet, he seemed oblivious to the hypocrisy attached to his belief that 'in sport ... there was no politics; it served a great purpose in building up the youth of the nation and unifying the two [white] peoples'.[7]

As an Afrikaner, Hofmeyr's espousal of English games had wide and deep political resonances. It foreshadowed his accommodation with Rhodes but also pointed towards its limits in that he used his political skills and influence not only to prevent the imperial games from becoming solely a vehicle for Englishness, but also to forge a place within them for the Afrikaner. It was a development that impacted on the Western Province CC's desire to keep its own little England intact. Milton's grip on the game was loosened as Hofmeyr's Cape Town CC – of which Simkins was captain – assumed a prominent role. An anxious, unsettled relationship developed within cricket, but rugby was largely unaffected as it encouraged both Afrikaner and English-speaking whites to play the game.

When Hofmeyr, the editor of the *Zuid-Afrikaan*, first entered the Cape Parliament as the member for Stellenbosch in 1879, rugby had just begun its role as the leading winter code and its clubs were grappling with the game's intricate rules. Surprisingly, supporters of association football – 'soccer' – did not make claims for recognition and did not challenge the rugby initiative. They were probably comfortable in the knowledge that Cape rules already incorporated a number of the association game's features. A soccer match arranged between the third and seventh companies of the Duke of Edinburgh's Rifles in 1879 was essentially a one-off encounter, although it signified that the movement towards abandoning Cape rules had created openings for other codes.

In Britain, the Football Association had become 'more proactive'. The introduction of competitive cup football changed the nature of the game. The idea was also advanced that soccer was 'just as manly but less rough than the rugby game'; an important argument for many young men who had to work for a living and could not afford to lose time due to injuries at football.[8] Such developments had no immediate influence on potential soccer players in the Cape Colony. Nor was there much interest in the achievements of Cape Town-born William Rawson who captained England and then played in the 1877 Football Association cup final alongside Port Elizabeth-born Owen Dunell.[9]

As rugby moved to centre stage, there were few references to association football being played at the Cape. One rare but revealing encounter was that between two district towns outside Cape Town – Wellington and Paarl – in September 1881. With the notable exception of Paarl's Welsh captain Llewellyn Powys-Jones, the players were almost entirely from Afrikaans stock. The 15-a-side match ended when 'a combined rush of the Paarl forwards secured the downfall of the visitors' fortress'. It resulted in the only goal of one of the last inter-town soccer matches before rugby prevailed and 'the association game became taboo'.[10]

Towards the end of 1881, Cape Town was affected by the onset of a severe depression accompanied by another serious smallpox epidemic. Years of prosperity ended dramatically. The press, notably the *Cape Times* and the *Lantern*, were particularly inclined to use the epidemic as a stick to beat the poor and indulge in negative stereotyping through blaming the Malay community. For a while, the whole question of housing and sanitation became the basis of political activity: 'the sooner the Malays are forced to reside in a separate district the better for all concerned'.[11]

The English-speaking population united behind the 'Clean' Party, which entered municipal politics and criticised the dangers of poor sanitation. Victory in the 1882 election, says historian, Vivian Bickford-Smith, 'signalled the emergence of a dominant class in Cape Town that was not only white and bourgeois but also predominantly English'.[12]

Rugby consolidated its position in 1883 when Hamilton's called a meeting to establish the first provincial union and discuss the uniformity of rules.[13] Advocate Shepstone Giddy, who was described as 'a very clever exponent of the game',[14] became president of the newly formed Western Province Rugby Football Union. William Milton did not make an appearance but was elected vice-president. Twenty-one-year-old Carlo Douglas de Fenzi, a product of Bedford Modern who had recently joined the Cape's civil service, was appointed as the secretary. The 'Englishness' of the committee was significant, as was the union's decision to affiliate with the Rugby Football Union (RFU). It accepted the parent body's authority and adhered closely to its directives. Frederick York St Leger played his part by publishing details of meetings of the RFU.[15]

In the light of recent political activity and the interest shown in rugby by the Malay community, the Western Province RFU was conscious of the position that it should adopt towards players of colour. It was agreed that 'any club desirous of affiliation to the Union shall be proposed by a member of one club and seconded by a member of another club, after which the application shall be submitted to the Committee for decision'.[16] Clubs fielding coloured players would find it difficult to surmount the series of checkpoints designed to safeguard a white-only status for establishment rugby.

The new committee immediately set about organising a 'Grand Challenge Cup' competition, an idea used successfully overseas when the Yorkshire Challenge Cup brought with it an influx of new players, new spectators and new playing methods.[17]

Success at the Cape owed much to the committee that attended regular meetings in Advocate Giddy's chambers. Teams were soon neatly attired in their club colours, which enabled spectators and players to distinguish clearly between sides, a situation that had been found wanting in previous seasons. Good crowds attended matches even to the extent that they sometimes hampered play by 'getting inside the flags and closing round when there happens to be a scrimmage on the goal-line'. Improvements in the playing conditions were still necessary and when one of the Versfeld brothers broke a leg it was noted that it had been 'caused solely by the faulty nature of the ground ... the Green Point Common abounds with mole-holes'.[18]

The Grand Challenge Cup – proudly displayed in a shop window on Adderley Street – changed the complexion of Western Province's rugby. New clubs were established and there was a greater intensity in the play. Hamilton's were the inaugural champions in 1883 but Villager's raised their game to secure the cup the following year. Milton was sufficiently enthused by his club's success to return as captain in 1885. He had rarely played in the preceding years – achieving little since a match against Hamilton's in 1880 when his towering drop-goal from the halfway line was 'received with great enthusiasm on both sides'.[19] After his stint as captain, he served as a rugby 'umpire' and Western Province vice-president for a few years, before withdrawing from active participation.

Colonial-born players dominated rugby in the 1880s. The game was popular in the schools. This ensured a steady supply of talent and, in no time, the competitions featured at least a dozen clubs, some fielding second and third fifteens. Colonial-born teams would defeat 'Mother Country' with customary ease and it became increasingly difficult to find players to represent the latter. After a year or two of Milton cajoling civil service colleagues into making up the required number, the fixture was dropped. It did not matter in a crowded rugby programme.

'Rugby,' concede Alfred Gibson and William Pickford had 'obtained a start on association in the most fertile soil for football'.[20] It was probably the formation of the provincial rugby union in 1883 that eventually galvanised soccer's followers into action. A letter, signed 'Crystal Palace', appeared in the *Cape Times* that year and a meeting was subsequently arranged at which the city's first club – the Wanderers – was formed.

A series of letters to the press reflected the frustration of soccer supporters concerning the game's inferior status within the white colonial community. Letters from 'Aston Villa', 'H. Mac.', 'Old Carthusian' and 'A Player' were eager to point out that the 'association game is infinitely superior in point of skill and science' while condemning rugby for its 'useless exhibitions of physical strength' and its reliance on brute force.

The aggressive tone of the letters upset 'Crystal Palace' who saw himself as the innocent cause of provoking a public outcry. 'When I first played rugby,' he reminisced, 'loose hacking, tripping, etc. were allowed [but] these atrocities are now done away with and I don't think you get more "shinners" in rugby than in association'. He also revealed he was Walter Foster and that when the Football Association had been formed in 1863, he had been a Crystal Palace delegate at its first meeting.[21]

No sooner were practices for Foster's new club underway than the relatively large Scottish community formed the Thistle club. The latter proceeded to thrash Wanderers 5–0 in the first inter-club fixture and then played Princess Louise's Argyll and Sutherland Highlanders in a game billed as the season's 'Grand Football Match'. Thistles won 2–0 and talked up their achievement by announcing that it was the first time their opponents had suffered defeat in any athletic competition since their arrival in the country.[22]

Set on building a reputation, Thistles requested the Western Province ground in late October for an out-of-season return match against Highlanders but were turned down because cricket had been arranged. They submitted a letter of complaint to the *Cape Times*: 'It was unfortunate the "WP" could not see their way to grant the use of their park at Wynberg, as with the attraction of the regimental band, the gate-money would have been considerable and have proved a welcome addition to the Relief of the Distressed'. There was no sympathy for Thistles: the band of the Argyll and Sutherland Highlanders played at the cricket whilst a nasty drizzling shower struck the soccer game at Green Point and reduced the expected crowd of 300 to 80.[23]

The deepening Depression of the 1880s exacerbated soccer's problems, particularly as many white artisans simply moved on to overseas destinations such as New Zealand.[24] The struggling Wanderers called for a reduction in rail fares to assist sports, noting that Members of Parliament could economise on their liberal travelling allowance and taking their wives on holiday with them.[25] In the meantime, Thistles placed announcements in the press in the hope of attracting new members but faced a losing battle.

Gibson and Pickford sum up early Cape soccer as 'years of irregular competition on bad grounds'.[26] That there was a revival at all could be attributed to the input of military teams and they (the Royal Artillery, East Yorkshire Regiment, North Staffordshire Regiment and Cape Town Highlanders) joined newly formed civilian teams, Pioneers and Commercial Recreation, in setting up a provincial union during 1890. At the end of the first season, the Western Province Football Association managed to purchase medals and 'had a balance of a few shillings but had been unable to raise a cup'. The weak financial position was surprising in that the governing body was able to boast (briefly) of having Cecil John Rhodes as president and James Sivewright as vice-president.[27]

Rugby benefited by attracting interest from both white groups. The surge in Afrikaner involvement in the game began at a time when the Transvaal Boers were gathering support from the Cape and elsewhere to help them reverse the annexation of 1877. The visit to Cape Town of the Boer leaders, Paul Kruger and General Piet Joubert in 1879, drew attention to their cause and it seemed as if 'the politically sluggish Western Cape had thus wakened from inertia to action'.[28] The situation gained momentum through Boer success in the War of Independence during 1880–81, but in the course of the next few years 'the Afrikaner mobilisation in defence of their "oppressed brothers" proved remarkably ephemeral'. Wealthy farmers who dominated the Afrikaner Bond under Hofmeyr were not hostile to the imperial connection but, says

Shula Marks, would regret its parochialism when gold was discovered on the Witwatersrand in 1886.[29]

With De Fenzi's encouragement in the 1880s, 'the young Boers took to [rugby] like ducks to water, which was not surprising, in view of their magnificent physique and virility'. Stellenbosch, already noted for its fine cricket reputation, came to the fore in the winter sport 'with the result that enthusiasm for the rugby game spread like wildfire into all the farming districts of the country'.[30] De Fenzi introduced the successful Country Challenge Cup and an area such as Paarl, where players had previously been forbidden to participate because the game was considered too rough, provided a powerful team.[31] When Stellenbosch hosted a Challenge Cup final in 1886, the *Cape Times* expressed amazement at the interest for rugby in the area: 'The whole world and his wife were present at the ground.'[32] Not unexpectedly, Stellenbosch entered Cape Town's premier competition in 1888.[33]

The support of Western Province RFU secretary De Fenzi for the country rugby teams contrasted sharply with the uneasiness that characterised Milton's communication with the Afrikaner over cricket. Despite Stellenbosch having the most powerful cricket side in the western Cape in the late 1870s, Milton and the Western Province CC did not see the country team as a priority when arranging matches. Seasons went by without the two sides meeting. Milton wrote of the 'native talent of South Africa which lacks nothing but opportunity for development' but did not appear to have the time nor inclination to attend to the needs of those clubs and players outside the suburbs.[34] He designed cricket's fixture list to suit the Cape elite.

Milton's refusal to cater satisfactorily for cricket in the country districts effectively meant a refusal to support the Afrikaner in his efforts to play the game. This contributed to the decline in their cricket, and the potential for a production line of great fast bowlers remained unfulfilled until the late twentieth century. The outstanding Louis Neethling and E.L. Schröder made rare appearances, while South Africa's fiery opening bowler Nicolaas Theunissen sparked interest in the press through his high-profile switch from cricket to rugby.

The Cape rugby clubs were given a boost by the visit of Kimberley to play a series of matches in 1884. 'They were the first rugby adventurers,' wrote Paul Dobson, 'the first tourists, the first, really, to play inter-provincial rugby in South Africa.' Their visit attracted great interest as 3 000 people watched them play Villager's and there was 'a sea of faces on every side of the enclosure' when they met a combined town side at Rondebosch. Interest was not confined to whites – or white males. Men of every shade and colour and position could be seen: 'The Malay and the Negro were there, as well as the elite of Cape Town society; and the varied and bright costumes of the ladies, set off as they were by the large white canvas enclosure and marquee, made quite a pretty sight.'[35] If such occasions were regarded as helping to emphasise the cultural superiority of whites, they also presented a goal for blacks to strive towards in the hope of being assimilated into colonial society.

The *Cape Times* drew attention to people of colour playing football during the 1870s when it referred to their games in the city's streets. The newspaper thought it 'highly dangerous to equestrians and troublesome to pedestrians'. For playing ball in Hope Street on a Sunday evening 'two coloured lads of tender age were severely cautioned by the Resident Magistrate.'[36] There was little sympathy for the young enthusiasts and in complimenting the magistrate for moving against street games, St Leger wrote that 'the European population would be glad of such action'.[37]

Nineteenth-century Cape Town had football and cricket teams of mixed race or Malay backgrounds, sometimes with a smattering of Europeans. The teams that featured players of colour were not, however, matched against the better-known establishment clubs that came from the southern suburbs. Those clubs belonged to the gentry – the white people – who were conscious of their power and privilege and looked to exclusionary segregation in protecting their white bourgeois status.

Numerous football and cricket teams existed within the precincts of the city with the Malay community conspicuous in the organisation of games. Contests played out at Green Point Common on Sundays and during the festive holidays. Large crowds attended the matches because they were popular social occasions, often with a band in attendance. Practices in both sports were held on the Parade from the 1870s until restrictions were introduced in the mid-1880s. Eventually, ball-playing was prohibited altogether. An article in the *Cape Argus* commented:

> The stern Town Council has decreed that little boys shan't play cricket or football on the Parade any longer. The old gentleman with the crutches and the 'bell topper' may now hobble across without fear of his 'bell topper' coming to grief, but possibly some of the youthful spirits of Cape Town, who have hitherto found cricket and football on the Parade an outlet for their exuberance, may now seek other means for letting off steam even more objectionable to the City Fathers. It is an unwise thing to place too heavy restrictions on youthful sports.[38]

Sport gave pride and identity to those immersed in a vibrant culture that involved numerous relatively small clubs and included players from the different population groups. Sport in the old Cape liberal context 'helped define communities, facilitated their interaction and promoted a common set of values'.[39]

During the 1880s, the press encouraged a hardening of attitudes. 'Inextricably linked with their mobilisation of English,' says Bickford-Smith, 'the *Cape Times* and *Lantern* portrayed problems of social control as problems about controlling blacks'. The *Cape Argus*, 'which had been less racist than the *Cape Times* and *Lantern* before the depression, now competed in this arena, with virulent diatribes talking of "Cape Town's Curse", and the "criminal and vicious tendencies of the human scum of this city, the offensive and aggressive half-breeds"'.[40] The British did not readily encourage the various ethnic groups to join their games, which were often used to divide them from the local populations.

Amidst the ill-feeling that prevailed, sport still provided hope for the people. 'Rugby gripped the coloured sportsmen of the eighties,' reported the *Cape Standard* many years later.[41] The 'Roslyns' rugby club was formed in 1882 in an area that had previously been established by freed slaves and became known as the sixth district of Cape Town or 'District Six'. Paul Dobson points out that:

> Clubs in those days were representative of tight bits of a community, even of streets within a community. For that reason, Roslyns no longer exists. It was after all a District Six club, and District Six no longer exists. Roslyns never had headquarters. It used Green Point Common and then the track and played matches at a variety of grounds – at Brooklyn, in Ndabeni, at Meide Vlei (now Lynfrae Estate), at a field in Claremont called the Kas which was up near Bowwood Road on a ground called Sambokland at Kromboom, in Crawford, on Rondebosch Common, on a piece of ground where Newlands swimming pool now is, and at Vygieskraal in Athlone.[42]

Other clubs – Arabian College and Good Hopes – began playing in the Bo-Kaap (the 'Upper' Cape) or Malay Quarter, which was already stretching in ragged formation up the side of Signal Hill. It was the traditional home of a working-class population that emerged through the influx of thousands of labourers, slaves and political exiles, transported in chains by Dutch settlers from the colonies that formed the East Indies.

Towards the end of March 1886, De Fenzi became conscious of the number of small one-team clubs that had formed in the region and were looking to play fixtures. Some were coloured or mixed-race teams. Reports exist of Pioneers, St John's, Eureka (from Woodstock) and St Saviour's Grammar School playing in 1883. Other sides, such as Progress and Rugby of Cape Town, Thistles of Rondebosch and St Marks of District Six, followed soon afterwards. The players of colour came from working-class communities and their passion for rugby rivalled that of their white compatriots. De Fenzi was interested in expanding rugby's base and, having had success in attracting interest in the country districts, he turned to the city. Fair Players, a racially mixed team formed in District Six from frequenters of Wells Square, had played friendlies against Hamilton's and St Saviour's played Villager's.[43]

Advocate Giddy chaired a meeting of the Western Province RFU on 6 April 1886 at which De Fenzi pointed out the importance of assisting the smaller clubs. In response, Simkins moved a resolution in favour of a junior challenge cup for clubs affiliated to the exclusively white union, and to restrict the competition to second teams of those clubs only. De Fenzi opposed this motion on behalf of smaller clubs that did not have second teams. He moved that the junior challenge cup be contested by 'teams which do not comprise any players who may at any time have taken part in contests for the Country or Grand Challenge trophies'. But when it came to a vote, Simkins' resolution was carried.[44] The predominantly English-speaking delegates were not blind to the implications of the ruling that they had backed. The door to non-racial rugby was shut and remained locked.

On 10 April 1886, a follower of the game wrote to the *Cape Times* to query the Western Province RFU's decision on the agreed structure of the junior challenge cup:

Sir

In Wednesday's edition of your valuable paper, I notice that a junior challenge cup is to be established to be open for competition to all second teams of clubs affiliated to the Western Province Rugby Football Union. Now I think this condition a great shame. There are several junior clubs in Cape Town and suburbs, for instance, the St John's, Loco and Eureka football clubs, which are not able to enter for the first team cup, but anticipated being able to join for the junior team cup and have been greatly disappointed at not being able to enter for it. So I think if Mr W.V. Simkins would change his motion, and allow all junior teams to enter, it would be a great improvement on the present regulation for the junior challenge cup. Trusting you will find room for this small letter

– I am, etc.

A Football Player.[45]

The letter was ignored. Simkins's action might initially have appeared innocent, but in reality, it was a deliberate ploy to ensure the Western Province RFU remained a white organisation. The issue was not new as the union had been committed to a policy of exclusivity since its formation in 1883. Sketchy reporting unfortunately left unanswered questions. There is no reference, for example, to Advocate Giddy's position in the union's decision. Some years later, Giddy invited Krom Hendricks to play for his cricket side, United Services, in the predominantly white first league. The fact that rugby was a contact game might have influenced him and others in the vote against De Fenzi. It is also possible that delegates were conscious of the overseas tour that Simkins was arranging in 1886. They would not have wished their men to compete with players of colour for places in the team.

Rejected rugby clubs were forced to fend for themselves and to consider forming a separate union. The predominantly Malay clubs reacted quickly to the establishment's ruling and founded the Western Province Coloured Rugby Football Union in 1886. It was made up of 'Roslyns from District Six; Violets from Claremont, Good Hopes and Arabian College from the Bo-Kaap', with matches played at Green Point Common and on the track.[46] Other clubs that played against these sides included Excelsior, Shamrocks and Royal Standards.

Roslyns spawned clubs such as Hamediehs, Royal Alberts, Caledonian Roses and Olympics. They also maintained a prestigious position within the union, which would play a role in the establishment of a national body in Kimberley in 1897. Surprisingly, it would take the Western Province Coloured RFU some time before it organised a competition for first league teams – the Fernwood Cup – and then stage the event just 28 times in 76 years. Its first winners in 1898 were Violets of Claremont, a club that would produce many fine players at the Kas, a field described as 'deplorable'.

A prominent club formed in 1886 – Wanderers – enjoyed their first victory of 3–0 the same year over Excelsior in Stellenbosch. Wanderers would be largely instrumental in establishing a second rugby organisation, the City and Suburban Union, founded in 1898. They were followed by the founding clubs of the new union, namely California (1888), Perseverance (1889), Thistles (1891), Woodstock Rangers (1892) and Retreat (1898). Primrose joined in 1901, Progress in 1906 and Universals in 1931 to form the core City and Suburban Union clubs until the 1960s. The new regional association also developed links with rugby teams and associations in the Boland area east of Cape Town.[47]

The need to have two unions reflected race and religious distinctions that operated within the coloured communities of the city. The Western Province Coloured RFU was an inner-city, working-class league that was dominated by

Muslims – but by no means exclusively – whereas the City and Suburban Union, which would move outside the city, excluded Muslims from playing until the early 1960s.

After 1886, the coloured and white Western Province unions followed parallel paths. Rugby had been the first sport to be affected by the new political order, which would see the ideology and practice of racial separation replace mid-nineteenth-century Cape liberal notions of opportunity and advancement for all races. In the 1890s, the Rhodes-Afrikaner Bond coalition that gained control of the Cape government was determined to promote white ethnicity and embarked on a process to exclude blacks from political involvement. Large-scale immigration had brought inevitable change in the urban context and the Afrikaner Bond, with strong support from the Dutch Reformed Church, were increasingly concerned by the poor-white problem. They believed it could be controlled not only with greater government expenditure on white education, but also through the social separation of whites and blacks.

Hofmeyr wielded great authority and was arguably the power behind the Cape government and Western Province cricket. He had been instrumental in setting up Rhodes as prime minister and Milton as president of the Western Province Cricket Union, and it no doubt suited him that they should 'share' the same office. The significance of sporting Test matches against unified South African teams – cricket (1888/89 and 1891/92) and rugby (1891) – was not lost on Hofmeyr or Rhodes. In late 1893, Hofmeyr told guests at a celebratory banquet that 'the sporting associations of this country, which for the most part represent combinations of sportsmen throughout the various states ... have set an example which politicians are all too slow to follow in the aim for a United South Africa'.[48]

The changing nature of Cape politics coincided with the process of sportsmen forming administrative bodies and arranging international tours. There is no clear indication as to the extent of Hofmeyr's influence because he preferred to work behind the scenes, using his 'natural gift for lobbying and for grass-roots organisation'.[49] It was Rhodes as prime minister of the Cape who blocked the selection of Krom Hendricks for the first South African cricket team to tour overseas in 1894. The decision impacted on all sport during the period leading up to the early 1900s. Hendricks was the first cricketer to be banned from playing the game at a senior level in South Africa, and probably the first in the world to be formally excluded from playing for his country because of his colour.

Edmund Garrett, the editor of the *Cape Times*, examined the Hendricks problem in a detailed leader article. He embraced the Rhodes-Milton view of the importance of the strict separation of the races, and asked 'the old persistent, inevitable question, "Where are you to draw the line?"':

> Our colour friends of all shades and of various classes in life have taken to the white man's athletics with great vigour ... young fellows ranging from the lightest of brown looks to the darkest of black ones, going forth to various open spaces of an afternoon ... Can the English who carry their cricket and football to the uttermost parts of the earth look with disfavour on such a phenomenon?

Garrett accepted 'a general free mixing of white and coloured youth in games nobody here is prepared to advocate ... a cleavage there must be'. There were separate places of residence 'so there may be white athletic clubs and coloured athletic clubs, keeping to themselves and using different grounds'. He then switched focus to stress the important role that the Mfengu (referred to in derogatory colonial terms as 'Cape boys') had played in quelling the recent Matabele uprising. Garrett reflected on the hypocrisy of using social and economic inferiors to defend the empire, querying whether the sports-loving 'Cape boys' ...

> though good enough to fight side by side with white men, are good enough to play side by side with them. And the answer – 'NO'! It may be objected that it is wrong to put forward these considerations, unless we are prepared to advocate the opposite answer. But we think it is just as well to show that we whites are not – many of us are not – blind to such considerations, even if we cannot in some particular matter carry them into action.[50]

Milton departed for Rhodesia in order to restructure its civil service. Simkins succeeded him at the forefront of the campaign against Hendricks and was immediately incensed when the fast bowler was allowed to play for All-comers against the Western Province CC. At a meeting of the Western Province Cricket Union, he complained that 'someone was guilty of a grave error in having selected Hendricks for the All-comers'. He told members that they should use 'all means at their disposal to ensure the two classes be kept distinctly separate'. It had been the policy of the rugby clubs and he believed cricket should follow suit.

G.A. Parker, writing in 1897, claimed that South African cricket had no need to include racial barriers in its constitution as social custom already achieved that.[51] The same year, the Western Province Cricket Union introduced a resolution to prevent Hendricks from playing 'championship' cricket. Simkins was involved in the imposition of the desperate measure – Bye-law 10 – drafted in October 1897: 'That this union will not object to any club employing a coloured professional in matches other than championship fixtures and no coloured professional or member shall be allowed to compete in championship matches.'[52]

Shortly afterwards, Simkins as president of the Western Province RFU would do the same for rugby. The union had earlier established its policy of exclusivity at its inaugural meeting in 1883 and confirmed it in 1886, the year the predominantly Muslim board was formed. Then, in 1898, further action coincided with the formation of the City and Suburban Union. When the Western Province Junior Rugby Football Union was formally constituted on 25 November 1898, a clause was inserted in its constitution stating: 'Affiliation to the Union shall be open only to such clubs as shall consist entirely of European players.'[53]

Western Province's white rugby and cricket authorities proved inflexible and insensitive. There would be no concessions. Hendricks was followed by thousands of black sportsmen who didn't fit into the establishment's stereotype of a South African. They suffered huge injustices, being denied access to opportunities, adequate facilities and the right to play representatively.

Rugby's approach towards its soccer counterparts gradually mellowed in the course of the 1890s. By then the soccerites had formed associations in other parts of the country, with a national body established in 1892. In May 1895, Simkins expressed sudden concern about 'progress being made by the socker [sic] game, and that it would not do for ruggers to sit still', but in August 1897, the Western Province RFU accepted that there was room for both codes of football to flourish side by side. The *Cape Times* suggested no love was lost in the past, commenting rightly or wrongly that 'to a great extent, the present strength of the rugby game in this province has, so to speak, been the outcome of the first attempt to instil the old socker [sic] game here.' The writer did not believe that soccer would again 'fall into the same state of decay as that which followed its introduction years ago and there is no wish that it should'.

'Rugby,' concluded the report, 'had established itself in too strong a position in every centre in South Africa where outdoor exercise is indulged in to wish the sister game harm.'[54]

Notes

1   Western Province RFU, *Rules of the Western Province Junior Rugby Football Union* (Cape Town: Western Province Junior Rugby Football Union, 1898), 2.
2   M. Tamarkin, *Cecil Rhodes and the Cape Afrikaners: The Imperial Colossus and the Colonial Parish Pump* (London: Routledge, 1996), 73. The quote refers to the May 1888 Bond Conference.
3   Tamarkin, *Cecil Rhodes and the Cape Afrikaners*, 63.
4   Ibid, 95–96.
5   J. Hofmeyr and F. Reitz, *The Life of Jan Hendrik Hofmeyr (Onze Jan)* (Cape Town: Van de Sandt De Villiers, 1913), 31.

6   C.F.J. Muller (ed.), *Five Hundred Years: A History of South Africa* (Pretoria: Academica, 1981), 190.

7   Hofmeyr and Reitz, *The Life of Jan Hendrik Hofmeyr*, 84.

8   C. Eisenberg, P. Lanfanchi, T. Mason and A. Wahl, (eds), *100 Years of Football: The FIFA Centennial Book* (London: Weidenfeld & Nicolson, 2004), 21.

9   On Dunell's return to South Africa, he became involved in rugby administration as vice-president of Crusader's in Port Elizabeth and was captain of South Africa's first cricket 'Test' team in March 1889.

10   *Cape Times*, 24 September 1881; P. van Schaik, 'Paarl RFC', in I. Difford (ed.), *The History of South African Rugby Football 1875–1932* (Wynberg: Speciality Press, 1933), 514.

11   *The Lantern*, 23 September 1882.

12   V. Bickford-Smith, *Ethnic Pride and Racial Prejudice in Victorian Cape Town: Group Identity and Social Practice 1875–1902* (Cambridge: Cambridge University Press, 1995), 39.

13   *Cape Times*, 29 May 1883.

14   Ibid., 30 March 1927.

15   Ibid., 29 May–31 May 1883.

16   Western Province RFU, *Bye-laws and Laws of the Game* (Cape Town: Western Province RFU, 1883), 19.

17   T. Collins, *A Social History of English Rugby Union* (Abingdon: Routledge, 2009), 25.

18   *Cape Times*, 9 July 1883.

19   Ibid., 26 June 1880.

20   A. Gibson and W. Pickford, *Football and the Men who Made it* (London: Caxton, 1906), 220.

21   *Cape Times*, 26 May–9 June 1883.

22   Ibid., 8 September 1883.

23   Ibid., 20 October 1883.

24   Bickford-Smith, *Ethnic Pride and Racial Prejudice*, 94.

25   *Cape Times*, 26 March 1884.

26   Gibson and Pickford, *Football*, 224.

27   *Cape Times*, 11 March 1891.

28   J. Benyon, 'The Cape Colony, 1854–1881', in T. Cameron and S.B. Spies (eds), *An Illustrated History of South Africa* (Johannesburg: Jonathan Ball, 1986), 170.

29   S. Marks, 'Class, Culture and Consciousness in South Africa, 1880–1899', in R. Ross, A. Mager and B. Nasson (eds), *The Cambridge History of South Africa, Volume 2, 1885–1994* (Cambridge: Cambridge University Press, 2011), 111.

30   Difford, *History of South African Rugby*, 15.

31   *Cape Times*, 10 April 1885.

32   Ibid., 7 September 1886.

33   Difford, *History of South African Rugby*, 514.

34   *Cape Argus*, 18 October 1879.

35   P. Dobson, *Rugby in South Africa: A History 1861–1988* (Cape Town: SARB, 1989), 26; A. Parker, *W.P. Rugby: Centenary 1883–1983* (Cape Town: WPRFU, 1983), 17.

36   *Cape Times*, 15 October 1878.

37   Bickford-Smith, *Ethnic Pride and Racial Prejudice*, 99.

38   *Cape Argus*, 1 November 1890.

39   R. Parry, 'Origins of Segregation at the Cape', in B. Murray and G. Vahed (eds), *Empire and Cricket: The South African Experience, 1884–1914* (Pretoria: Unisa, 2009), 37.

40   Bickford-Smith, *Ethnic Pride and Racial Prejudice*, 99, 118.

41   *Cape Standard*, 14 September 1936.

42   Dobson, *Rugby in South Africa*, 167.

43   Ibid.

44   *Cape Argus*, 7 April 1886; *Cape Times*, 7 April 1886.

45   *Cape Times*, 10 April 1886.

46   A. Odendaal, 'The Thing that is Not Round', in A. Grundlingh, A. Odendaal and B. Spies (eds), *Beyond the Tryline: Rugby and South African Society* (Johannesburg: Ravan Press, 1995), 27–28.

47   Dobson, *Rugby in South Africa*, 167–168.

48   *South African Review*, 1 December 1893.
49   P. Lewsen, *John X. Merriman: Paradoxical South African Statesman* (New Haven: Yale University Press, 1982), 83.
50   *Cape Times*, 13 November 1897. The Mfengu were black colonial soldiers from the eastern Cape.
51   G. Parker *South African Sports* (London: Sampson Low, Marston, 1897), 47.
52   The wording of the resolution is outlined in the *Cape Times*, 6 November 1897.
53   Western Province RFU, *Rules*, 2.
54   Minutes of the SA Rugby Football Board, 1 May 1895; *Cape Times*, 24 August 1897.

4

First Steps towards International Sport

Probably in no country in the world is anti-professionalism
in sport more strong than in South Africa.[1]

– Cape Times, 1888

The Cape newspapers marvelled at the success of the Australian cricket teams. The *Cape Times* noted that 'merchants in Australia think nothing of giving £10 or £20 each to send home a good eleven and have their appointments still open for them when they come back. Cape Town could not send a team to Port Elizabeth.'[2] In 1881, the *Cape Argus* wrote pessimistically that 'it will be a long time before South Africa will attain to the pitch of perfection already reached by some of the sister colonies in the Australian group'. A few months later, the same newspaper pointed to the financial success experienced by Australian touring teams and stressed 'it is time the Colony did something to show that it is not dead to sports and manly pastimes'.[3]

William Milton, the leading personality in Cape Town sporting circles, did not agree with the sentiments expressed. He opposed the growing clamour for an overseas tour by stating in the *Cape Argus* that the idea of sending a team to England capable of holding its own was a great impossibility until interest was taken in development and improving standards. He put the problem down to inadequate facilities, claiming the cricket ground at Wynberg was 'little better than the hard road and not quite so good as a Namaqualand saltpan'.[4]

Milton's desire to downplay the prevailing eagerness for international competition and to focus on improving playing conditions was a sound argument. It culminated in the construction of Newlands, a grand venue for international tours. Yet the interest being shown in competing against teams from overseas could not be ignored. Enthusiasm was fuelled by sportswriters in South Africa, most notably those from Kimberley's rival newspapers: Harry Cadwallader, an ambitious sports' administrator and reporter for the *Diamond Fields Advertiser*, and Charles Finlason, an erudite commentator on rugby and cricket and the *Daily Independent* 'Gossip'. The two journalists kept tour aspirations alive, with rugby making the first move.

The Western Province Rugby Football Union (RFU) caused surprise in early July 1886 when it announced plans to send 'a thoroughly representative football team from the Cape Colony to England in order to play a series of matches towards the end of [that] year'.[5] Advocate Shepstone Giddy had occupied the chair when representatives from clubs met at the Café Royal to discuss the rugby tour. Billy Simkins was the originator of the scheme. He estimated that the cost of the venture lasting 45 days would be £1 300, an amount he believed would be covered by gate takings. Simkins hoped 'Kimberley, Grahamstown, Port Elizabeth, King William's Town, East London and other centres would support the idea'.[6]

A subcommittee was appointed, and a proposal was drawn up and forwarded to the RFU. The idea created interest at that stage but did not have unanimous support. Finlason, writing in the *Daily Independent*, described the project as 'a very bold one ... South Africa has never sent a team of any kind to England' but thought it impractical as there were very few young men in the country who could leave their occupations for such a long period. Instead, he argued 'let the executive make arrangements for a strong team to come out from England to play the strongest team that can be picked from the different teams in the Colony'. He continued:

> The South African football players would then be able to arrive at a juster idea of their strength than they can possibly have at present. They could learn a good deal from the visitors and with practice under professional coaching, a team to play a weak county team might be sent to England in about five years. The same remarks apply to cricket.[7]

The *Port Elizabeth Telegraph* thought a cricket or shooting team would have more hope in Britain than a football side. The *Diamond Fields Advertiser* agreed, suggesting a shooting or athletic team might perform better.[8] The *Lantern* feared the Cape players were too light to make any show against English clubs but an old Capetonian argued, 'Surely South Africa can produce plenty of eleven-stone men which in my opinion is enough for forward play.' The writer added that 'the old style of tight scrimmages when it was beef versus beef is, happily an item of the past and has given place to fast and loose play with plenty of pedal work'. Yet, he too admitted that 'shooting men would be likely to gain more laurels than football men'.[9]

Rugby in southern Africa at that stage was confined largely to the western Cape and Kimberley, although the latter lagged in terms of producing young players to carry the game forward. Finlason complained that the lack of excellence 'may be found in the way colonial youths are brought up ... we have never seen them play football; and as for cricket, we doubt not that many Kimberley schoolboys do not know a bat from a ball'. He did not think there was a school in Kimberley that boasted a football or cricket team. The main problem behind such an unsatisfactory state of affairs was the lack of facilities: 'no ground has been secured for them and they are in consequence reduced to playing marbles in the streets'. The imperial games in Kimberley, he added, were sustained by adults from various parts of the world.[10]

On 17 March 1887, Rowland Hill, the secretary of the RFU, sent his reply to the Western Province RFU, stressing that the RFU did not think it 'wise to recommend you to undertake your project'. He did not see a way to guaranteeing any part of the expenses and had discouraged 'letters of similar character from New Zealand and other quarters'. He went into the reasons behind the decision, explaining carefully that in principle he accepted the arrangement whereby part of the gate should be given to a visiting team but that 'the amount to be derived from this source would depend very much on the strength of [that team]'.

The fear – in Hill's mind at least – was that the colonial sides would be 'unable to make good matches with our best clubs' and, as a consequence, the receipts would be very small. He went on to explain that the English climate was very uncertain and that they had just experienced a period of six or seven weeks during which football was impossible.

Hill fully understood the Cape's desire to emulate the Australian cricketers but pointed out that there was a fundamental difference in tours made by the two sports. Whilst a cricket tour had been more than able to pay its way, it did not follow that a rugby team would be similarly fortunate. The cricketers, he explained 'are able to play every day but it would be physically impossible for footballers to follow their example; in fact, even three matches a week for any length of time would be a serious strain on men'.[11]

Hill's essentially pragmatic approach did not touch on the fact that the RFU was preoccupied with the pressing problem of professionalism. At a general meeting in October 1886, the governing body of the game had 'officially banned all forms of payments and inducements, monetary or otherwise', with firm action taken in the subsequent suspension of several clubs for not following the amateur code.[12] They faced troubled times and Hill was wary of further complications. The Western Province RFU might have its house in order but they had opened the tour to other territories in southern Africa where little was known about the administration of the game and background of players.

The message from London was a blow to sports organisers at the Cape who had just seen a cricket tour slip through their fingers. The Australians had been keen to visit in the course of a return trip from an England tour in 1886 and had communicated with the Cape Court of the Indian and Colonial Exhibition in London in the hope of extending their stay at the Cape to play a few games. They received no reply and when they stopped over at Cape Town in October, they could do little more than leave the boat briefly before moving on to New Zealand for two weeks. Cadwallader was incensed by the missed opportunity and in an article for the *Whitehall Review*, he lamented the inability of Cape cricketers to 'organise something'.[13]

Cadwallader's report was to an extent misleading: the Australian cricketers were in fact met by Milton and members of the Western Province Cricket Club (CC) on the day after their arrival. They were escorted around the Houses of Parliament, Library and Museum before returning to the vessel at noon. It also emerged that Milton was not to blame for the communication breakdown; no message had been passed on by the Exhibition officials in London who had told the Australians that 'they would find no cricket worth paying attention to at the Cape'.[14]

The stop-over by the Australian touring side stimulated interest but did not short-cut the process towards establishing international links. Poor communications, financial implications, relative strengths of teams involved, time away from work and fears over professionalism were some of the emerging issues in planning cricket and rugby tours at that time.

In 1888, the South Africans were led to believe that the RFU had altered its stance with regard to hosting touring teams. The development arose over the English governing body's decision to accept a visit from a New Zealand team. The *Cape Times* argued that Hill had misrepresented the situation in his letter in 1887 and that the RFU's 'misapprehension of the Cape's 1886 proposals' had been its fear of 'professionalism'.[15] There was a general belief that if the New Zealanders had been accepted, then so should the Cape players who had always demonstrated their loyalty to RFU ideals.

Compounding the problem was the English rugby tour made to Australia and New Zealand in 1888 under the auspices of sporting entrepreneurs, Alfred Shaw and Arthur Shrewsbury. Their boat was scheduled to make a stop-over at the Cape and they asked for a match. Great excitement followed. Milton made Newlands cricket ground available for the historic fixture and local players were soon involved in training. It, therefore, came as a shock when the Western Province RFU suddenly decided to abandon the arrangement. The *Cape Times Weekly* published the message that 'the objection was based on the supposed unfriendly attitude of the RFU [towards the touring side]'. It was rumoured that members of the party were being paid and the Western Province RFU chose to steer clear of trouble. Carlo Douglas De Fenzi, in his role as secretary, thought it appropriate to address a letter to the touring team on board the SS *Kaikoura* expressing 'regret that such a match could not be arranged and wishing them success on their tour'.[16]

In the course of their stop-over in Cape Town, the British players 'emphatically repudiated any imputation of professionalism existing within their team'. They were travelling under an arrangement whereby 'each member shall receive no more than his legitimate expenses, and none to be paid for loss of time'. They readily accepted that one member had 'received an advance of some £15, balance for outfit, in reference to which instance an objection had been made, but if such objection was sustained it was intended that the player in question could not be included in the matches'.[17] Jack Clowes openly admitted to receiving the money and offered to pay it back, but the RFU declared him a professional and, as the touring party had already departed, he was 'in the unfortunate position of being a tourist yet unable to play in any games'.[18]

There was much confusion. The *Daily Independent* was scathing about Cape Town's 'scurvy conduct' towards the English players but later conceded 'the English sporting 'papers conclusively prove that the English football team which touched at Cape Town is not an amateur team. The action taken by the Western Province RFU therefore will be approved by all the football unions in the Colony.'[19] Whether the Western Province authorities had indeed made the right decision was dependent on the way the RFU interpreted a potentially awkward situation.

Money had changed hands. Andrew Stoddart, who at various times captained England at cricket and rugby, was offered 'a £50 down payment for the rugby tour for which two lesser-known players were offered £200 each and the sole Welshman, W.H. Thomas, of Cambridge University, received £90'. On their return, the RFU 'proved strangely uninterested in checking out widespread rumours of illicit payment'.[20] The ban was lifted on Clowes, and the rest of the tourists signed an affidavit, stating that they had not received benefits. The RFU had thus side-stepped the possibility of further adverse publicity.

Six thousand miles away, Western Province rugby officials had perhaps unnecessarily sacrificed their first international game. It was not the only published example of their commitment to the RFU's rigid amateur ideals. When Kimberley toured the western Cape in 1888, the visitors were refused a percentage of the gate money for travelling purposes 'on the grounds that the union deems such allowance to be inconsistent with the rules of the English

Rugby Football Union'.[21] The *Cape Times* stated that 'probably in no country in the world is anti-professionalism in sport more strong than in South Africa'.

There was a belief that the RFU would look favourably upon them if they formed a national governing body that would oversee arrangements for a representative team to 'go "home" with but little requirement in the way of pecuniary assistance'. Once that point was made clear, said the *Cape Times*, 'and the outcome placed above all suspicion of being a "gate-money" venture the English Union would no doubt gladly hold out the right hand of fellowship and welcome'.[22]

During the latter part of 1887 and for much of 1888 arrangements were set in place for a tour to England by a mixed 'Maori' and 'Pakeha [white or non-Maori]' rugby squad that became known as the New Zealand 'Native' football team. It promised to be a financially successful venture because the British public 'were fascinated with indigenous representatives of the colonies during the nineteenth century, and there were handsome profits to be made from their visits'.[23] The tour was compared with the visit made by the Australian Aboriginals in 1868 when cricket was accompanied by spear and boomerang throwing, sprint races and other sports. The venture, recorded Arthur Haygarth, a nineteenth-century historian on the game, 'was a very lucrative speculation'.[24]

Although Hill had previously questioned the number of games men could play every week, the New Zealanders were involved in 74 matches in less than 6 months. There were controversial moments, not least when Hill refereed the match against England at Blackheath. It was claimed that the fixture 'was marred by some appalling refereeing'.[25] One particular incident saw the visitors not only object to a try that was awarded but temporarily leave the field in protest. The RFU forced the tourists to apologise twice, the second time 'at Hill's dictation' as the governing body sought to reaffirm its power and 'protect the reputation of its leading official'.[26] Colonials were not in a position to contest the hypocrisy of the RFU, a body that selected Stoddart, the paid leader on tour to Australasia, to captain England in the international against the visiting team at Blackheath.

The Western Province RFU showed interest in the New Zealand 'Native' tour. At their annual general meeting, they discussed the possibility of communicating with the New Zealanders before they departed from Britain. It was determined upon the motion of George Richards 'that a challenge should be sent on board the steamer for the Maori team to play a match or matches in Cape Town, the necessary arrangements to be left to the committee'.[27] Whether it was followed up is unknown but the fact that Giddy stood down as president and was replaced by Simkins did not bode well for a multiracial sporting event. The two men would later clash over the coloured cricketer Krom Hendricks playing for Giddy's club at a time when the Western Province Cricket Union was determined to preserve its white identity.[28]

On 2 January, the Newlands cricket ground was opened. An aggressive demand followed for a cricket tour in either direction. It was supported by the press, with the *Empire* stating: 'It is time for South Africa to send home something besides gold, diamonds and millionaires.'[29] In his desire to make the English public aware of developments at the Cape, Cadwallader began inserting details of local cricket matches in overseas journals such as *Sporting Life* and *Cricket: A Weekly Record of the Game*. He was interested in attracting the Australians, who were visiting England again. He pointed out that two of their players, '[Jack] Blackham and [Sammy] Jones, were both here *en route* home in October 1886 and expressed much regret at their not being able to meet our representatives'.[30]

In England, the Australian manager, Charles Beal, was more concerned with the form of his inexperienced team in 1888 because they were without players such as Giffen, Spofforth, Bruce, Moses and Trumble. The task was exacerbated by Jones developing smallpox during the eighth match and 'his life was in danger for some time'.[31] When Beal eventually turned his attention to South Africa, he forwarded a terse reply in mid-August: 'Thousand. You pay expenses, travelling and hotels.'[32]

The leader of the Afrikaner Bond and president of the Cape Town CC, J.H. 'Onze Jan' Hofmeyr, chaired a meeting of Cape Town cricketers and sportsmen at the St George's Hotel to decide whether to invite the Australians, an issue complicated by an offer from Major Robert Warton to bring out an English team. Warton had served on the Western Province CC committee and it was with loyalty to an old comrade, as much as there was a desire to play the 'Mother Country', that the meeting voted almost unanimously in favour of the England visit.

It was to be the first official sporting tour, although passing boats had stopped over at the Cape and played matches. In 1869, the *Flying Squadron* met the Western Province CC at the Wynberg Ground, with His Excellency the Governor and other dignitaries in attendance; and a team made up of cricketing passengers on the *Norsemen* were well beaten when they stopped over in 1871 to play a coloured eleven at Southey's Field. Players of colour were for a long time part of the local cricket scene, but no matches were arranged for Warton's tourists against black teams.

The focus on an English cricket tour in 1888 nevertheless prompted several business entrepreneurs – 'gentlemen from England' – to pursue the idea of assembling a black South African touring team along similar lines to that of the Aborigines of 1861. They launched their plan through the black newspaper, *Imvo Zabantsundu*, claiming that they were 'wishful to ascertain as to whether there is sufficient enthusiasm and ability among the Natives in the game of cricket as to warrant them in getting up a team for a tour through Great Britain next season (say to leave here in April 1889)'.

The editor of *Imvo Zabantsundu*, John Tengo Jabavu, gave his support by saying that the tour to England would 'afford our friends there the opportunity of realising the tone that European civilisation gives to the society of Africans'.[33] Some of the cricketers they were looking at were very capable, but the idea of the promoters gathering together black players to parade them before a curious paying public was not questioned. Plans were discussed and enthusiasm existed, but it was an impossible assignment. There were too many practical problems and when the last of the English businessmen left the country in January 1889, the proposed project was subsequently forgotten.

Warton's tour by then was underway. Milton's grand achievement in organising matches across the vast southern African landscape was perhaps tinged with irony as he had, in preceding years, demonstrated a reluctance to build relationships with other centres. In making up for lost time, he showed an ability to succeed where others had failed in previous attempts to stage a tour. He conceded it was not a financial success but pointed out that it had given 'great impetus to cricket'.[34] The welcome that Warton's team received was of a magnitude not previously experienced in the region. It brought both cricket itself and the key personalities, whether players, administrators or journalists, into the public eye. Political leaders were not slow to realise its significance and were soon clambering on the bandwagon.

The South African team selected for the first 'Test' at Port Elizabeth represented the various parts of the fragmented southern African political map. The first 'national' team – albeit English-speaking and white – came before there was a nation, a significant but perhaps understated development at the time in that the majority of the cricket-playing population expected unification in due course under the British flag. The tour also brought to light many of the problems that had simmered below the surface for some years. It was intended to promote imperial solidarity and, whilst several Afrikaans-speaking cricketers played against the touring team, their involvement was generally limited. Divisions were also apparent within English-speaking communities and Finlason questioned the loyalty of groups who supported the tourists, stating:

Nothing that the Colony has can equal anything that the Old Country has, nothing that a Colonial-born man can do can equal what a Home-born man can do. Such are the unfortunate opinions which are held by many men who owe every farthing they have in the world to the Colony they milk systematically in and out of season.[35]

Insight was gained into the way the game was played in various outposts. In the eastern Cape, 'articulate, settled, westernised black families had emerged ... [and] Africans established cricket clubs',[36] but when they were encouraged to support the matches at King William's Town, 'the sympathies of the native spectators were with the English'.[37] The touring captain, Aubrey Smith, in turn was conscious of the need to provide opportunities for all races to play cricket in South Africa. 'Our visit, which, from all that I can see,' he told a gathering in Port Elizabeth,

is calculated to have so great an effect on the cricket of the Cape, not only amongst the white population, but even amongst the black [people] ... wherever you go in the colonies you will find that it is cricket which binds men together in the cause of sport and I hope it will always be so.[38]

The Cape's rugby authorities hoped to go one better and send the first team overseas. They had no option but to display trust in Hill and the RFU when making a further effort to secure the desired tour. The new president of the Griqualand West RFU, 24-year-old Percival Ross Frames, wrote to various newspapers in September 1888, to inform readers that 'an inter-colonial tournament would afford an opportunity of discovering whether football has reached a sufficient state of perfection to justify a team sent to England at a not far distant date'.[39]

At the end of 1888 – Monday, 31 December – a 'South African [rugby] football conference' was staged at Cape Town. It was attended by representatives from the Western Province, Eastern Province and Griqualand West. The aim was to organise a tournament from which a side could be selected to visit England during the 1889/90 season. In order to do this and plan for the future, it was agreed that a South African Rugby Football Board should be formed at the August 1889 tournament at Kimberley.[40] Four teams entered the tournament, with the Eastern Province side selected from just three clubs, and Transvaal at one stage unlikely to participate because of mounting injuries and withdrawals. It reflected a disappointing state of affairs in terms of rugby depth, but the naming of the side to tour overseas was expected to be a highlight of the Kimberley tournament.

Frames was elected the first president of the new SA [Rugby] Football Board when delegates met in Glover's Athletic Bar committee room on Tuesday, 27 August 1889.[41] It should have been an auspicious occasion, but everyone was in a sombre mood. News had been received that the RFU was not in a position to entertain a touring team from southern Africa.

Finlason commented that delegates 'naturally felt the snub keenly'. He was critical of the 'toplofty frigidity' which had always 'been exhibited by representative English sporting bodies towards South Africa'. He referred to rugby's two attempts to arrange a tour as having been 'repulsed in the same cold way'. In an analysis, which served to underline his contempt for imperial arrogance, Finlason believed the project had 'struck the English Union as nothing but a money-making theme formulated by certain South African adventurers'. It disappointed him that the RFU did not seem prepared to discuss the proposed tour in any other light and he wrote:

> Even when they passingly enquire as to the quality of the team which could be bought over, the money question again fills their mind, and in effect, we are told that unless your team is a very good one and able to hold its own against decent clubs here, your gate will not be large and hence (this we are left to infer) the *raison d'être* of your scheme, which, of course is merely a money-making one, is gone.[42]

One Kimberley representative expressed his disgust by stating that 'the local share market offers better inducements for making money than a trip on a football tour to England does'.[43] Ironically, South Africa would not be affected by professionalism until a decade later, and then because players from England's northern union were 'continually arriving in this country' and wanted to play club rugby. There was sympathy for the former rugby league players but the SA Rugby Football Board felt it 'must abide by the rules of the [Rugby Football] Union'.[44]

Hofmeyr attended the inter-provincial tournament at Kimberley in 1889. He presented a cup to an outstanding Western Province player (Charlie van der Byl) while 'taking occasion in an eloquent and lengthy speech to combat the fear of those who held football to be a dangerous game and drew a happy augury of future success from the advance made'.[45] A few months earlier, he had been impressed by Warton's cricket tour in the way it united the South African states. He looked to rugby replicating the exercise under the new Western Province RFU president, Billy Simkins.

The Western Province RFU subsequently agreed to invite a British team to South Africa and sought permission from the board. In a later memoir, Jack Heyneman recalled Frames having no objection: 'He was the sole representative in Kimberley at the time and bundled all the papers down to Cape Town, saying he was "snowed under with work". This was really the start of the board's regime in Cape Town.'[46]

The groundwork for the proposed British tour to southern Africa in 1891 was conducted by Joe Richards who, during a stay of several months in London, 'acted like a Trojan on behalf of South African sport'.[47] There was much to be done in setting up the tour, particularly as Hill hedged on the go-ahead. Heyneman recalled: 'We accordingly began to move in the matter ... The English Rugby Union eventually asked who would guarantee the tour?'[48]

The Western Province rugby authorities turned to Cecil John Rhodes. The political alliance with Hofmeyr had secured his premiership after the fall of the Sprigg Cabinet in mid-July 1890. Rhodes appeared to be fully converted to the Bond's point of view 'on vital issues affecting it, like agricultural protection and "native policy"'.[49] Hofmeyr had been content to turn down the opportunity to form a government, preferring to back 'men with good sound Afrikander views' who were able to make judgements themselves.'[50] But it rarely happened that 'a proposal was submitted to the House without having been placed before the Afrikander leader'.[51]

It is not inconceivable that Hofmeyr convinced Rhodes to underwrite the tour, but there is no evidence to that effect. Heyneman recalled: 'W.P. Schreiner and H.H. Castens went off to see Rhodes. They waited all afternoon and when Rhodes arrived and heard their quandary he immediately said, "I'll guarantee the tour."'[52] Schreiner knew Rhodes well, having worked with him, but it was several years before he became his attorney-general.

The last but all-important piece was thus in place and greeted with some relief by the rugby authorities. Negotiating with Hill was never straightforward, recounted Simkins, 'but when we cabled home, "Rhodes, Premier, guarantees expenses" the team came out [under tour captain Bill Maclagan]'.[53] Heyneman added: 'When they arrived, Maclagan, Ash, Simkins, Castens and I got together, and Maclagan asked: "What about the guarantee?" Simkins laughed and said, "Do you want Rhodes to sign a chit to that effect?" Laughingly, we dispersed.'[54]

It was the first tour sanctioned by the RFU and a committee had been formed to select a 21-strong side consisting of players from English and Scottish clubs. Eight were internationals and fourteen from Oxford and Cambridge universities.[55] The composition of the team differed considerably from the working-class, northern-based side that had toured Australasia in 1888.[56] There was also careful consideration given to the appointment of the manager – Edwin Ash, the first secretary-treasurer of the RFU – and to the programme of matches. Hill sent a telegram requesting the Transvaal arrangements be dropped because the varsity men 'find it impossible to extend their absence owing to previous engagements at home'.[57]

On their arrival at the Cape, the touring team immediately agreed to play in the Transvaal where the English-speaking residents were not slow to use the tour in promoting their cause. The guest speaker at one after-match dinner for the team was Advocate Charles Leonard who was about to establish an organised *Uitlander* – 'foreigner' – movement, and would later publish an extensive series of grievances that placed President Kruger's government in a negative light.[58] He wished to obtain equal political rights for *Uitlanders* and told the rugby tourists that while they 'hoped for political freedom ere long', he believed their 'common love of sport would materially hasten that desired union of races in South Africa'.[59]

Herbert Castens, born in the eastern Cape, educated at Rugby School and an Oxford blue, captained South Africa in the first Test at Port Elizabeth on Thursday, 30 July 1891. He was the son of Emil Castens, the president of the host union, Eastern Province. The South Africans, who played in the white jerseys of the local Crusader club, surprised everyone in that they were 'able for the greatest part of the game to more than hold their own against the Englishmen'.

South Africa lost by two tries and a conversion to nil, but their performance was encouraging. Castens 'fully justified his selection for he made frequent telling dribbles'. Alf Richards, who might earlier have been selected for England, was 'simply grand at half. He was ever on the ball, stopping rushes and putting in timely kicks.'[60] Castens was unlucky to be dropped but was called upon to referee the third Test in Cape Town, a match in which Richards captained the South African team.

There was no lack of involvement from Afrikaans-speakers in the rugby tour. The work that the Western Province RFU had undertaken in establishing a country league was paying dividends and Afrikaners were amongst the finest players that the tourists came across. A trip was made to the farming districts outside Cape Town where a game at Stellenbosch was added to the original itinerary. The challenge from the 'old Dutch settlement' very nearly produced a defeat for the tourists as Marthinus Daneel crossed their line but was tackled when heading inwards to the goalposts. He lost possession and the chance to score in a match that the British scraped home by two points to nil. It was an era when one point was awarded for a try and two for a conversion.

The British won all 20 matches on tour, scoring 226 points (including 89 tries) with just one point in reply. The team considered to have given the tourists their best game was awarded the Currie Cup. The trophy named after Sir Donald

Currie, head of the Castle Line shipping company, was presented to Griqualand West. It later became a floating trophy for inter-provincial competition.

Dignitaries and rugby organisers lunched on the *Garth Castle* where they bid farewell to the tourists. Rhodes and Hofmeyr were there, as were former and future prime ministers, Thomas Upington, William Schreiner and John X. Merriman. Nearly thirty years earlier, Merriman had been part of the historic first 'football' fixture in Cape Town. In proposing a toast, he informed guests that he not only remembered being knocked down and trampled on in scrummages but had not forgotten that 'physical endurance and the exercise of other good qualities formed a valuable part of the national character'.[61]

Many years later, one of the visiting players, Paul Clauss, wrote an article in which he analysed the benefits of the tour. He concluded that the measure of success was not in the matter of matches won or points scored. It was a case of what happened next. 'We little dreamt,' he remarked, 'that only fifteen years later the first team of Springboks to visit us would win 25 out of 28 games, beating Ireland and Wales, and drawing with England.'[62]

Simkins replaced Frames as president of the SA Rugby Football Board in July 1893, and Cadwallader, who had earlier founded the SA Cricket Association, was elected secretary/treasurer. They were the only office-bearers on a committee that was made up of two representatives from each 'state, colony or province'. The year they were in office together was regarded as productive, with the newly designated board proceeding towards a new constitution. Cadwallader was praised for getting the board into shape, financial and otherwise, but there was no reward for him.

The tenacious journalist clashed with Milton over the proposed selection of Krom Hendricks for the 1894 cricket tour to England. Milton was furious that Cadwallader not only championed Hendricks but repeatedly criticised Cape government interference. Although Cadwallader had organised the venture, Milton successfully campaigned against his appointment as manager and saw to it that he was removed from his posts of responsibility in cricket. Simkins was named tour manager and Castens captain. Both were under Milton's influence and happy to inform the English public that Hendricks was 'over-rated'.

Rugby officials demonstrated their support for the anti-Hendricks faction at the next general meeting by replacing Cadwallader as secretary. Effectively, the journalist had paid a heavy price for advocating the selection of a player of colour for a national team. Life became difficult for him in Cape Town and he was transferred to the *Licensed Victualler* in Johannesburg. He was 34 when he died three years later, a broken man.

A British side toured again in 1896, with reports reflecting widespread interest. In the first Test played at Port Elizabeth, it was noted:

A large number of country visitors journeyed down to view the proceedings, and when the kick-off was signalled upwards of 7500 spectators thronged the barricades, while both pavilions were filled to overfilling. Both teams came in for an enthusiastic reception and as Crean and Myburgh led the respective fifteens on to the ground a great roar of welcome greeted them from all sides.[63]

It was a typical tour scene, but it is odd that Francis Rudolph Myburgh has since been overlooked by historians as South Africa's captain. Apart from leading the team onto the field, he was named as the South African captain in pre-match newspaper team lists and later appeared as such on the Bishops' honours board.[64] It was also custom in the early years for the local union to nominate the captain of the Test side.

The British beat Eastern Province 18–0 on Tuesday, 28 July and South Africa 8–0 on Thursday, 30 July. In an often hectic tour, the visitors won the first three Tests. With each game, South Africa edged closer to an elusive win. They scored their first tries in international rugby in the second Test at Johannesburg where they were defeated 17–8. They opened the scoring in the third Test at Kimberley but lost 9–3. The British were able to counter strong South African packs by wheeling or 'screwing' the scrum – 'we won all our matches by it', wrote the British forward, Walter Carey. It was a tactic that referee Alf Richards ruled illegal in the fourth Test at Newlands. The visitors 'felt sore about this', while South Africa went on to win the match 5–0.[65] Alf Larard, born in Kingston-upon-Hull, scored the try, which was converted by Tommy Hepburn, born in Shoshong, Bechuanaland.

The victory was a key turning point in South Africa's rugby history. They would not lose another rugby series, home or away, for 60 years.

Notes

1   *Cape Times*, 27 August 1888.
2   Ibid., 13 September 1880; Cape Town had been unable to send a side to compete in the Champion Bat tournament, played at King William's Town in January 1880.
3   *Cape Argus*, 26 May 1881 and 4 July 1881.
4   A letter dated 4 July 1881, published in the *Cape Argus* the following day.
5   *Cape Times*, 10 July 1886.
6   Ibid., 14 July 1886.
7   *Daily Independent*, 14 July 1886.
8   *Port Elizabeth Telegraph & Eastern Province Standard*, 26 July 1886; *Diamond Fields Advertiser*; 15 July 1886.
9   *Lantern*, 3 September 1886.
10   *Daily Independent*, 7 August 1886.
11   Letter from Rowland Hill, RFU, 17 March 1887.

12   T. Collins, *A Social History of English Rugby Union* (Abingdon: Routledge, 2009), 27.
13   Report in *Whitehall Review* published in *Cape Times*, 25 December 1886.
14   *Cape Times Weekly*, 23 February 1887.
15   *Cape Times*, 27 August 1888.
16   Ibid., 28 March 1888.
17   *Cape Times Weekly*, 11 April 1888.
18   T. Collins, *Rugby's Great Split: Class, Culture and the Origins of Rugby League Football* (Frank Cass, London, 2003), 73–74.
19   *Daily Independent*, 12 and 17 April 1888.
20   H. Richards, *A Game for Hooligans: The History of Rugby Union* (Edinburgh: Mainstream Publishing, 2006), 65–66.
21   *Daily Independent*, 19 June 1888.
22   *Cape Times*, 27 August 1888.
23   G. Ryan, *Forerunners of the All Blacks: The 1888–89 New Zealand Native Football Team in Britain, Australia and New Zealand* (Christchurch: Canterbury University Press, 1993), 18.
24   P. Wynne Thomas, *The Complete History of Cricket Tours at Home and Abroad* (London: Hamlyn, 1989), 208–209.
25   Clifton Rugby Football Club history: www.cliftonrfchistory.co.uk; accessed 28 March 2020.
26   Ryan, *Forerunners of the All Blacks*, 85–87.
27   *Cape Times Weekly*, 10 April 1889.
28   *Cape Times*, 6 November 1897.
29   Report in *Empire* published in *Daily Independent*, 30 March 1888.
30   Report in *Lantern* published in *Daily Independent*, 14 June 1888.
31   Wynne-Thomas, *The Complete History of Cricket Tours*, 219.
32   *Cape Times*, 23 August 1888.
33   *Imvo Zabantsundu*, 3 November 1888.
34   *Cape Argus*, 3 September 1890.
35   *Daily Independent*, 21 January 1889.
36   S. Marks, 'Class, Culture and Consciousness in South Africa, 1880–1899', in R. Ross, A. Mager and B. Nasson (eds), *The Cambridge History of South Africa, Volume 2, 1885–1994* (Cambridge: Cambridge University Press, 2011), 141.
37   *Imvo Zabantsundu*, 28 February 1889.
38   *Port Elizabeth Telegraph & Eastern Province Standard*, 3 January 1889.
39   *Cape Times*, 21 September 1888.
40   Initially recorded as the SA Football Board, it would be confirmed as the SA Rugby Football Board in October 1893.
41   This is the first reference to the actual date that the SA [Rugby] Football Board was formed. The Board's centenary publication believed the establishment of the date and details of the meeting were 'beyond possibility' (P. Dobson, *Rugby in South Africa: A History 1861–1988* (Cape Town: SARB, 1989), 33. The *Daily Independent* (31 August 1889) is clear in naming the date and venue.
42   *Daily Independent*, 31 August 1889.
43   Ibid.
44   *Diamond Fields Advertiser*, 24 August 1897.
45   *Cape Times Weekly*, 9 October 1891.
46   *Cape Times*, 30 March 1927.
47   Ibid., 13 June 1889.
48   Ibid., 30 March 1927.
49   M. Tamarkin, *Cecil Rhodes and the Cape Afrikaners: The Imperial Colossus and the Colonial Parish Pump* (London: Routledge, 1996), 127.
50   R. Rotberg, *The Founder: Cecil Rhodes and the Pursuit of Power* (Oxford: Oxford University Press, 1988), 341.
51   J. Hofmeyr and F. Reitz, *The Life of Jan Hendrik Hofmeyr (Onze Jan)* (Cape Town: Van de Sandt De Villiers, 1913), 375.
52   *Cape Times*, 30 March 1927.
53   Ibid., 10 September 1891.

54   Ibid., 30 March 1927.
55   I. Difford (ed.), *The History of South African Football* (Wynberg: Speciality Press, 1933), 258–259. The internationals were W. Mitchell, R. Aston, W. Bromet, P. Hancock (England), P. Clauss, W. Maclagan, W. Wotherspoon and R. MacMillan (Scotland). A. Rotherham was later selected for England.
56   C. Thomas and G. Thomas, *125 Years of the British & Irish Lions: The Official History* (Edinburgh: Mainstream, 2013), 50.
57   *Cape Times*, 13 June 1891.
58   C. Muller, *Five Hundred Years: A History of South Africa* (Pretoria: Academica, 1981), 287–292.
59   *The Star*, 24 August 1891.
60   *Port Elizabeth Telegraph & Eastern Province Standard*, 1 August 1891.
61   *Cape Times*, 10 September 1891.
62   Difford, *History of South African Football*, 258–259. Clauss does not include the victory over France.
63   *The Star*, 31 July 1896.
64   For team list details in the week prior to the Test, see for example the *Port Elizabeth Telegraph & Eastern Province Standard*, the *Eastern Province Herald* and the *Cape Times Weekly*.
65   Difford, *History of South African Football*, 268–269.

5

'A Progressive of Progressives'

It seems that in the 1890s, Grendon saw interethnic
cooperation in sports associations as laying the groundwork
for cooperation in more important areas of life.[1]

– Grant Christison

Robert Grendon was the first president of the South African Coloured Rugby
Football Board. He was an extraordinary man – an intellectual, poet, teacher,
writer, musician, sportsman – who was born in pre-colonial Namibia and lived
from 1867 to 1949. 'The Owl' writing in the *Citizen* on 16 April 1898 described
Grendon as 'certainly a progressive of progressives'.

Grendon's unusual background would in part account for his later restless,
often confrontational ways. His Irish father, Joseph Grendon, fought in the
Indian Mutiny and went on to establish a trading post in central Damaraland
(Namibia). Joseph had three children with a Herero woman, Maria, reputedly
the daughter of Maherero (*c.*1820–1890), the ruler of the Otjohorongo clan.

Grendon's boyhood was spent at Otjimbingwe and Okahandja near
Maherero's court but after the death of his mother, he and his siblings, Mary
Ann and William, moved to Cape Town. The boys attended Zonnebloem College,
which had been founded by Robert Gray, the first Anglican bishop of Cape Town,
and Sir George Grey, governor and high commissioner of the Cape. The original
idea was to convert black children – notably the offspring of the chiefs – into
English gentlemen and women.[2]

Michael Lambert recognises weaknesses in a system where 'grand narratives'
of empire were constantly undermined by experiences of British colonial rule
in daily practice. 'Grendon's classical education and his socialisation into
"Englishness" at Zonnebloem,' writes Lambert, 'seems to have produced an
uneasy identity, characteristic of many "coloured" South Africans of this and
later periods.' He also thinks Grendon's classical education, 'embedded in a

treacherously idealistic view of British intentions in Africa, ultimately prepared him for an intellectual no-man's-land, forever betwixt and between, neither white nor black, at the whim of *Fortuna* disguised as Britannica.'[3]

Grendon would ultimately graduate as a schoolteacher with distinction from the University of the Cape of Good Hope in 1889. It was a fine achievement because much of his time had been devoted to playing sport.

Cricket was introduced at Zonnebloem in 1861 and had been taken up with obsessive enthusiasm by the boys. The college fielded four sides with matches played mid-week as well as on Saturdays. Grendon was an outstanding player and represented the College First XI for several years. His enthusiasm was such that he also played cricket for St Mark's and Progress clubs in Cape Town. At a time when centuries were rare, he compiled 110 out of 204 (H. Daniels 68, extras 14, no other double figures) for Progress against Royal Scots (who were dismissed for 74) at Fort Knokke in January 1886. He then made another century – 103 against the Army – in the same season.[4]

While at Zonnebloem, Grendon developed an interest in rugby and played the game when he obtained a teaching post at Beaconsfield, formerly Du Toit's Pan, in Kimberley. But it was at cricket that he excelled. He represented Kimberley when they hosted the third Malay inter-town tournament during March/April 1891. The desire to win the Glover Cup was such that Malay teams included coloured Christians; a tendency that also helped break down barriers. At his first tournament, Grendon's inspirational batting enabled Kimberley to emerge as champions. He scored 80 not out against Port Elizabeth and then a brilliant 111 out of 191 in the final against Cape Town. A combined side was selected to play against a Kimberley 'European' XI and Grendon continued his rich vein of form by striking 92 in a drawn encounter.

At the next inter-town tournament in December 1891, Grendon played arguably the finest innings yet seen on the diamond fields. Representing a combined tournament team against Kimberley's Europeans, he was on a different level from everyone else involved in the game. Batting first, Malay wickets fell at regular intervals but Grendon was in imperious form, striking the ball with 'considerable power and precision' to hammer 110 out of 149 for seven and ultimately a magnificent 187 to enable his team to reach 269. In reply, the Kimberley Europeans were 123 for seven when stumps were drawn.[5]

There was little doubt that Grendon would have been a strong contender for a place in a South African team at international level if he had not been a player of colour. Cricket, however, was just one of his many interests at a time of 'almost frenetic activity. In addition to teaching school, the days were a ceaseless whirl of cricket tournaments, rugby engagements, athletics meetings, sports administration, musical recitals, botanising, forays into literature, freelance newspaper work, and – always – politics'.[6]

Not long after he arrived in Kimberley, Grendon was appointed secretary of the executive committee of the Coloured People's Association, also referred to as the Griqualand West Agitation Committee. Their main concern was that white parliamentarians were placing legislative restrictions upon the non-racial franchise that had traditionally represented hope within racist South Africa. The ruling class at the Cape were in the process of subjecting inhabitants of the colony to increased formal separation through building on the Parliamentary Registration Bill that had been enacted in 1887.

The passage of the Franchise and Ballot Act of 16 August 1892, driven by the prime minister, Cecil John Rhodes, with support from the Afrikaner Bond, was accomplished by 47 votes to 13. Rhodes was happy to further weaken a liberal tradition that posed an obstacle in the way of creating a South African federation alongside the Transvaal and Orange Free State where there was no similar structure. 'Psychologically,' explains Robert I. Rotberg, 'Rhodes readied parliament and the colony for more far-reaching measures.'[7]

The Coloured People's Association opposed the Act, with Grendon fully involved in the resulting 'agitation'. He cherished the Cape's enlightened race policy, even if it 'was always a minority creed and a rather frail one at that'.[8] He wrote to the British prime minister, William E. Gladstone, on 22 August 1892, to inform him of the stand that the coloured people were taking against the Cape franchise bill. This included a large protest meeting convened in Cape Town to muster support for a petition.

By late September there were 10 341 signatures and Grendon returned to Cape Town to present the petition to the acting governor, Lieutenant General Cameron. At the same time, he wrote a letter to the *Diamond Fields Advertiser* in which he not only explained the wide support base of the protest movement but blamed its failure on the newspaper editor and politician, John Tengo Jabavu:

> The natives are beginning to see the mischief that will be caused by the alteration, for had the editor of *Imvo* done his duty as a man; had he looked at the matter in its proper light; had he interpreted the natives' opinion in its true form, instead of beating about the bush to secure the favour of both parties concerned in this question; had he considered his position as one in whom the voice of a people was centred; there would to-day have been no alteration in the Franchise.[9]

Literary and social historian Tim Couzens comments that 'here Grendon's early identification with the "natives" is as interesting as the uncompromising and outspoken stance he takes. These are the two most characteristic traits of his later life.'[10]

Grendon fought a determined battle on behalf of the Coloured People's Association but the agitation failed because the establishment had seen the organisation as being essentially Muslim. This was despite the 450 active members in Kimberley in early 1893 being drawn from Muslim, black African ('Native'), Indian, and coloured ('Cape Men') sectors of the community. They were united in their stated objective 'to make black voters more politically-aware, to campaign for political equality, to secure a higher standard of education for historically-disadvantaged groups, and to provide for better representation of coloured people on the jury lists.'[11]

The non-racial nature of the community was also reflected in its rugby. In 1894, the Griqualand West Colonial Rugby Football Union was constituted. It is described by André Odendaal as being 'one of the very first sports organisations in South Africa which was specifically non-racial'. The Xhosa columns of *Imvo Zabantsundu* noted that it did not discriminate on the basis of '*bala, luhhlanga, lulwimi, nalunqulo*' (colour, nationality, language or religion).[12] It consisted of coloured, Malay (Muslim) and African clubs. The four founding clubs – Universals, Violets, Excelsior from Beaconsfield and the Native Rovers Rugby Football Club – were joined the following year by Progress.

Grant Christison says that Grendon 'viewed black interethnic rugby as a wholesome stimulus to the formation of a more ethnically-inclusive communal spirit. Whereas black cricketers showed comparatively little resistance to playing against persons of a different ethnic and cultural background, rugby – being a contact sport – seems to have offended the scruples of not a few.'[13]

Kimberley was a forward-looking society but tension still existed. This was noted by Bud Mbelle, a product of Healdtown in the eastern Cape, who had been appointed clerk and interpreter for African languages at the Supreme Court of Griqualand West. In 1895, Mbelle reacted immediately when the *Diamond Fields Advertiser* reported on a case where three coloured clubs had withdrawn from the local cricket league because a black African was elected as a vice-president. He informed the newspaper that he could

> understand the objection of the clubs if it was based on the fact that a barbarous native, a street Malay, nay, even a stupid Cape coloured man had been elected to such a post. As far as ability, education, and all other things – except an almost white colour – are concerned, Mr Moss is far superior to any of the men composing the three clubs.[14]

As captain of the Native Rovers Rugby Football Club (RFC), Mbelle was aware of Kimberley's desire to form a national governing body for rugby. Its structure would be similar to that of the SA Rugby Football Board, which had been founded in Kimberley eight years earlier. Those involved wished to emulate the white example and to build on the progress made by the Griqualand West Colonial Rugby Football Union (RFU). Mbelle became a driving force and was instrumental in Cecil John Rhodes being approached in 1897 to donate a trophy for 'non-European rugby'. It would be for 'all the coloured sporting people of South Africa ... for competition amongst themselves on the same lines as the Currie Cup'.[15] Rhodes presented a handsome silver cup worth 50 guineas, with the stipulation that the headquarters of the national body remain in Kimberley.

On 19 August 1897, a meeting was held at the Savona Café in Kimberley to propose the formation of the SA Coloured Rugby Football Board. The Griqualand West Colonial RFU had circularised black clubs across the country, inviting them to send delegates to the meeting. Griqualand West officials attended, but Port Elizabeth (Rovers and Union) and African clubs in King Williams Town and Johannesburg were represented by proxies only. The secretary read the notice – a circular issued by the local union dated 21 July 1897 – convening the meeting. Joseph Joshua (Progress) proposed and Bud Mbelle (Rovers) seconded that a South African Coloured Rugby Football Board be formed – 'carried nem. con'.[16]

The meeting elected Grendon as president of the board, and Mbelle as its secretary. Daniel Lenders and Ed Heneke were elected auditors. All four of the office-bearers were from Kimberley and active in the town's political and social affairs. They were, says Odendaal, 'respected figures within the emerging black educated and political elite'.[17] Grendon addressed the audience, reporting that 'owing to a little difference in Cape Town and Port Elizabeth amongst the players', these centres had not been properly represented at this important first meeting. Separate competitions served the different ethnic groups, which created friction and made combined teams difficult to arrange. However, Grendon remained optimistic and 'hoped that time would vanish all differences from amongst all our sportsmen'.[18]

The printed competition rules of the Rhodes Cup, together with correspondence from all centres, were presented. The colours of the teams were also recorded. It was resolved that a tournament for the competition of the Rhodes Cup be held in Kimberley in August 1898. It was further resolved that the secretary inform the various centres of the proceedings of the board and also forward a copy of the rules when complete.

On the proposal of Mbelle, seconded by Grendon, it was unanimously resolved that the board express 'the gratitude and appreciation of the Coloured inhabitants of South Africa to the Rt Hon C.J. Rhodes for the fifty-guinea silver cup which he so generously presented to them; and also heartily thank Mr W. Pickering for the assistance he personally rendered to the Griqualand West Colonial RFU of Kimberley in procuring the cup'.[19]

Mbelle then read a letter from William Pickering in which the latter consented to become patron to the board. Pickering was the brother of Neville, who had been Rhodes's closest friend and sole heir. In 1886, William had watched over his dying brother's bed with Rhodes. He then became acting secretary to De Beers in his brother's place and later secretary and a director of the company.

The day before the meeting, the Kimberley rugby team, under the management of Daniel Lenders, had embarked on a rugby venture to Cape Town. It was the perfect opportunity to establish strong links with Western Province and to discuss the aims of a national body. On their return, the touring side was welcomed back at a gathering in September 1897 at the Mission Hall, Jones Street and 'almost every seat [was] occupied. A programme of music began the evening.'

Will P. Thompson, a black American, had been the touring party's secretary. He had also been the tenor with the Virginia Jubilee Singers, a group of African-American musicians who toured South Africa during the 1890s. The group was led by Orpheus McAdoo, who aimed 'to introduce to the theatrical and music-loving public the genuine American negro as a comedian, singer, dancer, banjoist and general mirth-maker'. They were transformed into 'the only true exponent of American Coon songs in South Africa'. Thompson, however, had his differences with the impresario, and in February 1897 decided to take up residence in Kimberley, alternatively performing with the Colonial Concert Company and the Philharmonic Society and directing the Diamond Minstrels.[20]

Grendon became a tenor in Kimberley's Colonial Concert Company of which the impresario was Thompson. A friendship developed, which proved beneficial for rugby. The Jubilee Singers were ambitious and innovative in various ways and in Kimberley established the *Citizen* newspaper in 1897, the earliest independent publication for coloureds.[21] Thompson was a leading light in the venture, and rugby not only benefited from the publicity received in the *Citizen* but also enjoyed live entertainment at club functions – and on the tour to Cape Town.

Lenders reported that during the Cape Town tour they had played eight, won three, lost four, and drawn one, but had been placed under considerable disadvantage by having to conform to the 1896 rules under which the Cape Town teams played. He then spoke generally about the tour and its aim 'to promote the game of rugby union amongst the coloured community without distinction

(Hear! Hear!)'. He thought that rugby 'had jumped by leaps and bounds in popularity and was pleased that they were in a good financial state – able to send a team to Cape Town'. With references to the Rhodes Cup, he anticipated 'there would be some difficulty in some parts as some of the coloured clubs had refused to meet others of other coloured races. King William's Town, Port Elizabeth, Griqualand West and Johannesburg were not amongst this class and he hoped that they would keep their present opinions.'[22]

According to the *Citizen*, Grendon responded to the points made by Lenders by stating that Rhodes 'had given the Cup to the coloured rugby football players of South Africa, and he hoped there would be uniformity of opinion on the matter'.[23]

Christison comments: 'It becomes apparent that racial prejudice impinged upon harmonious sporting relations, just as it did upon all other aspects of cultural interaction in South Africa ... Even within their own ranks, players "of colour" did not always relish playing with – or even against – others of differing ethnic background.' He pointed out that Grendon had assisted the Western Province Coloured RFU during 1897/98 and that this experience might well have encouraged him towards achieving the unity he envisaged:

> [It] seems likely that Grendon believed that as players encountered one another with increasing frequency on the sports fields, the old prejudices would break down ... It seems that in the 1890s, Grendon saw interethnic cooperation in sports associations as laying the groundwork for cooperation in more important areas of life.[24]

After Grendon's response, Mbelle then stepped onto the platform and reinforced Grendon's plea for greater unity amongst coloured sportsmen:

> He briefly referred to sport in Europe where no distinctions are made as to race, complexion and creed, instancing Prince [Ranjitsinhji] and others. In Cape Town, the native coloured man and the aboriginal native do not want to play with the Malay. In Port Elizabeth the native coloured man and the Malay do not want to play with the aboriginal native. In the border towns the aboriginal native and the Malay do not want to play with the native coloured man. But he was glad to say that Kimberley would have none of these absurd classifications. Kimberley has proved that by the representative team which they were welcoming that night and also the composition of the platform. Thus in the game of unity in sport Kimberley has already scored a 'try', and he trusted that before the next century dawned upon them that try would be converted into a goal of unity in sport throughout South Africa.[25]

79

Grendon and Mbelle were aware of the difficulties that confronted them. It would be nearly one hundred years before the 'game of unity in sport' was discussed by rival groups and the 'goal of unity' was achieved.

In March 1898, a *Citizen* columnist reported: 'I learn that that good sportsman, Mr Robert Grendon, will shortly leave Kimberley to take charge of a school in Uitenhage. "Bob" will be greatly missed ... his departure from our midst will be hailed with general regret.'[26] Grendon moved to Uitenhage where he briefly edited *Coloured South African*, later incorporated into the *South African Spectator*. He continued to head rugby's governing body, although Lenders chaired the annual general meeting in May, when representatives from the rugby unions of Western Province, Eastern Province, and Transvaal attended, along with the host Griqualand West Colonial RFU.

Grendon returned for the SA Coloured Rugby Football Board meeting in July. Its main purpose was to consider the application of the Eastern Province Coloured Rugby Union for affiliation to the board. Rovers and Union from Port Elizabeth were among the founders of the board and up to that stage had been recognised as the Eastern Province Union. The application of a second union representing the Eastern Province coloured body was discussed but agreement could not be reached, and it was decided the matter should be referred to the white Eastern Province RFU for arbitration.[27]

Grendon and Mbelle travelled widely, attending to grievances and ensuring the various areas established unions and registered with the national body. They were successful although divisions that existed in non-white rugby would be reflected in the sporting demographics of the teams that participated in the first Rhodes Cup during 20–27 August. These demographics indicated the coloured/Muslim composition of the Western Province and Transvaal teams, the African names of the Eastern Province squad, and the fully mixed Griqualand West side.[28]

Rugby coverage was prominent amidst important political developments taking place. In the period prior to the Anglo-Boer War, the coloured vote was important and attracted promises of equal rights. Rhodes altered his slogan of 'equal rights for every white man south of the Zambezi' to 'equal rights for every civilised man south of the Zambezi', and defined 'civilised' as a man white or black, 'who has sufficient education to write his name, has some property, or works. In fact, is not a loafer.'[29] The elections 'were fought with a ferocity and expenditure of money unexampled in the sober annals of the Cape Colony.'[30] Rhodes's Progressive party (38 seats) would lose to the Independent-Afrikaner Bond (40 seats), despite winning 53.1 per cent of the popular vote against 38.0 per cent. William Schreiner – an independent – was elected prime minister not long after informing Parliament that Rhodes 'was the cause of all the unrest and friction and race hatred in South Africa'.[31]

Rhodes Cup advertisements were placed in the *Diamond Fields Advertiser* and tickets were obtainable at Looney's in Dutoitspan Road. The tournament secretary Thomas Dooling asked the public to choose their 'Griqua XVs' and forward lists to him care of the *Diamond Field Advertiser* – he wished to allow readers the opportunity to give their opinions regarding selection. It was reported that spectators 'rolled up in good numbers'; admission was one shilling to the ground, three shillings to the pavilion and two shillings to the temporary pavilion. The mayor was in attendance; the South African rugby international, Chubb Vigne, was one of the referees, and the weather was far from pleasant – a strong wind blowing, with a dust accompaniment.[32]

Western Province defeated Eastern Province 19–3 in a largely one-sided encounter. R. Maher of Western Province was the first man to score a try in the Rhodes Cup, breaking from inside his half and crossing in the corner. A. Kamaldien and A. Kennie each scored a brace and A. Seldon provided two conversions. Finally, 'in the dying moments, Eastern Province took advantage from an intercept and forged their way deep into the Western Province territory from where P. Dalaza went over'.[33]

Griqualand West then defeated the Transvalers 19–0, P. Jampies scoring two tries. Although the victory margin flattered the home side, it did mean the second day – when Griquas played Western Province – would almost certainly decide the overall winner.

Griqualand West wore green jerseys with a yellow diamond on the left breast whilst Western Province were in navy blue and white. The result was in doubt until close to the finish in a stern forward battle. The Kimberley backs were superior but the heavy Western Province pack eventually wore down their lighter opponents. Kimberley were on top in the first half: 'W. Flooks, P. Jampies and J.H. Sikili had some dashing runs. Stellenburg eventually scored, securing the ball on the "25" and getting over in the corner to the delight of the crowd. Flooks couldn't convert.' After the interval, recounted the *Diamond Fields Advertiser*, 'Western Province and Griquas fought a great battle with Griquas 3–0 in the lead with moments to go, when H. Kennie ran half the length of the field to score a try which Seldon converted. Western Province won 5–3.'[34]

On the final day, the Rhodes Cup concluded in presence of a large crowd. Western Province beat Transvaal 8–0 while Griquas beat Eastern Province 11–6. 'Both matches were keenly contested – some capital play being witnessed ... Eastern Province played up splendidly and showed a great improvement on their previous form.'

In a summary of the Rhodes Cup tournament, the *Diamond Fields Advertiser* commented:

> The coloured players cannot complain of lack of support either on the part of their own people or Europeans and if they do not shine in rugby football in the future it will be their own fault ... The Western Province pack for instance is an excellent one, several of the men being first-class. Of the backs, Sikili, Jampies and H. Kennie have displayed capital form and would not have disgraced any team. The first named is perhaps entitled to the post of honour. His kicking and tackling are alike excellent, his one fault being that he does not appear to consider his colleagues sufficiently. This by the way is a fault that is common to the Kimberley backs who show a tendency to play too much on their own – too much 'gallery' play.[35]

The cup was presented to the winning team on the Saturday evening at the Woodley Street Hall by William Pickering, patron of the SA Coloured Rugby Football Board, in the presence of a fairly large gathering of footballers and their friends. 'The tournament,' observes Odendaal, 'was a significant achievement, predating formal political co-operation along inter-racial lines by nearly a decade; for it was only in 1907 that the South African Native Congress and the coloured APO held their first formal joint conference.'[36]

In 1899, the year after the first Rhodes Cup tournament, the Anglo-Boer War broke out and disrupted the normal activities of life, including rugby. The SA Coloured Rugby Football Board suspended its national tournament for the duration of the conflict. Grendon joined the war effort as a driver of the forge wagon of the 42nd Battery Royal Fleet Auxiliary and was present at the Battle of Bergendal in August 1900.

The high commissioner and governor, Sir Alfred Milner, asserted that the Transvaal's discrimination against blacks was a 'justification for intervention' while Joseph Chamberlain, the secretary of state for the colonies, told the British Parliament that victory would bring 'equal laws, equal liberty' to all.[37] Coloureds and Africans had little option but to take them at their word and hope for change and improved treatment in the event of a British victory. At the very least they thought they would retain the rights they had.

After the war, promises made by the British leaders were broken and there was bitter disappointment for coloureds and Africans who suffered huge casualties and were betrayed by a 'white man's' peace. Imperial rhetoric that the war had been fought to bring equal rights was a lie. Grendon remained loyal to the British but his attitude towards Milner changed and he likened the arrogant leader to King Herod, predicting that his popularity would not last and he would soon have throngs baying for his blood: 'To-day, whilst "fortune smiles", they hail their idol with a deafening "*Hosanna*". To-morrow, when fortune frowns – *as assuredly it must!* – their salutation will be changed to a furious "*Crucify!*"'[38]

Grendon became headmaster of the Wesleyan mission school Edendale, west of Pietermaritzburg from 1900 to 1903 before teaching at a school at KaLabutsheni, Swaziland and then serving as headmaster of John Dube's Ohlange Institute. While Dube (first president of the SA Native National Congress, later the African National Congress) was abroad during 1904–05, Grendon was influential as a lead writer for *Illanga*. He was also a private tutor to the Swazi princes, notably King Sobhuza, and became involved in the SA Native National Congress, serving as editor-in-chief of *Abantu-Batho*, the organisation's newspaper.

Mbelle was also involved in politics. He joined the SA Native National Congress while in Kimberley and became increasingly active after moving to Johannesburg. In 1917 he was elected as the party's general secretary and helped articulate the grievances of his fellow Africans against discriminatory measures, even though he could be considered conservative and moderate in his actions.

Lenders became vice-president of the African Political (later People's) Organisation (APO) when it was formed in September 1902. Establishing the pressure group was done reluctantly because coloured people saw the political dangers of setting themselves up as a 'racial' grouping, which would play into the hands of those who wished to deny them political rights on racial grounds. Nonetheless, it was recognised that the erosion of their rights required a focused opposition.

In 1909, Lenders was a member of the South African Native and Coloured Delegation that travelled to London to protest before the British Parliament against the new South African colour-bar Constitution. The delegation was led by William Schreiner, the former prime minister of the Cape Colony and future president of the SA Rugby Football Board. It was a futile bid to persuade the British Parliament not to ratify the Constitution for the new Union of South Africa until the discriminatory 'colour-bar' clauses in it were removed. The delegation marked a high point in the history of African political mobilisation and paved the way for the formation of the SA Native National Congress in 1912.

Lenders continued as president of the SA Coloured Rugby Football Board. Under his leadership, the Rhodes Cup increasingly became a coloured organisation with virtually no African participation. The second tournament took place in 1903, the year after the peace agreement was signed. This was the beginning of a run of six tournaments in seven years held at rotating venues but after 1909 the board went into decline. There were many reasons: the 1909 tournament ended in unpleasant controversy; Lenders died in 1912; the union did not have the financial resources to run a national organisation; and the governing body in Kimberley was located far from other centres of coloured rugby in Cape Town, the Boland area and Port Elizabeth.

As rugby was showing 'no sign of improvement' and 'no desire to develop the finer points of the game', there were desperate efforts in 1911 to promote interest through the promise of an overseas tour.[39] It was an idea that 'had frequently been discussed amongst prominent clubs' and the APO thought it 'quite possible to arrange a series of matches organised by the Northern English Rugby Union or the British Rugby Football Board'.[40] The tour planning appeared slipshod and if they did contact Rowland Hill, he would not have been impressed at their limited knowledge of the structure of English rugby.

The organiser was Maurice P. Epstein, who later styled himself as Captain Paddy Hepston. He was a 'large and red-faced beery moustached settler-farmer of Irish origin', who had arrived in South Africa to take part in the Anglo-Boer War. His entrepreneurial farming venture was unsuccessful and by 1911, he had moved to Selby Street in the Malay Camp, a multiracial part of Kimberley.[41] From there he conducted his rugby business.

Epstein forwarded a letter to the New Zealand RFU late in 1911, proposing a tour to be made by 'a South African team comprised of purely coloured colonials, all trained athletes and the majority international players'. The letter said that the team 'would pay all its own expenses but was purely independent, and would be composed of 27 players, more to follow if necessary'.

The New Zealand committee decided to pass on the correspondence to the SA Rugby Football Board while taking the opportunity to state that the New Zealand RFU would be pleased to receive a white South African representative team to tour the Dominion in 1912.[42]

Epstein also approached the New South Wales Rugby League and the Northern Rugby Football Union, but all attempts to arrange a tour were rebuffed.[43] Within weeks, he had dropped rugby and focused his efforts on Franz Taibosch – 'Clicko' – who would tour the world as the 'wild dancing bushman'. Said an English stage manager: 'I consider Epstein not a proper person to have charge of such a being, who is treated like an animal and is powerless to defend himself.'[44]

In 1912, the SA Coloured Rugby Football Board announced at its annual general meeting that a movement had begun the previous year to send a team overseas. It reported that 'a European gentleman of Kimberley [had] very generously offered to finance the scheme, but through some unavoidable circumstances the matter was dropped'.[45]

The board changed direction and revived the Rhodes Cup tournament in 1914, but Eastern Province, the holders, and Transvaal declined to take part. Eastern Province had unhappy memories of the way they had been treated in 1909. They had emerged top of the log, but the Kimberley-based board overruled a disallowed Griqualand West try in an earlier drawn match against Western Province. The revised log placed Griquas level with Eastern Province, and a 'play-off' was ordered to determine the winners. A large crowd turned out at Green Point, but Eastern Province stood their ground, refused to play and were eventually declared winners.

Griqualand West beat Western Province 3–0 to win the 1914 tournament. It gave rise to enthusiastic celebrations when the winning team was welcomed home by their mayor, Councillor Ernest Oppenheimer, at Kimberley station. From there, carriages transported the players to the town hall where H.A. Oliver, the Member of Parliament, received the heroes as an excited crowd roared its approval.[46]

It was the last tournament for 14 years, but the problems that rugby administrators experienced were not uncommon. Sport was not a priority at a time of great upheaval that encompassed the inequities of Union; the struggle over labour; involvement in the Great War; the 1918–20 pandemic, and continued efforts to entrench segregation.

Notes

1   G. Christison, 'African Jerusalem: The Vision of Robert Grendon' (unpublished PhD thesis; University of KwaZulu-Natal, Pietermaritzburg, 2007), 279.

2   G. Christison, 'Then Came the Whiteman: An African Poet and Polemicist on the Fateful Encounter', in P. Limb, N. Etherington and P. Midgley (eds), *Grappling with the Beast: Indigenous Southern African Responses to Colonialism 1840–1930* (Leiden: Brill, 2010), 279–280; Christison, 'African Jerusalem', 205–209; T. Couzens, 'Robert Grendon, Irish Traders, Cricket Scores and Paul Kruger's Dreams', in *English in Africa*, 15, 2 (1988), 63–64.

3   M. Lambert, *The Classics and South African Identities* (London: Bloomsbury, 2011), 109–110.

4   *Cape Times*, 12 January and 22 February 1886.

5   A. Odendaal, K. Reddy, C. Merrett and J. Winch, *Cricket & Conquest: The History of South African Cricket Retold 1795–1914 Volume 1* (Cape Town: HSRC, 2016), 233.

6   Christison, 'African Jerusalem', 258.

7   R. Rotberg, *The Founder: Cecil Rhodes and the Pursuit of Power* (Oxford: Oxford University Press, 1988), 368–369.

8   S. Marks, 'Class, Culture and Consciousness in South Africa, 1880–1899', in R. Ross, A. Kelk Mager and B. Nasson (eds), *The Cambridge History of South Africa, Volume 2, 1885–1994* (Cambridge: Cambridge University Press, 2011), 144.

9   *Diamond Field Advertiser*, 23 September 1892.

10   Couzens, 'Robert Grendon', 71.

11   Ibid., 297.

12   A. Odendaal, '"The Thing that is Not Round": The Untold History of Black Rugby in South Africa', in A. Grundlingh, A. Odendaal and B. Spies (eds), *Beyond the Tryline: Rugby and South African Society* (Johannesburg: Ravan Press, 1995), 37.

13   Christison, 'African Jerusalem', 277.

14   *Diamond Fields Advertiser*, 14 November 1895.
15   *Imvo Zabantsundu*, 29 July 1897.
16   *Diamond Fields Advertiser*, 20 August 1897.
17   A. Odendaal, *The Story of an African Game Black Cricketers and the Unmasking of One of Cricket's Greatest Myths, South Africa, 1850–2003* (Cape Town: David Philip, 2003), 78.
18   *Citizen*, 25 August 1897.
19   Ibid.
20   V. Erlmann, *African Stars: Studies in Black South African Performances* (Chicago: University of Chicago Press, 1991), 34–36.
21   J. Vann and R. van Arsdel (eds), *Periodicals of Queen Victoria's Empire* (Toronto: University of Toronto Press, 1996), 282.
22   *Diamond Fields Advertiser*, 10 September 1897.
23   *Citizen*, 22 September 1897.
24   Christison, 'African Jerusalem', 279.
25   *Citizen*, 12 January 1898.
26   Ibid., 26 March 1898.
27   *Diamond Fields Advertiser*, 21 July 1898.
28   Ibid., 19 August 1898.
29   Rotberg, *The Founder*, 610–612.
30   E. Walker, *W.P. Schreiner: A South African* (London: Oxford University Press, 1969), 113.
31   *Diamond Fields Advertiser*, 1 July 1898.
32   Ibid., 12 August and 22 August 1898.
33   Ibid., 22 August 1898.
34   Ibid., 25 August 1898.
35   Ibid., 26 August 1898.
36   Odendaal, 'The Thing that is Not Round', 42; A. Odendaal, *The Founders: The Origins of the ANC and the Struggle for Democracy in South Africa* (Johannesburg: Jacana, 2012), 339–340.
37   A. Marx, *Making Race and Nation: A Comparison of South Africa, the United States, and Brazil* (Cape Town: Cambridge University Press, 2003), 88.
38   Christison, 'African Jerusalem', 292.
39   *APO*, 17 June 1911.
40   Ibid., 15 July 1911. According to RFU minutes, 2 October 1906 and 15 March 1907, there was an application from Mr Woodcock to tour England with a 'kaffirs team'. It was subsequently rejected.
41   B. Lindfors, *Africans on Stage: Studies in Ethnological Show Business* (Cape Town: David Philip, 1999), 206.
42   *Manawatū Daily Times*, 10 November 1911; *Auckland Star*, Vol. XLII, Issue 268, 10 November 1911.
43   *Sydney Referee*, 22 November 1911.
44   Lindfors, *Africans on Stage*, 209.
45   *APO*, 1 June 1912.
46   S. Carmichael (ed.), *112 Years of Springbok Tests and Heroes* (Cape Town: SA Rugby Football Union, 2003), 352.

6

From Healdtown and Lovedale to the 'Amadoda' of Orlando

Thrills were provided ad infinitum. Kolisi (Eastern Province full-back) capping them with a 'Morkel' drop-goal from the centre.[1]

– Tatius I.N. Sondlo

André Odendaal describes the eastern Cape as an important cradle of black sport in South Africa. He points out that the dynamics were very different from those in the relatively cosmopolitan western Cape:

> This region was the home of hundreds and thousands of Africans brought under British rule during the nineteenth century as Xhosa chiefdoms were conquered and incorporated into the expanding Cape Colony ... A European system of administration was imposed over them and agents of imperialism such as missionaries, teachers, traders and farmers moved into the African territories.[2]

According to tradition, says historian Jeff Peires, rugby (*mboxo* = a thing which is not round) was introduced to the Xhosa by Reverend Robert Mullins.[3] The earliest black rugby teams were institutional, for example, the Kaffir Institute, Lovedale, Healdtown and St Matthews at Keiskammahoek. The often racially mixed mission schools provided education based on the English model and were the training grounds for black sportsmen. They were, explains Odendaal, encouraging 'the people to forego their "uncivilised" customs and obtain a western education, learn about Christianity and adopt British cultural values'.[4]

Africans were playing rugby from an early stage of the game's history in South Africa. Paul Dobson notes that St Andrew's College 'lays claim to be the oldest rugby-playing – as distinct from playing other forms of football – school in South Africa, first playing the game in 1878'.[5] Some pupils from the black townships went on to St Andrew's where the Kaffir Institute had been established. They were encouraged to play the game by the latter's headmaster, Reverend Mullins, a rugby enthusiast whose son represented the British side on tour to South Africa in 1896.

The earliest black rugby club was the Union Rugby Football Club, founded in 1887 at Port Elizabeth. According to records collected by rugby historian Braber Ngozi, the club was started by 'kitchen boys who learnt their rugby from whites'.[6] At first, Union's opponents were local coloured rugby teams but in 1894 a second African club, Orientals, was formed followed by the Morning Star, Rovers, Frontier and Spring Rose clubs. Rugby became a vital part of social life, especially in the smaller towns.

Manie Booley notes that white clergymen were active in coaching in the townships. Conspicuous in this regard was Reverend Whyte, who became the first president of the Winter Rose Rugby Football Club (RFC), founded in Grahamstown in 1890. Most of the club's players were old boys of St Philip's Mission School in Grahamstown, some of whom had played for Union in Port Elizabeth.[7]

Families were committed to particular clubs, and the walls of their houses were sometimes covered with photographs of great teams of the past. 'Black rugby,' says Peires, 'has always been more closely associated than its white counterpart with the central concerns of its community, much more than simply a recreation or an entertainment, rugby served as a vehicle of popular culture and as an outlet for personal achievement and ambition.'[8]

Such enthusiasm existed even though the game itself was played in appalling conditions. Material poverty and lack of facilities meant that black players struggled to find space for their games and yet rugby grew in popularity. Peires describes their plight:

> Most fields were without grass, and many were riven by ditches, located on slopes or acting as public thoroughfares. Boots were considered a luxury and each team had at most a single set of jerseys. Such circumstances bred dedication and selflessness: sacrificing one's wages to buy the team colours, walking all night to be at a match the following day. It also bred dependence on local whites.[9]

'The spread of the game,' continues Peires, was due to 'the zeal of the newly converted. Self-appointed rugby missionaries carried the oval ball to even the remoter towns.'[10] As a result, inter-town contests became a firm fixture of black rugby before the end of the nineteenth century. Odendaal records that challenges would 'sometimes take place via the press, as when Grahamstown challenged towns such as East London and King Williams Town in the columns of the

Imvo Zabantsundu in 1899. *Velani makwedini ase ma Xhoseni* (Come on, show yourselves, young boys of Xhosaland)'.[11]

Black South Africans who were fascinated by the cultural practices of the colonisers 'entertained high hopes that having accepted the way of the white man they would eventually be assimilated fully into the evolving Cape society'. Sport was integral to this whole process of assimilation and mobilisation.[12] In 1904, the black communities were in a position to organise the first inter-town tournament in Port Elizabeth. Teams from Grahamstown, East London and Port Elizabeth competed for the Wynne's Cup. By 1906, nine teams were playing in the competition: Oriental (the 1905 champions), Union and Rovers (all Port Elizabeth), Zebras Football Club (Uitenhage), Lions Football Club (Cradock) and Wanderers, Winter Rose, Lily White and Eastern Province Football Club (Grahamstown).

The following year – 1907 – they were joined by the Tigers Club from Somerset East.[13] The club was founded in 1895 and used to play against white sides in the area. To play rugby in those early years, players would walk to Cookhouse 40 kilometres away. When they acquired jerseys after the Anglo-Boer War, they chose red, white and blue in honour of the British victors.[14]

All the while, the game of rugby was spreading out from the western and eastern Cape to the mining centres of Kimberley and the Witwatersrand. Some young African men were assuming positions of social prominence and taking up administrative roles in cultural and sports associations. They were founder members of early provincial rugby unions and the non-racial SA Coloured Rugby Football Board, which was formed in 1897, and organised the Rhodes Cup. After the Anglo-Boer War, the national body became a largely coloured organisation and struggled to survive. The Rhodes Cup was suspended after 1914 and did not resume until 1928. Africans continued to play but most were not attached to the national body.

The eastern Cape became a preserve of African labour for the mines in the north. Mine managers encouraged migrant miners to play sport rather than explore the townships during their spare time. The Chamber of Mines newspaper, *Umteteli wa Bantu* reported that 'all kinds of sports are organised and in various other ways provision is made to keep the Natives amused'.[15] The black Transvaal Rugby Union was formed in 1923 at a time when enormous changes were taking place through rapid development in urbanisation, industrial expansion and increasing racial segregation. The Witwatersrand gold mines ensured massive growth in Johannesburg as Africans arrived from all parts of the Union and indeed southern Africa. The black population on the Witwatersrand more than doubled from 304 000 in 1921 to 620 000 in 1936.[16]

Odendaal records that new clubs, such as Swallows and United, were formed in Johannesburg by expatriates from the eastern Cape. Along with existing clubs and mine-based teams, an active league was established. E. Juno Nogaga (an *induna* – mine foreman – at Crown Mines) presented a cup that Swallows won in 1923 and 1924. In 1925, the Chamber of Mines donated the 25-guinea Native Recruiting Corporation (NRC) Grand Challenge Cup, and a team from Queenstown visited Johannesburg and Pretoria to 'baptise rugby in the Transvaal which had just started'. By 1934, the province had fifteen clubs playing in two divisions.[17]

Years later, a Transvaal rugby observer would recall the time when the game was 'looked upon as "No Man's Hobby". Even in the schools, the "oblong ball" was regarded as nothing more than a "leather watermelon".' Only when 'the famous 1935 Transvaal tour of the Cape was sponsored and followed by tournaments was the standard of rugby in the Transvaal 'brought up-to-date'.[18]

The 1935 tour was an ambitious venture, especially 'owing to the limited number of only eighteen [touring] players against fifteen fresh players at every centre'. The first section was the eastern Cape, starting in Aliwal North and stopping in Burgersdorp, Queenstown, East London, Alice, Grahamstown, and Port Elizabeth. Every game was a testing encounter. Tatius I.N. Sondlo reported: 'The fact that our Cape friends played rugby better than us was known to us before we left but we were surprised at the high standard of play we found at even small towns ... Playing the game as we do in the Transvaal, we were no match for the solid scrummaging of the Cape forwards.'[19]

The tour created considerable interest: 'Lovedale authorities rolled out the red carpet, matches were played on white-controlled grounds, referees included ex-international Jack Slater.'[20] The touring side played a combined students team (Fort Hare and Lovedale) at Alice and their match at Adelaide was viewed as a major event with strong European support. *Bantu World* recalled 'all classes were represented including the native commissioner, the mayor and mayoress, the legal fraternity, professional men, businessmen, sportsmen, as well as prominent farmers'. E.O. Kennedy, the popular Eastern Province scrum-half, officiated the match which Midlands won 8–3. Jimmie Msikinya was the touring side's star that day, but his fine performance was ultimately overshadowed by the local side's scrum-half 'Dwarfy' Nyarashe, who scored a magnificent try.[21]

The second leg of the tour consisted of a visit to Cape Town and a match against Griqualand West on the return trip to Johannesburg. Rain accompanied the team and players struggled to produce their best form. The conditions also affected the gates at several matches and financially the scheme proved disappointing.

Overall, the tourists won six matches, lost seven and drew one. 'The objects of the tour,' observed Sondlo, 'embraced a great deal more than the mere winning and losing of a few matches.' He explained:

The Transvaal Union was out to establish the game firmly and to extend its influence throughout the Union; to arouse and maintain a new interest in the lives of young people; to commend ourselves to our white fellow citizens by following up their example because imitation is the highest form of flattery; to enjoy the life that God gives us by uniting exercise to entertainment, and to deserve pleasure and pastime in the noble game of rugby football.[22]

The Chamber of Mines held a reception for the touring party at which their representative, J.B. Gedye, appealed to 'the educated native to try to get in touch with his raw brother in the mine [and] help bring him to a civilised state' through participation in sport. 'If you can take my advice,' he said, 'and organise your raw brothers, you will have the strongest team and one that can never be beaten in South Africa. You have a very good chance to do so, for the people of Johannesburg are very proud.'[23]

Perhaps the most important factor in arranging the tour was that it gave impetus to the formation of a national governing body. Effectively, this meant a clean break from the SA Coloured Rugby Football Board.

The eastern Cape led the movement towards establishing a governing body along the lines of the SA Bantu Cricket Board, which had been founded in 1932. In 1935, local administrators formed a committee to discuss the establishment of a new structure. Progress was made during that year's inter-town rugby tournament at East London and a new administrative body was formally launched at Port Elizabeth in December. It would be known as the South African Bantu Rugby Board and facilitate greater exposure for African players.

The first president was James Mawela Dippa, a well-known figure in Port Elizabeth. He had been the Industrial and Commercial Union (ICU) provincial secretary for the eastern Cape. The ICU was founded in post-war South Africa when prices rose but wages, especially for African and coloured workers, had not been increased since 1914. Dippa made a name for himself in 1926 through an article that attacked 'the white man's law which has branded the native worker an outcast'.[24] At the same time, he was recognised as a 'moderate' who represented the Cape liberal tradition, a man who had 'left the revolutionary camp and moved to the law and order camp'.[25]

By the 1930s, Dippa was a clerk in an attorney's office. Black rugby players and administrators were initially drawn primarily from the emerging black middle class. Halley Plaatje, the secretary, was the son of Sol Plaatje and nephew of Bud Mbelle. His assistant secretary was Tatius I.N. Sondlo from Johannesburg.

Plaatje was largely responsible for the first SA Bantu Rugby Board inter-provincial tournament at Kimberley in 1936. Other participants included the Northern Eastern Districts and Griqualand West. There were no teams from Western Province, Natal and Border. This was an unexpected development, as not long before, Natal had defeated Border 8–3 before 4 000 spectators at East London.

Trials were held at the various centres to select teams for the tournament. Queenstown hosted the North-Eastern Districts trials, which were held in unfavourable weather. Molteno played Burgersdorp, Lady Grey was up against Sterkstroom, and the main game featured Aliwal North against Queenstown. Wiwie Pahlane of Queenstown was described as 'a player in a class of his own'.[26] A similar structure was adopted for the Transvaal trials. Queen's Park, the cracks of Johannesburg met Cannibals of New States. All Blacks played Crusaders, with Olympics against Blue Bells.[27]

The SA Bantu Rugby Board arranged trophies. The NRC Cup was contested on a league system, and the Parton Purifying Pills Co. of Cape Town presented a cup for a knockout competition. *Bantu World* published an advice column over a couple of issues, headed 'J.L.B.C. Kwaza's "Just a Few Rugby Don'ts and Does"'. It was designed not only to assist a wider population that would not be familiar with the game, but also to provide a few tips on how to play winning rugby at a higher level.

The tournament, sponsored by the Chamber of Mines, was condensed into a single week's rugby played from 27 June to 4 July. *Bantu World* commented:

> Preparations for this big venture were flawless – visitors whose propensity is to look over other people's fences just for the sake of finding fault were obliged to admit the completeness of this organisation and its satisfactory administration. For simple though the catering was, from its tea-sipping to the square meal, things were well arranged. Accommodation, which is what most centres fail to provide, should be well remembered by all the visitors who were treated to such, as proper meals and sleep-in-comfort count first to be followed by other 'hospitality' – galore.[28]

The programme included addresses by the local magistrate and location superintendent, a speech by a Member of Parliament, a silent-picture house, music and sight-seeing.

The opening day of the tournament began with Transvaal playing the hosts, Griqualand West. The visitors were struck a severe blow when their captain,

Bob Sondlo, broke his collarbone in the first ten minutes of the NRC Cup match. Down to fourteen men and with the crowd firmly behind the home side, Transvaal dug deep to win 3–0 in the last minute of the contest. It was described as the most exciting and fastest of all the matches – a game that would be long remembered in the tournament's history.[29]

The following day, Eastern Province beat North-Eastern Districts 6–3 in an NRC encounter and on 1 July, Transvaal went down by three points to North-Easterns in the first of the Parton Cup knock-out fixtures. Wiwie Pahlane scored a spectacular try by 'side-stepping, swerving, and dummying his way through almost the whole Transvaal team'. Bob Sibenya, the Transvaal centre was also impressive. He made numerous forays into North-Easterns' territory and had he been supported it would almost certainly have changed the score tally. On the same day, Griquas met Eastern Province in the Chamber of Mines competition. *Bantu World* recorded:

> Thrills were provided ad infinitum. Kolisi (Eastern Province full-back) capping them with a 'Morkel' drop-goal from the centre. He and M. Hendricks (Griquas full-back) had some spectacular duels. But Kolisi has a 'larger foot' and accurate touch-finding. F. Louw from ten yards out wormed his way through the Eastern Province to score Griquas' only try. Gqomo the classical centre of the Eastern Province scored and Kolisi converted. Eastern Province 9; Griqualand West 3.[30]

Comparing Kolisi to Gerhard Morkel further revealed Tatius Sondlo's knowledge of the game. Morkel was one of the finest full-backs in the world during a career that spanned the First World War and kicked the vital second-half drop-goal (then worth four points) that gave South Africa a 9–5 victory over New Zealand in the second Test of 1921.

In the Parton Cup on 2 July, Eastern Province's heavier pack was decisive in their victory over Griquas. Manana, Gqomo, Nshekisa and Kolisi were mentioned as points-scorers in enabling Eastern Province to gain the ascendancy and win 16–0. Later in the day, Transvaal beat North-Eastern Districts 12–0 in an NRC Cup match – Kemka scored two tries while Jimmie Msikinya added a drop-goal when he 'secured the ball and took a running shot at the posts with his left foot'.

The tournament was ambitious in that separate tournaments – for the NRC and Parton Cups – ran concurrently. This resulted in a punishing schedule. Eastern Province qualified for two finals and therefore played on five successive days. On 3 July, they beat North-Easterns 6–0 in the final of the Parton Cup and the following day met Transvaal in the final of the NRC Cup. The match was a thrilling scoreless encounter:

From the start, the game was evenly balanced. Infringements by Transvaal resulted in Eastern Province being awarded two penalties. Kolisi, who in this game did not have things his own way as in previous matches, failed with both kicks. Fast three-quarter movements were adopted by both sides, but neither could cross the line owing to keen tackling. At half-time the scoreboard was clean. The second half brought even faster and more thrilling rugby than the first and it was evident that both teams played to win. Alternative forward rushes and three-quarter thrusts were tried – in vain. Accurate touch-finding, faultless three-quarter movements, fine foot-work and keen tackling were the feature of the game.[31]

Eastern Province and Transvaal became joint holders of the NRC Cup. This was the first of 28 inter-provincial tournaments to be held in the next 38 years up to 1974 when a new competition – played on a home-and-away basis – was started.[32]

Everyone was delighted with the success of the first tournament and the executive was re-elected en bloc. A further name was added: Johnie Moleke of Kimberley as treasurer. This was a significant appointment as finance – or lack of it – would be a major issue for the organisation. The 1936 tournament had been free of controversy and Tatius Sondlo praised those Kimberley gentlemen who 'added dignity to the whole affair by proving that honesty with "gate-takings" was their policy; very uncommon with our associations of today'.[33]

A few years later, an official of the Grahamstown Rugby Union commented on rugby under the jurisdiction of the SA Bantu Rugby Board. He thought the organisation 'outdated, old-fashioned, incapable of making the player give of his best and lends itself to corruption'. He added:

> The select committee can cite many occasions when, during the opening day of such tournaments, some officials were seen collecting money outside the grounds, armed with identical tickets, and pocketing the money! Almost invariably the officials of SA Bantu Rugby Board, some of whom had never touched a rugby ball in the field, or at best had never gone beyond the local second division, find themselves sleeping in cosy surroundings, dining and wining to their heart's content, while the poor players sleep on school desks, and literally starve.[34]

Eastern Province was the team to beat, in the early years winning eight of the tournaments between 1936 and 1953. In June 1937, Cape Town hosted the tournament, which Eastern Province won, although the NCR Cup did not arrive for presentation. They won again in Port Elizabeth in 1938 but did not participate in the tournament at Johannesburg in 1939.

In early 1938, 'Spotlight', writing in the *Bantu World,* lamented the fact that rugby and cricket had become 'strangers' in the Transvaal sporting community. He criticised soccer associations for playing their game in the 'off-season and the public who probably know no better, supporting them staunchly'. He commended the Cape for their example in encouraging an all-round interest. Even if rugby and cricket were almost a religion there, and they 'did little in the soccer world' they still encouraged the association game.[35]

Tatius Sondlo and tournament secretary Gilbert B. Makalima, a well-known Xhosa writer, led the organisation for the 1939 tournament. Considerable effort went into the preparations. The aim was to revive the game in a province 'where soccer has such a strong grip on the minds of sportsmen as to minimise the side of rugby'. The tournament itself was a great success, although disappointing for the Transvalers. They failed to win a trophy despite fielding a strong side, with Bob Sondlo and Sam Ndlazilwana, captain and vice-captain respectively for the third year in succession.

Four centres – Transvaal, Border, Griqualand West and North-Eastern Districts – took part. After a lively reception that featured the music of the Jazz Maniacs, play began the next day at the Springfield 'European' Sports Ground. As always, there was white involvement and the deputy-mayor, Councillor Tom Huddle, was called upon to declare proceedings open. There were to be several surprises in an entertaining week, most notably North-Easterns defeating Transvaal in the league to win the NCR Cup. The hosts were also beaten by Griquas 6–3 in the knock-out competition.[36]

Border won the tournament at East London in 1940. They included 'many students from the Native colleges of the Ciskei' and performed well to the delight of the 2 000 spectators in attendance. Each of the six teams, consisting of squads of 25 players, played every day for a week and the star wing Braber Ngozi scored 33 points to set a tournament record.[37]

Odendaal also notes the power relations in the wider society that were once again evident. When the mayor opened the tournament, it was reported 'with him will be the Native Commissioner D.G. Hartmann, the manager of urban native affairs R.C. Cook and the secretary of the white Border Rugby Football Union H.W. Wedd. There will be a separate entrance to the ground for Europeans.'[38]

The *Umteteli wa Bantu* newspaper described the condition of the ground at Rubusana Park as 'atrocious'. Hartmann acknowledged this when he said at the opening: 'I have heard the Bantu players are tough men. To play on a field like the one here they will have to be very tough.'

After Queenstown had hosted the tournament in 1941, there was a gap during the Second World War. When the tournament resumed, the NRC Cup was won by Transvaal at Cape Town in 1944 and at New Brighton in 1945 when seven teams participated: Western Province, Griqualand West, Border, North-Eastern Districts, Eastern Province, Transvaal and Midlands. The years that followed were unfortunately marred by boardroom fighting and financial controversy alongside the adversities already faced by black rugby.

The most dramatic tournament organised by the SA Bantu Rugby Board was that of 1947. Their Johannesburg-based president, A.B. Mathobela, probably had little idea of the problems that faced him when he departed early for Kimberley to oversee operations.[39] The tournament, won by Eastern Province, 'cost the SA Bantu Rugby Board its innocence and it was never on an even keel again as violence invaded the field and even dangerous weapons were brandished ... [it] was a financial and organisational flop, players resorting to theft of bread in their hunger'. It ended with the trophies being taken to the police station and Mathobela's abrupt dismissal – he was replaced by Sipho M. Siwisa in an organised coup.[40]

While this low point in African rugby was being played out, there was a bright glimmer of promise from within the heartland of Transvaal's black rugby. *Bantu World* reported in July 1947 that after a fortnight of trial games, a team was selected to represent Orlando High School on a rugby tour of the Cape.[41]

It was a major step forward in a determined campaign to establish rugby at the famous school, known by pupils and staff as 'The Rock'. A leading educationalist, Michael Morapeli, said that there was no rugby played when Victor Sondlo, the tour captain, enrolled at the school as a Form 1 pupil in 1943. Sondlo had played the game in Queenstown before he came to Johannesburg and was pleased to discover fellow enthusiasts in Francis Majambe and the Nziba brothers, Rosette and Russel. Together, they approached staff member Dunstan Dladla about introducing rugby at Orlando.[42]

Sondlo recalled the headmaster, Godfrey Nakene, being 'extremely enthusiastic' and prepared to lend his full support. At assembly, he referred to rugby as a sport of the *amadoda* – 'real men' – while Dladla, an outstanding player at Fort Hare, began organising practices almost immediately from March 1943. He entered a side into the 'B' Division of the Transvaal Bantu Rugby Football Union (RFU). The game 'quickly caught on in the school and an ever-increasing number of pupils joined the club'.[43]

Nakene was university trained. Through the intervention of Peter Raynes, the priest in charge of St Cyprian's in Johannesburg, he and Harry Madibane had been allowed to enrol as students at the University of the Witwatersrand. They became the first two Africans to receive a Bachelor degree and subsequently became headmasters of two new African non-residential secondary schools. Nakene was acknowledged as being 'highly gifted in motivating staff and students'. At assembly, he encouraged both players and spectators, and 'after the matches, whether the teams had been victorious or not, he would talk at length about the performance as well as the importance of giving of one's best in all endeavours ... The various extra-mural activities were used as an intellectual stimulus.'[44]

When Madibane became headmaster at Western High School, he introduced rugby. The coach was Lancelot Gama, who had been educated at St Peter's, Rosettenville, and Fort Hare. He and several ex-Peterians (Oliver Tambo, Congress Mbata and Joe Mokoena) had, as university students, 'styled themselves "The Syndicate" and pledged themselves to work for a better world'.[45] At the 1942 African National Congress (ANC) conference, Gama ...

> drew attention to the unrest among the youth at educational institutions around the country ... He argued that this unrest was a manifestation of the mood and militancy of the youth, and hence it was necessary to galvanise and direct it along proper political channels. At the end of the conference, the executive was authorised to institute an ANC youth league.[46]

Gama became a medical doctor in Springs and was King Sobhuza's Induuna General in South Africa. His legacy at Western High was a rugby rivalry with Orlando High, remembered as a great occasion between the 'Rock' and 'Dynamite'. Virtually the whole pupil bodies of both schools turned out in full force to witness these matches and to cheer their teams.[47]

Orlando High School won the 'B' league in 1943 and were presented with the Nogaga Trophy, which had been donated to the Transvaal Bantu RFU in 1923.

Benjamin Diphoko, a fine player from Kimberley, succeeded Dladla in 1946 as the rugby coach and was assisted by another new arrival, Grant Khomo, an exceptional all-rounder from Border, who would captain South Africa at rugby and soccer, and become the country's undisputed tennis champion. The circuit inspector, Japie Mentjies, was extremely impressed with developments at the school and, together with the sporting staff, helped 'to imbue the school rugby team with deep love and great respect for this game'. It was thought that Mentjies arranged for the former Springbok, Morris Zimerman, to train the school team at Ellis Park.[48]

Mentjies encouraged the school to broaden its horizons and the historic rugby tour to the Cape was arranged in June 1947. New kit was bought from school funds and a powerful team was selected under the direction of Grant Khomo. There were six Transvaal players in the touring side that embarked on a venture involving nine games in seventeen days from 11 July to 28 July. Matches were arranged in Kimberley (versus Gore Browne Training Institute), Uitenhage (versus Hamilton's), Port Elizabeth (two matches), Fort Beaufort (Healdtown), Alice (Lovedale and Fort Hare), East London (Welsh High School) and Queenstown (against the Breakers).

Bantu World gave generous coverage with comments on individual players, for example:

> Hobart Nolutshungu, Transvaal full-back, fields brilliantly and is a deadly tackler ... Ambition Brown the Transvaal wing is a versatile ruggerite with a vicious side-step. He is undoubtedly the greatest three-quarter Orlando High School has produced. He resembles lightning and thunder in his stride when an opportunity comes his way ... Simon Ntshepe is one of the best forwards playing in the Transvaal. He is strong, hard and a brilliant line-out forward.[49]

Orlando High had mixed fortunes in their campaign but what 'excited both the players and the whole school was that the "Rock" had managed a total of 129 points against the 115 gained by the more experienced teams visited, some of them with a whole history or tradition of rugby in their favour'.[50]

The standard of rugby at Orlando reached its peak after the 1947 tour. The following year, the Orlando boys were promoted to the 'A' section of the Union's rugby and continued their success, defeating mine sides – Rand Leases, Ventersport, Robinson Deep, Crown Mines, Simmer and Jack, and Anglo-Vaal – amongst others. Such teams, declares Morapeli, 'were subsequently reluctant to play against the *Amakhwenkhwe* (boys) for fear of being out-played and humiliated'.[51]

Many outstanding soccer players at the school, including Cecil Dinalane and Phineas Lehobo, switched over to rugby. In this way, soccer was ousted by rugby at Orlando High School towards the 1950s. Outstanding players of rugby – the *amadoda* – were school heroes, especially those who became regulars in the Transvaal team against other provinces. They included Victor Sondlo, Simon Ntshepe, Ambition Brown, Benjamin Rasmeni, Russel Nziba, Fred Sishaba and Hobart Nolutshungu.[52]

Vuyisa Qunta, a rugby writer, administrator and coach, supports Morapeli's viewpoint, stating that 'African rugby followers revered their provincial representatives ... rugby crowds also bestowed their own "Springbok colours" on players whom they thought were good enough to play for the white South African team. Thus, the prowess and strength of prop Wilson Bizo (1947–48) earned him the nickname "Bokwe, the Bok!"'[53]

In the 1940s, Transvaal was a major force in African rugby. They won the NRC Cup five times (twice shared) in six competitions between 1941 and 1949.

During the same period, they shared the Parton Cup three times. In the 1949 competition, Transvaal and Eastern Province fought an epic battle that ended in a draw. The match was replayed, but in bad weather. At the end of normal time there was still no score. Another ten minutes' extra-time made no difference and referee Bharayi 'blew the final whistle in the deepening dark'.[54]

The mighty struggle encapsulated the competitive nature of African rugby. Newspaper clippings also reveal the high standard achieved by these hardy players. One piece that created interest in *Bantu World* was written by S.B. Skenjana. He praised the individual talents of players from Villagers, a new team in the Transvaal league. And, above all else in the report, he singled out the play of Simon Ntshepe, the captain, 'an outstanding forward in the game who played like Hennie Muller'.

The article attracted the attention of Victor Sondlo, who had been Ntshepe's captain at Orlando High School. He responded by asking readers if they realised that there was 'a great deal of inferiority we have to eradicate'. He wrote:

> I think we unconsciously practise the slave state mentality and it is high time we did things consciously in all spheres of life ... This 'Hennie Muller' that Skenjana compares with Ntshepe is said to be a good Springbok number 8 forward because he has a keen eye in the land of the blind. He has never played against Ntshepe to show his real worth in the game. We are so mentally enslaved that we do not realise that we are poisoning the minds of young Africans to think that the best things can only be done by Europeans and not by any non-European ... [It] makes us underrate the great things we do as non-Europeans so much that we forget that we should compare our present good players with the brilliant players of the past.

Sondlo concluded by saying he had recently been much impressed by a young tennis player at Western Township who was having a practice with his friends there. The boy stood out for his fine play, not least because his service was excellent. When his friends praised him for the good work he showed, he smiled and remarked: 'I am Khomo himself.'[55]

Notes

1   *Bantu World*, 18 July 1936.
2   A. Odendaal, 'The Thing that is Not Round', in A. Grundlingh, A. Odendaal and B. Spies, *Beyond the Tryline: Rugby and South African Society* (Johannesburg: Ravan Press, 1995), 32.
3   J. Peires, 'Rugby in the Eastern Cape: A History', in *Work in Progress*, 17 (1981), 5.
4   Odendaal, 'The Thing that is Not Round', 32. The Kaffir Institution in Grahamstown, run by Anglicans, was subsequently moved to St Matthews College, Keiskamma hoek, under Charles Taberer.
5   P. Dobson, *Rugby in South Africa: A History 1861–1988* (Cape Town: SARB, 1989), 201.

6   B. Ngozi, 'History and Development of Non-White Rugby in South Africa' (bound source book), in Odendaal, 'The Thing that is Not Round', 32.

7   A. Booley, *Forgotten Heroes: History of Black Rugby 1882–1992* (Cape Town: Manie Booley Publications, 1998), 95.

8   Peires, 'Rugby in the Eastern Cape', 5.

9   J. Peires, '*Facta non Verba*: Towards a History of Black Rugby', History Workshop, University of the Witwatersrand, 1981, 5.

10   Peires, 'Rugby in the Eastern Cape', 5.

11   *Imvo Zabantsundu*, 29 May 1899, in Odendaal, 'The Thing that is Not Round', 35.

12   Odendaal, 'The Thing that is Not Round', 32.

13   Ibid., 35.

14   Booley, *Forgotten Heroes*, 96.

15   *Umteteli wa Bantu*, 13 October 1923.

16   B. Murray and A. Stadler, 'From the Pact to the Advent of Apartheid 1924–48', in T. Cameron (ed.), *An Illustrated History of South Africa* (Johannesburg: Jonathan Ball Publishers, 1986), 257.

17   M. Morapeli, 'The Rock: The History of Orlando High School 1939–1984' (unpublished master's thesis, University of the Witwatersrand, Johannesburg, 1984), 40; Odendaal, 'The Thing that is Not Round', 44.

18   *Bantu World*, 12 July 1947.

19   Ibid., 29 June 1935.

20   Odendaal, 'The Thing that is Not Round', 45.

21   *Bantu World*, 1 June 1935.

22   Ibid., 29 June 1935.

23   Ibid., 15 June 1935.

24   *Native Worker*, 26 October 1926, 5; L. Switzer, *South Africa's Alternative Press: Voices of Protest and Resistance* (Cambridge: Cambridge University Press, 1997), 172, 180.

25   A. Drew, *Discordant Comrades: Identities and Loyalties on the South African Left* (Abingdon: Routledge, 2000), 81.

26   *Bantu World*, 6 June 1936.

27   Ibid., 13 June 1936.

28   Ibid., 25 July 1936.

29   Ibid., 18 July 1936.

30   Ibid.

31   *Bantu World*, 18 July 1936.

32   Odendaal, 'The Thing that is Not Round', 47.

33   *Bantu World*, 25 July 1936.

34   Peires, 'Rugby in the Eastern Cape', 6.

35   *Bantu World*, 22 January 1938.

36   *Bantu World*, 1, 8, 15 July 1939.

37   Odendaal, 'The Thing that is Not Round', 47.

38   *Umteteli wa Bantu*, 2 and 8 June 1940.

39   *Bantu World*, 7 June 1947.

40   Dobson, *Rugby in South Africa*, 203–204; Booley, *Forgotten Heroes*, 96.

41   *Bantu World*, 12 July 1947.

42   Morapeli, 'The Rock', 39.

43   Ibid.

44   E. Verwey (ed.), *New Dictionary of South African Biography, Volume 1* (Pretoria: HSRC, 1995), 150–151, 200; Morapeli, 'The Rock', 40.

45   C. Woeber, "A Good Education Sets up a Divine Discontent": The Contribution of St Peter's School to Black South African Autobiography' (unpublished PhD thesis, University of the Witwatersrand, Johannesburg, 2000), 425.

46   E. Sisulu, *Walter and Albertina Sisulu: In Our Lifetime* (David Philip and New Africa Books, 2002), 98.

47   Morapeli, 'The Rock', 40. Western High was called 'Dynamite' by its pupils and teachers.

48   Morapeli, 'The Rock', 40, 41.

49   *Bantu World*, 12 July 1947.

50   Morapeli, 'The Rock', 41.

51   Ibid., 42.

52   Ibid.

53   V. Qunta, 'The African Springboks', in D. Cruywagen (ed.), *The Badge, a Centenary of the Springbok Emblem* (Newlands: SA Rugby, 2006), 143.

54   Dobson, *Rugby in South Africa*, 204.

55   *Bantu World*, 3 May 1952.

7

Establishing a South African Rugby Identity

[The Springboks] have by winning all the Test matches, reversed
the position and taught us how the game should be played.[1]

– Sir George Rowland Hill, January 1913

At a meeting of the SA Rugby Football Board at Algoa House Hotel in Port
Elizabeth on Friday, 20 August 1897, a letter was read from Rowland Hill of the
Rugby Football Union (RFU) to Jack Heyneman. It stated:

Greenwich, June 28, 1897

Dear Sir – I may say my Committee will be very pleased to have your Board
affiliated to the English Rugby Football Union. If you will kindly at your
convenience forward me entrance fee 10s 6d, and subscription 21s, and let
me know if there is anyone in England whom you wish should represent the
Board at our general meetings. As regards the delegation of power, that will be
considered by my Committee when it next meets. Would you kindly send me
particulars giving the present constitution, &c, of your Board – Yours faithfully,

G. Rowland Hill[2]

Affiliation to the RFU brought renewed optimism that South Africa would be
able to tour England. Johnny Hammond, a member of the 1891 British touring
side, and captain in 1896, became the South African representative on the English
union. He reported back that satisfactory arrangements could be made for the
1898/99 season. It was anticipated that the team would be in England for nearly
four months.

The board – with Barry Heatlie presiding – agreed to send a team to England for the 1898/99 season if suitable arrangements could be made there and if the various local centres contributed towards the guarantee. Some delegates were sceptical as one of Hill's letters had 'put forward the objection that there was not sufficient time to make arrangements'. Others were probably mindful of the manner in which the South African cricket team had been chosen to tour England three years earlier – 'a South African team with but few South Africans in it'.[3] Visiting English professionals were included, along with an Irishman who had been in South Africa for four months.

Philip Myburgh, the rugby delegate from the Eastern Province, told the meeting he had 'no doubt that an overseas tour would be a greater financial success if the players were South African-born'. If a 'team of colonials could not be picked, then he suggested players should have played at least three seasons in South Africa'. His proposal received immediate support from H.H. Strugnell (Griqualand West) who emphasised 'three full seasons'.[4]

Indecision over finance delayed progress over the year. At the SA Rugby Football Board's meeting of 26 August 1898, the Transvaal delegate, R.H. Blakely, moved that an England team be invited to tour South Africa in 1899 and that a South African team visit England after that year's Currie Cup tournament. His idea was that 'if they pooled the whole profits [for the English visit] no loss would be suffered. Any surplus would go towards paying the expenses of the South African team to England.'[5]

The motion to invite the English team to tour South Africa in 1899 was agreed to but the proposed tour to England was lost by five votes to four. Permission was granted to the Transvaal RFU to send a team, but this became impossible because of the political friction that existed. War appeared imminent and, as it turned out, the 1899 Currie Cup tournament at Kimberley was played without Western Province and Transvaal.

The British destroyed Boer farms, established concentration camps and inflicted appalling treatment on the women and children. But some rugby was played when Boers were incarcerated in camps at St Helena, Ceylon, Bermuda, India and Portugal, as well as at Simon's Town and Green Point.[6] It was a popular pastime in the camps and played until the fighting was eventually concluded with the Peace of Vereeniging in May 1902.

Efforts were made almost immediately to reconstruct the country; gold mines resumed operations and the Afrikaners returned to their land. A sense of normality prevailed but the divisions and bitterness exacerbated by the war would affect the country for a long time. Sports leaders played a part in trying to heal the wounds that were left by the war. White sports organisations were encouraged to create as many opportunities as possible for their members. Tours became increasingly important and wealthy benefactors provided generous financial assistance.

Mark Morrison's British rugby team toured South Africa in 1903. The team included players from all four home unions: eight Englishmen, seven Scots, five Irishmen, and a Welshman, Reg Skrimshire, who subsequently worked on the railway from Johannesburg to the Victoria Falls, a task that included the famous bridge at Livingstone.

From the outset, South Africans were conscious of the need to create an identity for their team. It had been normal practice in the past that the Test sides played in the colours of the local union where the match was staged, or in those of one of its clubs. At a meeting of the SA Rugby Football Board in March 1903, the Transvaal RFU requested the motion be tabled that the Test team wear 'olive-green jerseys, with gold collar, and on the left breast embroidered in natural colour, a springbok, navy-blue knickers, dark blue stockings, with green and gold band on the tops'.[7]

After these details were referred to a commission, a second meeting was arranged in May 1903. It was subsequently agreed that the South African colours be: 'green jersey with white collar and springbok in natural colours on left breast, black knickers and blue stockings with two white stripes at top'.[8]

The board failed to ensure green jerseys were worn in the 1903 Tests in Johannesburg and Kimberley, but they appeared for the match in Cape Town, albeit without the Springbok badge. The South African captain Barry Heatlie, who had provided green jerseys for South Africa's first-ever Test victory in 1896, claimed credit for the jerseys in 1903. Writing about it in 1933, he recalled: 'At that time I had on hand a supply of dark green jerseys, the colours of the defunct Old Diocesans' Club. It was decided to wear those jerseys at Newlands, and ever since South African fifteens have been clad in green.'[9]

Lappe Laubscher and Gideon Nieman pointed out an apparent contradiction in Heatlie's claim:

> The Old Diocesans' Club became defunct in 1899. When one compares the jerseys that the South Africans wore in the final Test in 1896 with those that they wore in the final Test in 1903 there is a definite difference in the cut. Was it possible that a team on the verge of becoming defunct would design new jerseys? Or was it possible that after almost forty years Heatlie confused the final Test in 1896 with the one in 1903?[10]

The problem over jerseys suggested South Africa's rugby authorities were struggling to get their house in order. The crucial question of who was a South African also remained unanswered in 1903. Selectors of the Test team included men who had arrived to fight in the Anglo-Boer War and were available for the internationals played shortly afterwards. As there were no agreed rules governing who was eligible, the Scotland internationals Alex Frew and 'Saxon' McEwan, the Ireland scrum-half Hugh Ferris, and Newport's 'Birdie' Partridge represented South Africa against the 1903 tourists.

The arrangement gave rise to a bizarre situation in the first Test at the Wanderers when the captains and referee were all Scottish internationals. Mark Morrison, the tour captain, had led Scotland to the Triple Crown in 1901. His opposite number, the South African captain Alex Frew had played under Morrison in the Triple Crown side before emigrating to the Transvaal. The referee, Bill Donaldson, played six times for Scotland during the 1890s.[11]

A memorable series began with two closely fought drawn matches. South Africa then won the third Test and the series at Newlands. Their rugby had progressed, and Morrison believed that they would be fully capable of testing any international side in the British Isles.[12]

South Africa's rugby authorities built on the success. Early the following year, it was agreed at a board meeting to introduce a green cap with gold trimmings and a 'springbuck head as badge'. The caps would be awarded retrospectively to players who had represented South Africa since 1891.[13] The choice of green and the use of the 'springbuck' were also confirmed in the course of meetings of the SA Rugby Football Board in September 1906, shortly before South Africa embarked on its first overseas tour.[14]

Tour organisers sought to assemble a team that was white, South African-born and, if possible, had equal representation of Afrikaans- and English-speaking players. They were aware that they might encounter black players on tour and would have noted that James Peters – whose father was Jamaican – had played in England's last two internationals of the 1905/06 season. There is no evidence that this posed a problem. The South African cricketers had in 1894 appreciated the opportunity to play against the outstanding Kumar Shri Ranjitsinhji. He scored 53 and 146 not out for C.W. Wright's XI against them at Portsmouth, prompting three of the tourists, George Glover, George Kempis and Dante Parkin, to rate him as the finest batsman that they came across: 'a prettier bat all-round the wickets it would be impossible to imagine'.[15]

Clarence Becker spent 'many months beforehand … obtaining confidential information, both as to the play and the characteristics of those players who would have to be seriously considered for their South African places'.[16] The board discussed qualifications for national selection at meetings during 1905. They did so largely with the Rhodesian Freddie Brooks in mind. Although Rhodesia had affiliated to the SA Rugby Football Board in 1895, there was a strong argument that Brooks was essentially an Englishman.

He had been the finest schoolboy sportsman in England, a dashing cricket captain at Bedford Grammar School and the public schools' athletic champion in four events, but it was at rugby that he excelled. In an England 'trial' match in 1901/02, he had as a schoolboy scored the only two tries for the South against the North. Thought to be 'the fastest man now playing football', he was surprisingly overlooked for England, causing 'a considerable measure of comment, for his play warranted his being considered a certainty'.[17]

Brooks played rugby with the Milton boys whose father, William Milton, was by then the administrator of Rhodesia. Arrangements were made for the family to immigrate to Rhodesia, with 19-year-old Freddie arriving in Salisbury at the start of the 1902/03 cricket season and scoring centuries in his first two innings in a new country. In 1904/05, he played against a powerful Transvaal team that included five of South Africa's leading Test players. Striking the ball fluently, he contributed 61 out of his side's total of 115. The *Rand Daily Mail* cricket correspondent agreed with Herbert Castens that Brooks 'was good enough to play for South Africa'.[18]

It was Rhodesia's first and last Currie Cup cricket match for 25 years. Brooks focused his efforts on rugby and returned to England over several Christmas periods to play for Bedford.[19] During Rhodesia's winters, he strengthened his defensive qualities on the dusty, thorn-scrub fields where inter-provincial clashes were likened to wars of attrition. He emerged 'a stronger, a more resourceful and in every way a better player' through such fixtures, which also paved the way for Rhodesia's return to the rugby Currie Cup in 1906.[20]

At SA Rugby Football Board meetings, Rhodesia was represented by proxy. In June 1905, Gerald Orpen (Transvaal) seconded by M.J. Louw (Rhodesia) moved that 'players who are not South African-born but who have three years residential qualification be eligible for selection'.[21] L.A. Myburgh (North-Eastern Districts) seconded by Leslie Cox (Griqualand West) moved an amendment that the residential qualification 'be five years instead of three'. The amendment was carried by eight votes to five. At the next meeting in August 1905, Edward Allen (Rhodesia) objected to 'the tentative resolution' having been passed but a second vote was lost by the same eight to five margin and the original resolution duly carried.[22] The board did not wish to select Rhodesia's 'Englishman', Freddie Brooks.

There was great interest in the Currie Cup tournament, which doubled as a trial to choose the first South African rugby side to tour overseas. Outstanding play by Brooks created early interest. Billy Millar, who would later captain South Africa, marvelled at the Rhodesian's 'tremendous pace' and how he swerved past the outstanding South African full-back, Arthur Marsberg.[23] With certain players lobbied for as likely contenders for the tour, *The Star* wrote of Brooks that he 'must surely be selected to go to England',[24] a view the *Rand Daily Mail* endorsed by stating that he was 'the best wing three-quarter who has taken part in the tournament'.[25] Their views did not matter; he was not chosen for the tour. He was a few months short of the five-year residential requirement.

In the selected squad of 29 players, only W.A. 'Piet' Neill was not South African-born. He had left Glasgow for South Africa when he was two years old. The touring side had slightly more Afrikaans-speaking players than English. The excellent forward from Stellenbosch, Paul Roos, was elected captain after an 'exhaustive ballot' with Paddy Carolin, the Villager half-back who became vice-captain.[26]

Following the resounding success and huge interest generated by the first All Blacks rugby tour to Great Britain and France in 1905/06, there was great anticipation in advance of the arrival of the side from South Africa. They travelled on the *Gascon*, which docked at Southampton on 19 September 1906, and hoped to emulate the All Black haka with a 'Zulu' war-cry. It never really took off, but the first 'Springbok' rugby jerseys, which arrived before the opening match, were a great success. The *Daily Mail* had spoken to Roos and gathered his preference for 'De Springbokken', which they shortened to 'Springboks':

> The team's colours will be myrtle green jerseys with gold collar. They will wear dark-blue shorts and dark blue stockings, and the jerseys will have embroidered in mouse-coloured silk on the left breast a Springbok, a small African antelope which is typical of Africa as the kangaroo is of Australia.[27]

That the *Daily Mail* should refer to 'gold collars' attracted comment. Laubscher and Nieman note that from 1906 to 1933 the South African jersey was 'a myrtle-green one with a white collar'. Only in 1937 did the collar change to gold. The two writers thought the white-collared jerseys might be a factory mistake that became part of the official design.[28]

The touring side made a fine start, winning their first six matches. They scored 187 points and conceded 4 through a dropped goal. It was not until their seventh match at Devon that their line was crossed by Ernest Roberts who had played for Villager's before the Anglo-Boer War and was well known to the South Africans. The match was mentioned by Anne Pallant in a self-published 1997 family history entitled *A Sporting Century 1863–1963*. Her brief and highly improbable account is as follows:

> During the 1906/07 season, the Springboks visited Devon as they were county champions. Jimmy Peters was a member of that Devon side, and being a coloured man the South Africans made a scene, even though they were told Peters was known to be one of the fairest men who ever wore a football boot. Their High Commissioner who had to come down from the stand at last persuaded the visitors to take the field. 'Well, all right,' they agreed, 'but we shall kill him.' Tom Kelly, Devon's captain replied, 'That's all right, we've been trying to for years.' The South Africans came off saying 'we give you best, he is a man.' Being a very elusive runner, Peters had the great quality of 'going away like a boxer' when he was tackled. [29]

Pallant did not realise that the appointment of a South African high commissioner in London did not take place until after Union in 1910. The first was Sir Richard Solomon who served from 1910–13. Her doubtful understanding of rugby history is also evident in the fact that it was Ernest Roberts who captained Devon and not Tom Kelly.

The careless piece had unfortunate repercussions. 'Every non-historical work on Peters produced after 1997,' says Tom Weir, 'repeated the story, making it part of common narrative of the tour'. In 2006, for example, Brendan Gallagher, writing in the *Daily Telegraph,* was happy to side with Pallant at the expense of factual reporting and claim that 'in the bowels of the changing rooms, a huge row had broken out. The tourists ... were seething at the presence of such a "savage" on the pitch ... the South African High Commissioner and local dignitaries ... feared a riot'. [30]

In a detailed investigation, Weir concludes that the historical view of the Springboks was likely to be embellished in a book crafted from family stories. He explains:

> Pallant's statement is extremely problematic, as in addition to not being able to attribute its source through lack of referencing, the facts are at odds with wider reporting of the game. No news coverage, either local or national, mentions so much as a delay at the start of the game: *The Times, Daily Chronicle,* the *Daily Mail,* the *Sportsman, The Field,* the *Yorkshire Post* and *Leeds Intelligencer, Western Times,* the *Plymouth Football Herald,* the *Nottinghamshire Guardian* – a cross-section of papers. [31]

Pallant's glowing picture of Peters' play is contradicted by reports stating that he did not have a good game. Newspaper accounts in the *Daily Chronicle,* the

Sportsman, *The Times*, and the *Plymouth Football Herald* indicate that Peters played poorly against the Springboks.[32] Although he partnered the accomplished Raphael Jago, there was little to commend in his play in a game described as 'Dobbin's match'.[33] The South African half-back, Fred 'Uncle' Dobbin, outplayed Peters and scored two tries in a dominant performance, 'his running and adroit passing being the most conspicuous feature of the game'.[34] He would become South Africa's first choice – ahead of vice-captain Carolin – in the Tests against Wales and England.

After defeating Somerset a few days later in their eighth successive victory, the Springboks struggled with injuries. It necessitated a telegram from the team manager, Cecil Carden, to 'W.V. Simkins, President, South African Rugby Football Board'. Dated 21 October 1906, it read: 'Morkel and Burmeister unavailable for a month x cable authorisation play Brooks of Rhodesia x end x.'

There were various developments behind the scenes. Milton had allowed Brooks sufficient leave to press for a place in the English team. In Milton's mind, an England jersey was probably preferable, although he might have stopped short of supporting the writer in awe of a team 'dressed in immaculate white, a modest emblem of the stainless purity of the national life'.[35] Two of Milton's sons, both South African-born, had played in recent internationals – Jumbo was selected for England against Scotland in 1905 and Cecil played against Ireland in early 1906, but was reported as being unavailable when approached to play in the South African match.[36] The youngest son Noel played against the Springboks for Oxford University.

An emergency meeting of the SA Rugby Football Board was held in late October at which the telegram concerning Brooks was discussed. According to the minutes: 'There was practically no discussion on this point as the chairman – [Billy Simkins] – referred to the resolution of the Board to the effect that no player be eligible for the team who was not South African born or had five years' residential qualification'. Simkins, who had been Milton's stooge in the 'Hendricks Affair', now asserted himself by preventing a Rhodesian with strong imperial ties from representing the Springboks. The secretary, Louis Smuts, immediately moved that 'Carden be not authorised to avail himself of Brooks's services' and that a replacement be sent from South Africa.[37]

The Springboks won their first fifteen matches leading up to the first international. They were then unexpectedly defeated by Scotland 6–0 on a muddy and uneven ground. In front of a passionate crowd, Scotland scored two tries, including a superb solo effort by their young winger Kenneth Macleod. The Springboks, who were already without the injured Roos, experienced further bad luck. As players were not allowed to be substituted – a rule that remained unchanged until 1969 – they found themselves in some difficulty. Carolin (who captained the side) sent home a letter that was not short on excuses but did paint a dismal picture:

> The game had not been in progress six minutes [when Dietlof] Maré had a finger broken in his left hand. He pluckily remained on the ground, but it was almost useless as he was in great agony and unable to pack. In ten minutes time [Koei] Brink was carried off with a sprained ankle and though he returned after an absence of 15 or 20 minutes, he was also useless as he could only manage to limp about ... Twenty minutes before time, Arthur Marsberg was carried off the ground unconscious.[38]

A week later the Springboks played Ireland in Belfast and narrowly won a tight encounter 15–12. The dry conditions were favourable, Roos was back, and South Africa led 12–3 at half-time. After the interval, the Springboks seemed on course for victory, Bob Loubser was twice tackled with the try-line beckoning. However, a tremendous rally by Ireland was inspired by a memorable length-of-the-field try from their wing Basil Maclear. The scores were levelled at 12–12 soon afterwards, but the Springboks kept attacking and their wing Anton Stegmann scored after gathering a cross-kick from Japie Krige ten minutes from time.

The tour moved on to Wales where team manager Cecil Carden described interest as being 'enormous in a country simply devoted to rugby'.[39] Wales had beaten the All Blacks a year earlier under the same captain, the centre Gwyn Nicholls, and an estimated 50 000 spectators gathered in the Swansea ground. This was expected to be the Springboks' greatest challenge, but the Welsh were never in contention. After leading 6–0 at half-time, the Springboks scored a further converted try to secure the match comfortably by 11 points to nil.

The final international fixture awaited South Africa a week later at Crystal Palace in London. England selected Adrian Stoop and Raphael Jago at half-back. The roles of the half-backs had become increasingly specialised in the mid-1900s. The 'left' and 'right' method was being replaced by 'scrum-halves' (Jago) and outside halves (Stoop/Peters). Some sportswriters have since seen Stoop as being fortunate to be chosen ahead of Peters, with a *Daily Telegraph* writer imagining the latter to be 'left fuming back home in Plymouth, putting in an extra shift as a carpenter at the Devonport naval dockyards to sweat off his anger and humiliation'.[40] But as Peters was not part of the trial prior to the Test, he was not being considered for the side to play the Springboks.

The English selectors had good reason not to select him as Dobbin clearly had the measure of Peters when the Springboks played Devon. On that occasion, Peters had tried desperately to exert pressure on his opponent, but reports stated he was frequently caught off-side.[41] Billy Millar saw Dobbin as pivotal to South Africa's success:

> Dobbin is essentially a 'stand-off' half-back and not a 'scrum' half-back, and he is cleverness personified, always drawing a section of the defence before passing, and his feinting repeatedly deceived opponents. South Africa owes more to Dobbin than to any other single player.[42]

To blame South Africa for any racial controversy that prevailed over Peters is ill-considered. The English had been engaged in racial accusations involving Peters for several years. Weir wrote that when living in Bristol, Peters experienced 'the most blatant and overt racist attitudes'. He then moved to Plymouth where Weir and the *Guardian's* Andy Bull list examples of the treatment he received before the arrival of the Springboks. The *Plymouth Football Herald* reported 'racist convention' prevented selection against Wales. After continued non-selection against Ireland, with Jago and Gent again favoured, the *Western Times* was blunt in its opinion: 'Peters is sacrificed. Colour is the difficulty.'[43]

Complicating the issue was the class prejudice that existed in Britain. The RFU was not opposed to selecting working-class players – such as Jago – but they would have been delighted in Stoop's enthusiasm for the game. After all, he was Rugby- and Oxford-educated and for his 21st birthday, 'his father had given him a marble mine on the Turkish island of Marmara'.[44] He would become one of England's greatest players.

England also selected the India-born Brooks. His country of residence, Southern Rhodesia, was affiliated to the SA Rugby Football Board, which in turn was affiliated to the RFU. Through these slightly tenuous links, Brooks was eligible for South Africa and England. Given first choice, the governing body in Cape Town wouldn't select him because he wasn't a true South African – a perennial problem for Rhodesians.

In the build-up to the Test, Brooks was in wonderful form for Bedford, scoring nine tries in four matches. Selection followed for the South against North when he 'was the best man on the field ... his four tries were equally masterly in conception'.[45] He represented an England XV against the Rest at Coventry in a final trial, scoring again through 'a grand run down the left wing ... without doubt the effort of the match'.[46] Selection for England came against South Africa at Crystal Palace on a soft and greasy ground, with play being hampered by showers of rain. It was for good reason that the South Africans feared the Rhodesian speedster who was quite at home in such conditions. Concern swept through their ranks when Brooks became the first player to stir the partisan 40 000 crowd. According to the *Morning Post*, 'he put everyone on the tip-toe of expectancy in the first few minutes by a dashing run', which took play into the South African '22'.[47]

The tight marking that ensued drew comment from the *Daily Telegraph* that several of the touring team had fought with the Boers and 'doubtless showed the same dogged and brilliant qualities'.[48] The Springboks led 3–0 – a try by Millar – at half-time but the English equalised in the second half through a mixture of skill and opportunism. It was Brooks who dribbled the ball into the South African half. Raphael Jago and Harry Shewring became involved, then the forwards joined the action and a ruck developed. At the right moment, recalled the *Morning Post*, the ball was quickly heeled:

> Jago gave an excellent pass to Stoop; the latter gently kicked over the defensive wall and the speedy Brooks, waiting for something to turn up went for the leather like a shot from a gun. He was there first; a storm proclaimed his try. Yes, his deed was done; the scores were equal.[49]

The English *Sunday Times* recalled Brooks's ability to outsprint two South Africans to score: 'The try roused the sodden crowd to wild excitement. Cheer after cheer boomed out on the heavy air.'[50] E.H.D. Sewell commented in the *Daily Graphic* that Brooks, 'who is the best player living at seeing half a chance and making the most of it, "went", to use Roos's own words, "past me like a flash just as I was going to kick dead"'.[51]

In the last part of play, the match became 'a succession of thrills'. Stoop and Brooks were both nearly over but the South Africans held on for the draw.[52]

The Springbok captain thought the game 'had shown them all as equals' and that the tour had united the (white) South African nation. 'From Cape Agulhas to the Zambesi,' he said, 'South Africa was one and all differences have been forgotten.'[53] He had obviously missed the significance of the Brooks debate – the only player from the territory immediately south of the Zambezi had played for England.

The 1906/07 Springboks enjoyed a dinner at the Café Royal, London, after their match against England. It was presided over by Rowland Hill (president, RFU), and attended by members of the 1891, 1896 and 1903 British teams that had visited South Africa, many of whom travelled very long distances to be present. It was not as yet the end of the tour as the South Africans had another eight matches to play. They would visit Paris and defeat France 55–6 to complete an itinerary in which they played 29; won 26; drew 1 and lost 2 matches.

The English press were unstinting in their praise. *The Times* commented:

> Their code of ethics leaves nothing to be desired. They are the most generous of opponents ... It would be idle to pretend that the New Zealanders, great as was the admiration which their extraordinary skill excited, engendered in England the same feeling of respect which the South Africans engendered. The latest visitors have successfully appealed to the best feelings of the sportsmanlike community. They have done more than that. They have proved without preaching that the greatest possible is consistent with the fairest possible play, and it is to be hoped that the lesson taught will be practically learnt ... They leave behind them only feelings of gratitude and admiration. They have played the game.[54]

The *Guardian* also compared the South African game to that of the New Zealanders: 'Men who have played against both sides confess that for the sheer pleasure of sport the South African matches have been unequalled. They have no system of tricks for execution when the referee was not close at hand, and the penalties against them for infringing the rules have been surprisingly few in number.'[55]

The Springboks became the first of the southern hemisphere teams to be invited to make a second tour. Billy Millar's 1912/13 side would be even more successful than the 1906/07 team in that they achieved the first 'grand slam' by winning all their internationals. They defeated Scotland 16–0, Ireland 38–0, Wales 3–0, England 9–3 and France 38–5. The game against Wales was a mighty battle on a water logged field in which Millar remembered Boet McHardy 'playing the game of his life' in defence. Three weeks later, England's Ronnie Poulton scored the most magnificent try Millar had ever seen, but when he set off 'on his own again, and seemed a certain scorer, McHardy came like a bolt from the blue and saved us'.[56]

South African rugby had come a long way since the 1880s when administrators made their initial unsuccessful attempts to arrange an overseas tour. It was therefore fitting that Sir Rowland Hill should address the 1912/13 Springboks at a farewell luncheon on the *Armadale Castle* at Southampton. For many years, he had appeared to have reservations about South Africa's ambitions to play international rugby, but on this occasion, he spoke with deep emotion, 'tears trickling down his cheeks':

I have bidden farewell to every representative rugby side that has left our shores for the colonies and welcomed them home bringing the spoils of victory. I have also welcomed teams from the colonies and followed with keen interest their splendid achievements on our fields, showing how well they had learned the grand game we set out to teach them. On this occasion, however, they have by winning all the Test matches, reversed the position and taught us how the game should be played.[57]

Notes

1   W. Millar, 'The Springboks in Great Britain 1912/13', in I. Difford (ed.), *The History of South African Rugby Football 1875–1932* (Wynberg: Speciality Press, 1933), 378–379.
2   Minutes of the SA Rugby Football Board, 20, 23 August 1897.
3   *Bloemfontein Express*, 9 March 1894.
4   *Diamond Fields Advertiser*, 25 August 1897.
5   Ibid., 29 August 1898.
6   See F. van der Merwe, 'Rugby in the Prisoner-of-War Camps during the Anglo-Boer War of 1899–1902', Department of Human Movement Studies, University of Stellenbosch.
7   Minutes of the SA Rugby Football Board Special General Meeting, 24 March 1903. Gerald Orpen represented the Transvaal and tabled the motion. South African cyclists and athletes had made use of the green vest and springbok badge in the late 1890s, so the Transvaal RFU could not lay claim to be the first to suggest the identity.
8   P. van der Schyff, 'Birth of an African legend', in D. Cruywagen (ed.), *The Badge: A Centenary of the Springbok Emblem* (Newlands: SA Rugby, 2006), 28; Minutes of the SA Rugby Football Special General Meeting, 6 May 1903.
9   Difford, *History of South African Rugby Football*, 291.
10 L. Laubscher and G. Nieman (eds), *The Carolin Papers: A Diary of the 1906–07 Springbok Tour* (Pretoria: Rugbyana, 1990), 50.
11 J. Griffiths, *Rugby's Strangest Matches: Extraordinary but True Stories from Over a Century of Rugby* (London: Portico, 2000), 39.
12 P. Dobson, *Rugby in South Africa: A History 1861–1988* (Cape Town: SARB, 1989), 59.
13 Minutes of the SA Rugby Football Board Special General Meeting, 26 February 1904.
14 Minutes of the SA Rugby Football Board, 5 and 12 September 1906.
15 *Cape Times*, 17 September 1894; *Standard and Diggers News*, 15 September 1894.
16 C. Becker, 'The Selection of the Team', in L. Laubscher and G. Nieman (eds), *The Carolin Papers: A Diary of the 1906–07 Springbok Tour* (Pretoria: Rugbyana, 1990), 38.
17 'Journal of Bedford Grammar School', *The Ousel*, 1901–02.
18 *Rand Daily Mail*, 16 March 1905.
19 N. Roy (ed.), *100 Years of the Blues: The Bedfordshire Times Centenary History of Bedford RUFC, 1886–1986* (Bedford: Bedford County Press, 1986) records that Brooks represented the club in the 1901/02; 1902/03; 1903/04 and 1906/07 seasons.
20 *Morning Post*, 8 November 1906.
21 Minutes of the SA Rugby Football Board, 30 June 1905.
22 Minutes of the SA Rugby Football Board, 18 August 1905.
23 W. Millar, *My Recollections and Reminiscences* (Cape Town: Juta, 1926), 84.
24 *The Star*, 21 July 1906.
25 *Rand Daily Mail*, 21 July 1906.
26 Laubscher and Nieman, *The Carolin Papers*, 47–48.
27 *Daily Mail*, 20 September 1906.
28 Laubscher and Nieman, *The Carolin Papers*, 49. The SA Rugby Football Board would later make their colours and emblem available to all sports.
29 A. Pallant, *A Sporting Century 1863–1963* (Callington: self-published, 1997), 93, 97.

30   T. Weir, 'James Peters: The Man They Wouldn't Play. England›s First Black International and the 1906 Springboks' (unpublished master's thesis, De Montfort University, Leicester, 2015); *Daily Telegraph*, 17 November 2006.
31   Weir, 'James Peters'.
32   Ibid.
33   Laubscher and Nieman, *The Carolin Papers*, 105.
34   *The Star* (Johannesburg), 18 October 1906.
35   A. Hales in the *Sunday Times* (London), 6 January 1907.
36   J. Thompson, *The Story of Rhodesian Sport: 1889–1935* (Bulawayo: Rhodesia P&P, 1935), 141.
37   Minutes of the SA Rugby Football Board, 25 October 1905; Laubscher and Nieman, *Carolin Papers*, 109 and 114.
38   P. Carolin letter to L. Cox, 23 November 1906, in Laubscher and Nieman, *The Carolin Papers*, 163.
39   C. Carden, manager's report to W.V. Simkins, 30 November 1906.
40   *Daily Telegraph*, 17 November 2006.
41   Weir, 'James Peters', 32–33: He cited the *Daily Chronicle, the Sportsman, The Times* (all 18 October 1906) and the *Plymouth Football Herald*, 27 October 1906.
42   F. Keating, *The Great Number Tens: A Century of Rugby's Pivots and Playmakers* (London: Corgi, 1999), 59.
43   Weir, 'James Peters', 17: A. Bull, 'Jimmy Peters: Race Pioneer of English Rugby who Emerged from the Circus', in *The Guardian*, 26 December 2018; *Plymouth Football Herald*, 13 January 1906; *Western Times*, Exeter, 5 February 1906.
44   T. Collins, *The Oval World: A Global History of Rugby* (London: Bloomsbury, 2015), 208.
45   The *Morning Post* in 'scrap books' titled 'Adrian Stoop, His Playing Days, 1902–1912', RFU Museum of Rugby, Twickenham.
46   Scrap books ... Adrian Stoop, Museum of Rugby, Twickenham.
47   *Morning Post*, 9 December 1906.
48   *Daily Telegraph*, 9 December 1906, reported in Laubscher and Nieman, *The Carolin Papers*, 192. Conditions deteriorated to the extent that the match was described as 'mud-larking'. One notable scribe, C.B. Fry, thought that 'only play of the most brilliant order saved the game under such conditions from bathos'.
49   *Morning Post*, 9 December 1906; *Sportsman*, Scrap books ... Adrian Stoop, Museum of Rugby, Twickenham.
50   A. Hales in the *Sunday Times* (London), 6 January 1907.
51   *Daily Graphic*, 10 December 1906.
52   *Morning Post*, 9 December 1906.
53   B. Spies, 'The Imperial Heritage', in A. Grundlingh, A. Odendaal and B. Spies (eds), *Beyond the Tryline: Rugby and South African Society* (Johannesburg: Ravan Press, 1995), 75.
54   *The Times*, 28 January 1907.
55   *The Guardian*, 17 December 1906.
56   Millar, 'The Springboks' 375–376.
57   Ibid., 378–379.

8

'Most Unfortunate Match Ever Played'

It would be unfair to suggest that the injuries were
the result of intentionally foul or unnecessarily
rough play. The Maoris merely threw their weight
about regardless of the niceties of the game.

– The Star, 8 September 1921

'Everything comes to him who waits,' announced the *Cape Times* on 8 July 1919.
The newspaper was referring to the confirmation received that the New Zealand
Services team – fresh from their King's Cup rugby victory in London – would
be arriving on a full-scale tour. It continued: 'South Africa stands indebted to
that great pillar of the rugby game, the late Hon W.P. Schreiner – we are keenly
expecting a visit from a great New Zealand side.'[1]

Much, in fact, had happened in three months since 2 April 1919. That was the
day when Schreiner, the South African high commissioner in London, received a
cable from the SA Rugby Football Board. They requested his assistance:

> Would it be possible to arrange representative Australian or New Zealand
> Army Rugby Team break journey Cape Town Stop Tour Union for six weeks
> or less Stop Travelling and hotel expenses paid Stop Pardon liberty Stop Reply
> paid Stop and end.[2]

Schreiner was struggling with his health. Early in May 1919, he visited his doctor
who was of the opinion: 'Why not chuck your job with all its exactions and
constant worries?'[3] The high commissioner was reluctant to leave his work but
agreed to see a heart specialist. In the meantime, he responded to the board on
19 May 1919: 'Arrangements now provisionally completed successful Stop New
Zealand Services team personnel twenty-nine visit Union six weeks'[4]

Then, on Monday 2 June, Schreiner requested details of fixtures for the New Zealand team and presumed a union official would accompany the touring team as a local manager. It seems unlikely that he was of any further assistance in tour preparations as he was in the process of leaving work. According to his biographer, 'the result of the [specialist's] examination was so disquieting that the doctors decided to get him away at once'. Schreiner sent for the 'senior members of his staff, one by one and bade them farewell'.[5]

In this, the first week of June, he also informed his office that he would be away 'for some weeks, possibly for as much as three months'. Accompanied by his wife, he went to stay in Llandrindod Wells in Central Wales. He died there on 28 June 1919, the day the Treaty of Versailles was signed.

In the meantime, the SA Rugby Football Board met on 2 June to reconsider and discuss aspects of the tour arrangements. The question was raised as to whether there would be Maori players in the visiting team. After a lengthy discussion, it was eventually decided by eight votes to six – on the motion of Ronnie McIntyre, seconded by Bill Schreiner (the high commissioner's son) – that the following cable be sent to London: 'Confidential if visitors include Maoris tour would be wrecked and immense harm politically and otherwise would follow. Please explain position fully and try arrange exclusion.'[6]

The behaviour of the younger Schreiner was extraordinary in his taking a lead role in a decision that would have upset his ailing father.[7] Moreover, would the tour have been 'wrecked' and 'immense harm' occurred? Six members of the board appeared to think not. They were almost certainly correct. Ron Palenski records that 'at least two Maoris played in South Africa in 1917 when teams from two troopships bound for England played in Durban during a refuelling stop'. He said that John Grace from Gisborne scored one of the tries for the winning team from the *Turakina*. A team-mate was Paraine ('Friday') Pirihi – both were with the Maori contingent in the seventeenth reinforcement draft.[8]

Two Maori players who had been members of the team that won the King's Cup were left out of the side to tour South Africa. They were Parekura Tureia and Arthur 'Ranji' Wilson, who was given his nickname after the famous cricketer of that time, Kumar Shri Ranjitsinhji. To cover Tureia's non-appearance, it was announced that he had missed the *Cap Polonio*, but Wilson was fully aware of what was happening. He helped to select the team of which he could not be a part.[9]

Charlie Brown, a player from Taranaki, was named as captain of a touring squad of 26. Some years later, it was noted that he 'was in fact part-Maori – he just did not look the part'.[10] South Africa's sports administrators would struggle to work out how the line of colour should be drawn, but were happy nevertheless to call the tourists, the 'All Blacks'. Nobody seemed to mind that this was not the official team and no Tests were played. The imperial services wore black on their tour with a silver fern on the left breast. And of the players selected, seventeen were All Blacks or became so in the future.

They were not the first New Zealand team to play in southern Africa. A New Zealand Services XV visited Rhodesia during the Anglo-Boer War and played an historic match against Matabeleland in Bulawayo on 28 July 1900. Although the Rhodesians had affiliated to the SA Rugby Football Board in 1895, this was the first time a rugby side had visited the colony and it did so despite severe military restrictions. The Matabeles were led by Tommy Hepburn, the son of missionary parents from Bechuanaland. He was an outstanding player who had converted Alf Larard's try in South Africa's 5–0 victory over the British in 1896. He scored a try against the New Zealand tourists but this time his team went down 10–3; the visitors celebrating with a war cry that presented 'a strange and weird ending to a most exciting tussle'.[11]

A South African team played against the combined New Zealand forces at Johannesburg in 1902. As a consequence, several attempts were made to arrange an official tour. They did not succeed for logistical reasons, but the First World War brought the two countries together in an inter-services tournament in England in 1919. New Zealand beat South Africa and went on to win the King's Cup, thus creating further interest in establishing international competition.

Teams from Australia were already playing matches in South Africa in 1919, prior to the arrival of the New Zealanders on 17 July. A side from HMAT *Orits* led by Lieutenant Ernest Grimstone arranged a fixture against Gardens at Green Point track. Bitterly cold conditions accompanied by driving rain made handling difficult, but the visitors were in excellent shape although lacking in practice as they were just off the ship. They were beaten by three tries to two, but 'finished the game in rare style, continually rushing Gardens' lines and were beaten off with difficulty'.[12]

Australian troops from the TSS *Themistocles* also played matches as they were cooling their heels at Wynberg while repairs were being effected to their ship. A testing fixture was arranged for them against a combined Villager and Gardens team at Newlands on 19 July. The match was advertised, only for the ship to be declared fit to sail and the departure time fixed hours before the game could be played.

Frantic organisers hurried to Cape Town harbour where the HMAT *Giessen*, carrying New Zealand troops, had just arrived. The soldiers were more than happy to fill the breach, 'welcoming the opportunity of having a game at Newlands – a ground of which they had heard much'. The rumour that the 'All Blacks' would be playing spread quickly and attracted a large crowd. There were useful players among the visitors, notably full-back Henry Capper MM who had played for the New Zealand army team in their narrow 5–3 victory over the French military at Parc de Princes in February 1918.

The town team won because they were better prepared and match fit. There was no score at half-time, but the local side eventually emerged on top 19–0.[13]

Charlie Brown's New Zealand Services team were at Newlands to watch the game. They had arrived on the seized German liner, the *Cap Polonio*, and played their first match against Western Province Country on Thursday 24 July. They were also scheduled to play their last match in Cape Town but as the ship was leaving from Durban, an extra match was organised against Natal on Tuesday 16 September. They then set sail on the Thursday after fifteen matches in 54 days. They won eleven, drew one and lost three.

Wilson – whose father was West Indian and mother British – did in fact get to South Africa and met up with the touring team in Durban. He left on the troopship *Cordoba* on 18 July and, some five weeks later, the *Natal Witness* let it be known that 'amongst the troops on the New Zealand transport is their great forward Ranji Wilson who has already met and fraternised with his old comrades'. A later report added: 'The Pacific Islander, Wilson, just arrived from England, is perhaps the greatest player in the service team and it would be a good thing if his inclusion could be arranged. He was a very popular player in the Home matches.'[14]

The machinations of the SA Rugby Football Board were not common knowledge. Two years later, the Springbok rugby side toured New Zealand for the first time. 'The 1921 Springbok tour,' says Mike Buckley, 'was an occasion which emphasised empire solidarity. The South African players were welcomed in a manner similar to royalty.' For most New Zealanders, it was a case of two nations strengthening intra-imperial relations, having recently fought together in the First World War.[15]

New Zealand won the inaugural Test and the second Test was won by South Africa. Shortly before the deciding international, a match was played against the Maori that would create great controversy. Accounts written some years afterwards have stated there were problems even before play started. 'Insensitive Afrikaners in the team,' claim New Zealand writers R.H. Chester and N.A.C. McMillan, 'deliberately turned their backs upon a group of Maori girls who were performing a poi dance of welcome.' It is a farcical statement. How did the two men manage to identify the 'Afrikaners' in the team? And how did they reach the conclusion that the described action – if it did occur – was deliberate?[16]

Buckley says about the same occasion:

> The incident was overlooked by the sporting press, which presumed that nothing untoward had taken place. The Maori XV players did not publicly remark at the time that they were offended. Moreover, photographs of the haka which appeared in the *Otago Witness* failed to indicate that the Springbok players had turned their backs. It was only in the mid-to-late twentieth century, when New Zealand's rugby contacts with South Africa were opposed by many on racial grounds, that the Springbok back-turning incident was mentioned.[17]

There were 6 000 spectators to witness an historic encounter on Wednesday 7 September. The Maori team was captained by Parekura Tureia who had not been allowed to tour South Africa two years earlier. That might have contributed to the prevailing tension and the home side's determination to defeat the visitors. There were scenes of emotion throughout, especially when two crucial refereeing decisions went against the Maori. Jack Blake claimed a fair catch or 'mark' in front of the posts from which he would almost certainly have kicked a goal, but the referee ruled the ball had come off a player. Local supporters were then convinced that the South African wing, Bill Zeller, had put a foot into touch before delivering a pass that led to a try.

Feelings ran high amongst both spectators and players, with the Springboks winning a ferocious encounter 9–8. The victory was perhaps deserved because they had scored three tries (Zeller, Van Heerden and Townsend) to one (Garlick).

The drama, however, had only just begun. Not long after the match was played a scandal erupted. The journalist travelling with the Springboks, Mortimer Charles 'Mort' Blackett, cabled a report to South Africa that allegedly shocked a telegraphist at the Napier Post Office, J.T. Evans. He and two of his colleagues then 'illegally typed a copy of the cablegram and forwarded it to the Napier *Daily Telegraph*'.[18] Other reports claimed that one of Evans's copies turned up in a billiards saloon where a reporter of the Napier *Daily Telegraph* was playing. When published in the *Daily Telegraph*, it stated:

> Most unfortunate match ever played. Only result great pressure being brought to bear on Bennett induced them to meet Maoris, who assisted largely entertainment Springboks. Bad enough having play team officially designated 'New Zealand natives', but spectacle thousands Europeans frantically cheering

on band of coloured men to defeat members of own race was too much for Springboks, who frankly disgusted. That was not the worst. The crowd was most unsportsmanlike experienced on the tour, especially section who lost all control of their feelings. When not booing the referee, they indulged in sarcastic remarks at his expense. On many occasions Africans were hurt. Crowd, without waiting for possibility of immediate recovery, shouted 'Take him off!' 'Take him off!' Their faithful coloured allies proved loyal to New Zealand, for, in addition to serious injury to Kruger's leg, Van Heerden had to stay off field for fifteen minutes. Others were limping badly. Maoris flung their weight about regardless of niceties of the game.[19]

Greg Ryan states that the three men were subsequently dismissed for their part in this 'media leak'. Elsewhere it was noted that the telegraph operators were reinstated.[20]

The public's critical response was initially aimed at the Springbok players because Blackett was not immediately named as the cablegram's author. *The Sun* (Christchurch) reported rumours that a number of the Springboks 'strongly resented having to play the Maoris'.[21] The *Daily Telegraph* accused the Springboks of hypocrisy in that they had accepted Maori hospitality, but subsequently thought Maori rugby players were racially inferior.[22]

The *Christchurch Press*, in an editorial, commented that it was absurd to place black South Africans as equals with Maoris. It stated:

> There are no doubt good reasons why European South Africans should draw a hard and fast colour line against Kaffirs and Zulus, but no one in his senses would dream of placing the latter on an equality with the Maoris ... If now [the Maori] feels that he has been insulted because a party of visitors are made to appear unable or unwilling to recognise the essential differences between him and the Kaffir or the Hottentot, who can wonder?[23]

Buckley comments on the fact that 'Maori and Pakeha spokespeople took issue with the cablegram's implication of racial parity between Maori and black South Africans':

> Publicised Maori protests against the Blackett cablegram were as social Darwinist in nature as those of Pakeha. Nonetheless, they were confined publicly to the Arawa tribal confederation (Bay of Plenty) and the renowned doctor, Te Rangi Hiroa (Dr Peter Buck).[24]

The Hawke's Bay Rugby Union, host of the Maori match, telegraphed the Springbok manager Harold Bennett, and asked him to disassociate himself and his team from the reported comments but did express regret at the action of a section of the crowd.

The manager of the Maori team, W.T. 'Ned' Parata, also expressed regret that the conduct of a certain section of the mixed crowd should have left room for complaint.[25] He added that there was no ill-feeling between the Springboks and Maori players and that his son had been a Springbok mascot for several of their games.

Bennett sent a cable in which he stated: 'The whole of my team and officials are very much hurt, because the Maoris have been particularly hospitable towards us. They were certainly not guilty of any dirty play, and we have certainly not been a party to hurting their feelings in any way.'[26]

Blackett, who announced that he had sent the cable, was surprised that Bennett had issued an apology. He pointed out that he was selectively quoted and that it was never his intention to insult the New Zealanders. Blackett informed the New Zealand press:

What I do regret, apart from the unfortunate manner in which the message was disclosed at this end, is the mutilated and abridged form in which it was published in certain papers for reasons best known to themselves. Persons who surreptitiously obtained and disseminated the cable only published those passages which could be construed as an attack on the Maoris.[27]

The Maori confederation, Te Arawa, through prominent leaders Henry Taiporutu (Tai) Mitchell and Henare Mete (Kiwi) Amohau, reacted to the Blackett cablegram by accusing the Springboks of ungentlemanly behaviour. They asked Bennett to 'convey to the Boers in your team' their regret at offering courtesies to the Springboks during their Rotorua visit: 'To accept the welcome, and to break bread with our people, and then, later, to insult them as you have done, is not, according to Maoris, the code honourable adopted by gentlemen.'

Bennett replied:

Thanks for the telegram ... We are not responsible for the alleged cable, which does not in any way represent our views. Regret you should have telegraphed in such an insulting strain without making proper inquiry.[28]

There was considerable tension before the deciding Test. The newspaper *Truth* appeared on the morning of the final Test 'with its usual eloquent outrage and its unidentified writer said the cabled message was "too bad for words" and that its writer should be "severely set upon and silenced"'.[29] This was not contested, although most newspapers took the line of the *New Zealand Herald,* which stated that the visitors came from a country where 'the colour line is drawn very clearly and their acquaintance with New Zealand has not been sufficiently long for them to understand the status for the Maoris in this country'.[30]

It seems incredible that nobody at the time bothered to find out anything about Blackett. Or, if they did, thought it best to keep quiet. The irony of the cable issue was that the writer of the telegram was not South African. The Johannesburg newspaper, *The Star*, would later record that Blackett was brought up in New Zealand:

He was born in Tasmania in 1881 and he went to New Zealand at an early age. He came to South Africa with a New Zealand contingent to serve in the South African war. In June 1904 he joined the editorial staff of *The Star* ... In the Great War, he served in South-West Africa as a lieutenant in the Natal Light Horse and was wounded at Gibeon. He then went to England and joined the Australian Forces in which he served as a captain on the headquarters staff of General [John] Monash. He was awarded the OBE.[31]

Blackett was a brave and intelligent man and knew New Zealand well. Any comments on his cable might therefore be viewed in a different light from the approach that was taken in 1921 and by commentators over the years. His war record suggests that he was a man who commanded respect and perhaps did not deserve the criticism that he received.

A second strange aspect of the unhappy saga was that no one bothered to investigate whether Blackett's report of the game was published in South Africa. It was – on Thursday, 8 September – at the same time as the *Daily Telegraph* first published news about the cable. *The Star's* report stated:

It was perhaps unfortunate that today's match between the Springboks and Maoris was played. Only as a result of great pressure being brought to bear, was Mr Bennett, the manager induced to meet the Maoris, who had certainly assisted largely in the entertainment of the Springboks. It was bad enough that South Africans were playing a team officially designated New Zealand Natives, but the spectacle of thousands of Europeans frantically cheering on a band of non-Europeans to defeat members of their own race was too much for the Springboks. The crowd, too, was the least sportsmanlike experienced during the tour, especially the European section, which seemed to lose control of its feelings, and when not booing the referee, indulged in sarcastic remarks at his expense. On occasions when South Africans were hurt, the crowd, without waiting the possibility of immediate recovery, shouted, 'Take him off.' In addition to the serious injury to Kruger's leg, which may incapacitate him for the tour, Van Heerden was off the field for fifteen minutes and half a dozen others were limping badly. It would be unfair to suggest that the injuries were the result of intentionally foul or unnecessarily rough play. The Maoris merely threw their weight about regardless of the niceties of the game.[32]

The version published by *The Star* differed from that which appeared in New Zealand newspapers. It is possible that the piece was edited in Johannesburg, a normal process that would have been understood by those involved in both reporting and sub-editing. Blackett had every right to be annoyed that someone in New Zealand should have intercepted the text and then distributed what he alleged to be an altered version. The action of the post office officials was a crime that reflected poorly on their country. Both Bennett and George Slade, the chairman of the New Zealand Rugby Football Union (RFU) management committee, 'were highly critical of the breach of trust on the part of post and telegraph authorities and the New Zealand press for publishing the cable'.[33]

Blackett's report served warnings to rugby's officialdom. He was not the 'ignorant' participant in the scandal that rocked New Zealand rugby. Far from it, he was the one person who understood the lay of the land in both countries. He – and no doubt Bennett – feared that a contest featuring 'white' Springboks versus the New Zealand 'Natives' could have resulted in a bloodbath. It was understandable that the Maori should resent South Africa's segregationist policy and the behind-the-scenes activity that had led to two of their players being barred from the 1919 tour.

In Blackett's mind, these problems were further compounded by early tour experiences. The Springboks' match against Manawatu District at Palmerston North was reputedly the first against a team to contain Maori players in any numbers and it gave the first real indication of the conflict that would follow. 'There can be no doubt,' observed Blackett, 'that when the play became rather willing as the result of weak control by the referee, the Springboks were more disposed to retaliate against the natives than they had in those rough matches down south when their opponents were exclusively Europeans.'[34]

Blackett drew attention to the fixture at Napier where 'private funds brought Maoris from all parts of the dominion, a fortnight previously'. He asserted 'they were perfectly trained under an expert coach. The match was invested with a Test atmosphere and was preceded by a war-like haka (dance) by men and women.'[35] He was concerned that this was more than just a mid-week tour match. There was a point to prove.

Once play was underway, Blackett saw the antagonism that he knew existed. In his report which sparked the outrage, he dwelt on the injuries the Springboks had suffered in the course of the match. He was not going to abide by the 'protective' policy that the New Zealand establishment had adopted towards Maori players, nor was he going to hold back from unleashing a scathing attack on the behaviour of the host crowd. He aimed to produce an objective report, based on what he saw at the game.

The Blackett 'scandal' raged on for ten days until the third Test and then festered for a good part of the twentieth century. The Test itself captured much attention. Special arrangements were made to expedite the result not only to England and France, but also America, 'while steps were taken to acquaint South Africa of the fateful news before breakfast'. *The Star* thought it doubtful if, apart from an occasional glove contest, a sporting fixture ever gave rise to such 'tremendous worldwide interest as the final meeting for rugby supremacy between New Zealand and South Africa'.[36]

'It was throughout,' said Blackett, 'a terrific battle. There was no score in the first half, and in the second half, despite the desperate efforts on each side neither line was crossed, so that the game ended in a draw.'[37]

There remained one other major point of contention. The South African manager had commented during a conversation with Ned Parata, that it was unlikely Maori rugby players would be able to tour South Africa.[38] Bennett's stance stemmed from the decision made by the SA Rugby Football Board in 1919. He was fully aware of the board's attitude and, in recognising their intransigence, was honest in his assessment of the situation.

The Springboks departed in the belief that the tour had been a success. Capacity crowds had watched the nineteen matches and the New Zealand RFU recorded a profit of £7 170. The SA Rugby Football Board learnt nothing from the unpleasantness over the Maori issue. They were quietly content that Blackett should be made a scapegoat for a scandal that went a great deal deeper than his relatively brief rugby report.

The New Zealanders felt the need to tour South Africa in 1928, largely for financial reasons. They argued that the recent tour had materially assisted their rugby and it was only right that the South Africans were able to generate a similar profit. Balanced against this was the Maori question. Important developments had taken place: a Maori Advisory Board was formed in 1922 with Ned Parata as chairman, while Maori players contributed impressively to the unbeaten overseas tour to the United Kingdom, Ireland, France and Canada by the 1924/25 New Zealand 'Invincibles'.

According to Ryan, the New Zealand RFU 'confidentially informed its provincial affiliates in June 1927 that no Maori should be included in trials to select the 1928 All Black touring team'. The 'decision had been made in full consultation with its Maori Advisory Board ... there was a general desire to "protect" Maori from potential "incidents" and insult in a country with different racial circumstances from those enjoyed in New Zealand'.[39]

When the New Zealand RFU selected their side to tour South Africa in 1928, they reluctantly excluded two of their best players – George Nepia and Jimmy Mill – on grounds of race. In New Zealand, it aroused some feelings of frustration and anger. The Akarana Maori Association described the decision as a slur on the dignity and manhood of the Maori and the All Black team as not truly representative of New Zealand.[40]

Maori exclusion from the 1928 tour, explains Buckley, directly contradicted the inclusionist tradition of New Zealand sport and society, based on the equal citizenship of Maori and Pakeha. It did not mean that the status of Maori in relation to Pakeha in the wider society was equal, although the Reform government had during the 1920s attempted to narrow the social and economic gap between Maori and Pakeha.[41]

The decision not to include Maoris was hailed in South Africa as a diplomatic triumph for the rugby authorities.[42] It came in the wake of determined efforts on the part of prime minister General J.B.M. Hertzog to ensure white supremacy. He had introduced the Mines and Works Amendment Act (1926) to prevent blacks from obtaining skilled mining trades and the Native Administration Act (1927), which gave management wide powers over individuals. He provided sheltered employment for 'poor whites' in state enterprises and moved to extend the vote to all white men and women while leaving the Cape 'non-white' vote in a form that was restricted to men who possessed property and educational qualifications.

Buckley draws attention to the fact that the exclusion of Maori rugby players from the 1928 tour did not produce debate in New Zealand on the wider question of racial discrimination against black South Africans: 'The All Black players generally remained silent over inequalities between black and white South Africans. Their main focus was to play rugby, and they stood aloof from social and political questions.'[43]

This attitude proved unfortunate as the New Zealanders arrived at a time when the coloured community in Cape Town were not only protesting that Maoris had been excluded from the All Black team, but that the Western Province RFU was in the process of restricting the right of entry of the coloured community to all parts of Newlands ground. This was not the first time the establishment had acted in this way. Four years earlier a similar attempt at the restriction of non-Europeans had been withdrawn after a deputation from the coloured peoples had threatened to forsake the ground. The money factor had weighed then with the rugby union.

A prominent figure in the African Political/People's Organisation (APO), Stephen Reagon, addressed coloured representatives 'who came from Sea Point to Simon's Town' to fill the Draper Hall, Claremont, on Tuesday night, 22 May 1928. He reiterated the view that the coloured community

> felt very keenly the extra stigma thrown upon it by the Western Province RFU. This stigma was familiar to them in ordinary life, but it was the last thing they expected in sport ... Matters had now come to the stage when the Western Province RFU considered that anything could be done to the coloured community with impunity. ... In the building up of the Newlands rugby ground the coloured folk could take as much credit as anyone else ... It had taken the Rugby Union thirty years to reach its present strong position – a position which it had attained largely by the aid of the people whom it now insulted and decried.[44]

The Western Province RFU had recently announced its finances were in a sound and healthy condition and appeared to relish the opportunity to follow the lead of its parent body by tightening colour-bar restrictions.[45]

New Zealanders did not react to the coloured rugby protest, although journalist F.M. Howard was keen to emphasise that the touring team had been weakened by the exclusion of the Maori players. In a guest article, he told readers of the *Cape Times* that Maurice Brownlie ranked the missing Mill as the finest scrum-half ever produced by New Zealand. Howard recalled: 'I was told that [Mill] had retired from the game at the end of the past season. But I imagine that had he not been a Maori, he would still have been chosen, and that he would easily have been persuaded to turn out again.'[46]

Leaving out the brilliant Nepia created the greatest outcry of all. When the All Blacks toured Europe in 1924, they were unbeaten and Nepia played in every match. He was powerfully built with thighs like young tree trunks. 'His head was fit for the prow of a Viking longship,' says Denzil Batchelor, 'with its passionless, sculpted bronzed features and plume of blue-black hair. Behind the game he slunk from side to side like a panther on the prowl: but not like a black panther behind bars – like a lord of the jungle on the prowl for a kill.'[47]

Many years later, Spiro Zavos was moved to ask the question: 'Might the sight of the great Nepia, so godlike on the rugby field, have turned perhaps one or two influential South Africans from their hatred of the black population?'[48]

While the Springboks played the Maori in New Zealand, there was no thought given to the All Blacks playing against a black team in South Africa. The one socio-political complaint the New Zealanders had in the course of their 1928 tour was that one of the players, Neil McGregor, was struck by a brick as he was driven through Cape Town. It was the occasion of the raising of the flags on 30 May 1928, a day the English *Daily Telegraph* described as full of promise for the future because it would reaffirm South Africa's association with the British Empire. Unfortunately, the speeches went on far too long on a hot day and men of all races became extremely thirsty and later rowdy. The *Cape Times* concluded that the ugly little disturbance was 'an ominous reminder of the native problem that white South Africa has to face'.[49]

The rugby series was drawn 2–2. The Springboks led 2–1 with the Newlands match still to play. Their forwards had dominated and they were firm favourites to take the series. But it rained all week and in the muddy conditions, the All Blacks were unquestionably the best side, winning 13–5. 'What capped the surprise,' wrote 'Olympic', 'was the clear ocular evidence that there was more push and devil in the All Blacks' scrum work than the Springboks could ever bring to bear.'[50]

South Africa toured New Zealand again in 1937. The tour was not free from protest but much of the antagonism over race was fought out a year in advance. South Africa's racism had become a deep-seated grievance. It led to the first organised nationwide protest against the New Zealand-South Africa rugby relationship, with Te Arawa seeking a social and sporting boycott.

On 24 July 1936, *The Press* published a memorial conveyed by Tai Mitchell of Te Arawa to the New Zealand RFU. Its aim was:

> To protect the Maori race from any possible recurrence of the unpleasant incidents which occurred during the previous visit of a South African rugby football team when members of the race had to endure on the field many epithets cast at them by some of the visitors resulting in frayed tempers on both sides, together with the reported objectionable treatment some of our womenfolk received during the tribal reception tendered to them.[51]

As a consequence of the memorial, Te Arawa requested no Maori player be called upon to play against the Springboks during their tour in 1937 and no Maori representative match be played against the tourists. For the same reasons, the Maori did not wish to be invited to take part in any official receptions arranged for the Springboks.

Tai Mitchell was determined to revive memories of 1921. Ryan wonders whether the memorial was 'entirely a product of Te Arawa or whether Mitchell might not have consulted a wider circle of influence as to the consequences of issuing such a potentially provocative statement'. It was also unknown why 'long-held grievances were not expressed before 1936'.[52]

Stan Dean, chairman of the New Zealand RFU, arranged to meet with the protesting group in mid-September 1936. The Te Arawa grievances were then forwarded to the SA Rugby Football Board to seek their assurance that the 1937 Springboks would respect the inclusionist custom of New Zealand and treat the Maori as equals.

It should have been a straightforward task for the South Africans but was held up by Johan D. de Villiers of Western Province who was opposed to playing against Maoris. The minutes of the meeting record that he requested:

> The Board should take steps to ensure the prohibition of Maoris taking part in matches. He was of the opinion that if players were asked to play against Maoris, they would refuse to go at all costs. Players would definitely not play against coloured people. Parents would not allow their sons to do so.[53]

His outburst was dismissed as lacking a dignified and Christian spirit, with the SA Rugby Football Board deciding in favour of a match against the Maori team.

Tai Mitchell was reported to be satisfied with the outcome of the Te Arawa memorial and entertained the Springboks at Rotorua. Maoris played against the Springboks in provincial teams and several were included in the All Black side. But the New Zealand RFU decided that in a shortened programme there would not be a match against the representative Maori team. The decision was seen by Ryan as 'surely a product of Dean's desire to avoid any further controversy'.[54]

Nearly twenty years after it was written, Blackett's match report of 1921 still played on the minds of those associated with rugby.

Notes

1   *Cape Times*, 8 July 1919.
2   G. Nieman and L. Laubscher, 'W.P. Schreiner and His Role in the 1919 New Zealand Services Tour of South Africa', in *Points Unlimited*, 7, 2 (2000).
3   E. Walker, *W.P. Schreiner: A South African* (London: Oxford University Press, 1969), 379–380.
4   Nieman and Laubscher, 'W.P. Schreiner and His Role'.
5
6   Minutes of a special general meeting of the SA Rugby Football Board, 2 June 1919.
7   Bill Schreiner lived in the shadow of his brother Oliver who was awarded the Military Cross and Trinity Cambridge Fellowship in the same year. In later years, Oliver was twice passed over as Chief Justice for his role in the coloured vote crisis, when he refused to endorse the attempts of the National Party government to remove coloured voters from the Cape Province's roll.
8   R. Palenski, *Rugby: A New Zealand History* (Auckland: Auckland University Press, 2015), 178.
9   F. Boshier, the editor of the *Evening Post*, quoted in Palenski, *Rugby*: 175–176.
10 Palenski, *Rugby*, 180 – he quoted Wiremu 'Ned' Parata as 'the single most influential person in the fostering of Maori rugby in the twentieth century'. Brown played for a Maori XV in 1913.
11 *Bulawayo Chronicle*, 4 August 1900.
12 *Cape Times*, 17 July 1919.
13 *Cape Times*, 21 July 1919. The New Zealand team was: full-back Capper; three-quarters Williams, Paine and Nissen; five-eighths McKenzie and Klerck; half back Mair; forwards Murray, Ciochetto, Hugo, Still, Martin, Maddock, Fisher and Spence.

14   *Natal Witness*, 26 and 27 August 1919.
15   M. Buckley '"A Colour Line Affair": Race, Imperialism and Rugby Football Contacts between New Zealand and South Africa to 1950' (unpublished master's thesis, University of Canterbury, 1996), 7.
16   R. Chester and N. McMillan, *The Visitors: The History of International Rugby Teams in New Zealand* (Auckland: Moa Publications 1990), 113.
17   Buckley, 'A Colour Line Affair', 18.
18   Ibid., 20.
19   *Daily Telegraph* (New Zealand), 9 September 1921.
20   G. Ryan, 'Maori and the 1937 Springbok Tour of New Zealand', in *New Zealand Journal of History*, 34, 1 (2000), 62.
21   *The Sun* (Christchurch), 13 September 1921.
22   Buckley, 'A Colour Line Affair', 20.
23   *The Press* (Christchurch), 15 September 1921 (Papers Past: Volume LVII, Issue 17 251).
24   Buckley, 'A Colour Line Affair', 21.
25   *Evening Post*, 15 September 1921.
26   *The Shannon News*, 16 September 1921.
27   *Auckland Star*, 15 September 1921.
28   *The Shannon News*, 16 September 1921.
29   Palenski, *Rugby*, refers to *New Zealand Truth*, 17 September 1921.
30   *New Zealand Herald*, 13 September 1921.
31   *The Star*, 10 August 1938.
32   Ibid., 8 September 1921.
33   Ryan, 'Maori and the 1937 Springbok Tour', 62.
34   *The Star*, 21 October 1921.
35   Ibid., 8 September 1921.
36   Ibid., 16 September 1921.
37   Ibid., 17 September 1921.
38   *Daily Telegraph*, 9 and 10 September 1921.
39   Ryan, 'Maori and the 1937 Springbok Tour', 65.
40   *The Sun* (Christchurch), 8, 10 October 1927; Buckley, 'A Colour Line Affair', 40.
41   Buckley, 'A Colour Line Affair', 36.
42   T. Richards, *Dancing on Our Bones: New Zealand, South Africa, Rugby and Racism* (Wellington: Bridget Williams Books, 2012), 12.
43   Buckley, 'A Colour Line Affair', 43.
44   *Cape Times*, 26 May 1928.
45   A. Parker, *WP Rugby: Centenary 1883–1983* (Cape Town: WPRFU, 1983), 38.
46   F. Howard, 'Men Who Will be Missed', *Cape Times*, 29 May 1928.
47   D. Batchelor, *Days Without Sunset* (London: Eyre & Spottiswoode, 1949), 214–215.
48   S. Zavos, *Winters of Revenge: The Bitter Rivalry between the All Blacks and the Springboks* (Auckland: Viking, 1997), 56. In 1986, the SA Rugby Board elected George Nepia an honorary life vice-president.
49   *Cape Times*, 1 and 2 June 1928.
50   *The Star*, 3 September 1928.
51   *The Press* (Christchurch), 24 July 1936; Ryan, 'Maori and the 1937 Springbok Tour'.
52   Ryan, 'Maori and the 1937 Springbok Tour', 69.
53   P. Dobson, *Doc: The Life of Danie Craven* (Cape Town: Human & Rousseau, 1994), 157–158.
54   Ryan, 'Maori and the 1937 Springbok Tour', 76.

9

Rhodes, Rugby and the Road to Springboxford, 1903–1953

It is expected of our territories that they should
despatch something upstanding and freckled. We
have enough, brainy, spectacled youth at home.[1]

– Morning Post, 1936

In 1891, Cecil John Rhodes declared, 'I find I am human and should like to be living after my death.'[2] In the years that followed, he gave thought to living on through his scholarship scheme, which would be established at Oxford University and used to promote imperial unity and interest. According to the Zimbabwean historian Robert Challiss, the scholarships originated in the founder's belief that 'Anglo-Saxons were "the finest race in the world" and … that the world could only benefit from unity under their sway'.[3]

The plan went beyond empire. The importance Rhodes attached to Anglo-American partnership meant an initial 32 scholarships for the United States, whilst a further 5 for the Germans came in the belief that 'an understanding between the three great powers will render war impossible'.[4] There were twenty for the Commonwealth, of which eight were awarded to southern Africa: three to Rhodesia, one to Natal, and four to designated secondary schools in the Cape, namely the Diocesan College (Bishops); St Andrew's College, Grahamstown; Boys High School, Stellenbosch (now Paul Roos Gymnasium), and the South African College School (SACS). Elsewhere, Australia received six and New Zealand one.

Rhodes advocated support for the all-rounder, reflecting the 'special admiration he had conceived second-hand of the British public school'. His criteria drew from concepts of manliness 'associated with the rigours of the games field and the cadet corps, and the hardness, even brutality, of much of school life'.[5] He noted as guidance that a proportion of four-tenths should be attached to 'literary and scholastic attainments', and two-tenths to 'fondness for, and success in, manly outdoor sports, such as cricket, football and the like'. He then suggested two-tenths to 'qualities of manhood', and a similar share to 'moral force of character' through which he expected the ideal candidate to have demonstrated 'instincts to lead' and to 'esteem the performance of public duties as his highest aim'.

When the scheme came into operation in October 1903, the opportunity to play in the Oxbridge contests proved to be a great attraction to young sportsmen from southern Africa. They were able to demonstrate their sporting skills and in doing so strengthen the games at Oxford University. 'The last thing' Rhodes wanted was 'a bookworm' – no Greek and Latin 'swots'. Under the usual modern system of competitive examinations, he asked: 'Do we ... get the best man for the world's fight?'

'I think not,' he answered.[6]

Rhodes did not specifically refer to colour when he directed his trustees to establish 'colonial scholarships' for 'male students'. The scheme included the provision that 'no student shall be qualified or disqualified ... on account of his race or religious opinions'. Robert Rotberg, who wrote perhaps the most detailed survey of Rhodes's life, believed that his subject was thinking of the English-Dutch division, 'not of overcoming colour bars'.[7] Philip Ziegler, a British biographer and historian, comments that while black South Africans 'were not specifically ruled out; they were simply not in the frame as potential candidates'.[8] That was essentially the case of Richard Msimang, a fine half-back with Taunton for five years, a law student at Queen's College, and later legal advisor to the African National Congress. He was described as 'one of the most gentlemanly players that ever donned a jersey'.[9]

'The issue which most perplexed trustees and selectors,' asserts Ziegler, 'was that of "brains against brawn". From the outset, some challenged the importance attached to sports, notably George Parkin, a Canadian who served as secretary of the Rhodes Trust from 1902 to 1920. He interpreted success in manly outdoor sports such as cricket and rugby as 'thinking not of runs or goals or cups for championships but of the moral qualities inspired by team games'. These he saw as 'the training in fair play, the absence of all trickery, the chivalrous yielding of advantage to an opponent and acceptance of defeat with cheerfulness'. Ziegler was critical of the idea, arguing 'it would be hard to conceive any set of characteristics more remote from Rhodes's own practices in politics or business'.[10]

A rugby football club had been formed at Oxford on 2 November 1869, and the inaugural inter-varsity – a twenty-a-side fixture – was played three years later at the Parks. Oxford won this match but Cambridge gained their revenge a year later at the Oval. The occasion grew in significance and contributed greatly to the development and refinement of the game. By the early 1880s, rugby had become popular and an Oxford captain, Harry Vassall, wrote: 'With excellent grounds in the Parks close at hand, crowds of men ready to play six times a week if given the chance, the difficulty was rather to stop them from getting too much practice.'[11]

A South African, James Sutherland, who was from Pietermaritzburg but educated at Fettes in Edinburgh, played in the 1885 inter-varsity, a year when shorts replaced breeches fastened at the knee. Sutherland was followed by Herbert Castens from Port Elizabeth, who attended Rugby School, received a 'blue' for his selection to play in the Cambridge match in 1886 and 1887, and became South Africa's first rugby captain when he led his country against the British in 1891. Thereafter, St Andrew's College, Grahamstown, produced Henry Taberer who in 1892 became the first South African-educated blue, and Cuthbert Mullins, whose form at Oxford earned him a place in the British side that toured South Africa in 1896.

The period mirrored social changes taking place as well as evolving attitudes to the sport. Tony Collins advances the view that 'for its supporters, rugby union had a higher moral purpose than mere recreation: its goal was to train young men to be leaders of the empire, to demonstrate the superiority of the Anglo-Saxon race in peace and war'.[12] In effect, the game of rugby and Rhodes's scholarship scheme shared the same ideals at the time Oxford University welcomed the first of the founder's Scholars in 1903.

Of further relevance from a rugby perspective is that the introduction of the scheme coincided with a period when Oxford and Cambridge produced some of the most famous players in the history of British rugby, such as Kenneth MacLeod, Adrian Stoop, Vincent Cartwright, Henry Vassall, John Raphael and Ronnie Poulton.[13] 'It is difficult,' wrote James Corsan in *Poulton and England*, 'to overstate the position of Oxbridge within the Edwardian rugby scene,' adding, 'in terms of lifetime achievement, a blue was regarded as next after an international cap'.[14]

It was in this era of advancement that South Africans had considerable influence on the game at Oxford. Prowess in rugby was an integral part of the make-up of young men elected Rhodes Scholars by two of the South African schools, St Andrew's College, Grahamstown, and the Diocesan College (Bishops), Cape Town. Parkin complained that at St Andrew's College, Grahamstown, 'the boys practically controlled the election, which was "decided almost entirely by the result of play on the [rugby] football ground!"' This method of voting was originally suggested by Rhodes who believed pupils should decide on 'marks for "athletics" and "manhood", ... "scholarship" to be decided by examination, and "leadership" by the headmaster'.[15]

Parkin thought his Canadian compatriots were 'a fine set of fellows', but made the bizarre claim that South African Rhodes Scholars 'were inadequate not so much because most of them were picked from the restricted field offered by the four schools as because "the stimulating air of the high veldt and plateau country tends to nervous exhaustion"'. He also believed their reliance on black people meant they were ill-prepared for Oxford and further argued that 'parents with clever boys' had told him at St Andrew's, Grahamstown, that 'they had given up all hope of competition with the sporting interest'.[16] All but one of the pre-war Rhodes Scholars from St Andrew's won rugby blues by playing for Oxford against Cambridge. Yet from this group emerged a judge, a professor, a vice-principal of the alma mater, a couple of barristers, a mine manager and Lennox Broster OBE, 'a very eminent surgeon in Harley Street'.[17]

The story of one of the barristers, Stephanus Cronjé, certainly creates a positive image of the scholarship scheme and rugby. During the period of reconstruction after the Anglo-Boer War, Alfred Milner decided something should be done for the sons of Boer leaders returning to their homes, and arranged for a number of them to be admitted to St Andrew's, Grahamstown. Cronjé, the son of Commandant Andries Cronjé and nephew of General Piet Cronjé, the Boer Commander at Paardeberg, was one of 'a fine group of youngsters [who] made a great contribution to the life of the school'.[18] In 1907, he was elected as the St Andrew's Rhodes Scholar, going on to excel as a law student and rugby player. He represented South Africa during their highly successful 'grand-slam' tour of 1912/13 and was awarded the Military Cross for gallantry during the First World War.

Parkin questioned the contribution of South Africans to college life and claimed they 'found the problems of adjustment harder than did most colonials'.[19] He overlooked the bonds that developed between rugby players who would spend some eight weeks channelling everything towards beating Cambridge. Another St Andrew's product, Rupert 'Mop' Williamson, who had been a reserve for Paul Roos's 1906 Springboks, was described as 'definitely the "find" of the 1907/08 season as far as England were concerned'. Against Wales, he was partnered by the black fly-half James Peters when, significantly, 'the English halves, Williamson and Peters, showed splendid combination and made many openings for their three-quarters'.[20]

Sportswriter Frank Keating refers to the 'brilliance and originality at half-back' of Williamson and Wal Flemmer, two Rhodes Scholars from St Andrew's, Grahamstown. They did not take it 'in turns to put the ball into the scrum, or play "left" and "right", and thus became the first authentic fly-half and scrum-half to play in a "University Match"'.[21] Ironically, the two South Africans did not support the innovation and there was much grumbling, 'nearly a mutiny'.[22]

Seven of the first eight Rhodes Scholars from St Andrew's earned rugby blues. Of these, six played for the Barbarians and Williamson for England. Bishops had a similarly impressive record with six of their Scholars earning blues; three representing the Barbarians, and Reginald Hands (England) and Stephen Steyn (Scotland) achieving international honours. There were no fewer than seven southern Africans – six Rhodes Scholars – in Oxford University's match against the 1906/07 Springboks at Iffley Road.

There were South Africans who gained Oxford blues but were not Rhodes Scholars, including Mike Dickson who played for Scotland in 1912–13. Some southern African Scholars came from schools outside the country. Noel Milton and the England international Ronald Lagden were educated at Marlborough. The former was the son of Sir William Milton, an England international and administrator of Southern Rhodesia who had previously served Rhodes as head of the Cape's prime minister's department. Lagden's father, Sir Godfrey, chaired the Lagden Commission, which built on the work Rhodes's government had initiated in respect of land ownership and control through the Glen Grey Act.

A Rhodesian, Eric Thomas, the grandson of missionaries, was the first Rhodes Scholar blue (1911–12) from SACS. He was awarded the Military Cross in the First World War and later knighted.

It was a grand adventure for the boys from southern Africa, with many arriving straight from school, as Rhodes intended. J.E. 'Jenny' Greenwood, who captained Cambridge in an inter-varsity at the age of 27, criticised Oxford because they 'always had a very unfair advantage' in that '[Rhodes Scholars] were of course, much older than freshmen at the university'.[23] Worthington Hoskin from St Andrew's College, Grahamstown, was nineteen years old and the youngest member of the Oxford team when in 1904 he became the first Rhodes Scholar to be awarded a rugby blue. The following year, Milton was the youngest at eighteen years old. The average age of the pre-First World War Oxford teams was twenty-one years old but, of the thirteen blue-winning Rhodes Scholars from St Andrew's and Bishops, nine were twenty years old or younger when they were first selected for the 'University Match'.[24]

Oxford did not lose to Cambridge between 1906 and 1911, by which time 16 000 spectators were packing into the Queen's ground. There was a draw in

1908 but Oxford scored nine tries and won 35–3 in 1909, despite playing one man short for most of the match. Cambridge also fielded South Africans, and Dirk de Villiers – a member of the Springbok team that defeated the British in 1910 – assisted them in their victory of 1913. He was one of several Afrikaans-speaking players who appeared in the Oxbridge matches at that time. There might have been more but Stellenbosch Boys' High tended to emphasise academic ability in the selection of their Rhodes Scholars. There were also reservations about the scheme; the first Stellenbosch Scholar to be selected, Toby Muller, turned down the opportunity because 'he disapproved so strongly of Rhodes'.[25]

Before the war, 19 southern Africans – 15 Rhodes Scholars – won 34 Oxford University Rugby blues. They made a favourable impression at a time when Springbok tours were consolidating links between 'mother country' and empire.

The southern African rugby record at Oxford was all the more remarkable because their cricketers struggled to make an impression during the same period. Five students – 'Plum' Lewis, Norman Reid and the three Hands brothers – went on to play Test cricket for South Africa but were unable to secure a place in the university side. Turf wickets counted against the success of cricketers who were used to playing on matting, whilst achievements on the public-school circuit generally gave English players a head start when it came to selection for university teams.

Rhodes Scholars were amongst rugby's conspicuous contribution to the 1914–18 war. Three Rhodes Scholars who played international rugby paid the supreme sacrifice: Captain Ronald Lagden was killed in the Ypres salient early in 1915 when leading his men over the top against well-established German trenches; Lieutenant Stephen Steyn lost his life when entering the gates of Jerusalem on 8 December 1917, and Captain Reginald Hands was in the South African heavy artillery when he died of wounds and gas poisoning on 20 April 1918. South Africa's Scottish full-back Mike Dickson, who had 'saved his side time and again' against the 1912/13 Springboks, was killed at Loos whilst serving in the Argyll and Sutherland Highlanders.[26]

After the war, three additional Rhodes Scholarships were allocated to South Africa. These were awarded to Kimberley, the Orange Free State and the Transvaal. Further scholarships were provided for the Cape Province in 1922 and then Eastern Province in 1933. As it was decided that the Kimberley and Eastern Province scholars should be elected in alternate years, the annual South African allocation had effectively risen to nine.

In the early 1920s, Oxford blues were awarded to two fine players from the Transvaal – 'Boet' Neser (Potchefstroom and SACS) and the 'phenomenally tough' English trialist Arthur Shacksnovis (King Edward, Johannesburg).[27]

The 1920 inter-varsity – the last to be played at Queen's – is known as 'Neser's match'. Oxford lost their fly-half shortly before the game so their captain, Denoon Duncan – a South African who played for Scotland – pulled the Transvaal Rhodes Scholar, 'Boet' Neser, out of the scrum. 'There can never have been a more powerful stand-off half,' remarked journalist Howard Marshall, 'he had the physique of a heavyweight boxer'.[28] Neser was also a man of action who had won the Military Cross on the Western Front, and 'was quick moving and quick thinking – he got a first – [and] was likely to rise to such a challenge'.[29] The gamble succeeded – Neser set up two tries, one of which he scored, and Oxford won comfortably.

Others to gain blues in the early 1920s included Ernest van der Riet; George Macdonald; Thomas 'Pax' Theron and Milner Humphrey – but there were none in 1924 and 1925 and one in the sides of 1926 and 1927. Greenwood observes that the only time that Cambridge had a run of four successive victories (1925–28) was when Oxford had fewer overseas players than in any other period.[30]

It was a temporary respite because Oxford regained the ascendancy. They could start drawing on one of the finest sides to emerge from St Andrew's, Grahamstown – that of 1926 – which included five players who would win Oxford blues. They were Brian Black, who played for England and the British Isles; Thomas Gubb, who toured Argentina with the British; John Rowley, who became governor of Darfur province in Sudan, the 'Land of Blacks ruled by Blues';[31] Paul Alexander, and Harland Rees 'who was asked to play for Wales but declined … partly because he hoped for a call (which never came) from England'.[32] In 1929, Gubb – with five other South Africans to assist him including the Springbok Willie Rousseau – led his side to a 9–0 victory.[33] Mike Robson, one of just four players from England in that year's team, remembered that 'it was quite an achievement for an Englishman to get into the Oxford side – the few places left after the South Africans had picked themselves were normally filled by Scots, Welsh, Irish and New Zealanders'.[34]

Oxford extended their undefeated record to five years, with the only check to their supremacy coming in 1930 when Steve Hofmeyr's side drew 3–3. A year later, Stanley Osler, who had played for the Springboks against the 1928 All Blacks, was elected a Cape Province Rhodes Scholar and turned out for Oxford against his brother when the famous Bennie Osler brought the 1931/32 Springboks to Iffley Road. Stanley Osler and the Welshman Vivian Jenkins were a formidable partnership in Oxford's 10–3 victory over Cambridge. The former, who was praised for 'appearing time and again to carry on a dying movement', was unfortunate to sustain an injury in the match, which put an end to his playing career.[35]

A colourful era was memorable for Oxbridge players posing 'for "society" photographs in over-illustrated weeklies', and travelling to Twickenham in Rolls Royces decked out with dark and light-blue ribbons.[36] A player who always stood out was a Bishops' Rhodes Scholar, 'Tuppy' Owen-Smith who had played cricket for South Africa and scored a century before lunch against England at Leeds. The Telegraph's Jim Swanton described him as 'the most remarkable all-rounder of my time … inimitable, a genius – and he did everything with a grin'.[37]

In 1933, Owen-Smith's sustained brilliance was the main reason a powerful Cambridge side did not win the inter-varsity. The Welsh international Wilf Wooller recalled kicking ahead and running hard at the Oxford full-back who would have to gather a ball falling short of him. Owen-Smith 'trapped it in an extraordinary way with one hand on the ground, picked it up with the same hand, side-stepped me and kicked the ball a good 70-yards back on to our 25-yard line'. For Wooller, it was the game's defining moment: 'When that ball went sailing over my head and I had to go back another 50 or 60 yards, I remember thinking "we're never going to win this match".'[38]

Owen-Smith went on to captain England in a triumphant 1937 season, which included the Triple Crown and their first-ever win at Murrayfield. Although 'not heavily built, he was wonderfully tough, and could take any amount of punishment … His value in morale alone was invaluable'.[39] Vivian Jenkins, who was Oxford's wicket-keeper in the same cricket side as Owen-Smith, recalled an occasion when they were opposing full-backs during a Wales versus England match at Twickenham:

> Tuppy and I played cricket together at Oxford … I used to keep wicket and he used to field at cover-point and would throw in at me like a bullet. I remember playing against him at Twickenham, when I was full-back for Wales, and he was full-back for England. It was 0-0 at half-time and we had been trying to outdo each other all half. As the referee blew to start the second half, I happened to catch his eye across the pitch from about thirty yards away. He threw his lemon at me exactly as he would have done from cover point and I caught the thing like a wicket-keeper, then off we went to play like hell for the second half.[40]

A fellow South African, H.D. 'Trilby' Freakes – an Eastern Province cricketer who focused on rugby – succeeded Owen-Smith as England's full-back. He was largely instrumental in the 1937 inter-varsity match producing an Oxford triumph against the odds and in the presence of King George VI. He was brought up to centre to smother the strong Cambridge backline before it could get going. The dangerman was a Rhodesian, J.G.S. 'Springy' Forrest who 'was like a gazelle and became one of the great Scottish wing three-quarters'.[41] As Marshall reports,

'Freakes was clearly a man with a mission that day, and he carried it out in the opening minutes of the game when he hurled himself through the air to hit Forrest with one of the most devastating and shaking tackles I have ever seen. It knocked the light-blue centre out and set the pattern for the game', with Oxford winning easily.[42]

The leaders that Rhodes expected appeared both on and off the sports field. Freakes, who captained Oxford, played rugby alongside Rhodes Scholars such as Gideon Roos, son of the legendary Springbok rugby captain and later director-general of the South African Broadcasting Corporation; (Sir) Richard 'Dick' Luyt, who became governor-general of Guyana, and Hilgard Muller who was South Africa's first ambassador in London, and thereafter minister of foreign affairs. The year after Freakes left, a Rhodes Scholar, Michael Davies, was selected as Wilf Wooller's partner in the Welsh team, and after the war became a cabinet minister in the government of Tanganyika.

'By 1939,' says Ziegler, Rhodes Scholars 'were established as a major force'. The number of overseas students at Oxford 'veered between 525 and 600 of which a third were Rhodes Scholars who made a notable contribution to the colleges to which they were assigned'.[43] Between the wars, 24 South Africans – 19 Rhodes Scholars – had earned 38 rugby blues. As a result of the new Rhodes Scholarships, more South African schools were represented amongst those who played for Oxford during this period. The favoured schools – SACS (4), St Andrew's (4) and Bishops (3) – still headed the list of blues, but Grey, Port Elizabeth (2), Rondebosch (2), Maritzburg, Hoër Volkskool, Potchefstroom and King Edward School also featured.

Sport thrived at the university and encouragement was received from staff members. An Oxford don of some standing started a campaign urging the Trust 'to abandon the intellectual qualification and to select good rugger toughs, as they are the people the empire really wants'.[44] The idea came, despite the academic results of some South African Scholars being of concern to the Trust: the warden of Rhodes House, Sir Carleton Allen, noted in his 1937 report that 'St Andrew's scholars were undistinguished by comparison with the other schools'.[45]

The debate was shelved as the empire was about to face its greatest challenge, the Second World War. Freakes and Forrest, the 'mighty opposites in a well-remembered tackle', were killed in air crashes,[46] as was Brian Black who had 'spent many hours a week practising place-kicking with the result that he became perhaps one of the greatest place kicks of modern times'.[47] Black played in all five Tests on the British tour of Australasia in 1930 before winning gold medals for British bobsleigh teams at World Championships in Cortina and St Moritz.

In the aftermath of the fighting, credit is often given to both universities for doing much to galvanise the game during a period of rebuilding. Ross McWhirter and Sir Andrew Noble wrote of 'war-time experiences, pressure of work, and the greatest earnestness of the post-war world [all contributing] to make the players of this period more sober, in every sense of the word'.[48] Statistics indicate that rugby at Oxford had probably never been stronger.

Few epitomised the spirit of the period quite as much as Ossie Newton Thompson, a Rhodes Scholar who had served in the forces during the previous four years; an experience which involved 'flying Spitfires, winning the DFC and reaching the rank of Wing Commander'.[49] He captained and coached Oxford in 1946, with one of the front row moved to recall 'he was a divine creation under whose spell we all were to some degree'.[50] Newton Thompson's side arrived at Twickenham having won all their eleven games, with a record 53 tries to three and a points difference of 260–22. 'Oxford's success,' explains Marshall, 'was built upon their ability to have the ball back quickly and fast to Newton Thompson, a strong and indefatigable scrum-half whose passes were long, fast and accurate'.[51] He also left nothing to chance, drilling the laws and going 'thoroughly into all tactical situations, with the aid of blackboard demonstrations; some of the home players thought it all a bit too "professional"'.

In the inter-varsity, 'Oxford's all-round excellence was not to be denied and, before a record intervarsity crowd of 50 000, [Mickey Steele-Bodger's] Cambridge were beaten 15-5 in a match fit to rank among the most compelling of the series'.[52]

Seven of the Oxford team – four Rhodes Scholars – played for England or Scotland, including Syd Newman, who had been captured at the fall of Tobruk and spent three years as a prisoner of war. After being demobilised, he was able to take up his scholarship and experience the excitement of a tense 3–3 draw against Wales in 1948 before 73 000 Twickenham spectators. He landed a towering 50-yard goal in the opening minutes and then brought off a breathtaking tackle to prevent Jack Matthews, the Welsh wing, from scoring at the corner flag.

One of the most exciting of the sportsmen playing for Oxford at this time was Martin Donnelly – also a world-class cricketer – who was turned down by a New Zealand selection committee more concerned with academic achievement. The Trust, however, did not wish a double international with a distinguished war record to slip by unrewarded and provided Donnelly with a grant, despite the fact that he 'planned to do as much work as was necessary to scrape a pass'.[53]

New Zealand – and to an extent, Australian selection committees – differed in attitude from most of their South African counterparts insofar as emphasis on sport was concerned. This was brought home by a report in the *Cape Times* in 1946 which stated that only 9.3 per cent of South Africa's Rhodes Scholars took firsts (as opposed to New Zealand's 34.2 per cent and Australia's 32.9 per cent) and 5.2 per cent failed to get any degree (compared to no failures for New Zealand and 0.7 per cent for Australia).

Some of the South African scholarship selection committees were reluctant to tamper with an apparent bias towards sport. Apart from the positive publicity received, they believed the selection of the 'all-rounder' was in the spirit of Rhodes's will. The founder would have approved of scholars from different parts of the world uniting in the success of Oxford University rugby and gaining selection for home union teams. In the post-war period, Ossie Newton Thompson, Syd Newman, Clive van Ryneveld, Murray Hofmeyr, Harry Small (all South Africa) and 'Jika' Travers (Australia) played for England, and Pat MacLachlan (Rhodesia) and George Cawkwell (New Zealand) represented Scotland.

'The game saw itself as part of an imperial British network,' explains Collins, 'through which players, like businessmen and members of the professional classes, could move without restriction.' He put it down to 'the shared sense of Britishness of the "home" unions and the white dominions of the empire'.[54]

The outstanding Clive van Ryneveld was not British and admitted that he was not sure how he qualified for England other than he was playing his rugby there and 'nobody asked any questions'. He was of Dutch, German and French origin but for England, his 'penetrating run made him an exceptionally attractive centre'.[55] He also secured Oxford's victory in 1948 with a piece of brilliant opportunism. The *Daily Express* described him as 'undoubtedly the best centre in the four home countries' yet Van Ryneveld reconsidered his availability for a second year.[56] 'It will be a thousand pities,' lamented the *Cape Times*, 'if he sticks to his determination to give up rugby after Christmas owing to exams.'[57] Van Ryneveld later admitted his withdrawal was a poor decision.[58]

Country Life wrote of 'gentle grumbles at there being five South Africans in [the 1949] Oxford fifteen'. It argued that they are not only 'very fine players and greatly contributed to their team's victory in a very hard-fought match, but are as much undergraduates as anyone else at Oxford or Cambridge, and it is unthinkable that they should not be allowed to play'. The writer then felt it necessary to add that Rhodes Scholars were 'a little older and stronger and more experienced as athletes and game players than most of their contemporaries'.[59]

In the 1949 side, there were five South Africans, one New Zealander and nine from the British Isles. The two youngest players were both 21 years old – England's Brian Boobbyer being a month older than Clive van Ryneveld, who was playing in his third inter-varsity match. Of the next six youngest players in the side, three were South Africans: the captain Nelles Vintcent, who turned down an England trial to concentrate on his studies, Willem Hefer and Murray Hofmeyr.

John Kendall-Carpenter, who captained Oxford in 1950, wrote of his being up at the university at one of the best times for their rugby. It was a period of 'much activity and thinking [with] the players to put theory into action'. He pointed to the coaching manual which the Rugby Football Union (RFU) produced and said it was the result of the thinking done by the 1945–49 players at Oxford with all their home and particularly dominion experience.[60]

The side Kendall-Carpenter led in 1950 included five southern Africans, with two of the Rhodes Scholars – Murray Hofmeyr and Harry Small – playing that year for England. The dark-blues were nevertheless hard pressed to win the inter-varsity, partly because Hofmeyr the fly-half, was injured early in the match and had to alternate with Rhodesia's David Lewis at full-back. Oxford did not quite find their rhythm, but that thirteen of the side played for the Barbarians reflected the quality of players that the university was producing.

Not everyone was satisfied with Oxford's rugby. Dudley Wood, who would become a long-serving secretary of the RFU, recalled participating in the 'freshmen's' trials at Oxford in 1951: 'It was very strange because at that time varsity rugby was very much dominated by South Africans. I packed down with so many of them that often they would speak to each other in Afrikaans and I felt totally left out of it.'[61]

Wood was also left out of the Oxford team, which gained a fourth successive intervarsity win in 1951, putting them seven games ahead of Cambridge in the series, a statistical high-water mark in the whole history of this fixture.[62] The South African involvement at the club had become an integral part of Oxford's rugby reputation, accentuated perhaps by the Springboks becoming world leaders.

One of South Africa's 1951/52 grand-slam heroes, Paul Johnstone, arrived at Oxford a few months later. He had played in all five internationals on the tour as a wing, but Oxford used him at centre. The Rhodesian Denis Robinson who had attended Hilton College, and Chick Henderson from nearby Michaelhouse were also in the university side. They created interest as they had been trialists for the all-conquering Springboks. The Scots, who were thrashed 44–0 in the 'Murrayfield massacre', were not slow to select Henderson, a loose forward who had previously formed an outstanding Transvaal back-row triumvirate with Springbok stars Basie van Wyk and Hennie Muller.

Oxford were firm favourites to take the 1952 inter-varsity. They were also confident, having just beaten Cardiff, but Cambridge won 6–5. Oxford were perhaps unfortunate. Wood, who was chosen as a lock-forward when he hoped to play at number 8, believed they had scored from a push-over try when the selected number 8, Henderson, touched down. Swanton's report in the *Telegraph* supported this view as 'Henderson got up with the ball' but the referee gave a five-yard scrum instead.[63]

Oxford should also have won in 1953. They had been unlucky against the All Blacks in going down 5–14, but disappointed in the inter-varsity when a huge penalty goal from the halfway by Robinson and an individualist try by Johnstone secured no more than a 6–6 draw. The Oxford team included eight southern Africans and a New Zealander. Wood was playing in his favoured position, but the press were concerned by the selection of only four Englishmen. Such was the South African presence that the dark-blues were referred to as 'Springboxford'.[64]

McWhirter and Noble thought the press were 'following a subtle change in social mood, perhaps a dawning recognition of the smaller part being played by the British Isles in world affairs'. As a consequence, they became 'sensitive about the Commonwealth element creeping into university sport [and] took umbrage at the reflection on "home-bred" players. This led to a quick count to see if there were a majority of South Africans each time that Oxford announced a team.'[65]

In the first 50 years of the scholarship scheme, southern Africa produced 64 players – 47 Rhodes Scholars – in 40 inter-varsity matches. This achievement effectively amounted to 114 blues. In addition, 15 southern Africans – of whom 12 were Rhodes Scholars – played international rugby during their time in Britain, and 34 – of whom 28 were Rhodes Scholars – were invited to play for the Barbarians. Of the southern Africans who represented Oxford in inter-varsity matches during 1903–53, two schools dominated: there were 33 players from St Andrew's, Grahamstown, and Bishops, of whom 26 were Rhodes Scholars – 13 from each school.

If a full picture is to be gained of Rhodes's influence on the game, it is also necessary to consider the 24 Australians and New Zealanders – 16 Rhodes Scholars – who won 47 blues. Seven of the Rhodes Scholars played international rugby for the Home Unions. In addition, the student interaction that Rhodes desired resulted in American Scholars taking up rugby and winning blues: Donald Herring was the first in 1909, followed by Alan Valentine, who was not only the recipient of three blues (1923 to 1925), but also represented the United States gold medal-winning rugby team at the 1924 Olympic Games in Paris. Then came Frederick Hovde who scored the decisive try in the 1931 inter-varsity.

There was pride in the impact that Rhodes Scholars had on Oxford University rugby, but some selection committees, such as that of Stellenbosch Boys' High School, continued to emphasise academic distinction. The school's leading players looked to represent Stellenbosch University. To them, the real 'inter-varsity' was that played against the University of Cape Town, a contest that featured numerous Springbok players over the years. Bennie Osler did not think one 'could find a keener sporting rivalry anywhere in the world ... Ikey and Maties were temporarily at war'.[66]

In the end, decisions made off the field ultimately limited the influence Rhodes Scholars had on inter-varsity rugby in England. Changes to the system became inevitable when Oxford colleges began to look towards awarding places to young men and women with academic talent rather than sporting prowess. It made the task confronting selection committees increasingly difficult. They were looking not for mere bookworms, but for future leaders and yet Oxford Colleges seemed to be interested only in academic potential. Sir Carleton Allen, warden of Rhodes House from 1931 to 1952, and his successor, Sir Edgar Williams, felt that 'the selectors were going too far in favouring academic achievement over other qualifications'.[67]

In time, one report pointed to 'growing tension between the narrow professionalism increasingly valued by Oxford tutors and the requirements specified in the founder's will'.[68] Williams was obliged in 1961 to 'dress the founder's aspirations in modern garb' and rewrite the memorandum for selection committees. He stated that 'physical vigour is an essential qualification for a Rhodes Scholar, but athletic prowess is less important than the moral qualities which can be developed in sports'.[69]

Fewer quality sportsmen arrived at Oxford from the former empire and notably South Africa,[70] a development that is represented by a decline in the number of southern African Rhodes Scholars who achieved rugby blues. Over the next forty inter-varsities during 1954–93, southern Africa produced 42 players – 16 Rhodes Scholars – who gained 69 blues.

The era of 'Springboxford' faded as the empire unravelled. So did Rhodes's aim to create a white male Anglo-Saxon hegemony that would dominate the world. Yet the scholarship scheme survived and continues to attract a range of talent, whilst its products have made a positive contribution to the world. The English-speaking world to which Rhodes attached so much importance has enabled him to live on through his scheme. Success has been achieved by men and women of all races, effectively 'in defiance of the design of their founder', an outcome seen by Rotberg as 'an ironic tribute to the final workings of his uncommon genius'.[71]

Notes

1   Quoted in the *Rand Daily Mail*, 5 February 1936. The article in the *Morning Post* was in response to a call from Sir Herbert Stanley, governor of Southern Rhodesia, for 'more brainy Rhodes Scholars'.

2   R. Rotberg, *The Founder: Cecil Rhodes and the Pursuit of Power* (Oxford: Oxford University Press, 1988), 663.

3   R. Challiss, 'The Rhodes Trust', in I.P. MacLaren (ed.), *Some Renowned Rhodesian Senior Schools 1892–1979* (Bulawayo: Books of Zimbabwe, 1981), 336.

4   Rotberg, *The Founder*, 663.

5   J. Honey, *Tom Brown in South Africa* (Grahamstown: Rhodes University, 1972), 16–17.

6   Rotberg, *The Founder*, 666–667, 669.

7   Ibid, 668.

8   P. Ziegler, *Legacy: Cecil Rhodes, the Rhodes Trust and Rhodes Scholarships* (New Haven: Yale University Press, 2008), 138.

9   B. Willan, 'One of the Most Gentlemanly Players that Ever Donned a Jersey', in *Quarterly Bulletin of the National Library of South Africa*, 66, 3 (2012).

10   Ziegler, *Legacy*, 33–34.

11   H. Richards, *A Game for Hooligans: The History of Rugby Union* (Edinburgh: Mainstream Publishing, 2006), 77.

12   T. Collins, 'English Rugby Union and the First World War', in *The Historical Journal*, 45, 4 (2002), 798.

13   D. Frost, *The Bowring Story of the Varsity Match* (London: Macdonald Queen Anne Press, 1988), 39.

14   J. Corsan, *Poulton and England: The Life and Times of an Edwardian Rugby Hero* (Leicester: Matador, 2009), 143–144.

15   Ziegler, *Legacy*, 34; Rotberg, *The Founder*, 667.

16   Ziegler, *Legacy*, 77–78.

17   R. McWhirter and Sir A. Noble, *Centenary History of Oxford University Rugby Football Club 1869–1969* (Oxford: OURFC, 1969), 213.

18   R. Currey, *St Andrew's College. Grahamstown, 1855–1955* (Oxford: Basil Blackwell, 1955), 81.

19   Ziegler, *Legacy*, 78.

20   J. Griffiths, *The Book of English International Rugby 1871–1982* (London: Willow Books, 1982), 116.

21   F. Keating, *The Great Number Tens: A Century of Rugby's Pivots and Playmakers* (London: Corgi, 1999), 73.

22   McWhirter and Noble, *Centenary History*, 97.

23   J. Greenwood, *A Cap for Boots: An Autobiography* (London: Hutchinson Benham, 1977), 100.

24   McWhirter and Noble, *Centenary History*, 213.

25   Ziegler, *Legacy*, 42.

26   W. Millar, *My Recollections and Reminiscences* (Cape Town: Juta, 1926), 36.

27   H. Marshall in collaboration with Lieut.-Col. J. Jordan, *Oxford v Cambridge: The Story of the University Match* (London: Clerke & Cockeran, 1951), 163.

28   Marshall and Jordan, *Oxford v Cambridge*, 148.

29   McWhirter and Noble, *Centenary History*, 125–126.

30   Greenwood, *A Cap for Boots*, 101.

31   J. Mangan, *The Games Ethic and Imperialism* (Harmondsworth: Viking, 1985), 74–75.

32   *Daily Telegraph*, 8 August 2002.

33   Gubb toured Argentina with the British side in 1929.

34   McWhirter and Noble, *Centenary History*, 141.

35   Frost, *The Bowring Story*, 71.

36   R. Harding, *Rugby, Reminiscences and Opinions* (London: Pilot Press, 1929), 103.

37   E. Swanton, *As I Said at the Time: A Lifetime of Cricket* (London: Unwin Paperbacks, 1986), 86.

38   Frost, *The Bowring Story*, 76.

39   Marshall and Jordan, *Oxford v Cambridge*, 197, 202.

40   Frost, *The Bowring Story*, 72; *Lions versus Barbarians* programme, 10 September 1977, 6.

41   Ibid., 80.
42   Marshall and Jordon, *Oxford v Cambridge*, 218.
43   Ziegler, *Legacy*, 110.
44   Ibid., 110, 151.
45   Ibid., 77.
46   *The Scotsman*, 29 September 1942.
47   P. Kettlewell (Headmaster), 'St Andrew's College RFC, Grahamstown', in I. Difford (ed.), *The History of South African Rugby Football, 1875–1932* (Wynberg: Speciality Press, 1933), 601.
48   McWhirter and Noble, *Centenary History*, 154.
49   Frost, *The Bowring Story*, 86.
50   R. Nye, *Martin Donnelly: New Zealand Cricket's Master Craftsman* (Auckland: Harper Collins, 1998), 149.
51   Marshall and Jordon, *Oxford v Cambridge*, 229.
52   Frost, *The Bowring Story*, 86.
53   Ziegler, *Legacy*, 240.
54   T. Collins, *A Social History of English Rugby Union* (Abingdon: Routledge, 2009), 165.
55   H. Schulze, *South Africa's Cricketing Lawyers: Biographical Notes on the 32 Lawyers Who Represented South Africa in Cricket* (Halfway House: Interdoc Consultants, 1999), 151–157; O. Owen, *The History of the RFU* (London: Playfair Books, 1955), 165.
56   P. Dobson, *Bishops Rugby: A History* (Cape Town: Don Nelson, 1990), 225–226.
57   *Cape Times*, 23 December 1948.
58   C. van Ryneveld, *20th Century All-rounder: Reminiscences and Reflections of Clive van Ryneveld* (Cape Town: Pretext, 2011), 61.
59   *Country Life*, 16–23 December 1949; Greenwood, *A Cap for Boots*, 100–101.
60   McWhirter and Noble, *Centenary History*, 213.
61   Frost, *The Bowring Story*, 104.
62   McWhirter and Noble, *Centenary History*, 141.
63   *Daily Telegraph*, 10 December 1952.
64   Frost, *The Bowring Story*, 104; McWhirter and Noble, *Centenary History*, 182.
65   McWhirter and Noble, *Centenary History*, 182.
66   C. Greyvenstein, *The Bennie Osler Story* (Cape Town: Howard Timmins, 1970), 54.
67   Ziegler, *Legacy*, 243–244.
68   Ibid., 244.
69   Ibid., 239.
70   See P. Davies, *From Magdalen to Merger: A Short History of Oxford University Cricket Club* (Buxton: Church in the Market Place Publications, 2004), 76.
71   Rotberg, *The Founder*, 692.

10

'Men Worthy of Springbok Chance'

They used to say that I could be likened to Bennie [Osler] in every way on the rugby field. Only my colour was different.[1]

– Dol Freeman

'Coloured Athletes Beat the World' – the headline was splashed across the front page of the 10 August 1936 issue of the *Cape Standard*.

A subheading followed: 'Jesse Owens the Greatest Living Sprinter'. And then a second subheading: 'Brown Men Collar Title after Title'.

The article began: 'Coloured athletes are leading the world at the Olympic Games in Berlin [1–16 August 1936], headed by Jesse Owens, the "Ohio Express".'[2]

Owens' feat of winning four gold medals and setting two world records not only challenged Adolf Hitler's notions of racial supremacy but also asked questions of America's implacable racial divide. Apart from his medal and record success, Owens was a particularly good role model for black Americans because of when and where he succeeded. Moreover, the aftermath prompted Owens' telling statement on American society:

After all those stories about Hitler and his snub, I came back to my native country, and I couldn't ride in the front of the bus. I had to go to the back door. I couldn't live where I wanted. Now what's the difference?[3]

In South Africa, the timing and setting of Owens' athletic dominance had an immediate impact. News of his success inspired local coloured sports administrators who realised what could be achieved on the international stage. The *Cape Standard* reported 'plans for coloured sports development on a firmer basis were rapidly taking shape and would run parallel with an Olympic committee's scheme ... to secure the South African coloured man's participation in the next Olympic Games to be held in Tokyo, Japan'.

Projected developments outlined in the same edition of the *Cape Standard* included a plan for a coloured rugby team to tour overseas at the end of the 1938 season. Members of the SA Coloured Rugby Football Board had discussed ideas during the previous week's Rhodes Cup tournament. A rugby official, Charles Calvert, told the newspaper that 'the whole coloured community will enjoy an improved status if a strong team of manly sportsmen tours overseas, especially if it proves successful in a fair proportion of its matches'.[4]

Calvert expressed concern that outside of South Africa little was known of the coloured community. People in Britain, for instance, usually thought of South Africa as populated 'only by English, Dutch and Natives: they do not know that there is a virile coloured community 600 000 strong waiting to show the world that it also has a claim for a place in the sun alongside the nations overseas'.

The *Cape Standard's* special correspondent, George Golding, was conscious of the need for public diplomacy. A successful project was not only a case of performing well and displaying high levels of sportsmanship on the sports field. He hoped the proposed tour would be acknowledged by the ruling class and that it would 'make the European South African as proud of the coloured man's prowess in international competition as the coloured man is of the Springbok teams that have competed successfully overseas'.

'Men Worthy of Springbok Chance' was another eye-catching headline to appear in the 10 August edition of the *Cape Standard*. In his review of the 1936 Rhodes Cup, Golding was perhaps deliberately ambiguous in exploring the issue of the 'springbok' and the coloured rugby player's right to represent his country. There were players at the tournament who deserved to represent a coloured 'Springbok' team, but Golding went further to suggest they possessed the right gentlemanly qualities to represent the white side. 'The conduct of players had been exemplary,' he remarked, 'and created a most favourable impression. It served as an illustration of manliness to our coloured youths, while to Europeans it was proof of our people's ability to observe discipline.'[5]

The Rhodes Cup tournament in 1936 was hosted by South-Western Districts and played at Mossel Bay, Swellendam and Riversdale. The local organising committee had struggled to complete preparations. They approached the European sports club at Riversdale in order to use their ground but were informed that a clause in the grant forbade its use by coloured players. It had also been subsequently booked for European matches between Heidelberg and Riversdale. The coloured players would have to rely on their ground at Riversdale, which was not regulation size and its surface was of such a nature as to be dangerous for players.

At a very late hour, the desperate organising committee called on Golding and asked him to intervene. Their predicament was referred to in the course of a letter subsequently written to the *Cape Standard* by Charles Calvert, president of the SA Coloured Rugby Football Board:

> We fully realised the hopelessness of the situation, but Mr Golding sportingly agreed to do his best. How he succeeded may best be related by himself, but the Heidelberg-Riversdale match was postponed by telephone ... Riversdale's sporting Europeans have earned the gratitude of all coloured football fans.[6]

Golding was a product of Zonnebloem College and had served as a teacher and school principal in Oudtshoorn, Heidelberg, and then Cape Town. He believed in the old-guard African Political/People's Organisation (APO) policy of collaboration with whites, a stance he would maintain as he became increasingly involved in politics. He would, however, vehemently oppose the policies of Dr D.F. Malan, who was coincidentally quoted in the same *Cape Standard* edition of 10 August 1936. The future prime minister was visiting Mossel Bay at the time and took the opportunity to tell a local audience: 'It was a shame that European students should sit on the same benches as natives and coloured students at the University of Cape Town.'[7]

South Africa was undergoing a period in which segregation was further entrenched through the 'native' acts of 1936. The bill relating to the coloured franchise was dropped but the resurgence of coloured radicalism led to the formation of the National Liberation League. Coloured politicians had traditionally been reluctant to support ethnic organisations in that they feared their chances of assimilation into European society would be affected. Only when it became obvious that white politicians were not going to accommodate their aspirations did they begin to organise along ethnic lines 'to provide a springboard by which the group could launch its campaign for inclusion in the white society'.[8]

Despite the setbacks, rugby remained integral to the coloured man's way of life. Five more Rhodes Cup tournaments – 1931, 1932, 1935, 1936 and 1938 – were held in various parts of the country during an active decade in coloured rugby development. Again, this is put into perspective through a comparison with the SA Rugby Football Board, which arranged just four Currie Cup tournaments during the same period.

By the 1930s, more than 200 rugby clubs catered for players of colour in the Western Province, which included Cape Town, Lambert's Bay, Worcester, Caledon and Gordon's Bay – and towns within that arc.[9] Clubs were encouraged to join or form unions, with rugby proving to be the dominant winter sport since the early 1900s. Male teachers among Cape Town's elite coloured schools promoted the game as an ideal way to encourage discipline and generate social solidarity. As Golding indicated, it became a perfect means to shape manly and character-forming behaviour.

But rugby did not remain unaffected by old problems. André Odendaal outlines developments where 'a major realignment of forces in the Western Cape led to the formation of a new Western Province League'. The founder members of this new union were City and Suburban, whose vice-chairman, Fred Russouw, had initiated the move. Parow, Paarl and teams from the country districts joined the breakaway, which was caused by ethnic and religious differences, as well as leadership tensions, within the communities. Says Odendaal, 'the cultural-religious divides that had become clear in Cape Town by the turn of the century were accentuated, and two Western Province teams took part in the 1936 Rhodes Cup tournament'.[10]

Rugby was also played against a background of political change. After three decades, the APO had not, 'as promised, been able to "lead" civilised coloured people back into the European camp'.[11] Although the coloured community shared the culture of Afrikaans-speaking whites – and to an extent that of the English – they had been socially rejected by them. The APO's dominant figure, Dr Abdullah Abdurahman, was considered too moderate by young and disillusioned coloureds who opposed the organisation's tactics of collaboration with white political parties. By the mid-1930s, a determined opposition had begun to exert a powerful influence.

Further division between races became inevitable as the African National Congress (ANC) in the Western Cape and elsewhere was seen to be devoted to African interests. The racial rift taking place in the wider political environment was replicated in rugby where African administrators engineered a breakaway from the SA Coloured Rugby Football Board. Their efforts reached fruition in late 1935 with the establishment of a separate governing body, the SA Bantu Rugby Board. This paved the way to hold a separate tournament in 1936.

Stephen Reagon appealed to the coloured community 'to support coloured sport more and not to flock to European sporting grounds where they were merely tolerated. They should have a little more race-pride and build up something worthwhile of their own.'[12] His comments were significant in the year when the famous Wanderers Rugby Football Club (RFC) celebrated 50 years of rugby. Articles appeared in the press that drew attention to the establishment of the club in 1886 and its contribution to the formation of the City and Suburban Union just before the Anglo-Boer War.[13]

There were commemorative events, beginning with a festival match on the Mowbray field against California RFC. Wanderers defeated California 10–6 in a match in which former players participated in the celebrations: 'Jacobus Marneveld, the veteran Wanderers player, was given the honour of getting the match underway ... the sturdy kick he gave the ball was applauded from touch by greyheads who had seen the day when his kicking was known far and wide in coloured rugby circles.'[14]

The club selected a party of twenty-nine men to tour the Transvaal – chiefly Pretoria – for fourteen days. A highlight was beating the Northern Transvaal Coloured Union 9–3 at the Police Ground, the same venue at which they lost to Young Standards of Pretoria 14–12. The *Cape Standard* reported: 'Hundreds of Europeans flocked to watch the matches. They were also attended by a large proportion of Pretoria's coloured population, by lorry-loads of visitors from Johannesburg and by a fair number of natives.'[15]

The end-of-season rugby also featured an extraordinary Grand Challenge final between Marines and Caledonian Roses. They played three times and on each occasion, the match was drawn 0–0. One report commented: 'Three successive weeks of pointless draws in the Marines-Caledonian Roses clash at Maitland ended on Saturday ... Four hours of rugby without a try or a successful penalty.' Officials initially decided to award the cup jointly to both teams, but the clubs objected to a shared outcome and a fourth match was arranged two weeks later.[16]

Not unexpectedly, further drama marred a titanic battle. Five minutes before time, Marines were leading 6–3 when Roses forced play up to the opposition line. Frantic movements were countered by a desperate Marines' defence. The *Cape Standard* report recalled:

> When a Roses' player was about to dash over the Marines' line, Mr de Goede whistled for a free kick. The player continued his dash and touched down. Some of the Roses' players disputed de Goede's decision and claimed the try. De Goede blew off the match and announced the matter would be brought before a union meeting at the first opportunity ... the disputed decision, if conceded, would have given Roses three points for a try and possibly the lead if the try was converted.[17]

The reporter sympathised with the players. Ill-temper had been caused by their keen anxiety for a decision after the agony of the pointless draws. If the fourth match had not been tarnished by the fateful final controversy, it 'would have been the best of the season'.[18]

The coloured players' passion for the game never diminished despite perennial problems of lack of finance and inferior facilities. There were hard-fought clashes, such as the afternoon in June 1936 when 'twenty players were injured in robust games at Maitland sports ground ... the Rahmanieh Division of the St John's Ambulance rushed assistance to all the hurt men – three went to hospital'.[19] The article did not, however, refer to the number of games played and it would be unfair speculation to suggest a lack of control. 'In 1933,' according to Timothy Chandler and John Nauright, 'eight players were suspended or reprimanded, four for "foul play", three for "disturbance on ground" and one for striking a referee.' But as the City and Suburban Union 'had over 1 100 registered members at the time and ran three grades of competition among its nine clubs so instances of violent or disorderly behaviour at matches were minimal.'[20]

In fact, coloured rugby administrators were determined to demonstrate 'respectable' behaviour through asserting their Christian backgrounds and beliefs. Meetings were held in English even though the majority of members spoke in Afrikaans, Xhosa or another first language.[21] Despite such efforts, the various pressures and prejudiced policies of white administrators led at times to decline and dissension. The frustrations of ambitious rugby enthusiasts were understandably immense.

Harold Wilson, a rugby administrator for more than sixty years, referred to a protest that took place in Kimberley. J.C. September, a former president of the SA Coloured Rugby Football Board, objected to the fact that the 1937 Springboks on tour to Australia and New Zealand were not a fully representative South African team. He stated that players of the SA Coloured Rugby Football Board and the SA Bantu Rugby Board were not given an opportunity to participate in trials for the selection of the touring team.[22] As expected, white rugby authorities were unmoved.

'By 1938,' observes Ian Goldin, 'the face of coloured politics had been altered. The leadership had passed into the hands of radicals, such as James la Guma, Johnny Gomas and Goolam and Cissie Gool, the daughter of Abdurahman. These people exercised a decisive influence over a wide cross-section of the coloured community of the Western Cape.' The National Liberation League was firmly committed to the establishment of united, non-racial opposition and in March 1938 initiated the Non-European United Front. From the outset, 'it aimed to provide mass opposition ... seeking to embrace working-class as well as petty-bourgeois coloureds and Africans'.[23]

The decision to select a rugby team to tour South Africa and then Britain was a positive attempt by coloured rugby to assert itself. At the same time, the organisers were determined not to rock the boat by upsetting conservative rugby establishments at home and overseas. Simultaneously, white civic leaders feared the radical rhetoric of new political developments and moved to assist and placate the coloured community at the Cape. In July, the mayor of Cape Town,

William C. Foster, opened the new Wynberg sports field in the presence of six fellow coloured and white councillors.[24]

There was strong white representation at the opening of the 1938 Rhodes Cup tournament. Foster was again the guest of honour and he stated he was pleased 'to hear that the European community have done much to support the tournament as the coloured people by their regular attendance and enthusiasm at Newlands have done much to place the European Western Province RFU in the proud position which it occupies in the South African rugby world today.'[25]

A.V. True of Swellendam was alert to the hypocrisy that existed and was keen to put the record straight in a letter to the *Cape Times*. He 'deplored the non-support of the Europeans at the Rhodes Cup tournament', stating that their involvement did not compare with that received in Johannesburg, Kimberley and South-Western Districts.[26]

The opening match resulted in a 16–13 defeat for the Western Province League against South-Western Districts, followed by a gripping encounter in which the Western Province Board were perhaps fortunate to beat Transvaal 9–8. The *Cape Standard* recorded 'notable features of the day's play were the magnificence of the South-Western Districts' forwards, the brilliance of the Western Province League's backs and the great kicking of the Transvaal and Western Province Board'.

Western Province Board, the cup holders, remained unbeaten. They went on to defeat South-Western Districts 11–3, Griqualand West 18–0 and Western Province League 11–9. As anticipated, there was a huge crowd for the match between the two sides from Western Province. The League played the better rugby, but the Board came back from 3–9 down to emerge triumphant.

At the end-of-tournament function at Salt River, Dr Abdurahman, leader of the virtually defunct APO and a city and provincial councillor, spoke to the assembled guests. He maintained that without the coloured people's love for their church and for their sport, 'they would have been in a worse position than they were at that time'. He praised the community's 'deep and sustaining love of rugby which went largely unrecognised and unrecorded, but which survived severe trials through its sheer love of the game and flourished in its striving for better things'. He urged the two Western Province unions to amalgamate and form one centre.

Abdurahman also remarked that it was fitting that the teams should be playing for the Rhodes Cup at a time when there was increasing agitation against racial discrimination because Rhodes was 'the man who laid down the slogan of equal rights to all civilised people from the Cape to the Zambezi. The attempt to introduce segregation is the very opposite of what this man wished.'

Abdurahman, who had been studying overseas when Krom Hendricks was barred by Rhodes from representing South Africa, appeared blissfully unaware of the Cape government's influence in the establishment of segregated sport at the Cape.

There were two highlights in the course of the evening. The first was the presentation of the Rhodes Cup to the Western Province Board. The captain, Dol Freeman, was a gracious recipient. He felt proud to have captained the winning team but congratulated Western Province League on their fine display, concluding with the remark: 'Personally, I say they were better, and we were lucky.'[27]

The second highlight was the naming of players selected for the Springboks' internal tour in June/July 1939. They would be accompanied by selectors on the lookout for talent with a view to a British tour at the end of the year:

Full backs: B. Walbrugh (Western Province League), D. van Heerden (Transvaal); Wings: M. Botha (Western Province League), F. Schilder (Western Province League), M. Philander (Western Province Board); Centres: I. Kiewietz (Western Province League), A. Julius (Western Province League), A. Padiachy (South Western Districts), P. Olivier (Western Province Board); Halves: J. Niels, captain (Western Province League), A. Freeman (Western Province Board), G. Almacin (Western Province League); Forwards: J. Goetham (Western Province Board), L. Goetham (Western Province Board), F. Marquard (Western Province Board), S. Appolis (Western Province League), A. Jacobs (Western Province League), V. Marinus (Western Province League), E. Brown (Transvaal), A. Caster (Transvaal), J. Kinnear (Griqualand West), A. Ebden (Griqualand West), S. Hopley (South Western Districts), T. Cupido (South Western Districts), S. Booysen (Western Province League), F. Pietersen (Western Province Board).

Selectors: P.M. Jampies, J.C. Jasson, A.F. Pietersen.

The selected team did not win unanimous approval. In a letter to the *Cape Standard*, Gedaar Moosa, the manager of the Western Province Board, lamented the non-selection of 'such outstanding players as I. Frieslaar, T. Davids (Carnera) and S. Nel'. He was also surprised that no recognised hooker was selected. The first man to have been nominated for the pack, he argued 'should have been Adams – the most outstanding hooker of the whole tournament'.[28] Abdullah 'Meneer' Adams, who played in the Western Province from 1928 to 1948, was 50 years old when he stopped playing rugby. He was called 'Meneer' Adams because he was a schoolmaster and for many years (1950 to 1976) the principal of Rahmaniyeh Institute in District Six. It was a school founded by Dr Abdurahman in 1913 and eventually named after him.[29]

Only one scrum-half was selected. He was Gonsalez 'Saal' Almacin. It was reported that 'his family were originally Spanish-speaking from the Philippines, shipwrecked off the Cape and setting up a church named for Spain's patron saint, St James. They were fisherfolk and Almacin played for Thistles, a club formed by Rogge Bay fishermen who frequented the Thistle Bar.'

There were two outstanding fly-halves in the team. Johnny Niels, who was named as tour captain, was a proven outside half, fast and elusive, a master tactician and schemer, and with the temperament to shine on the big occasion. Like many good fly-halves, he was also a fine cricketer. Dave Nourse, the great Springbok cricketer, thought him 'the most stylish stroke-maker I have ever played against'.[30] Niels had struck 57 in a comprehensive victory by Stephen Reagon's XI (204–2) over Nourse's XI (189) in 1937.[31]

Not long after the rugby touring team was named, Niels became an instant hero when he dropped the goal which gave Temperance a 4–3 win over Universals in the Grand Challenge Final at Mowbray. The *Cape Standard* recorded adverse conditions but a fine crowd nonetheless to see

> a terrific struggle in which players were drenched to the skin from the heavy downpours … With one minute to go, Niels received the ball on the Universals '25' and from a right angle he put over a beautiful drop which rose higher than the uprights. It sent Temperance supporters wild with delight. Niels was carried shoulder-high from the field.[32]

The team was fortunate to have another quality fly-half in Abdollah 'Dol' Freeman who went from Rahmaniyeh to Trafalgar High School. He was a great all-rounder – a fly-half who could kick with either foot and a splendid cricketer. He was described as Bennie Osler's coloured counterpart, Freeman conceding: 'Yes, I suppose I was in a sense his understudy.' Ironically, Freeman, who became a headmaster, could never be a replacement for Osler. The two players were great friends but were not allowed to play in the same match: 'They used to say that I could be likened to Bennie in every way on the rugby field. Only my colour was different. I knew his style so well that when I played for my team at fly-half, I drop-kicked after the Osler fashion with effortless ease.'[33]

The publicity given to the tour reached the SA Rugby Football Board meeting in October 1938. S.F. du Toit referred to reports that arrangements were being made for the visit to England of a coloured rugby team from South Africa. This project, he proclaimed, 'was causing considerable misgivings with many people here and he wanted to know from the president whether the board or the English Rugby Football Union to which it was affiliated had at any time been consulted on or informed of it, and whether therefore the board could in time to come to be held to have been in any way connected with the enterprise'.[34]

Harold Wilson recalled cordial relations existed between governing bodies and that A.J. 'Sport' Pienaar, president of the SA Rugby Football Board, assisted with the organisation of the scheduled 1939 tour to Britain 'as well as fitting the team out'. Yet, in response to Du Toit's question, Pienaar had no knowledge whatever of the scheme: 'Such a tour could not be carried out without the blessing of the English authorities, and if there is any truth in the report, the board would have been informed about it.'[35]

If the various statements were correct, then it would appear that Pienaar became involved at some stage after the SA Rugby Football Board meeting. Wilson noted that 'Pienaar was called upon to present the players with their colours', and that a stamp of approval came through Prime Minister Hertzog contributing five guineas towards the tour. The 'Springboks' were presented with their colours – a tie, muffler, and a blazer, which was green with a leaping springbok and ball on the badge – at the Salt River function in 1938.[36]

'Sound familiar?' asks historian Hendrik Snyders. 'The white Springboks only added a rugby ball to their logo some twenty-five years later.'[37]

By the time the national coloured team departed on their 1939 internal tour, there were several changes. Six players dropped out – Van Heerden, Botha, Schilder, Padiachy, Niels and Marinus – and three came into the side – Pinky Julius, Meneer Adams and Tiny Davids. The greatest loss was the tour captain, Johnny Niels, particularly as 'Dol' Freeman was hampered by injury problems. Freeman and Jaai Goetham were given opportunities to captain a side in which players were frequently forced to play out of position.

A Transvaal correspondent wrote to say how pleased he was with the final composition of the tour party. He regretted, however, that Reggie Mulder, had been excluded because the fly-half had earned a great name for himself at the last Rhodes Cup tournament when playing for Western Province and had since become 'the most brilliant and consistent player in the Transvaal'.[38] The observation was fair as Mulder proved to be in great form and was reportedly called upon to assist the national side during the tour.

A big crowd gave the Western Province representatives of the touring team a hearty send-off at the Cape Town railway station on Thursday night, 22 June.[39] The side arrived in Johannesburg the next day and were accommodated in a clubhouse in the centre of the city. The opening game against Transvaal was played at the Natalspruit Indian Sports Ground, normally used for soccer matches. It was a well-organised occasion during which the teams were introduced to the mayor, Dan Corlett, who then kicked off for the home team.

Transvaal gave the national side a fright in the opening half and were unfortunate not to open their account. Fly-half Reggie Mulder had a grand game, being mainly responsible for frustrating many South African backline movements. The Transvaal forwards were also impressive but because of over-eagerness in the backs, they could not drive home an early advantage. There was no score at the change-over.

It was always going to be difficult for the tourists with men from the different centres being an unknown quantity to one another. It was not until late in the second half that they managed to score. Ivan Kiewietz played a prominent part in the national side's victory, kicking a penalty to put his team ahead 3–0 and then scoring his side's first try. Bailey Walbrugh converted (8–0). Before Transvaal could recover, the South African team scored again. Silvester 'Vessie' Booysen cross-kicked and Flip Olivier fielded before knifing through a gap to score a try which was not converted (11–0).[40]

Two days later on Monday, 26 June, the touring side played Transvaal again, winning 25–7. The national team settled down quickly, combined well and for the greater part of the match had matters all their own way. Mulder maintained his form and had an outstanding game for Transvaal despite an injury sustained in the first half. Pinky Julius on the wing scored a hat-trick of tries for the tourists; Kiewietz again starred, and Archie 'Eier' Jacobs gave a sound display at full-back.[41]

The national team then travelled south by train, staying in private homes. On Wednesday 28 June, they defeated Griqualand West 13–11 at Kimberley. 'Of the tour matches played so far,' said the *Cape Times*, 'this was the most interesting and exciting.'[42] Although outweighed in the scrums the light Griqualand West pack played with tigerish ferocity in the loose, their flanks foiling many of the opposing side's back movements. The national team played open rugby, but handling lapses allowed the Griquas to profit from mistakes and score two excellent tries. The *Cape Standard* argued that the home players were allowed too much latitude. They naturally took advantage of this and spoiled what should otherwise have been a good game. Weight in the end told and Griquas 'had to put in some heroic defence during the closing stages to keep the visitors at bay'.[43]

In De Aar on 1 July, the touring side beat Midlands 28–5 and in Paarl, a day later, they were hard-pressed to defeat Paarl and Country 11–5. They were still unbeaten after five matches in eight days. Not surprisingly, injuries had taken their toll, and eight Paarl players – L. Kermis, J. Arendse, M. Adams, J. Thomas, C. Carollsse, J. MacKleim, Oranje and I. Sampson – were called upon for the tourists' next two matches. In a bizarre arrangement, the selectors split the available 30 players in order to take part in two matches on Monday 3

July. Half the team travelled to Worcester and lost 11–12. The other half played against the Western Province Union at the Green Point Track and were well beaten 18–5.

The stronger side played at Worcester where they were introduced to the mayor who kicked off for the home team before a crowd of 300. Worcester's backs were excellent, especially Jac Job the fly-half who scored the opening try, having ghosted through the opposing defence to touch down beneath the posts. Worcester also kicked a penalty, but Dol Freeman reduced the leeway with a try in the corner which Jaai Goetham converted through a great kick. Worcester led 8–5 at the interval. Archie Jacobs and Goetham scored tries in the second half but the conversions were missed. In reply, Job kicked a drop-goal to win the game for Worcester 12–11. The tourists were unlucky to lose a fast, bright open match, having scored three tries to Worcester's one. Played under the modern scoring system, they would have won 17–13.[44]

On the same day, the tourists' 'second string' played a Western Province Board team that was assisted at the eleventh hour by Caledonian Roses' players. The press appeared confused about arrangements, but the *Cape Times* gave the Western Province Board full credit for their 18–5 victory: 'The team rose to the occasion and played the South African side to a standstill. They played as one man and their back movements which were at all times orthodox were well rounded off.' In contrast, the national team 'appeared a moderate side and whatever movements they attempted fizzled out'.[45]

When the full touring party assembled in Cape Town as scheduled on Wednesday 5 July, they fielded a depleted side and lost again. They were beaten 16–12 by a combined Western Province side on the City and Suburban ground at Mowbray. The *Cape Standard* was critical, stating that 'the display given by the tourists was far from what can be expected from a national side'. It did concede, however, that the team 'probably suffered from staleness and most of the better players were not playing'.[46]

The tourists were back to full strength for their final match against Western Province League at Mowbray on 8 July 1939. The teams were presented to Dr Abdullah Abdurahman who kicked off for the League. Meneer Adams led many forward rushes, which kept the League on the defence, while there was a stern duel at scrum-half between the brothers Saal and Pablo Almacin. The former was described as the more polished and scored a trade mark try after a five-yard scrum. It was the only score of the first half, and it was anyone's game until Jaai Goetham, the captain that day, obtained possession from a loose melee and bullocked his way over to score a try. 'Vessie' Booysen converted to register an 8–0 victory.[47] It was the national team's finest performance, a fitting conclusion to a challenging tour. According to the *Cape Standard*, the team played ten matches between 24 June and 8 July, of which seven were won and three lost. They scored 142 points and conceded 75. The fixture against the Western Province Union was ruled as unofficial, being played on the same day as the official match at Worcester, and the statistics for this encounter might be removed from the record. The *Cape Standard* also referred to a tenth fixture staged in Cape Town and won 18–6. It was possibly played by the strongest fifteen on Wednesday 5 July, which would suggest the defeat against a combined Western Province side was also unofficial. The *Cape Standard* felt the tour served its purpose. The selectors had seen leading rugby centres in action, and they had been able to observe and assess the standard of the national team. Probably the best player was Flip Olivier, a centre of international class. Ivan Kiewietz was an ideal partner for him but had been injured at Kimberley. Saal Almacin was a hardy scrum-half and operated efficiently behind forwards not lacking in bulk. Seven members of the tour party were selected to play in seven out of the possible eight matches: S. Almacin, S. Appolis, A. Jacobs, M. Philander, L. Goetham, F. Pietersen and S. Booysen. Six played in six matches: B. Walbrugh, A. Julius, C. Julius, A. Adams, F. Marquard and J. Goetham.

The idea of an overseas tour fell away with the advent of the Second World War. Many of the players volunteered for active service but on their return, some became involved in rugby again. Western Province won the Rhodes Cup in Johannesburg in 1946. The cup was shared by Western Province, Eastern Province and Griqualand West at Kimberley in 1947, the fiftieth anniversary of the SA Coloured Rugby Football Board. Western Province League were champions for the first time in 1948 when they conceded just one try in five matches. It was then decided that the Rhodes Cup should continue through a biennial format from 1950.

The war brought home the contradiction between the plight of non-Europeans in their lack of political rights, and the causes for which the Allies were fighting. Abdurahman died in 1940 and his successor Dr F.H. Gow urged the APO to accept the government's support. Those opposed formed the Anti-Coloured Affairs Department (Anti-CAD) organisation in May 1943. They claimed the support of the majority of coloured people but were conscious of the need to broaden their base. A new liberation movement became necessary.

The Non-European Unity Movement, the first countrywide Trotskyist organisation, was established in late 1943. Its aim was to draw the community into a shared struggle with the African people. They were not as successful as hoped because resistance to the government was increasingly divided along racial lines. The ANC pursued a path to liberation that excluded coloureds, while the

Anti-CAD and Non-European Unity Movement – although in theory non-racial – were in practice preoccupied with issues of immediate concern to coloured people.

These political developments filtered down to the rugby administrations, with the coloured and African boards seeking opportunities to meet. By 1950 they had arranged to play internal Test matches and, for a relatively short period, the Non-European Rugby Football Federation served as a joint board. They hoped to organise an overseas tour and went so far as to select a combined team for this purpose.

George Golding, who had assisted coloured rugby before the war, became a founding member of the Coloured Peoples National Union in 1944, an organisation that superseded the APO. Under his leadership, they supported the Jan Smuts administration and collaborated with the Coloured Affairs Department. Golding was bitterly criticised by radical coloureds, but he remained influential and played a lead role in challenging government efforts in the 1950s to remove coloured voters from the common voters' roll.

Notes

1   C. Greyvenstein, *The Bennie Osler Story* (Cape Town: Howard Timmins, 1970), 65.
2   *Cape Standard*, 10 August 1936.
3   J. Vecchione (ed.), *New York Times: Book of Sport Legends* (New York: Simon & Schuster, 1992), 235.
4   *Cape Standard*, 10 August 1936.
5   Ibid.
6   Ibid.
7   Ibid.
8   I. Goldin, *Making Race: The Politics and Economics of Coloured Identity in South Africa* (London: Longman, 1987), 26.
9   P. Dobson, *Rugby in South Africa: A History 1861–1988* (Cape Town: SARB, 1989), 170.
10   A. Odendaal, 'The Thing that is Not Round', in A. Grundlingh, A. Odendaal and B. Spies (eds), *Beyond the Tryline: Rugby and South African Society* (Johannesburg: Ravan Press, 1995), 43.
11   Goldin, *Making Race*, 54.
12   *Cape Standard*, 11 May 1936.
13   See, for example, *Cape Standard*, 14 September 1936.
14   *Cape Standard*, 7 September 1936.
15   Ibid., 6 October 1936.
16   Ibid., 7 September 1936.
17   Ibid., 21 September 1936.
18   Ibid.
19   Ibid., 15 June 1936.
20   T. Chandler and J. Nauright, *Making the Rugby World: Race, Gender, Commerce* (London: Frank Cass, 1999), 38.
21   Chandler and Nauright, *Making the Rugby World*, 30.
22   H. Wilson, 'Separated by Race', in *The Badge: A Centenary of the Springbok Emblem* (Newlands: SA Rugby, 2006), 124–125.
23   Goldin, *Making Race*, 55, 56.
24   *Cape Standard*, 19 July 1938.
25   Ibid., 30 August 1938.

26   *Cape Times*, 31 August 1938.
27   *Cape Standard*, 6 September 1938.
28   *Cape Standard*, 27 September 1938. Davids resembled Primo Carnera the Italian world heavyweight boxing champion.
29   *Weekend Argus*, 8 October 2011.
30   Ibid.
31   *Cape Standard*, 6 October 1937.
32   *Cape Standard*, 27 September 1938.
33   Greyvenstein, *The Bennie Osler Story*, 65.
34   Minutes of the South African Rugby Football Board meeting, October 1938.
35   Wilson, 'Separated by Race', 124–125; Minutes of the South African Rugby Football Board meeting, October 1938.
36   Dobson, *Rugby in South Africa*, 175; Wilson, 'Separated by Race', 124–125. The presentation might have occurred later as the players did not wear official uniform in pictures taken during the internal tour.
37   N. Dall, 'South Africa's history of black rugby dates back more than a century', in *OZY*, 8 November 2019.
38   *Cape Standard*, 13 June 1939.
39   Ibid., 27 June 1939.
40   *Cape Times*, 26 June 1939; *Cape Standard*, 4 July 1939.
41   *Cape Times*, 27 June 1939.
42   Ibid., 29 June 1939.
43   *Cape Standard*, 4 July 1939.
44   Ibid., 11 July 1939.
45   *Cape Times*, 6 July 1939.
46   *Cape Standard*, 11 July 1939.
47   *Cape Times*, 10 July 1939; *Cape Standard*, 11 July 1939.

11

The IRB and Interchangeable National Identities

The ultimate aim was to establish a world rugby board
in opposition to the International Rugby Board.[1]

– Harold Wilson, South African non-racial rugby administrator

South Africa's famous rugby captain, Barry Heatlie, left the Cape dramatically in 1905. Villager rugby supporters rowed him out to a waiting ship in Table Bay from where he set sail for Argentina. Heatlie had become immersed in serious financial difficulties and his departure was a desperate bid to avoid arrest. Five years later, at Flores, Buenos Aires, he played for the River Plate Rugby Football Union (RFU) in Argentina's first-ever rugby Test match. The game against John Raphael's pioneer British touring team on 12 June 1910 enabled Heatlie, a 38-year-old fugitive, to become a double international. He avoided the team photograph, but returned to South Africa after twenty years, having supposedly paid his debts.

The day before the Test match in Buenos Aires, another British side was scheduled to play its opening fixture in South Africa. One source recalled the tour had come close to being abandoned, even before the team left England. The problem boiled down to confusion over whether South Africans could continue to represent a nation they had adopted temporarily for study purposes once they had returned home. Shortly before the 1910 team departed for Cape Town, the Transvaal RFU reported to the SA Rugby Football Board that two players, 'Messrs Williamson and Flemmer, ex-Rhodes Scholars residing in the Transvaal, had been approached by the International Rugby Football Board (IRB) to play for the English [British] team.'

The SA Rugby Football Board was 'strongly opposed to their inclusion' and their argument against the IRB won the day.[2] Rupert Williamson had played five times for England and Wal Flemmer attended a trial, but both were back in South Africa in 1910. Williamson was a brilliant scrum-half, good enough to be selected for Adrian Stoop's World XV, chosen from the best players the former England captain had seen up to 1927.[3]

Once the British tour to South Africa had started, the manager, William Cail, drew attention to mounting injuries and indicated that it was 'imperative to have the assistance of another forward'. The RFU claimed the only player available was Reginald Hands, who had played twice in the 1910 Five Nations Championship but had since completed his studies and was back in Cape Town. As in the case of the other two Rhodes Scholars, the SA Rugby Football Board did not agree with interchangeable national identities and opposed the selection of Hands.[4]

Appeals on national qualification had been made at various stages, but the IRB demonstrated a reluctance if not an inability to deal with issues involving the game in the wider world. This was not surprising. When Ireland, Scotland and Wales had formed an exclusive 'international' body in 1886, its membership was in effect tasked with little more than overseeing the standard rules of rugby football. No one was bothered much by this new body, except for the English who refused to accept them as being the ultimate authority and promptly complicated the issue by introducing a new points system.

A result of the squabbling was that the IRB member countries refused to play against England in 1888 and 1889. Eventually, arbitrators were appointed in late 1889 to settle the stalemate. They agreed to an arrangement whereby the IRB would be responsible for framing the laws of the game but England should have a controlling influence on the committee. The RFU was given six seats on the IRB, the other unions two each. A rule change required a three-quarters majority.

For 60 years, the IRB refused to allocate seats to any additional rugby-playing country. This effectively meant they controlled games played by the four home countries and had a remote, often strained relationship with the New Zealanders, and New South Wales in particular. When Charles Wade represented New South Wales against the British in 1888, having previously appeared for England against Scotland, the matter was of little interest. But when (Dr) James Marsh played for Scotland in 1889 and then for England against Ireland in 1892, a ruling needed to be made. It was subsequently resolved that no man could play for two home countries.

South African interest in the IRB in the late nineteenth century was largely limited to a *Cape Times* report in March 1888 that Alf Richards was showing fine form for Old Leysians. The article said, 'He seems to be making his mark and qualifying for his international colours if the IRB will only see the folly of their ways and not continue to boycott England on the point-scoring question.'[5] Richards was living with his mother but when she died later in the year, he gave up his England ambitions; returned to the Cape, and captained South Africa against the touring British in 1891.

It was not until Rhodes Scholars arrived at Oxford University that a wider international ruling needed to be made. Many of the Scholars were fine rugby players, as were other young men from the southern hemisphere who were attending various universities and colleges. England rugby benefited enormously, but Scotland also kept an eye open for potential international representatives. When the Scots defeated England at Richmond in 1903, their three-quarter line was made up of Jimmy Macdonald from Stellenbosch; Hugh Orr, born in Dineliquin, New South Wales; Alec Timms, from Geelong; and Nolan Fell, a former Otago University player born in Nelson.

Such was the influx of players that the IRB adopted the following resolution in 1911:

> No player except of home-born parentage is eligible to play for any country until he has resided for a period of two years in that country. Any player born abroad, one of whose parents is home-born, shall however be eligible to play for the country of such parent.

It suited England and Scotland that the resolution was largely ineffectual. They were reluctant to place restrictions on a rich supply of talent from the colonies. A year later, in 1912, Ireland called on the IRB to follow South Africa's lead in requesting 'no player except of home-born parentage is eligible to play for any country until he has resided for a period of at least five years in that country'. It is significant that Eric Watts Moses should note in his *History of the International Rugby Football Board* that there was 'no record of any discussion' concerning the Irish proposal.[6]

The rugby correspondent of the *Athletic News* summed up the situation by writing just before the First World War that there were no formal guidelines for national selection:

> Sentiment enters the process of qualification to a very great extent and if the stranger from afar has a reasonable sort of association with the land wherein he is domiciled he may, if he possesses no previous national distinction, be picked for that very land of temporary residence.[7]

It was a fair assessment but there were always going to be complications, even in cases where players possessed some national distinction. Colin Gilray, who was born in Scotland, represented New Zealand against New South Wales in 1905. On taking up his Rhodes Scholarship, he played four internationals for Scotland during 1908–12. This seemed fair enough, but the South African, Rupert Williamson went from reserve for the Springboks in 1906/07 to the England team the following year.

The SA Rugby Football Board's relationship with the IRB was strained, largely because William Cail headed their international committee. He had upset the South Africans on the 1910 tour over players and fixtures, eventually forcing the hosts to cancel two matches. Problems continued during the South African overseas tour in 1912/13 when Cail's communication was 'ill-judged and discourteous'. The tour manager, Max Honnet, contacted South Africa's representative on the RFU and was shocked to discover:

> [Donaldson] knew absolutely nothing about the tour, and on being asked what
> he represented had replied that he represented nothing at all! ... As things now
> stood, [his] position is positively ridiculous and none felt this more than Mr.
> Donaldson himself. [8]

Honnet discovered that several leading men in Britain were averse to giving the colonies direct representation on the English union, while the SA Rugby Football Board had little idea of the terms of its RFU affiliation. Historian Wouter de Wet notes that while the board 'did not necessarily feel entitled to a vote on the RFU, it felt that "the time had arrived when the scheme for the formation of some higher body than the English union should be considered"'. [9]

The New Zealand authorities had been clamouring for representation on the IRB since 1908, and eleven years later joined forces with the Australians in calling for an 'Imperial Board of Control'. They wanted equal representation for the three southern hemisphere countries and four home unions. They had given considerable support to Britain during the war and their standard of play on the rugby field was impressive. But the IRB resolutely opposed the idea of the colonies playing a part in the game's decision-making.

New Zealand rugby's London representative, C.J. Wray, might have had Jan Smuts in mind when he argued in 1921, 'if dominions were consulted over imperial defence and premiers invited to London for conferences, why not in rugby union?' [10]

IRB members had become concerned about the key issues of professionalism and rule changes. In 1920, the antipodeans submitted a joint document questioning aspects of the prevailing strict amateurism and 'proposing thirteen rule changes, many of which were modelled on rugby league rules'. According to Tony Collins: 'On all substantive issues, the [IRB] voted to reject the proposals but a "dispensation" was granted to the Australasian unions to allow them to ban direct kicking into touch from outside the kicking team's twenty-five-yard line.'[11]

There were no seats on the IRB for the colonies but the RFU offered places on its committee from 1921 as a form of compensation. The rugby establishment was awash with hypocrisy as the RFU strove to strengthen its rugby side by including southern hemisphere players and Welshmen. Huw Richards explains: 'England's inclusiveness was perhaps best seen in the context of the recent war and the fellow-feeling that had been rooted in a common cause. If South Africans and Australasians had fought for England ... why should they not play for it?'

The Welsh asked the RFU for 'clarification on qualification rules ... None was forthcoming'.

Richards concedes nevertheless that 'Welsh puzzlement at England's policy was equally understandable – why should a nation that already had more players than any other insist on chasing players whose Englishness was debatable?'[12]

South Africans at Oxford were frequently called to England trials. At a time when the England selectors were following Oxford's 'Boet' Neser in the early 1920s, there was interest in the rugby ranks of Guy's Hospital. Neser's brother was in their First XV alongside fellow Afrikaans-speaking South Africans, W. Olivier, S.L. Steyn, J. Krige, J. van Schalkwijk, A. Daneel, F. Bekker, F.W. Reitz, A. Marais, A. van Zyl, and A. Pauw. Seven of them played for the Barbarians and one, Jannie Krige – brother of the famous 1906/07 Springbok, Japie – was selected for England against Wales in 1920.[13]

Jannie Krige's international career was affected by events that were described as a 'trifle Gilbertian'.[14] To give two examples, Ernest Fahmy was selected for Scotland having attended a Welsh trial, and Newport's Ernest Hammett was chosen in the same week for both England and Wales. Hammett stood by the English for making the first offer but would have preferred to be with his club-mates. There was concern at the ease with which players were able to switch their national allegiance. *The Times* argued that England had complicated the issue by being prepared to select Krige, 'a colonial by birth, who in the course of his studies in this country is also able to take part in our games'. The newspaper believed that if England could select someone who had no real qualification to represent the country, then the Welsh should have been allowed to choose those who played for their clubs.[15]

John Hughes, an Australian playing for Harlequins, wrote: 'The international qualification is becoming a burning question, yet no lead is given.'[16] In 1921, the IRB was asked for a ruling but 'no action was taken'.[17] The same year, Cape Town-born Frank Mellish, who was awarded the Military Cross at Ypres, was allowed to play for both England and South Africa. He played his last of six Tests for England against Ireland at Twickenham on 12 February 1921 and the first of six Tests for South Africa six months later against New Zealand at Dunedin on 13 August.

While the South Africans were in New Zealand in 1921, it was an opportunity for their hosts to clarify where the SA Rugby Football Board stood in matters related to the IRB. 'First of all,' explained Harold Bennett the South African manager and a member of the board, 'we stand by the English rugby union. We have always stuck fast to it. And we hold dearly to amateurism.'[18]

Despite the Krige controversy, the RFU remained comfortable that the British imperial mission paved the way for them to select Afrikaners. They endeavoured to attract Pierre Albertyn, who had made an immediate impression at Guy's Hospital. He was a gifted exponent of the game, one of three players that the legendary coach A.F. Markotter regarded as 'truly great'; the other two being Japie Krige and Bob Loubser. Albertyn duly received a card from the RFU inviting him to play in a trial match, but he was too busy with his studies and replied accordingly. On his return to South Africa, he captained the Springboks against the touring British side in 1924.

Scotland also showed interest in players from the southern hemisphere. Denoon Duncan, a South African College School (SACS) old boy, who captained Transvaal in 1922 – a year in which they won the Currie Cup – played four times for the Scots. They also had a famous backline that included Australian-born, New Zealand-educated Ian Smith, an all-time great wing who later captained Scotland; George Aitken who had led the All Blacks against the Springboks in 1921; and Johnnie Wallace, an outstanding Australian wing.

Interchangeable identities were not discussed when the IRB eventually agreed to convene a meeting in London on 12 December 1924. The 'Imperial Rugby Conference' coincided with the All Blacks rugby tour and was chaired by Rowland Hill. Representatives of the IRB countries and the southern hemisphere rugby unions attended. The Australasian contingent was particularly well versed on rugby matters: Dr L.G. 'Bruno' Brown and Johnnie Wallace (New South Wales) were rugby internationals; Stan Dean was the manager of the 1924/25 'Invincibles' and S.F. Wilson the New Zealand RFU president in 1923.

Points raised were subsequently noted by the New Zealand Rugby Museum in their analysis of a 90-page verbatim report of the gathering. The minutes recorded that Hill was under instructions not to provide a forum for New Zealand's remit on 'professionalism'. Various other remits submitted to the conference by New Zealand and/or New South Wales, saw delegates consider rules that had been played under dispensation for some years. The Museum report observed that remits advocating changes in 1924 would in some cases become rugby law after the Second World War and, in certain instances, even later.

Examples included remit number 9, which was described by Hill as 'rather a controversial one'. It stated: 'If a player knocks the ball on and recovers it before it reaches the ground the referee shall not blow for a knock-on.' It took nearly fifty years, until 1973, before it was adopted. At the time, the Welsh delegate 'hoped Mr Wilson (of New Zealand) will not press this matter' and Hill responded, 'I do not see how you are going to alter the rule.' They then moved on to the next business.[19]

The developments of 1924 reinforced the view that the IRB was highly resistant to change. They also confirmed South Africa's blind loyalty to the RFU, which rendered them hopelessly inadequate in terms of defending and improving their position. The problem stemmed from a reliance on representatives who were resident in England and barely acquainted with South African rugby.

According to the Museum report, the recorded remarks of South Africa's two delegates, Vincent Cartwright and R.P. Fitzgerald suggested 'them to be more British than the British'. That was not surprising as Cartwright was a former England captain who served the interests of the RFU. Fitzgerald, a cricket official, informed delegates that 'the majority of our young players are Dutchmen ... any proposition or alteration might have come from people not of the same blood as yourselves'. He then reaffirmed his country's loyalty, stating: 'There is no movement in South Africa to do anything else but follow the lead of the home unions.'[20]

South Africa's devotion meant little as the IRB were less than encouraging in their dismissive attitude towards the dominions. Their 'best offer' is described by Richards as falling 'just short of insulting: a conference on the laws held every five years in London, with each union responsible for its own expenses and the IRB free to ignore its conclusions'.[21]

Major political developments in South Africa during the mid-twenties would influence the SA Rugby Football Board to realign its position and support the proposed imperial advisory board, which the New South Wales RFU believed should provide 'uniform international government' for rugby union.[22] The IRB debated the issue and in 1925 agreed to an 'imperial rugby conference' to be held every three years in London. They did not, however, have any intention of allowing rugby to follow the example of the politicians.

The South African prime minister, General Hertzog, assumed a prominent role in the Imperial Conference held in November 1926. Making use of a memorandum drawn up by Jan Smuts, he clearly defined a proposed equality of status with Britain within the empire and Commonwealth. According to the subsequent Balfour Declaration, Britain and the dominions were 'autonomous communities within the British Empire, equal in status, in no way subordinate to one another in any aspect of their domestic or external affairs, though united by a common allegiance to the Crown and freely associated as members of the British Commonwealth of Nations'.

The agreement reached was not quite everything that Hertzog wanted. His Canadian counterpart, William Lyon Mackenzie King, opposed his wish to describe the dominions as 'independent states', preferring the emphasis on 'equality of status'. The implications would be worked out over the next few years, leading to the later Statute of Westminster.[23]

The RFU delegates in 1926 went so far as to propose that a conference should be held to establish an imperial advisory board, with two delegates each from the four home countries and the three rugby-playing dominions. But when the conference began in November of that year, the IRB did not place 'an imperial advisory board' on the agenda. Proposals by South Africa and New Zealand for its formation were deemed to be 'outside the scope of the invitation issued to them and therefore not matters for the agenda'.[24]

The South African and New Zealand authorities anticipated the board's intransigence and had advised their representatives accordingly. Unfortunately for South Africa, they made a serious mistake in appointing Cecil Carden as a representative. He chose to ignore the instructions he was given and proceeded to tackle the situation as he saw best:

> While in England, I received a cable to represent South Africa at the Imperial Rugby Conference along with Major Cartwright. There was nothing on the agenda, and the South African board did the most foolish thing possible by cabling Major Cartwright and myself to walk out of the room if discussion were not allowed re the formation of an advisory board. The same thing was cabled to the New Zealand representatives and they allowed it to get into the press and it created a most rotten feeling ... the Scotsman raised an objection at the conference to informal discussions about matters not advised on the agenda, but Mr Baxter the chairman in a very conciliatory speech soothed matters. New Zealand was left with a rotten smirch and I saved South Africa from this, and the board can be jolly thankful.

Carden who thrived on his moment of fame as manager of the 1906/07 Springboks, was speaking to delegates at the North Eastern Districts RFU annual general meeting in 1927. He told them: 'South Africans are considered the best sportsmen that have visited the shores of England.' He was determined to find out who was responsible for the cablegram which he had in his possession. 'Why should England be insulted in this way? ... The matter is not going to rest where it is. I intend taking it up.'[25]

The dominions were nevertheless merging into a united group. The IRB was possibly aware of its intransigence when it adopted a plan to build on the Imperial Rugby Football Conference by inviting the dominions 'to express their views as to the frequency of meetings and state if they would be represented thereat'. New Zealand declined to attend any further conferences, while no replies were received from New South Wales and South Africa.[26]

The RFU's James Baxter endeavoured to repair some of the damage by stating that he had intended to announce that 'as a result of the recent meeting of the IRB, the formation of an imperial advisory board was an accomplished fact'. He did not wish to give up and hoped that the dominions would take the resolutions in a patient spirit. If they did, he added, 'there was no doubt that they would obtain their desire and the wish of the English union. It was bound to come for the English RFU could not and would not be tied down by other people.'[27]

At the thirty-seventh annual general meeting of the SA Rugby Football Board held in the *Cape Argus* boardroom in 1927, there were important developments. Jack Heyneman declined to stand again as president on account of old age and failing health. A.J. 'Sport' Pienaar, a lawyer and respected sports administrator, was unanimously elected to that office. M.J. Louw also retired as vice-president and Paul Roos was elected in his stead. South Africa would begin to shrug off its image as the most deferential of all the rugby-playing dominions.

Late 1928 was deemed an opportune time for Roos to take up what he termed 'the question of an imperial rugby board'. He met with Cartwright, who had as South Africa's representative, progressed to the position of RFU president during 1928/29. The two men had been opposing captains in the clash at Crystal Palace in 1906. Roos also met with Baxter, his vice-presidents Walter Pearce and Adrian Stoop, and Scotland's formidable James Aikman Smith. He was reportedly 'satisfied with negotiations', which ultimately led to agreement on a consultative body, 'provided the dominions accepted the IRB's rules of the game'.[28]

The rules were accepted but the four home unions stalled, and the issue lapsed after 1932.[29] Progress was derailed when it became 'abundantly clear that certain home union representatives were averse to [southern hemisphere] admission to the board under any circumstances'.[30] The Scots, in particular, had no time for colonial rugby, the Scotland RFU declaring in 1928 that 'it must always be second in importance to home football, which is their first consideration, and they cannot be party to any arrangement whereby any dominion is to have a say in the government of rugby at home'.[31]

The drama taking place over seats on the IRB continued to be played out against political developments where Hertzog pursued his quest to secure full sovereign independence. The provisions of the Statute of Westminster of 1931 formalised the position of the dominions as self-governing, separate states, effectively removing nearly all of the British Parliament's authority to legislate for them.

There was still no rugby equivalent granting the dominions representation on the governing body of the game. At a meeting of delegates from the four home unions held in July 1931, they decided that they would consent to the formation of a 'Rugby Football Commission'. The proposal was rejected, with New Zealand regretting it was unable to accept the commission in its proposed form. The home unions' 'final word on the subject until the reopening of negotiations in 1947 was the decision to advise South Africa that "as New Zealand and New South Wales have not accepted the suggested commission the matter will not be proceeded with"'.[32]

After years of lobbying and negotiating, efforts to secure admission to the IRB were to a large extent dropped. One reason was that 'the whole position of the dominions became the intimate concern of the RFU'. Within such an arrangement, the eligibility of overseas players representing England continued to be an issue during the 1930s through to the 1950s. It was highlighted almost immediately by the case of 'Tuppy' Owen-Smith, a well-known South African cricketer who was named one of *Wisden's* five 'Cricketers of the Year' in 1930.

Grand performances for his Oxford rugby side earned Owen-Smith an England trial, only for the *Guardian* to state that it 'revived an ancient controversy'. The report referred to London newspapers being divided over whether a player 'South African born, of South African parents and [having] played for South Africa at cricket' should be entitled to the 'hospitable gesture'. Compounding the problem, Owen-Smith also fell into a category with which the *Guardian* expressed concern: that of 'men who come to an English university or hospital and then return to their own country'. The RFU was unperturbed; rugby was a game of the empire and they subsequently appointed Owen-Smith as England captain.

English rugby authorities were a little more bothered over whether to select Owen-Smith's Russian team-mate, Prince Alexander Obolensky. Several members of the RFU committee opposed his selection, but when the prince was asked by the future Edward VIII as to his right to play for England, he replied, 'I attend Oxford University ... *sir*'.[33] The 73 000 spectators at Twickenham were delighted to acclaim his two memorable tries in the 13–0 defeat of the All Blacks, and he became a great favourite.

During the period in which the RFU assumed responsibility for the southern hemisphere countries, Bruno Brown, a surgeon, was determined to achieve seats for them on the IRB. He had been an Australian Rhodes Scholar who represented England at rugby before and after the First World War. He was awarded the Military Cross in 1917 and went on to captain England in 1922. In the course of representing New South Wales on the RFU committee during 1922–48, he became familiar with the IRB's resolute opposition to the idea of colonials playing a part in the game's decision-making. He would nevertheless succeed in the end in obtaining a seat for each of the three countries.

At a conference in London in December 1947 and a meeting in Dublin on 27 February 1948, the way was paved to facilitate the admission of the new members to the IRB at its annual meeting in Edinburgh on 19 March 1948 under the chairmanship of J.C.H. Ireland (Scotland). In attendance were Colonel B.C. Hartley, Admiral Sir P.M.R. Royds, L.G. Brown, E. Watts Moses (England), R.K. Cuthbertson (Scotland), J.R. Ramsey (Ireland), T.H. Vile, Dan Jones (Wales) and H. Thrift (honorary secretary). There was full agreement on the suggested constitution when the following resolution was unanimously adopted:

> The Home Unions having intimated their approval of the proposal to widen the constitution of the International Rugby Football Board to include representatives of the Dominions it is resolved that the Dominions be informed that the Board will welcome with great pleasure the appointment of their representatives in accordance with the bye-laws of the Board as now amended and set out hereafter, subject so far as concerns the Dominion of Australia to the formation of an Australian RFU.[34]

'The changed attitude of the Home Unions,' says Watts Moses, 'arose in part from the closer ties forged under wartime conditions, but perhaps, even more, the retirement of administrators who were strongly opposed to any widening of the Board's constitution.' He praised the efforts of the New South Wales representative:

> No individual strove more keenly on the Dominions' behalf than Dr L.G. Brown ... whilst attaching the greatest value to the bonds uniting [the RFU] to the dominions persuaded many home union administrators (before his death in 1949) of the genuineness of the dominions' aspirations and their potential value as full members of the board.[35]

The first meeting of the newly constituted board was held on 18 March 1949 under the chairmanship of Admiral Sir P.M.R. Royds (England). Watts Moses notes that England had been the most closely affected by the changes that had taken place, having given up two seats in 1909 and two more in 1948. Representatives of the new member countries expressed their appreciation in obtaining admission to the board and thanked the RFU for making it possible.

H.H. Roos, a long-serving Boland delegate later informed a meeting of the SA Rugby Football Board that he had his own thoughts on why membership of the IRB was eventually achieved:

> I see the whole thing. The international board was constituted to govern the four home unions. They did not legislate for us, but we accepted their legislation from our part. When we applied for membership of the board, England had four votes, Scotland, Ireland and Wales had two votes each. They objected to the dominions coming on the international board because they said that one vote each of the three dominions together with four votes of the English Rugby Union would make seven against six. Only when the England authorities gave up two votes did they agree to the dominions coming in. That constitutes the international board which now governs rugby in the world.[36]

Ironically, when the decision to widen the constitution was taken, South Africa was preparing for an election that would see the National Party sweep to power and open the way to severing links with Britain. Paul Roos, who had patiently promoted South Africa's aspirations to be represented in world rugby, was elected the National Party Member of Parliament for Stellenbosch. He died five months later: 'a relic of another age' opines journalist Michael Green, who does not believe that Roos 'would ever have subscribed to the cruelties and crudities of the apartheid policy as it evolved under his party'.[37]

In February 1950, the home unions' committee was unanimous that the resolution of 1892 – 'no man should play for two home countries' – was applicable to the dominions from the date on which they attained membership of the board. They based this decision on the circumstances of Dr Doug Keller who played six Tests for Australia during 1947/48 before representing Scotland (through his Scottish grandmother) in seven Tests – four as captain – during the 1949 and 1950 'five nations' championships. The IRB then reversed the decision in 1951, deciding that the resolution of 1892 applied to the four home unions only, and made no regulations as regards the qualifications of players in international matches.[38]

Players from the southern hemisphere were a feature of home union teams in the late 1940s and early 1950s. Syd Newman, Harry Small, Clive van Ryneveld, Murray Hofmeyr, Robert Kennedy, Nic Labuschagne, Ossie Newton-Thompson (all England), Chick Henderson, Kim Elgie, Keith McMillan and Pat MacLachlan (Scotland) were southern Africans who played 'Tests' for the home unions.

In 1952, the New Zealand RFU sought to increase the membership of the board from eleven to fourteen to permit each dominion to hold two seats. Discussion on the issue was deferred until 1954. These proposals were revived in 1954 but again deferred. Eventually, the all-important alteration to the board's constitution was made in 1958 at the annual meeting in Edinburgh. The bye-laws were amended to provide for two representatives from each of the seven-member unions, enabling the dominions to attain full and equal membership. 'The great change,' concludes Watts Moses, 'was not made without difficulties and anxious consideration, the balance of power and long hegemony of the home unions being at issue.'[39]

South Africa's relationship with international rugby began to change as the Afrikaner gained a foothold in the game's administration and as a consequence of domestic and foreign politics. There were also other significant governing bodies for rugby within South Africa. They catered for the non-European population and sought international contact. They had made contact with Fiji and Singapore and had hoped to meet in the latter country. A leading South African administrator, Harold Wilson commented:

> The ultimate aim was to establish a world rugby board in opposition to the International Rugby Board. The latter operated exclusively for members of the British Commonwealth. It had refused to accept another affiliate from South Africa by claiming that its constitution allowed only one affiliate from a country. The International Rugby Board was fully aware of the fact that its South African affiliate practised discrimination against the SA Bantu Rugby Football Board and the SA Coloured Rugby Football Board, but they were quite satisfied with the state of affairs.

At that stage, France was the only associate member. It was envisaged that if the French 'could be enticed to join the new organisation, she could influence other European countries to link up with the new world body'. Unfortunately, says Wilson, 'the attempt remained a dream because visas could not be obtained to travel to Singapore ... rugby officials were known to the [South African] authorities and the chances of securing travelling documents were remote'.[40]

Notes

1   H. Wilson, 'Separated by Race', in *The Badge: A Centenary of the Springbok Emblem* (Newlands: SA Rugby, 2006), 130.
2   C. Thomas and G. Thomas, *125 Years of the British & Irish Lions: The Official History* (London: Mainstream, 2005), 117.

3   *Cape Times*, 29 March 1927: Stoop's team consisted of W.J. Wallace, E.T. Morgan, G. Nicholls (captain), H. Vassall, A. Stegmann, P. Munro, R.H. Williamson, E.D. Simson, J. Daniell, V.H. Cartwright, W.W. Wakefield, C. Seeling, M. Brownlie, A. Tedford, and L.A.N. Slocock.
4   Minutes of the SA Rugby Football Board, 27 June 1910.
5   *Cape Times*, 7 March 1888.
6   E. Watts Moses, *History of the International Rugby Football Board* (London: IRB, 1960), 19.
7   *Athletic News*, 1 December 1913.
8   Minutes of the SA Rugby Football Board, 14 February 1913.
9   W. de Wet, 'A History of the South African Rugby Football Board: Early Years 1889–1914', in *Sport in History*, published online 25 September 2020.
10   H. Richards, *A Game for Hooligans: The History of Rugby Union* (Edinburgh: Mainstream Publishing, 2006), 111. Early in 1917, Smuts was invited to join the imperial war cabinet and the war policy committee.
11   T. Collins, *A Social History of English Rugby Union* (Abingdon: Routledge, 2009), 170–171.
12   H. Richards, *The Red and the White: A History of England versus Wales Rugby* (London: Aurum Press, 2010), 74–75.
13   N. Starmer-Smith, *The Barbarians: The Official History of the Barbarian Football Club* (London: Futura Publications, 1977), 217–233. Matches listed in *Sporting Life*, January–March 1920.
14   *Sporting Life*, 8 January 1920.
15   *The Times*, 8 January 1920.
16   Ibid., 24 January 1920.
17   Watts Moses, *History of the IRFB*, 20.
18   *New Zealand Herald*, 8 July 1921.
19   New Zealand Rugby Museum: Report of the Imperial Rugby Conference, London, 12 December 1924.
20   Report of the Imperial Rugby Conference, 12 December 1924.
21   Richards, *A Game for Hooligans*, 112.
22   Collins, *A Social History of English Rugby Union*, 173.
23   W. Kaufman and H. Slettedahl Macpherson (eds), *Britain and the Americas: Culture, Politics and History* (Santa Barbara: ABC-Clio, 2005), 137.
24   Watts Moses, *History of the IRFB*, 12; Collins, *A Social History of English Rugby Union*, 173.
25   *Cape Times*, 30 March 1927.
26   Watts Moses, *History of the IRFB*, 12.
27   *Cape Times*, 2 April 1927.
28   Ibid., 21 December 1928.
29   Richards, *A Game for Hooligans*, 112.
30   Watts Moses, *History of the IRFB*, 13; *Cape Times*, 21 December 1928.
31   Collins, *A Social History of English Rugby Union*, 173.
32   Watts Moses, *History of the IRFB*, 13.
33   Richards, *A Game for Hooligans*, 136.
34   Watts Moses, *History of the IRFB*, 14–15. Paul Roos and Bill Schreiner represented South Africa at the 1947 conference in London.
35   Watts Moses, *History of the IRFB*, 15.
36   Minutes of a special meeting of the SA Rugby Football Board, 21 May 1954.
37   M. Green, *Around and About: The Memoirs of a South African Newspaperman* (Claremont: David Philip, 2004), 59.
38   Watts Moses, *History of the IRFB*, 20.
39   Ibid., 17.
40   H. Wilson, 'Separated by Race', 130–131.

12

The Quest for World Rugby Supremacy

Skrum, skrum, skrum.[1]

– Paul Roos

The importance of Springbok rugby was brought home to Danie Craven in August 1921. He was ten years old and living on Steeton, the large family farm at Lindley in the eastern Free State. A bitterly cold spell had engulfed the area and he had been trudging slowly through the snow-covered veld, behind his father and older brother, John. They spent the morning looking for sheep trapped by the abrupt change in weather conditions. Later, they collected the local paper, *The Friend*, from Malan's Post in Lindley.

The headline news was the 13–5 defeat suffered by the Springboks in the first Test against New Zealand at Dunedin. Young Danie noticed a sense of gloom overtake his father and brother. He wanted to know more. 'Pa? How could the Springboks have lost the match?' he asked. 'We have such a good side ... what could have gone wrong?' His father explained as best he could that New Zealand 'which was many, many thousands of miles away in the South Pacific, was the nation second only to South Africa in the world at playing rugby'.[2]

The reputations built up by the Springboks and All Blacks were based on their achievements in Britain, Ireland and France. In two tours, the South Africans won 49 and drew one of their 55 games. Paul Roos's 1906/07 South African side defeated Ireland 15–12 and Wales 11–0, drew with England 3–3, and lost to Scotland 0–6. Billy Millar's 1912/13 team achieved the first-ever 'grand slam', beating Scotland 16–0, Ireland 38–0, Wales 3–0 and England 9–3. They conceded one score in four Tests, Ronnie Poulton getting a try for England at Twickenham.

The All Blacks – the 'Originals' – played 32 matches in the British Isles during 1905/06, of which they won 31. They defeated Scotland, Ireland and England but lost 3–0 to Wales at Cardiff Arms Park. It was generally felt that Wales deserved to win the match, but during the second half, a try was claimed by the New

Zealand wing Bob Deans. It was argued he was 'pulled back by Welshmen before [the] referee arrived'.[3] Scotsman John Dallas, who was refereeing the match, had fallen 30 yards behind play.

The 1921 Springboks won all five matches in Australia before arriving in New Zealand. Despite their continued success, the locals did not contemplate the possibility of defeat. 'People in New Zealand,' observed Mort Blackett, 'appear to be obsessed with the idea that the land which produced the All Blacks can have no peer at the game.' He wrote: 'Despite the fact that the idols they set up are being shattered week by week ... they are not the least impressed by the fact that the Springboks are unbeaten and that they were vastly superior in every department of the game to the Wellington side.'

At the same time, Blackett noted that the South African players were viewing 'the Test match with equanimity and are gradually concluding that the standard of rugby football in the dominion is vastly overrated'.[4]

The All Blacks won 13–5 at Dunedin and then lost narrowly 9–5 at Auckland. The second Test was decided by Gerhard Morkel's drop-goal (then worth four points), a spectacular second-half effort after the teams had been locked 5–5 at the interval. The interest by that stage was unprecedented; no one under-estimated the significance of winning the series.

The *Evening Post* announced: 'We simply cannot afford to lose the third Test.'[5] Determined to succeed, the New Zealand selectors included their former rugby league captain Karl Ifwersen in the side at five-eighth. 'According to the rules of the game,' says Tony Collins in a recent publication, this was 'completely illegal'.[6] But having been denied representation on the International Rugby Football Board (IRB), the New Zealanders felt torn between 'wanting to do one thing for the perceived good of New Zealand rugby, but having to do another to obey the dictates of the English union'.[7]

The deciding match was played in Wellington in appalling weather and produced a scoreless draw, the first and only occasion the All Blacks had failed to score at home. The *Press*'s special correspondent declared that 'two great teams had met, and the rugby superiority of the world was undecided'.[8]

It was deemed wise to leave Ifwersen out of the All Black team to tour Britain, Ireland, France and Canada in 1924/25. It did not matter as the 'Invincibles' played 32 matches and won them all, including 4 Tests against Ireland, England, Wales and France. The Scots refused to be part of the tour because the Rugby Football Union (RFU), not the IRB, had invited the All Blacks.

The British Isles visited South Africa in 1924. The Springboks scraped home in the first Test 7–3 at Durban thanks to a drop-goal by Bennie Osler. They were more convincing in winning the second Test 17–0 at Ellis Park. The British might have won the third encounter at Port Elizabeth, but Scotland's Dan Drysdale missed a penalty from in front of the posts with the scores level at 3–3. The last Test was won 16–9 by the Springboks, but there was splendid rugby from both sides.

Pierre Albertyn, one of 'Oubaas' Markötter's finest Stellenbosch products, was singularly influential in the series success. The touring captain, Ronald Cove-Smith, rated Albertyn highly as he was always 'able to produce the requisite thrust at the right moments'.[9] Another report described Albertyn as 'a devastating centre three-quarter with a lethal, blindingly fast sidestep'.[10]

In 1928, the Springboks resumed their rivalry against the touring All Blacks. There were nine players from the 'Invincibles' but the Maori stars George Nepia and Jimmy Mill were left out of the side.

Crucial decisions were made ahead of a series that attracted considerable interest. The All Blacks reacted to early defeats by abandoning the 2-3-2 scrum formation in favour of the three-man front row that the Springboks used.[11] They also refused to select Mark Nicholls who, with his 131 points, had been the leading points-scorer on the 'Invincibles' tour overseas. He had reputedly fallen out of favour with senior All Black players, notably the captain Maurice Brownlie.

The *Sydney Morning Herald* commented before the first Test: 'Tomorrow the eyes of the rugby world will be centred on Durban ... a struggle for the world's rugby supremacy.'[12] The Springbok forwards and Osler controlled the game. The fly-half was the hero of the day, kicking fourteen points and setting up a 17–0 victory. It was a desperate time for New Zealand, but in the second Test at Ellis Park, they edged ahead 7–6 through a penalty and drop-goal to two penalties. The Springboks came back with an 11–6 victory in the third Test at Port Elizabeth to establish a 2–1 series lead.

Nicholls watched the first three Tests from the grandstand. He wrote later that Osler 'was easily the best fly-half I ever saw. In fact, he was the best back I ever saw. He is great because he dominates the game.'[13]

A week before the fourth Test, an Osler-inspired Western Province beat the All Blacks 10–3. Eleven of the Western Province players returned to Newlands to play an important Test in determining the battle for the mythical world championship. The home side were firm favourites. The *Cape Argus* saw little hope for the visitors: 'With two Tests lost and the narrowest of victories in one, their form makes it impossible to predict anything but a South African victory.'[14]

It rained for most of the week before the 'Umbrella Test' and conditions on the day were atrocious. Nicholls was suddenly recalled. Most people – including the Springboks – had been baffled by his non-selection. As fate would have it, he played a major role in the outcome, scoring all New Zealand's points in a 13–5 triumph.

'Boy Bekkies' de Villiers, a 1906/07 Springbok and prominent coach, summed up the drawn series: 'Like the forwards and Bennie won the first Test match so did the [All Black] forwards and Nicholls win the last Test match.'[15]

The following year, Danie Craven began his studies at Stellenbosch. The coach, Markötter, saw him play and reputedly told colleagues: 'Well *kêrels* (fellows), you are looking at the Springbok scrum-half for the next tour to Britain in two years' time.'[16] He was right. Craven was selected for the 1931/32 overseas venture under the captaincy of a player he called 'Mr Osler'.[17]

Craven made his Test debut in the opening international at Cardiff Arms Park. It rained heavily and Osler changed tactics several times. At one stage, he ordered the Springboks to let Wales win the heavy, slippery ball from scrums and line-outs and then capitalise on their mistakes. South Africa won 8–3 in the end, a match Craven described as the 'most awesome, exciting and rewarding game of his rugby life'.

Further victories were achieved against Ireland 8–3, England 7–0 and Scotland 6–3. The single most memorable moment was Gerry Brand's drop-goal against England from the halfway line and near touch. One critic wrote: 'Brand's drop, two minutes from the finish, was a thing of beauty, a perfect parabola, taken calmly with the left foot, a fraction before the charging English forwards arrived.'[18] It was measured at 85 yards.

The second 'grand slam' reinforced the superiority of southern hemisphere rugby. The home unions criticised Osler for excessive kicking, yet they had made no real effort to introduce the restricted touch-kicking dispensation when it was proposed earlier by the New Zealanders and Australians. The SA Rugby Football Board – of which Osler's father was a member – also favoured experimenting with this aspect of the rules, which forbade kicking into touch on the full outside the kicker's quarter of the field. They requested permission to experiment, the IRB responding by cable: 'Approval given limited number of games'.[19]

D.R. Gent's assessment of Osler's kicking in the victory over England was that it 'prevented his backs from developing their attacks, but it always gained ground, and the result was that though the Springboks rarely looked like scoring, the game for practically the whole of the second half was in the English half of the field, more often than not, dangerously near the English line'.[20]

Some acknowledged the genius of Osler. O.L. Owen of *The Times* observed the South African fly-half's ability to 'plant the ball exactly in the spot most awkward for the other side'. A report in the same newspaper stated: 'One will always think of Osler as a great conductor of a band that his cool genius also made great. Without him, the South Africans might have developed into a more brilliant team. But it is doubtful if they would have won more than one international.'[21]

Osler accepted he might have kicked too much on the tour but believed he had little choice. 'Playing conditions were often very bad,' he countered, 'and to have tried to play the open game would have been to court disaster ... the latitude allowed wing-forwards coupled with the lack of control of the off-side law in Britain at that time, gave our backs no chance to attack in the orthodox manner.' As backline movements were blocked as soon as they were initiated, the Springboks relied on driving through with the forwards.[22]

Between 1928 and 1937, South Africa lost two out of nine Tests. After the 1931/32 British tour, they had one series that they won 3–2 against Australia in 1933. The All Blacks played more Tests during the same period, but experienced a modest record, winning ten and drawing one of their nineteen international matches. On their overseas tour in 1935/36, they defeated Scotland and Ireland but were beaten by Wales and England.

Statistics alone suggested that the All Blacks were perhaps not the fearsome force projected by the 'Originals' and the 'Invincibles'. The 1937 Springbok touring side, however, would have been aware that the All Blacks had thumped Australia 38–13 in a Bledisloe Cup match at Dunedin, towards the end of the previous season.

The Springboks played eleven matches in Australia in 1937 and won ten. They had few problems in their opening games, but then came up against New South Wales. It was raining and muddy, conditions similar to those experienced in Wales six years earlier. The Springboks attempted to replicate the tactics employed at Cardiff Arms Park but came unstuck. They had no Bennie Osler to guide them and lost 17–6. They were, nevertheless, able to win both Tests, 9–5 and 26–17.

After four matches and four victories in New Zealand, the Springboks prepared to play the All Blacks in the first Test at Athletic Park in Wellington. It was sixteen years after Craven's father had first enlightened him on Springbok-All Black rugby rivalry.

In an extraordinary move, the selectors – all players – dropped tour captain Philip Nel and fly-half, Tony Harris. Craven, who had played number 8 in the second Test against Australia, was named as captain and fly-half. The thinking behind the decision was that Craven had a strong boot, a key asset in the likelihood of rain the next day. The Springboks were beaten 13–7. They had badly erred in playing Craven at fly-half, his slowness off the mark was seen as a major reason for the defeat. One report opined 'his game was neither one thing nor the other ... he lacked the sharpness of Harris'.[23]

For the second Test at Christchurch. Nel was recalled and Harris was named as fly-half. New Zealand were beaten 13–6, with the South African forwards maintaining tight control despite the All Blacks taking an early lead. Jack Sullivan scored two opportunistic tries to give New Zealand a 6–0 lead, but South Africa fought back strongly in the second half. Freddie Turner demonstrated his pace to score a fine try, which Brand converted. The full-back then kicked a crucial penalty from inside his own half to put the Springboks 8–6 ahead. A grand try from Ebbo Bastard confirmed the victory in a game where the scoring was invariably against the run of play.

The Springboks were on the road for almost five months. Yet everything boiled down to the third and final Test at Eden Park. Ron Palenski comments that the prospect of New Zealand being beaten 'went to the front of minds'. The All Blacks were dispatched to Days Bay across the harbour from Wellington for 'five days of intensive training. It was as concentrated and organised as anything that could be devised by any of the professional coaches of the twenty-first century.'[24]

Tension mounted in South Africa. A *Cape Times* editorial recorded 'the misplacing of Craven in the first Test has left a deep and dark scar on local confidence'. It accepted that the New Zealanders were favourites for the deciding Test, but underlying 'the dubiousness about [the] result, is a genuine faith that our forwards will be up to the ordeal and will pull the match out of the fire, if needs be'. After careful analysis, the editor concluded: 'To blazes with the experts! The *Cape Times*, which has predicted rightly in these columns, the results of the other two Tests, plumps for a Springbok victory today.'[25]

Great uncertainty again affected selection, with Harris named in the side provided the weather was fine. Jimmy White, regarded as the 'world's best tackler', withdrew with a thigh muscle injury and was replaced by Flappie Lochner.[26] Fellow centre, Louis Babrow, was uncertain whether he could play. The match was on Yom Kippur, one of the most sacred Jewish holidays. Eventually, he convinced himself that because of the time difference Yom Kippur would not start in South Africa until after the match ended – and he was, of course, South African.

The weather proved unexpectedly kind for the match. A telegram arrived from Paul Roos with its famous message: 'Skrum, skrum, skrum'. Following the laws of the day, the Springboks chose scrums instead of line-outs. It created an initial psychological advantage. New Zealand's most obvious weakness lay in the front row and they were penalised at the fourth scrum. Brand's kick from the halfway fell short, but momentum favoured South Africa.

The first try resulted from a bad pass by Harris to Lochner. The latter had great difficulty in gathering the ball behind his back, so much so that All Black Jack Hooper thought he had dropped it, leaving a gap through which Lochner streaked.[27] He then off-loaded to Babrow who scored. Brand narrowly missed the conversion (3–0).

The Springbok full-back had a disastrous day with his boot. The All Blacks were penalised in front of the goal but, said one sarcastic report, 'Brand miraculously missed the kick.'[28] The next scoring movement began when Babrow broke through the All Black defence, beating 'Brushy' Mitchell, and placing a well-judged cross-kick. Ferdie Bergh gathered to score the Springboks' second try. On this occasion, Brand converted (8–0).

Up until then, the Springbok forwards were in command with Bergh, Bastard and Strachan prominent. But during the last fifteen minutes of the first half, the All Blacks had much the better of the game. A forward rush was courageously stopped by Turner. Eventually, the All Blacks scored through David Trevathan kicking a penalty from 50 yards out (8–3). It roused the record 58 000 crowd to wild enthusiasm.

Immediately after half-time, Craven decided on a pre-planned move from a scrum on the halfway line. He signalled to his fly-half Harris to move out further – and further ... The All Blacks feared the Craven dive-pass and adjusted their positioning to maintain alignment with the Springbok backs. A gap was created. The Springboks won the scrum. Craven lobbed a short pass to Turner who came from the blindside and raced through. He drew the full-back, passed to Lochner, and then on to Babrow who scored (11 3).

The All Blacks made positional changes. Mitchell, who appeared to carry an injury into the match, went on the wing in place of Pat Caughey who moved to centre to partner Hooper. Doug Dalton took Artie Lambourn's place at hooker.

It became clear that Mitchell was unable to cope with wing Dai Williams who made ground every time he received the ball. From a scrum 30 metres out, the Springbok backs swung the ball quickly to Williams who beat Mitchell and Jack Taylor to score a brilliant try. Brand again missed the conversion (14–3).

Harris had been in sublime form, his brilliant handling and pace off the mark having an impact on the Springbok line. The fifth try came from a scrum, with Harris knifing through the All Black defence before transferring to Babrow. The centre held on too long but, after being brought down by Taylor, recovered well. He regained the ball and threw it infield to Louis Strachan who, in turn, sent a long overhead pass to Turner. The wing dashed for the corner flag and crossed for the try (17–3).

New Zealand flung everything into attack. Hooper came close to scoring but Harris covering was able to rescue the situation. When the Springbok forwards were penalised for off-side, Trevathan added three points to the All Blacks' score with a penalty goal (17–6).

Taylor launched further All Black attacks as the crowd edged closer to the playing area. In the last five minutes, the referee moved them back, but the ground and corner flags were taken even before the final whistle. Sailors climbed the poles to secure South African flags, and they subsequently visited the Springbok hotel to ask the team to autograph them.

The vanquished were generous in their praise. 'New Zealand is bitterly disappointed,' admitted the *New Zealand Herald*, 'but the victory went to those having a much better right to it. This is acknowledged without the slightest grudge.'[29]

The *Cape Times* headline proclaimed: 'All Blacks Scrummaged to Stand-Still', but the editorial hoped South Africans would be responsible in celebration:

> With the rugby Test rubber won, a decent rejoicing is permissible, especially if it is tempered by admiration for the sporting spirit in which New Zealanders have taken the Springbok triumph ... there are, moreover, peculiar grounds for satisfaction in the clean and friendly way in which the final Test was fought ... the absence of rough play on Saturday was all the more remarkable because so much depended on its result.[30]

South Africa's success had been achieved more by fine teamwork than by individual brilliance and was acknowledged as a splendid vindication of orthodox methods in rugby. 'It is good, honest scrumming that counts after all,' remarked the *Cape Times*. 'The pack that consistently gets possession of the ball by really hard work in the scrum wears down its opponents and gives its own three-quarter line an inestimable advantage.'

Craven's performance was perhaps the best individual effort. He despatched 'the backs so swiftly with long accurate dive passes that the New Zealand breakaway forwards were unable to harass the Springbok inside backs'. His only fault was 'a tendency to throw high passes, but this was offset by Harris's superb handling. He never dropped a ball all day.'[31]

It was announced that 'the captain Mr Nel has decided to celebrate his retirement from the game by throwing his rugby boots into the Indian Ocean'. Babrow left for overseas to study but eleven of the team played in the first Test against Sam Walker's British Lions in 1938. Craven became captain.

Queues gathered before dawn to see the match at Ellis Park. Extra seating was provided to accommodate the 36 000 crowd, which spilt onto the perimeter around the field. They were treated to a thrilling contest that South Africa won 26–12. Sam Walker remarked: 'They told me the Springbok forwards were old and past their best, but I have never seen forwards play better.'[32]

A heatwave marred the second Test, which the Springboks won 19–0 at Port Elizabeth. The teams then travelled together to Cape Town on the *Windsor Castle*. Walker spoke to Markötter about the matches and the Springbok selector scribbled down the Lions team he would choose for the third Test. When the official announcement was made, the side was believed to be that which Markötterr had chosen. The inclusion of all eight Irishmen was just one of several significant changes.[33]

The Springboks led 13–3 at the interval, but the strong wind blew in favour of the tourists in the second half. A rousing fight-back saw the Lions playing their best rugby of the tour. The inspirational Paddy Mayne was pivotal in an incredible turnaround, which saw the tourists edge ahead 14–13. The lead then changed again but eventually, the Lions triumphed 21–16. They scored eighteen second-half points; Walker recalling the greatest thrill of his career occurring when 'Ben du Toit and Louis Strachan and others hoisted me on their shoulders and chaired me off'.

It would be eleven years before South Africa played international rugby again. Craven was 'sorry for the team in the future that loses the "rubber" in a series of Test matches. But we must remember that we cannot always win.'[34]

The All Blacks' tour of 1940 was cancelled because of the Second World War. When a South African tour was planned for 1949, rumours spread that New Zealand would be including Maori players in the team. *Die Transvaler* promptly warned the SA Rugby Football Board 'not to allow the game to be misused for an attempt by New Zealand to carry on a sort of political propaganda ... Such a team would not be acceptable to South Africa and the New Zealand authorities should know it.'[35]

In New Zealand, there was concerned debate. No comment received more publicity than that made by Major-General Sir Howard Kippenberger at an informal gathering of the Returned Servicemen's Association. 'The Maoris had fought for and earned their citizenship,' he thundered. 'I had the Maoris under my command for two years, and in that time, they had 1 500 casualties, and I am not going to acquiesce in any damned Afrikanders [*sic*] saying that they cannot go. To hell with them.'[36]

Kippenberger's strongly worded comments triggered an immediate reaction. In New Zealand, Maoris sent messages of thanks. There were also those who opposed Kippenberger. A former minister of education saw the tour as purely a rugby matter and deplored the suggestion that because some Maoris were excluded 'other young players should be deprived of the trip'. One sports' editor described opposition to the tour as the result of 'the sinister activities of a rival code, presumably rugby league, and the communist party'.[37]

The New Zealand RFU confirmed its decision to exclude Maori players from the 1949 tour at a meeting with the Maori Advisory Board in October 1948. It stated that the board gave its unanimous support to the rugby union in a resolution signed by Ned Parata and Kingi Tahiwi.[38]

There were divisions in South Africa in the aftermath of the war. Dr Louis Babrow recalled that Maori soldiers saved 'many young South African lives' at Sidi Rezegh (North Africa) during 1941. He also commented that the Springboks who had enjoyed Maori hospitality in New Zealand would be keen to play against them in South Africa. Babrow did not have the support of the SA Rugby Football Board. The president, 'Sport' Pienaar, dismissed New Zealand protests against Maori exclusion as originating from 'people in the pavilion and on the rope'.[39]

The 1949 All Blacks were expected to do well. They had strength in depth, so much so that they also organised a parallel Test series against Australia, a side they had beaten 4–0 two years earlier. Unfortunately for them, they disappointed in South Africa as they suffered seven defeats (including all four Tests) in twenty-four matches. Against Australia, they were beaten in both Tests at home. On the 3 September 1949, New Zealand played two Tests on the same day and lost both: 9–3 at Kingsmead, Durban, and 11–6 at Athletic Park, Wellington.

It might be added that they lost a 'series' to a third country – Rhodesia – as they were beaten 10–8 at Bulawayo and drew 3–3 at Salisbury.

The Springboks had the ascendancy in the scrum. Indeed, their superiority was such that their coach Danie Craven offered to assist the tourists. The All Black backline suffered from the exclusion of the talented Maori backs, Vince Bevan, Johnny Smith and Ben Couch. 'It was a tough break for us,' admitted Allen, 'that Bevan was a Maori. The 'Boks are hard enough to beat anyway. When they've got race on their side, they're even harder.'[40]

It was an absurd situation. 'Bevan would have toured,' argues Spiro Zavos, 'if the Maori Advisory Council had not informed the New Zealand RFU that he was Maori. Bevan did not consider himself Maori, although his mother was a quarter Maori.'[41]

The Springboks were indisputably the best side in world rugby when they embarked on their 1951/52 tour to the United Kingdom and France. After losing their captain, Basil Kenyon, to a serious eye injury, Hennie Muller took over as a highly successful replacement. The tourists lost the tenth match of the tour against London Counties at Twickenham, but the home unions gasped in horror at the news of the 'Murrayfield Massacre'. Jack Gage, who had played for Ireland and the Springboks, stated: 'Never during a quarter of a century of playing and watching international rugby have I seen such a complete eclipse by one team of another as we saw when the Springboks beat Scotland by 44 points to nil on Saturday.'[42]

The People claimed 'they toyed with the Scots'. *The Graphic* commented 'this was rugby murder'. Edinburgh's *Evening Dispatch* said, 'The South Africans proved themselves 100% worthy of the title of international champions of the world.' The *News of the World* recalled, 'The home defence appeared mesmerised … the South African forwards bullocked and barged, side-stepped and dummied until we thought we were watching a team of 14 three-quarters'.[43] The nine-try thrashing would be worth a 62–0 score-line under the modern points system.

Victory over Ireland was not as easily won. It was a show of strength in adversity, especially as the Springboks played into the face of a blustering half-gale with fourteen men for thirty-four minutes of the first half. Centre Ryk van Schoor was carried off the field unconscious after six minutes' play. The half-time whistle blew with the Irish leading 5–3.[44]

Van Schoor arrived back on the field six minutes into the second half, having disregarded the doctor's orders. The fact that flank Stephen Fry could then re-join the line-out enabled South Africa to take command in that area. The Springboks also became more assertive in the loose and Hansie Brewis directed play to advantage. In the last five minutes, Basie van Wyk, who was magnificent throughout, scored his second try and then Van Schoor added 'a brilliant winding solo effort that left five recumbent opponents in his wake. He remembered nothing of it afterwards.'[45] It was a hard-won 17–5 victory.

The Welsh had been preparing for some time for what was hailed as the 'rugby match of the century'. A month before, J.B.G. Thomas had written that the Welsh must prove their power as a rugby nation by beating South Africa to 'wipe out the stain of her three previous defeats in 1906, 1912 and 1931'.[46]

It was a close call before a crowd of 55 000 at Cardiff Arms Park. The *Cape Times* sensed 'opportunism, the game's most telling weapon, won this match for the Springboks who were outplayed in their most powerful quarter – at forward'. Just before the interval, Chum Ochse scored a try 'rather in the fashion of lightning suddenly illuminating a sullen sky'.[47] Later, seven minutes before the end, Brewis cleverly manoeuvred himself into a position where he could drop for goal to give the Springboks a 6–0 lead. They eventually scraped home 6–3.

Gage wrote of the Cardiff experience as 'one of the tensest atmospheres in which I have ever seen a rugby international take place'. He put it down to the rugby supremacy of the world being at stake. As a result, the Springboks, instead of playing their natural open game, played a safety-first type of rugby.

An 8–3 victory over England secured the grand slam. Gage described England's challenge as 'magnificent and rather unexpected ... Territorially the Springboks had 75% of the game but England fought superbly to keep the might of South Africa at bay for 80 minutes of truly glorious rugby.'

There was one further international, against France, played for the most part amidst an amazing cacophony of booing and whistling. The Springboks had thrashed the French in 1906/07 and in 1912/13, and again won comfortably 25–3. The 1951/52 side carved out their victory through 'outstanding teamwork and disciplined execution of a preconceived plan which made the fullest use of the side's greatest strength – the exceptional momentum of the forwards'.[48] The French had fifteen players intent on making a personal success of the game – there was much to learn from the Springboks' keen backing up and swift inter-passing.

R.C. Robertson-Glasgow, one of the finest writers in British journalism, paid tribute in the *Observer* to 'a team and its two managers, who showed us all that is best in rugby; clever in plan, brilliant in execution':

> Individually there have been games-players from overseas of so consummate a skill and so winning a personality that they have outsoared the glare, and the shadows, of national rivalry. Such a one was the American golfer, R.T. [Bobby] Jones. And now a whole team, the Springboks have done likewise. They leave behind them new ideas, new standards, and thousands of friends who have never shaken them by the hand ... Opponents found themselves trying to cope with men who combined the power of a heavyweight boxer with the speed of a hundred-yarder.[49]

The tour was the most successful a South African team had undertaken. The final record saw 31 matches played, with South Africa winning 30 and losing only one game. Harry Cleaver, president of the RFU, praised their rugby as being imaginative and virile, and noted their matches attracted probably the biggest crowds that have ever watched a touring side. 'That, perhaps, is the greatest tribute that has been paid them.'[50]

But, despite the praise they received, there was also resentment. The British were not 'entirely happy with all this coaching, smacking as it did of professionalism'.[51] Ironically, there was a history of planning tactics and strategies in their own rugby. Wavell Wakefield had employed a 'professional' attitude towards the game at Cambridge between the wars whilst the far-sightedness of Oxford leaders such as Newton-Thompson, Travers and Kendall-Carpenter often gave their teams a crucial advantage. Chick Henderson thought the preparation for the inter-varsity to be at odds with the approach taken by the home unions at international level. When selected for Scotland in the wake of the 'Murrayfield Massacre', he was advised to 'arrive in Edinburgh if possible in time for a run-around with the rest of the team on the Friday afternoon'.[52] Clive van Ryneveld would write in a similar vein of England's 'archaic' preparations.[53]

Different worlds clashed in the post-war period. On the way to England, Kenyon informed Frank Mellish, the 'double' international and manager of the 1951/52 Springboks, that Craven would coach the Springboks. Mellish reacted later by writing an open letter, 'My Dear Danie', in which he stated 'rugby is a young man's game … It is against the spirit of the game to go on to the field with a set plan drawn up by someone who is not taking an active part.'[54]

Notes

1   Telegram from Paul Roos to the 1937 Springboks.
2   T. Partridge, *A Life in Rugby* (Halfway House: Southern Book Publishers, 1991), 29–30.
3   Telegram to the London *Daily Mail*: T. McLean, 'The Greatest Match of All', in G. Williams, *Sport: A Literary Anthology* (Cardigan: Parthian, 2008), 322–323.
4   *Daily Mail*, 28 July 1921.
5   *Evening Post*, 30 August 1921.
6   T. Collins, *The Oval World: A Global History of Rugby* (London: Bloomsbury, 2015), 235.
7   R. Palenski, *Rugby: A New Zealand History* (Auckland: Auckland University Press, 2015), 193.
8   T. Richards, *Dancing on Our Bones: New Zealand, South Africa, Rugby and Racism* (Wellington: Bridget Williams Books, 2012), 10.
9   I. Difford (ed.), *The History of South African Rugby Football 1875–1932* (Wynberg: Speciality Press, 1933), 310.
10   C. Thomas and G. Thomas, *125 Years of the British & Irish Lions: The Official History* (London: Mainstream, 2005), 136.
11   They also lost 6–0 to the Transvaal at Ellis Park in their fourth game.
12   *Sydney Morning Herald*, 29 June 1928.
13   NZ 'Free Lance', November 1931.
14   *Cape Argus*, 31 August 1928.
15   M. Nicholls, *The All Blacks in Springbokland* (Wellington: L.T. Watkins, 1928), 168.
16   Partridge, *A Life in Rugby*, 28.
17   The *Friend* criticised the selection and Craven's father cancelled his subscription to the newspaper.
18   *Cape Times*, 5 January 1952.
19   P. Dobson, *Rugby in South Africa: A History 1861–1988* (Cape Town: SARB, 1989), 71. The Cape universities played the 1928 All Blacks under the rule of 'no kicking into touch on the full outside the 25-yard (22-metre) area during free play'.
20   *Sunday Times* (London), 3 January 1932.
21   H. Richards, *A Game for Hooligans: The History of Rugby Union* (Edinburgh: Mainstream Publishing, 2006), 138.
22   C. Greyvenstein, *The Bennie Osler Story* (Cape Town: Howard Timmins, 1970), 114.
23   *Cape Times*, 16 August 1937.
24   Palenski, *Rugby*, 189.
25   *Cape Times* editorial, 27 September 1937.
26   A New Zealand opinion: T. Meredith, president of the New Zealand Rugby Council who thought the Springbok defence had been a revelation.
27   *Cape Times*, 27 September 1937.
28   Ibid.

29   *New Zealand Herald*, 27 September 1937.
30   *Cape Times*, 27 and 28 September 1937.
31   Ibid., 27 September 1937.
32   *The Star*, 6 August 1938.
33   S. Lewis, *Last of the Blue Lions: The 1938 British Lions Tour of South Africa* (Cheltenham: Sports Books Limited, 2009), 209, 213–214.
34   P. Dobson, *Doc: The Life of Danie Craven* (Cape Town: Human & Rousseau, 1994), 72–73.
35   R. Thompson, *Retreat from Apartheid: New Zealand's Sporting Contacts with South Africa* (London: Oxford University Press, 1975), 14.
36   Thompson, *Retreat from Apartheid*, 16.
37   Ibid., 17. Kippenberger was subsequently forced to concede his remarks were 'quite improper'; M. Buckley '"A Colour Line Affair": Race, Imperialism and Rugby Football Contacts between New Zealand and South Africa to 1950' (unpublished master's thesis, University of Canterbury, 1996), 99.
38   *The Press*, 2 October 1948; Buckley, 'A Colour Line Affair', 99.
39   *The Press*, 4 September 1948; Buckley, 'A Colour Line Affair', 98.
40   T. McLean, *The All Blacks* (London: Sidgwick & Jackson, 1991), 59.
41   S. Zavos, *Winters of Revenge: The Bitter Rivalry between the All Blacks and the Springboks* (Auckland: Viking, 1997), 107–108.
42   *Cape Times*, 26 November 1951.
43   Ibid.
44   R. Stent, *The Fourth Springboks 1951–52* (London: Longmans, 1952), 150.
45   Stent, *The Fourth Springboks*, 151.
46   *Western Mail*, 22 November 1951.
47   *Cape Times*, 23 November 1951.
48   Ibid., 18 February 1952.
49   R.C. Robertson-Glasgow, *The Observer*, 27 January 1952.
50   *Cape Times*, 7 January 1952.
51   Dobson, *Doc: The Life of Danie Craven*, 106.
52   Interview with Chick Henderson, *Wits Sport*, Johannesburg, 2, 6 (1985), 39.
53   C. van Ryneveld, *20th Century All-rounder: Reminiscences and Reflections of Clive van Ryneveld* (Cape Town: Pretext, 2011), 42–43.
54   F. Mellish, *My Dear Danie – An Open Letter to Danie Craven* (Cape Town: Maskew Miller, 1960).

13

'The Fight for the Control of Rugby'

> Rugby is an English game which had been fostered in this
> country by all sections of the community: English, Afrikaans,
> Jews, Gentiles and coloured people, and the dissentients'
> views were not the only views that could be expressed.[1]

– A.J. Pienaar, President of the SA Rugby Football Board

A sharply divided South Africa entered the Second World War on
6 September 1939. The prime minister, General Hertzog, had been adamant
that his country should not interfere in a European quarrel and was in favour
of remaining neutral. His deputy, Jan Smuts, opposed this view, believing it was
impossible for South Africa to reconcile neutrality with its commitments to
Britain and the Commonwealth.

After a day of intense debate in the House of Assembly, Hertzog's motion was
defeated by 80 votes to 67 and he was forced to resign. Smuts formed a coalition
government with a Cabinet made up of an almost equal number of English-
and Afrikaans-speaking members. The decision to enter the war precipitated
widespread conflict between those who supported South Africa's war effort and
those who opposed it.

All the English were behind Smuts, records historian Frank Welsh, 'as well
as a substantial minority of Afrikaners, and all those "non-whites" who could
afford to take an interest in anything so far removed from their daily struggles.'
He notes there had been enthusiasm among non-whites for the British cause
in 1914 but that was absent in 1939. Imperial goodwill and power 'had long
evaporated, and the hundred thousand blacks and coloureds who volunteered for
service were often inspired only by hopes of better pay'.[2]

South African troops became heavily engaged in battle in East Africa,
Madagascar, North Africa and Italy. The fall of Tobruk was one of the war's
worst defeats, but South African soldiers were also prominent in the victory at El

Alamein and participated in the invasion of Europe. With a regular army of less than five thousand, they placed great reliance on volunteers. Over a third of the country's eligible European population – both Afrikaans and English speaking – served in the armed services.[3]

Political differences that erupted over South Africa's participation filtered down to rugby unions and clubs. Hostility permeated the administrative chambers, but arguments leading to breakaways and divisions did not focus on who was or wasn't fighting. They centred on whether rugby should be played for war funds or for any other charity. Debates were bitter and time-consuming and dominated rugby meetings for nearly four years. The anti-war faction argued that money collected in an amateur game should be used only for the improvement of rugby facilities. They objected to financial support being given to Ouma's Gifts and Comforts Fund – Ouma being Issie Smuts, wife of the prime minister, Field Marshal Jan Smuts.

The Afrikaner desire to play a greater role in the administration of the game compounded the problem. No other sport or cultural pursuit became so closely tied up with both their identity and the rise of Afrikaner nationalism than rugby. Although they were prominent within the SA Rugby Football Board, there were other governing bodies – most notably the Transvaal Rugby Football Union (RFU) – that were in the hands of English-speaking South Africans. This state of affairs would be challenged during the 1940s, with the Broederbond attempting to influence the administrative structures of the game at provincial level.

The Transvaal RFU was the scene of bitter in-fighting during the war. Initially, the selection committee was ordered to limit the choice of players to those who were either in the army or had received an exemption from the military authorities. Seven players who usually represented Transvaal in inter-provincial matches were allegedly not prepared to take the 'Africa-oath' and were therefore not eligible for service. There were objections voiced when players were left out of the provincial team as a result of their principles. The situation caused discord and dissension and soon focused on the symbolic issue of whether gate money should be used for war funds.

Rumblings of discontent were heard in other provinces. In December 1940, the president of the South African Board, Major A.J. 'Sport' Pienaar, warned the unions that the matter of rugby matches for charity had taken on a political colouring. 'The game must not be used as a bazaar,' he said, 'where any local institution might make use of the rugby game to raise money.' He did, however, accept that respective committees could do what they wished with funds, provided it was within their own rules.[4]

With so many players in the forces, clubs from the Transvaal and Northern Transvaal established a combined league in 1941. It did not last more than a couple of weeks as complications arose over charity games. The Transvaal authorities were conscious the war had divided the Afrikaner population. A compromise was sought. Permission was given for a match at Ellis Park to assist the SA Vroue Federasie (Women's Federation) and the Armsorgraad (Care for the Poor) of the Dutch Reformed Church, but a game in aid of Reddingsdaad Fonds (Rescue Fund) was denied because the organisation was seen to be a business enterprise. There were immediate repercussions.

Pretoria Rugby Football Club (RFC) protested by choosing not to fulfil a fixture against the Transvaal side, East Rand Proprietary Mines (ERPM). A mass meeting of several hundred rugby players was held in Pretoria where several speakers addressed the audience and a resolution was drawn up, unanimously adopted, and published in *Die Transvaler*. It objected to the Transvaal RFU's political bias and stated its intention to protest directly to the SA Rugby Football Board. The resolution praised the Pretoria RFC and requested that the Northern Transvaal RFU dissolve the combined league and establish its own competition.[5]

The *Star* pointed out that the sponsors of the resolution 'apparently did not take the trouble to ascertain the true facts dealing with the charity match staged at Ellis Park on 14 April 1941'. It had been played in aid of the funds for the Vroue Federasie and the Armsorgraad.[6] The Northern Transvaal RFU subsequently received a full apology from the Pretoria RFC, but it was not the end of the matter.[7]

The Northern Transvaal's anti-war activists – led by Springboks Ferdie Bergh and Ben du Toit – held a meeting in Johannesburg. The pro-war Transvaal president, H.J. 'Sandy' Sanderson noted their intention 'to divide the players on racial lines which is something the Transvaal RFU deprecates very strongly'.[8] The gathering encouraged members of a leading Transvaal club, Diggers, to boycott a fixture against New State Areas at Brakpan. When Diggers assembled in Johannesburg, four players declined to go to the match and they influenced a fifth to join them. Two were Transvaal representatives. The Diggers players were punished for coming 'under influences foreign to rugby'.[9]

Considerable damage had been done and the combined league was discontinued. Northern Transvaal's president, Professor H.B. Davel, cautioned the unions: 'It had to be remembered that just as there were people in parliament who opposed the government's war policy, so there were many rugby players who opposed it and if an effort were made to stage matches for war funds, the game would be split asunder.'[10] A match was nevertheless held on 21 June 1941 at Ellis Park with the proceeds divided between the Reddingsdaadfonds and the Transvaal RFU.[11]

Sanderson viewed the situation differently from his northern counterpart. He had been president since 1934 and liked to have his way. At his union's annual general meeting in early 1942, he strongly denounced the infiltration of politics into sport, 'an unwelcome innovation which should never again be allowed to obtrude itself into the game'.[12] His argument meant little as both sides – the 'pro-war' and 'anti-war' – accused the other of introducing politics into rugby.

The rugby crisis was widespread. At the Cape, the president, Johan D. de Villiers, had initially taken the line in April 1941 that 'this union resolves that its grounds be used exclusively for the purpose of the game of rugby football and that no matches be played on the grounds, in respect of which the gate takings are specifically devoted to any other purposes, whether of a charitable nature or not'.[13]

In June 1942, South Africa suffered its greatest military defeat when thousands of her troops were taken prisoner by Rommel at Tobruk. De Villiers changed his attitude. On 15 September 1942, he said:

> The hardships and sufferings of the hundreds and thousands of rugby players fighting in defence of South Africa has now reached such a stage that I can no longer allow the minority on the union to act on the advice of those miserable politicians to withhold from our Springboks the little comforts which their comrades who are enjoying the game at leisure in the Western Province ought to send up to them without further delay.[14]

De Villiers asked his union 'to adopt with effect from 1 September 1942 three teams (45) of rugby soldiers at 7s 6d per month per soldier in accordance with the condition laid down in the South African Gifts and Comforts section of Ouma's Funds'. *Die Burger* was critical, stating 'the fact remains that the fund, like all the others, is closely linked up with the general war policy, and that support, therefore, is to be interpreted as approval of that policy'.[15] The *Cape Times* responded in a lengthy editorial:

> We are at war and the fact is that there are scores of splendid fellows who have played rugby football in all the teams of the Western Province throughout South Africa who are now volunteers at the front and who are doing noble service there ... We would like to believe that tonight's meeting will show that *Die Burger*'s estimate is wrong and that the proposals will be accepted without opposition and with enthusiasm. Showing that the men who play rugby today

are not less sportsmen, even if they have been unable, for political reasons to do their duty at the front, than the men who there are doing their duty.[16]

De Villiers's resolution was carried but the Stellenbosch delegates, Sid C. Harvey and D.J. Conradie warned that the adoption of such a motion could lead to 'serious consequences'.[17]

Several 'anti-war' clubs seceded from the union. On 6 October 1942, the Western Province RFU was informed that at a general meeting of the Stellenbosch RFC, the club decided against further participation in rugby organised by the Western Province RFU, as long as the decision of 15 September remained in force.[18]

The loss of Stellenbosch created shock waves through Western Province rugby and, according to the *Cape Times*, the union 'placed the club in quarantine as punishment for their withdrawal'.[19] The university explained that it was

> fully aware of the difficult position which arose as a result of its decision, but even if during the next ten years the club does not take part in competitions, it still does not intend to surrender the principle that every situation of politics should be avoided in our national game. Further as long as a rugby ball is procurable, rugby will be played at Stellenbosch.[20]

The University of Cape Town's rugby club initially sided with its Stellenbosch counterparts. After a lively discussion, it passed a resolution at its annual general meeting on 10 March 1943, expressing the opinion of the playing members that the Western Province RFU 'should not contribute to any charitable organisation for the duration of the war'. The president of the club, Professor Theo le Roux, intervened by emphasising that the resolution could not go forward to the union as 'an expression of the feeling of the University of Cape Town RFC' because the matter had first to be considered by the University of Cape Town Council, the governing body of all university associations.[21]

The matter was debated further over the next two weeks. The Springbok fullback Gerry Brand deplored the resolution adopted by playing members of the club but was prepared to continue to coach there. On 26 March 1943, a special general meeting of the university's rugby club was held at which a new resolution was unanimously adopted: 'That the playing members of the University of Cape Town RFC state that they desire to abide by the Western Province RFU's decision and they offer their fullest support to the Western Province RFU.'

A.D. Knott Craig had chaired the gathering as Professor le Roux was at the SA Rugby Football Board meeting. Voting was by ballot and only members of the previous year were entitled to take part. It was noted that four anti-war members of the committee, 'Messrs S. de Jongh, P. Neethling, J.T. Oosthuizen and S. van der Spuy had resigned'.[22] They joined a relatively large group of Cape Town students that formed the Groote Schuur RFC.

An open meeting was called by those members of the Western Province RFU who were opposed to the resolution that supported the Ouma's Gifts and Comforts Fund. The gathering, which took place at Bellville, included representatives from Stellenbosch, Paarl, Gardens, Bellville, Goodwood, Groote Schuur and other clubs. They agreed in principle to secede from the parent body and form the Stellenbosch-based Wes-Kaaplandse Rugbybond. Delegates were advised by Dr E.T. 'Ebbie' Stegmann, who was elected chairman, that a new rugby union was not being formed, but an association to oversee 'rugby for the sake of rugby, and that as soon as the Western Province RFU altered its declared policy all the clubs affiliated to the new association would come back'.[23]

Not all members of the dissentient clubs agreed with the decision to secede. Members of Gardens and Maitland RFCs decided to call a meeting at the Long St YMCA for the purpose of forming a new senior club to enter the Western Province RFU league in the new season. The Union RFC was formed with two leading Springboks, Boy Louw and Mauritz van der Berg, in their ranks. They won the Grand Challenge in 1943.

The situation became progressively polarised between the pro-war and anti-war elements. Prime Minister Smuts became involved in the controversy when Justice H.S. van Zyl – the judge-president of the Cape and vice-chancellor of Stellenbosch University – interviewed him and presented the Stellenbosch and other dissident clubs' viewpoint. At the same time, Van Zyl expressed the fear that the split might extend to South African rugby as a whole.[24] At the request of Smuts, the administrator of the Cape, Major Gideon Brand van Zyl, met with J.D. de Villiers, as well as A.J. Pienaar and Paul Roos, president and vice-president respectively of the SA Rugby Football Board.

Little progress was made. De Villiers submitted nine points to the administrator in support of his union's stand. One of the nine points was that a large proportion of members – some 200 in the case of Gardens – were away with the fighting forces and therefore unable to vote at their clubs' annual meetings. The line taken by the SA Rugby Football Board spokesmen was that the Western Province RFU should adopt a 'magnanimous' attitude and 'try to come to a suitable accommodation with the dissident clubs, believing this to be in the best interests of South African rugby as a whole'. Van Zyl, the honest broker, was mainly concerned over implications for the schools. He did not want the education department to become involved in the dispute.[25]

The next development was the calling of a special general meeting of the SA Rugby Football Board in Cape Town on 17 May 1943 to consider the resolution by the Western Province RFU 'that no union shall authorise any club within the area of its jurisdiction to play a match against any club within the area of another union unless the consent of such union has been obtained'. The Western Province RFU had been influenced in this step with a view to preventing a game between Stellenbosch and Pretoria universities which had been approved by the Northern Transvaal RFU.

It emerged that only Transvaal and Natal delegates positively supported the resolution and the SA Rugby Football Board in effect decided to postpone action by appointing a commission of five to go into the whole question. Pienaar condemned the situation in which South African rugby found itself:

> The dissentient clubs should also remember that rugby is an English game which had been fostered in this country by all sections of the community: English, Afrikaans, Jews, Gentiles and coloured people, and the dissentients' views were not the only views that could be expressed. Rugby was a common heritage and with tolerance and willingness a way could be found without loss of self-respect and with no compulsion from either side.[26]

The independent committee was unable to reconcile the differences and bring about a compromise between the Western Province RFU and the clubs that seceded from the union. It reported that all efforts made to arrive at some compromise had been 'unavailing and the committee has failed in its efforts'. It did warn both sides that if a solution was not found it would mean that 'no player connected with the dissentient groups would be eligible to represent South Africa – to wear a Springbok jersey – an intolerable state of affairs'.

It was almost inevitable that Eastern Province would follow a similar direction to that of the Western Cape. The chairman, R. St Leger Searle, invited conflict when he proposed cup competitions be cancelled and replaced by friendly fixtures between players who had volunteered for military service. He claimed such a competition enjoyed the wholehearted support of the inhabitants of Port Elizabeth because only men willing to serve their country would take part. First Graaff-Reinet and then Parks objected to the proposal. The recently inaugurated Kwagga club from Cradock thought Searle's plan discriminated against one section of sportsmen.

After a period of uncertainty, Parks broke away in October 1942. Their delegate gave notice at a union meeting, explaining that his club disassociated itself from the decision of the Eastern Province RFU to contribute to war funds. They supported the decision made earlier by Stellenbosch. Other clubs followed Parks's lead and formed the Oos-Kaaplandse Rugbybond. They organised friendlies against South-Western Districts and Boland.

The focus of the crisis had by this stage moved to the Transvaal. The union had done well to make a profit of £1 378 1s 11d in 1943. There was no admission charge at league games but Red Cross collections were allowed and they benefited to the extent of £918. The *Rand Daily Mail* commented:

> It would be well here, perhaps, to remind any critics of the union's policy in this matter that while it is recognised that rugby is mainly a game for players, it can only survive and flourish with public support, and your committee would be failing in its duty to the game if it ignored the strong and insistent demand from its supporting public to identify the union with the common war effort, more specially as so many of its players are on military service.[27]

Willem Stork, the schools' representative on the Transvaal RFU and a history teacher at Helpmekaar, objected to the support being given to war funds. He decided he would topple the Sanderson-controlled rugby establishment. Stork had already discussed the question of rugby matches for the benefit of war funds with Dr H.F. Verwoerd, who was then editor-in-chief of *Die Transvaler*, and informed him: 'Give a year or two and I'll fix the problem.'[28]

According to rugby journalist Gert Kotzé, it 'marked the beginning of one of the biggest underground movements in the history of South African sport'. Stork mentioned his plan to end English rule in Transvaal rugby with his headmaster 'Oubaas' Jan Brink. The latter was in immediate agreement and, over two years, their organisation – *Boere Beesblaasbond* (the Boer Cattle Bonds Association) – attempted to undermine the administration of certain clubs through conducting operations from the inside. Stork studied methods by which the desired revolution might take place and managed to obtain constitutions from virtually all the clubs and sub-unions affiliated to the Transvaal RFU.[29]

Wits University, situated over the road from Helpmekaar, was a relatively easy target. Their rugby club was dominated by Afrikaans-speaking students whose sympathies were with the Afrikaanse Nasionale Studentebond (ANS). At the time, students from English-speaking universities affiliated to the National Union of South African Students (NUSAS) and perceived themselves as being pro-war, anti-Nazi and fighting racialism. Their ANS opponents were anti-war and seen by some to associate with the pro-Nazi Ossewabrandwag (Ox-wagon Sentinel).

The Wits Student Representative Council (SRC) did not recognise the ANS because of its racial exclusiveness but the latter organisation had an active branch at the university with headquarters off-campus in Braamfontein. It played a part in encouraging the Pretoria SRC to refuse an inter-varsity in Johannesburg at the end of August 1941 and break off all relations 'until the intolerable liberal policy of the students of Wits has been so modified that it opens the door for the restoration of normal relations'. Potchefstroom, Bloemfontein and Stellenbosch universities endorsed the proclamation by severing formal relations – chiefly in the field of sport – with Wits.[30]

A medical student, Carel de Wet, later minister of health, and South Africa's ambassador to London, was Stork's main link at Wits but others infiltrated the club and obtained key positions. The most important of these was Dan de Villiers, an advocate, who offered to coach the under-19 team and used that as a platform upon which he was able to rise through the ranks, promoting his own rugby ambitions and political views. Shortly before the 1944 annual general meeting of the Transvaal RFU, Wits RFC announced posts of responsibility that included 'representatives on the TRFU (Messrs van Heerden, de Villiers and Rautenbach), and delegates to the junior sub-union (Mr C de Wet) and senior sub-union (Mr van Heerden with Mr de Villiers as an alternative)'.[31] These men could be relied upon to support Stork.

The operation that the Helpmekaar history teacher masterminded began to take effect as contacts were established. Using Diggers RFC as his rugby base, Stork encouraged supporters to seek positions of power in as many clubs as possible. Two prominent men in education circles, P.A.M. Brink from the East Rand and Martin Brink, principal of Monument High School in Krugersdorp, were staunch allies, as was former Springbok Ben du Toit. In time, the sports editor of the *Rand Daily Mail*, Ted Nelson, and the management of the Transvaal RFU became suspicious. Nelson asked: 'What was happening because club management was tumbling left and right.'[32]

Stork was so confident in converting ERPM to his way of thinking that he quipped: 'Keep a few of the English, then they will not notice any further fuss.' Simmer and Jack was the last club to be tackled. There were some tense moments, not least in the club election where a massive crowd attended. Ted Nelson had 'christened the insurgents as the South African League of Hitler's Pals and warned against another "takeover" ... there was an open confrontation between Afrikaner and "Rooinek".'[33]

Transvaal RFU nominations were submitted three weeks before the annual general meeting. Stork's headmaster, 'Oubaas' Brink was backed by Diggers and stood against Sanderson. Others nominated for management included P.A.M. Brink, Martin Brink and Dan de Villiers.

The Sanderson regime had planned countermoves. They were meticulous and ruthless, with Sanderson's trump card being the votes of New States Areas. At the end of the 1941 season, New States had been suspended for two years, following incidents in the final of a senior regional competition. One member of the side had been sent off for illegal play; others left the field in protest, and spectators attacked the referee.[34] Sanderson was able to locate three representatives from the club to vote for him at the annual general meeting on 21 March 1944.

The gathering at the Carlton Hotel in central Johannesburg was the most well attended and controversial meeting in many years. Business started amidst challenges about the credibility of the voting powers of certain clubs and bodies. At one stage, one of the vice-presidents, Harry Rissik, burst into a discussion with the remark: 'In all my experience I have never seen anything like this. What are we? Rugby lovers or a lot of politicians? What is going on here tonight?'

According to the *Star*, it was 'the fight for the control of rugby in the Transvaal between the old administration and the new faction in the game which has sprung up in recent years'. It came to a head when Sanderson was re-elected president by defeating Oubaas Brink by 25 votes to 22. The result was greeted enthusiastically by the singing of 'For he's a jolly good fellow'.[35]

The heated political battle raged on almost to midnight with the anti-war delegates highly critical of old men administering the union. Dan de Villiers, who had worked closely with Stork, challenged the validity of the evening's voting. He listed his objections against both individuals and clubs, stating that the delegates of the New State Areas, Wanderers, Pirates and the Junior Rugby Sub-Union were not constitutionally present as members of the meeting and that Benoni and Brakpan had been unconstitutionally refuted the right of sending delegates to the meeting. He requested that the voting papers be kept and followed up on the matter at the first meeting of the newly elected committee.

Nelson lamented the fact that 'the three Wits delegates saw fit to side with the so-called "Nazi sympathisers" who had dragged the game into such disrepute during the war years'. He added: 'No worse start to any new season could possibly have been made and few would be sorry if the game were closed up altogether, until those thousands of splendid young rugby players who saw where their duty lay return to take charge as they assuredly will do.'[36]

At the end of March 1944, Diggers forwarded a letter to the union in which it was alleged that the election of office-bearers was unlawful and invalid, and asked the union 'to declare as elected those persons who would have been elected if there had not been an illegality, or to call a properly constituted meeting'.[37] On 3 April, a committee of the union decided by thirteen votes to seven not to accede to demands put forward by Dan de Villiers on behalf of Diggers.[38]

At a special meeting of the Diggers club held on 17 May, it was agreed by an overwhelming majority of votes to take steps to test the validity of the election of officials by the Transvaal RFU. Three representatives of the club, headed by the president, J.H. Lourens, were given power of attorney to act on behalf of the club and to take the issue to court if necessary. However, no financial obligations would be carried by Diggers and the three men themselves would carry costs.[39] Legal petitions to the Supreme Court for setting aside the elections at the annual meeting on 21 March were served on the president, vice-presidents and the Transvaal RFU by the Diggers RFC.[40]

The applicants were Lourens and 112 others. They contended that the election on 21 March of Sanderson as president and five others as vice-presidents was invalid. The respondents were the Transvaal RFU (Incorporated), Sanderson (president), I.G.C. Wright, I.B. de Villiers, M.A. Cooper, H. Rissik and C. Rose-Innes (vice-presidents) plus J.K. Jankowitz, I.J. Sendin and others.[41]

On 31 October 1944, an application came before Justice William H. Ramsbottom in the Supreme Court, Pretoria, to set aside the election of office bearers of the Transvaal RFU and to direct the union to hold a special meeting within a month to elect new office-bearers. G.A. Mulligan KC, with him J.F. Ludorf and P. Cillie (instructed by Messrs de Villiers and Gouws, Johannesburg, and Roger Dyason and Gie), appeared for the applicants. N.E. Rosenberg KC, with him A.F. Williamson (instructed by Hayman, Godfrey and Sanderson, Johannesburg, and Kraut, Hazelhurst and Hutchinson, Pretoria) represented the respondents.[42]

In his judgement on 22 December 1944, Justice Ramsbottom outlined the affairs of the union and how it was managed by a committee entrusted with wide powers. He went over the structure of the meeting of 21 March 1944 and noted the grounds on which the applicants were dissatisfied. He also pointed out that by order of the court the applicants had been given leave to amend the application by inserting the allegation that they were acting 'on behalf of themselves and of all members of the Transvaal Rugby Football Union' other than the respondents and by joining as the ninth respondents certain persons who were alleged to be members of New States Areas club.

Step by step, Justice Ramsbottom destroyed the applicants' case, as reported by the *Rand Daily Mail*:

Before the application came on for hearing, it was ascertained that many of the applicants were minors. There was nothing on the papers to show that any of these minors had the assistance or authority of his guardian to join in these proceedings. The applicants did not bring the proceedings in the name of the Diggers RFC and there was nothing to show that they were authorised to act for the club.

There was also nothing on the papers to support the allegation made by the amendment that the applicants were acting on behalf of 'all members of the Transvaal Rugby Union other than the respondents'.

The applicants claimed the right to prove that 'the Benoni and Brakpan clubs were senior affiliated clubs and that their delegates had the right to vote'. The judge was 'unable to understand how the applicants possess any such right' ... Whether or not such a claim should be persisted in is entirely a matter for the clubs concerned.

Concerning the complaint that the chairman had accepted the votes of the wrong Pirates delegates, the judge held that if this were correct the applicants did not have the right to have the election set aside on that ground. The complaint was not that the Pirates club ought to have been refused permission to vote, but that the wrong persons had exercised its voting rights. That seemed to be a domestic matter for the members of the Pirates Club.

Of H.B. Hockley of the junior sub-union, whether he was elected regularly or not, he was in fact elected chairman, and he remains chairman, until his election is set aside. Whether or not steps should be taken to set aside his election is a matter for the sub-union and apparently that body is satisfied with his election.

Regarding New State Areas, some of the members of the club were overseas on active service and could not easily be served. That may be the result and it may be unfortunate for the applicants, but if the rules of procedure and justice of the case require that the persons whose rights are being attacked should be parties to the litigation, and if the applicants are unable to bring them before the court, the litigation must fail. The addition of the ninth respondents in terms of the amendment to the petition does not constitute a joinder of the New States Club.[43]

On 23 December 1944, the application by J.H. Lourens and 112 other members of the Diggers RFC was dismissed with costs by Justice Ramsbottom.

A leader article in the *Rand Daily Mail* commented on the law and rugby:

It may even be that the frequency with which [the most eminent judges] are being called on to take part in South Africa's national sport is giving them a certain zest for a game which many of them had long thought to be beyond their reach. Rugby players should be warned that the process of taking rugby to court can easily become reciprocal, and that the law, in time, may go in for rugby.[44]

Two days after the judgement, 'the Boer Cattle Bonds Association received its first bill. It had to pay 650 pounds but had only 150 pounds in the bank.' They sought help from Dr Frikkie Kritzinger who paid the entire 650 pounds.[45] The rest of the debt was to be collected by Stork and his helpers through the Boer

Cattle Bonds. It took ten years, but there was compensation in that Diggers honoured Stork with life membership.

In the meantime, Pienaar had become impatient with the Western Province RFU and had taken steps towards accommodating dissentient clubs at the soonest possible opportunity. In early October 1944, a resolution was adopted by the SA Rugby Football Board which accepted the fact that unions 'who in accordance with their constitution have contributed to war funds were entirely within their rights'. But 'from 1 April 1945 no rugby funds shall be devoted to or contributed to any object save the game of rugby, its upkeep and development'. One day in a season, however, 'may be devoted to charitable objects and/ or war funds provided that no club or player shall be forced to participate'.

Pienaar's actions could have been influenced by his suggestion that 'the war might end before the beginning of the next season'.[46] The Western Province RFU initially opposed Pienaar's attempts to intervene on behalf of the secessionists but when the war ended, De Villiers did not adopt a vindictive attitude. At their meeting on 3 April 1945, he appealed for 'no dirty linen to be washed'.[47] Stellenbosch, Gardens, Paarl and Maitland were accordingly re-admitted to the Grand Challenge and Belville and False Bay were granted senior status.

For their part, Wits University's SRC had during 1944 undertaken an enquiry. Its president, Ian Welsh, said the impression created had been that the rugby club was associated with the Ossewabrandwag and that its representatives had acted unpleasantly at Transvaal RFU meetings. Correspondence had been received from prominent members of the club that Wits's representatives on the Transvaal RFU were not members of the university; that they sided with the anti-war faction at the general meeting; that a so-called Afrikaans caucus meeting involving Wits representatives was held at Helpmekaar before the union meeting of 21 March; and that Dan de Villiers participated prominently in a meeting of the Pirates Club.[48]

The SRC under Welsh was known to be 'anxious to appease the substantial, conservative, rugby-playing elements in its constituency' and had been involved in attempts to restore relations with Pretoria.[49] It was therefore keen to adopt a conciliatory stance in which allegations involving the Transvaal RFU would be considered unproven and forgotten.

De Villiers announced his resignation from the Wits committee on 21 March 1945. He was later appointed as Danie Craven's assistant manager on the Springbok team that toured Australia and New Zealand in 1956. Craven remained convinced that 'De Villiers had been put there by the Broederbond to keep an eye on him'.[50] The two men did not get on and one article stated De Villiers 'was christened "Dangerous Dan" by the media due to his unfriendly demeanour and his open attacks on both South African and New Zealand media for their reporting of the tour'.[51]

Sanderson would continue as president of the Transvaal RFU for another twenty years. When he retired at the age of seventy-five, he was succeeded by Jannie le Roux, one of Stork's former school pupils.

Notes

1   *Cape Times*, 18 May 1943.
2   F. Welsh, *A History of South Africa* (London: Harper Collins, 2000), 419.
3   *The Official Yearbook of the Union of South Africa 1946, XXIX* states 'a total of 334 324 South Africans were involved, made up of 211 193 whites and 123 131 coloureds, Indians and Africans'. Around 9 500 were killed in action.
4   *Cape Times*, 12 December 1940.
5   *The Star*, 23 April 1941.
6   Ibid., 24 April 1941.
7   Ibid., 29 April 1941.
8   Ibid., 25 April 1941.
9   *Rand Daily Mail*, 6 May 1941.
10   Ibid., 17 March 1942.
11   *The Star*, 21 June 1941. Transvaal won 27–11.
12   *The Star*, 24 March 1942.
13   A. Parker, *W.P. Rugby: Centenary 1883–1983* (Cape Town: WPRFU, 1983), 50.
14   Ibid.
15   *Die Burger*, 14 September 1942 (translated).
16   *Cape Times*, 15 September 1942.
17   Parker, *W.P. Rugby*, 50–51.
18   Ibid., 51.
19   *Cape Times*, 9 October 1942.
20   Ibid., 13 October 1942.
21   Ibid., 11 March 1943.
22   Ibid., 11 and 27 March 1943.
23   Ibid., 19 March 1944.
24   Parker, *W.P. Rugby*, 52.
25   Ibid., 52–53.
26   *Cape Times*, 18 May 1943; A. Grundlingh commented on Pienaar's statement: 'Although unintended, implicit in this was an important message for Afrikaners: unless they had full control of the various bodies involved in rugby, they would be unable to influence the wider social and political dimensions of the sport in South Africa'. A. Grundlingh, 'Playing for Power: Rugby, Afrikaner Nationalism and Masculinity in South Africa', in A. Grundlingh, A. Odendaal and B. Spies (eds), *Beyond the Tryline: Rugby and South African Society* (Johannesburg: Ravan Press, 1995), 121.
27   *Rand Daily Mail*, 29 March 1944.
28   G. Kotzé, 'Sportrevolusie en die Beesblaasbond', in Sport en Politiek, *Gelofteland*, 4 April 2012.
29   Ibid.
30   B. Murray, *Wits: The Open Years: A History of the University of the Witwatersrand, Johannesburg 1939–1959* (Johannesburg: Witwatersrand University Press, 1997), 89–90.
31   Minutes of the Wits University RFC, 15 March 1944. De Villiers became coach of the Under 19 side on 19 March 1942.
32   Kotzé, 'Sportrevolusie en die Beesblaasbond'.
33   Ibid. A 'rooinek' – 'red-neck' – originally referred to the sunburnt British soldier in the Anglo-Boer War but became a derogatory term for an English person or English-speaking South African.
34   *Rand Daily Mail*, 4 October and 24 November 1941.

35   *The Star*, 23 March 1944; *Rand Daily Mail*, 22 March 1944.
36   *Sunday Times*, 26 March 1944.
37   *The Star*, 1 April 1944.
38   Ibid., 17 April 1944.
39   J. Ferreira, J. Blignaut, P. Landman and J. du Toit, *Transvaal Rugby Football Union 100 Years* (Johannesburg: TRFU, 1989), 61.
40   *The Star*, 13 June 1944.
41   *Rand Daily Mail*, 23 December 1944.
42   *The Star*, 31 October 1944.
43   *Rand Daily Mail*, 23 December 1944.
44   Ibid., 25 December 1944.
45   Kotzé, 'Sportrevolusie en die Beesblaasbond'.
46   *Cape Times*, 6 October 1944.
47   Parker, *W.P. Rugby*, 57.
48   Minutes of the meeting of the Wits University RFC, 3 August 1944, during which Welsh spoke to club members. Minutes of club meetings in 1944 were recorded in Afrikaans.
49   Murray, *Wits: The Open Years*, 90.
50   P. Dobson, *Doc: The Life of Danie Craven* (Cape Town: Human & Rousseau, 1994), 115.
51   The 'McLook rugby collection' springbokrugby.webs.com; Introduction, 56; accessed 27 April 2020.

14

The Black Springboks

7 October 1950 breaks the dawn of a new era ... the
first Bantu XV in action against the first Coloured
XV – a milestone in the careers of both unions ...
a step of this nature has been long overdue.[1]

– Sipho M. Siwisa, President of the SA Bantu Rugby Board

The SA Coloured Rugby Football Board decided at its annual general meeting
in 1950 that it would like to play a match against the SA Bantu Rugby Board. It
was proposed that the fixture should take place in Port Elizabeth after the 1950
Rhodes Cup tournament.

The SA Bantu Rugby Board was keen to accept an arrangement that Vuyisa
Qunta described as rugby's 'turning point amongst people of colour'.[2] It not
only provided players with the opportunity to achieve national honours but also
served as preparation for the planned entry into formal international competition.

The SA Bantu Rugby Board's annual inter-provincial championship in July
1950 acted as an early trial for places in the national team. The selection process
was thorough and in the weeks before the Test at Port Elizabeth, two members of
the national rugby selection committee – Wilson Ximinya of Port Elizabeth and
L.P. Siya of East London – scoured the country in search of rugby talent.

A further trial for the Bantu team was held at Crown Mines on 24 September.
The full selection committee gathered: Ximinya; Siya; president of the SA Bantu
Rugby Board, Sipho M. Siwisa; the national secretary, Victor K. Ntshona; and
the appointed captain, Grant Khomo. They named the players for the final trial
at Port Elizabeth on Monday 2 October. After this last intensive examination, the
Bantu side was announced and remained in Port Elizabeth from 2 to 7 October
to prepare for the Test.[3]

Khomo was a respected figure in the sporting world. A Fort Hare graduate
and Border rugby player, he joined Orlando High School as a teacher and set

new standards for games. He 'lived and breathed sport. He believed in constant physical training.'[4] One of South Africa's finest all-rounders, he captained the national rugby and soccer teams and established himself as the country's tennis champion from 1945 to 1961.[5] Rugby's 'Rubber Man', Khomo was described as 'the one player to keep the spectators in the grandstand on their feet and opposition backs in particular on tenterhooks'.[6] In 1961, a *Zonk* magazine poll named him 'the greatest rugby player ever'.

The SA Coloured Rugby Football Board relied on the Rhodes Cup tournament to select their side. The competition was held in Port Elizabeth over six days, ending on Thursday 5 October. Immediately following the tournament, a civic reception was held at the New Brighton Social Centre where the representative team was announced.

The respective governing bodies introduced elaborate blazer badges. The SA Coloured Rugby Football Board chose two springboks in gold leaping towards the King Protea. The SA Bantu Rugby Board's emblem was the continent of Africa in black imposed upon a golden background. The springbok in gold was boldly featured across the continent.

A message from Sipho Siwisa was published on the eve of the match. In his enthusiasm he believed the event represented a chance 'to go into action, to save civilisation'. One reporter quoted part of Siwisa's statesmanlike address 'because it serves to show the approach of the African towards sport and the aim behind it':

> Genuine sportsmanship calls each nation like each individual to its highest destiny, breaks down the barriers of fear and greed, of suspicion and hatred. It can transcend conflicting political systems, and reconcile order and freedom, can rekindle true patriotism, can unite all citizens in the nation and all nations in the service of mankind.[7]

The historic first non-European Test match took place between the Coloured Springboks and the Bantu Springboks on 7 October 1950. Staging the game in Port Elizabeth was to the advantage of the Bantu XV as the city had been at the heart of the African game for more than sixty years. There were six Eastern Province and three Border players in their side. In contrast, the Coloured XV was drawn largely from the western Cape.[8]

The Test match started at 4.15 p.m. at Sydenham's agricultural showground. The slight wind was a welcome relief in the oppressive heat of the summer afternoon. The arena was packed, with hundreds of white rugby followers readily joining the record 13 000-strong crowd.

The coloured team wore green and gold and the Bantu XV players were resplendent in black and gold jerseys donated by the African Mutual Credit Association of Port Elizabeth. 'Both sides,' commented *Bantu World*, 'looked smart and confident as they lined up to be introduced to the mayor of Port Elizabeth, Boet Erasmus.' It was also the mayor's task to kick off the match.

In the first half, the two sides played with great caution. The coloured players led by Lawrence Erasmus were superior at forward and dominated the scrums. Their backline received a generous supply of possession but failed to take advantage. A reappraisal of tactics during the half-time huddle appeared to rectify the problem. Immediately after the resumption of play, their rapid wing Johnny Neethling scored a fine try that was not converted.

The Bantu Springboks equalised soon afterwards when full-back Frank Koka kicked a drop-goal. The pace of the game quickened, and each side opened up. Bantu winger Winty Pandle angled a grubber towards the opposition goal area. The crowd rose in anticipation but as he ran to touch down he was tackled without the ball. The referee awarded a penalty try, which was converted, taking the score to 8–3.

The coloured Springboks rallied and attacked strongly, making penetrative forays into the Bantu '25' area. Grant Khomo calmly marshalled his defence and they held on heroically. A relieving kick eventually enabled the Bantu Springboks to progress deep into their opponents' territory. Ngxatha Njengele, the well-built scrum-half, received the ball from a line-out on the coloured 25-yard line and forced his way through a phalanx of defenders to score a try, which was not converted. The coloured side were down 3–11 and it seemed as if a hard week of tournament rugby was beginning to tell.

Sensing a momentous victory, the Bantu XV dominated the last quarter with flashes of brilliant back-line play that caused considerable excitement amongst the spectators. A fine dash from mid-field by wing Foreman Skunana rounded off a neat line movement and secured another try for the Bantu. The conversion failed but the match was won 14–3.

The *Bantu World* report singled out the 'hefty forward, [Ben] Malamba, who was impressive and Koka at full-back gave a splendid performance which brought waves of applause from the crowd. The captain of the Bantu side Khomo was in solid form.'[9] There was also praise for Pandle, an attacking wing who would later play professional rugby league overseas. He was described as Port Elizabeth's 'master of the sidestep and the dance who had a reputation for living the high life in New Brighton township ... he set the local jazz evenings alight with his prowess in the local Kwela jive'.[10]

The SA Bantu Rugby Board believed the next step was international competition and that there should be a big drive to send a South African non-European representative team to meet the Maoris in New Zealand. *Bantu World* built up the excitement in heightened language:

> When the South African Bantu RFB met last month the eyes of the rugby sporting world were fixed on Port Elizabeth which was the venue of the meeting. The world awaited the decision of the Bantu board with anxiety. They wanted to know about the contemplated tour of New Zealand to play against the Maoris. The board had to decide whether in the light of the year's activities it was satisfied to carry on with the arrangements for the tour or not. It was also for the board to decide whether it was going to send a purely African side or a truly representative side of the non-European of this country.[11]

The coloured board indicated its readiness to cooperate and a jointly planned trip to New Zealand was scheduled to come off in 1952 if the necessary funds were available. *Bantu World* reported that 'donations were already forthcoming from sympathetic Europeans in the Cape and a good response was expected from the Rand'.[12]

By 1951, however, plans had changed, and the focus was no longer on a tour to New Zealand. Vuyisa Qunta reports that 'Eastern Province's Alfred Zilindile Lamani popularly known as "AZ" was involved in moves to send a black Springbok team to the South Pacific to play Fiji'. Officials anticipated that 1951 was going to be 'a big year for black Springbok rugby with the rugby hub that was Port Elizabeth being the venue for both the provincial tournament and the [second match of the] Test series'.[13]

The Manhattan Brothers, later to tour the world with Miriam Makeba, travelled from Johannesburg to entertain the crowds during the opening ceremony of the thirteenth inter-provincial tournament. A 'Golden Oldies' match featuring the Eastern Province African team of 1936 versus the Eastern Province Coloured XV of 1936 was also part of the celebrations. The tournament was held at New Brighton, Port Elizabeth from 30 June to 7 July, and was said to be the biggest ever staged by the board. Visitors booked their seats in advance of the opening day: season tickets were available at fifteen shillings from A.Z. Lamani of 12 Ruta Street.[14]

The rugby was a great success, especially for the home crowd. They saw Eastern Province win the Parton Cup knockout competition, beating Western Province 3–0 in the final, and then account for Transvaal 9–3 in the Native Recruiting Corporation (NRC) final, which was a curtain-raiser to the South African Bantu XV versus South African Coloured XV Test.

A crowd of 10 000 saw the second Test played between the two non-European boards. The SA Coloured Rugby Football Board had chosen their team after trials at Robertson. The team scored a decisive 12–3 victory at Port Elizabeth and scored four tries – two apiece by scrum-half Tommy Musson and wing Tony Lewis. On this occasion, the Bantu players found it difficult to play a Test immediately after a tournament.

A letter to the press complained about the team selection of the Bantu Springboks. It noted that the composition of the side favoured the eastern Cape players: there were nine Eastern Province representatives and three from Border, while Transvaal had two and Western Province one. The writer questioned whether it could be called a representative team.[15] The matter was at least partly addressed by the team's improved display in the return match, the first to be played at Green Point Track in Cape Town. Siwisa thought it 'was a grand finale to the season', the game being drawn 6–6 before 8 000 people.[16]

In 1952, the two non-European national boards formed the unified Non-European Rugby Football Federation, an inter-racial umbrella organisation. A constitution was drawn up and a joint board of control was established, with three officials from each of the two organisations. Sipho Siwisa was elected as president, with John Kester of the coloured board as vice-president. It was agreed that members from both boards should meet as a coordinating committee to select a representative side to tour Fiji and manage the £10 000 budget.

The newly formed Federation used the two Tests of 1952 – at the De Beers showgrounds, Kimberley, and Sydenham showgrounds, Port Elizabeth – as trial matches. After a thrilling 3–3 draw on the diamond fields, excitement surrounded the fifth rugby Test at Port Elizabeth in August 1952.[17] The coloured Springboks won 5–3 in front of a multiracial crowd of 15 000 to lead the series 2–1 with two drawn matches. A combined national team was chosen to tour South Africa in 1953 to raise funds for a Fijian venture. Heneke 'Baard' Daniels was named as captain with Jack Abrahams as manager. 'Pinky' Julius, who had taken part in the internal tour in 1939, was chosen as fly-half. An itinerary was drawn up for the tour, which was aimed at showcasing the talent of a unified non-racial team.

Progress had been made but the tour did not take place. In Qunta's assessment, the most common explanation 'amongst veterans is that of the combination of the newly-elected National Party, and increased participation by African "volunteers" in the defiance campaign against unjust laws organised by the ANC [African National Congress]'.[18] Rugby historian Harold Wilson saw the reason as being black opposition to tercentenary celebrations that commemorated the arrival of Jan van Riebeeck in 1652. He says this led to internal unrest, but he also blames the minister of internal affairs, Dr Eben Donges, for the cancellation of the tour as it was 'decreed that no team or person of colour would either enter South Africa or leave the shores of South Africa to participate in sport'.[19]

There were other factors to be considered. 'When the authorities denied A.Z. Lamani, the Non-European Rugby Football Federation organiser, a passport,' says Hendrik Snyders, 'the project was stopped in its tracks.'[20] The £8 000 tour guarantee demanded by the Fijians also posed a problem. Jeff Peires suggests that 'the career of Mr A.Z. Lamani of Port Elizabeth is illuminating. In 1951, Mr Lamani was assistant secretary of the SA Bantu Rugby Board. Two years later he was suspended following "discrepancies in the financial statement" of the 1951 tournament.'[21]

The scandal over finance contributed to the announcement that there would be no SA Bantu Rugby Board tournament in 1952. Siwisa asserted the decision was made by mutual consent of the parties involved. *Bantu World* responded: 'That in itself implies inter-alia, the long-desired rest from the strenuous journeys that delve deeply into the unwilling pockets of empty-handed provinces. It affords a period of reconstruction.'[22]

In 1954, Lamani challenged his suspension in the Supreme Court and since his application was unopposed, he was reinstated. 'Sadly enough,' says Peires, 'in that very year of his triumph, he was forced to resign from the presidency of his province when a financial statement tabled by him was declared by the treasurer S.T. Tshangana to be fraudulent.'[23]

A general meeting of the SA Coloured Rugby Football Board in 1954 urged the Non-European Rugby Football Federation to 'adopt a progressive policy by making its existence known by seeking formal recognition'. An attempt was made to contact Singapore, but little progress was made. It was 'further mandated to investigate the establishment of a formal relationship with Japanese rugby with a view to establish the "embryo of a new organisation" for those rugby-playing countries not affiliated to the IRB'.[24]

Evidence exists that Fiji was contacted through a J. Griffiths but generally the South Africans were unable to gain a foothold.[25] In an interesting assessment of the situation, Snyders concludes that 'the SA Coloured Rugby Football Board and SA Bantu Rugby Board followed a strategy of publicising their touring plans in order to raise awareness of their initiative [and] generate interest amongst both players and sponsors before initiating actual tour arrangements'.[26]

Non-European rugby suffered a series of rebuffs, but they were not the only sports body hoping to build unity whilst seeking to establish international contacts. During the same period, black cricket and soccer bodies started playing inter-racial matches and respectively formed the South African Cricket Board of Control (SACBOC) and the South African Soccer Federation. 'These moves,' explains André Odendaal, 'were in many ways similar to the multi-racial cooperation happening on a political level in the Congress Alliance during the 1950s.'[27]

SACBOC organised the Dadabhay Trophy tournaments, which were attended by African, coloured, Indian and Malay cricketers. There were some outstanding players, and during the early 1950s, SACBOC sought opportunities in the way of international contact. There were a series of disappointments before they eventually arranged international competition for their players against Kenya. Tests were played at home and then away when Basil D'Oliveira's South African side embarked on an historic tour to East Africa and Rhodesia.

According to Odendaal, rugby did not achieve 'the same level of inter-race cooperation as cricket in the 1950s and 1960s'. The Non-European Rugby Football Federation failed largely because of the lack of support from Kester and the coloured board's entrenched racial attitudes. Odendaal discloses:

> There were complaints that SA Coloured Rugby Board people were even unwilling to share change rooms and showers. Despite growing anti-apartheid struggles, ethnic feelings and an awareness of the other were still deeply ingrained. This also applied to the African rugby players.[28]

There were other grievances. The Western Province League was unhappy with the way the national body was controlled by its Kimberley-based leadership. They disliked the format of the unwieldy biennial mass tournament, and they called for a home-and-away system. The League was in itself a powerful organisation with 14 unions, nearly 200 clubs and 10 000 players, and it believed the time had come to gather support for a new national body.

During the same period, the SA Bantu Rugby Board faced up to its own challenging circumstances. The Native Recruitment Cup, the premier inter-provincial rugby trophy, was 'abandoned on the grounds that the mines were exploiting black labour'. It was replaced by the Zonk Trophy, presented by A.G. Lee of *Zonk* magazine, and played for the first time in Johannesburg in 1955 when Eastern Province defeated North-Eastern Districts 12–6 in extra-time.[29] The Parton Cup was competed for in all the inter-provincial tournaments, a total of 28 competitions between 1936 and 1973.

Govan Mbeki, writing in the *New Age* under the heading 'Special Branch Spied on Rugby Players', reported that the 1956 tournament arrangements in Port Elizabeth were upset by half a day when Native Affairs Department officials demanded that the 300-odd players 'had to straighten out their passes under the provisions of Section 10'. An official expounded: 'It is just a formality to comply with the regulations.' Yet Security Branch members had suspiciously booked into the same compartments as players from Transvaal and North Eastern Transvaal on the train journey to Port Elizabeth.[30] Petty apartheid was endured but did not curtail enthusiasm for the game.

Mbeki's son Thabo – the future president – was at school in the eastern Cape. Author Mark Gevisser provides a glimpse of the importance of rugby to young Africans by recalling Thabo Mbeki's determination to play the game:

> When he arrived at Lovedale, he was placed, along with the other Transkeians, in Shaw House. The Transkei boys were known as *moegoes* – country bumpkins – by the more sophisticated Eastern Cape city boys in other houses. The Transkei boys played soccer, the eastern Cape boys were devoted to rugby. Determined to shuck his *moegoeness*, Thabo Mbeki chose rugby, and doggedly stuck to it throughout his time at Lovedale, despite the fact that he was never very good at it; he never made it beyond the lower division.[31]

In 1957, the Africans staged their tournament in a reserve. 'That is taking the game to the people,' commented Robert Resha in the *New Age*. The venue was Umtata, Transkei, where Siwisa revealed the catering committee could get all it wanted 'from the local traders and farmers, from meat to vegetables – Umtata people are very generous'. The one disappointment was that Transvaal could not participate: 'They were suspended at the last tournament in Port Elizabeth pending payment of monies which the Board claimed they owed.'[32]

Despite Siwisa's efforts, all was not well in African rugby. An unsatisfactory state of affairs was summed up in a letter to *New Age* in August 1958:

> Sir
>
> When in 1956 S.M. Siwisa president of the Bantu Rugby Board said it was too soon for the Bantu Board to seek international recognition as they still required intensive organisation, I didn't know what he meant.
>
> But since attending a few of their meetings I find myself in agreement with his views ...
>
> Arguments at the meetings left one with the feeling that perhaps delegates came to tournaments with deep-seated wrath and vengeance against somebody or other.
>
> A great deal of lobbying goes on; telegrams, and trunk calls are used extensively and personal caucusing guides discussions.

The fate of our rugby is definitely not in the best hands. There is a great deal of emotion, but no constructive discussion. It is a case of support me here and I'll support you there. Western Province has a grudge against Eastern Province because they are the champions and the president came from Eastern Province.

If they cannot run their own board, how can they aspire to a higher organisation. So before we follow the cricket, soccer and table tennis unions we shall have to get fresh administration in various provinces.

VERA

New Brighton.[33]

Change was inevitable when Louis Leo Mtshizana, an East London lawyer, became president of the SA Bantu Rugby Board in 1958. He was an active opponent of racial segregation and objected to racial epithets, such as the derogatory reference to 'Bantu' in his organisation's name. At the NRC Cup inter-provincial tournament at Queenstown in 1959, he led the process of reconstituting the governing body as the SA African Rugby Board.

In the meantime, the Western Province League kept to their promise to form a new governing body. They boycotted the 1957 Rhodes Cup tournament and on 25 April 1958 disaffiliated from the SA Coloured Rugby Football Board. Led by Cuthbert Loriston, they formed the SA Rugby Football Federation at Paarl in January 1959. The new organisation started its own Gold Cup inter-provincial competition to run alongside the Zonk Trophy and the Rhodes Cup. The different competitions reinforced the divided landscape of South African rugby.

The overseas tour project was all but shelved but there was a sixth Test in 1957, which the coloured Springboks won 18–11 at Port Elizabeth. It was reported that the 'coloured forwards, spearheaded by the lively Eastern Province hooker Ralph Carolus, harassed the African backs and San King Mawing and Goolam Abed ran rings around their opponents'.[34]

Two dramatic and controversial encounters followed in 1959. The seventh match in the series was held at the Green Point stadium, Cape Town where there were more than 10 000 spectators. One report stated that 'play was of a high standard: brilliant long runs from the full-backs, a lot of burly bustling from the forwards and some classic passing movements by the backs'. The score was 3–3 at half-time with the Africans' best movement coming early in the second half. Jagger Nyamakazi burst through the ranks of the coloured forwards to set up Ntsikelelo Plaatjie who scored under the posts. Eric Majola converted, the score was 8–3 and the African supporters were confident of victory.

Play swung from one side to the other until Freddie Fredericks kicked the ball over the goal-line. Two players dived on the ball. The Africans thought that Modi Soga had touched down but the referee awarded Mawing a try. Players and spectators protested but the referee was not prepared to change his mind. The conversion was missed so the Africans were still in the lead 8–6. The next try was also controversial. Johnny Neethling was racing down the left wing when it seemed as if Majola had pushed him into touch. Neething kept running, the linesman's flag stayed down and the referee awarded the try. The angry crowd poured onto the field, but linesman Ismail 'Fatty' Bohardien was adamant that Neethling had not stepped out. Spectators, he said, had encroached on the field and shuffled back as Neethling approached. It gave the wrong impression: 'He wasn't out.'[35]

The second of the 1959 Tests was played in Johannesburg at the Western Native Township Oval. Hlanganyana Booi was magnificent at full-back for the Africans, but the match was marred by unpleasant fighting and a gale that blew over one set of goal-posts. There was also considerable excitement as the Africans strove mightily to match their opponents' score. Eventually, Thembile Sizani was able to score the equalising try late in the second half, but the conversion was missed and the honours were shared 3–3.

While rugby maintained its policy of inter-racial Tests, the cricket authorities had changed direction. A meeting of all affiliate boards of the parent SACBOC adopted a system of integrated provincialism that would result in racialism being abolished in 'non-white' cricket. It was argued that fragmentation of sides into Bantu, coloureds, Indians and Malays weakened black sport and played into the hands of pro-apartheid white bodies.

The newly formed SA Sports Association under Dennis Brutus observed the success of the SACBOC meeting and then used it against them. Brutus's fledgling organisation was able to prevent the West Indian tour that SACBOC had scheduled for 1959. Brutus believed the event was tacit acceptance of apartheid. If they accepted the West Indians, he thought they would lose credibility in their fight for a unified, non-racial cricket body in South Africa. The counter-argument projected by C.L.R. James was that a tour would have exposed weaknesses in the apartheid structure, thereby creating serious difficulties and embarrassment for the South African government.[36]

Rugby officials revived their efforts to organise an overseas tour. In 1960, legendary rugby figure Noortjie Khan and members of the Western Province Coloured Rugby Football Union (RFU) met informally with representatives of the All Blacks' touring team, including the assistant manager Jack Sullivan. They discussed the possibility of a tour to New Zealand and Fiji and were informed the matter would be taken up with the manager, Tom Pearce. He subsequently denied that talks were held.[37] John Kester, president of the SA Coloured Rugby Football Board, later met with Danie Craven but they were unable to make headway on the issue of a tour.

There were no rugby Tests in 1960, largely because Mtshizana was preoccupied with more pressing matters. Following the shootings at Sharpeville and the declaration of a state of emergency, he was involved in representing political detainees. Brutus also urged him not to play inter-racial matches, a view that he supported. In 1961, Mtshizana argued that the only way forward was to 'emerge from our racial kraals and form a truly representative organisation, an organisation open to all racial groups on this basis of equality'.[38] His plea went unanswered. In the same way that Basil D'Oliveira and SACBOC opposed Brutus, so did the majority of black rugby players when it came to internal Test matches.

Wilson suggests that the 1960s 'ushered in a period of friendlier relations' in matters concerning rugby. After the internal conflict of the past few years, it was encouraging that the four national bodies entered into negotiations in order to establish one unified rugby organisation. 'The SA Coloured Rugby Football Board,' recounts Wilson, 'could have succeeded in merging with the SA Bantu Rugby Board but it was too obsessed with luring the Federation back into its fold and thus missed a golden opportunity to forge a powerful disadvantaged bloc.'[39]

When the ninth Test was played at Green Point in 1961, the African Springboks emerged triumphant 12–6 in front of another large crowd of 12 000. After the provincial success in the previous year, the national victory was a welcome boost for African rugby. It was also significant that Eric Majola should play a lead role. An *Imvo Zabantsundu* report claimed their Eastern Province star was regarded by most South African critics as the country's best fly-half since the days of Hansie Brewis.[40]

Also impressive was Majola's trusted half-back partner, Simo Mjo, a talented member of the community. He started the East London Harmony Set, which performed compositions of African musical greats as well as European classics, and became the first black actor to feature in East London's Guild Theatre when he participated in a drama adapted from John Steinbeck's *Of Mice and Men*.[41] Interested in politics, he developed an early loyalty to the ANC and was imprisoned for furthering the aims of the banned organisation.

There were some grand players in the eastern Cape at that time, such as centre Jimmy Nomo, wing Phildon Kona and Mjo's fellow political activist, Sobhizana Mngqikana, who was later incarcerated on Robben Island. The story goes that when Mngqikana once ran at the Eastern Province defence in the closing stages of a tense final at Walter Rubusana Park, the crowd swayed in unison with his 'outward jink, his inward jink ... and as he beat the defence on the outside, they danced with such gusto that the scaffolding stand collapsed'.[42]

Some notable forwards appeared during the same period. Dumile Kondile, later a judge, and Mpenduli Ntshongwana were brilliant performers for Border and Fanie Headbush, who was especially effective in combination with Robert Maduba, Melody Madikane and Eric Rula, was a feared opponent from Eastern Province.[43]

The 1961 season saw the return of A.Z. Lamani, who had maintained his involvement in African rugby through the Port Elizabeth and Districts Rugby Board. This allowed him to secure his former secretarial position in which he could oversee the 1961 inter-provincial tournament. 'Strangely,' says Peires, 'at the end of the tournament he failed to present a financial statement. That finally ended his career in rugby administration ... but his talents were not altogether lost to his people. He subsequently became a minister in the Ciskeian government.'[44]

In 1963, the three black national bodies held discussions about unity, but there was little progress. Mtshizana's involvement in politics as a member of the Non-European Unity Movement caused complications as he was being closely monitored. In June 1963, he was served with three banning orders and confined to the East London Magisterial District. This led to his suspension from the SA African Rugby Board by nine votes to six. By 1965, Mtshizana was arrested under the Suppression of Communism Act and sentenced to imprisonment on Robben Island as prisoner 369/65.[45]

In the meantime, the Springbok sides of the SA Coloured Rugby Football Board and the SA African Rugby Board played their tenth Test in 1963. Danie Craven was at Green Point amidst 'rows and rows of red fezzes' to see the talented Newell High schoolboy Glenn Scott feature in a sparkling African backline that was instrumental in the side winning 9–3. Craven was impressed by 'the handling and passing of the Africans and their joyful exuberance after scoring a try. He was particularly taken with the play of Wete Nqontsi and Phakamile Lubambo and the speed of Phildon Kona on the wing.'[46]

Thereafter the African Springboks revelled in an unprecedented flurry of Test matches in the latter part of the 1960s. This resulted from the additional involvement of the SA Rugby Football Federation. Damoo 'Benny' Bansda, writing in the *Cape Times*, in 1964, thought the Federation had 'proved themselves to be a strong body in their five years of existence and this was aptly proved in their Test win against the Africans'.[47] The Federation's 25–8 victory on a Wednesday in late September was followed by a weekend match when they met the SA Coloured Rugby Football Board. The contest between 'coloured' teams drew considerable interest amidst the ongoing tension that emanated from the Federation's breakaway.

The Board, with eleven Western Province players, wore their traditional green and gold; the Federation appeared in gold with green collars and cuffs. The latter, spearheaded by Jack Juries, delighted the record crowd with their rugby and were clearly the better side on the day. Paul Dobson noted:

> The star of the match was Hannes Ontong on the right wing for the Federation. He scored three tries, two of them from runs of over 60 yards. When he scored the third in the second half, he was kicked on the head and taken to hospital. He never recovered fully. The score was only 14-9, but in fact Federation scored four tries, the fourth by Maurice Heemro, to the one by Ismail Arendse after a break by Dennis Jacobs.[48]

The two sides did not meet again, but the Africans were unaffected by this decision. They continued to meet both coloured teams in keenly contested encounters. During an eventful long weekend in September 1965, Rex Giladile at full-back starred for the Africans on the Saturday but they went down 14–11 to the SA Coloureds who were inspired by Salie Fredericks. The Africans made five changes to their team and outclassed the Federation 20–6 on the Monday. They played adventurous rugby with Phildon Kona, Goods Lonzi and Stanford Mzanywa scoring memorable tries. Peter Mkata, a talented twenty-year-old from Port Elizabeth, fast and elusive at fly-half, centre or full-back, made his debut when the African Springboks were beaten 8–6 in their twelfth match against the SA Coloured Rugby Football Board at East London in October 1965. The conditions were dreadful after three days of continuous rain, but there was a large crowd as a Test had not previously been played in East London. Permission to play the match was obtained from the Department of Community Development, but white spectators were turned away because they had not been issued permits.[49]

The same season, the City and Suburban union expressed their opposition to the concept of racial matches. They were suspended for a year by the Federation for 'deliberate defiance of authority'. Although that sentence was suspended, City and Suburban decided to leave the parent body. They joined the SA Coloured Rugby Football Board, which changed its name to the SA Rugby Union (SARU) in 1966. It dropped the racial designation it had carried since its foundation in 1897 and, in a significant move, forbade its clubs to play those of the Federation.

In 1966, the Federation defeated the Africans 11–8 in the sand of the Huguenot sports field at Paarl and 24–6 at New Brighton. Finding somewhere to play in Port Elizabeth posed a problem because the Group Areas Act had designated the preferred venue, the showgrounds, as a white area and there was a jazz festival at Wolfson Stadium. Eventually, the match was played at Kwaford Stadium, New Brighton, where drum majorettes created a festive atmosphere.[50]

The Africans came back with a vengeance in 1967. Under the captaincy of Western Province loose-head Phillip Danster, they made a clean sweep of three Tests, two against the Federation (8–6 at Paarl and 13–6 at Port Elizabeth) and one against the newly named SARU (9–3 at Green Point).[51] A brilliant drop-goal from the halfway line by Federation's Vernon Brinkhuis was a highlight before 15 000 spectators at Paarl. But Norman Mbiko's drop-goal seven minutes before the final whistle won the match for the Africans. Wonder Nqxila scored a hat-trick of tries at Port Elizabeth in a season in which the African Springboks were better prepared, a development also reflected by the decision to take the field with badges on their jerseys. The reason they had not done so in the past was purely financial.

The SA African Rugby Board produced a new emblem in 1968 with the springbok leaping across a map of South Africa. They played seven further Tests against teams from the Federation and SARU from 1968 to 1969. The Africans won five of the matches. They went down heavily 40–19 to SARU at Green Point in 1969 but won the return fixture 9–8 at Wolfson Stadium, Port Elizabeth. Similarly, they defeated Federation 28–15 at Wolfson Stadium in 1968 and 14–8 at the same venue the following year but were well beaten 28–3 at Paarl in 1969.

The last meeting between the Africans and SARU was played under floodlights at Green Point at the end of August 1970. Snyders suggests that their intention was to win the respect of the New Zealand All Blacks, who were touring South Africa at the time. The fixture was arranged to coincide with the visit of the tourists to Cape Town, but the event did not unfold as planned. The All Blacks failed to make an appearance and the rugby was summed up by the *Cape Herald* headline 'SARU Beat Africans in Very Poor Game'. The newspaper commented: 'If this was supposed to be a demonstration to the visiting All Blacks of our non-white rugby strength, thank heaven the All Blacks did not turn up.'[52]

The failure of the 'exhibition' Test and the subsequent press coverage resulted in SARU reassessing its position in rugby. They questioned their own participation in the playing of ethnic Tests and firmly committed themselves to non-racial rugby. This involved the targeted principle of a non-racial representative South African team based on merit selection. By severing links, SARU ended hopes of a united non-racial bloc to challenge establishment rugby. The SA African Rugby Board and the SA Rugby Football Federation continued to play Test matches until 1978.

The Rhodes Cup tournament was played through the 1950s and 1960s. The format changed at various stages but for the most part, a biennial competition was maintained. The winning teams were Eastern Province (1950, 1965), South-Western Districts (1953), Western Province (1955, 1959, 1961, 1963 shared, 1969), Transvaal (1957), North Western Cape (1963 shared) and City and Suburban (1967). As a result of City and Suburban's criticism of Rhodes for his 'discriminatory and unfair' practices, the Rhodes Cup was withdrawn after 1969.[53] The SA Cup was introduced in 1971, although one further Rhodes Cup tournament was played in 1980 for 'second-tier' teams. It was won by Western Province Country.

The Tests played during the 1950s and 1960s were remarkable as they were staged at a time when the apartheid government enforced segregation and set up separate political institutions for the so-called coloured, Indian and African 'nations'. They were also years of repression, with the National Party creating widespread resentment through the forced removals under the Group Areas Act. That communities should be uprooted and resettled in areas such as the Cape Flats had a severe impact on sport as clubhouses and playing fields were lost and long-settled communities broken up.

Notes

1   Message from S.M. Siwisa in the 1950 Rhodes Cup brochure; *Bantu World*, 27 January 1951.
2   V. Qunta, 'The African Springboks', D. Cruywagen (ed.), in *The Badge: A Centenary of the Springbok Emblem* (Newlands: SA Rugby, 2006), 146.
3   *Bantu World*, 30 September 1950.
4   J. Schadeberg (ed.), *The Fifties People of South Africa* (Johannesburg: J.R.A. Bailey, 1987), 132.
5   M. Morapeli, 'The Rock: The History of Orlando High School 1939–1984' (unpublished master's thesis, University of the Witwatersrand, Johannesburg, 1984), 40.
6   *Bantu World*, 12 July 1947.
7   *Bantu World*, 27 January 1951; the quote was taken from the 1950 Rhodes Cup brochure.
8   The crowd has also been quoted as 13 000 and 15 000. The teams were as follows:
Coloured: R. Poggenpoel, A. Abed, J. Neethling, E. Clarke, A. Lewis, L. Erasmus (captain), A. Samaai, R. Malghas, S. Jacobs, I. Davids, J. Julius, M. Daniels, C. Said (vice-captain), S. Hopley and M. Agherdien.
Bantu: F. Koka, F. Skunana, G. Khomo (captain), R. Kota, W. Pandle, A. Tsendze, N. Njengele, M. Zinto, S. Ntshepe, G. Mnyute, E. Hini, M. Vabaza, D. Mbane, B. Malamba and S. Dingaan (vice-captain).
9   *Bantu World*, 14 October 1950. 'Khomo' was at times spelt 'Kgomo'.
10   Qunta, 'The African Springboks', 148, 150. 'Pandle' was at times spelt 'Phandle'.
11   *Bantu World*, 27 January 1951.
12   Ibid., 30 September 1951.
13   Qunta, 'The African Springboks', 147.
14   *Bantu World*, 19 May 1951.
15   Ibid., 15 September 1951.
16   Ibid., 5 April 1952.
17   On leaving Kimberley, the Bantu Springboks beat Transvaal 11–0 in a fund-raising match during a short tour.
18   Qunta, 'The African Springboks', 148.

19 H. Wilson, 'Separated by Race', in D. Cruywagen (ed.), *The Badge: A Centenary of the Springbok Emblem* (Newlands: SA Rugby, 2006), 127, 130.
20 H. Snyders, 'Rugby, National Pride and the Struggle of the Black South Africans for Recognition, 1897–1992', in *Sporting Traditions*, 32, 1 (2015), 108.
21 J. Peires, 'Rugby in the Eastern Cape: A History', in *Work in Progress*, 17 (1981), 6.
22 *Bantu World*, 5 April 1952.
23 Peires, 'Rugby in the Eastern Cape', 6.
24 Snyders, 'Rugby, National Pride and the Struggle', 108.
25 Wilson, 'Separated by Race', 127.
26 Snyders, 'Rugby, National Pride and the Struggle', 107, Note 43.
27 A. Odendaal, 'The Thing that is Not Round', in A. Grundlingh, A. Odendaal and B. Spies (eds), *Beyond the Tryline: Rugby and South African Society* (Johannesburg: Ravan Press, 1995), 51. The ANC had formed the Congress Alliance with pro-democracy Indian, coloured and white groups in order to create a broader front against apartheid.
28 A. Odendaal, *The Story of an African Game: Black Cricketers and the Unmasking of One of Cricket's Greatest Myths, South Africa, 1850–2003* (Cape Town: David Philip, 2003), 157; Odendaal, 'The Thing that is Not Round', 52.
29 P. Dobson, *Rugby in South Africa: A History 1861–1988* (Cape Town: SARB, 1989), 203.
30 Odendaal, *The Story of an African Game*, 160; *New Age*, 12 July 1956.
31 M. Gevisser, *Thabo Mbeki: The Dream Deferred* (Johannesburg: Jonathan Ball, 2007), 90.
32 *New Age*, 20 June 1957. The tournament was played during 29 June to 7 July.
33 Ibid., 14 August 1958.
34 S. Carmichael (ed.), *112 Years of Springbok Tests and Heroes* (Cape Town: SA Rugby Football Union, 2003), 96.
35 Odendaal, *The Story of an African Game*, 157–158; A. Booley, *Forgotten Heroes: History of Black Rugby 1882–1992* (Cape Town: Manie Booley Publications, 1998), 20; Carmichael, *112 Years of Springbok Tests*, 102.
36 J. Winch, 'Should the West Indies have Toured South Africa in 1959? C.L.R. James versus Learie Constantine', in B. Murray, R. Parry and J. Winch (eds), *Cricket & Society in South Africa 1910–1971; From Union to Isolation* (London: Palgrave Macmillan, 2018), 275–306.
37 *The Star*, 2 and 5 August 1960.
38 Odendaal, 'The Thing that is Not Round', 54.
39 Wilson, 'Separated by Race', 134.
40 Odendaal, *The Story of an African Game*, 157; *Imvo Zabantsundu*, 17 January 1959.
41 *Grassroots Rugby*, 18 June 2013.
42 Qunta, 'The African Springboks', 155–156.
43 *Weekend Argus*, 8 October 2011.
44 Peires, 'Rugby in the Eastern Cape', 6.
45 Dobson, *Rugby in South Africa*, 211; Odendaal, 'The Thing that is Not Round', 54.
46 Carmichael, *112 Years of Springbok Tests*, 126.
47 *Cape Times*, 1 October 1964.
48 Dobson, *Rugby in South Africa*, 179.
49 Carmichael, *112 Years of Springbok Tests*, 141.
50 Ibid., 143.
51 Dobson, *Rugby in South Africa*, 213; Qunta, 'The African Springboks', 157.
52 Snyders, 'Rugby, National Pride and the Struggle', 112; *Cape Herald*, 29 August 1970.
53 Carmichael, *112 Years of Springbok Tests*, 353, 357.

15

Veritable Tom Browns to Springboks

> It is an evil day for South African rugby when the
> country has had to seek its rugby captain from beyond
> its borders in the territory of a strange land.[1]
>
> – *Die Transvaler*

In 1890, the British South Africa Company established a new colony in the region between the Limpopo and Zambezi rivers. It became known as Rhodesia and represented further expansion of the English-speaking world. Robert Blake describes the 1890 pioneers as the heirs to a tradition of European adventure that began in the fifteenth century. If these men had been 'endowed with the gift of prevision,' he says, 'they would have seen themselves as the last European colony of settlement ever to be established – unless one counts Israel, as some people might.'[2] The Pioneer Column aimed to take advantage of the fabled riches of ancient Ophir in the course of a venture that Cecil John Rhodes hoped would redress the balance of power in the subcontinent by tilting it in favour of the Cape and against the Transvaal.

Rhodes asked Frederick Courteney Selous to guide the expeditionary force. The famous hunter had entered Rugby School in 1866 and was, says his biographer, Stephen Taylor, 'a veritable Tom Brown'.[3] At Rugby, Selous was a member of the first cricket team and the youngest boy ever to be honoured with a (football) house cap.[4] For nearly twenty years, he travelled extensively north of the Limpopo River and knew the area better than anyone. Robert Cary describes him as 'an excellent publicity factor. A national figure of almost transparent honesty, he gave the whole expedition that aura of respectability which Rhodes needed so badly in his dealings with the British government and the liberal elements in London.'[5]

There was disagreement over the hunter's view that 'a large sector of Mashonaland was not within [King] Lobengula Khumalo's gift ... [the Matabele] are no more aborigines of the country they now occupy than the Romans were aborigines of Britain'.[6] It was a view that Rhodes had to oppose because the Moffat Treaty 'made it a matter of record that Lobengula's domain consisted not of Matabeleland but also of Mashonaland'. Rhodes argued that if 'the Mashona were independent of Lobengula, then it made matters a great deal easier for the Portuguese to move in'.[7]

The full expeditionary force amounted to about 1 000 men as the pioneers were accompanied by a police escort. There were 2 000 applicants for the Pioneer Column's 200 places. Athletic distinction was especially valued in the selection process, with early advertisements also calling for men 'who could ride and shoot'. Rhodes wanted the right balance of people; a community prepared to settle and build up the country. It suited him that young men from 'good families' supported his venture. He told Frank Johnson, leader of the Pioneer Corps, that if there was an attack by the feared Matabele, it would be 'the influential fathers of the young men' who would exert pressure on the British government to provide support.[8]

The first game of rugby to be played in the northern hinterland was staged on the eve of the great undertaking, and at the mercy of King Lobengula.[9] It was played on the dry riverbed of the Shashi, a sandy stretch some 500 yards wide. The 'B' Troop under Skipper Hoste challenged the rest who were made up of the general Pioneer Corps and the 'A' Troop of the Police. There were some fine players involved: Louis Vintcent had played for Transvaal and Adrian Darter and Charlie van der Byl for Western Province in the first inter-provincial tournament to be held in South Africa in 1889. The 'overseas' contingent included Edward Pocock, who had represented Scotland in a rugby victory over England in their first fifteen-a-side international in 1876/77.[10]

A field was quickly marked out, and sweating bodies were soon floundering in ankle-deep sand. It was hard work but failed to detract from the enjoyment. Darter wrote about the match in *Pioneers of Mashonaland*: 'Louis Vintcent captained the Pioneers and Charlie van der Byl the Police. It was a well-contested game and we ['B' Troop] won by a try which I secured for our side. I endeavoured to convert, but my place-kick was a hopeless failure.'[11]

The next day the column entered Matabele territory. 'In the eyes of the local Shona and Ndebele,' says James Muzondidya, 'it was an 'invading force.'[12]

Blake comments that there were at least those who 'had a streak of idealism … The concept of timid Mashona being in a perpetual state of terror from Matabele raids, however partial a picture this now seems, did have its effects. Some of the Pioneers believed that they were bringing progress and protection to depressed and downtrodden races.' Some of them, in the words of Philip Mason, 'were romantics with the strenuous Puritan romanticism of the Victorians, of Charles Kingsley and Arnold of Rugby'.[13]

On receiving news that the Pioneers had reached Fort Salisbury, Rhodes handed a telegram to his secretary, William Milton, with the characteristic remark, 'My young men have got the country.'[14] The 'invaders' were just in time for a horrific rainy season accompanied by swarms of mosquitoes and men succumbed to malaria. Rugby was not played until 1892 when Captain H.J. Borrow and his brother-in-law, Jack Spreckley, organised Fort Salisbury's first fixture between Home-born and Colonials at the 'Ranche' in Johnson's backyard.

In 1893, Dr Leander Jameson decided not only to stop the bloodshed caused by inter-tribal strife but to open up Matabeleland. It would 'give us a tremendous lift in shares and everything else'. The Matabele were easily conquered through the use of the Maxim gun, and Jameson's triumphant force entered their deserted kingdom.[15]

Most of the white troops stayed on in Bulawayo and a burgeoning town emerged. Within months, rugby and cricket were thriving on land generously allocated to newly formed clubs. The organisation of games was quickly institutionalised through the clubs and regular competitions. Bulawayo citizens presumptuously set up the Rhodesian Rugby Cup competition and awaited Salisbury's entry. They also asserted their growing authority by forming the Rhodesia Rugby Football Union (RFU) and affiliating to the SA Rugby Football Board in 1895.

Progress was interrupted by the disastrous Jameson Raid of 1895/96. The repercussions for all concerned were immense because the defeat of the raiders led to members of the Rhodesian police force being trapped in the Transvaal. The Matabele were not slow to take advantage. They were an unhappy people because calamities such as drought, swarms of locusts and an epidemic of the dreaded rinderpest occurred at a time when they were 'chafing under the man-made exactions' of the English-speaking intruders from the south.[16] They struck suddenly and dramatically in late March 1896. The town retreated into a laager for two months whilst more than 5 000 Matabele warriors infiltrated the neighbourhood.

Late in May, Rhodes's reinforcements linked up with a column sent out from Bulawayo. The Matabele fled to the Matopos hills, but even before their resistance had been quelled, Rhodes was making moves to restructure the administration. Milton was contacted to reorganise the civil service.[17] In 1897, he was appointed Rhodesia's acting administrator, and within four years the entire administrative establishment was unified in his hands. The Order in Council gave the administrator considerable authority as he presided over both the executive and legislative councils. Milton also headed the civil service and native affairs and was, therefore 'responsible for two separate administrative systems which corresponded with the division of the country into "two nations"'.[18]

As Rhodesia was in many respects a northward expansion of the Cape, Milton took advantage of the situation in importing experienced men. The new arrivals who modelled the Rhodesian civil service on that of the Cape 'soon gave an entirely different tone to the administration', one that 'lacked the distinctive British upper-class background which came to characterise the administrative machine in tropical dependencies like Nyasaland'.[19] It was observed that sport was the principal qualification of Milton's civil service appointees, a development that stemmed from his belief that 'employers and heads of department would find that if they have a good player in their employ, he will be a good worker as well'.[20] His methods were justified by the strong administrative and judicial systems that were created.[21]

The arrival of the railway line at Bulawayo in 1897 opened new opportunities for the sporting community. The following year, Rhodesia entered the Currie Cup rugby competition. The venture owed much to the inspirational Tom Brown Hepburn whose parents had been drawn to the moral fervour of Thomas Hughes's famous story when christening their son. The Reverend James Hepburn was an influential missionary to Chief Khama in Bechuanaland and young Tommy was brought up in Shoshong but learnt to play rugby at George Watson's College, Edinburgh.[22] After representing South Africa in 1896, he moved to Bulawayo and joined the Native Affairs Department. Several South African players who had participated in the same Test series against the British followed Hepburn. They included Francis Myburgh, Hamish 'Spanner' Forbes, Sonny Taberer, Ben Andrews and 'Patats' Cloete. There was no coordinated plan to strengthen Rhodesian rugby and the players branched out far and wide on arrival, making their homes in Bulawayo, Selukwe, Salisbury and Umtali.

The 1898 Rhodesian touring team exceeded expectations, drawing with the mighty Transvaal and defeating Eastern Province and the Orange Free State. Glowing accounts of their achievements appeared in the local press and sporting heroes emerged. Hepburn was a tower of strength, ably assisted by Colin Duff, a former Western Province player whose transfer to Rhodesia had been arranged by Milton. A huge welcoming reception greeted the side on their return to Bulawayo station. It was headed by Percy Ross Frames, the first president of the SA Rugby Football Board, (1889–93) and later a member of Milton's legislative council.[23]

A Rhodesian rugby team entered the Currie Cup again in 1899. The shadow of the Anglo-Boer War was already spreading across the country and a somewhat depleted entry of four teams competed in the rugby. It was a tournament that

Balfour Helm – son of Hope Fountain missionaries – might have helped the Rhodesians win. The opening match against Eastern Province was lost 9–11 but the final whistle went as Helm failed to gather a pass with the line at his mercy. Rhodesia subsequently beat Border 31–0 (Colin Duff kicking four drop-goals) and drew 0–0 against Griqualand West.[24]

The protracted Anglo-Boer War that 'tarnished the glamour of empire' was largely peripheral because Rhodesia was never invaded.[25] There was nevertheless terrible uncertainty within the country where 1 000 Afrikaners were viewed with suspicion, and there was general relief that war did not appeal to African leaders.[26] Rhodesia 'contained a very high proportion of young men trained in the use of arms, familiar with horsemanship and veld-lore, with the result that by 1900 something like 1 700 men had gone to war, out of a total white population of little more than 11 000'.[27]

Rugby continued nonetheless and Milton was elected president of the Rhodesia RFU in 1900. During the year, a New Zealand team drawn from men in the services visited Bulawayo and beat a Matabeleland XV 10–3.[28] Milton then established inter-provincial rugby in 1901 when tribal imagery was invoked through Hepburn's Matabeleland challenging Mashonaland. Ten days were allocated to the outward journey of the last sporting trip made by mule-drawn coaches. The Mashonaland side included two South African internationals, fly-half Francis Myburgh (four years later, a member of the legislative council) and centre Sonny Taberer (the chief native commissioner). In a hard-fought clash, Hepburn proved the difference between the teams. He scored three tries, the last from an intercept on his 25-yard line, to help Matabeleland win 16–0.[29]

The Anglo-Boer War ended on 31 May 1902. Rhodesia struggled financially in its aftermath, presenting a difficult period for Milton who had been appointed administrator in January 1901. After twelve years of Company administration, the lack of commercial and industrial development in the territory could not be disguised and there were difficulties in recruiting and retaining labour at cheap enough rates. There was also the serious task of overcoming the loss of Rhodes, who had died on 26 March 1902. The territory had 'become virtually an absolute monarchy with [Rhodes] as king'.[30]

Although Milton rarely had time to take an interest in sporting matters, he was happy to attend a game in Bulawayo in 1903. It was Freddie Brooks's first inter-provincial appearance for Mashonaland and partnering him at centre was Milton's son Cecil, who was home for the summer holiday before moving on to the Camborne School of Mines. The matches were played against Matabeleland on a Saturday and Monday, with the opening game highlighted by Cecil Milton making 'the most brilliant dash of the day three minutes before the end to seal victory'. Two days later, offices and stores closed as people streamed into Queens to witness a second epic struggle that was decided by an individualistic try from Brooks.[31]

Three years later, Brooks and Cecil Milton played for England. The former had not met South Africa's new five-year residential qualification and, instead, played against the Springboks at Twickenham. Brooks's achievement was a talking point when the imperial government applied pressure on Milton senior to merge Rhodesia with the powerful neighbour in the 'Union of South Africa'. Milton deflected their demands, stating that he was unable to express a firm opinion.[32] Unification was an important issue but Rhodesia's interest in joining the union was at best marginal.[33]

The SA Rugby Football Board put forward its plan for accelerating the 'unification' process by making the impractical suggestion that Rhodesia should be merged into Griqualand West's rugby.[34] The board paid little heed to the fact that the game gave white Rhodesia a sense of national worth and that its teams travelled great distances to hold their own against South Africa's best sides. Within Rhodesia, there was widespread diffusion of a sport that appealed to the aggressive masculinity of the rural white settlements. Comment on a match at the mining town of Eiffel Flats, for example, recalled that wagon journeys might force men to inhale 'several cubic yards of dust and defeats might be heavy against men of unexpected physique, but a bath, a good dinner, drinks, speeches and songs made for an enjoyable day'.[35]

When the British rugby team visited Bulawayo in 1910, the Rhodesian captain, H.O. Coker, was openly critical of the SA Rugby Football Board. His main objection was that Rhodesia had played just one match against the visiting British team. The tourists readily supported him in stressing the lack of 'fair play from the strongest centres in South Africa' – an argument that might have been justified but Rhodesians were reliant on their neighbour.[36] Profits accrued through rugby's Currie Cup participation and international tours were of great importance to their limited sporting coffers.[37]

In 1911, Milton established a 'responsible position' in the Company for Anthony Henniker-Gotley who arrived in Bulawayo a matter of weeks after captaining England to victory over Scotland.[38] By the end of June, the *Bulawayo Chronicle* boasted, 'South Africa has no half to show of the English crack's quality.'[39] At the same time, John Hopley, the former English forward, played for Mashonaland. He had attended Harrow and Cambridge and gained further fame when he won the British amateur heavyweight boxing title – Denzil Batchelor described him as 'the most outstanding heavyweight boxer of his day, amateur or professional'.[40]

Mashonaland defeated Matabeleland 23–3 in their first encounter of the 1911 season. Hopley 'went into the fray like a gladiator' in a match won by the forwards. Bulawayo, however, emerged on top in the return fixture 5–4 – Gotley 'transferring to his backs with beautiful precision'. The *Bulawayo Chronicle* proffered the view that it was 'a pity we couldn't send a side to Newlands for it is beyond question that at the moment rugger here is better than it has ever been'.[41]

Prospects continued to improve in other areas as the Company's annual report showed a substantial surplus in revenue over expenditure. That was the condition defined by Rhodes as justifying the white population's claim to responsible government, although it was considered advisable 'to abide under Company rule till they had won political independence'.[42] The country was increasingly known as Southern Rhodesia, the designation adopted in 1901 as a result of developments taking place in the two territories north of the Zambezi. They were amalgamated in 1911 and, at the end of the rugby season, Gotley was transferred to Northern Rhodesia.[43]

In 1912, the Currie Cup gave way to a week's trials in Cape Town from which a Springbok side was selected to tour overseas.[44] It became apparent that Grahamstown-born Hopley was looked upon as a possible captain of the touring squad. He led sides during the week and played in the main game on the last day. Letters to the press also indicated that he was favoured for selection but, when the team was announced, he was named as one of eight reserves. It provided a way out for selectors who might otherwise have subjected rugby to an awkward debate on Southern Rhodesia's relationship with South Africa.

By the advent of the First World War in 1914, Southern Rhodesia's destiny was very much in the hands of the country's white citizens, but the future of its rugby and cricket was through South Africa.

In 1922, a referendum was held in which white Southern Rhodesians voted for 'responsible government', thereby rejecting the idea of being incorporated into the Union of South Africa. Local historian Frank Clements thought that they 'voted not so much against South Africa as against the Afrikaners'. He pointed out that 'social prejudice against the "Dutchmen"', as they were called was overwhelming ... and kept them out of all positions of influence, even in the farming community where their numbers were strongest'.[45] During the referendum, Jan Smuts stated pessimistically that Rhodesians were 'afraid of our bilingualism, our nationalism ... In short, they are little jingoes'.[46] In hindsight, Ian Smith, the prime minister during the last colonial era, argued that Rhodesians made the wrong decision in 1922. Apart from practical and economic benefits, they could have 'significantly influenced the outcome of the crucial first post-Second World War election in South Africa'.[47]

The white population in Southern Rhodesia increased slowly but steadily from 49 910 in 1931 to 68 954 in 1941 with the prime minister, Godfrey Huggins, striving to maintain the British character of the colony: 'the immigrant was feared as a competitor and a potential disrupter of privilege much more than the African'.[48]

After Rhodesia's unsuccessful 1923 venture into the rugby Currie Cup, the game was placed on hold at provincial level. Ten years elapsed before a national rugby conference was held in 1933 at which representatives of the Rhodesian provinces discussed progress. They concluded that the standard of rugby in the country did not warrant the entry of a side in the Currie Cup. Interest was sustained through visits by the British (1924 and 1938), the All Blacks (1928) and the Wallabies (1933) but defeats were heavy. Afrikaners in rural areas were invariably precluded by distance from playing the game and national teams were almost entirely English-speaking.

There were an estimated 10 000 Afrikaners in Southern Rhodesia by the outbreak of the Second World War, an ethnic and social minority of some political significance. In a study that examines the social and economic foundations of white immigration, Colin Leys indicates strengths within the Afrikaner community at that time, notably their possession of a separate language and a common religion, which preserved their group solidarity. Ties with Afrikaner nationalism in the Union also kept 'alive the idea that they [had] a racial and cultural heritage separate from that of the rest of the white community'.[49]

In the years immediately after the war, Southern Rhodesia experienced an 'agricultural revolution'. It resulted largely from a period of wartime industrialisation where Rhodesians had been forced to manufacture items previously imported and was based on technological advances in manufactured fertilisers, herbicides and pesticides as well as the use of efficient motorised machinery and new crop strains. The switch from burley and Turkish to Virginia tobacco also provided white farmers with the reliable and highly profitable cash crop they had been seeking for the past 40 years.[50]

The *Rhodesia Herald* announced a record tobacco crop for 1944/45 as agriculture entered a period of unprecedented growth.[51] The value of tobacco sales rose from £3.9 million in 1945 to £29.5 million in 1960, thereby creating employment. The number of white men working on or owning farms almost doubled from 4 673 in 1945 to 8 632 in 1960.[52]

Wealthy farmers saw an opportunity to improve the standard of rugby in their respective districts by making the game a condition in the appointment of farm managers. Contacts at the University of Stellenbosch helped attract capable players to the tobacco areas, especially Rusape, Inyazura and Odzi.

Immigration changed the character of white farming. Many of the newcomers to the tobacco districts – both English- and Afrikaans-speakers – were young servicemen or recent university graduates. They gave 'a vitality, a new confidence and indeed a new impatient aggressiveness'. The acceptance of risk 'permeated what had been a cautious, conservative, backward rather than forward-looking community ... the newcomers began to dominate'.[53]

In early 1946, it was announced that Northern Rhodesia had agreed to join Southern Rhodesia in an expanded Rhodesia RFU, a significant development insofar as it preceded political amalgamation by seven years. Rapid rugby progress in the north had been achieved primarily through the migration of engineers and artisans from the Witwatersrand to the copper mines. Many of them came from the hard school of Transvaal rugby and they not only provided skills and expertise but injected a robustness not previously seen in Rhodesian sides. The strong rugby base that developed on the Northern Rhodesian Copperbelt was generously assisted by the mines in the construction of first-class rugby facilities.[54]

In Northern Rhodesia, a 'modern, highly mechanised industry [was] superimposed on a rural, backward economy'.[55] Smuts recorded Winston Churchill as saying if the Southern Rhodesian vote had favoured South Africa at the 1922 referendum, 'Northern Rhodesia would be thrown in as a gift'.[56] By 1949, Northern Rhodesia's exports 'exceeded the value of Southern Rhodesia's [and] in 1953 they were more than double since copper was in huge demand for post-war global reconstruction'.[57]

The British were alarmed by the northward expansion of the Union but their efforts to check immigration were neither supported nor practical. The Copperbelt 'relied on white South Africans because Britain could not supply comparably qualified workers, whilst it was not thought practicable to replace whites with Africans except over a considerable period of time'.[58]

The arrival of quality rugby players from South Africa encouraged the Rhodesians to field a side in the first Currie Cup tournament after the war. A trial match was played in Bulawayo which saw Northern Rhodesia surprise their hosts by holding them to a 6–6 draw. The combined side chosen for the 1946 tour was a mix of returning servicemen and new arrivals from South Africa who were seeking opportunities in the colonies. The Afrikaans-speaking contingent was made up of four players from the north and three from the south. They were conspicuous contributors in spirited displays on tour and whilst there was just one victory – over Griqualand West at Kimberley – defeats were by narrow margins except for Northern Transvaal. The success of the venture saw Afrikaner influence gather momentum over the next few years. They provided outstanding players and generated mutual respect in communities associated with the game.

Schalk de Villiers, a former Western Province player who was farming in the Makoni district, was the outstanding player in 1946 and the following season became the first of a series of Afrikaners to captain the colony. It was under his guidance that Rhodesia gained two of its most famous victories. The first was against Western Province at Newlands in 1947 when they played there for the first time in 39 years. The Rhodesian tackling was deadly, enabling them to gain a 10–6 victory. *Die Burger* commented on the spectacle of the home crowd rising and applauding a visiting team on their unexpected victory over a side destined to become that year's Currie Cup champions. 'This is a Rhodesian team,' said the *Port Elizabeth Advertiser* that is 'fit, eager, quietly confident, willing to learn, inspired by the leadership of Schalk de Villiers – a team which, in the space of a few short days, has become "big news" wherever rugby is understood in this country'.[59]

Success at Newlands drew further attention to Rhodesia at a time when Afrikaners were starting to invest in tobacco farms. In an article on their involvement in the industry, Gustav Hendrich suggests that 1947 marked an upsurge in interest by the Afrikaner in the potentially rich agricultural lands between Salisbury and Umtali. The 'cheque-book farmers', as they became known, spent considerable sums of money in purchasing land in the area. Senator Daantjie Viljoen, for example, bought the farm Sysalvale at Odzi in 1948 for about £48 000 and enjoyed a remarkable first harvest of £27 000. The South Africans were men who not only had capital but also had knowledge of farming.[60]

Two Manicaland farmers, Schalk de Villiers and Daantjie Viljoen, the son of the South African senator, were selected as captain and vice-captain respectively of the 1948 Rhodesian touring side. Viljoen was an experienced campaigner, having represented Western Province and then Boland. Also in the team was another tobacco farmer, 'Bubbles' Koch, who had made his debut for Boland in 1942, and had then moved to Western Province where he was a regular eighth man for three seasons before he arrived in Rhodesia.

The might of Northern Transvaal stood before the Rhodesians as the ominous first obstacle on their tour. Outweighed, outhooked and beaten in the line-outs, the Rhodesians seized every opportunity and were down narrowly 10–14 in the second half. The idea that Northerns would eventually coast to victory was countered by a side led efficiently by De Villiers and inspired on this occasion by Koch. The latter rounded off his efforts with a try that fly-half Edmund Karg converted to seal Northern Transvaal's fate 15–14; three tries to one made the win more convincing than the scoreboard suggested. The Rhodesians had again proved themselves in South Africa, but inconsistency prevented them from making a serious challenge for Currie Cup honours.

The All Blacks visited in 1949 for the first time since Maurice Brownlie's side had played in Bulawayo in 1928. In an editorial, the *Rhodesia Herald* made the customary observation that international visits 'bind the bonds of empire closer together'. It then observed that the local team reflected 'a cross-section of modern Rhodesia ... Not only did it include northern representation, but it was composed of Rhodesians born and bred and Rhodesians by adoption – a fair sample of the people who today are working together to send this country ahead.'[61] It did not mention that more than half of the players were Afrikaans-speaking.

The four Inyazura farmers on debut for Rhodesia were the new captain John Morkel, who had previously led Stellenbosch and represented Western Province; the wing, Koos Brink; flank, 'Salty' du Rand, who had similarly played for Stellenbosch and Western Province; and centre, Ryk van Schoor, who had at various stages gained selection for Western Province. The other Southern Rhodesians to be selected were two soldiers, a salesman, a boilermaker, a plumber and a fitter-and-turner, a reflection on the working-class nature of rugby in the colony at that time. There were also five Northern Rhodesians in the team – a clerk, a surveyor and three miners – with three having had provincial experience: Waldemar Brune (Griqualand West), Wilhelm 'Billy' Viljoen (Transvaal) and 245-pound lock, Michiel 'Kleintjie' Prinsloo (Orange Free State).

A large crowd descended on Hartsfield, Bulawayo, to witness an historic match in which the All Blacks, fresh from victory over Transvaal, included nine players who had taken part in the first Test. The game began dramatically when Viljoen punted the ball across the New Zealand try-line and Brink won the race to touch down in the corner. The latter converted his own try. Then, in the second half, Morkel secured possession to set up a try by Claude Jones which Karg converted. The Rhodesians led 10–0. Although New Zealand scored twice, Joe Pretorius was outstandingly dependable at full-back, and centres Van Schoor and Brune flew into their tackles to blot out the tourists' attempts to run the ball. Rhodesia emerged victorious 10–8 and an ecstatic crowd carried Morkel and his team shoulder-high to the pavilion.

Another Inyazura farmer and former Western Province player, John Slabbert, joined the Rhodesian team for the second match at Salisbury. The capital city, with its accommodation problem acute at the best of times in those days, crammed in visitors from all parts of southern Africa. The greatest concentration of people to have gathered in the colony up to then numbered close to 13 000 and covered every square metre of available room. Rhodesia's only score in a tense struggle was a Karg drop-goal, achieved with split-second timing to give them the initial lead. A year earlier, it would have meant victory because it was only in 1948 that the value of a drop-goal was reduced from four to three points. The 3–3 draw, nevertheless, gave Rhodesia an unofficial 'series' win over the All Blacks.

Van Schoor and Du Rand were named in the Springbok side for the next Test. They were the first Rhodesian players to achieve this honour but, behind the scenes, efforts were ongoing to restrict Afrikaner immigration. They were being driven at the highest level in colonial administration, notably by the governor of Northern Rhodesia, Sir Gilbert Rennie, who pointed out that 'if Afrikaners are not to dominate the scene here in the near future, remedial steps will have to be taken without delay'. He believed the 'partnership' policy between whites and blacks was being threatened because it 'is likely to become increasingly distasteful to Afrikaners as their numbers here increase'. Secret discussions were planned with politicians to keep Northern Rhodesia 'a British territory, deeply appreciative of the British connection and valuing highly the British way of life'.[62]

The governor of Southern Rhodesia, Sir John Kennedy, said that in his three years in office he had noticed a slight deterioration in Southern Rhodesia's spirit of friendliness with Britain, while also observing Afrikaners 'are coming up here from the Union in increasing numbers ... attracted to a great extent by the money to be made out of tobacco'. He wrote cautiously, perhaps naively in the light of the Afrikaner involvement in rugby:

> They do not assimilate with other Europeans at all. They live mostly in the country, and often in groups, where farms are owned by them in great blocks ... There is a great deal of coming and going between them and the Union for higher education and so forth, and there is no doubt that their sympathies and loyalties are all with the Union.[63]

The influence that Afrikaners wielded in Central Africa during the 1950s could not be ignored. Leys says that 'without the presence of the Afrikaner community, the balance of European race attitudes would be appreciably more liberal'.[64] Blake argues that the Afrikaner might not count socially, but they constituted 13.5% of the white population in 1951 and significantly one-quarter of the white rural population. They were even more influential than their numbers suggested because 'electoral boundaries, thanks to the power of the agricultural interests, were drawn in a way which over-weighted the rural vote'.[65]

Important developments were taking place on the political front as the Central African colonies moved towards Federation in 1953. Hopes to incorporate Southern Rhodesia within the Union of South Africa had all but disappeared, despite support from the Salisbury-based newspaper, *Die Volksgenoot*, and Afrikaners living in the colony. Imperial opinion 'still dreaded the growing power of South Africa', believing Afrikaner nationalists coveted the colony for her land and labour. It was thought a federation in the heart of Africa would counterbalance the growing economic strength of South Africa.[66]

It was claimed that virtually all the British representatives on the spot – high commissioners and governors – believed the South African threat could not be ignored, especially 'if Afrikaners became a majority of the European population in Northern Rhodesia and if Southern Rhodesia suffered an economic depression'.[67]

British journalist John Parker maintained that 'the South African way of doing things was rather infra dig for Rhodesians steeped as they were in the British tradition'.[68] But opinions were changing as white interactions across national boundaries in southern Africa increased. Newspapers in Rhodesia highlighted South African news to a greater extent than before, with considerable space allocated to sporting achievements from school sides to the Springboks. Other writers drew attention to strong business, family and social links, with holidays spent at South Africa's numerous coastal venues.

'This is a *British* Colony' was for 'the best part of forty years to remain a proud – and towards South Africa – almost a provocative boast.'[69] Yet Rhodesians were firmly behind the 1951/52 Springboks when they wanted one more victory – against England – to complete the grand slam. 'The fourth international,' said the *Rhodesia Herald* editorial on the morning of the match, 'will bring thousands of Rhodesians to their wireless sets this afternoon.' Then, perhaps conscious of the mood that existed at the time and the strong possibility of a Springbok victory, the pro-English editorial played down the importance of the result, stating in a subtle reflection: 'Strange as it may seem, there are quite a few English in Rhodesia. Even the London accent may sometimes be heard. They have no divided loyalties – they will be content if the better team wins.'[70]

Rhodesians took pride in sharing the Springboks' 8–3 victory and South Africa's position as the world's best rugby nation. Delight was expressed in the reproduction of comments such as those which appeared in the London *Sunday Express*: 'It was a game dominated by the thudding tackle in all its robust glory, the most deadly exponent was the Rhodesian Van Schoor.'[71]

Rhodesia had been involved in preparations for the tour, having hosted the Junior Springboks. Seven of the players in that side were chosen to travel overseas, with a further three playing for the Springboks in later encounters. In Umtali, a combined Manicaland/Mashonaland XV side exposed previously unknown shortcomings in the Junior Springboks' play through inflicting a 26–14 defeat on their opponents, but Rhodesians were unable to convince the

Springbok selectors that they deserved increased representation in the national squad.

Du Rand was named as the new Rhodesian captain for the 1952 season but was injured early on and, soon after his marriage in Umtali, he accepted a position at the Cape. Van Schoor also departed but there were new arrivals with provincial experience who allowed Rhodesia to continue to field competitive sides. The constant coming and going was not ideal, but it reflected a population that was shifting in nature, with 125 000 whites arriving in Southern Rhodesia and 53 000 leaving during the post-war decade, 1946–56.[72]

The selection process for the Rhodesian team was never easy and based to a large extent on the Clark Cup, an annual competition of two matches played between the colonies over a long weekend. Rugby relations improved, partly because of club tours and through players such as the experienced Des van Jaarsveldt and Alan Poole moving between the two colonies. Disadvantages were also countered by the annual South African tour – up to four weeks in duration – which helped the Rhodesians build spirit and cohesion.

Rhodesia defeated Natal 11–3 in heavy, windy weather in Durban in 1950 and twice at home the following year. Eastern Province were beaten 24–6 in Port Elizabeth in 1952 and stirring performances against the 1953 Wallabies saw Rhodesia go down 15–18 at Bulawayo but draw 8–8 at Kitwe. A memorable 14–11 victory was achieved over Transvaal at Ellis Park in 1954 and the Rhodesians acquitted themselves well in a 12–16 loss against the 1955 Lions in Salisbury. The best-ever Currie Cup season occurred in 1957 when five victories were earned, and Rhodesia was unfortunate that a 'disputed' try should deny them another win against Transvaal. 'Virile, full of fire, tenacious, they almost carried the day,' reported Johannesburg's *Sunday Express*.[73]

The 1957 season was essentially the last in which Afrikaner influence was a dominant force in Rhodesian rugby. Between 1946 and 1957 they had made up 38 per cent of the players – 73 out of 194 – who represented the combined Rhodesias. The progress made was also largely driven by Afrikaans-speaking team captains, beginning with De Villiers, Morkel and Du Rand. They were followed by the relatively unknown 'Soks' Grobler, described as 'an inspiration to the Rhodesians'.[74] Daantjie van der Spuy, the vice-captain of the Junior Springboks, led Rhodesia at various times, with Attie Botha captaining the side in 1956 and Wickus de Kock in 1957. The Rhodesian side in 1958 was a mere shadow of previous years. The departure of leading players coincided with concerns over decolonisation across Africa and growing opposition to Federation. African leaders in Nyasaland and Northern Rhodesia were critical that the 'partnership' ideal had failed to ensure black advancement. They were also wary of white Southern Rhodesians extending their political and economic influence northwards. A black Southern Rhodesian journalist, Lawrence Vambe, opposed the Federal government's demands for dominion status and believed it preferable to assist the northern territories achieve independence so that 'they, in turn, would assist us to achieve our freedom'.[75]

Rhodesians, it seems, never questioned the extraordinary arrangement whereby they were qualified to play for South Africa. They might have criticised the selection of Springbok teams from the 1950s onwards, but it remained the greatest sporting honour to wear the green and gold, even if South Africa was a 'foreign' country, soon to become a republic, and its rugby was strongly associated with a nationalist ideology.

One Rhodesian player, the enduring Des van Jaarsveldt, was extremely unlucky not to be chosen for Springbok tours in 1951/52 and 1956. But when he captained the Rest of South Africa to victory over the Currie Cup champions Western Province in 1959, it paved the way for his selection as Springbok captain against Scotland in the opening international of 1960. *Die Transvaler* commented that 'it is an evil day for South African rugby when the country has had to seek its rugby captain from beyond its borders in the territory of a strange land'.[76]

South Africa won the Test 18–10, with Van Jaarsveldt scoring his side's final try after outpacing the Scots' defence in a 50-metre dash to the posts. He was not selected again but fellow Rhodesians Ronnie Hill and Andy Macdonald were named in Springbok sides over the next five years. The case of Macdonald, who was selected to tour New Zealand with the Springbok side in 1965, gave rise to political debate as he was farming in the newly independent Zambia. The Federation had been formally dissolved, and the new dispensation warned him that he would face 'certain consequences' if he represented South Africa.[77] Macdonald ignored the threat and toured; his loyalty firmly with a land in which he had no real desire to live.

Events were moving quickly. When the conservative Rhodesian Front acceded to power in 1962, there was a noticeable trend away from racial partnership towards the idea of racial separation. English-Afrikaans inter-ethnic hostility gave way to racial unity. A Zimbabwean historian, Alois Mlambo, questions British settlers in the way they had looked down upon other whites and treated them with hostility and contempt but were prepared to join forces 'in the face of the greater threat of a possible future African domination'. According to Mlambo, barriers were also broken down because 'non-British settlers became economically more powerful and socially and politically more acceptable'.[78]

Afrikaners worked hard and became influential in local government as well as organisations such as the Rhodesian Tobacco Association and the Rhodesian

National Farmers' Union. Some were involved in politics; the minister of immigration post was held for varying periods by two Afrikaners.

The appointment of Wickus de Kock, a third-generation Rhodesian and former national rugby captain, as a cabinet minister was significant at a time when the South African prime minister, John Vorster, attempted to impress upon the Rhodesian prime minister, Ian Smith, the need to address the issue of majority rule. When negotiations between the two countries broke down, the South African government sought an alternative 'channel of communication'. De Kock was invited to Pretoria in early 1975 to attend a meeting at which Vorster spelt out his country's future policy towards Rhodesia.

'It dawned on Wickus de Kock,' says Mordechai Tamarkin, 'that Rhodesia, as he had known it, was gone forever.'[79]

Piet Greyling had left Rhodesia by then in his quest to represent the Springboks and later captained the side. Ian Robertson toured France in 1974 and played against the All Blacks at home in 1976. Ray Mordt and David Smith were selected for the Tests against the British Lions in 1980. By then Rhodesia had become independent Zimbabwe and rugby ties were severed at the end of the season. In subsequent years, numerous Rhodesian/Zimbabwean-born players crossed the Limpopo. Some, such as Chris Rogers, Adrian Garvey, Gary Teichmann, Bob Skinstad, Tendai Mtawarira, Brian Mujati and Tonderai Chavhanga, represented the Springboks. Teichmann and Skinstad captained the side.[80]

Notes

1 The English translation appeared in the *Rhodesia Herald*, 28 April 1960.
2 R. Blake, 'The Pioneer Column – Its Origins and Implications' (Fourth Dugmore Memorial Lecture, Rhodes University), Grahamstown, 1970.
3 S. Taylor, *The Mighty Nimrod: A Life of Frederick Courteney Selous, African Hunter and Adventurer 1851–1917* (London: Collins, 1989), heading to opening chapter.
4 Taylor, *The Mighty Nimrod*, 15.
5 R. Cary, *Charter Royal* (Cape Town: Howard Timmins, 1970), 49.
6 Taylor, *The Mighty Nimrod*, 56. Selous was of the opinion that the Matabele 'were invaders and have almost utterly exterminated the original population'.
7 Cary, *Charter Royal*, 49.
8 F. Johnson, *Great Days* (Bulawayo: Books of Rhodesia, 1972), 109.
9 A. Darter, *Pioneers of Mashonaland* (Bulawayo: Books of Rhodesia, 1977), 65.
10 R. Cary, *The Pioneer Corps* (Salisbury: Galaxie Press, 1975), 64, 95. Pocock played in two internationals, scoring a try against Ireland.
11 Darter, *Pioneers of Mashonaland*, 65.
12 J. Muzondidya, 'Towards a Historical Understanding of the Making of the Coloured Community in Zimbabwe 1890–1920', in *Identity, Culture and Politics*, 3, 2 (2002), 84.
13 Blake, 'The Pioneer Column'; P. Mason, *The Birth of a Dilemma: The Conquest and Settlement of Rhodesia* (London: Oxford University Press, 1958).
14 *Rhodesia Herald*, 18 September 1914.
15 R. Rotberg, *The Founder: Cecil Rhodes and the Pursuit of Power* (Oxford: Oxford University Press, 1988), 435–436.

16   Rotberg, *The Founder*, 554.
17   Rhodes to Milton, 13 July 1896 (MI 1/1/1, NAZ).
18   R. Blake, *A History of Rhodesia* (London: Eyre Methuen, 1977), 151.
19   L. Gann, *A History of Southern Rhodesia: Early Days to 1934* (London: Chatto & Windus, 1965), 146.
20   *Cape Times Weekly*, 2 September 1896.
21   Blake, *A History of Rhodesia*, 147–152.
22   See J. Hepburn, *Twenty Years in Khama's Country and Pioneering among the Bataunga of Lake Ngami* (London: Hodder and Stoughton, 1895). The Reverend James Hepburn had always opposed Dutch interference in Bechuanaland.
23   *Bulawayo Chronicle*, 1, 3 September 1898.
24   I. Difford (ed.), *The History of South African Rugby Football 1875–1932* (Wynberg: Speciality Press, 1933), 223.
25   A. Keppel-Jones, *Rhodes and Rhodesia*, (Kingston: McGill-Queen's University Press, 1983), 589; Gann, *A History of Southern Rhodesia*, 140.
26   'Sikhombo expressed astonishment that the Boers had dared to fight the queen for "if a man tries to catch the sun, surely he will burn his fingers"' (Keppel-Jones, *Rhodes and Rhodesia*, 602).
27   Gann, *A History of Southern Rhodesia*, 151.
28   *Bulawayo Chronicle*, 4 August 1900. The match was played on 28 July 1900.
29   *Rhodesia Herald*, 28 September 1901. Matabeleland won the second match 25–0.
30   J. Wallis, *One Man's Hand* (Bulawayo: Books of Rhodesia, 1972), 61.
31   *Rhodesia Herald*, 17 and 18 August 1903.
32   Administrator to High Commissioner, 14 December 1906, in papers of the Gell family of Hopton, Derbyshire Record Office (D3287 BSA/4/221).
33   T. Davenport, *South Africa: A Modern History* (Johannesburg: Southern Book Publishers, 1989), 246.
34   *Rhodesia Herald*, 26 May 1911.
35   Ibid., 25 June 1910.
36   *Bulawayo Chronicle*, 25 July 1910.
37   £400 was received from profits of the 1906 Currie Cup tournament and Springbok tour (*Rhodesia Herald*, 19 August 1907).
38   *Rhodesia Herald*, 17 February 1911.
39   *Bulawayo Chronicle*, 30 June 1911.
40   D. Batchelor, 'British Boxing, London, 1948', in S. Macdonald (ed.), *Winter Cricket: The Spirit of Wedza* (Harare: Self-published, 2003), 145–146.
41   *Bulawayo Chronicle*, 20 and 21 August 1911. The Currie Cup tournament was held at Cape Town in 1911.
42   Gann, *A History of Southern Rhodesia*, 118; Wallis, *One Man's Hand*, 147.
43   Gotley was appointed as a native commissioner. He served in the Northern Rhodesian Police from 18 August 1915 to 11 January 1917 (Archives reference S 2300/1/1).
44   Four Rhodesians were nominated for the trials: John Hopley, Phil and Ben Rabinson, and Tom Louw.
45   F. Clements, 'Rhodesia: Afrikanderdom bids for power', *The Spectator*, 24 August 1967, 4.
46   R. Hyam, *The Failure of South African Expansion 1908–1948* (London: Macmillan, 1972), 185.
47   I. Smith, *The Great Betrayal* (London: Blake, 1997), 4.
48   F. Clements, *Rhodesia: The Course to Collision* (London: Pall Mall Press, 1969), 76.
49   C. Leys, *European Politics in Southern Rhodesia* (London: Clarendon Press, 1959), 93.
50   R. Palmer, *Land & Racial Domination in Rhodesia* (Berkeley: University of California Press, 1977), 242, 247.
51   *Rhodesia Herald*, 8 March 1946.
52   Palmer, *Land & Racial Domination*, 242–243.
53   Clements, *Rhodesia: The Course to Collision*, 83.
54   The Roan Antelope club at one time boasted the tallest rugby posts in the world (33.54 metres).
55   R. Baldwin, *Economic Development and Export Growth: A Study of Northern Rhodesia 1920–1960* (Berkeley: University of California Press, 1966), 40.

56   Sir R. Welensky, *Welensky's 4 000 Days: The Life and Death of the Federation of Rhodesia and Nyasaland* (London: Collins, 1964), 56.
57   A. Roscoe, *The Columbia Guide to Central African Literature in English since 1945* (New York: Columbia University Press, 2007), 24.
58   R. Hyam and P. Henshaw, *The Lion and the Springbok: Britain and South Africa since the Boer War* (Cambridge: Cambridge University Press, 2003), 211.
59   *Rhodesia Herald*, 14 August 1947.
60   G. Hendrich, 'The History of Afrikaner Involvement in the Rhodesian Tobacco Industry, 1890–1980', in *Historia*, 56, 2 (2011), 53.
61   *Rhodesia Herald*, 29 July 1949.
62   Sir G. Rennie to A.B. Cohen (3 December 1949), in P. Murphy (ed.), *Central Africa: British Documents on the End of Empire 1945–58, Part 1* (London: Stationery Office Books, 2005), 127.
63   Sir J. Kennedy to Sir P. Liesching (11 January 1950), in Murphy, *Central Africa: British Documents*, 129.
64   Leys, *European Politics in Southern Rhodesia*, 97.
65   Blake, *A History of Rhodesia*, 279.
66   J. Parker, *Little White Island* (London: Pitman Publishing, 1972), 37.
67   Hyam and Henshaw, *The Lion and the Springbok*, 223.
68   Parker, *Little White Island*, 37.
69   Clements, *Rhodesia: The Course to Collision*, 43.
70   *Rhodesia Herald*, January 5, 1952.
71   *Sunday Express*, quoted in the *Rhodesia Herald*, 7 January 1952.
72   Blake, *A History of Rhodesia*, 274.
73   J. Winch, *Rhodesia Rugby: A History of the National Side 1898–1979* (Salisbury: ZRRFU, 1979), 44.
74   Interview with John Barritt, May 1979.
75   L. Vambe, *An Ill-Fated People: Zimbabwe before and after Rhodes* (Pittsburgh: University of Pittsburgh Press, 1972), 267.
76   The English translation appeared in the *Rhodesia Herald*, 28 April 1960.
77   G. Byrom, *Rhodesian Sports Profiles 1907–1979* (Bulawayo: Books of Zimbabwe, 1980), 73.
78   A. Mlambo, '"Some Are More White than Others": Racial Chauvinism as a Factor in Rhodesian Immigration Policy, 1890 to 1963', in *Zambezia*, 27, 2 (2000), 160.
79   M. Tamarkin, *The Making of Zimbabwe: Decolonisation in Regional and International Politics* (London: Frank Cass, 1990), 50.
80   Other players from Rhodesia/Zimbabwe won international honours overseas. They include: David Pocock, Kyle Godwin (both Australia), David Curtis (Ireland), David Denton, Thom Evans, Scott Gray (all Scotland), Don Armand (England), Andy Marinos (Wales), Sebastian Negri (Italy) and Takudzwa Ngwenya (United States).

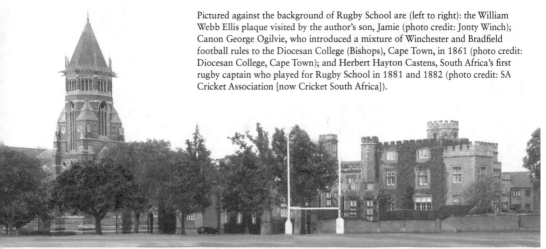

Pictured against the background of Rugby School are (left to right): the William Webb Ellis plaque visited by the author's son, Jamie (photo credit: Jonty Winch); Canon George Ogilvie, who introduced a mixture of Winchester and Bradfield football rules to the Diocesan College (Bishops), Cape Town, in 1861 (photo credit: Diocesan College, Cape Town); and Herbert Hayton Castens, South Africa's first rugby captain who played for Rugby School in 1881 and 1882 (photo credit: SA Cricket Association [now Cricket South Africa]).

The earliest recorded football match to have been staged in South Africa was played between 'colonial-born' and 'home-born' on 23 May 1862 in Port Elizabeth. The 'colonial-born' team was (left to right – standing): Smuts, Castleman, Pearson, Cloete, Loubser, W. Smith, R. Pakenham, Palmer, H. Smith, Dellamore (in front): Brown, Riches, Solomon, Morkel, Heugh, Van Reenen, Reis, C. Pakenham (photo credit: Cape Archives).

There were several crucial developments that influenced the switch to rugby at the Cape. In 1879, William Milton (left), a product of Marlborough College and an England player during 1874–75, persuaded the Cape to switch to rugby (photo credit: National Archives of Rhodesia [now Zimbabwe]). He was joined by John Graham (centre) who, in 1873, established a uniform code of laws for playing 'foot-ball' in Cape Town and its suburbs (photo credit: SA Law Journal). Influential support for the rugby code was also received from Frederick York St Leger (right), the editor of the *Cape Times*, who realised South Africa could forge highly visible links with the Mother Country and become part of an imperial sporting network (photo credit: University of the Witwatersrand).

Several unsuccessful attempts were made to arrange an international tour before the British arrived in 1891. This rugby scene is from the third 'Test' played that year at Newlands (photo credit: SA Rugby Football Board [now SA Rugby Union]).

People of all races developed an interest in rugby at the Cape. Roslyns from District Six was formed in 1882 (photo credit: Cape Archives), and Arabian College (above) from Bo-Kaap (or the Malay Quarter) followed in 1883 (photo credit: Arabian College: SA Rugby Football Board [now SA Rugby Union]). They were founding clubs of the Western Province Coloured Rugby Football Union, along with Violets from Claremont and Good Hopes from Bo-Kaap.

Bud Mbelle (below left) and Robert Grendon established the SA Coloured Rugby Football Board in 1897 (photo credit: University of the Witwatersrand). Daniel Lenders (centre) led the governing body of this organisation into the twentieth century (photo credit: University of the Witwatersrand). London-born Billy Simkins (right) was president of the SA Rugby Football Board for 23 years from 1890 to 1913 (photo credit: SA Rugby Football Board [now SA Rugby Union]). He was determined to keep the races separate in both rugby and cricket; his intransigence was largely responsible for separate provincial and national rugby boards.

South Africa's rugby team became known as the 'Springboks' when they toured overseas for the first time in 1906/07. The selection committee raised the residential requirement to five years to keep out the Rhodesian Freddie Brooks (above left) (photo credit: A.P. Singleton). England, however, chose Brooks and he outpaced the South African defence to score the equalising try in a tense 3–3 draw at Crystal Palace. In scenes from the tour, Springbok captain Paul Roos in the centre of the line-out anticipates winning the ball against Wales (photo credit: SA Rugby Football Board [now SA Rugby Union]) and (below) Anton Stegmann eludes the Glamorgan defence, as Dougie Morkel, Cocky Brooks, 'Uncle' Dobbin and Paul Roos move up in support (photo credit: SA Rugby Football Board [now SA Rugby Union])

In 1912/13, Billy Millar (left) led South Africa to their first 'grand slam', winning all four Tests against the Home Nations, as well as defeating France (photo credit: SA Rugby Football Board [now SA Rugby Union]). Boy Morkel (centre) captained the Springboks in their first Test series against New Zealand in 1921 (photo credit: SA Rugby Football Board [now SA Rugby Union]). It was a tour marred by controversy over a report by Mort Blackett (right) on the 'most unfortunate match ever played' (photo credit: *The Star*).

The Springboks and All Blacks drew 1–1 in 1921 and 2–2 in 1928. By then it was generally acknowledged that they were playing for the 'world championship'.

Above: Danie Craven played an important role during a decade in which the Springboks achieved their second 'grand-slam' in 1931/32; defeated Australia in 1933 and 1937; the All Blacks in 1937, and the visiting British Lions in 1938 (photo credit: SA Rugby Football Board [now SA Rugby Union]).

Left: Bennie Osler was influential in the late 1920s and early 1930s (photo credit: SA Rugby Football Board [now SA Rugby Union]).

Right: Flappie Lochner made the break to set up the first of the Springboks' five tries against the All Blacks at Eden Park in 1937. (photo credit: SA Rugby Football Board [now SA Rugby Union])

Left: The unofficial world champions in 1937 (left to right – back row): T.A. Harris, D.F. van de Vyver, S.R. Hofmeyr, J. White, A.D. Lawton, L. Babrow (second row): W.E. Bastard, J.W. Lotz, J.L.A. Bester, G.P. Lochner, H.J. Martin, D.O. Williams, J.A. Broodryk (third row): C.B. Jennings, S.C. Louw, M.A. van den Berg, F. Bergh, G.L. van Reenen, A.R. Sherriff, B.A. du Toit, H.H. Watt (front row): F.G. Turner, P.J. Lyster, P.W. Day (manager), M.M. Louw, P.J. Nel (captain), D.H. Craven (vice-captain), A. de Villiers (assistant manager), G.H. Brand, L.C. Strachan (in front): P. du P. de Villiers. (photo credit: SA Rugby Football Board [now SA Rugby Union])

The SA Coloured Rugby Football Board chose a national team and arranged an internal tour in 1939. They hoped to arrange sufficient funds to travel overseas, but the venture was dashed by the Second World War.

Pinky Julius (above) is pictured in the scarf and blazer – with Springbok badge – that were designed for the tour (photo credit: SA Rugby Football Board [now SA Rugby Union]). A brochure (right) was produced and the *Cape Standard* gave prominent coverage to the tour (photo credit: *Cape Standard*)

BOARD OFFICIALS

RHODES CUP.

C.A.F. CALVERT. PRESIDENT.

THE LATE HON. CECIL J. RHODES.

J. W. KAY. LIFE VICE-PRESIDENT.

P. M. JAMPIES. Vice-President & Selector.

P. A. DANIELS. SECRETARY.

J. J. KEMM. TREASURER.

EVERY WEEK 45,000 PEOPLE READ THE

Read in Every Town in the Cape Province—Also in all parts of Union & Rhodesia

Cape Standard

TUESDAY, SEPTEMBER 19, 1938 Registered at the G.P.O. as a Newspaper

S.A. RUGBY TEAM
Proposed Tour in June

THE following South African (Coloured) rugby team has been chosen to tour the Union in June, 1939. The team will be accompanied by the selectors, who will be on the look-out for talent.

FULL-BACKS :
B. Walbrugh (W.P. League).
D. Van Heerden (Transvaal).

WINGS :
M. G. Botha (W.P. League).
F. Schilder (W.P. League).
M. Philander (W.P. Board).

CENTRES :
I. Kienrty (W.P. League).
A. Julius (W.P. League).
A. Padiachy (S.W.D.).
T. Oliver (W.P. Board).

HALVES :

Thanks from Namaqualand

NATIONAL TEAM IN TRANSVAAL

S.A. Wins Both Games

Transvaal gave a great display against a powerful South Afri...

African side showed a marked superiority in ...

NATIONAL TOURING RUGBY TEAM LEAVES FOR THE NORTH

Some of the Western Province representatives for the National Rugby Touring side, who left Cape Town by train on Thursday night for Johannesburg, where the first match will be played.

In 1950, the SA Coloured Rugby Football Board and the SA Bantu Rugby Board agreed to play Test matches. The arrangement not only provided players with the opportunity to achieve national honours but also served as preparation for the planned entry of a team of colour into formal international competition. They were later joined by the SA Rugby Football Federation.

Above: Sing Kan 'Sam' Mawing dive passing in the 1959 Test against the SA Africans. Strong and innovative, his elusive running made him a popular player (photo credit: SA Rugby Union).

Right: Grant Khomo was one of South Africa's most outstanding sportsmen: in the early 1950s; he captained the national rugby and football teams and was the country's leading tennis player (photo credit: A. Bailey African Photo Archives).

Below: The SA Coloured Rugby Football Board team that won the second Test at Port Elizabeth in 1951 (left to right – back row): E. Moore, A. Lewis, C. Sharpe, A.R. Hermanus, W.H. Basson, S. Ruiters (middle row): Y. Kannemeyer, P. Hopley, D. Josephs, C. Saaid, M. Bohardien, J. Jephta, S. Baster, (front row): T. Musson, G.D. Davids (manager), H.M. Daniels (captain), J.D. Kester (president), L. Matthews (vice-captain), A. Abass (secretary) and C.J. Julius (photo credit: SA Rugby Union).

South Africans – and, in particular, Rhodes Scholars – made an impact on Oxford University and Home Union rugby from the beginning of the twentieth century. One of the most famous of these was 'Tuppy' Owen-Smith, pictured directing a practice (photo credit: Jonty Winch Collection). He had already represented South Africa at cricket and stood out as one of Oxford University's most exciting players in both sports. He captained England at rugby when they won the Triple Crown in 1937.

Right: Tom Bedford, who captained Oxford University and the Springboks, was an outspoken opponent of apartheid (photo credit: *Die Huisgenoot*).

Below left: Clive van Ryneveld had at 21-years old won three Oxford rugby blues and represented England. Here he evades a tackle against Scotland in 1949 (photo credit: C.B. van Ryneveld).

Centre: Chick Henderson was selected for Oxford and Scotland, and later influenced the game as president of the SA Barbarians (photo credit: J.H. Henderson).

Right: There were other reasons for playing overseas. With opportunities restricted in South Africa, some talented players of colour turned to rugby league. David Barends, who represented SARU in 1970, later played for Great Britain in Tests against Australia.

In 1949, Rhodesia won 10–8 and drew 3–3 against the All Blacks, after which Ryk van Schoor and Salty du Rand were selected for the Springbok team. The Rhodesians that won at Bulawayo were (left to right – standing): F. Eksteen (referee), C. Jones, K. Brink, P. Greaves, E. Painting, J. du Rand, J. Morkel (captain), W. Brune, K. Prinsloo, A. Birkin (in front): J. Pretorius, I. Brownlee, R. van Schoor, E. Karg, W. Kidd, W. Viljoen (photo credit: Rhodesia [now Zimbabwe] RFU).

Above (left to right): Andy Macdonald was farming in independent Zambia when selected to tour Australasia with the Springbok team in 1965 (photo credit: Rhodesia [now Zimbabwe] RFU); David Smith and Ray Mordt played for independent Zimbabwe and South Africa in 1980 (photo credit: John Rubython); Des van Jaarsveldt was Springbok captain against Scotland in 1960, prompting a Rand newspaper to comment: 'Stranger must not lead South Africa' (photo credit: Rhodesia [now Zimbabwe] RFU).

Left: Richard Tsimba was Zimbabwe's first black representative, playing impressively at the 1987 and 1991 World Cups (photo credit: Rhodesia [now Zimbabwe] RFU).

Right: Ian Robertson was a classy Rhodesian Springbok who represented a World XV at Cardiff in 1976 (photo credit: Rhodesia [now Zimbabwe] RFU).

South Africa's reign as unofficial world champions continued into the 1950s. They defeated the All Blacks 4–0 in 1949; achieved a third 'grand slam' in Europe in 1951/52, and accounted for the Australians 3–1 in 1953. Hansie Brewis (above left) was on the winning side in all ten of the Tests he played, while Hennie Muller (right) – known as the 'Windhond' because of his great pace – led South Africa with distinction (photo credits: SA Rugby Football Board [now SA Rugby Union]).

Right: The South Africans were given a scare in 1955 when they had to come from behind to square the Test series 2–2 against the 1955 British Lions. They lost the opening Test 23–22 before more than 90 000 spectators at Ellis Park, Johannesburg. The unlucky Jack van der Schyff missed the crucial conversion of Theuns Briers's second try with the last kick of the match. Photographer Ivor Hanes captured the famous moment on film.

Springbok wing Tom van Vollenhoven was photographed beside a 'World Champions' banner at the team's Sydney hotel in 1956 (photo credit: SA Rugby Football Board [now SA Rugby Union]). Not long afterwards, the Springboks were beaten for the first time in a twentieth-century series when they went down to the All Blacks in New Zealand. A further defeat followed against the French at home in 1958, but a series win over the All Blacks in 1960 and a fourth 'grand slam' in 1960/61 helped restore South African pride.

...aba Jali, the SA African XV wing (left) is pictured with Milase Majola and team-mate ...bulelo Twaku. Wearing their distinctive Springbok blazers, the SA African players were ...elebrating a fine 12–6 victory over the SA Coloured XV at Cape Town in 1961 (photo ...redit: SA Rugby Union).

...epresentative Test matches were ...taged from 1950 by the SA Coloured ...ugby Football Board (later SARU) ...nd the SA African Rugby Board. In ...959, the Western Province League ...isaffiliated from its governing body ...nd formed the SA Rugby Football ...ederation. They competed against the ...A Africans over nearly twenty years, ...ut SARU ended their participation in ...thnic Tests in 1970, and committed ...hemselves to non-racial rugby. They ...roduced some fine players over the ...ears such as (below – left to right): ...eter Mkata, Cassiem Jabaar, Salie ...redericks and Pieter Jooste (photo ...redit: SA Rugby Union).

The successful 1961 South African African Rugby Board team (left to right – back row): S. McDonald, H.M. Madikane, H.C. Lebakeng, B.N. Malamba, E. Rula, J.M. Mbize, B. Phillips (middle row): C. Mvinjelwa, G.M. Mashinqana, F.J. Mtyeku (captain), C.M. Scott (manager), E. Majola (vice-captain), M.H. Bafana, S.M. Mjo (in front): C.M. Twaku, S.B. Jali (photo credit: SA Rugby Union).

International matches involving South Africa continued to be played despite the worldwide anti-apartheid movement. Many well-known personalities were amongst those demonstrators (above) who made their way to Twickenham during the Springboks' tour to Britain in 1969/70 (photo credit: Unknown source – Jonty Winch Collection). Peter Hain, who made use of direct action to disrupt matches and stop tours, was arrested at Twickenham (below) and ejected from the stadium (photo credit: SA Rugby Football Board [now SA Rugby Union])

Left: The 1969/70 tour produced disappointing results for the besieged Springboks, but Dawie de Villiers was chaired off the field by Mike Gibson and Gareth Edwards after his team had defeated the Barbarians 21–12 in their final tour match (photo credit: Barbarian FC).

Right: Frik du Preez, who was voted South Africa's 'player of the twentieth century', was one of five South Africans invited to participate in the RFU's centenary celebrations in April 1971. Du Preez, Dawie de Villiers, Joggie Jansen and Hannes Marais were included in the President's XV that defeated an England XV 28–11 at Twickenham, while Ian McCallum was a member of the touring party (photo credit: SA Rugby Football Board [now SA Rugby Union]).

Above: Dr Piet Koornhof (right, interviewed by the author) was arguably the country's most enlightened cabinet minister, but he was unable to accept the 1977 agreement reached by the SA Rugby Football Board and SARU (photo credit: Jonty Winch Collection). There were changes nevertheless in the country's rugby structure, leading to the selection of Errol Tobias (right) for the SA Barbarians, and subsequently for the Springboks during the 1980s (photo credit: Jonty Winch).

WHEN Wynand Claasen's Springbok rugby team landed in New Zealand in July 1981 at the start of a three-month tour, their presence in the "land of the long white cloud" caused bitter tensions and violent confrontation in a society that had a long-held reputation for being – at least superficially – non-violent, polite and laid-back.

Many commentators agree that political disagreement about the ill-conceived tour, the accompanying protests, retaliation by angry and frustrated rugby supporters, and heavy-handed police action, collectively constituted one of the formative moments in New Zealand's history.

It has been variously described as "a coming of age" for that young country and "the year we lost our innocence".

Above: An article published in the *Cape Argus* commented on the highly controversial Springbok rugby tour to New Zealand in 1981 (photo credit: African News Agency). **Below:** The establishment of the National Sports Congress in 1989 was crucial to South Africa's return to international sport. Key figures in the movement included (left to right) Steve Tshwete, Mluleki George and Ngconde Balfour who was interviewed by Minisha Patel (photo credits: Jonty Winch).

The establishment of the unified SA Rugby Football Union (SARFU) was celebrated at Kimberley on 20 March 1992. Danie Craven (above left) and Ebrahim Patel (centre) initially shared the presidency (photo credits: SA Rugby Football Board [now SA Rugby Union] and Jonty Winch). Unity was a welcome development at all levels. St Martin's pupils, Alan Botha, Sule Arnautovic, Deon Rebello and David Buhlungu, joined the Springbok captain Naas Botha at a festival dinner (above right), while Daniel Changwa, Steven Becker, Thokozani Dlamlenze, Nkhensani Tlakula and Wilson Modiba (below) were coached by one of the world's greatest centres, Danie Gerber (photo credits: Jonty Winch).

All South Africans – both men and women – became increasingly interested in the game. Members of the Gauteng schoolgirls' touch-rugby team, Vidette Steenkamp and Louise Botha (left), received encouragement from Rassie Erasmus who, twenty years later, became World Rugby's 'Coach of the Year' (photo credit: Jonty Winch). Tsoanelo Pholo (right) was selected for the South African team to compete in the 1999 Touch Rugby World Cup, before concentrating on hockey and participating in the 2004 Olympic Games (photo credit: Jonty Winch).

The Springboks won the Rugby World Cup at their first attempt when François Pienaar (left) led the team to victory over the All Blacks at Ellis Park, Johannesburg, in 1995. John Smit's team beat England in the 2007 final in Paris and Siya Kolisi (right) was captain of the winning side at Yokohama in 2019 (photo credit: Matthew Winch).

World Rugby – formerly the International Rugby Board – has made annual awards since 2001. Three South Africans have received the 'Player of the Year' award: Schalk Burger in 2007; Bryan Habana 2004, and Pieter-Steph du Toit in 2019. The 'Team of the Year' award was won in 2004, 2007, 2009 and 2019. Jake White won 'Coach of the Year 'in 2004 and 2007, and Rassie Erasmus was similarly honoured in 2019.

'Players of the Year', Schalk Burger (left) and Bryan Habana (right) are pictured either side of World Cup heroes Joost van der Westhuizen, outstanding in 1995, and Victor Matfield, 'Man of the Match' in the 2007 final (photo credits: Jonty Winch).

South Africa's 32-12 victory over England in the 2019 World Cup final was given prominent coverage in the British press: (top row left) Cheslin Kolbe and (right) Makazole Mapimpi scored South Africa's first World Cup final tries; (top row centre) Pieter-Steph du Toit emerged as World Rugby's 'Player of the Year'; (middle row left) Handré Pollard contributed 22 points, and (right) Duane Vermeulen was 'Man of the Match'; (bottom row left) Eben Etzebeth played in his 85th Test and (right) Tendai Mtawarira in his 117th (photo credits: Matthew Winch).

16

Wind of Change

It is difficult to discover exactly what the Government's sports
policy is at present. D'Oliveira was refused admission as part
of a team, but admitted as an individual. Arthur Ashe was
refused entry as an individual, but would have been admitted
as a member of a team. Japanese people could come to South
Africa in a swimming team or to buy iron, but not as jockeys.[1]

– Sir de Villiers Graaff, leader of the United Party, 1970

In February 1960, the British prime minister, Harold Macmillan, made what
became known as his 'Wind of Change' speech to the South African Parliament.
'The most striking of all impressions I have formed since I left London a month
ago,' he intoned, 'is of the strength of this African national consciousness. The
wind of change is blowing through this continent and, whether we like it or not,
this growth of national consciousness is a political fact. We must all accept it as a
fact, and our national policies must take account of it.'[2]

The speech had a great effect on South Africans. Whites felt let down in that
they believed the British were abdicating their responsibilities. A hardening of
attitudes led to increased support for then prime minister, Dr H.F. Verwoerd,
who was moving towards declaring the republic that would finally be enacted
in 1961. Verwoerd had concluded that only in a republic would there be unity
between white English- and Afrikaans-speaking South Africans.

On 21 March 1960, black people in various parts of the country burnt their
passes and then went to police stations and asked to be arrested. About 10 000
blacks assembled at Sharpeville. The police felt threatened and opened fire with
machine guns, leaving 69 dead and 178 injured. A post-mortem enquiry later
revealed that most of those killed were shot from behind while fleeing the scene.

The world was incensed and, within a week, thousands of people demonstrated in London. In South Africa, the resistance campaign continued and protests were held throughout the country. The government declared a state of emergency. Parliament passed the Unlawful Organisations Act by which means the government was able to ban the African National Congress (ANC) and Pan Africanist Congress (PAC). On 9 April, Verwoerd survived being shot twice in the head at close range by a wealthy Transvaal farmer, David Pratt.

It was against this background that South Africa embarked on one of its busiest sporting years. The All Blacks toured South Africa; the Springbok cricketers visited England and the Olympic Games were staged in Rome (the last at which South Africa took part until 1992). But increasingly there were questions about racial discrimination in the country's sport.

A major issue was whether Maori players were permitted to tour with the All Black team. 'Some time ago,' commented *The Star* (Johannesburg), 'the New Zealand Council referred the matter to the South African Board and asked many detailed questions. According to informed sources, the South African Board replied in effect, "Do as you think best. Of course, you will be well aware of the laws of our country."'[3]

Selection for the tour was still confined to whites. This time, however, there was concerted opposition in New Zealand, notably from the Citizens' All Black Tour Association. It campaigned with the slogan, 'No Maoris – No Tour' and more than 150 000 people signed a petition.

Their efforts, however, were unsuccessful. Walter Nash's Labour government paid little attention to the protests and granted a state farewell to the players. Parliamentarians argued that they would not like to see Maoris in a racially torn South Africa, while rugby authorities claimed that they were honouring a promise to send a team. Tour manager Tom Pearce believed that the decision to select a whites-only team 'sprang only from love of the Maoris – those gentle people. We wouldn't want to hurt them in the least.'[4]

Dennis Brutus's SA Sports Association demonstrated against the All Blacks on their arrival in South Africa, but police monitored the situation and the anti-tour protests made little impression. The greatest stir was created by black support given to the tourists. The 8 000-strong crowd in the coloured area at the second Test match at Newlands drew comment from *Die Burger*:

> They jeered every move made by the Springboks, and whenever the All Blacks scored, the non-Europeans' stand literally vibrated with excitement. It was obvious to everyone else in the crowd that there could not have been a single non-European spectator who wanted the Springboks to win. When the final

whistle blew, the cheers and screams from the non-Europeans' stand were thunderous and no-one left the ground without the feeling of the political undertones of their demonstration.[5]

The New Zealand manager was not influenced. 'The colour question,' he remarked, 'never cropped up during the tour.'[6]

The All Blacks' visit was pronounced a great success, making a clear profit of over £100 000. Everything went the way of the SA Rugby Football Board, including a narrow 2–1 victory in the four-match series. Anti-apartheid leaders voiced their disapproval that the New Zealand rugby administrators had again been manoeuvred into serving the South African political system and its sporting showpiece, rugby. In his triumph, Danie Craven did make one concession. At the end of the tour, he joined New Zealand officials in talks, after which they were able to report that the way was open for the inclusion of Maori in future tours of South Africa. It pacified some tour detractors but meant little as later political developments proved.

The 1960 South African cricket side was expected to be a soft target for demonstrators in England. That the sporadic demonstrations were mild was surprising considering the huge anti-apartheid protests in the aftermath of Sharpeville. The answer, according to political scientist Adrian Guelke, was that sport was then regarded as being insignificant in comparison with trade which was the main target of opponents of apartheid. A deeper reason was 'simply an assumption that sport lay basically outside the realm of politics'.[7]

The tour made by Avril Malan's 1960/61 Springbok rugby team began in October, 'the wettest month recorded in Britain in the wettest five-month period since 1877'.[8] They were unaffected by the anti-apartheid movement, but British reporters asked politically based questions to which manager Ferdie Bergh responded with the unhelpful 'we have come here to play rugger'.[9] The Springboks coped better with the often appalling weather through their powerful, efficient forward play, allied to a well-organised defence. They built up a formidable record, playing thirty-four matches and losing just one, against the Barbarians in their last fixture in Britain. They achieved another 'grand slam', defeating Wales 3–0, Ireland 8–3, England 5–0 and Scotland 12–5. They drew 0–0 against France.[10]

That the Springboks scored 132 tries on tour and conceded just 25 is a revealing statistic. They were determined to win every match, while there was an obsessive desire on the part of the British to see them beaten. This aggressive competitiveness ensured the tour's overwhelming financial success. The third match at Cardiff Arms Park was particularly unpleasant, with local prop Dai

Hayward punching Doug Hopwood at the first line-out. Bryn Thomas's emotive piece in the *Western Mail* fanned the flames. 'To the Springboks the victory,' he wrote, 'to Cardiff the glory ... Cardiff were battered into submission by the most vigorous South African pack.'[11]

Terry O'Connor, like many of the British journalists, was critical of the Springboks because they 'play Test matches to win, and they avoid risks. No wonder they won few friends at Twickenham.'[12] Frustration at the visitors' forward dominance became evident when 'the Springbok team were booed because the English forwards could not win the ball'.[13] *The Times* denounced elements in the 70 000 crowd for their poor behaviour: 'to whistle and give the slow handicap to a player as he runs up for a place kick is worse than lack of sportsmanship; it is rank bad manners'.[14]

The outstanding Springbok centre John Gainsford enjoyed the tour immensely, but was aware of the side being 'lashed unmercifully by a one-eye British press who couldn't seem to stand the sight of us winning and winning and winning'.[15] Bergh observed 'when England score eight runs an hour and win a cricket Test, then all is well ... and had the English forwards beaten us, and Risman's kicking brought success ... all would have been well'.[16] Dirk Kamfer, writing in *Die Burger*, expressed his reservations about the tour: 'The Britons do not like our rugby because they do not like us, and they do not like us because we do not want to be Britons.'[17]

In March 1961, Verwoerd withdrew South Africa from the Commonwealth, a move later endorsed by an all-white referendum, and the Republic of South Africa came into being. His government moved quickly: 'Mandela was arrested in 1962 and *uMkhonto weSizwe*'s key Rivonia personnel were arrested in 1963 ... By the end of 1963, the ANC leadership was jailed or banned.' Oliver Tambo, in exile, found himself heading a demoralised organisation, 'its strategy discredited [and] its goals unmet'.[18]

Brutus appealed to white South African sports bodies to reject race discrimination and to form genuinely national and non-racial organisations. The minister of the interior, Jan de Klerk (father of F.W., later the country's state president), warned sporting bodies that they would not be allowed to send mixed teams to represent South Africa in international events. If they did not comply with government policy, legislation would be introduced to compel them to do so. He left white sports administrators with little room to manoeuvre.[19]

The persecution of those involved in the non-racial sports movement was such that the South African Non-Racial Olympic Committee (SANROC) found it almost impossible to function. The body's credibility also suffered when its president, John Harris, was arrested for sabotage, having planted a bomb in the concourse of Johannesburg station. It exploded, injuring twenty-three people, one of whom later died. Harris was executed in April 1965. The following year, Brutus left South Africa and, together with Chris de Broglio and Reg Hlongwane, both prominent weightlifters, set up an office in London.

In exile, Brutus monitored the situation closely, sending delegates to international sports conferences to lobby against white South African sport. The establishment of a controlling sports body in Africa ensured the future success of the anti-apartheid movement. In 1963 the Organisation of African Unity (OAU) was established and, three years later, the Supreme Council of Sport in Africa (SCSA) came into being. It became clear that pressure from Africa would begin to assume new proportions.

Virtually every tour involving a South African team was fraught with controversy. During the visit of the Springbok rugby side to New Zealand in the winter of 1965, the question arose as to whether the next All Blacks team to tour South Africa would be permitted to include Maori. The New Zealand Rugby Football Union (RFU) was no longer prepared to omit some of its best players and give South Africa an unfair advantage. They had made this clear to the South African authorities, and Craven responded by saying that Maori would be acceptable. He was in New Zealand with the rugby side when the worst possible news was received.

Verwoerd delivered his fateful Loskop Dam address on 4 September 1965:

> At present we are engaged in an argument in a sphere which I should prefer not to discuss, namely, in regard to our rugby team in New Zealand. But I am compelled to talk about it because of late so much is openly being written and said in opposition newspapers, which has compelled me to state my own and the government's attitude very clearly and unequivocally ... We have not changed our attitude. As we behave in other countries, we expect them to behave here, in accordance with our customs, and I want to add this: everyone knows what they are.[20]

The New Zealand prime minister, Keith Holyoake, stated that it appeared to him that the South African prime minister was telling the New Zealand selectors which players to include in their team. He was not prepared to accept such interference and told Parliament, 'In this country we are one people ... we cannot be fully and truly represented by a team chosen on racial lines.' The New Zealand RFU agreed to postpone the proposed tour to South Africa in 1967.[21]

It was a serious error of judgement by Verwoerd and contributed to South Africa's rapidly developing isolation. Future sports minister Piet Koornhof recalled Verwoerd later confessing to John Vorster that he bitterly regretted banning the

All Blacks' tour of South Africa. Koornhof further claimed that Verwoerd began looking for an opportunity to make amends but the chance never came. In 1966, he was stabbed to death by a parliamentary messenger, Demetrios Tsafendas.[22]

Verwoerd's successor, John Vorster, appreciated the danger of isolation and endeavoured to change his predecessor's sport policy. He had to move cautiously because of the fear of not meeting with the approval of his party's right wing. On 11 April 1967, he told the House of Assembly that he would not dictate to countries with which South Africa had traditional sports ties as to who they may or may not include in their teams. The new policy was designed to allow South Africa to be represented by a mixed team at the Mexico Olympic Games in 1968 and for Maori to be included in the New Zealand rugby side in 1970.

At an International Olympic Committee (IOC) meeting in May 1967, South African delegates spoke enthusiastically about the changes that were taking place in their country. There was initial support but protests led by the SCSA resulted in approximately forty countries, as well as the black members of the United States team, threatening to boycott the Games if South Africa participated. The invitation was withdrawn by forty-seven votes to sixteen, with eight abstentions.

Vorster's initiative had collapsed at the first hurdle. He then blundered a few months later by refusing to allow Basil D'Oliveira, the South African-born coloured cricketer, to accompany the 1968/69 England team in South Africa. The tour was cancelled, leaving South Africans to face the consequences.

Nineteen-year-old Peter Hain entered the fray. He had four years earlier given the funeral oration for John Harris who was hanged for placing the bomb at Johannesburg's railway station. Hain had since followed his parents overseas and, in August 1969, formed the Stop the Seventy Tour Committee (STST). The idea was to prevent the South African cricketers from touring England in 1970. They decided to build their campaign on the foundation of direct action tactics aimed at physically stopping the cricket matches. But before long, its initiators realised the significance of other tours and began gathering 'momentum from a position of almost no coherent overall organisation'.[23]

One intention was to show the conditions to which the cricket tour would be subject if it took place. It was also hoped to demonstrate the strength of opposition and feeling towards apartheid. Selected events served as training grounds. Tennis was the scene of early demonstrations at the Great Britain versus South Africa clash at Bristol. Organisers looked on horrified as demonstrators invaded the court and held up play. The Wilf Isaacs XI tour of England – sponsored by a Johannesburg property magnate and cricket benefactor – was also targeted. In the opening match at Basildon, where the tourists were playing against Essex, demonstrators ran on to the field and waved banners. They then sat down until the police arrived. At Oxford, they were more innovative, encircling the wicket and making speeches. Mirrors were flashed into batsmen's eyes; there were frequent calls of 'no-ball' as the bowler delivered a ball, and the pitch was dug up.[24]

By the time the rugby tourists arrived, the STST campaign 'had reached a position of amazing depth of support and commitment'.[25] The Springboks knew that they were going to come across demonstrators during their three-month tour but had little idea as to the strength of the campaign. 'Even before we left Johannesburg,' said team captain, Dawie de Villiers, 'we encouraged the players not to take any notice of the demonstrators because by taking notice we would fail in our aim to play rugby.'[26]

The demonstrators hounded the Springboks from the beginning of the tour, interfering with practices and functions. On the night they attended a reception given by the South African ambassador, they were delayed when trying to leave because demonstrators had cut them off from their bus.

Hain later saw the opening match against Oxford University as crucial to his eventual success. The organisers decided to switch venues for the match, and this sparked off immediate public interest in the campaign. Wallace Reyburn, who had been a war correspondent, says that arrangements for the Oxford match took on 'all the cloak-and-dagger aspects of a wartime arrangement ... the ground at which it would be played was known only to those of the High Command and when I set off to join the team I was reminded very much of going off on the Dieppe Raid'.[27]

The uncertainty that existed affected the Springboks. They did not know until the day of the match that the game would be played and that it would be at Twickenham. De Villiers admitted to 'the unnerving effect the demonstrators had on us already – we tried to create the impression that it was normal, but it wasn't'. Throughout the game, the players were subjected to a verbal barrage of 'Sieg Heil!' and 'Fascist pigs!' Several demonstrators managed to invade the field and one climbed a goal post.[28]

Bill McLaren was asked to commentate at the next match against the Midland Counties (East) at Welford Road. He described his experience:

> I remember having to walk the gauntlet up a narrow channel lined on each side by policemen holding back the mob. Those policemen were covered in spittle, had hats knocked off, were kicked in places where no man should be kicked, and yet took it all with stoic calm. I couldn't believe that people in the British Isles would behave in that manner ... Constant noise outside the South

Africans' hotels to try and prevent them sleeping was another unbelievable ploy that sickened decent people.[29]

Demonstrations took place at every game the Springboks played, capturing the attention of the general public. The political aspect of the tour made daily front-page news and was often the lead story on television. Demonstrators threw smoke bombs, ran onto the fields, chained themselves to uprights or crossbars, and scattered drawing-pins on the field of play. Matches were only possible because of a huge police presence and the use of brawny stewards drawn from local rugby clubs.

Over-zealous demonstrators were always a danger. 'I and my committee have no time for those who want to dig up pitches or throw glass onto rugby fields,' explained Hain in an interview during the tour. 'It's strictly banned and it's not in my code book at all.'[30]

The worst scenes occurred in the fourth game at Swansea. The whole field became a mass of people running and fighting. 'It was a snarling brutal fight,' says Reyburn. 'The ardent Welsh rugby fan like the official stewards, was having his keenly awaited go at the long hairs.'[31] After the first month of the three-month itinerary, Hain says 'the grounds were enveloped by a network of security. Then the barbed wire went up around the perimeter of some tour venues – until, finally, the grounds began to assume the appearance of armed camps.'[32]

The Springboks did not know where the demonstrators would strike next. There were demonstrations outside the hotels, usually at night. Fire alarms were set off, threatening telephone calls were made. On the morning of the international against England at Twickenham, a young man from Belfast jumped aboard the vehicle, chained himself to the steering column and tried to take off to an unknown destination. He took a number of players some 40 metres down Piccadilly before crashing into a van and then a pneumatic drill. Thereafter, he was quickly overpowered and handed to the police. It was an incident that greatly upset the Springboks. 'This is going too far,' complained manager Corrie Bornman. 'The boys' lives were in danger. This chap couldn't even drive.'[33]

Hain's influence was remarkable, the more so because he ran the campaign from his bedroom in Putney. He had no central fund from which to operate. 'We have very little money at all,' he acknowledged at the time. 'The university groups in the centres where demos are being arranged, pay all their own expenses. It is as simple as that.'[34]

More than 10 000 demonstrators and a record 2 300 police turned out in Dublin for the international at Lansdowne Road. In a match played behind barbed wire, Ireland snatched a draw in the eighth minute of injury time. It helped ensure that the Springboks had one of the worst records in international matches of any touring side to Britain. They did not win one of their four internationals and lost two of them, to England and Scotland; they lost five of their other tour matches.

Hain's campaign created a powerful mass movement. In the course of the 24 tour matches, he mobilised more than 50 000 people. 'In a few months,' he proclaimed, 'we have revitalised the anti-apartheid campaign in Britain, and whether people agree with us or not about mass demonstrations and the disruption of matches, we have forced everyone in Britain to think more about apartheid and what it means.'

After all the damage and disruption, Hain did not believe the campaign would affect South Africa's sports policy: 'There are signs of a change of heart among sportsmen, but I doubt if they can make an impression on the Nationalist government.'[35] The Springboks themselves provided mixed reactions. Corrie Bornman was quoted as stating: 'All this trouble could have been stopped right at the beginning. If the rugby fans had gone at these people, given them a real going-over, they'd have very soon stopped.'[36] Captain Dawie de Villiers recognised that Springbok rugby would never be the same again: 'Changes would have to be made if we were to compete freely at international level.'[37]

White South Africans were bitter at Hain's success and the SA Cricket Association continued with their plans for 1970. They announced that the team to tour England would be selected on merit – but this was crushed by Vorster's New Year message that no multi-racial teams from South Africa could tour overseas. On 22 May 1970, then home secretary James Callaghan forced a withdrawal of the invitation to South Africa 'on grounds of broad public policy'. Cricket contact with South Africa was effectively severed.

By June 1970, the country had been expelled from the IOC and expelled or suspended from international athletics, basketball, boxing, cycling, fencing, football, gymnastics, judo, netball, pentathlon, swimming, volleyball, weightlifting, wrestling, tennis (Davis Cup), table-tennis and big-game fishing. They were about to be cast out of international cricket and massive demonstrations had been staged against their rugby side. The government had bungled Arthur Ashe's request to play in South Africa and prevented a Japanese jockey, Sueo Masuzawa, from riding in a race in Pietermaritzburg.

The most important event for white South African sportsmen in 1970 was the All Blacks' rugby tour. It also brought to a head the question of whether or not to accept Maori players. The problem, more than any other issue, had plagued Vorster. When he had carefully enunciated his new sports policy in April 1967, he had aimed at paving the way for Maori to tour the country. He had even based his announcement on the astonishing premise that the acceptance of Maori was not a departure from tradition. He told the House of Assembly that 'the 1928 New Zealand rugby team that visited South Africa had included two Maoris or people of Maori extraction, while there had been at least three in each of the teams that had come to South Africa in 1949 and 1960'.

Vorster continued:

We received these people [the Maori] and treated them as we treated any members of the New Zealand touring side. There were no problems or troubles in this regard. South Africa would not try to prescribe to New Zealand what the composition of New Zealand teams should be; it had not tried to prescribe in the past.

A stern warning followed: 'But I want to point out clearly that if politics creeps in with the purpose of disturbing relations between the countries, or of creating internal difficulties here, I shall not hesitate to act as my predecessor acted at Loskop Dam.'[38]

Reference to Verwoerd's disastrous intervention simply added to the confusion already created by Vorster's address. Throughout his speech, he kept one eye on the right-wing element of his party, which resulted in ambiguities and qualifying comments watering down any positive statements. The sports editor of the *Dominion*, Wellington's morning newspaper, stated euphemistically that much of what Vorster said, 'leans away from fact'.[39]

Rugby administrators responded by denying any knowledge of the Maori players referred to by Vorster. Press reports reminded readers that the day before Vorster made his address, his minister of sport and former Springbok Frank Waring had asserted, 'There has never been a Maori, as far as I know, in a team which has come to South Africa.'[40]

While the undignified debate continued, South African cabinet ministers referred frequently to Maori players who had visited the country. Dr Connie Mulder noted that 'in 1919 a visiting All Black team had two Maoris and an Indian'. Dr Carel de Wet, the minister of mines opined, 'It has been traditional for South Africa since 1928 to allow the New Zealand All Blacks to come to South Africa and to have within that team people of Maori descent or even Maoris.' Waring also suddenly 'remembered' that Maori had toured South Africa and added his support to the argument.[41]

Two members of the National Party, Dr Albert Hertzog (minister of posts and telegraphs) and Jaap Marais (Member of Parliament for Innesdal) were adamant that they did not want Maori to accompany the New Zealand team. They were against everything that could threaten the Afrikaner's identity. They would rather do without international sporting contact than put up with any mixing between races.

At the Transvaal Congress of the National Party in September 1969, Hertzog was troubled that Maori on a rugby tour would take part in social events with white South Africans. 'They will sit at tables with our young men and girls,' he lamented, 'and they will dance with our girls.'[42]

When the congress was called to vote on the much-maligned sports policy, a handful of delegates opposed it. They were championed by Hertzog 'in a speech that strongly attacked Vorster for departing from the stance on sports policy taken by Verwoerd'.[43] The reprisals were swift. Vorster expelled Hertzog, Marais and Cape member Louis Stofberg from the National Party. The rebels formed the Herstigte Nasionale Party (HNP, Reconstituted National Party).

Vorster announced a general election in April 1970, a year ahead of schedule, with a key issue being the HNP's fierce opposition to non-racial sport. The strength of the new party's support was an unknown factor but the National Party chose to devote most of its attention to them. At the end of a bitter campaign, the HNP did not win a single seat while the moderate United Party captured eight National Party seats. The results helped convince the South African government that the majority of whites were in favour of concessions being made to facilitate participation in international sport.

The New Zealand side to tour South Africa in 1970 included three part-Maori (Syd Going, Buff Milner and Blair Furlong) and a player of Samoan extraction (Bryan Williams). There was still tremendous opposition in New Zealand to playing rugby against South Africa. An application was made to the Supreme Court that the proposed tour would be prejudicial to the interests of New Zealand. On 8 June, five days before the team was due to leave, the case was heard by Justice Michael Boys Hardie and the application was turned down.

All Blacks' scrum-half Chris Laidlaw outlines the alternatives he faced as follows: 'Should New Zealand refuse to tour South Africa at all in the hope that enforced isolation would provoke the breakdown of apartheid, or should contact be maintained in order that direct persuasion could take place with rugby acting as a catalyst?' Laidlaw chose the latter option but was aware that many people, including friends, opposed his decision. He concedes that he and several other All Blacks were very uneasy about the consequences. In their favour was the fact that this was the first multiracial tour to South Africa and that that was a step in the right direction. 'I saw it as a chink in the armour of apartheid,' adds Laidlaw, 'through which a wedge could be driven.'[44]

The Springboks won the Test series 3–1, but for the New Zealand RFU there was satisfaction that they had at last made demands on their South African counterparts. It was impossible to measure the psychological impact a multiracial side made on those South Africans who supported apartheid. A follow-up was seen as essential with South Africa expected to make further concessions, the most important being the selection of a Springbok side on merit. This would necessitate mixed trials, something the Vorster government would not tolerate.

Five Springboks were included in a President's Overseas XV that toured England in April 1971 to celebrate the centenary of the Rugby Football Union, a rugby administration to which South Africa was once affiliated. Joggie Jansen, Dawie de Villiers, Hannes Marais, Frik du Preez and Ian McCallum were honoured through their selection for the tour. The highlight was the match against England at Twickenham, a game that the President's Overseas XV won 28–11, with the All Blacks' wing Bryan Williams scoring a hat-trick of tries. Also memorable was the selection of Du Preez and New Zealand's Colin Meads to form the lock partnership. Many years later, they would be named 'Players of the Century' for their respective countries.

Du Preez's last appearances for the Springboks came during the controversial tour to Australia in 1971. The Australian Council of Trade Unions boycotted the visit, which meant the South Africans travelled on private aircraft. Peter Hain flew to Australia specifically to help coordinate the demonstrations. He teamed up with the Australian anti-apartheid leaders, a radical student Meredith Burgmann, a communist journalist Denis Freney, and a teacher Peter McGregor, arguably something of a loose cannon who inexplicably smashed windows and glass doors of a Sydney clubhouse in the middle of the night.[45]

Seven former Australian players were opposed to the tour and gave credibility to the cause. They believed that by playing against South Africa they were endorsing racial sport and effectively accepting apartheid. The players joined forces with opposition leader Gough Whitlam in publishing a leaflet that would be distributed by the anti-apartheid movement at matches and rallies. While they aimed to stop the tour, they also provided the following assurance: 'We stress that we would never condone violent action or demonstrations which might infringe the civil liberties of the individual citizen.'[46]

They could not have imagined that demonstrators would be so keen to push protest to the limit. Hundreds were arrested, with disruptions described as being on a scale even greater than they had been in Britain. Matches were played behind police cordons and barbed wire, with onlookers stunned by the violence. That all matches were completed was largely attributed to the professionalism of the police.

Meredith Burgmann gained satisfaction from the demonstrations because 'generally speaking, rugby union was played by toffs and that's why they got on well with the white South Africans'. Demonstrators damaged property; provoked and attacked the police; spread tacks and glass on the fields; and threw fireworks, flares and balloons filled with 'sharp metal discs that were capable of slicing open the arm or leg of any player who fell on them'. Police were bombarded with golf balls, cans of beer and flying bottles and some had their heads split open.[47]

Australian Reg Smith, who played in the opening Test, was astounded: 'They kept trying to get on the pitch, they were throwing smoke bombs – it was bloody mayhem.'[48] When the Springboks were seated in the bus to take them to the Sydney Cricket Ground for the third Test, a demonstrator tossed a glass phial of tear-gas through a window. The tube shattered and players were engulfed in the unpleasant gas.

The demonstrators complained about the way they were treated. The riot at Olympic Park, Melbourne, was a frightening experience and in Queensland, a 'state of emergency' was declared. When Sir Henry Bolte, the Victorian prime minister, was asked if he was perturbed at the number of protestors who were injured, he responded: 'They put themselves in harm's way and then they squeal.'[49]

'For the Springboks' part,' says Sydney-based journalist Larry Writer,

> there is no doubt that in their rugby and personal conduct on tour, they were beyond reproach ... To win the Test series and remain unbeaten under the pressures they faced every day was a special achievement. These men, under siege from the moment they arrived in Australia, proved themselves to be as mentally strong as they were physically powerful ... they continued to play the brand of rugby that made them world champions, at one beautiful and brutal, with its quicksilver attack and relentless, teeming, jolting defence.[50]

The Springboks won all 13 of their matches, scoring an astonishing 76 tries in the process. But the protestors claimed victory in that South Africa's scheduled cricket tour would not take place in 1971/72.

Tom Bedford, the tour vice-captain, was critical of rugby officials and the South African management as they had not engaged with the Australian media in reasoned debate. The manager Flappie Lochner and his assistant Johan Claassen were clearly not comfortable in taking on the task, whilst the players were generally kept hidden, sneaking in out of the back doors of hotels, stadia and airports.

Sport was being punished by the South African government's intransigence.

Notes

1   *Rand Daily Mail*, 1 April 1970.
2   L. Butler and S. Stockwell (eds), *The Wind of Change: Harold Macmillan and British Decolonization* (London: Palgrave Macmillan, 2013), 1.
3   *The Star*, 19 February 1959.
4   R. Thompson, *Retreat from Apartheid: New Zealand's Sporting Contacts with South Africa* (London: Oxford University Press, 1975), 24.
5   *Die Burger*, 25 July 1960 (translated).
6   Thompson, *Retreat from Apartheid*, 25.
7   A. Guelke, 'The Politicisation of South African Sport', in L. Allison (ed.), *The Politics of Sport* (Manchester: Manchester University Press, 1986), 123.
8   S. Carmichael, *112 Years of Springbok Tests and Heroes* (Cape Town: SA Rugby Football Union, 2003), 108.
9   Carmichael (ed.), *112 Years of Springbok Tests and Heroes*, 107–108.
10 On their way back to Johannesburg, the Springboks had a four-day stop-over in Nairobi where they defeated East Africa. This was the first match between South Africa and another African 'nation'.
11 B. Thomas, *Springbok Glory* (London: Stanley Paul, 1961), 49.
12 *Daily Mail*, 9 January 1961.
13 D. Kamfer, *Die Burger*, quoted in Thomas, *Springbok Glory*, 26.
14 *The Times*, 9 January 1961.
15 J. Gainsford with N. Leck, *Nice Guys Come Second* (Cape Town: Don Nelson, 1974), 71–72.
16 Quoted in Thomas, *Springbok Glory*, 139.
17 Ibid., 26.
18 E. Louw, *The Rise, Fall and Legacy of Apartheid* (Westport: Praeger, 2004), 121.
19 Guelke, 'The Politicisation of South African Sport', 123–124.
20 *Sunday Times*, 5 September 1965.
21 A. Campbell, 'Right or Wrong – Let the Games Begin?', in *Australia and New Zealand Sports Law Journal*, 5, 1 (2010), 33; *New Zealand Hansard*, 7 September 1965, 2527.
22 J. Winch and M. Patel, interview with P. Koornhof, in 'Playing the Game: The Unification of South African Sport' (unpublished M-Net project, 2000).
23 P. Hain, 'Direct Action and the Springbok Tours', in R. Benewick and T. Smith (eds), *Direct Action and Democratic Politics* (London: Allen and Unwin, 1972), 193.
24 B. Murray, R. Parry and J. Winch (eds), *Cricket and Society in South Africa 1910–1971: From Union to Isolation* (London: Palgrave Macmillan, 2018), 22, 158.
25 Hain, 'Direct Action and the Springbok Tours', 193.
26 D. Humphry, *The Cricket Conspiracy* (London: National Council for Civil Liberties, 1972), 37–38.
27 W. Reyburn, *There Was Also Some Rugby: The Sixth Springboks in Britain* (London: Stanley Paul, 1970), 16.
28 Humphry, *The Cricket Conspiracy*, 37–38.
29 B. McLaren, *Talking of Rugby: An Autobiography* (London: Stanley Paul, 1991), 137–138.
30 *Daily Dispatch*, 5 January 1970.
31 Reyburn, *There Was Also Some Rugby*, 26.
32 Hain, 'Direct Action and the Springbok Tours', 194.
33 *Sunday Times* (Johannesburg), 21 December 1969.
34 *Daily Dispatch*, 5 January 1970.
35 Ibid.
36 Reyburn, *There Was Also Some Rugby*, 81.
37 C. Rea, 'Our Man in London', *Rugby World*, November 1979, 18.
38 *Rand Daily Mail*, 12 April 1967.
39 *Dominion*, 11 April 1967.
40 *Rand Daily Mail*, 11 April 1967.
41 Thompson, *Retreat from Apartheid*, 52.
42 Ibid.

43   A. Guelke, *Rethinking the Rise and Fall of Apartheid: South Africa and World Politics* (London: Palgrave Macmillan, 2005), 121.

44   C. Laidlaw, *Mud in Your Eye: A Worm's Eye View of the Changing World of Rugby* (London: Pelham Books, 1974), 190.

45   L. Writer, *Pitched Battle: In the Frontline of the 1971 Springbok Tour of Australia* (Melbourne: Scribe, 2016), 88–90, 113.

46   J. Boyce, J. Roxburgh, B. McDonald, P. Darveniza, B. Taafe and T. Forman, 'Non-White Rugby in South Africa', in a leaflet, *Australia-South Africa: An Appeal from Some Wallabies*; Writer, *Pitched Battle*, 74–76.

47   Writer, *Pitched Battle*, 115, 217.

48   C. Doran, Fox Sports, 8 September 2016.

49   Writer, *Pitched Battle*, 196.

50   Ibid., 234, 280.

17

SARU, SACOS and Multinationalism

The South African Rugby Union said that non-racialism
is a principle not peculiar or not particularly exclusive to
any political organisation. In SARU, we hold the view that
non-racialism is enshrined in morality. We believe with all
our hearts that our non-racial ethic comes from the Bible and
it comes from the Koran and it comes from God. It is from
that premise that we believe anything that militates against
true non-racialism to be false. The South African Rugby
Union from that particular ideology believes in a non-racial
democratic South Africa in which all men shall be free.[1]

– Ebrahim Patel (SARU AGM, 1987)

Ebrahim Patel, the last-serving president of the SA Rugby Union, believes rugby's
unification process in South Africa began when John Kester, president of the SA
Coloured Rugby Football Board, met Danie Craven in April 1962. They signed
an agreement aimed at fostering closer cooperation and, three years later, Craven
went to Kimberley to hold further talks. By that stage, Patel had become involved
in rugby administration and noted that Craven's attempt to create support for an
amalgamation was turned down. 'The coloured board,' explained Patel, 'objected
to the suggestion of a white representing them on the SA Rugby Football Board.'[2]

In 1966, the SA Coloured Rugby Football Board reaffirmed its desire to be a
non-racial body. It changed its name to the SA Rugby Union – popularly referred
to as 'SARU' – but its national team continued to be known as 'Springboks'. The
same year, the City and Suburban Union left the SA Rugby Football Federation
for SARU because they were unhappy with Cuthbert Loriston's leadership and
the direction he was taking. Loriston's support base was largely situated in
the Boland area of the Western Cape, while SARU was a national body, with
provincial unions across the country.

In 1967, John Kester departed for Canada and was succeeded as SARU president by Abdullah Abass. The latter was greatly respected by both SARU and the SA Rugby Football Board. His secretary was Patel, who had developed a love for rugby at an early age and was president of the Transvaal Rugby Union.[3] 'In the past,' says Paul Dobson, 'Kester had done the talking; now it would be Patel. And increasingly, in those stressful times, the talking would be aimed at apartheid.'[4]

Patel appreciated the opportunity to work under Abass: 'It was initially a professional working arrangement but developed into a great friendship – a father-son relationship.'[5] Patel addressed the day-to-day matters and corresponded with representatives from rugby organisations at home and overseas. In addition, he accompanied Abass to rugby gatherings in various parts of the country.

In 1970, SARU – represented by Abass and Patel – attended a meeting of four rugby administrations at Newlands. Also taking part were the SA Rugby Football Board under Craven, the SA Rugby Football Federation under Loriston and the SA African Rugby Board under Grant Khomo. At the meeting, SARU objected to the SA Rugby Football Federation and the SA African Rugby Board being given equal status as they were not national organisations and only represented limited constituencies. Their argument appeared to be partly in conflict with a survey conducted by the South African Institute of Race Relations in 1971. The survey notes: 'The SA African Rugby Board (with some 50 000 African members), the SA Rugby Union (with some 18 000 coloured and Indian members) and the SA Rugby Football Federation (with some 7 000–9 000 coloured members).'[6]

When Craven endeavoured to proceed with a shared advisory committee, SARU refused to cooperate. It did not want to be part of any such arrangement until the SA Rugby Football Board accepted the principles of non-racialism and merit selection. SARU dropped the annual match against the national African team and established the SA Cup, initially as a tournament but then on a home and away basis. They also rejected the introduction of 'multinational sport', a new concept that the South African government – together with the Broederbond – had come up with in April 1971.

The government believed multinationalism would satisfy international opinion and yet allow the policy of separate development to be maintained. Blacks and whites playing in the same team was still forbidden, but multinational sport, involving blacks and whites competing against each other in separate teams, became permissible at international level. While South Africa would continue to be represented abroad only by all-white teams, John Vorster made several concessions. He indicated that multiracial teams could be sent to four events – the Olympic Games, the Canada Cup (golf), the Federation Cup (tennis) and the Davis Cup (tennis). A condition of this arrangement was that the Springbok symbol could not be used.

In announcing these changes, Vorster was keen to demonstrate to his right-wingers that he was following a progressive line of thought and not deviating from National Party principles. Under apartheid, South Africa was made up of separate nations – there were eight national 'homelands' – and the government believed that these nations had matured to the extent that they were ready to become involved in 'international' competition.

The cabinet minister tasked with the responsibility of implementing the new policy was Dr Piet Koornhof, a Rhodes Scholar who had made his way up the ranks of the Broederbond and the National Party. He recalled: 'Mr Vorster was very conscious of the mistakes that had been made in sport. And when I was appointed minister, he called me in and said: "See what you can do to remedy the situation."'

Critics were quick to point out that multinationalism was a contradictory and hopelessly inadequate approach, one that served to emphasise rather than disguise racial imbalances. It was uncertain, for example, how the government intended to cater for the coloured and Indian 'nations'. 'Yes, of course multinationalism could not work,' explained Koornhof. 'The thinking was that everyone [black, white, coloured and Indian] would get a physical homeland, but that remained a theory.'[7] This was naturally not admitted at the time.

Craven wanted SARU to join plans he had for a 'coloured' tour overseas in December 1971 and for a match against a touring England team in 1972. He was very persuasive, but Patel and his committee were suspicious from the outset that Craven was only interested in selecting blacks for the sake of expediency. Loriston opposed SARU's stance, believing that it was better to accept what advantages they could obtain. However, he was realistic enough to accept that 'for purposes of the convenience of international rugby relationships, it has now pleased them to treat us as equals. But when the need of convenience is no longer there, we shall go back to our life of sub-humanity.'[8]

Some black communities expressed their objection to links with white rugby by switching allegiance. They included Port Elizabeth's Kwazakhele Rugby Union, which brought a strong African influence into SARU. From a strengthened position, Abass repeatedly asked the SA Rugby Football Board to allow black players to participate in trials, thereby meeting their demand for a merit-based, non-racial selection.[9] According to Patel, Craven became frustrated by these requests, claiming, 'There are stages in life, through which everything develops. You crawl, you walk, you run; every plant grows up. Evolution is in stages.'[10]

SARU members were scornful of the stages that Craven envisaged. 'We were not a developing organisation,' explained Patel, 'but one that had been in existence for 80 years.' He outlined SARU's position and emphasised that they did not want to be part of any tour or to play against touring white teams because such participation would be 'blatant opportunism'. It served the interest of a few black sportsmen but did nothing for the wider community. He described the SA Rugby Football Board's action in propping up the Federation as 'utterly detestable'.[11] At a later meeting, Patel spoke of the Federation 'being backed by propaganda, money and support and any other assistance which is necessary to produce a coloured front in South Africa'.[12]

In 1971, the SA African Rugby Board beat the Federation twice – 10–3 at Athlone Stadium and 13–6 at Wolfson Stadium. They were a side of limited strength but happy to seize the opportunity to tour Britain and the Netherlands during 1971/72. SARU dismissed the tour because it advanced multinationalism but Loriston argued that it was an experiment designed 'to test our strength'. The Proteas, who were subjected to anti-apartheid protests, won three, lost three and drew one of their matches. Mixed fortunes were experienced against sides such as Hertfordshire, Berkshire, Oxfordshire and Buckinghamshire before they went on to beat the Netherlands 28–23.

Proteas player Errol Tobias saw the team as trailblazers: 'We largely turned our backs on politics and apartheid laws, and were prepared to play rugby against anyone ... as long as it was within the context of human dignity.' He described the tour as an eye-opener, with players startled to see mixed black and white couples in Britain: 'The group talked about it for days ... surely this is how it should be; surely this is how things should work in South Africa.'[13]

The following year, the Proteas played against England in Cape Town. In a short seven-match tour, the English beat the Springboks in a Test match at Ellis Park but struggled to defeat the Proteas 11–6 in Cape Town. The latter was an historic match, the first reported occasion in which a team of colour had played against whites in South Africa. It was a tough, physical encounter, during which Errol Tobias, Green Vigo, Johnny Noble and Jack Juries showed glimpses of genuine class. Former All Blacks scrum-half Chris Laidlaw viewed the game as 'finally putting to rest the myth that non-whites were not yet ready for the big stuff'.

Although impressed by the performance of the Proteas, Laidlaw was not taken in by the concept of multinationalism. It would not be long before 'other rugby countries realise that initiating matches with the differing rugby bodies in South Africa amounts no more or less to confederacy in apartheid'. He believed that black rugby was still in the wilderness. 'No African or coloured player,' he comments, 'can hope to become a Springbok, still less represent his country, the Republic. The greatest indignity, however, is that he cannot test his strength against European players. Coloured against African is quite permissible, non-white against European is taboo.'[14]

The SA African Rugby Board was also given opportunities to play touring sides, beginning with defeats against England 36–3 in 1972 and Italy 24–4 the following year. John Reason of the *Daily Telegraph* recalls the England side driving 'seemingly for miles through thousands of African well-wishers on route to the stadium in Port Elizabeth'.[15] They were to meet the SA African Rugby Board's 'Leopards', a name choice that did not come from the Africans. Vuyisa Qunta condemned it as a patronising move by whites, who wished to appropriate the springbok for their rugby only. 'Black rugby-supporting committees rejected and denigrated the leopard emblem', which they associated with the sorghum beer sold by white-run municipalities.[16]

SARU leaders viewed their rival organisations as being 'sell-outs' but were also concerned that their members might be tempted by international glory and defect to where the grass was greener. Patel warned his organisation of the need to stand up for its stance against multinationalism, arguing that 'while Rome is burning, SARU is sitting in an ideological position of holiness'. He believed that 'the holiness must be emanated and activated to a positive force of opposition, otherwise South Africa will definitely and is definitely moving to multinationalism and, by its silence, SARU will definitely assist this process'.[17]

The South African tour to New Zealand in 1973 was under discussion for some months. The political correspondent of *Die Transvaler* expressed concern that attention should be given to inviting coloured players to trials: 'In top rugby circles there is strong pressure for such a step.' A few days later, Koornhof rejected mixed trials. 'The government's policy remained unchanged,' he explained.[18] To demonstrate solidarity on the matter, the prime minister and ministers of economic affairs, labour, and transport also made a point of opposing mixed trials.[19]

Leaders of HART (Halt All Racist Tours) and CARE (Citizens' Association for Racial Equality) in New Zealand told Craven in a telephone conversation that they would drop all plans to disrupt the tour if he could persuade the government to give coloured players a fair chance to make the team. The SA Rugby Football

Board asked the government for permission to include players on merit, but their request was refused.

New Zealand prime minister Norman Kirk reacted by telling his rugby union that they should cancel the tour. Kirk referred to a police report that predicted 'the greatest eruption of violence this country has known'.[20] The tour was cancelled.

'On moral grounds,' recorded the *Christchurch Star*, 'the tour could not possibly have taken place. It would have spelt out to the world, contrary to our professions, that our racially harmonious society condoned racial separation in South Africa.'[21]

SARU met with Koornhof in early 1973. The meeting aroused considerable speculation and suspicion that SARU had compromised or abandoned its non-racial principles. In reply, Patel argued that the discussions had emphasised SARU's 'willingness to cooperate with anybody, including the government, in working towards integrated and non-racial sport'.[22] This commitment was reaffirmed later in the year when SARU became a member and leading force behind the establishment of the South African Council on Sport (SACOS). The latter body, which coined the slogan, 'No normal sport in an abnormal society', aimed to unify the various non-racial organisations and was determined to fight the policy of multinationalism. It followed a rigid policy of non-collaboration, a strategy that Patel did not strictly adhere to in subsequent years.

Despite politics impinging increasingly on rugby, the Leopards embarked on a tour to Italy in May 1974. The side, financed by the SA Rugby Football Board, won one and drew one of their seven matches. The defeats were by no more than five points, except for the Test against Italy which was lost 25–10. The tour highlight was the 4–0 victory over the Zebre, an invitation team in north-west Italy that included the England player Jeremy Janion and several New Zealanders.

Craven continued to ask SARU to play matches against touring sides. The British Lions were scheduled to visit from May to July 1974, and fixtures against black teams were expected to gain considerable exposure. The inclusion of SARU players would have provided a clearer indication of the strength of black rugby. With the Springboks down 2–0 prior to the third Test against the Lions at Port Elizabeth, one leading newspaper suggested SARU's outstanding half-backs Peter Mkata and Cassiem Jabaar might be the solution to South Africa's woes.[23]

Patel was annoyed that the views expressed by his union two years earlier had been forgotten. He described matches played by black teams against touring sides as 'a mere sop for overseas consumption' and 'where goodwill towards the underprivileged players of South Africa is a mere afterthought'. There was no interest in playing visiting white sides, 'whilst we are denied and debarred from playing rugby with and against white rugby players from our own country'. Patel emphasised the need 'to create a position whereby a South African team would be welcome to play rugby throughout the free world'.[24]

One important factor that offered hope was that Craven had insisted he was in favour of merit selection. Admittedly, the situation was confused by his statement that Springbok colours should be for whites only. 'If we give the Springbok away,' he allegedly stated, 'what will be left for us whites?'[25]

Willie-John McBride's triumphant 1974 Lions defeated the Proteas 37–6 at Cape Town and Leopards 56–10 at East London. The matches were characterised by robust play. John Reason was encouraged that teams from overseas wanted to help the advance of rugby in non-white communities but believed it to be 'time that the non-whites stopped making political points and started playing rugby'. He claims that 'neither England nor the Lions enjoyed their games against the Proteas and that is the whole point of playing any sport'.[26]

The match against the Leopards at the Mdantsane Stadium, East London, saw local captain Thompson Magxala upstage the Lions by holding aloft a live leopard cub as he entered the field. But the most dramatic moment occurred when Mbulelo Maqosha punched Chris Ralston unconscious shortly after half-time. McBride chose not to make use of the Lions' infamous '99' call,[27] possibly because Maqosha had already taken off with his horrified team after him.[28] The Leopards lost 56–10 – ten tries to one – with great excitement reserved for a rare try scored against the Lions late in the game. Morgan Cushe, who had been outstanding throughout, gathered a stray pass, rapidly made ground and created space for Charles Mgweba on the left wing. Mgweba did the rest, sprinting 40 metres to score.

Sport was riddled with problems during this period and there seemed to be no long-term plan. Rugby-wise, one-off matches against vastly more experienced opponents encouraged desperate tactics to prevent runaway victories.[29] The government struggled to keep the faltering multinational policy in place, and Craven grasped the opportunity to make a breakthrough. He visited Prime Minister Vorster to request permission for a mixed South African team to play against the French in 1975 – and for mixed trials. Vorster began by berating Craven and it was not surprising that the request for mixed trials was turned down.

When Craven pushed for a mixed team, the meeting took a dramatic turn. 'He was furious again,' observed Craven. 'But it was a strange, almost controlled fury':

> At one time, at the height of his fury, I really thought I was about to see the prime minister of South Africa have a heart attack right in front of me but I now reasoned as I sat there, 'Wait for it ... I think we're going to hear something dramatic!' Then the prime minister's astute legal brain simply started to dictate his words. It was almost as if he knew he had lost and that he was about to make a major concession: 'All right,' he conceded, 'have your mixed President's XV and choose whom you like, but no mixed trials ... no mixed trials!'[30]

Vorster attended the match in which Morné du Plessis led the President's XV against the French at Newlands. Four black players – John Noble, Toto Tsotsobe, Turkey Shields and Morgan Cushe – were included in the team, which wore black and white jerseys. Right-wing Noble scored the opening try of the match to set the President's XV on their way. They won 18–3, with black spectators in the crowd for once supporting the home side.

The following year, the All Blacks were assisted by the New Zealand prime minister Robert Muldoon, who supported rugby links with South Africa. The touring team, captained by Andy Leslie, gathered in Auckland amidst huge security restrictions. As they departed for the airport, demonstrators threw paint at the bus. The players were driven straight to their aircraft and then embarked on a long roundabout route because the Australian government refused transit to a national team heading for South Africa.

The All Blacks played against the Proteas in the third match of their tour. Terry McLean praises 'two magnificent coloured teams who played an enthralling 15-all curtain-raiser in wet conditions. They proved the ball could be handled securely by players with the right technical skill.' The main game followed the pattern of previous matches against international teams where the Proteas practised 'the kind of illegalities which are common the rugby world over when a team without hope, but endless enthusiasm takes on a crack side'.

McLean says the sad feature was that 'the Proteas had enough ability to play tidy rugby efficiently and effectively. They were amazingly quick. Eddie Gillion and Charles Williams moved to quell those attacks by [the New Zealand backs] with shattering speed. Ronnie Louw behind them was genuinely quick, too, and as a full-back would be greeted with joy by many New Zealand provincial selectors.' The Proteas were defeated 25–3 but their style of 'swarming and amazingly swift defence was undoubtedly deucedly difficult to combat'.[31]

In the fourth match of the tour, the SA Rugby Board fielded a mixed SA Invitation XV against the All Blacks at Newlands. Four black players were chosen – but there was a shock withdrawal of the white captain of the side and one of the country's greatest players, flanker Jan Ellis. He was reported to be unwell, but the *Sunday Times* revealed that he had refused to play in a mixed-race team:

> Multiracial sport anywhere in the world is okay. I have played against and socialised with Fijians, Maoris and all other kinds – but that was overseas. When in Rome, you do as the Romans tell you. Here in South Africa, the same thing holds – and I am a white South African.[32]

A glorious day was nevertheless experienced at Newlands. The Proteas played the Leopards in a curtain-raiser that impressed McLean: 'At least four of the Protea backs, Lategan at scrumhalf, Williams in the centre, Gillion and Davids on the wings, and one forward, Jack Juries, the number 8 ... and two Leopard backs, Sonto and Gawulayo, looked good enough to play in All Black trials.'

In the main game, the All Blacks demonstrated admirable resilience to defeat the Invitation XV 31–24 in a thrilling encounter. The latter included massive forwards from the SA Rugby Board such as Louis Moolman, Moaner van Heerden, Theuns Stofberg and Richard Prentis – 'the only Slim Jim was the black flanker, Morgan Cushe'. They played alongside the likes of Carel Fourie, Gavin Cowley and Divan Serfontein. At the back was the Protea star Ronnie Louw, fielding the ball 'like a player who had served a long time in the best of company'.[33]

Later in the tour, the All Blacks accounted for the Leopards. An army helicopter patrolled the townships, armed police guarded the gates and escorted coaches carried the players and the press. Cushe, fellow flank Lilee Jonas, fly-half Norman Mbiko, lock Thompson Magxala (a laboratory technician in the Groote Schuur Hospital), and props William Diba and Broadness Cona showed up well but

> questionable, though understandable, were the tactics devised for the Leopards by their coach, Sipho Nozewu [who] had recently spent six weeks at a coaching course run by the RFU at Twickenham ... Pretty well everyone was off-side at some time or other. Pretty well everyone tackled head high ... a real need of black rugby was education in the laws, starting at the very young.[34]

It was not the happiest of tours for the All Blacks as it was played at a time of bitter racial unrest.

In June that year, police had violently quelled a demonstration by thousands of black schoolchildren in Soweto, triggering an upsurge of protest marches and riots throughout the country with concomitant retaliation by the state. There was no escaping reality and two of the visiting players, Ian Kirkpatrick and Bryan Williams, were teargassed in Cape Town.

The New Zealanders were also unhappy with the controversial refereeing in the final Test which possibly denied them a share of the series. By the same token, they could not match the kicking qualities of Springbok Gerald Bosch, although he was not everyone's choice at fly-half. Former *Daily Dispatch* editor Donald Woods recalled discussing the issue with the imprisoned black consciousness leader, Steve Biko:

> His interrogators had been astonished by his interest in what they regarded as exclusively 'white' matters ... The security police asked if he was following the tour. He told them he was. What did he think of the Springbok team? Steve replied, 'I wouldn't have Bosch at fly-half, I'd pick Gavin Cowley.' This, he said, appeared to flabbergast them. Such black knowledge of white sport.[35]

Opposition to the tour was widespread and All Blacks players were questioned about taking part. The part-Samoan wing Bryan Williams told the *Auckland Star*:

> Apartheid gets me down. Knowing that I'd probably be in the same situation as South Africa's blacks is not a very nice thought. I do get depressed. But if you fight the problem by boycotts, by bullying someone, I think you get resented. If you go there, and discuss it with people, you get communication.[36]

Some developments in the course of the tour served to support Williams' viewpoint. The New Zealand management eventually realised that South Africa's insistence on an all-white Test team could no longer be tolerated. Tour manager Noel Stanley announced two days before the last Test that merit selection had to be implemented before the next Springbok team could be accepted into New Zealand. From a South African perspective, Koornhof asserted that the tour had an impact on the formulation of a new sports policy that he introduced not long afterwards.

Statements made for the media had no effect on mounting opposition from the Supreme Council of Sport in Africa. Twenty African countries, and Guinea and Iraq, announced that in accordance with a resolution of the Organisation of African Unity (OAU), they would boycott the 1976 Montreal Olympic Games if New Zealand took part. The boycott was announced less than 48 hours before the Games were due to begin. The Olympic leaders were stunned. It was a problem that they could not solve; rugby had not been an Olympic sport since 1924 and they had no jurisdiction over it. The president of the International Olympic Committee, Lord Killanin, supported by his entire executive board, rejected the ultimatum. Twenty-two countries withdrew 441 athletes in 14 events.

Inevitably, the events of 1976 had an impact on South Africa. Adrian Guelke believes the 'serious rioting in Soweto in June 1976 and subsequent black unrest elsewhere ... had shaken white self-confidence and increased white receptivity to reform in this and other areas of policy ... The boycott of the Olympic Games forced many western countries to re-examine their attitude towards apartheid sport.'[37]

In September 1976, Koornhof announced further adjustments to South Africa's sports policy. They amounted to multinational sport being extended to club level, allowing black and white clubs to play against one another. About two months later, Koornhof stated that all South African teams would in future be selected on merit and that multiracial trials would be held. In a further concession, he agreed that blacks could obtain Springbok colours.

It was a substantial shift in sports policy, but the anti-apartheid movement claimed it was too little too late. SACOS declared that South Africa could not participate in international sport until apartheid itself was dismantled. This meant that the moratorium Dennis Brutus had imposed when he prevented the West Indies cricket team from touring in 1959 would continue indefinitely. Norman Middleton, SACOS's inaugural president stated:

> We need to remember that whatever movements are made by the white sports bodies are only to safeguard their own positions and add more camouflage for overseas. The same thing is happening in the political arena. Everyone is saying we are moving away from discrimination, which is not true, and I must challenge the white administrators because I feel there is no sincerity in their approach.[38]

Resolutions were passed in the United Nations and in the 1977 Gleneagles Agreement among Commonwealth leaders, condemning and discouraging sporting contacts with South Africa. Koornhof looked for ways to counter the opposition. He hoped to establish contact with leading anti-apartheid activists such as Dennis Brutus and Peter Hain. Donald Woods let Hain know that Koornhof was keen to meet him, but the initiative was abruptly halted. General Hendrik van den Bergh, head of the Bureau of State Security, entered the picture, claiming that Koornhof was moving too quickly and that he wanted to 'protect' him.[39] Woods decided to opt out of the plans that were taking place and, not long afterwards, was forced to flee the country as a result of his investigating the death of Steve Biko.

Throughout the seventies, SARU kept in touch with the SA Rugby Football Board. SACOS members opposed this link and demanded the total isolation of white South African rugby. In 1977, SACOS introduced their 'double standards resolution' which effectively banned persons from their sports organisation who were in any way linked to white establishment or government bodies or events. A rigid commitment to non-collaboration saw SACOS spend time punishing and expelling members who stepped out of line. Their founding president, Norman Middleton, a respected fighter for non-racialism, was forced to step down over his ties to the Coloured Representative Council,[40] and the resolution was extended beyond the sports field to include schools, universities and hotels.

SARU was aware of the need for SACOS to adopt a more flexible approach and to build a broader base in catering for the requirements of its sports bodies. Some SARU officials suggested consideration be given to an application for membership of the International Rugby Football Board (IRB), but Patel was against such a move. He explained that the 'affiliation of SARU to the IRB, as a so-called "coloured" body will be the fulfilment of separate development as the union will then be arranging its own tours as well as touring abroad separately'.[41]

Despite obvious differences in policy between 'multinationalism' and 'non-racialism', delegations from the rival rugby administrations, the SA Rugby Football Board and SARU, saw an opportunity to push for unity. In 1977, an agreement was reached. A formal document was drawn up in the form of four points which, Craven acknowledged, 'although counter to the then government policy, weren't entirely revolutionary or so terribly controversial':

1) That we need one non-racial controlling body for rugby in South Africa, which means that we must amalgamate.
2) Their union boundaries and our union boundaries must be the same.
3) All the clubs must be open.
4) A player must be able to play wherever he wants to play.

Delegates from the rugby administrations travelled to the Union Buildings in Pretoria where a meeting was arranged with Koornhof. Craven had promised Abass that if they went together, they could not be ignored and would get a good reception. It was nevertheless a tense moment when the document was formally presented. Craven described the scene:

The Minister read the document very carefully. Perhaps even a couple of times. And then, I swear, I could almost see him start to shake. His face went bright red and, as if we were errant little schoolboys, he turned to us – turned on us, would perhaps be the better word – and snarled: 'You are asking me to acknowledge the impossible. I will not have anything to do with this agreement. You know that what you are asking is totally against the policy of this government.'[42]

Sport had moved too quickly for the government. Koornhof, who was arguably the country's most enlightened cabinet minister, ended any hope of a breakthrough in the South African rugby impasse. 'Stunned,' remarked Craven, 'we turned on our heels.'[43]

'We stopped to talk on the steps of the Union Buildings,' recalled Patel. 'Mr Abass was extremely upset. Never again would he give a white minister the opportunity to insult him.'

It had been a critical meeting. 'The SA Rugby Union,' reaffirmed Patel, 'had demonstrated beyond all reasonable doubt that it had done everything conceivably possible to unite South African rugby. It was clear that the government of the day was the impediment to progress. We now had no alternative but to officially engage in the isolation of South African sport.'[44] Both delegations knew that the division between whites and blacks, one which they had hoped to have bridged through their agreement, had widened.

Further talks were considered a waste of time. 'It was extremely difficult for us,' Patel explained. 'As disenfranchised people there was no political means at our disposal to change the government. It was up to those with the franchise – if they were serious about change – to do something.' He would later add with a sense of irony: 'It was evident, from our recent experience in Mr Koornhof's office that the SA Rugby Football Board was as powerless as we were to normalise the game.'[45]

Craven was determined to demonstrate to the IRB that the developments that had taken place were not entirely wasted. Ironically, they would be without SARU. In November 1977, the SA Rugby Association (formerly the SA African Rugby Board) and the SA Rugby Football Federation merged with the SA Rugby Football Board. They formed the SA Rugby Board, with black members appearing on the executive of the board and on the national panel of selectors. It was also keenly anticipated that Timothy Konki would become the first black Springbok; he had recently travelled with Morné du Plessis to play for a World XV as part of the 75th anniversary celebrations of the French Rugby Federation.

The new SA Rugby Board struggled to find opposition for the Springboks and, without the support of SARU, the amalgamation with the SA Rugby Association and SA Rugby Football Federation could never be more than partial unification. It was rejected as 'one of convenience and not of substance'.[46]

Abass died a few years later and Patel took over as president of SARU in 1983. Craven believed it would be more difficult for his organisation to have their way. 'Mr Patel, I often think,' grumbled Craven, 'is more of a politician than a rugby administrator – but so be it.' He then admitted to his biographer, Ted Partridge, 'I'm sure that if I had been born black in South Africa, I too would have been a militant – possibly even more radical than the elegant, and always quietly articulate and efficient Johannesburg-based, Mr Patel.'[47]

The image that Craven presented of Patel as head of an organisation bent on obstructing South Africa's return to international rugby was adopted by the white mainstream press. It was largely correct. Patel as the union's secretary, spokesman and then president performed a key role in isolating the rugby establishment during the apartheid era.

It was thought that Patel 'intensified the pressure' in South Africa's rugby structure and, as a consequence, there was reason for the government to eye the SA Rugby Union with suspicion.[48] Professor Jakes Gerwel, rector of the University of the Western Cape, stated in an address to a SA Rugby Union meeting: 'I am aware that just being a member of the SA Rugby Union is regarded as being subversive ... we have been called a bunch or a nest of Marxist opportunists by one cabinet minister. I know that we must be doing something right to have been called that.'[49]

The SA Rugby Union continued to run its affairs in much the same way as it had always done. It was a community-based organisation with very little financial support and largely primitive facilities. In 1982 'the white 15% of the population controlled 82% of the country's rugby fields'.[50] SARU nevertheless had a membership of 26 000 in 26 provincial unions and its three-tiered national league was well supported. Even though it received no television coverage and limited support from the establishment press, its organisation thrived and the SA Cup final was a major occasion.

'The game of rugby was a luxury in the face of poverty,' contended Patel, 'Gate-takings would be used to buy food for the people.' He frequently spoke about the people, rarely about players and matches. 'The SA Rugby Union,' he declared, 'provided an escape mechanism from a dull life under apartheid. The few hours of glorious entertainment on a Saturday afternoon helped people forget the slavery of the other six days of the week.' He concluded: 'The people loved "SARU" and "SARU" loved the people.'[51]

Rugby heroes emerged. In an ideal world, some would have played international rugby ahead of whites who were selected. There were 'many a supporter and player' commented Manie Booley, 'who will acknowledge that, with the passing years, they had seen similar or even better talent among the disadvantaged during their lifetime'.[52] Forwards Salie Fredericks and Peter Jooste and scrum-half Julian Smith were noted by their contemporaries as capable of playing at the highest level.

During the 1980s, there was great racial tension in South Africa. The SA Rugby Board continued to arrange international tours – including the 1981 demonstration-marred trip to New Zealand – and the rift with SARU widened. According to Hendrik Snyders, the selection of black players Errol Tobias and Avril Williams for South Africa was 'seen as a "sell-out" and a betrayal of the principles of non-racialism, merit and true freedom and therefore no cause for celebration'.[53]

Throughout the years of division, the SA Cup featured fine exponents of the game, large crowds, and generated great passion amongst players and supporters. Emotions ran high in difficult times and a later SA Rugby Football Union publication was at pains to emphasise the competition 'was not always savoury'. It provided a series of examples, the most dramatic probably being the 1985 final between fierce rivals Western Province and Tygerberg. A massive fight involving players and spectators erupted seven minutes into the match. The Tygerberg captain subsequently took his players off the field; irate spectators invaded the playing area, and the referee was chased away by an intruder wielding a knife. Ebrahim Patel spent 35 minutes persuading the players to restart the match.[54]

Patel's responsibilities were never-ending. When Springbok loose-forward Rob Louw attended an SA Cup semi-final match at Green Point in 1985, news spread quickly and a mood of hostility surfaced. Louw was worried that 'a riot might develop'. Patel went to his rescue by speaking to the crowd over the microphone before escorting him to safety. 'I stated with regret, but very understandably, that Rob Louw would be leaving. I asked that no one should try to harm him in any way. There was thunderous applause.' Once at the gate, Patel apologised for the situation and admitted to Louw, 'There's a lot of white hatred.'[55]

Throughout this turbulent period of disunity, the two pillars of South African rugby were as rigidly divided as ever. The liberal-minded former Springbok rugby player Tommy Bedford was 'reluctant to concede that SARU was non-racial: it was really for black and brown, hardly any whites. Let us say it aspired to be non-racial but wasn't.'[56] His viewpoint was supported by the case of Dan 'Cheeky' Watson and his brother Valence who turned their backs on the white

SA Rugby Football Board in 1976 to play rugby in the Kwazakhele league, a sub-division of SARU. Seven years later in 1983, the Watsons severed links with SARU, because they 'found it riddled with racism ... the problem stems from a rift between the different groups – Muslims, coloureds, blacks and ourselves'.[57]

That the Watsons became disenchanted was disappointing because they had made a brave and dramatic attempt to challenge the apartheid system. Most memorable was the celebrated mixed-race match played at the Dan Qeqe Stadium in Veeplaas, Zwide, on 10 October 1976. The government issued a series of threats and roadblocks were set up around the black township. The white players were forced to use a back road and side streets, but when they arrived at the stadium the 10 000-strong crowd erupted in wild excitement. 'The blacks had heard the media warnings. They did not think the whites would have the courage to play.'[58] Eight whites were amongst the thirty players who took part in the match in which Kwazakhele defeated South-Eastern Districts Rugby Union 23–13. Newspaper headlines recorded: 'Non-Race Rugby is Born'.[59]

The Watson brothers and Colin Snodgrass were chaired off the field. Cheeky Watson remembered the moment:

> It isn't just breaking the barriers of non-racial sport. You are on these guys' shoulders. They are lifting their fists. You suddenly feel that these guys have taken you in amongst them. You are part and parcel of them. You suddenly begin to feel their heartbeat. It is a deep, deep emotional thing.[60]

Notes

1   Minutes of the SARU Annual General Meeting, 1987.
2   J. Winch and M. Patel, interview with E. Patel, in 'Playing the Game: The Unification of South African Sport' (unpublished M-Net project, 2000).
3   G. Vahed, *Muslim Portraits: The Anti-Apartheid Struggle* (Durban: Madiba Publishers, 2012), 306.
4   P. Dobson, *Rugby in South Africa: A History 1861–1988* (Cape Town: SARB, 1989), 182.
5   Winch and Patel, interview with Patel, in 'Playing the Game'.
6   M. Horrell, D. Horner, J. Kane-Berman (eds), *A Survey of Race Relations in South Africa 1971* (Johannesburg: South African Institute of Race Relations, 1972), 321.
7   J. Winch and M. Patel, interview with P. Koornhof, in 'Playing the Game: The Unification of South African Sport' (unpublished M-Net project, 2000).
8   T. McLean, *Goodbye to Glory: The 1976 All Black Tour to South Africa* (Wellington: Pelham Books, 1976), 73.
9   *Rand Daily Mail*, 17 April, 12 and 18 May 1971.
10   Winch and Patel, interview with Patel, in 'Playing the Game'.
11   Minutes of the SARU meeting at Kimberley, May 1971.
12   Minutes of the SARU meeting, July 1975.
13   E. Tobias, *Errol Tobias: Pure Gold* (Cape Town: Tafelberg, 2015), kindle edition.
14   C. Laidlaw, *Mud in Your Eye: A Worm's Eye View of the Changing World of Rugby* (London: Pelham Books, 1974), 189.
15   J. Reason, *The Unbeaten Lions: The 1974 British Isles Rugby Union Tour of South Africa* (London: Rugby Books, 1974), 169.

16   V. Qunta, 'The African Springboks', in D. Cruywagen (ed.), *The Badge, a Centenary of the Springbok Emblem* (Newlands: SA Rugby, 2006), 158–159.
17   Address to the SARU Council, 1973.
18   *Rand Daily Mail*, 23 August 1972.
19   *The Star*, 4 and 9 September 1972; *Rand Daily Mail*, 13 and 16 September 1972.
20   D. Grant, *The Mighty Totara: The Life and Times of Norman Kirk* (Auckland: Random House New Zealand, 2014), 140.
21   *Christchurch Star*, 9 April 1973.
22   Secretarial report to SARU General Meeting, 1973.
23   S. Carmichael (ed.), *112 Years of Springbok Tests and Heroes* (Cape Town: SA Rugby Football Union, 2003), 357–358.
24   Letter from Ebrahim Patel to the SA Rugby Football Board, July 1973.
25   P. Dobson, *Doc: The Life of Danie Craven* (Cape Town: Human & Rousseau, 1994), 204.
26   Reason, *The Unbeaten Lions*, 61.
27   In explaining the '99' call, McBride had stated: 'If anybody gets into trouble, you all get involved wherever you are ... the referee can't send off the whole team' (*Independent*, 15 May 2009).
28   Reason, *The Unbeaten Lions*, 173.
29   The French beat the Leopards 39–9.
30   T. Partridge, *A Life in Rugby* (Halfway House: Southern Book Publishers, 1991), 102.
31   McLean, *Goodbye to Glory*, 86–87.
32   *Sunday Times*, 11 July 1976.
33   McLean, *Goodbye to Glory*, 88–90.
34   Ibid., 133–134.
35   D. Woods, *Biko* (London: Penguin, 1978), 130.
36   McLean, *Goodbye to Glory*, 71.
37   A. Guelke, 'The Politicisation of South African Sport', in L. Allison (ed.), *The Politics of Sport* (Manchester: Manchester University Press, 1986), 118.
38   J. Brickhill, *Race against Race, South Africa's 'Multinational' Sport Fraud* (London: International Defence and Aid Fund, 1976), 58.
39   Winch and Patel, interview with Koornhof, in 'Playing the Game'.
40   See *Natalia* No. 45 (Natal Society Foundation: 2015).
41   Minutes of the SARU meeting, July 1975.
42   Partridge, *A Life in Rugby*, 103–104.
43   Ibid., 104.
44   Winch and Patel, interview with Patel, in 'Playing the Game'.
45   Ibid.
46   H. Snyders, 'Rugby, National Pride and the Struggle of Black South Africans for International Recognition, 1897–1992', in *Sporting Traditions*, 32, 1 (2015), 119.
47   Partridge, *A Life in Rugby*, 139.
48   L. Luyt, *Walking Proud: The Louis Luyt Autobiography* (Cape Town: Don Nelson, 2003), 177.
49   Address to SARU at Peninsula Technikon, Cape Town, 1986.
50   D. Black and J. Nauright, *Rugby and the South African Nation: Sport, Cultures, Politics and Power in the Old and New South Africa* (Manchester: Manchester University Press, 1998), 110–111.
51   Winch and Patel, interview with Patel, in 'Playing the Game'.
52   A. Booley, *Forgotten Heroes: History of Black Rugby 1882–1992* (Cape Town: Manie Booley Publications, 1998), 11.
53   Snyders, 'Rugby, National Pride and the Struggle', 121–122.
54   Carmichael, *112 Years of Springbok Tests and Heroes*, 357–358.
55   R. Louw (with J. Cameron-Dow), *For the Love of Rugby* (Johannesburg: Hans Strydom Publishers, 1987), 166–167; Winch and Patel, interview with Patel, in 'Playing the Game'.
56   M. Bose, *Sporting Colours: Sport and Politics in South Africa* (London: Robson Books, 1994), 186.
57   M. Channer, 'Watson turns other Cheek', *Sunday Times*, 3 July 1983.

58   K. Williamson, *Brothers to Us: The Story of a Remarkable Family's Fight against Apartheid* (Ringwood: Viking, 1997), 37–40. The white players involved were Cheeky and Valence Watson and Colin Snodgrass (all Crusaders who played for Kwazakhele) and Mark Rowles, Kevin Purcell, Al Weakley, Derek Barter and Graham Bell (all Rhodes University who played for South-Eastern Districts Rugby Union).

59   The *Evening Post* (Port Elizabeth), 11 October 1976.

60   Williamson, *Brothers to Us*, 40.

18

The Last British Influence

There were rugby men in high places who viewed
them as a threat of some sort, a sort of foreign
body in the indigenous rugby system.[1]

– Reg Sweet

The formation of a South African 'invitation' rugby club was inspired by the visit
of the 1955 British Lions. 'We proved that you must throw the ball about to win
matches,' said fly-half, Cliff Morgan, as the Lions accounted for South Africa's
top provincial sides and forced the Springboks to come from behind to level the
series 2–2.[2] There was a record crowd of 90 000 to watch them play the opening
Test at Ellis Park. It was one of the greatest games in the history of rugby, won
23–22 by the Lions.

Not long afterwards, in early November 1955, a meeting was called at the
Country Club, Auckland Park, Johannesburg. A group of businessmen met
to discuss the tour and the impact it had made on rugby in the country. They
were there at the invitation of Cyril Briggs, described by the well-known cricket
commentator Charles Fortune as being 'typically English, of course: English of
an era now all but forgotten'.[3] Briggs informed the gathering that he wanted to
recapture the rugby spirit displayed by the Lions and allow it to live on in South
African rugby. 'The aim,' he explained, 'is to form an invitation rugby club.'

Cyril Briggs, Dave Brown, Thys du Plessis, Charles Fortune, C.J.L. Griffith,
Doug Low, Jack Phelan, W.C. Powell, Harry Willis, Jack Wright, Dr D.H.
Drummond and Dr Dennis Oberholzer attended the meeting. They acknowledged
there were important issues that had to be overcome. For a start, they had to
obtain permission from the Transvaal Rugby Football Union (RFU) to form a
club and would need to confirm whether sufficient funds could be raised to make

it viable. It was mentioned that Frank Mellish had tried to establish a Barbarian club but the SA Rugby Football Board rejected the idea as being too British.[4]

Mellish had suggested 'the formation of a rugby football club under the aegis of the board' but there was no objection to the concept being 'too British'. As chairman of the previous year's selection committee, he had concluded that 'there were many young players whom we would have liked to see a bit more of in the right type of company'. A national club would create opportunities to see 'these young players and in that way get a better idea of their capabilities before having to select a South African side'.

Mellish's proposal received support from delegates: 'They were not against [the idea] but rather inclined to consider it favourably.' Discussion took place on the suggestion that some sort of junior team would 'play a few matches each season rather on the lines of the Barbarian Football Club overseas'. Norman Lacey reminded delegates that they had already fielded Junior Springboks teams, a point supported by Professor H.B. Davel who asked: 'Why do we want to abandon the side? There is much merit in their existence.'[5]

Biggs believed there was a place in South Africa for the Barbarians, a club which owed its origin to a 'scratch' team raised by Percy 'Tottie' Capmael to tour the north of England in 1890. 'A unique club, a unique style,' says Nigel Starmer-Smith, adding, 'it is the most revered rugby touring club in the history of rugby football … it has no ground, no clubhouse, no entry fee, no subscription and virtually no money; the expenses for players and three of the committee are paid by the clubs they visit.'[6]

Great players, memorable matches and wonderful stories make up the history of the Barbarians. But the overriding factor in the club's success is the attractive rugby played. 'I came to love the Barbarians,' Cliff Morgan reminisced,

> in particular for their insistence on playing a recklessly attacking game, even if it cost defeat – not that winning or losing meant a great deal to them. It was the kind of rugby I enjoyed and, as you discovered when you got to know them, enjoyment and entertainment were what they were promoting.[7]

Biggs arranged meetings early in 1956. The question of constitution, name and colours became a matter of urgency. Members steered clear of 'Barbarian' because of the myth that Mellish had experienced problems. Initial suggestions for a name included Achilles, Corinthians, Wasps, Hornets, Kudus, Wildebeests, Spartans, Voyagers, Musketeers, Hercules, Isis, Pericles, Bohemians, Vandals and Tigers. After some discussion it was thought that the name should be typically South African; if possible, a word that had the same meaning in both Afrikaans and English. This quickly limited the field and Simba, Quagga and Zebra were suggested. At a further meeting, the die-hard English element went for Freebooter and it was only after a re-vote that Quagga edged ahead 6–4.[8]

In April 1956, the first formal meeting was held, and Biggs was elected chairman. He reported that the Quagga Rugby Football Club had been officially accepted by the Transvaal RFU, an important step forward although the provincial body was not always accommodating in the early years. The problem was largely one of provincial sub-committees dealing with matters in a high-handed manner. Fortunately, the president, Harold Sanderson, was firmly behind the Quagga and complaints never amounted to much.[9]

The election as president of former Cambridge Blue and leading businessman, C.S. 'Punch' Barlow, was a shrewd move but there were, nevertheless, endless problems for the fledgling organisation. There was the matter of administering club funds, which proved to be time-consuming. Two letters were sent out, the first to rich members who would be given a Quagga tie and asked for a minimum of £25. A second was sent to 'fellows of ordinary standing, from whom [the club] would not expect more than two guineas each'.[10]

Committee members were naturally keen to get their side onto the field. In 1956, all six matches failed to materialise despite the Quagga being prepared to travel to Pretoria, Pietermaritzburg and Bloemfontein. The club realised the need to be better organised and a committee was formed that included men who could use their influence to ensure the club did at least play its first match. In 1957, fixtures were played against a Lowveld XV and Natal Duikers. Biggs was relieved after 'many trials and tribulations ... that the players to whom invitations were extended appeared to regard playing for Quagga as an honour – their enthusiasm gave us much heart and stimulation'.[11]

In 1958, matches were played against Duikers, Lowveld, Germiston, the Free State Riemlanders, an Eastern Transvaal XV, Vereeniging and District, and Diggers (the winners of Transvaal's Pirates Grand Challenge). Scottish international Chick Henderson captained the side in most of the matches, during which 68 players represented the Quagga, some going on to play for Transvaal. 'All our matches were played in absolutely the right spirit,' remarked Biggs who was adamant that match scores should never be mentioned.[12]

The highlight of the season was the tour made by the (British) Barbarian Football Club. The Quagga were granted a match against Natal Duikers as a curtain-raiser to the Transvaal versus British Barbarians game watched by 60 000. The lasting memory of the main encounter was the famous Lion Tony O'Reilly running into a jittery photographer and being forced to ground the ball midway between the posts and touchline instead of under the posts. The conversion was missed and the match was ultimately drawn 17–17.

The success of the Barbarian visit prompted discussion in the national press. 'What about South Africa returning the compliment,' asked Vivian Jenkins in the *Sunday Times*, 'and sending the equivalent of a Barbarian team of their own to play a short tour in Britain in October? I gather that the Baa-Baas' visit has put something like £65 000 into the pockets of South African rugby. Some of the clubs over here could do with that kind of money.'

The *Sunday Times* called upon 'ex-members of the Barbarians living in South Africa to get together and form their own branch of the club'.[13] The newspaper unwittingly shed some light on the problems facing the Quagga committee. Their product was largely unknown, certainly not the national club they desired. The question of raising the club's profile by inviting top players from outside the province was discussed with the Transvaal RFU but members did not wish an upstart invitation club to play an influential role at a higher level, while provincial coaches were wary of Quagga officials encroaching on their territory.

In the course of the 1950s, several invitation clubs operated in South Africa. There were the Natal Duikers, Border Baa-Baas and Free State Riemlanders, but the Quagga regarded themselves as being different in that they wished to be known as a 'national' club. Jack Wright noted in 1959 that they harboured an ambition 'to become the equivalent of the Barbarian FC in South Africa but we cannot reach the standard without one hundred per cent support from the Transvaal RFU'.[14]

In September 1959, the Quagga arranged a trip to Rhodesia. Two players were invited from Natal – Peter Taylor who was named as captain and former England international Nick Labuschagne. The Quagga defeated Mashonaland 36–10 but struggled to overcome Matabeleland where the local newspaper dismissed Paul Johnstone's winning try as being a score that 'nine referees out of ten would have disallowed'.[15]

Taylor saw the importance of the work being undertaken by the Quagga committee and suggested that if the club had been formed in Natal it would have received greater support from its provincial union.

On 19 July 1960, Taylor sent a letter to Harry Stacey, then president of the Natal RFU. Nine days later, Stacey, Taylor, Labuschagne, Basil Medway, Izak van Heerden and Leo Smithers attended an historic meeting on 28 July. Stacey was elected president of the SA Barbarians and signalled his intention to establish a club on a national basis with individuals from all parts of the country being co-opted on the committee. An article in a prominent Johannesburg newspaper described the formation of the club as 'one of the most significant moves in South African rugby of recent years'.[16]

The new club obtained the blessing of the parent Barbarians in Britain and by the end of October had adopted a constitution that was 'short, precise and with very few trimmings'.[17] The SA Rugby Football Board gave permission to stage a match involving the invitation team and Natal. The touring All Blacks gave their support, and eight New Zealanders and seven South Africans made up a side that chose to wear a quartered Oxford/Cambridge blue jersey featuring the gambolling lamb from the traditional Baa-Baa badge.

The Quagga had been upstaged and were well aware of this when members met to reassess their position in early November 1960. In an atmosphere of pessimism and gloom, the question arose as to whether the Quagga Rugby Football Club (RFC) should be disbanded. The idea was solemnly debated but 'it was unanimously decided that this should not happen and that we should carry on as in the past and remain an entity on our own. It was important, however, that we expand our circle of players and become more national in outlook and selection.'

Biggs pointed out that the Quagga committee had a responsibility to a flourishing club, noting that there were 200 honorary members with a waiting list, as well as 167 ordinary members. He had also discussed the possibility of an overseas tour with Brigadier Glyn Hughes of the Barbarian Football Club who 'was delighted to hear it and that they would be pleased to have us'.[18]

The founder-president and chairman of the SA Barbarians, Harry Stacey, died within a year of his club being formed. Frank Mellish succeeded him as president and in 1937, Springbok Pat Lyster was elected chairman. It was the club's intention 'to give opportunities to promising young players to play with experienced internationals and to arrange fixtures in centres where stars of the game were seldom if ever seen'. But as early as the second year of its existence it became obvious that the Barbarians would struggle to survive for reasons that were not dissimilar to those experienced by the Quagga. With no professional administrative staff and little help and encouragement from the national body, it was going to be a hard slog. 'Perhaps they were too successful for their own good,' says Reg Sweet, 'for it is undeniable that there were rugby men in high places who viewed them as a threat of some sort, a sort of foreign body in the indigenous rugby system.'[19]

Basil Medway, the president of the Natal Rugby Union, put it down to 'a mistake at the time in not making Danie Craven a member of our committee ... the feeling was that we did not want the SA Board involved in Barbarian affairs'.[20]

Because of the commitment and cost involved in running an invitation club, the SA Barbarians settled on a policy of playing one major match a year. They lost to Northern Transvaal 16–32 in 1961, and Combined Cape Universities 19–28 in

1962, before gaining their first victory over an Eastern Province Invitation XV 33–11 in 1963. There was an 18–30 defeat against a Combined Transvaal XV in 1964, but satisfaction in beating Western Province 'in the worst conditions possible' in 1965.[21] There was no fixture the following year, but a Rhodesian tour and Keith Oxlee's 'farewell' match took place in 1967.

The advent of the SA Barbarians created greater urgency within Quagga ranks to assert themselves. There were tours to various parts of South Africa and Rhodesia. Curtain-raisers to the Lions (1962 and 1968), Wallabies (1963) and France (1967) gave the club a chance to showcase its brand of rugby. 'This is rugby,' enthused Lions' fly-half, Richard Sharp, when the Quagga defeated Northern Universities 45–31 at Ellis Park in 1962.[22] The game contrasted sharply with the 3–3 draw in the Test match that followed.

Biggs saw an overseas tour being necessary to place the Quagga on the map. The SA Rugby Football Board blocked its efforts by announcing a ban on 'non-registered' clubs being allowed to tour overseas and then, at the end of August 1963, refusing the official Quagga application. The *Sunday Times* expressed its dismay: 'The board would not give their approval even though the Quagga had acted on earlier assurances that they could go ahead and complete arrangements. Three years of planning fell down and they let down the British clubs.'[23]

South Africa's rugby authorities adopted a different stance over the next few years as the anti-apartheid movement gained in stature. With South Africa barred from the Olympic Games in 1964 and cultural sanctions steadily expanding, sporting bodies faced expulsion from international events. Tours were targeted and maintenance of rugby links became crucial. The Quagga's fine showing in defeating Transvaal as part of the national body's seventy-fifth anniversary celebrations in 1964 was followed by a *Sunday Times* report that 'informed sources said if [the Quagga] made another approach to the SA Rugby Football Board for permission to make the overseas trip, it would be heard favourably'.[24]

The Quagga influence in rugby circles gained further support when, in 1965, club stalwart Jannie le Roux became the first Afrikaner president of the Transvaal RFU. He ensured a generous sponsorship the following year to enable the club to play and defeat London Harlequins at Ellis Park. Then, in 1968, the Quagga campaigned strongly for a tour. After energetic lobbying by Le Roux, the SA Rugby Football Board reversed the decision by the tours committee in a unanimous vote. The Transvaal RFU offered to back the tour financially and act as guarantors at a time when South African sport was under immense pressure.

The D'Oliveira 'Affair' in 1968 focused attention on the country's rigid adherence to a policy of apartheid in its sport. The International Rugby Football

Board (IRB) ruled that two sides from one country would not be allowed to visit another country in the same season. As the Springboks were playing in Britain in 1969/70, the Quagga tour had to be postponed until October 1970. They would be offered the opportunity to play at Twickenham and Cardiff Arms Park, with matches against Richmond, Newport, Harlequins, Bristol, Coventry, Northampton and Cardiff.

In the meantime, the British Barbarians toured South Africa in 1969, a year after Tom Kiernan's Lions had been well beaten. Sportswriter Fred Labuschagne claimed the Baa-Baas had decided 'to salvage some of the Lions' tattered honour' and hoped the Springbok selectors would look upon the tour as 'a serious overseas challenge'.[25] Clearly, the Barbarian ideal was not fully understood in South Africa, a theme taken up by the former Springbok centre Wilf Rosenberg. 'Players,' he asserted, 'lacked the 'carefree, dare-devil approach [because] they were being closely watched by the national selectors – and played accordingly.'[26]

The 'Demo' tour to the British Isles in 1969/70 ended all hope that the Quagga entertained of making their trip in October 1970. The shock waves generated from the disastrous Springbok visit played a part in the 1970 season being one of relatively little activity. The year also ended with the passing of Cyril Biggs. Sanderson became 'caretaker' chairman until Chick Henderson was appointed.

The Quagga consolidated their role in Transvaal rugby through playing curtain-raisers to matches against France in 1971 and England the following year. The most exciting development occurred in 1974 when they were granted a match against Willie-John McBride's British Lions. The tourists had just beaten the Springboks 28–9 in the second Test to go 2–0 up in the series. The team spent a few days in the Kruger National Park before returning to play the Quagga in Johannesburg on a Thursday and Free State in Bloemfontein on the Saturday. They then opposed Northern Transvaal before the third Test.

The match against the Quagga suddenly assumed greater importance than had been first anticipated. Every white South African wanted to see the Lions beaten. If the Quagga could do it, it might well encourage the Springboks to save the series. The selection of the Quagga side became everyone's concern. The most serious consequence of meddling in the selection process resulted in the Quagga committee being unable to include two black players in their line-up. They believed that if they handled the matter discreetly it would be allowed. But the story was leaked to a Johannesburg newspaper in the week before the game and the government stopped the plan.[27]

The public sensed that an interesting contest was on the cards at Ellis Park and there was a rush for tickets. The first print was 40 000, but by the time the match started, there were 55 000 people in Ellis Park, a world record for a mid-week game. The Quagga rose to the occasion, with fly-half Peter Kirsten in good form. They were down 13–16 with ten minutes remaining and the light fading. The Lions were awarded their third try after Tom Davids had appeared to knock-on. The crowd was incensed and threw naartjies and everything they could find at referee Ian Gourlay. The game went on, Kirsten kicked another penalty (16–20) and play was in the corner furthest away from the players' tunnel when Gourlay blew his final whistle.

'Whatever else one might have said of Mr Gourlay,' says John Reason, 'he certainly proved himself to be a brave man ... in no time, the crowd had jumped over the fences and had streamed on to the field to besiege him.'[28] One of the spectators attacked him and bowled him over. Gourlay lay on his back covering his head with his arms while numerous people went to his assistance. Gavin Cowley recalls that Kevin de Klerk 'grabbed the spectator and hauled him off Gourlay'.[29] Scottish lock Gordon Brown apprehended the man as he tried to escape and handed him over to the police, while Peter Cronje stood by Gourlay as he was assisted off the field.

The Quagga had achieved the recognition they desired by playing against the Lions, but the SA Barbarians had been struggling. Their first match in four years was against the Orange Free State in 1973. Not long afterwards, the Quagga and the SA Barbarians merged, with the headquarters being in Johannesburg. Henderson reported that the latter club's officials were happy to have the name changed to the Quagga-Barbarian RFC and they did not object to the springbok on their badge being replaced by the quagga.

The 1976 season marked the twenty-first anniversary of the Quagga RFC and they celebrated with a well-publicised fixture against Andy Leslie's All Blacks. Visiting journalists were quick to note that the absence of colour represented another opportunity missed. 'This time,' comments Terry McLean, 'the club had sounded out the possibility of other than the two Irishmen, Grace and Slattery, being invited and had been coldly warned. Such a pity. A multiracial team against a multiracial team could have meant more icing on this fabulous cake which the two teams offered at Ellis Park this day.'

There was some astonishing rugby. With Fergus Slattery in inspirational form and Gavin Cowley not only producing 'the great back display of the tour' but also booting kicks over from all angles, the Quagga-Barbarians roared into a virtually unassailable lead of 31–9. 'It was even conceivable,' wrote McLean, 'that Quagga-Barbarians could carry on to score fifty points, an unimaginable slight or insult to all of the traditions of New Zealand in international rugby'. But suddenly, for no apparent reason, the game turned around. An angled kick across the field led to Terry Mitchell's converted try; then came a penalty, Alan Sutherland scored a try and Lawrie Knight added another, which Laurie Mains goaled. The All Blacks were three points behind – 31–28 – but the game was in injury time. Play was swirling about but a kick downfield from skipper Leslie was chased by the All Blacks who secured possession and moved onwards nearer the home side's line.

'Fifty-five thousand people were going crazy, starkers. A ruck. A heel. Mains, Davis, Duncan Robertson, Mitchell. The last pass. Mitchell clear. A spurt. The goal-line. The try! It was the most shattering, superhuman, sensational comeback which could ever be imagined.'[30]

There was talk of the Quagga-Barbarians touring overseas but more needed to be done to include black players in teams at various levels throughout the country. The club wrote to the minister of sport and recreation, Dr Piet Koornhof, requesting permission to field mixed teams in fixtures against Goshawks and Buffaloes in 1977. Success here contributed to a new stage of the club's history.

In April 1979, Henderson informed the Quagga-Barbarian committee that he had been advised verbally that the SA Rugby Football Board were 'proposing to send a team overseas comprising one-third whites, one-third coloured and one-third blacks'. It would be selected by the board and would travel as the SA Barbarians.

Henderson asked the Quagga committee for their views on such an arrangement. Their reply was unequivocal; they 'were unanimous in rejecting the proposal'.[31]

Henderson and Jannie le Roux then met with Craven. Henderson told him that his committee could not agree to their name being used for issues over which they had no say. Craven argued that he had given an assurance to the IRB that everything possible would be done 'to promote rugby amongst the non-whites at all levels and to progress with the integration of clubs, etc.'.[32] He believed the platform to build on was the Barbarians. The touring side would make use of the SA Rugby Association (formerly the SA African Rugby Board) and the coloured SA Rugby Football Federation, the two black organisations that had amalgamated with the SA Rugby Football Board to form the SA Rugby Board.

The SA Rugby Union (SARU) provided outspoken opposition to the venture but it had little impact. Quagga-Barbarian committee members agreed to support Craven on the understanding that they were weakening apartheid's grip on rugby through creating opportunities for two black rugby organisations, and this was preferable to doing nothing. Former Springbok Paul Johnstone advised his colleagues to tread carefully. 'We must not allow ourselves to be dictated to by the SA Rugby Board,' he stressed, 'nor allow them to take control otherwise the tour could be in jeopardy.'[33]

The day after the 1979 Currie Cup final, 24 SA Barbarian players gathered at a Cape Town hotel. 'We realised that we were guinea pigs,' recounts Rob Louw.

'We would soon find out whether or not we could live, tour and play together as an integrated unit.'[34] The players settled down and enjoyed an unforgettable experience. Not only did they play some outstanding rugby, but they mixed freely, while chatting in Afrikaans, English and Xhosa. For South Africans, it was a rare opportunity to see how the other side thought and reacted. It made a favourable impression on a large section of the British media; one newspaper headline read: 'Blacks Share Bedrooms with White Barbarians'.[35]

Peter Hain and the anti-apartheid campaigners criticised the tour. During a television debate, Hain found Henderson, the Barbarians' manager, a formidable opponent. Team coach Dougie Dyers appeared on the live BBC radio programme, 'You, the Judge', alongside anti-apartheid campaigners, Hain, Donald Woods and Chris de Broglio. According to Louw, 'the studio audience voted in favour of Dougie by an overwhelming majority. After these debates, we didn't hear a word from Peter Hain for the rest of the tour.'[36] Protestors still gathered at various matches, but there were relatively few incidents. Journalist John Hopkins points out that 'sophisticated police methods, which cost the tax-payer and the Rugby Union over £300 000, ensured the tour's comparative peacefulness'.[37]

The Barbarians enjoyed a pleasing record, winning four and drawing one of their seven fixtures. A powerful Llanelli side – with Derek Quinnell, Roy Bergiers, Ray Gravell, J.J. Williams, Peter Morgan and Paul Ringer – was beaten. It allowed Henderson to respond smartly to a BBC question on the cosmetic nature of the team's selection: 'Anyone who can beat Llanelli 15–6 with a cosmetic side must be a bloody genius.'[38]

A leading South African rugby writer, Dan Retief, found the tour process fascinating to watch. As the players faced 'difficult matches and strong opponents, they discovered common cause and began to bond'. After the tour, Retief visited the highly promising full-back Solomon Mhlaba at his home in Hanover, mid-way between Johannesburg and Cape Town. Having rubbed shoulders with the likes of Gareth Edwards and Phil Bennett, and surprising everyone with his skill, Mhlaba had returned to his 'location' where the lavatory was outside and there was no running water. When they went to purchase a cool drink, Retief was disturbed that Mhlaba was expected to wait on the pavement by a window because 'the inside of the shop was a "net blankes" [whites only] preserve'.[39]

The tour had raised the profile of the SA Barbarians but had not improved the lives of those who had assisted South African rugby in circumventing anti-apartheid boycotts. Quagga-Barbarian members felt uneasy about being used by the SA Rugby Board but they were at least providing fly-half Errol Tobias and other black players with a platform on which to demonstrate their skills. It was a sad indictment of the extraordinary South African situation that for a time there were no other stepping-stones to the elite level for good black players.

When it came to the important fixture against the British Lions in 1980, the national selectors expected to be involved in choosing the Quagga-Barbarian side. Not unexpectedly, the club objected. Johnstone, supported by Eddie Orsmond pointed out that 'it was bad for our image overseas as no other Barbarian clubs had any involvement with their respective unions'.[40] Ultimately, good sense prevailed and the team, containing the electrifying Argentinian stand-off Hugo Porta and 'a catholic and welcoming smattering of white and non-white players was acclaimed when it was announced'.[41]

Porta brought a touch of class to the game that was not equalled in the course of the season. His ability to make something out of nothing, the variance of the angle at which he chose to run and how he brought the best out of those around him astonished the crowd of 30 000 at King's Park, Durban, and, indeed, the players. His changes of pace were a constant puzzle to the Lions' back-row, but they played well to win 25–14.

British rugby authorities paid little heed to political opinion and continued to maintain links with South Africa. In 1983, three South Africans – Hennie Bekker, Danie Gerber and Errol Tobias – were invited to play for the Baa-Baas against Scotland in a match to celebrate the opening of the new stand at Murrayfield. Gerber scored twice and then stayed on with Tobias for the Easter tour – one of the club's great traditions. He recorded a further four tries in the 32-all draw with Cardiff. The first began when Tobias broke from his own goal-line and ran 45 metres, before passing to Gerber who scored.

The South African desire to tour overseas resulted in a bizarre exercise that bordered on a state of desperation. A squad of 25 players was selected for a trip to West Germany in 1984. 'It was undertaken at short notice,' said the manager, Air Vice-Marshal Harold Hawkins, 'and was in the nature of a "missionary tour".'[42] Organised by the Bonn Sports Club with the support of the president of the German Rugby Board, it had been given the go-ahead by the Deutscher Sportbund.

The Germans were overwhelmed, even when they resorted to including British soldiers stationed in the vicinity. Peter Hubner, writing in the *Frankfurter Allegmeine Zeitung*, questioned the 322–27 points difference and asked whether 'four worthless wins' had made the tour a worthwhile exercise. He considered all points of view, including the extent to which the tour had broken down South Africa's sporting isolation, and concluded by saying: 'The question remains – who did it benefit?'[43]

Some Quagga-Barbarians – with founder member Dave Brown prominent – objected to the convenience role they were being forced to play. Others were beginning to relish the spotlight. In the 1985 season, the SA Rugby Board asked them to host four matches over two weeks in August against a Springbok side that would be making an internal tour. 'It was compensation,' announced Craven, 'for the matches that should have been played against the All Blacks.'[44] Complaints were raised as to how the club was forced into using regional titles, namely in the Transvaal, Cape and Central Barbarians.[45]

The Cape Barbarians beat the Springboks 18–13 at Newlands, a game that questioned the value of an internal tour. 'Many did not like the antagonism of the crowds when they played against local Barbarian sides,' disclosed Paul Dobson. 'Springboks, after all, expected support when they played in South Africa.'[46]

Henderson referred to the lack of courtesy towards the Barbarians by all provinces concerned except for Natal. 'We were very much the "poor relations",' he admitted. While Barbarian committee members did not expect recognition for their efforts and shrugged off the fact that they were not extended invitations to after-match festivities, they were concerned that the club did not benefit materially from the tour. 'Our club was desperately in need of funds,' protested Brown. He thought the Barbarians should have received a donation of R100 000 out of funds raised during the tour. A request made to the board was unsuccessful.[47]

The Quagga-Barbarians fell still deeper into the clutches of the SA Rugby Board. In 1986 they were included in the itinerary arranged for the New Zealand Cavaliers. The rebel tour involved most of the All Blacks side that had been selected for the cancelled trip of the previous year. It was seen to be counter-productive but white South Africans gave their enthusiastic support. Pre-match publicity for the Quagga-Barbarian game against the All Blacks almost inevitably centred on the spectacle ten years earlier. The Cavaliers, however, dominated all aspects of the game to win 42–13.

A year later, the South Pacific Barbarians arrived in South Africa. Eyebrows were raised because the SA Rugby Board had promised the IRB that they would not allow another rebel tour. The Fijian authorities made a formal request that their players return home, but Craven adopted a dubious stance. He claimed it 'would be wrong to cancel a tour of "non-white" players after allowing the Cavaliers' tour the year before'.[48] It was originally intended that the South Pacific team should oppose the Springboks in 'Tests' at Johannesburg and Durban. But, with South Africa's position on the IRB under fire, Craven's executive voted – by a slender margin – against Test match status for the matches. Instead, the SA Barbarians would take over the fixtures originally allocated to the Springboks.

The late change in arrangement meant the Quagga-Barbarians were not given the opportunity to thrash out the implications of their involvement. The South Pacific Barbarians played some exhilarating rugby, but the matches served little purpose, other than creating exposure for Craven's 'feeder-team' system where seven experienced whites played alongside eight blacks against the touring side. Quagga-Barbarian members were concerned about the deeper moral implications of what was happening. There were no black players, for example, in the SA Barbarian teams that opposed their South Pacific counterparts, a surprising departure from club policy at that time.

The SA Barbarians were rewarded for their loyalty to the board by being invited to play against a South African President's XV at Kimberley to celebrate the centenary of the SA Rugby Board. The Barbarians won 23–10 but the occasion created further concern for the invitation club in the irony that the President's XV should field five black players and the Barbarians none. The *Star*'s Deon Viljoen thought the match 'neither a showpiece nor a triumph for the true tradition of Barbarian rugby'. His criticism was encapsulated in his concluding question, 'Why did the Barbarians who are known internationally for exuberant play, opt to kick at posts when awarded a penalty three minutes from full-time and leading 19–10?'[49]

Such developments reflected poorly on the club. A decade under the wing of the SA Rugby Board had tainted the image of a well-meaning organisation. There was some compensation when they were given the enormous boost of an overseas tour in October–November 1993. Preparations included a testing clash against Wales in Windhoek and several games against provincial sides. Once overseas, outstanding players emerged who coped admirably with the conditions, type of rugby played and a tight schedule of eight matches in eighteen days. A leading rugby writer, Steve Bale, was impressed. He wrote of the 'liberated brand of rugby they have espoused ... at their less exalted level the Barbarians have managed to do what the Springboks have not; successfully combine huge forwards of a typical South African kind with backs unencumbered by the dictates of hidebound coaching'.[50]

The team averaged 37 points per game, scoring 44 tries against 11. Henderson was delighted: 'We took twenty-eight players with us and there wasn't a dud amongst them.'[51] Seven members of the Barbarian side that toured overseas in 1993 were included in the Springbok squad for the World Cup.

It was the last crowning glory for the SA Barbarians, although there was still some rugby to come. They played a role in building interest in sevens rugby during the late 1990s. In 1999, the Quagga went down narrowly 23–29 to Tonga and the SA Barbarians drew 24–24 with a Namibian President's XV in matches that assisted those countries in their World Cup preparations. There was the 42–11 victory against Italy in 2001; a match against Saracens in London in May 2012 and provincial 'Barbarian' teams played against England in 2013.

The SA Barbarians became a fading, nostalgic memory, the ideal an anachronism in a professional era. Even in Britain, it was suggested 'their longevity depends on the allure of a glittering past and a future where they evolve into rugby's equivalent of the Harlem Globetrotters'.[52]

Notes

1   R. Sweet, *Natal 100: Centenary of Natal Rugby Union* (Durban: Natal RFU, 1990), 205.

2   C. Morgan and G. Nicholson, *The Autobiography – Beyond the Fields of Play* (London: Hodder and Stoughton, 1996), 141.

3   *Quagga Rugby Football Club 21 1955–1976* (Johannesburg: Quagga RFC, 1976).

4   Minutes of the Quagga RFC, 2 November 1955.

5   Minutes of the SA Rugby Football Board, 21 May and 12 November 1954.

6   N. Starmer-Smith, *The Barbarians: The Official History of the Barbarian Football Club* (London: Futura Publications, 1977), 9.

7   Morgan, *The Autobiography*, 159–160.

8   *Quagga Rugby Football Club*, 21; Minutes of the Quagga RFC, 23 January and 10 February 1956.

9   Minutes of the Quagga RFC, 26 April 1956.

10   Ibid., 5 July 1957.

11   Ibid., 11 October 1957.

12   Ibid., various club minutes/ reports 1956–1958.

13   *Sunday Times*, 25 May 1958.

14   Minutes of the Quagga RFC, 10 April 1959.

15   *Bulawayo Chronicle*, 15 September 1959.

16   *The Star*, 29 July 1960; C. Medworth, *The Battle of the Giants* (Cape Town: Howard Timmins, 1960), 186.

17   Sweet, *Natal 100*, 204.

18   Minutes of the Quagga RFC, 4 November 1960.

19   Sweet, *Natal 100*, 205.

20   Letter from Basil Medway to Chick Henderson, 13 September 1984.

21   *Cape Times*, 26 August 1965.

22   *Sunday Times*, 24 June 1962.

23   Minutes of the Quagga RFC, 12 October 1962; *Sunday Times*, 25 August 1963.

24   *Sunday Times*, 10 May 1964.

25   Ibid., 20 April 1969.

26   Ibid., 25 May 1969.

27   Interview with Chick Henderson for *Wits Sport*, July 1985.

28   J. Reason, *The Unbeaten Lions: The 1974 British Isles Rugby Union Tour of South Africa* (London: Rugby Books, 1974), 135, 140–141.

29   G. Cowley, *Having a Ball* (Port Elizabeth: SA Sporting Publications, 1983), 20.

30   T. McLean, *Goodbye to Glory: the 1976 All Black Tour to South Africa* (Wellington: Pelham Books, 1976), 122–124.

31   Minutes of the Quagga-Barbarian RFC, 6 April 1979.

32   Ibid.

33   Minutes of the Quagga-Barbarian RFC, 25 May 1979.

34   R. Louw, with J. Cameron-Dow, *For the Love of Rugby* (Johannesburg: Hans Strydom, Publishers 1987), 47.

35   Louw, *For the Love of Rugby*, 48.

36   Ibid., 50.

37   J. Hopkins, *British Lions 1980* (Worthing: Littlehampton Book Service, 1980), 32.
38   Louw, *For the Love of Rugby*, 52, 54.
39   D. Retief, 'Mind games: Early black players had tough time', *City Press*, 21 October 2013.
40   Minutes of the Quagga-Barbarian RFC, 16 May 1980; later, it was resolved that Barbarian teams must be selected by the club and not by 'non-members' (Minutes of the Quagga-Barbarian RFC, 28 November 1982).
41   Hopkins, *British Lions*, 135–136.
42   Minutes of the Quagga-Barbarian RFC, 12 October 1984.
43   *Frankfurter Allegmeine Zeitung*, 26 September 1984.
44   *Sunday Times*, 25 August 1985.
45   Minutes of the Quagga-Barbarian RFC, 2 August 1985.
46   P. Dobson, *Rugby in South Africa: A History 1861–1988* (Cape Town: SARB, 1989), 146.
47   Minutes of the Quagga-Barbarian RFC, 2 August 1985.
48   P. Dobson, *Doc: The Life of Danie Craven* (Cape Town: Human & Rousseau, 1994), 146.
49   *The Star*, 7 April 1989.
50   *The Independent*, 10 November 1993.
51   *The Star*, 10 November 1993.
52   P. Ackford in *The Telegraph*, 30 May 2004.

19

Tours of the 1980s: Politics, Protestors and Payments

The only part of life in South Africa where people
are the same, where they wear the same jersey and
come under the same rules is on a rugby field.[1]

– Jean-Pierre Rives

By the late 1970s, anti-apartheid forces seemed in control of rugby links with South Africa. The sports boycott had influenced political leaders and rugby administrators to the extent that Scotland cancelled their tour to South Africa in 1978 and no invitation was issued for the scheduled Springbok visit to Britain in 1978/79. The Australians were prevented from making a tour to South Africa in 1979, and the French government soon afterwards banned the Springboks from playing in France.

Contact was nevertheless maintained with South Africa. During 1979, top sides visited the country, notably Middlesex, the English county champions, Surrey, North-West Counties, Cardiff, Llanelli and Newport. They reported favourably on developments taking place: 'South Africa had gone a long way towards fulfilling the demands of the politically-minded.'[2]

The SA Barbarians' tour to Britain in 1979/80 was nevertheless a high-risk gamble. Their arrival was marked by intense but effective security controls. Plainclothes policemen and uniformed officers mingled with travellers and searched cars at Heathrow's terminal 3. Demonstrators shouted, 'Racist Barbarians go home', with their disapproval echoed in a *Guardian* editorial. In contrast, the *Daily Telegraph* believed 'like every group of visitors to this country the team deserves our welcome'.[3]

Blacks and coloureds played with whites in a tour designed to reflect the progress that had been made in South Africa. They played some fine rugby and helped the SA Rugby Board gain a temporary respite from isolation. John Reason claimed, 'It would be no exaggeration to say that [Chick] Henderson's success in handling the difficult and critical elements in the British press and on television, not only turned the SA Barbarians tour into a triumph but also made possible the subsequent tour of South Africa by the British Lions.'[4]

The Scottish, Irish and English rugby officials were unanimous in their decision to proceed with the tour to South Africa. The Welsh were uncertain but in the end gave their support by a narrow thirteen votes to twelve.

In 1980, the Springboks played nine internationals. There were two early victories at home over the South American Jaguars. The British Lions arrived in mid-season to play a four match-series which the Springboks won 3–1. In October, the South Africans toured for the first time since 1974, playing fixtures in Paraguay, Chile and Uruguay. The season ended in November with the French arriving for a Test at Loftus Versfeld. Despite the heat, the match was played at a thrilling pace with South Africa winning 37–15.

The anti-apartheid movement was particularly upset that matches were played against the Lions and the French. Part of the problem for the movement was that it found itself playing second fiddle to the international boycott of the Moscow Olympic Games. While the British people argued over whether it was right to compete in Moscow, the Lions were able to visit South Africa with relatively little opposition.

The French leadership supported South Africa's efforts to establish non-racial rugby. The president, Albert Ferasse, proclaimed: 'I always relied on rugby ... to defeat apartheid.' And the legendary team captain, Jean-Pierre Rives – although avowedly hostile to apartheid itself – believed that 'such was the white South Africans' love of sport that more could be done to encourage change through continuing sporting relations with them than by ostracising their country'.[5]

The anti-apartheid movement discovered European governments were prepared to support the Gleneagles Agreement but would not deny travel facilities to their people travelling abroad. Margaret Thatcher's argument over the next few years was that her government did not have the power to prevent the country's sportsmen and women from visiting South Africa or anywhere else. 'If we did,' she insisted, 'we would no longer be a free country.'[6]

Billy Beaumont's British and Irish Lions touring side of 1980 praised South Africa's efforts towards integration. When they defeated a Proteas XV 15–6 at the Danie Craven Stadium, Stellenbosch, the local side included notable coloured players such as Ronnie Louw, John Noble, Hennie Shields, Charles Williams,

Frankie Davids, Errol Tobias and Attie Lategan. The forward pack's front five was composed of white Western Province players. A similar structure occurred when the Lions beat a mixed-race Leopards XV 28–6.

'Our coming here,' explained the Lions' team manager Syd Millar,

> was, if you like, a recognition that changes are taking place and people must be encouraged to make changes. I've always maintained that one must communicate. I learn of further changes ahead to ensure complete multi-racial rugby at all levels – I would like to think that some of these happened because of us coming to South Africa.[7]

Not everyone agreed with Millar. 'At the end of the day,' contended the Irish fly-half Tony Ward,

> you and I play a game and then we go to the bar for a pint. If you are black in South Africa that is not possible. I go to the bar and you go to the township or wherever ... and I'm alone in the bar with my pint. That's neither rugby, sporting nor moral.[8]

After the Lions' tour, the star coloured fly-half Errol Tobias was included in the Springboks' tour party to South America where two Tests were played and won against the Jaguars (effectively the Pumas) in Montevideo and Santiago. Tobias kicked ten successive conversions against a Chilean Invitation XV in a 78–12 victory but did not play in the Tests. He would make his international debut the following year.

There was considerable opposition to Ireland's tour to South Africa in May 1981. Most Irish newspapers criticised contact with South Africa and there were heated demonstrations. Twelve leading players withdrew from the tour for one reason or another. Fergus Slattery's tour party left Ireland incognito and gathered in London for their flight to Johannesburg.

In South Africa, there was opposition to the inclusion of Tobias in the Springbok team. In his autobiography, the player outlines the battles fought against selectors, players and administrators, but stresses that Danie Craven was unwavering in his support over a long time. Tobias acknowledges the opposition he faced from the SA Rugby Union (SARU), although there was some understanding between players. They would tell him, 'We really want you to play well, but in our hearts, we still hope and pray the Boks lose.' He in turn supported SARU politically in their fight for equal rights but was not prepared to stray from his commitment to destroy the myth that people of colour were not good enough to represent the Springboks at rugby.[9]

Tobias was capped for South Africa at outside centre in the two Tests against the Irish team. It had been a dream to play a Test at Newlands and he settled quickly into the role, making a 40-metre break to set up the first try. The Springboks won both Tests but not without a struggle – 23–15 at Newlands and 12–10 at Durban.

The tour to New Zealand followed shortly afterwards in July 1981, creating a huge public protest. 'The SA Rugby Board abetted the blunder,' says Terry McLean, 'by appointing, as manager of the team, a great lock forward of the 1950s, Johan Claassen. Slow-speaking and sometimes, it seemed, slow-witted, Claassen was cut to pieces, mainly by tough Aussie reporters, at his first Press conference.'[10]

'Years ago we played rugby without interference and without involvement in politics,' maintained Claassen, 'I cannot see why it should not be so now.'[11]

The tour shocked and divided a nation. The All Blacks captain, Graham Mourie, chose not to play against the Springboks. Apart from his opposition to apartheid, he was concerned with the deep divisions being created in New Zealand society. He was worried that New Zealand's international relationships – political, economic, as well as sporting – were being affected by continued support for South Africa.

In the 56 days in which the Springboks were in New Zealand, there were more than 200 demonstrations in 28 centres involving 150 000 people.[12] Spiro Zavos describes 'an underlying cultural revolution within the protest movement, in that young people, church people, Maoris and women linked the protest against apartheid in South Africa with their exclusion from the establishment and the mainstream of New Zealand life. They were victims, they claimed, of a form of social and cultural apartheid.'[13]

Street battles were fought; police wore helmets, carried shields and wielded batons. Robert Archer and Antoine Bouillon wrote of scenes where 'men and women were beaten, attacked with bottles, kicked upon the ground; and the police themselves used aggressive riot techniques and were increasingly guilty of unjustified physical violence.'[14] The Springbok fly-half Naas Botha remembered nearly being run over by a 'wild-eyed woman who swerved her car towards a group of players out walking'.[15]

The second match (at Hamilton) did not take place. In a dramatic scene, 3 000 protestors suddenly broke away from a march. Several hundred pulled down a fence and stormed onto the ground. They regrouped on the field, linked arms and sat down. Riot police, wearing dark-blue helmets and carrying long batons, were unable to move them. Commissioner Bob Walton tried to negotiate with the demonstrators but was unsuccessful. Adding to Walton's problems was the news that a light plane piloted by a demonstrator might attempt to crash into the crowded stadium. It seemed a genuine threat and Walton was reluctant to risk antagonising the man.

Tension increased. The police had lost face because of the cancellation and were determined to put matters right. In contrast, the anti-apartheid campaigners were bucked at their victory and were keen to bring an abrupt end to the tour. The Red Squad – a special force – became increasingly conspicuous in quelling riots and looking after the Springboks.

Watching the first-ever live coverage of a Springbok side playing overseas was an absorbing experience for South African tour supporters. Yet few appreciated the extent to which New Zealand was being torn apart. Most of them saw the tour as a chance to prove to the world that rugby could not do without the Springboks.

> The SA Rugby Board failed or refused to take heed of the wider implications of the tour,' conceded the Springbok captain, Wynand Claassen. 'So much was written and said about the damage it could do to New Zealand, about the plans of the protestors, and yet the board chose to doggedly view our visit as no more than a rugby tour.'[16]

New Zealand writers were astonished that the South African management did not make use of its trump card, the two black members, Errol Tobias at centre and Abe Williams as assistant manager. 'Their presence,' observes McLean, 'argued that the South African authorities implicitly accepted their national team must be non-racial.'[17]

McLean might not have been aware that some members of the South African tour party and media contingent resented the inclusion of Errol Tobias in the team. It was generally known that coach Nelie Smith had been opposed to the selection of coloured Springboks and did not support Tobias's inclusion in the tour party.[18] There was also no support for Tobias from manager Johan Claassen, who allegedly claimed the player's grievances 'were typical of coloured people who weren't properly educated and couldn't handle pressure either'.[19]

The strain on Tobias was immense. Apart from the unpleasantness on tour, he was worried about the safety of his wife at home in the Cape. At one stage, he wanted to go back to South Africa. Rob Louw talked the matter over with him and convinced Tobias to stay: 'If he had, in fact, returned I have no doubt that the tour would have ended there and then.'[20]

The most dramatic demonstration was saved for the third Test at Eden Park. Each country had won one Test, which made this game an emotionally charged climax to the series. Unusual accommodation arrangements again followed, with the Springboks spending the eve of the Test sleeping in the grandstand.

A crowd of 49 000 witnessed an occasion of emotional intensity and real physical danger. During the game, a Cessna aircraft passed recklessly over the stadium more than 60 times, often close to the open grandstand behind the goalposts. The crew of the aircraft dropped flour bombs, flares and smoke canisters into the crowd and onto the field. One flour bomb struck All Blacks prop Gary Knight and knocked him to the ground.

By half-time, the Springboks were 16–3 down, partly because they played the first half facing the direction from which the plane kept appearing. 'I was afraid,' recalled the outstanding centre Danie Gerber, 'especially when we saw the plane coming low over the ground ... It didn't seem much higher than the top of the goalposts. When we played with our backs to it in the second half, we could focus more on the rugby.'[21]

Not unexpectedly, the referee Clive Norling wanted to call off the match. 'I answered, "No way",' says Wynand Claassen. 'We were trailing at that point ... I also felt no referee should have the power to call off an international match before it had run its course.'[22]

In the end, the All Blacks won narrowly through a penalty in injury time by Allan Hewson. The Springboks complained that the referee had engineered the result and All Blacks' Murray Mexted acknowledged his team had 'won it in controversial circumstances'.[23] It was nevertheless an epic encounter. Said one New Zealand report: 'Under unimaginable pressure, the Springboks had done remarkably well to force such a late conclusion. Some of them still bristle over Norling's penalty call, and they were a touch unlucky.'[24]

Ray Mordt scored a brilliant hat-trick of tries at Eden Park. He would score another three in the next Springbok Test, which was played on the way home from New Zealand. It was a bizarre encounter against the United States and created more controversy. A group of Springbok players visited a museum the day before the scheduled Test. On their return to the hotel, they were amazed to see a television report that the Springboks had defeated the United States 38–7 on a muddy polo field in Albany before 75 New York State troopers and no more than 40 spectators.

'The dirtiest of dirty tricks had been played on us,' declared Louw. 'Our management had simply betrayed us. We were members of an official Springbok touring team and we didn't even know that a Test match had been played that afternoon.' The president of the USA Rugby Football Association, who was on his way by air from Texas while the match was being played, was also disappointed.

The International Rugby Football Board (IRB), motivated by sentiment and traditional ties as well as the need to keep balance in a small pool of top rugby nations, kept South Africa in the fold. Critics who blamed the 'old-boy' network did not fully appreciate the danger of completely isolating South African rugby. There was the real fear that isolation would result in a rival professional movement, a development that would have a huge impact on rugby worldwide.

South Africa's white rugby administrators did not follow the rebel route for some time. The South American Jaguars (essentially Argentina) created a huge upset in a two-match visit in 1982. They were well beaten 50–18 in the first Test at Pretoria but shocked the Springboks 21–12 in Bloemfontein. Their success came through a vastly improved pack and a magnificent individual performance by Hugo Porta who scored all 21 points via a try, conversion, four penalty goals and a drop-goal.

England made an official tour in 1984, followed by a visit from a squad known as 'South America and Spain'. Naas Botha was unavailable as he had decided to try professional football with the Dallas Cowboys. The fly-half position was filled by Errol Tobias after he had excelled for the Federation against England. His instinctive running play prompted the English coach, Dick Greenwood, to say, 'Errol Tobias is not coloured – he's pure gold.'[25]

'Finally, South Africa has a fly-half that can catch, pass and break,' commented Boland Coetzee in *Die Burger*.[26] Tobias undoubtedly influenced the Springbok side's magnificent backline displays against the English. Danie Gerber, John Villet, Carel du Plessis and a second player of colour, Avril Williams, ran with pace and power. The Springboks won 33–15 at Port Elizabeth and then by a record-breaking 35–9 margin at Ellis Park. Gerber was unstoppable in registering a hat-trick of tries before half-time in the second Test, with Tobias adding another in a memorable performance.

The New Zealand Rugby Football Union (RFU) accepted an invitation to tour South Africa in 1985, against the unanimous resolution of the New Zealand Parliament. John Minto's Halt All Racist Tours (HART) movement, a New Zealand-based anti-apartheid organisation, promised that the 'wheels of the aircraft carrying the All Blacks will never get off the tarmac'.[27] Nearly 100 000 people took part in a day of nationwide protest marches. They had little effect: the rugby side's travel arrangements had been booked; invitations to functions in South Africa were sent out; tour memorabilia was on sale, and the All Blacks assembled in Auckland.

Minto's desperate efforts included a debate with one of the All Blacks players, Murray Mexted. The protest leader achieved little, especially as Mexted made no effort to disguise the problems that existed in South Africa. He argued:

The Afrikaner had his head buried in the sand. When I first went to South Africa, I could not believe how insular and naive they are. In my view a boycott would hinder change rather than bring it about ... South Africa is a country of inequality – between men and women, English and Afrikaner, blacks and whites and, most of all, between blacks and blacks. The All Black tour can only help to foster change.[28]

While Minto and Mexted vehemently disagreed, two rugby-playing lawyers, Patrick Thomas Finnigan and Phillip James Recordan, brought legal action against the New Zealand RFU by claiming that the tour was invalid because it went against the union's constitutional objectives of promoting, fostering and developing rugby. They pointed to the widespread opposition to the tour in New Zealand and the prospect of international sports boycotts and other repercussions if the tour proceeded.

No one took them seriously and there was relatively little coverage. This was not surprising because their application was dismissed by the chief justice, Sir Ronald Davidson. But then they exercised their right to appeal, which resulted in a decision by the Full Court of Appeal that the plaintiffs had the right to proceed. Suddenly, everyone sat up and took notice.

The hearing began on Monday 8 July. Two days later, the plaintiffs sought an interim injunction because the proceedings were unlikely to conclude before the rugby side's scheduled departure. Douglas White, counsel for the defendants – the Rugby Union and members of the Union Council – pointed out that the granting of an interim injunction would prevent the departure of the All Blacks team in time to play their first match on 24 July. He also stated that it would mean that the tour would have to be called off as alternative arrangements for departure could not be made until at least 2 August.

The Auckland lawyers were worried that if the New Zealand RFU eventually won the case, it would be in a position to sue for damages. Sam Ramsamy of the South African Non-Racial Olympic Committee (SANROC) was contacted in London and, with the assistance of Bishop Trevor Huddleston, obtained a guarantee of up to a million dollars from the Defence and Aid Fund.

Back in court, there was a surprise witness from South Africa. He was the Reverend Makhenkesi Arnold Stofile, a lecturer in theology at the University of Fort Hare, an executive member of the United Democratic Front and a long-serving rugby player and administrator. Stofile was a trump card. He told the court that he knew his people would be killed and injured in clashes with the security forces while protesting against the tour.

In recounting the injustices of South African society, Stofile asserted that the 'unrest' in South Africa had been escalating, especially during the previous nine months. 'Before I came here,' he remarked, 'I was at Kimberley on the weekend of 8–9 June when the police and army, with their dogs and their rifles, surrounded us in a church building.'[29]

Stofile said that the actual structure of rugby in South Africa was such that there was no 'normalisation of sport'. A system prevailed whereby permits were necessary for persons of a different colour to play against one another. He could not accept that as 'integration'. At the highest level, he continued, there were separate associations, each having a racially defined membership. Within such an arrangement, 'there is no integration of sport at community level. Sports clubs, with only a few exceptions, are racially segregated. There is definitely no integrated sport at school level.'[30]

On Saturday, 13 July, Justice Casey stunned the rugby-playing world when he upheld an interim interdict preventing the players from leaving New Zealand as the official New Zealand RFU touring team. He noted that the plaintiffs had put forward a strong prima facie case that the tour would tarnish the image of rugby in the community and would thus be against the union's constitutional objectives. He stated that the plaintiffs could not be dismissed as 'irresponsible trouble-makers'.

Casey informed the New Zealand RFU that it was obliged to act in accordance with its constitution. He emphasised the importance of adhering to two points in particular. He referred to rule 2a of the constitution, which stated that it was the duty of the Union to 'promote, foster and develop rugby'. He also mentioned rule 2b which provided for the union to arrange any 'desirable' international tours.

Referring to the latter rule, Justice Casey noted that the last Springbok tour of New Zealand did not seem to fit into the category 'desirable'. Although there was no need to enlarge on that tour, he did note that it was a disaster for both rugby football and the community.

While an interim injunction would not necessarily lead to a cancellation of the tour, the New Zealand RFU believed that they had no option but to call it off. It seemed incongruous that a New Zealand court had achieved what demonstrations had failed to manage.

Stofile emerged from the court case a respected figure in New Zealand. Justice Casey had set considerable store in his assertions and acknowledged that he had 'eloquently testified' to the risk of black African bloodshed.[31] On Stofile's return to South Africa, the government detained him for more than three hours after he had landed at East London. 'I was asked why I had lied in New Zealand and why I didn't want to watch a beautiful game of rugby on television.'[32]

The cancelled rugby tour reduced a portion of the white South African population to a mood of gloom and bitterness. A despondent Danie Craven spoke of running a 'rebel' World Cup in 1987 to challenge the inaugural official competition to be held in Australia and New Zealand. The Johannesburg *Sunday Times* gave Craven its full backing: 'South Africans are tired of being messed around. They are fed up with the pussyfooting and hypocrisy that has become the hallmark of international sports relations. The SA Rugby Board should give Danie Craven its whole-hearted backing for his plan.'[33]

Few white South Africans spoke out against Craven's bravado. Dr Beyers Naudé, the general secretary of the South African Council of Churches, referred cautiously to the tour. His council did not want to deny rugby supporters their international tours but there were larger issues at stake than 'mere sporting links ... we cannot afford the luxury of a sporting tour that will heighten the tension and give credibility to a system that cannot be justified by any stretch of the imagination. When will white South Africa understand the nature of the catastrophe that is upon it?'[34]

White South Africa was simply not ready – nor willing – to accept that there might be another viewpoint. There was no thought, for example, to seek out the Reverend Stofile and discuss the issue with him. The majority of whites were indignant that a black South African had been allowed to state his views. What right had he to speak on behalf of South African rugby? And why wasn't there someone from the SA Rugby Board to give contrary evidence to the court?

Rugby authorities talked of a new era in the South African game based on rebel-type tours similar to those staged by the country's cricket leaders. Rumours persisted that New Zealand rugby players were ready and waiting to fly to South Africa. Entrepreneurs were supposedly tying up the loose ends. It wasn't a surprising revelation because a number of the players had been left stranded by the cancellation of the 1985 tour.

In 1986, Craven was attending an IRB meeting at the East India Club when news broke of a 'rebel' tour to South Africa. Members of the board were fearful that it was a 'professional' enterprise; they turned on Craven who denied all knowledge of the venture. He left for South Africa with instructions to stop the tour but, on returning to Cape Town, he informed the SA Rugby Board that they should take control of the operation.

Louis Luyt tells a different story. It was Craven who had 'sanctioned a full rebel tour'. He had informed Luyt that a private company, involving Volkskas, the owners of Ellis Park Stadium, had taken on the role to bring out a New Zealand team as individuals. The SA Rugby Board assisted them in their clandestine arrangements by circulating two sets of minutes. Those on pink paper informed all members of the board that the executive had called off the tour. Another set of minutes on white paper informed a select group about new plans in progress, noting '29 of the 30 [All Blacks] players, including Mr B. Lochore, are still interested in touring South Africa'.[35]

Luyt, then president of the Transvaal RFU, was stunned by the 'sheer audacity' of Volkskas in embarking on such a plan without his knowledge. However, the All Blacks players had reservations about dealing with the bank and their representative, Robert Denton. Craven wanted Luyt to take control and the Transvaal RFU to act as hosts. A meeting was arranged in Hong Kong where Luyt and Volkskas representatives met the New Zealand delegation, namely, Ian Kirkpatrick, Andy Haden and Andy Dalton. Yellow Pages had agreed to sponsor the tour and Luyt undertook to extend official invitations on Transvaal RFU letterheads to every player.[36]

Craven's handling of the issue infuriated the New Zealand RFU. They had already been humiliated by their players who were secretly contracted to play twelve matches, including four Tests. All but two of the official side selected for the aborted 1985 tour turned out for the 1986 rebels – only wing John Kirwan, and scrum-half David Kirk were unavailable. The touring team became known as the New Zealand Cavaliers, although the South African rugby media, keen to legitimise the contest, frequently referred to them as the All Blacks. And, to the delight of the Ellis Park crowd, they performed the haka.

Spiro Zavos blames New Zealand prime minister, David Lange, for giving the tour organisers a loophole through which they could arrange the tour. 'Lange, garrulous and know-all as ever,' says Zavos, 'sowed the seed of a rebel Cavaliers tour by pointing out to the media when defending his approach to individual rights that there was nothing to prevent the All Blacks going to South Africa as individuals.'[37]

The SA Rugby Board designated the 'Tests' as official and Springbok colours were awarded. There were numerous contrasting opinions on a series that the Springboks won 3–1. 'It was a frustrating tour,' admitted Mexted, 'because we were encouraged by the New Zealand Rugby Union off the record, then the moment we went we were black-listed. It was a great tour because for an amateur rugby player it was a challenge to play against the best.'[38]

The All Blacks' captain Andy Dalton, who had played an important role in organising the trip, was unable to play in the Tests. He was on the field for just 37 minutes of the match against Northern Transvaal when Burger Geldenhuys broke his jaw with 'the most notorious punch in the history of South African rugby'.[39]

Andy Haden, a fellow organiser and player, was frustrated and disappointed, stating, 'We thought we had made a major effort to get there and then [Geldenhuys] hit Dalton from behind ... The thought that went through your mind was that they didn't deserve the opportunity to play us – they were in isolation, we weren't.'[40]

Rugby tours did not stop. In 1987, SARU visited South-West Africa, although many people were referring to it then as Namibia. The SARU team had played matches against provincial teams during the 1980s, defeating a President's XV in 1982, Western Cape in 1984, Eastern Cape in 1985 and Northern Zone in 1986. The team to play Namibia was chosen after a day of rugby to celebrate the founding of the Griqualand West Coloured Rugby Union in 1887. The side proved far too strong for the Namibians, winning 72–3. Wing Newton Kennedy scored five tries on his debut, Yagya Sakier recorded a hat-trick and full-back Irven October added a further 24 points.

The same year, the rebel South Pacific Barbarians arrived in South Africa. Arthur Jennings, a 1967 All Black, managed the side, which comprised twenty Fijians, four Tongans, four Western Samoans and one Canadian. Thirteen of the squad had participated in the previous year's World Cup. They played some entertaining rugby but, as it turned out, there was skulduggery involved. When the Fijian Rugby Union requested the team return immediately, it transpired that the manager had failed to obtain permission to tour because he had 'run out of time'.

Rumours were rife that the tourists were paid amounts beyond those stipulated by the IRB. The situation became messy when local players selected for the SA Barbarians wanted to be paid. They argued that they were obliged to wear the First National Bank logo on their kit and deserved to be compensated. Meetings were held and threats made but when it counted the South Africans were unable to present a united front. The Irish, British Lions and SA Barbarian scrum-half John Robbie opposed the blackmail and believed that 'brinkmanship, especially against Chick Henderson and his Barbarian committee, who have always played to the traditional rules, was very unfair'.[41]

Craven lamented the inability of the IRB to understand his position. 'Everything that had been demanded of us, as a group of sports organisers, we had done ... but we could not convince Mr P.W. Botha to scrap apartheid, no matter how many times we tried.' Craven did not attend another IRB meeting after the embarrassment of 1986. His representatives at the November 1987 meeting assured the governing body that there would be no more 'rebel' tours. It was known that the Australians were keen to visit South Africa and players met Craven in an effort to persuade him to agree to a tour similar to that made by the

Cavaliers. He refused to accede to their request and the IRB tried to compensate him in some way. Promises of matches in 1988 did not materialise but a World XV toured the following year as part of the SA Rugby Board's centenary celebrations.

The struggle to assemble a First National Bank-sponsored international side strong enough to play the Springboks reflected a rugby world wary of dealing with South Africa. The New Zealand RFU had forgiven the Cavaliers – who were to play a significant role in New Zealand winning the World Cup in 1987 – but not South Africa. There were no All Blacks in the World XV that played and lost 'two unsatisfactory Tests' at Newlands (20–19) and Ellis Park (22–16) in 1989.[42]

Sandwiched between the two Tests was a match featuring SARU and a Transvaal XV at Longdale Stadium, Johannesburg. Described as 'a thriller', it was the highlight of the centenary celebrations of the Transvaal Independent Rugby Union.[43] Although SARU led 10–6 at the break, Transvaal dominated much of the second half with an enterprising display of running rugby. Shrewd use of the boot kept SARU in the picture, but Transvaal's fourth try by Ebrahim Ganief put them ahead 22–19 shortly before the end. Victory appeared imminent for the home side, only for it to be cruelly snatched away. Lock Richard Britton burst dramatically across the line for the winning try, and SARU emerged triumphant 23–22.

As the decade drew to a close and despite a privileged rugby position, there was undeniable frustration on the other side of the rugby divide. The Currie Cup competition maintained a relatively high standard but the Springboks needed the stimulus of regular competition. Mark Smit wrote in the *Sunday Times* that the narrow victory over the World XV at Newlands brought home an unpalatable truth: 'Without the cross-pollination of regular international tours, the Springbok game has become staid, cumbersome and unimaginative – lacking in thrust and authority, and terribly vulnerable to quick-thinking, fleet-footed attacks.'[44]

Dealing with South Africa was not simply a political issue, but one in which allegations of player payments were widespread. There was a Welsh Rugby Union enquiry into the World XV tour, leading to the claim that players were paid in the region of £30 000. 'More generally,' says Tony Collins, 'the Welsh inquiry found cynicism and deceit to be widespread in the sport.'[45]

In the strange world of rugby, Fritz Eloff served as the IRB chairman during 1989, the year of the SA Rugby Board's centenary. It did not seem to have bothered the world body that they should be led that year by a member of the Broederbond.[46]

Notes

1   P. Bills, *Jean Pierre Rives: A Modern Corinthian* (London: Allen and Unwin, 1986), 137.
2   C. James and C. Rea, *Injured Pride: The Lions in South Africa* (London: Arthur Barker, 1980), 3.
3   J. Hopkins, *British Lions 1980* (Worthing: Littlehampton Book Service, 1980), 24.
4   J. Reason in *Sunday Times*, 15 March 1981.
5   P. Dine, *French Rugby Football: A Cultural History* (Oxford: Berg, 2001), 165.
6   J. Stern and M. Williams (eds), *The Essential Wisden: An Anthology of 150 Years of Wisden Cricketers' Almanack* (London: Bloomsbury, 2013), 9.
7   J. Rubython and M. Bishop (eds), *Springbok Triumph: Lions Tour of South Africa* (Cape Town: Howard Timmins, 1980), 4.
8   S. Ramsamy, *Apartheid: The Real Hurdle* (London: International Defence and Aid Fund, 1982), 68.
9   E. Tobias, *Errol Tobias: Pure Gold* (Cape Town: Tafelberg, 2015), kindle edition.
10   T. McLean, *The All Blacks* (London: Sidgwick & Jackson, 1991), 119.
11   A. Veysey, *New Zealand Times*, cited in C. Bryden and M. Colby (eds), *Springboks under Siege* (Johannesburg: Now Publications, 1981), 34.
12   T. Richards, *Dancing on Our Bones: New Zealand, South Africa, Rugby and Racism* (Wellington: Bridget Williams Books, 2012), 3.
13   S. Zavos, *Winters of Revenge: The Bitter Rivalry between the All Blacks and the Springboks* (Auckland: Viking, 1997), 192.
14   R. Archer and A. Bouillon, *The South African Game: Sport and Racism* (London: Zed Press, 1982), 197–198.
15   M. Geenty, '1981 Springbok tour horrors recalled', *New Zealand Herald*, 31 August 2006.
16   W. Claassen and D. Retief, *More than Just Rugby* (Johannesburg: Hans Strydom, 1985), 122.
17   McLean, *The All Blacks*, 120.
18   Claassen and Retief, *More than Just Rugby*, 152.
19   Tobias, *Pure Gold*, kindle edition.
20   R. Louw, with J. Cameron-Dow, *For the Love of Rugby* (Johannesburg: Hans Strydom Publishers, 1987), 148.
21   *The Star*, 18 October 2011.
22   Claassen and Retief, *More than Just Rugby*, 188.
23   T. Johnson and L. McConnell, *Behind the Silver Fern: The Players Speak* (Edinburgh: Polaris Publishing, 2016), 255.
24   Johnson and McConnell, *Behind the Silver Fern*, 252.
25   Louw, *For the Love of Rugby*, 149.
26   *Die Burger*, 24 May 1984; Tobias, *Pure Gold*, kindle edition.
27   *The Star*, 13 July 1985.
28   Report by T. McLean, *The Star*, 13 July 1985.
29   *The Star*, 10 July 1985.
30   Ibid.
31   Reports referring to the granting of the injunction, *Sunday Times*, 14 July 1985 and *The Star*, 15 July 1985.
32   *The Star*, 16 July 1985.
33   *Sunday Times*, 21 July 1985.
34   *The Star*, 15 July 1985.
35   L. Luyt, *Walking Proud: The Louis Luyt Autobiography* (Cape Town: Don Nelson, 2003), 165.
36   Ibid., 166–167.
37   Zavos, *Winters of Revenge*, 206.
38   Johnson and McConnell, *Behind the Silver Fern*, 280.
39   P. Dobson, *Doc: The Life of Danie Craven* (Cape Town: Human & Rousseau, 1994), 128.
40   Johnson and McConnell, *Behind the Silver Fern*, 280. Craven barred Geldenhuys from playing in the Tests.
41   J. Robbie, *The Game of My Life* (London: Pelham Books, 1989), 149–150.
42   S. Carmichael (ed.), *112 Years of Springbok Tests and Heroes* (Cape Town: SA Rugby Football Union, 2003), 254.
43   Carmichael, *112 Years of Springbok Tests*, 254.
44   M. Smit in *Sunday Times*, 27 August 1989.
45   T. Collins, *The Oval World: A Global History of Rugby* (London: Bloomsbury, 2015), 465.
46   Dobson, *Doc: The Life*, 156.

20

'Front Runners in the Formation of the NSC'

The boycott campaigns, from their inception in the late 'fifties, were aimed at the total isolation of apartheid South Africa ... At the same time, we must take into account the changes that have taken place ... There has emerged a definable, alternative, democratic culture – the People's Culture – permeated with and giving expression to the deepest aspirations of our people in the struggle ... This is taking place within the context of the emergent alternative democratic power whose duty it is to draw on the academic and cultural resources and heritage of the world community to advance the democratic perspective in our country. For it is only with the realisation of a non-racial, democratic and united South Africa that such a People's Culture shall be able to flourish in full glory.[1]

– Oliver Tambo

In 1982, the African National Congress (ANC) created a new position at their Lusaka headquarters. They appointed Barbara Masekela as an administrative secretary for Arts and Culture, with special responsibility for the cultural boycott. An interesting feature of the appointment was that sport was regarded as part of 'culture'. It had not previously been an interest of hers. 'I've never been a jock,' she laughed, although she did play tennis at school to a reasonably good standard.

She matriculated from the Inanda Seminary in Natal in 1961. Universities had recently been segregated and on principle, Masekela did not want to attend a 'Bantu' institution. She worked in a factory for a year, during which time she endured the humiliation of being arrested for living illegally in Berea. In 1963, she went into exile, beginning her new life in Ghana.

She spent some time in America with her brother Hugh, the famous jazz musician, and worked hard to build a successful career in education. She became an assistant professor of English at the State University of New Jersey – Rutgers University – and was also chairperson of the North American branch of the ANC. She recalled becoming actively involved 'after being so incensed by the Soweto Riots of 1976'.

Mongane Wally Serote, a leading poet, had attended to the ANC's cultural affairs prior to Masekela's arrival. Involvement in sport was relatively new, but the ANC had realised that it could play an important role in normalising the political situation. As its administration was traditionally a male preserve, Masekela's appointment raised eyebrows. She had no illusions about the difficulties facing her, 'I don't think sports bodies were thrilled to deal with a woman.'

Masekela was grateful to have the chance to work under Thabo Mbeki, whom she saw as the 'core' to unifying South African sport. 'I was given the platform and both Mbeki and my immediate supervisor, Steve Tshwete, provided support'.[2] Her formidable powers of organisation were soon recognised.

While Masekela was establishing her office in Lusaka, Tshwete was helping to set up the United Democratic Front (UDF) in South Africa. Unlike Masekela, he had been deeply involved in sport all his life. His father was an active player and administrator, and the young Tshwete, who was brought up in the Eastern Cape village of Peelton, became passionately interested in rugby. When he had money, he would watch white matches from 'cages' reserved for 'non-whites'. Otherwise, he would climb a tree outside the ground to catch a glimpse of the game, always trying his best 'to see how these guys were playing. We had our own heroes among them, even though they didn't want anything to do with us.'[3]

Tshwete became increasingly angry at the inequalities of everyday life in South Africa. He became involved in the ANC where his courage and determination were soon obvious. His commitment led to a period with the ANC's military wing and his eventual arrest. He was tried and convicted of belonging to the banned organisation and, in April 1964, was sent to Robben Island in handcuffs and leg-irons. He described his first eight years on the island as being 'hell on earth'. The prisoners were locked in their cells from five o'clock in the afternoon until seven the following morning and had to sleep on little more than a bare floor. Throughout the day, they broke rocks, were regularly sjambokked and came to think of their survival in terms of hours.[4]

Tensions between the authorities and the prisoners were beginning to ease in 1969 and, to Tshwete's delight, he was able to start rugby on the island. A ground was established within the prison yard and prisoners were at first given permission to play 'touch' rugby. The warders did not want contact between players because of the possible inconvenience and expense of injuries. The arrangement lasted only a few weeks: the desire to play properly was too great. They founded the Island Rugby Board – 'the IRB' – and formed clubs, each of which had their own divisions.[5]

Tshwete, who was elected president of the IRB and served as chairman of his club, was so enthusiastic that he wrote a constitution of nineteen pages and started a newspaper to record details of matches. 'We built our own facility, complete with beautiful green turf. We discovered a hidden tap that we would leave running overnight. The prison authorities could never work out how we managed to develop such a lush field.'[6] He added:

> At the spearhead of the whole venture were May Speelman, Sedick Isaacs (the general secretary of the IRB), Ndikho Mnyute (a one-time regular Border utility back before arrest), myself and many other rugby enthusiasts ... I played flank, number 8 and at times centre ... matches were played on Saturdays – kit was bought from Logan's in Cape Town.[7]

Tshwete was released in 1979 and taken to King William's Town where he was served with banning orders. His new punishment lasted two years and, on its completion, he became involved in underground activities. By 1985, his life was in danger – the government death squads had him on their list – and he was forced into exile. He made his way to Lusaka and from there travelled widely on anti-apartheid business. As a member of the ANC's military wing, he trained in East Germany and eventually became second-in-command to Chris Hani.

Tshwete was sorry to leave South Africa, describing the mass upsurge of the mid-1980s as being 'unbelievable'.[8] He saw that non-racialism in sport had gathered momentum and that it needed support.

The same year that Tshwete went into exile, another Eastern Cape rugby enthusiast, Makhenkesi Stofile, visited New Zealand in a successful bid to stop the 1985 All Blacks from touring South Africa. His achievement and its political impact on whites gave the UDF much food for thought. Before long, delegates were discussing the establishment of a sports wing. A prime mover was Bill Jardine, a seasoned political activist, rugby administrator and executive member of the Lions Rugby Club in Eldorado Park.

Krish Naidoo recalled Jardine arriving in his office. The latter had just returned from Lusaka where he met Thabo Mbeki, Steve Tshwete and Barbara Masekela. He showed Naidoo a document that set out proposals on how they could mobilise sportspersons across the colour line and provide facilities and programmes to develop them, especially black sportspersons, in the goal of a creating a disciplined sports movement.

Jardine wanted Naidoo to be involved: 'We will call our organisation the National Sports Congress. Mluleki George will be the president.' Naidoo protested: 'I was running a busy law practice under a state of emergency ... I knew very little about the politics of sport [but] Bill was having nothing of it ... I relented to the burly man. It was much easier than to argue with Bill.'[9]

First, a South African sports and culture 'desk' was formed to get rid of apartheid in sport. Then, in 1987, the 'desk' split and the National Sports Congress (NSC) emerged as an interim structure. The establishment of the non-racial internal body influenced significant policy changes by the external ANC. In May 1987, president Oliver Tambo gave his Canon Collins Memorial Lecture, which Masekela referred to as 'a ground-breaking address':

> Indeed the moment is upon us when we shall have to deal with alternative structures that our people have created and are creating through struggle and sacrifice as the genuine representatives of these masses in all fields of human activity. Not only should these not be boycotted, but more, they should be supported, encouraged and treated as the democratic counterparts within South Africa of similar institutions and organisations internationally. This means that the ANC, the broad democratic movement in its various formations within South Africa and the international solidarity movement need to act together.[10]

The address was a turning point in the ANC's approach. 'We started to rethink our tactics,' said Masekela. 'The boycott had also disadvantaged the oppressed. It, therefore, became necessary to prepare people inside South Africa to cope with the post-liberation period.'[11]

Tshwete added that they decided to ask the international community to support the non-racial, democratic sports structure that was beginning to emerge, 'and to provide it with the expertise it required and with moral and material support so that it could grow and itself become a prominent force against apartheid. We resolved that if non-racial democratic sport was going to take its place in the international community, we felt we must eat into the body of racist sport to weaken it.'[12]

The matter was discussed with Sam Ramsamy's South African Non-Racial Olympic Committee (SANROC). Masekela remembered:

> We met with Ramsamy one afternoon at Thabo Mbeki's residence in Lusaka and explained that it was time to change and that it would be necessary to call off the sports boycott. It was not easy for him, particularly as there were so

many people and countries involved. But he had no alternative – if he did not accept the change, he would become obsolete.

Thabo Mbeki was the key figure in the change. 'He was responsible,' said Masekela,

> for taking the ANC from an underground organisation to one on the surface that was open, friendly and keen to show its face. The time had arrived for South Africans to see that we were not 'terrorists' but a liberation movement made up of human beings who were interested in the activities in which humans take part.[13]

Collaboration between Tshwete and Masekela with underground activists in South Africa became increasingly important. It was their task to convince those involved in sport to adopt the new outlook.

Naidoo recalled the non-racial rugby administrators were 'the front runners in the formation of the NSC'.[14] Mluleki George, a personnel officer from Zwelitsha in the Ciskei, spearheaded the group of officials involved. A former Robben Island detainee, he was both a sports administrator and politician. He succeeded Tshwete as president of the Border region of the UDF and was president of the Border Rugby Union. He was also a member of the interim committee of the Border region of the ANC.

George linked up with Sefako Nyaka in Gauteng and Smuts Ngonyama, Phila Ngquumba and Richard Fonti in East London. 'They needed somewhere to meet,' recalled Mthobi Tyamzashe, then a personnel administration manager from East London and general secretary of the Border Rugby Union. 'So Mluleki asked if they could use my house in Buffalo Flats. Next thing, I was drawn into the discussions.'[15]

Ngconde Balfour, who had captained Victoria East in rugby and cricket, was also involved in the NSC at an early stage of its development: 'I met Mluleki George one evening after he had returned from a trip to Lusaka. We discussed the formation of a new organisation – the NSC – and it was agreed that I should promote it in the Western Cape. It wasn't an easy task as the area was a [South African Council on Sports]SACOS stronghold.'[16] The *Sowetan* was impressed by Balfour, describing him as 'your typical streetwise administrator who has all his facts regarding sports policy and current affairs at his fingertips – but insists he is still very much "a rural boykie"'.[17]

George knew his actions could lead to a split within SACOS. As a serving member of that organisation, he was aware that its rigid approach was adversely affecting the progress of non-racial sport. He became involved in heated discussions within SACOS as early as 1984. 'The slogan "No normal sport in an abnormal society" was fine,' he conceded, 'but it was not a solution. It was a cul-de-sac. Just to repeat the slogan was a weakness.' He realised SACOS policy did not come out with any position. 'You went to a meeting, condemned apartheid and waited for the next meeting. We were not progressing. We had to do something to normalise sport.'[18]

The ANC's shift in strategic thinking impacted everyone involved in sport. The NSC stated what it 'stood for, rather than against', explains Martin Keech, whereas SACOS 'was seen as having been locked into a political struggle whose forms and identities had been set by the agendas of the white authorities'.[19] It was an awkward position for SACOS – a largely Indian and coloured organisation – especially as their uncompromising stand on non-racialism always had limited support from the townships.

Ebrahim Patel, president of the SACOS-affiliated SA Rugby Union, thought the parent body's approach had 'served the cause admirably but, after successfully isolating South African sport, there was no longer a need to use it'. He expressed concern over how the organisation turned the slogan 'no normal sport in an abnormal society' into a principle rather than a strategy and then applied it to their own people through the double standards resolution. 'That was a colossal misjudgement,' he acknowledged, 'it should never have been used against the oppressed.' A person seen at a white sports establishment or in the company of a white official would be reported and ostracised. 'The community was conditioned to regard the convicted person as a sell-out. No worse stigma could be attached to someone. It could destroy a life.'[20]

Naidoo saw nothing wrong with the SACOS slogan but was concerned that steps should be taken to create a normal, working society. He believed the solution for SACOS was 'to relax or abandon the double standards resolution and the policy of non-collaboration. But it was unwilling to do so.'[21] It became too rigidly ideological and therefore hamstrung its ability to achieve its own goals. Naidoo summed up the NSC's approach to the issue with a play on the words first coined by Hassan Howa: 'We are normalising society through the normalisation of sport.'[22]

In May 1988, the NSC announced its formation and, five months later, released a 'Statement of Intent'. At a meeting in Durban, it was decided to lay the foundation for a mass-based democratic organisation within sport. It was seen as 'an integral participant in the struggle to abolish apartheid and would mobilise sportspersons into a broad democratic non-racial movement'. While the processes of normal sport could only be finalised once apartheid was completely destroyed, the NSC agreed that membership should be open to 'all mass-based sports organisations striving for a non-racial, democratic and unitary South Africa'.[23]

To keep things simple, the NSC based their approach on three principles – unity, development and preparation. This involved the unity of all participants in sport and the sharing of all structures and facilities, with the development of skills and the necessary preparation to run sport in the post-apartheid era.

The NSC also clarified its attitude to SACOS by accepting the latter as 'the authentic sports body in South Africa'. It was a major concession, but it lent credibility to their claim that they were trying to change SACOS from within.

Sections of the media thought there was enough common ground for the two organisations to reach consensus; they were both committed to the struggle and both supported a moratorium on international tours. But there were serious doubts that they could work together. That the NSC was prepared to talk to all sporting bodies was a major ideological difference. Furthermore, after sixteen years as the voice of anti-apartheid sport, SACOS opposed a rival organisation entering the scene. Executive members of SACOS were proud of their part in isolating the establishment sports bodies and were content to await the dismantling of apartheid by the politicians. They seemed oblivious to some of their members being disgruntled with the lack of progress.

Initially, SACOS hoped the NSC would operate in a complementary way. They wanted the NSC to mobilise support in the townships and the rural areas. This did not happen. The NSC worked hard to drum up support, but for their own policies. Conflict was inevitable. SACOS leaders accused the NSC of going behind their backs.

It was a complex situation because many SACOS members were sympathetic towards the NSC and – unofficially – had dual membership. SACOS insisted on being regarded as 'politically non-aligned', but were supported by several black consciousness groups, Azapo, the New Unity Movement and, later, the Pan African Congress. The NSC was described as the creation of the Congress of South African Trade Unions (COSATU) and the UDF, and openly aligned itself with the Mass Democratic Movement (MDM).

SACOS described the NSC's insistence on political alignment in sport to be 'foolish, divisive and politically arrogant' but the latter argued that sport in South Africa could only be played in a political context.[24] The NSC was keen to create an opening for otherwise restricted political associations to express themselves.

Vivian Reddiar wrote in the New Nation of the NSC: 'In some ways – for example, the fact that freedom songs, poetry reading, and toyi-toying have been a feature of many of its meetings – it has politicised sport to an extent not witnessed before.'[25] Tyamzashe recalled that 'we were dubbed as the ANC in tracksuits. It was a little ironic because we always packed our tracksuits when travelling, just in case we were arrested.'[26]

The National Union of Mineworkers commented bitterly on the tactics of the NSC. It described the new organisation as

> a product of political opportunism, set amongst the oppressed like a wooden horse – to undermine and divide SACOS ... it is our contention that the NSC has been brought into being with the express purpose of holding SACOS to ransom. Non-racial sports codes are being blackmailed into accepting the Freedom Charter and joining up with populist forces.[27]

Despite such efforts to discredit them, popular support for the NSC increased. A crucial shift occurred when key SACOS figures such as Krish Mackerdhuj and Errol Vawda did not seek re-election to the executive. SACOS remained defiant but seemed to be losing the battle for the allegiance of players and administrators. Its president, Joe Ebrahim, stated: 'There can be no question of our watering down our principles to make it easier for others to join us. Surely if they believe in what we stand for they must make the adjustment in their thinking.'[28]

By April 1989, the NSC had decided the time had come to take a lead role by building a base amongst sportspeople. George published an open letter to all sportsmen and women in which he explained the policy and objectives of the NSC. The organisation then staged a huge sports conference at the University of the Witwatersrand in July 1989. The conference was seen as the first step towards unifying sport and an impressive 475 delegates attended, representing a wide range of sporting codes and other community organisations.

In the build-up to the Wits conference, members of the NSC liaised closely with the ANC. Trips were made to Lusaka for discussions with Masekela. 'Barbara was constantly urging us on to launch the NSC,' recounted Tyamzashe, 'she virtually planned the conference from Lusaka.'

Masekela remembered:

> It was an exciting time for us and our staff were fully extended. Thabo Mbeki and Steve Tshwete could not always give their attention or advice to sports matters; they were busy much of the time meeting businessmen or attending conferences and were often out of the country. I had to take on a greater responsibility and came into contact with so many people, a great number of organisations and sports codes ... even students from Stellenbosch University![29]

The SA Cricket Union and the SA Rugby Board did not receive invitations to the Wits Conference because of their involvement in 'rebel' tours. SACOS was invited but the organisation's executive were conspicuous by their absence. They objected to the expected presence of officials such as Anthony Willcox (soccer) and Issy Kramer (swimming), arguing that it would 'gravely compromise non-racial sportspersons and affect the double standards resolution'.[30] But it was a no-win situation for SACOS because the conference simply emphasised the split in their ranks. Many SACOS members attended – notably from rugby, cricket and soccer. Leading figures, such as Krish Mackerdhuj, Ebrahim Patel and Errol Vawda, agreed to speak.

The rector of the University of the Western Cape, Jakes Gerwel, spoke on the theme of the conference, which was 'Towards a disciplined, healthy sports movement in preparation for a post-apartheid South Africa'. He told delegates that after their success in isolating racial sport, they should re-examine the whole issue of the moratorium on international tours. He saw such a move as being an ideological victory because it would 'convince those who organise and participate in racial sports of the advantages that could accrue by being part of the non-racial democratic sports movement'.

Gerwel added, 'The Mass Democratic Movement has been able to win over significant numbers of whites to the democratic fold. The success and prestige that they have gained has to be paralleled by the sports wing.'[31]

The conference was largely exploratory in nature, but it confirmed that the NSC was on the right track. Not only were they able to move into the townships to identify with people that SACOS had never been able to reach, but they had also made an effort to woo white supporters. They wanted all South African sportsmen and women who opposed the apartheid system to be brought together.

Naidoo recalled a delicate balance in maintaining support from all sides. The intention was 'to wean established white sports bodies away from the political agenda of apartheid, to widen fractures in the apartheid structures and lessen the influence of the National Party, and to make the point that only a non-racial demographic government could deliver international participation for athletes'.[32]

When the question, 'Should we launch the NSC?' was asked, there was a resounding 'Yes!'

Speakers at the conference urged a conciliatory stance towards SACOS and a meeting was set for mid-September in Port Elizabeth. SACOS was keen to settle the question as to which of its affiliates had joined the NSC. Tyamzashe observed:

> They forced the issue by requesting members to sit on opposite sides of the room; I can vividly remember Krish Mackerdhuj gathering his papers under his arm and slowly making his way across to our side. Errol Vawdra and Silas

Nkununu also joined us. Ebrahim Patel sat in the middle, between the two organisations – a significant decision.[33]

SACOS president Joe Ebrahim then accused the NSC of reneging on their agreements, primarily that the NSC should recognise SACOS as the authentic, non-racial coordinating sports body in the country, and that the two bodies should complement each other. He was convinced that the NSC was bent on destroying SACOS.[34] He pressed Mluleki George to say whether the NSC still regarded SACOS as the authentic sports wing of the liberation movement. George tried to evade the issue, explaining that the answer would emerge in the course of the meeting, but eventually was forced into replying, 'The answer is "No".'[35]

The meeting ended abruptly without compromise. Ronnie Govender recalled:

For many in SACOS, like long-standing stalwart Krish Mackerdhuj, the crunch came at the Port Elizabeth meeting. SACOS had insisted it was neutral in terms of the various anti-apartheid political groupings. It had vehemently supported non-alignment, yet its delegation to meet the NSC consisted of representation from Azapo, and the Pan Africanist Congress ... The irony, of course, is that to many loyal SACOS supporters, the perspectives have become blurred to the extent that they have become unwitting pawns in a power game that can only harm the cause of true liberation.[36]

The NSC became the most powerful of the non-racial movements. Their significance was recognised overseas and they received the support of the United Nations Special Committee against Apartheid, the Supreme Council of Sport in Africa, SANROC and other international organisations. They were complimented on their vision and ability to see the larger picture. 'SACOS was still propagating an outdated all-or-nothing approach,' claimed Tyamazashe, 'while the NSC was being more open-minded. An example is the ultimatum SACOS gave their members, who are also members of the NSC, that they have to choose between one or the other. We had no objection to dual membership because both sports bodies were non-racial.'[37]

Govender wrote mockingly of the situation: 'Now we're landed with a problem which has become so clouded by a distortion of the facts that faithful supporters of the cause are somewhat bemused at the spectacle of two progressive sporting organisations, SACOS and NSC, looking set for a bloody showdown at sun-up.' He asked:

Who are the good guys and who are the bad guys? Before we try to sort out that question, there's another question: aren't these guys supposed to be up against the baddest guys of them all – guys like Danie Craven, Ali Bacher, Abdul Bhamjee, and a host of such apologists for a system of privilege, once nakedly racist but now cosmeticised to be beguilingly seductive and yet just as supportive of elitist empowerment?[38]

In the opening months of 1990, the NSC took on the 'bad guys'. The SA Cricket Union had gone ahead with Mike Gatting's 'rebel' cricket tour despite several warnings. Shortly after being released from detention for political activities, Ngconde Balfour joined Murphy Morobe, Mi Hlatshwayo (both MDM) and Krish Mackerdhuj (NSC) in speaking to Gatting and tour manager David Graveney in London. The English cricket representatives had made up their minds that they would be touring. On his return to South Africa, Balfour was part of the NSC delegation (Mluleki George, Mthobi Tyamzashe, Harry Naidu, Bill Jardine, Krish Naidoo and Balfour) that met with the SA Cricket Union at the Johannesburg Sun in November 1989.

Tyamzashe remembered two aspects standing out during the discussions: 'Bill Jardine's emotive contributions and Ngconde Balfour's organised responses to counter Ali Bacher's claims. Balfour did his homework and helped give us credibility on cricket matters – we were not seen simply as a bunch of politicians.'[39] At the same time, Naidoo admitted: 'I didn't think the SA Cricket Union took us seriously. As expected, the union decided to proceed with the tour.'

The anticipated confrontation aroused tremendous interest and representatives of the British tabloids appeared in full force. It turned into an assignment of a lifetime because the cricket venture coincided with Nelson Mandela's release and the major political changes that swept South Africa. Angry demonstrations were staged at airports, hotels and cricket grounds, and the national political temperature rose steadily.

That the NSC was running sport in the country was underlined by their taking control in determining the outcome of the tour and resolving the impasse. Naidoo met with Bacher at the home of Professor Michael Katz, the honorary legal counsel to the SA Cricket Union. The NSC agreed to allow the union to play four one-day games in exchange for calling off protest action. The second leg of the tour would be cancelled.[40]

More than 300 delegates attended the formal inauguration of the NSC held at Langa in the Cape from 31 May to 1 June 1990. Special guest Steve Tshwete delivered the keynote address in which he urged the NSC to persuade sponsors to join it in its campaign to change South African sport. 'The sports movement should not only ask sponsors for financial aid but try to make them active partners in the process of transforming sport.'[41]

'Black sportspersons also had aspirations to compete and excel internationally,' says Naidoo. 'Our role as the NSC was to create an appropriate environment for black sportspersons to be prepared for that eventuality.'[42]

Mluleki George was elected the first president of the NSC, which changed its name to the National Olympic and Sports Congress (NOSC) as it would be required to establish a special committee for Olympic disciplines. The change of name was made specifically at the suggestion of the African National Olympic Committees Association (ANOCA).

Soon after his election, George travelled to New York to address the United Nations Commission against Apartheid in Sport. George told reporters, 'We talk about entering international sport, not re-entering, because we were never there. White South Africa was.'[43]

David Miller wrote from Sweden that 'the speed at which attitudes within Africa were being revised, indeed reversed, was leaving some outposts of the anti-apartheid empire ethically isolated'. Some foreign ideologists were still intent on pursuing absolute political liberation within South Africa at a time 'when Africans together with South Africans were seeking an interim solution that might keep international sport alive in advance of the establishment of one-man-one-vote ... some of the Scandinavians could scarcely believe what they were hearing'.[44]

According to South African newspapers, the optimism was tempered only by the fact that the NSC and SACOS could agree on very little. Over the next few months, SACOS pressed for the retention of the international sports boycott and slowed progress in certain areas. Jean-Claude Ganga, the president of ANOCA was unsympathetic towards this lack of cooperation. He asserted, 'SACOS is a very small minority ... I told them in Harare that if they wanted to wait until there were no black people in prison in South Africa until there was no marijuana on the streets, they would only see that in heaven.'[45]

Ganga had called a meeting in November 1990 to deal with the question as to when South Africa should be allowed back into the Olympic movement. The aims of this 'Harare Indaba' were threefold: to agree on a programme designed to unite South African sport; to accelerate the end of apartheid and to establish a National Olympic Committee for South Africa. Officials from various internal sports bodies attended the conference. A seating plan was arranged whereby old adversaries were placed together – Craven and Patel for rugby, Dakin and Mackerdhuj for cricket, and so on. It did not upset delegates because the meeting took place at a time of unprecedented consensus in South African sport. Craven was one of the very few people unwilling to abide by the moratorium.

Everyone listened intently to Ganga's explanation of the conditions necessary for South African sport to gain international acceptability: unity among the country's fractious sports bodies and sufficient movement on the political front to end apartheid.

To assist progress, a ten-man committee was appointed. This comprised two members each from SANROC, NSC, SACOS, the Confederation of SA Sport and the South Africa National Olympic Committee SANOC. Chaired by Ramsamy, it became the Interim National Olympic Committee of South Africa and, finally, the National Olympic Committee of South Africa (NOCSA). On the formation of NOCSA, the National Olympic Sports Congress (NOSC) became known as the National Sports Council (NSC).

Notes

1   O. Tambo, 'South Africa at the Crossroads': Canon Collins Memorial Lecture, May 1987.
2   J. Winch and M. Patel, interview with B. Masekela, in 'Playing the Game: The Unification of South African Sport' (unpublished M-Net project, 2000).
3   M. Bose, *Sporting Colours: Sport and Politics in South Africa* (London: Robson Books, 1994), 166; *The Star*, 22 August 1992.
4   J. Winch and M. Patel, interview with S. Tshwete, in 'Playing the Game: The Unification of South African Sport' (unpublished M-Net project, 2000).
5   *SA Rugby*, 1, 1 (April 1995); Winch and Patel, interview with Tshwete, in 'Playing the Game'.
6   *Business Day*, 9 October 1992.
7   *SA Rugby*, 1, 1 (April 1995).
8   *Pace*, October 1992, 40.
9   K. Naidoo, *Krish: Struggle Lawyer* (Crown Mines: Self-published, 2019), 148–149.
10   Tambo, 'South Africa at the Crossroads'.
11   Winch and Patel, interview with Masekela, in 'Playing the Game'.
12   Bose, *Sporting Colours*, 178.
13   Winch and Patel, interview with Masekela, in 'Playing the Game'.
14   J. Winch and M. Patel, interview with K. Naidoo, in 'Playing the Game: The Unification of South African Sport' (unpublished M-Net project, 2000); Naidoo, *Krish: Struggle Lawyer*, 166.
15   J. Winch and M. Patel, interview with M. Tyamzashe, in 'Playing the Game: The Unification of South African Sport' (unpublished M-Net project, 2000).
16   J. Winch and M. Patel, interview with N. Balfour, in 'Playing the Game: The Unification of South African Sport' (unpublished M-Net project, 2000).
17   *Sowetan*, 30 June 1999.
18   Bose, *Sporting Colours*, 178. J. Winch and M. Patel, interview with M. George, in 'Playing the Game: The Unification of South African Sport' (unpublished M-Net project, 2000).
19   M. Keech, 'One Nation, One Soul, One Dream, One Goal?', in A. Smith and D. Porter (eds), *Sport and National Identity in the Post-War World* (London: Routledge, 2004), 116.
20   J. Winch and M. Patel, interview with E. Patel, in 'Playing the Game: The Unification of South African Sport' (unpublished M-Net project, 2000).
21   Naidoo, *Krish: Struggle Lawyer*, 152.
22   Introductory notes prepared for a book on reconciliation of sport (Department of Sport and Recreation), 10 October 1996.
23   *Daily Dispatch*, 12 May 1988.
24   *City Press*, 3 December 1989.
25   *The New Nation*, 20 July 1989.
26   Winch and Patel, interview with Tyamzashe, in 'Playing the Game'.
27   National Union of Mineworkers (NUM) bulletin, December 1988.

28   *City Press*, 23 July 1989.
29   Winch and Patel, interview with Masekela, in 'Playing the Game'.
30   *Eastern Province Herald*, 18 September 1989.
31   *Post Natal*, 27 September 1989.
32   Naidoo, *Krish: Struggle Lawyer*, 156.
33   Winch and Patel, interview with Tyamzashe, in 'Playing the Game'.
34   *Post Natal*, 22 September 1989.
35   *Weekly Mail*, 21 December 1989.
36   *Weekend Argus*, 2 June 1990.
37   *Leadership SA*, October 1990.
38   *Post Natal*, 22 November 1989.
39   Winch and Patel, interview with Tyamzashe, in 'Playing the Game'.
40   Naidoo, *Krish: Struggle Lawyer*, 184-185.
41   D. Miller, *Olympic Revolution: The Olympic Biography of Juan Antonio Samaranch* (London: Pavilion Books, 1994), 209.
42   Naidoo, *Krish: Struggle Lawyer*, 155.
43   Miller, *Olympic Revolution*, 208–209.
44   *Post Natal*, 22 November 1989.
45   Miller, *Olympic Revolution*, 218.

21

The Unification of Rugby

There are many variables in establishing the unity that we have in mind. These include the redressing of the imbalances that presently exist between non-racial sport and establishment sport that apartheid has created. We are not calling for establishment sports to drop levels to those of non-racial sports but wish to highlight the establishment sports' responsibility towards non-racial sport. We all need each other irrespective of the disparities in resources and facilities.[1]

– Mthobi Tyamzashe

In the latter part of the 1980s, concerted efforts were made to reopen discussions between rival sports bodies. When the former Springbok cricketer and Transvaal rugby player Eddie Barlow served as an unofficial sports 'ambassador' in London, he was able to establish some contacts. By 1986, he had set up the first of a series of 'secret' meetings for South Africa's sports administrators.

The SA Rugby Union (SARU) did not support the meetings, but they gave Danie Craven an opportunity to assess the views of other black sports personalities. It worried him that they wanted to impose a moratorium of up to four years, but he was optimistic that progress could be made towards a solution. He was left in no doubt that the way back to international sport was through Africa, which meant negotiating with the African National Congress (ANC). He resolved to meet the banned organisation, despite the knowledge that he would face fierce opposition, even within his own executive.

Craven's good intentions were shelved when it was announced that the rebel New Zealand Cavaliers would tour South Africa in 1986. Ebrahim Patel condemned the 'deceit and secrecy' with which arrangements were made and the callous disregard they showed for the 'feelings and political realities of the oppressed people in South Africa'.[2]

Craven was later assisted by political developments. In 1987, former Springbok rugby star Tom Bedford travelled to Dakar in Senegal to meet members of the ANC. He was part of the pioneering group, the Institute for Democratic Alternatives in South Africa (IDASA), led by Frederik van Zyl Slabbert, the former leader of the opposition in Parliament. Their expedition was to have an important influence in encouraging South African politicians to move in a new direction. Bedford confirmed that the ANC was prepared to talk to South Africa's sports administrators.

Two meetings were arranged in the first few months of 1988. Craven was unable to attend them because he was recovering from open-heart surgery. He asked Dr Louis Luyt and Professor Johan Claassen to attend but the latter withdrew.

Craven was happy to send Luyt because of the progress that Transvaal had made with regard to rugby in Soweto and Eldorado Park. 'I was proud to nominate him [Luyt] to represent me because I knew that he could walk into that meeting with his head held high.'[3]

Craven did not agree with some of his other board members. He had confronted them on the issue: 'Would they have been able to name just one junior team in a single mixed competition in their provinces which they had introduced as their bit for integrated rugby? As I turned towards them, their eyes switched down to the table in front of them.'[4]

Steve Tshwete remembered,

> Luyt rang me himself and I met him in London and Frankfurt. It was provoked by the desire to get back to international competition. They realised that the key to that lay with the ANC. As far as we were concerned the issue was a single rugby-controlling body ... Once that was achieved the prospects of South Africa competing internationally would be brighter.[5]

The ANC held the upper hand and Luyt found the negotiations hard going. However, after long conversations with ANC representatives, including Thabo Mbeki, it was decided on Luyt's return to send a report to the foreign minister, Pik Botha. The latter was impressed but could not find a way to submit the report to state president, P.W. Botha, who would not tolerate any contact with the ANC. As a result, nothing came of it.

Luyt was determined not to give up and an effort was made to set up another meeting. The ANC wanted to speak to Craven and were prepared to meet him in Harare in October 1988, which obviated a long journey for the ailing rugby chief. 'We thought that the unification of rugby would be the toughest,' explained Barbara Masekela, 'and we were keen to make progress in our discussions with them. We also wanted SARU under Ebrahim Patel to attend.'[6]

Although his loyalties were divided, Patel was concerned by the South African Council on Sports' (SACOS's) inflexibility and realised the need to align SARU with the broader democratic movement that was being driven by the ANC. He had observed developments taking place, as well as the more enlightened approach that had become visible in white politics and sport.[7]

Craven was delighted to be meeting the ANC, claiming 'this old heart of mine really came alive. The adrenalin is what keeps you young and I felt like I did back in 1931 when I first played for the Springboks in Swansea.'[8]

'The night before the meeting,' recalled Patel, 'Craven received a telephone call from Pik Botha, asking him to return to South Africa. Craven refused.'[9]

The ANC's Alfred Nzo chaired the meeting, which was attended by Thabo Mbeki, Barbara Masekela, Steve Tshwete and Stanley Mabizela, a former rugby player for Border. Luyt thought Craven was not at his best and 'might have been thrown off balance by the professional preparedness of the other side, or perhaps by the unexpected respect and warmth that came across the table from Mbeki, who insisted on calling him "Oom Danie"'.[10]

Craven liked Nzo from the outset and admired his handling of the meeting. Discussions moved at a lively pace and delegates were not allowed to become bogged down on petty issues. There were still heated arguments. Craven, for example, claimed his board had more right than SARU to regard itself as a non-racial organisation.[11]

Luyt claimed the SARU leader often sought advice from Mbeki and Tshwete, but Craven reported the situation differently. He saw the aggression coming from the SARU delegation comprising Patel; Sas Bailey, the general secretary; Ismail Jakoet, the treasurer; and Lex Mpati, a lawyer who later became chancellor of Rhodes University. Craven was surprised at 'the conviviality and total lack of antagonism from the ANC ... the hostile vibes came not from the ANC people, but from the SARU delegates'.[12] He did not take into account that the ANC were there to mediate between the governing bodies and that the awkward questions would inevitably come from the very organised SARU representatives.

Luyt used the opportunity to question the ANC as to whether they had been responsible for a bomb blast outside Ellis Park earlier that year. The ANC replied that they had made extensive enquiries as to who was responsible and were certain that it had not been the work of their military wing. Later Craven would maintain that he and Luyt were responsible for 'an almost complete cessation of violence in white urban areas from that time on'.[13]

At the end of the meeting, the ANC, the SA Rugby Board and SARU drew up a joint statement which Patel read to the media. They agreed that rugby should come under one non-racial controlling body. The document was signed by Mbeki, Craven and Patel and stated: 'The leaders ... met the ANC solely because of their belief that it can play a positive role to achieve common objectives ... These leaders are ready to meet at all times, and shall meet any other parties or groups that may also play such a role.'[14]

It was a good start in which rugby's representatives had demonstrated their commitment to unification. 'Craven was a brave man,' said Masekela, 'to buck the powers-that-be by visiting us in Lusaka. He was motivated by survival but, at the same time, had the courage to stick his neck out.' Craven did not believe that 'the unity of rugby was an overnight transformation, frequently comparing South African society with the human body, in which sick cells die off as a small group of healthy ones start spreading'.

Masekela also spoke highly of Patel: 'It was more difficult for him to join hands than anyone else. He represented the most excluded part of the rugby community.'[15]

The rugby leaders returned home to face a barrage of questions. Security police visited Patel at his home, and he was also called upon to pacify SACOS members who were understandably concerned. Patel remained firm: 'Our [SARU's] attitude was that we would talk to whoever we chose. No one would prescribe to us.'[16]

Craven and Luyt were criticised by a wide range of people. F.W. de Klerk, then minister of education with responsibility for sport, called the rugby men 'traitors'. Although he was to talk to the ANC not long afterwards, De Klerk expressed his shock that 'the president of one of South Africa's national sports bypasses the government and turns to a terrorist organisation that is engaged in terrorist attacks on innocent civilians every day'.[17]

Something of a compromise was made to pacify the government, but Craven was not prepared to accept the National Sport Council's (NSC's) imposition of a moratorium that would prevent international tours taking place whilst sports bodies were involved in sensitive negotiations.[18] After the apparent breakthrough in Harare, he proceeded to place everything at risk by negotiating a tour for 1989. He antagonised SARU and rendered further talks difficult to arrange.

The rugby bodies suddenly found themselves lagging in the unity talks, particularly in the context of President de Klerk's lifting of the ban on the ANC and the Pan African Congress and the start of serious negotiations. When South African sports administrators attended the Harare Indaba in November 1990, Craven was very much a lone voice in his insistence on defying the moratorium, a stance directly opposed to Patel's view that it was a key condition if talks were to continue.

The various sports codes were given targets by the National Olympic and Sports Congress (NOSC) – formerly the NSC. They were asked to establish a unified non-racial body, create a development programme and attempt to address historical imbalances. Certain sports were more enthusiastic than others in their support for the unification process. Many were sceptical of the NOSC, doubting whether it had the power to carry out its promises. The sports moratorium, in particular, became an emotional issue and there were heated arguments over political interference in sport.

The moratorium was self-imposed. It had been called by Dennis Brutus some 30 years previously and had been in existence in various forms ever since. Mthobi Tyamzashe said that the NOSC had decided to use it 'as a tool to ensure that the imbalances were addressed as a matter of urgency'. He thought that the moratorium struck a blow against establishment sports bodies and that it made people listen. 'We do not see the moratorium as a permanent fixture,' he maintained at the time, 'it is presently working to direct focus to what needs to be done by South Africa.'[19]

After the awkward relationship in Harare, the NOSC resolved to sort out rugby's problems on their return to South Africa. A delegation, comprising Makhenkesi Stofile, Mluleki George and Mthobi Tyamzashe, met Craven, Johan Claassen and Jan Pickard at Newlands. Fresh from its success in uniting cricket, the NOSC arrived with every good intention but its mission was doomed to fail. Craven was in an irascible mood and saw no reason why he should negotiate with a group of people whose rugby credentials he doubted.

He set out to intimidate his visitors. 'He had something to say to each of us,' recounted Tyamzashe, 'when it came to my turn, he asked me my name and what position I used to play. I told him and he snapped back, "Never heard of you ... but I'm sure you've heard of me."'[20] Although Craven claimed that he 'tried to co-operate but got nothing in return', he was obviously not interested in the other side's viewpoint.

It was a frustrating three hours for the NOSC. Craven was determined to dominate proceedings. At one point he told them that apartheid had hurt him as much as anyone else, which produced laughter. In the end, the NOSC withdrew, saying that it had discharged its responsibility by voicing its standpoint to the SA

Rugby Board. Craven complained: 'Where do the NOSC fit in anyway? Who do they represent? They have no rugby constituency.'[21]

It was more practical for the rugby bodies to take responsibility for the negotiations. If the NOSC had decided to take part, Patel would probably have found himself negotiating with men who were part of his SARU rugby structure – administrators such as George, Stofile and Tyamzashe. At the same time, getting the talks back on track was going to be difficult, with historian Albert Grundlingh noting that they had 'ground to a halt amidst accusations and counter-accusations of intransigence, insensitivity and opportunism'.[22]

Luyt intimated that 'there were simply too many in the SA Rugby Board who were opposed, and the demands from SARU were hardly reasonable'. Yet Patel found a way of breaking the impasse. He called Luyt early in 1991 in order to bring the provincial administrations together and agree to a 'newly-formed non-racial structure as a concrete example' for the national body. Luyt then invited the provincial heads of white rugby to his office where 'with Patel at my side in his newly appointed position as deputy president of the Transvaal RFU [Rugby Football Union], we started twisting arms. Why, we asked, don't we apply the Transvaal RFU model and make the SA Rugby Board truly representative of all rugby in South Africa?'

In reality, the formation of a single body to govern rugby in South Africa was far more complex than an agreement between the two Transvaal organisations. No other sporting unification captured public interest to the same extent. Its significance went beyond an agreement between sporting bodies. 'It was seen by many as the ANC and NSC versus the National Party and the SA Rugby Board,' explained Patel.[23]

Nelson Mandela invited delegations from the SA Rugby Board and SARU to ANC headquarters in Shell House, Johannesburg. He urged rugby's leaders 'to find a way to come together'. Luyt recollected that he 'warned us not to, during our discussions, make remarks or insult each other as that would only serve to make negotiations difficult'.[24]

Following his success in the unification of cricket, the ANC's Steve Tshwete – 'Mr Fix-it' – was brought in as the facilitator to give direction to rugby's rocky unity talks.[25] Throughout the discussions, Craven kept fuelling the fires by insisting that his board would not observe the moratorium. He was looking forward to 1992 as the International Rugby Football Board (IRB) had diarised fixtures for him. But, despite the distractions, the show was kept on the road. By December 1991, it was announced that agreement had been reached, and the South African Rugby Football Union came into being on 19 January 1992.

The rugby world looked on nervously. Grundlingh describes the arrangement as 'an uneasy unity; both parties were driven to it by circumstances rather than conviction'.[26] Officials of the former bodies, the SA Rugby Board and SARU, would initially be given an equal say in all matters pertaining to the control of rugby. It was accepted that the presidency should be shared over the first two years, with Craven taking the first term in office (up to March 1993) and Patel the second (to March 1994).

Craven was one of South Africa's best-known citizens, but Patel was comparatively unknown to white rugby followers save for references to him in the national press when he resisted the advances of the SA Rugby Board. Patel had endured negative publicity but was always well aware of his responsibilities. He knew that rugby was a powerful social force and that he had been right in advocating non-racial sport and merit selection. He had also been flexible enough to talk to white rugby authorities even though they were committed to acting along lines acceptable to the government.

Patel would later say that the four points he and Craven had drawn up in 1978 were at the core of the final unification. There was a sense of pride in a partnership that had maintained an understanding over the years. Patel was adamant that it was he and Craven who achieved the unity – not the NSC nor anyone else – and that they did so despite interruptions and interference.[27] That SARU should arrive as an equal partner with the SA Rugby Board was achieved to the dismay of the SA African Rugby Association and the SA Rugby Football Federation. These organisations felt slighted in the 50-50 deals which were struck with unification.

Despite the criticism, the establishment of the SA Rugby Football Union (SARFU) was celebrated in style. Kimberley was chosen for a special function on 20 March 1992 because it was the birthplace of the SA Rugby Football Board and the SA Coloured Rugby Football Board. The occasion was followed by an important development. Tshwete had been moved by Craven's desperation to see the Springboks play the All Blacks just one more time. He spoke to Mluleki George and, in a remarkable conciliatory gesture, the two men agreed to matches being played against the All Blacks and the Wallabies.[28]

Others did not fall into the spirit of the occasion. When the first post-unity Test match was played against the All Blacks in August 1992, the rugby authorities at Ellis Park – led by Luyt – displayed blatant indifference to the good faith shown by Tshwete and George. They were joined by a section of the crowd that destroyed almost all the goodwill that had been established in months of sensitive negotiation. Spiro Zavos says: 'The white tribe's response was to break an agreement made by the SA Rugby Football Union by singing *Die Stem*, the provocative white anthem.' The former All Black Chris Laidlaw was there and noticed 'you could almost see the glitter in the eyes of those who sang loudest during the minute of silence for the loss of life in the townships'. He also mentioned glancing across at Tshwete, who 'sat "impassive, unreadable" during this snub to the new order'.[29]

Luyt responded proudly: 'Craven and Patel apologised in their capacity as joint presidents of SARFU. I stood firm.' Joe French, of the visiting Australian Rugby Football Union, accused Luyt of having acted with 'malice afterthought'.[30] There were also thoughts of the Aussies returning home, but this did not happen. Tshwete threatened the game's authorities that if *Die Stem* was sung at the Test against the Wallabies at Cape Town, South African rugby would return to the wilderness. 'Verwoerd,' he warned, 'will not be allowed to rule this nation from his grave.'[31] The warning was heeded, and on the instruction of Craven and Patel, there was no anthem at Newlands.

The behaviour of the crowd at Newlands satisfied Tshwete, 'there were 42 000 saying they recognise the need for peace and democracy in our country'.[32] Yet some NSC officials admitted the unification process had been pushed through too quickly. Mluleki George was uncomfortable with developments: 'We have been taken for a ride. Certain people were never interested in unity. They were more interested in international competition.' The NSC and the ANC considered re-imposing the boycott. Douglas Booth, however, notes:

> They quickly learned that you cannot turn an international boycott on and off like a tap. Sponsors, local and international sports administrators, and foreign governments rejected a new boycott and the ANC backtracked. It realised that a boycott would drain resources and undermine its strategy of social reform through reconciliation.[33]

With the Springboks doing badly on the field of play, there were calls in the media for Craven to go. Luyt reacted at SARFU's special general meeting in November 1992, by proposing a change to the constitution that would make the presidency an honorary position, whilst a chairman administered the affairs of the union. His effort failed, says Paul Dobson, 'not because the delegates rallied behind Craven, but because Ebrahim Patel threatened the fragile fabric of unity would be rent asunder by such a move'. Patel saw Luyt's proposal as 'undemocratic and likely to cause uncertainty amongst the men who had previously been part of SARU'.[34] Luyt's challenge was countered but his desire to implement change so soon was an early warning to Patel as the latter prepared for his stint in overseeing an unsettled boardroom.

Craven did not complete his term of office. After a bad fall, he was in no condition to continue his work. Patel covered for him through awkward moments, such as when Craven fell asleep during meetings. In a difficult period, Patel told SARFU: 'You will neither oust him nor humiliate him. I can cover for him. That is the least we can do after all the man has done for rugby.'[35] Patel understood his former rival better than most people. He respected the fact that Craven had dedicated his life to the game, even though they disagreed on numerous issues. 'Such was Craven's consuming, passionate love for rugby,' said Patel, 'that he made errors of judgement. He was blind to the real aspirations of the oppressed.'[36]

Patel did not merely hold the fort during the early part of transformation. His leadership was vital in a critical formative period for the new united board. He confronted important issues and instituted change. He believed that rugby should move closer to other sports and thereby fall under the aegis of the NSC. 'Traditionally,' explains Dobson, 'rugby football had paddled its own course, not being part of the Olympic or any other movement.'[37] That was possible in the apartheid era but, under the new dispensation, greater credibility would be gained by moving towards the NSC. Patel's view was backed by a SARFU executive, which unanimously decided to seek affiliation.

The development programme was launched in March 1993, thereby coinciding with the beginning of Patel's term in office. It had been a key aspect of the unity agreement and the first year was marked by a concerted effort to set a standard in terms of financial support, facilities and coaching for the more than 100 000 players who attended. Nevertheless, Patel and others were not convinced by the sincerity of the process. Sports historians David Black and John Nauright thought 'early efforts tended to support the views of those critics who asserted that unity was, by and large, a shallow and elite-driven process dominated by the priorities of the old SA Rugby Board'.[38]

For some time, the 'springbok' as an emblem was a contentious issue. Patel favoured its retention, pointing out that SARU's emblem had incorporated two springbok heads flanking a protea. He was quoted as saying: 'It is eyewash to suggest that a mixed South African side abroad would want to play under any emblem but the springbok.'[39] His determination to retain the status quo was crucial to the cause at that stage but not fully appreciated by Craven and Luyt, amongst others. There was a particularly tense period when Patel was unable to get NSC officials – most notably George – to grant their approval. Craven 'fumed' but the others worked on a suitable emblem 'deep into the early morning hours'.[40]

Perhaps the greatest challenge for Patel was to convince the rugby world that he was indeed worthy of the responsibility that had been bestowed on him. It was his task to make an impression on the IRB – a body he described as 'an elite, snobbish, very British' organisation.

'I was a non-white member, a rare occurrence in the more than one-hundred-year history of the IRB,' he recalled. 'I remember watching the reaction of people attending the opening function of my first meeting. I was obviously going to be matched against Craven. They were trying to sum me up, and I was endeavouring to sum them up. Suddenly, halfway through the meeting, everything evaporated through the windows.'[41]

It was a poignant moment in the history of rugby. The IRB accepted that Patel had every right to be there. He was a highly experienced rugby administrator who had served the game for nearly thirty years. He was also very aware of how South Africa had evolved during a complex period in its development. Before long, Patel was asked to chair IRB committees and address the press on their behalf. He became a key figure in promoting South Africa's changing image among rugby nations.

At home, Patel was aware of the difficulties involved in being accepted by the domineering white rugby fraternity; a situation that involved overcoming deep-rooted legacies of discrimination and segregation. It was, for example, customary for the heads of international rugby unions to make appearances during their teams' tours abroad. When Patel visited Australia in 1993, the youthful captain, François Pienaar, was pleased to see him because he 'seemed well-placed to establish and maintain a kinder, more conciliatory tone and approach'.[42] The Springbok manager Jannie Engelbrecht saw Patel as a model ambassador for the game but was unhappy that the latter should make the speech at the post-game dinner after a Test match in Australia – 'a task Engelbrecht argued, that was best left to the manager who knows more about rugby'.[43]

It was Luyt, however, who posed the greatest threat to Patel. In his autobiography, the wealthy businessman-turned-rugby-administrator seemed intent on portraying Patel as being of inferior status in the game. He was 'the good cop' as long as he did as he was told, but when he asserted his viewpoint, he became 'the bad cop'.[44] Then, when Patel assumed the office of president of SARFU, Luyt dismissed him as 'another interim caretaker'.[45] The autobiography goes further. In Australia, Luyt discovered the hotel management had made a mistake in allocating his room to Patel, but instead of addressing the matter in the expected manner, he and a fellow official took delight in entering Patel's suite and emptying the liquor cabinet, 'much to the obvious unease of this devout Muslim'.[46]

Patel was aware for some time of Luyt's aspirations and influence. As chairman of the organising committee for the Rugby World Cup, Luyt held a position of growing prominence. It bothered Patel who thought SARFU should play a greater role in the running of the World Cup. When the matter was placed before the union's committee, Luyt was given its full backing. Even more ominous for Patel was Luyt's interest in the presidency with all the lobbying and canvassing done on his behalf by the Transvaal RFU. André Markgraaff and Mauritz Meyer were praised for working 'round the clock' to make sure Luyt received the vote as the next president.[47]

A South African rugby magazine thought Patel was 'nice to know' but lacked the 'guts and thunder bona fides' to take rugby forward. It was an article that did not take into account the courage and commitment he had shown over twenty-plus years in arguing the SARU case against a dictatorial government-backed SA Rugby Board. One of the aims of the article was to convey the impression that if there was a white man who could stand up to the politically inspired changes in South Africa's rugby structure, no one better fitted the job description than Luyt.[48]

In 1994, Patel announced that he would not be standing for re-election as president of SARFU, citing the greater demands of his school, the Lenasia Moslem Primary School. It caused surprise. Black and Nauright comment: 'Why his dual responsibilities should have now become untenable after the years of complex and time-consuming unity talks is not clear.'[49] Patel did not add to the reason given for his withdrawal and did not point fingers. The structures had been in place for some time to ensure a resurgence of white dominance and, as a consequence, Luyt's election was relatively uneventful.

The death of Craven in 1993 and the withdrawal of Patel the following year meant South African rugby lost its two most experienced administrators. They had represented opposing views for nearly three decades, a stalemate eventually concluded by a transformation process that was designed to bring both an end to discrimination and set up an administration that would redress past inequities. Significantly, the careers of the two men spanned the last era of the amateur game, with new leaders ushering in the dramatic changes which brought about professionalism.

Reflecting on past events, Patel regretted the fact that sacrifices had to be made in the name of unification. He was completely satisfied that SARU had to contribute to the broader liberation struggle and the ultimate democracy of South Africa. However, he was not satisfied that the high price that SARU had to pay – the death of its rugby – was justifiable. He believed in unity but the unification achieved favoured the continued dominance of white administrators who controlled the game's finances, sponsorships and facilities.

The legacy of apartheid was a tremendous imbalance, with black rugby largely absorbed by the wealthy white organisations. 'A disadvantaged community could never compete in a meaningful sense,' said Patel. 'The needs and priorities were different; it was more important for black people to pursue education and jobs than play rugby.' He concluded: 'Rugby lost the community-based game which meant so much to the people. The advent of professionalism turned rugby into a business, and it needed a new movement to rectify the wrongs that had taken place.' He did not think 'development' as it was implemented was the answer. 'How do you develop a dead thing?' he asked not long after leaving the game. 'We needed to coin a new word – something like "resurrection".'[50]

Notes

1   *Weekend Argus*, 26 January 1991. Tyamzashe was then national secretary of the NOSC.
2   *Cape Times*, 1 May 1989.
3   T. Partridge, *A Life in Rugby* (Halfway House: Southern Book Publishers, 1991), 136.
4   Partridge, *A Life in Rugby*, 136–137.
5   M. Bose, *Sporting Colours: Sport and Politics in South Africa* (London: Robson Books, 1994), 184.
6   J. Winch and M. Patel, interview with B. Masekela, in 'Playing the Game: The Unification of South African Sport' (unpublished M-Net project, 2000).
7   J. Winch and M. Patel, interview with E. Patel, in 'Playing the Game: The Unification of South African Sport' (unpublished M-Net project, 2000).
8   Partridge, *A Life in Rugby*, 138.
9   Winch and Patel, interview with Patel, in 'Playing the Game'.
10   L. Luyt, *Walking Proud: The Louis Luyt Autobiography* (Cape Town: Don Nelson, 2003), 177.
11   Partridge, *A Life in Rugby*, 140.
12   Ibid., 139.
13   Ibid., 142.
14   Ibid., 139.
15   Winch and Patel, interview with Masekela, in 'Playing the Game'; Partridge, *A Life in Rugby*, 139.
16   Winch and Patel, interview with Patel, in 'Playing the Game'.
17   Bose, *Sporting Colours*, 187.
18   Partridge, *A Life in Rugby*, 144.
19   J. Winch and M. Patel, interview with M. Tyamzashe, in 'Playing the Game: The Unification of South African Sport' (unpublished M-Net project, 2000).
20   Winch and Patel, interview with Tyamzashe, in 'Playing the Game'.
21   *Sunday Times*, 2 December 1990.
22   A. Grundlingh, 'The New Politics of Rugby', in A. Grundlingh, A. Odendaal and B.Spies, *Beyond the Tryline: Rugby and South African Society* (Johannesburg: Ravan Press, 1995), 3.
23   Winch and Patel, interview with Patel, in 'Playing the Game'.
24   Luyt, *Walking Proud*, 208.
25   *Sunday Star*, 3 February 1991.
26   A. Grundlingh, 'The New Politics of Rugby', 5.

27 Winch and Patel, interview with Patel, in 'Playing the Game'.
28 J. Winch and M. Patel, interviews with S. Tshwete, M. George and M. Tyamzashe, in 'Playing the Game: The Unification of South African Sport' (unpublished M-Net project, 2000).
29 S. Zavos, *Winters of Revenge: The Bitter Rivalry between the All Blacks and the Springboks* (Auckland: Viking, 1997), 207–208.
30 Luyt, *Walking Proud*, 198–199.
31 Zavos, *Winters of Revenge*, 208.
32 Quoted in S. Jones, *Endless Winter: The Inside Story of the Rugby Revolution* (London: Mainstream Publishing, 1993), 98.
33 D. Booth, 'Recapturing the Moment? Global Rugby, Economics and the Politics of Nation in Post-Apartheid South Africa', in T. Chandler and J. Nauright (eds), *Making the Rugby World, Race, Gender, Commerce* (London: Frank Cass, 1999), 186.
34 P. Dobson, *Doc: The Life of Danie Craven* (Cape Town: Human & Rousseau, 1994), 192.
35 Ibid.
36 Winch and Patel, interview with Patel, in 'Playing the Game'.
37 Ibid.; Dobson, *Doc: The Life*, 193–194.
38 D. Black and J. Nauright, *Rugby and the South African Nation: Sport, Cultures, Politics and Power in the Old and New South Africa* (Manchester: Manchester University Press, 1998), 113.
39 Dobson, *Doc: The Life*, 203.
40 Luyt, *Walking Proud*, 184.
41 Winch and Patel, interview with Patel, in 'Playing the Game'.
42 F. Pienaar, *Rainbow Warrior* (London: Harper/Collins, 1999), 106.
43 Luyt, *Walking Proud*, 207.
44 Ibid., 183.
45 Ibid., 206.
46 Ibid., 226.
47 Ibid., 204.
48 *Rugby 15*, April 1994; Grundlingh, 'The New Politics of Rugby', 14.
49 Grundlingh, 'The New Politics of Rugby', 4.
50 Winch and Patel, interview with Patel, in 'Playing the Game'.

22

'Madiba Magic'

> Up to now rugby has been the application of apartheid in the
> sports field. But now things are changing. We must use sport
> for the purpose of nation-building and promoting all the ideas
> which we think will lead to peace and stability in the country.[1]
>
> – Nelson Mandela

Nelson Mandela made a calculated decision to use the 1995 Rugby World Cup as a means to galvanise the process of national unification. He believed the third edition of the rugby extravaganza presented an opportunity to create something for all South Africans to celebrate. He also accepted the formidable role of winning over the support of the different population groups at a time when fears, uncertainty and racial divisions between blacks and whites in South Africa had still to be conquered.

To achieve success, millions of black South Africans would have to be persuaded to stand behind a team that had for so many years represented white supremacy. Mandela believed the time had come to abandon old perceptions and look at the bigger picture. He intended to use rugby for the purpose of nation-building and to promote a tournament that could shake off bitterness and prejudice and unite the people of South Africa. He believed the game could act as a metaphor for a new South Africa.

Mandela also reached out to whites in a remarkable way. He endeavoured to placate Afrikaners in particular through actively sharing in their support for the Springboks. It was an extraordinary mission as it came in the wake of an earlier demonstration by whites opposed to transformation. The country's fragile unification structure had been undermined at Ellis Park in August 1992 when 'it seemed like a besieged tribe had gathered to take strength in their numbers and to send a message of defiance to their perceived persecutors'.[2]

That the International Rugby Football Board (IRB) should award the World Cup to South Africa in the same year was arguably a gamble rather than a stroke of opportunism. Rugby leaders in Australia and New Zealand had not forgotten Danie Craven's support for the inaugural Rugby World Cup in 1987 – even though the Springboks were unable to participate. They owed him a favour, although he would not live to see the tournament in 1995.

South Africa nearly lost the right to host the tournament. Escalating unrest and political violence in the early 1990s put the IRB under pressure to make contingency plans. There were rumours of England and Wales being lined up to stage the event if the violence worsened. Mluleki George attended a meeting at Louis Luyt's house to discuss the situation with members of the IRB.

George remembered:

Dr Luyt was very worried and pleaded for assistance. I told the IRB members that New Zealand and Australia had visited us to play rugby in 1992 at the height of the violence; the matches had taken place without any disruption. I also mentioned that the unrest would subside after the 1994 elections. They accepted that view.[3]

Mandela was inaugurated as president on 10 May 1994 and less than a month later, on 4 June, attended the first Test against England at Loftus Versfeld. The English had lost four out of five matches on their tour but, after eighteen minutes, led 20–0 and went on to win 32–15. It was a disaster for the over-confident Springboks, but they won the second Test convincingly at Cape Town 27–9. They then toured New Zealand, losing their first two Test matches against the All Blacks, but scored two tries to nil in drawing the last 18–18. At the end of the year, they toured Britain, winning the two Tests played against Scotland 34–10 and Wales 20–12.

Preparations were on course for the Springboks although Kitch Christie replaced Ian McIntosh as coach after the New Zealand tour. Other new key appointments were Edward Griffiths as chief executive officer of the SA Rugby Football Union (SARFU) and Morné du Plessis as manager of the Springbok side. They would make important contributions, as New Zealand journalist, Spiro Zavos indicates:

The nation, the rugby community and the political community was put on a virtual war footing to ensure a South African victory. The PR campaigns during the First World War with the posters of a grim-faced Lord Kitchener insisting 'Your Country Needs You' were matched by the hype in South Africa around the – unlikely – theme, 'One Country, One Team'. Rugby, the historical force for divisiveness in South African life, was used shrewdly and without remorse to support the new political order.[4]

The African National Congress (ANC) leadership recognised the importance of staging such an event in South Africa but, says Professor Albert Grundlingh, 'the Springboks probably stood more to gain by the association with Mandela than the other way around'. He was a leader with an established international reputation reputation 'and his strategic appearances and his identification with the team helped elevate them, a virtually all-white team, to a symbol of nationhood.'[5]

When the Springbok badge became an issue, Mandela responded quickly: 'I decided to act. I made a statement. I suggested that we must retain the Springbok.' According to John Carlin, the president called in those who disagreed with him: 'one by one ... [he] imposed his will once again. In time for the World Cup, the Springbok had been saved.'

Mandela visited the team the day before their opening match against Australia. They had just completed a training session at the Silvermine military base when a large helicopter descended towards the field. Mandela had arrived to chat to 'his boys' and told them, 'You now have the opportunity of serving South Africa and uniting our people ... Just remember, all of us, black and white, are behind you.' Morné du Plessis recalled, 'What was amazing was the chemistry. The players were drawn to him immediately ... and [as he departed] they were like young boys waving, so full of this ... excitement.'

Luyt and his management provided positive support for the new political environment that had emerged after the 1994 election. Grundlingh notes that the Springboks 'willingly played along, not fully realising that at a meta-level they were small players in a far greater political drama than the World Cup. Wrapped up in their own limited sporting concerns, they were feted and momentarily ensnared by "Madiba magic".'[6]

Nine countries were automatic qualifiers for the 1995 World Cup: Australia (as champions), South Africa (as hosts) and the remaining quarter-finalists from 1991: Canada, England, France, Ireland, New Zealand, Scotland and Western Samoa. Pre-tournament rankings generally recognised Australia, England, South Africa and New Zealand as the favoured teams.

South Africa's splendid facilities made it possible for the World Cup to be played in a single country for the first time. The opening ceremony at Newlands – 'with its manufactured magic of unity' – featured different aspects of South African life, including traditional gumboot dancers and warriors in tribal regalia. Special highlights were the emotional welcome given by a mainly white crowd to the president and the coming together of the dancers to form a human map of South

Africa. Mandela opened rugby's global showpiece, stating that 'through it we shall also contribute to the promotion of excellence, world peace and friendship'.[7]

The Springboks were well prepared for the singing of the African hymn, 'Nkosi Sikelel' iAfrica' (God Bless Africa) which was sung as one of South Africa's two national anthems at the time. Morné du Plessis had enlisted the help of a Cape Town music teacher, Anne Munnik. The Springbok management attended to every detail, but it was also important for the players to win their matches.

The tournament's opening encounter was between hosts South Africa and the reigning champions, Australia. The winning team would gain an easier passage towards the final. Not surprisingly, it developed into a compelling struggle for supremacy. The South Africans led 14–13 at the interval thanks to Joel Stransky, who was on target with his boot, and wing Pieter Hendricks, who stormed past David Campese to score a wildly applauded try. The Australian fly-half, Michael Lynagh, missed a couple of easy penalty kicks but made amends with a well-judged try.

As the game progressed, the Springboks played some inspired rugby and forced the Australians into a succession of errors. The pressure 'seemed to get to us,' admitted Lynagh, but conceded that his opponents were in great form.[8] Stransky stamped his authority on proceedings, and a match-winning try from a planned and practised move gave him 22 points in his side's 27–18 victory.

The *Sowetan's* support arrived at a vital stage. Their front-page coverage of the match against Australia hailed the great victory of the Amabokoboko – 'the boks, the boks'. The headline that captured the imagination of the people and linguistically 'Africanised' the Springboks was the idea of sub-editor Sy Makaringe. It was endorsed by his editor Aggrey Klaaste who noted that he had joined his Springbok-supporting sons in watching the match.

Morné du Plessis ensured the players were kept aware of the significance of growing African support by taking them and their partners to Robben Island. They visited the cell where the apartheid government had kept Mandela for eighteen of the twenty-seven years he spent in prison.

Victories over unfancied Romania (21–8) and Canada (20–0) followed although the Springboks were unconvincing in both matches. The Romanians harassed them into making mistakes and, on a night when the lights went out temporarily because of an electrical fault, the match against Canada produced some nasty incidents. Three players were sent off – including the South African hooker James Dalton. The Canadian manager commented ruefully, 'The game started in the dark and finished pretty black.'[9]

Before the match against Canada, the Springboks were taken to Zwide, a township outside Port Elizabeth. Siya Kolisi, who was then four years old, was too young to join some three hundred children who gathered around a dusty field for a coaching clinic in which Mark Andrews was prominent because he spoke isiXhosa. The same evening, Morné du Plessis took the players to the stadium where local black teams were playing. The attendance of the Springboks was appreciated and they were soon signing autographs.

In the quarter-final, South Africa beat Western Samoa 42–14. Chester Williams, a player of colour who featured in many advertising billboards, returned from injury and scored a record four tries for the Springboks. It was a hard, physical game. The South African media was shocked by Western Samoa's liberal indulgence in stiff-arm and late tackles. They spoilt an exciting game and it resulted in injuries. The most serious was André Joubert's broken hand, which led to sessions in a decompression chamber and a protective glove being flown out from Ireland.

As the Springboks kept winning, they could feel the country uniting behind them. The day before the semi-final against France at Durban, Mandela spoke in the former Zulu homeland of KwaZulu. Wearing his Springbok cap, he stated that the time had come for all South Africa to get behind 'our boys'. The Rainbow Nation waved the colourful flag, provided renditions of the anthem and gathered behind the 'One team, One country' slogan in generating unprecedented support.

Heavy rain in Durban nearly prevented the match between South Africa and France from taking place. Conditions were so bad that there was a 90-minute delay. If the game had been called off, the Springboks would have been knocked out because of their disciplinary record in earlier matches. When referee Derek Bevan decided play could commence, the decision was made in the nick of time, as rain came down again soon after play started.

In atrocious conditions, South Africa established a 10–0 lead thanks to a try by Ruben Kruger and the boot of Stransky. Two penalties by Thierry Lacroix kept the French in the picture and the score was 10–6 at the interval. In the second half, Stransky and Lacroix were responsible for three penalties apiece. The last five minutes were undoubtedly the most thrilling of the match as the Springboks clung desperately to a 19–15 lead. The French threw everything at them in a dramatic do-or-die attempt to score a try. With scrums collapsing on the Springboks' muddy try-line, there was the fear of a penalty try being given away. It was gripping stuff and the French came tantalisingly close to winning the match when the big forward Abdelatif Benazzi dived towards the line. He was convinced he had scored but the referee signalled for a five-metre scrum.

Chester Williams confessed: 'That day our destiny was decided: we would win the World Cup. Morné du Plessis was convinced that there had been a greater force at play. Most of the team felt the same way.'[10]

New Zealand won the other semi-final, blasting England aside in a devastating opening session. The huge wing Jonah Lomu scored four tries. He had become the central figure in an All Blacks side that emerged as clear favourites to win the final. They had played some terrific rugby – but they did not bargain for the incredible build-up to the match on 24 June 1995.

Louis Luyt was determined that the final at Ellis Park would outdo the opening ceremony at Newlands. Dan Moyane, a well-known broadcaster led the crowd in renditions of 'Shosholoza', originally sung by black migrant workers who travelled from the rural areas of southern Africa to work on the gold mines. Merle McKenna, who had also organised the Newlands event, decided to take the show to the air in Johannesburg. A spectacular afternoon involved 500 performers and 15 aircraft, the highlight being the breathtaking arrival of a 285-seater Boeing 747, commanded by Captain Laurie Kay. It flew just 200 feet above the grandstand to display the message 'Good Luck Bokke' on its undercarriage.

A dramatic addition to the programme was conceived by Linga Moonsamy, a former ANC guerrilla and member of the presidential protection unit. On the morning of the rugby final, he was chatting with other members of the presidential guard outside Mandela's house in Houghton, Johannesburg, 'when in the middle of it all the idea popped out that it would be great if the president wore the green-and-gold Springbok jersey to the stadium'. Moonsamy entered the house to speak to Mandela. The president's secretary was asked to contact Luyt who had the jersey and cap delivered to Mandela's home within the hour.

'We looked at him in that green rugby jersey,' Moonsamy told Carlin, 'and we felt so proud because he himself looked so proud.'[11]

Mandela was at the ground at three o'clock. 'I would like to wish my boys the best of luck,' he remarked and was invited to the dressing room before kick-off.[12] 'A Test-match dressing room,' advised the manager, Morné du Plessis, 'is a very serious place and the tension can be unbearable ... And then Madiba arrives with that glow that seems to surround him.'[13]

Five minutes before kick-off, Mandela entered the field to meet the players. A crowd of more than 60 000 was initially stunned but then broke into a chant. 'Nel-son! Nel-son! Nel-son!' reverberated around the stadium. The broadly smiling Mandela acknowledged the cheering by waving his Springbok cap.

'The All Blacks,' wrote Spiro Zavos, in his dramatic assessment, 'were psyched out by the South African authorities who forced every bit of passion from the supporters until the combined will of the Ellis Park Stadium was so powerful for a South African victory, nothing could stop it from being fulfilled.' The greatest trump card was the president in a replica of Springbok captain François Pienaar's number 6 jersey. Zavos admitted that only Mandela 'could have got away with it' but claimed it 'placed the All Blacks under enormous psychological pressure, for the crowd, always fervent in their support for the Springboks, became rabid'.[14]

Up until the advent of the World Cup in 1987, South Africans and New Zealanders had looked upon their rivalry as one which decided the 'unofficial' world championship. This was their forty-second meeting: South Africa had twenty wins, New Zealand eighteen, and three games were drawn. The clash in 1995 was the first official challenge for world supremacy. In an enthralling duel, the New Zealanders ran the ball and the South Africans tackled superbly. An oil company had offered cash incentives to those Springboks who tackled Jonah Lomu and the huge wing was held up every time he came into the line. 'Lomu got the ball eight times,' remarked Kitch Christie the Springbok coach, 'and we took him out eight times.'[15] There were especially memorable tackles by Japie Mulder and Joost van der Westhuizen.

Ruben Kruger was certain he had scored a try after being powered over the line from a scrum. Pienaar later commented that one can always see whether a try has been scored by looking at the facial expressions of one's opponents. 'In this instance, the All Blacks on the scene certainly appeared resigned to the fact. But [Ed] Morrison decided otherwise.'[16] The referee claimed he was unsighted, although he admitted years later Kruger probably did score the try that he disallowed: 'Nobody said anything, because they won!'[17]

There were no tries in the match. The Springboks led 9–6 at half-time, Stransky kicking two penalties and a drop-goal against two penalties from Andrew Mehrtens. A lone drop from Mehrtens was the only score in the second half, enabling New Zealand to draw level. Mehrtens missed another attempt when Josh Kronfeld wandered into his sights and forced him to hook the ball.

The match went into extra time. Mehrtens kicked a penalty and Stransky replied for the Springboks, bringing the score to 12-all. Play entered the final session with the teams locked into one of the most uncompromising battles in rugby history. According to the rules, if the teams could not be separated in score or tries at the end of extra-time, then the number of red cards would come into play. Dalton's dismissal at Port Elizabeth again became relevant.

With seven minutes remaining, the Springboks earned a scrum in an attacking position. Pienaar called a blindside move from where they would be able to establish a solid forward platform. The scrum wheeled and was reset. Stransky cancelled Pienaar's call from fly-half. He wanted the ball immediately. Van der Westhuizen sent it spinning to Stransky. The fly-half struck it perfectly and as the ball soared high above the posts, the crowd erupted in joyous celebration. The giant screen recorded: South Africa 15; New Zealand 12.

Springbok captain François Pienaar was promptly guided towards SABC's David van der Sandt to conduct a live interview to a worldwide television audience of 500 million. Van der Sandt began by stating: 'François, fantastic support from 63 000 South Africans today?' Pienaar reacted quickly: 'David, we didn't have the support of 63 000 South Africans today. We had the support of 42 million South Africans.'[18]

Euphoric scenes followed as Pienaar then approached the podium where President Mandela was waiting to present him with the Webb Ellis Cup. He thanked the president, before taking the trophy and raising it above his head. 'This is the pinnacle,' declared Kitch Christie, adding: 'It could have gone either way and we must feel for the New Zealanders. They could be where we are now with a little bit of luck.'[19]

Lomu's threat had been nullified. 'Dogged, unremitting defence,' maintained Dan Retief. 'That is what finally made South Africa champions of the world.'[20] Pienaar agreed, expressing his pleasure that his team had not conceded a try in either the semi-final or the final. 'We knew we had won the World Cup largely because of our outstanding defensive pattern, and we felt we had not scraped the surface of our attacking potential.'[21]

South Africa had returned triumphantly to the sporting arena, a glorious victory for the new 'rainbow nation.' Mandela led the country in its celebrations, a dramatic achievement that saw black people toyi-toying through the townships, singing the theme song 'Shosholoza', and shouting *'viva amabokoboko'*. These were moments that would stay with those who had followed an unforgettable event.

Frederick Van Zyl Slabbert wrote of Mandela being the 'master at exploiting the appropriate moment ... Nobody must underestimate his performance at the Rugby World Cup final ... This was one of the final blows to exclusive rightwing Afrikaner nationalism. I saw and heard one of the pot-bellied brigade whisper through his tears: "That is my president."[22]

Rugby World Cup 1995 had provided a platform on which to drive the transformation process. In an ideal world, this might have become the main focus of attention for rugby's leaders, but the dawn of a new era was dominated by the advent of professionalism. On the eve of the World Cup final, the rugby unions of Australia, New Zealand and South Africa (SANZAR) announced that they had sold their combined television rights to Rupert Murdoch's News Corporation for US$555 million over ten years. The amount to be administered by SANZAR would pay for an annual Tri-Nations championship between the three unions, and a 'Super 12' competition involving regional teams from each nation.

Amidst the excitement, the Springbok squad, as well as many of their counterparts in New Zealand and Australia, became engaged in talks with a rival group, the World Rugby Corporation (WRC). This organisation, led by a leading figure in Australian rugby, Ross Turnbull, was bankrolled by Kerry Packer.[23] Pienaar was offered $300 000 to sign up the South African team for the WRC. He explained, 'We had found ourselves in a position where two groups wanted our services. We considered their respective offers and reached our decision. It was as simple as that.'[24]

It was a little more complex. As the NewsCorp offer allowed rugby to continue operating as before, it suited the establishment. The awkwardness lay with the WRC offering to pay the players 20 per cent more than any other offer received at any stage of negotiations. Their rugby would operate through a global conference system, with fewer matches and taking the game to new markets, such as the United States and Japan. Pienaar, as the recruiting agent, believed the circuit 'could catapult rugby union into a fresh, honest and professional era where the game would be marketed on a level, and to an audience, far beyond its traditional frontiers'.[25]

Dan Retief had reservations. What he saw of WRC's confidential plans convinced him that the scheme was unworkable: 'The document enumerated on crowds numbering 40 000 in Houston and Tokyo, and even bigger numbers at established venues.' He had doubts over whether composite teams made up of various nationalities could attract the anticipated interest.[26]

NewsCorp became anxious that leading players were being signed up by their media rivals. Sam Chisholm, head of NewsCorp, London, contacted Pienaar and the Springbok captain effectively switched allegiance when promised a similar deal to that of WRC. Chisholm also contacted Luyt and it was agreed that SARFU would effectively act as NewsCorp's agents.[27]

On 4 August 1995, the Springboks gathered at the Midrand Protea hotel to make their final decision. All but three players voted to sign up with SARFU and NewsCorp. It was a triumph for the establishment. Pienaar, Hennie le Roux and James Small voted for WRC but then joined their team-mates in signing three-year contracts. Within weeks, the WRC – 'an amorphous international league' according to Luyt – had folded.[28] World Cup Springboks were accused of looking after themselves at the expense of leading players around the world and their team-mates at provincial level.[29]

In Paris, on 27 August 1995, SARFU president Louis Luyt attended the first IRB meeting since the signing of the NewsCorp contract. He addressed delegates and asked the other countries whether they had ever paid their players in one way or another. He said he began with England: 'You could hear a pin drop in the ornate conference room ... One after another, everyone admitted to some form of payment – except Argentina, where a rare breed of players was still willing to be bruised and battered for the sheer joy of it.'[30]

The IRB agreed to do away with rugby union's amateur status at that meeting. According to the Australian captain, Nick Farr-Jones, delegates resembled men emerging from their own funeral.[31]

The remaining matches in 1995 were successful for the Springboks. They defeated Wales 40–11 at Ellis Park and then won both Tests on an overseas tour. They were down against Italy with fifteen minutes remaining but finished strongly to win 40–21. It was good preparation for the match against England at Twickenham where the Springboks were more convincing than the 24–10 victory reflected. By the end of 1995, rugby's public image in Pienaar's eyes had never been better: 'The Springboks were well paid, safely contracted and winning; the development programme was finally discovering real momentum ... We were bringing the country together, we were making a difference.'[32]

The following year was to be vastly different. The first full professional season based on the Super 12 and Tri-Nations added enormous pressure to the players' workload. Luyt encouraged Kitch Christie, who had been battling illness, to step down. Christie had been the most successful coach in South African history, winning all fourteen Tests during his term in office. André Markgraaff, who had been instrumental in Luyt becoming president of SARFU and had since revitalised Griqualand West rugby, was appointed the new Springboks' coach.

Much went wrong in 1996, with the All Blacks proving themselves a superior side. Markgraaff invited controversy by including Henry Tromp in the South African team. Three years earlier, the player and his father had beaten a sixteen-year-old black youth who had stolen from a farm labourer. The youth died from his injuries and the Tromps were jailed. When advice was sought from the government, it was ruled that Tromp had served his punishment. Jon Swift reflected on a struggling Springbok team during the series against the All Blacks, and in an article titled 'Blame Those in Power, Not The Players' questioned the game's administration: 'Tromp – a selection that did so much to alienate the largest portion of this polyglot and still-fractured nation – did not live up to his pre-match billing and one wonders why Sarfu risked the national ire to include him in the first place.'[33]

Further controversy was created when Pienaar was dropped. It came after a poor campaign had seen the Springboks win just one out of four matches in the Tri-Nations tournament and thereafter become the first side to lose to New Zealand in a home series. They defeated the All Blacks once in five matches, beating them 32–22 at Ellis Park.

A tour to Argentina, France and Wales in the latter part of the year did provide an opportunity to regain some confidence. All five Tests were won – two each against Argentina and France and one against Wales. In addition, a South African 'A' side confirmed the country's depth in the course of a six-week tour of the British Isles. After losing to Scotland 'A' and Ireland 'A' in early November, they concluded their visit with convincing victories over England 'A' and Wales 'A' in their last two matches in December.

As the Springboks reasserted themselves in international rugby, so Louis Luyt attracted unfavourable press coverage. In October 1996, Brian van Rooyen, representing the 'coloured' club Eldoronians, objected to the fact that he was not privy to the finances of the Golden Lions (formerly Transvaal) Rugby Union. He also complained that not enough was done to promote the development of rugby among 'non-whites'. Van Rooyen opposed Luyt's re-election as president but was defeated by an overwhelming margin. Luyt then turned on him, informing Van Rooyen he was 'too stupid' to ask intelligent questions about the union's financial affairs.[34]

Van Rooyen reacted by supplying sports minister Steve Tshwete with a document that warranted a government inquiry into rugby. It would take a while to set the process in motion, not least because Luyt was initially denied access to Van Rooyen's dossier. On eventually receiving a copy, Luyt realised that the government was keen to get rid of him. In one letter to Van Rooyen, Cabinet minister Kader Asmal had written: 'Luyt is rooted in an era in which it was expected of people like him to do execrable things for the established order ... He is having a grievously divisive effect on our public life.'[35]

In February 1997 it was announced that Markgraaff had been caught uttering shocking and insulting remarks about black South Africans. André Bester, who harboured a grievance against Markgraaff, had spoken to him about the state of South African rugby. The Springbok coach did not realise a hidden tape recorder was running as he repeatedly used the word 'kaffir'. In directing his derogatory language towards a number of public figures including Pienaar, he described Mluleki George as a 'f------ kaffir'. The tape was subsequently leaked to the media, became headline news and Markgraaff resigned.[36]

Carel du Plessis, an outstanding wing from the 1980s, was chosen to replace Markgraaff. His main challenge in 1997 was the tour by Martin Johnson's British Lions. The Springboks were strongly favoured to win the series but lost the first two of three Tests. They also lost their first three matches in the Tri-Nations series and pressure mounted for Du Plessis to be removed as coach. Ironically, in his eighth and last Test in control, the Springboks scored a record 61–22 win over the Wallabies at Loftus Versfeld.

In the meantime, the government planned their inquiry into rugby. On 6 August, the director-general of sport, Mthobi Tyamzashe, issued a press release, stating Mandela had told Tshwete that 'a commission is yours if, in your best judgement, it is opportune'. On 22 September, Mandela announced a commission of inquiry under the chairmanship of Acting Judge Jules Browde, and the following month SARFU filed their opposition to the commission. On 4 November, the union firmly backed Luyt's re-election in a secret ballot: thirty-three votes against the fourteen equally shared by Keith Parkinson and Mluleki George.

The atmosphere was tense both off and on the field when Nick Mallett – the third coach in nine months – succeeded du Plessis. His first assignment – a demanding European tour at the end of 1997 – did not receive the support that one might expect from a sports minister. Tshwete commented:

> When we won the Rugby World Cup in 1995, never once in the history of our country, never for a single moment before, were the people so solidly united. Never! That was a remarkable, remarkable moment ... When the Springboks arrive in Edinburgh in November, I can tell you there is going to be jubilation at home every time they lose, make no mistake about that. We have lost the moment. It is sad.[37]

The Springboks were in magnificent form on tour, scoring 247 points and emerging unbeaten in five Tests. They defeated Italy 62–31; France 36–32 and 52–10; England 29–11, and Scotland 68–10. Mallett's impact was enormous. 'Watching this team play with such passion and power,' observes captain Gary Teichmann, 'I found it impossible to understand how essentially the same group of players had seemed so abject and abysmal losing to the Lions earlier in the year.' Being hailed as heroes by Parisians, adds Teichmann 'was a bizarre, incredible experience ... Twickenham was quiet and the chariot stopped swinging ... and [at Murrayfield] the result of our cold efficiency was a one-sided match in which the Scots collapsed after half-time.'[38]

Success continued well into 1998, with the Springboks defeating Ireland twice, England and Wales in warm-up internationals for the Tri-Nations. The Springboks scored 184 points and conceded a mere 26 in four internationals. Fifteen tries were scored in thrashing Wales 96–13 at Loftus Versfeld.

Mallett's men began the Tri-nations by narrowly defeating the Wallabies 14–13 at Perth. The All Blacks were then beaten 13–3 in Wellington in the fiftieth Test between rugby's greatest rivals. The Springbok defence – with Pieter Müller claiming more than twenty tackles – was remarkable. In the return game in Durban, the South Africans trailed 5–23 with twenty minutes to go. They then 'unleashed some of the best rugby they had ever produced to score tries through Joost van der Westhuizen, Bob Skinstad and James Dalton to snatch a wonderful 24–23 victory'.[39]

A week later at Ellis Park, the Springboks defeated Australia 29–15 to clinch the Tri-Nations trophy. Skinstad's try was highlighted by an extravagant swallow dive: 'It put the smile on the face of an often dour, brutal sport [and] summed up the buoyant mood in the country.'[40] The Springboks had triumphed, winning all four of their matches, and had taken their winning streak to fourteen matches. At that stage, they were three short of the All Black' record of seventeen, achieved from 1965 to 1969.

Mallett described his Tri-Nations victors as the greatest Springbok team of all time:

> In the past, I've downplayed it, but I can say it now: on the 22nd of August 1998, South Africa are the best team in the world ... This is just a fantastic achievement. We've beaten France away twice, we've beaten England home and away, Australia and New Zealand home and away. I challenge anyone to go back in the history of South African rugby ever to find results like that in a one-year period.[41]

Off the field, Louis Luyt's legal wrangle with the government was played out in court. Mandela confirmed he was not going to back down. The president's office issued a statement saying that 'the cloud hanging over South African rugby needs to be lifted and the president is confident that the inquiry presents an opportunity to do so, and to dispel any impression that ... it is retreating into a laager of racial chauvinism'.[42]

SARFU contested the validity of the inquiry into its private affairs, alleging that Mandela had acted unconstitutionally by simply 'rubber-stamping' Tshwete's wish to implement the investigation. A key piece of evidence was Tyamzashe's press release of 6 August. Mandela denied making the remarks attributed to him, and Tshwete was forced to concede that they were inaccurate and had not been corrected. Tyamzashe was asked to explain the press statement he had made but was unable to do so, claiming he could not find a copy. After a member of the press produced one, Tyamzashe said that he had wanted to give rugby a fright by threatening them with the possibility of a commission of inquiry ... tactics to make SARFU comply with the government's demands. He admitted he had not been truthful under oath but that his statements had been an 'honest lie'.[43]

When Mandela was called upon to make an appearance, he informed the court that he alone had made the decision to establish a commission. He believed that a sport which had played such a huge role in nation-building could not be seen as a private matter and 'the SA Rugby Football Union could not be left to regulate itself when internal democracy seemed lacking'. Mandela let it be known that he had risked his political future after his release by promoting 'the game of the enemy', but the situation had changed.

Mandela asked whether Luyt was resisting transparency as he gave 'the message he is hiding something ... The feeling is that Louis is a pitiless dictator. No one can stand up to him.'[44]

Luyt won the court battle when Judge William de Villiers set aside Mandela's appointment of a judicial commission into rugby. The Browde commission of inquiry into rugby never resumed. The government appealed to the Constitutional Court but by the time it had ruled in their favour, Luyt had been forced to resign. Blacks and whites were angry that Mandela was forced to testify. When Luyt was replaced by Silas Nkanunu, rugby's governing body sent a delegation to apologise to Mandela.

There had been problems in building on the momentum of the World Cup victory, but Professor Albert Grundlingh pointed out 'it does not necessarily follow that rugby returned to its former Afrikaner and apartheid enclave ... even if rugby wanted to return to the past, it would have been difficult to find a home at all.'[45]

'Public ownership' of rugby had been 'symbolically democratised and extended' by Mandela's involvement with the Springbok team. The game, said Grundlingh, was no longer 'a predominantly Afrikaner preserve ... [their] claims of possession were compromised with Mandela's anointment of the game; the metaphorical message was that the game belonged to the new South Africa and the old order had passed.'[46]

Moreover, in a changing world, rugby was moving rapidly towards the globalised sport of the twenty-first century ... 'ownership had now to a greater extent than before shifted to large television corporations and sponsors'.[47]

Some years later, the Springbok team gathered at Le Meurice Hotel, Paris. They were there to celebrate a special award made by the IRB to the former South African president. The inscription read: 'Presented by the IRB to Mr Nelson Mandela who, during Rugby World Cup 1995, united his nation under the banner of rugby – Paris, September 6, 2007'.

Notes

1   J. Carlin, *Playing the Enemy: Nelson Mandela and the Game that Made a Nation* (London: Atlantic Books, 2008), 113.

2   *The Star*, 17 August 1992.

3   J. Winch and M. Patel, interview with M. George, in 'Playing the Game: The Unification of South African Sport' (unpublished M-Net project, 2000).

4   S. Zavos, *Winters of Revenge: The Bitter Rivalry between the All Blacks and the Springboks* (Auckland: Viking, 1997), 229.
5   A. Grundlingh, *Potent Pastimes: Sport and Leisure Practices in Modern Afrikaner History* (Pretoria: Protea Book House, 2013), 143.
6   L. Luyt, *Walking Proud: The Louis Luyt Autobiography* (Cape Town: Don Nelson, 2003), 242; Carlin, *Playing the Enemy*, 185; Grundlingh, *Potent Pastimes*, 145.
7   *The Star*, 26 May 1995.
8   Ibid.
9   Ibid., 26 June 1995.
10   M. Keohane, *Chester: A Biography of Courage* (Cape Town: Don Nelson, 2002), 30.
11   Carlin, *Playing the Enemy*, 205–206.
12   Luyt, *Walking Proud*, 257.
13   D. Retief, *The Springboks and the Holy Grail: Behind the Scenes at the Rugby World Cup 1995–2007* (Cape Town: Zebra Press, 2011), 65.
14   Zavos, *Winters of Revenge*, 229.
15   Ibid., 230.
16   F. Pienaar, *Rainbow Warrior* (London: Harper/Collins: 1999), 170.
17   *World Rugby*, 15 July 2015.
18   Pienaar, *Rainbow Warrior*, 182.
19   *The Star*, 26 June 1995.
20   *Sunday Times*, 25 June 1995.
21   E. Griffiths, *The Captains* (Johannesburg: Jonathan Ball, 2001), 447.
22   Quoted in Grundlingh, *Potent Pastimes*, 145.
23   Pienaar, *Rainbow Warrior*, 188.
24   Griffiths, *The Captains*, 446.
25   Pienaar, *Rainbow Warrior*, 188–189, 205, 207–208.
26   Retief, *The Springboks and the Holy Grail*, 91.
27   Pienaar, *Rainbow Warrior*, 204.
28   Luyt, *Walking Proud*, 278.
29   Pienaar, *Rainbow Warrior*, 209.
30   Luyt, *Walking Proud*, 280.
31   R. Steen, *Floodlights and Touchlines: A History of Spectator Sport* (London: Bloomsbury, 2014), 226.
32   Pienaar, *Rainbow Warrior*, 213.
33   *Mail & Guardian*, 23 August 1996.
34   *The Citizen* quoted in Luyt, *Walking Proud*, 286.
35   Luyt, *Walking Proud*, 288, 291.
36   K. Ritchie in *Saturday Star*, 30 November 2013.
37   *Mail & Guardian*, 31 October 1997.
38   G. Teichmann, *For the Record* (Johannesburg: Jonathan Ball, 2000), 171, 173–174.
39   Retief, *The Springboks and the Holy Grail*, 96.
40   I. McIntosh with J. Bishop, *Mac: The Face of Rugby* (Cape Town: Don Nelson, 2000), 212–213.
41   G. Growden in *The Guardian*, 24 August 1998.
42   N. Mandela and M. Langa, *Dare Not Linger: The Presidential Years* (London: Macmillan, 2017), 1812.
43   Keohane, *Chester: A Biography of Courage* 112; Luyt, *Walking Proud*, 298–299; *Sunday Times*, 6 August 1998.
44   M. Braid in *The Independent*, 20 March 1998.
45   Grundlingh, *Potent Pastimes*, 153.
46   Ibid., 144–145.
47   Ibid., 154.

23

Balancing Transformation with a Winning Team

I've believed for a long time that we're going to win the World
Cup. There is a sense of destiny about this team because
no other side in world rugby plays with this pressure.[1]

– Jake White

The departure of Louis Luyt in 1998 brought important changes for rugby. The
South African sports ministry and the SA Rugby Football Union (SARFU) became
increasingly active in the implementation of a policy of racially integrating rugby.
They aimed to push transformation that essentially focused on the creation of
opportunities for black players to become Springboks.

According to academics Christopher Merrett, Colin Tatz and Daryl Adair, the
adoption of race quotas coincided with 'a marked shift in the fundamentals of
South African politics: the end of Nelson Mandela's era of non-racialism and the
introduction of Thabo Mbeki's race populism. Emphasis was placed upon black
African hegemony over a diverse nation.'[2]

One journalist pointed out that 'the notion that race might actually be a
consideration in team selection is not a new one – it is as old as Springbok teams.
Once upon a time, the quota was 100% white – never 100% of the best rugby
players in the country.'[3]

Silas Nkanunu, the first black African president of SARFU, promoted 'merit
with bias', a concept designed to fast-track black players in those instances where
they were only marginally less talented than their white counterparts.[4] While
implementing affirmative action, government officials and the union would also
see it as their right to influence team selection.

There was resistance from white and black coaches and players. The white
trade union Mineworkers' Union (MWU)-Solidarity publication stated that

players were being selected 'based on their skin colour to play at a level for which they were not ready'.[5] In turn, black players objected to being tainted with the 'quota' stigma – no one wanted his selection to be based on a demographic formula. Chester Williams admitted: 'I absolutely hate the term "quota player" ... It implied that black was inferior to white.'[6]

As the African National Congress (ANC) strove to transform the racial composition of the teams and the existing white culture of rugby, Merrett, Tatz and Adair question the development from a non-racial perspective:

> In the South African case, the strongest argument against quotas is that they are not about redress and transformation, but rather about reinforcing the political dominance of a national government dominated by a black elite. This has meant nationalist politicians looking for quick-fix glory on the international sports field are opportunistic ideologues: they want largely black teams to represent the country and win trophies that reflect the ascendancy of black athletes representing a 'new' South Africa.[7]

Credible cases were put for and against quotas. The system was initially introduced in the selection of age-group teams, often with positive results. Some progress was made in breaking down barriers, facilitating a realistic shift in the racial make-up of rugby. But to be successful, greater investment was necessary in community and school facilities, particularly in the construction of playing fields. It was argued that the government's 'inordinate fascination with the politics of race and representation at the elite level [resulted in] insufficient attention to programmes and resources needed to improve sports participation at grassroots level'.[8]

The Springbok coach Nick Mallett saw 'a lack of logic in the clamour for racial representation in top-level teams'. Rugby required big, fast and strong players, which resulted in the well-built Afrikaner with 'a freakish genetic make-up' tending to dominate ahead of both white English speakers and black players. He told rugby-writer Gavin Rich that players such as Pierre Spies, Juan Smith, Schalk Burger, François Steyn and Jean de Villiers had the attributes and genetics required to be Springboks. That they should be chosen ahead of black players was not racist, just as it was not racist that players with Pacific island backgrounds were more prominent in New Zealand backlines.[9]

When Mallett first asked SARFU whether he had 'to choose a quota of non-whites in the national team', he was informed that the requirement was only for teams lower down. He recalled selecting his strongest side at a time when its only player of colour, Breyton Paulse, was injured. On forwarding the team names to the union, it was accepted he had the right to choose the side, but they 'disowned it ... it was Nick Mallett's team, not theirs'.[10]

Mallett, who coached one of South Africa's greatest sides – the 1997/98 Springboks – was against 'transformation at the cost of quality'. He thought it would be counter-productive 'to weaken the national side for short-term political breathing space ... The best advert for rugby was a winning Springbok team'.[11] Before the 1998 tour to England, he questioned SARFU on the racial composition of the team. Their answer revealed a new target: 'They said I had some coloureds in the team, but they wanted an African.'[12]

Owen Nkumane was a promising choice. He had attended St John's College, Johannesburg, from where his rugby coach, Steve McFarland, encouraged him to join the Wits University club in 1995. Nkumane played for the Wits under-21 team for two years, and in 1997 progressed to the open ranks, captaining the side early in the season. By 1998, he was playing for the Golden Lions in the Vodacom Cup. He recalled:

> The first time it hit me that I could be a Springbok was when I was picked for the South Africa Under-21 side ... I can't say that it was an overriding dream of mine ... Then when I became a Bok it was the reaction of an aunt of mine that really drove home what an achievement it was. She said to me, 'You've just done what every young white Afrikaner boy dreams of. You've done something people said would never happen in this country.'[13]

Nkumane's aunt recognised the immensity of the breakthrough. An overseas newspaper added, 'Those who wish to see the development of the game could have no greater champion than a fully-fledged Springbok who hails from Soweto.'[14] The significance of Nkumane's selection was important even if his international career was short-lived. He played mid-week matches in the course of a tour that saw the Springboks ultimately achieve seventeen successive Test victories to equal the existing world record. Mallett's side was highly successful, although they lost the chance to establish a new record and secure the 'grand slam' when they went down 7–13 to England in the final tour match.

Despite Mallett's efforts, tension surrounded transformation in 1999 and could be partly blamed for a sudden and dramatic change in the mood and fortunes of the Springboks. Particularly unfortunate was a misguided report prior to a match against Wales in June to mark the official opening of the Millennium Stadium. An interview with Mallett resulted in a Cape newspaper projecting the view that he had requested ANC politicians to refrain from interfering.[15]

CEO Rian Oberholzer intervened. He told the players in Cardiff 'that if they were not prepared to accept the realities of the new South Africa and of transformation then they might as well go and seek employment elsewhere'.[16] Players and management were alarmed, prompting Dan Retief to comment on their naivety as they 'seemed to think that they could remain sublimely isolated from the problems of a country that for years had gone under the yoke of a repressive racist system'.[17]

Nkanunu informed Mallett that he had to take four black players to the 1999 Rugby World Cup. The long-term future of Springbok rugby was crucial and young players of colour had to be convinced that opportunities existed. Nkanunu's request seemed reasonable, particularly as World Cup squads were enlarged from 26 to 30 players. Mallett named Paulse and Deon Kayser who had already played for South Africa, alongside new caps: Kaya Malotana, who was the second black African player to be honoured, and Wayne Julies.

The colour issue was overshadowed by Mallett's decision not to take Gary Teichmann as his captain. The coach gambled on Bob Skinstad in the hope that the young star would add another dimension to the team. His decision misfired as it became clear that Skinstad had not fully recovered from injury. A further blow occurred when fly-half Henry Honiball suffered a hamstring problem early on in the World Cup campaign. Much of the Springboks' game plan had been built around him.

Jannie de Beer was thrust into the pivotal role for the quarter-final against the fancied English. The Springboks led narrowly 16–12 at the interval but De Beer and Brendan Venter had studied the way their opponents defended.[18] Three drop goals in eleven minutes after the break demoralised England. De Beer dropped a record five in 31 minutes in the second half – no one in the history of the game had managed more than three in a Test match. He also kicked five penalties and two conversions to set a record of 34 points in a Test. The Springboks won comfortably 44–21.

A week later, the South Africans were unlucky to lose to Australia in the semi-final, going down 27–21 in the second half of extra time. They went on to finish third, defeating the All Blacks 22–18 in the battle for the bronze medal. Breyton Paulse produced a piece of individual brilliance to score the only try of the match, while Montgomery kicked two drop-goals in a consolation victory.

Springbok loose-forward Corné Krige thought Mallett was beginning to feel the pressures of the Springbok coaching job. 'The more the pressure, the more he demanded results from his players, and that put additional pressure on them. In the end, something had to give.'[19] Mallett spent his last season developing a more expansive game. The Springboks scored six tries in beating the All Blacks 46–40 in a breathtaking encounter at Ellis Park. A little more than a week later, Mallett departed. Amongst other achievements, he had beaten the All Blacks more times than he had lost to them.

Harry Viljoen, a skilled scrum-half in his day, was appointed to take over from Mallett as Springbok coach. He was told to select eight players of colour in his 40-man squad for the end-of-year tour of Argentina and Britain. Rugby appeared to be progressing in its desire to become truly representative of the demographics of the rugby-playing population. The process, however, was sometimes complex and required sympathetic understanding. Thando Manana, the third black African Springbok and a rugged loose-forward created headline news when he refused to participate in the team initiation, the 'kontiki'. As a Xhosa who had been initiated into manhood, he was critical of those who organised the initiation ritual. He claimed 'all they wanted was for us to conform to their norms. We were a multicultural team and we wanted to promote multicultural values ... I was happy to have stood my ground throughout the entire ordeal.'[20]

During the tour, the Springboks defeated Argentina, Ireland and Wales but lost to England. It was a promising start for Viljoen but he had a short stay as coach. He had decided to model aspects of his team's play on the game the Wallabies had developed – not a popular innovation as South Africans baulked at being drawn into unfamiliar territory. Viljoen brought in three Australian coaches – Tim Lane, Les Kiss and Mick Byrne – but he then resigned in January 2002. He blamed the unrelenting pressure of the media for his departure.

Rudolf Straeuli, who succeeded Viljoen, preferred to play to South Africa's traditional strengths. He was unfortunate in the 2002 Tri-Nations campaign as the Springboks were narrowly beaten in some hard-fought clashes. An all-important match was the Test against the All Blacks in Durban. New Zealand scrum-half Justin Marshall commented: 'The crowd were pretty wound up. Every time [David] McHugh blew his whistle there was a massive reaction. It was really intense. We were getting the rub of the green.'[21]

Eventually, it was too much for pot-bellied fan Piet van Zyl who charged onto the field and tackled McHugh as he re-set a scrum. All Blacks' lock Chris Jack told *Radio Sport*: 'We saw "AJ" Venter and Richie McCaw on top of someone ... we tried to pull the poor referee out and I think we may have dislocated his shoulder ... we got a new referee.' After being locked on 23–23, the All Blacks scored a late try to win 30–23.[22]

The South Africans finished last in the Tri-Nations and then endured a dreadful overseas tour. Defeats were suffered at the hands of France 10–30, Scotland 6–21 and England 3–53. It was arguably the lowest point in South Africa's rugby history. Krige was recovering from a dislocated thumb and did not want to take part but Straeuli needed him to captain a side blighted by withdrawals. The worst day on tour was the match against England. After 23 minutes, referee Paddy O'Brien gave Jannes Labuschagne a red card for a late tackle on Jonny Wilkinson. Krige thought it unfair: 'From then on, we were on the back foot ... I knew that we were going to lose, but I made up my mind to take a few people down with me.' He later apologised and regretted going on the tour.[23]

Straeuli's reign was rocked by one crisis after another, not least being the pre-World Cup training camp that began at the University of Pretoria. Lock forward Geo Cronjé – 'a folk hero among conservative Afrikaners because of his unreconstructed Boer image' – did not wish to share a room with a coloured player, Quinton Davids.[24] Straeuli had purposely put them in the same room and he ordered Cronjé to return, which he did.

The story was leaked to the press and became worldwide news. Oberholzer ordered an investigation into whether Cronjé had breached the code of conduct. It subsequently found no conclusive evidence of racism. Mark Keohane resigned his position as the team's media officer and produced a critical report which reignited the furore. Oberholzer announced an inquiry under Judge Edwin King, which was then postponed because of World Cup preparations.[25]

Both Cronjé and Davids were left out of the Springboks' World Cup squad. Krige, the tour captain, thought the judgement was 'flawed ... in Quinton's case, the decision to exclude him from the World Cup was totally unacceptable. After all, what had he done wrong? Absolutely nothing ... his situation was handled very badly.'[26]

Worse followed as Straeuli sought to boost the sagging morale of his side. He and Oberholzer arranged a military-style pre-tournament boot camp. Its aim was based on the theory of breaking down players mentally and physically in order to rebuild them into a strong, close-knit unit. Kamp Staaldraad – or 'Camp Barbed Wire' – was given the go-ahead by Rian Oberholzer who appointed Adriaan Heijns, a former police task force commander, to run the camp.

The players were told that Heijns and two of his men would have total control of them for three days. Players were forced naked into a freezing lake to pump up water-sodden rugby balls. Krige recalls that when they rejected the torture and climbed out, shots were fired on either side of them.[27] There were also endless physically gruelling exercises, alternating with sessions during which they ripped heads off chickens and hammered one another in boxing bouts. The Springbok management looked on, ostensibly gathering intelligence on how their players reacted in such situations.

One of the players, John Smit, summed up the Kamp Staaldraad experience by stating: 'None of it helped me or South Africa in the 2003 World Cup.'[28] Krige, as captain, regretted that he hadn't stopped 'the verbal, mental and physical abuse'.

Above all, he added, 'Kamp Staaldraad allowed certain people's bizarre ideas to hold sway over common sense and the sanctity of others' human rights.'[29]

The troubled build-up to the World Cup undoubtedly had an impact on South Africa's disappointing performance. The Springboks lost to England in their pool encounter and were then knocked out of the tournament, comprehensively beaten 29–9 by the All Blacks in the quarter-final at the Telstra Dome, Melbourne. To add to their misery, the first pictures of Kamp Staaldraad – featuring naked, disillusioned Springboks – appeared in the international press on the day of the World Cup final.[30]

The repercussions were enormous. Oberholzer and Straeuli lost their jobs. Twenty-four hours later, Nkanunu announced he would not be standing for re-election. He stated: 'I have to regretfully submit that we have failed at least with the Springboks.'[31]

South African rugby had gone backwards – they were ranked a lowly sixth in the world. Part of the problem was the inconsistency created through ten 'head coach' appointments in twelve years.

Jake White was well placed to take over from Straeuli in 2004 but was not on the original shortlist. His name was added when André Markgraaff and Heyneke Meyer pulled out. The newly appointed president Brian van Rooyen wanted Chester Williams as coach, but White was so far ahead in the tests and presentation that he became the obvious choice.[32]

White had served as a Springbok coach under Mallett and Viljoen but had also spent many years coaching age groups up to under-21 level. In 1999, he was assistant coach to Eric Sauls when John Smit led South Africa to victory in the SANZAR/UAR tournament in Buenos Aires. This was the forerunner to the under-21 World Championships which White's team won in 2002.

As Springbok coach, White's first move was to install John Smit as captain. The partnership began with two victories over Ireland. The next Test at Loftus Versveld was the first attended by Nelson Mandela since the World Cup final of 1995. On a day when Wales were thrashed 53–18, White offered encouragement in the sensitive area of transformation. He had six players of colour in his side – Breyton Paulse, Wayne Julies, Bolla Conradie, Hanyani Shimange, Quinton Davids and Eddie Andrews – the greatest number yet to play in a Test. Three – Paulse, Julies and Conradie – scored tries.

White's first real test was against the All Blacks in the 2004 Tri-Nations at Christchurch. The Springboks were probably the better team on the night. They led 21–12 at half-time after scoring three tries but lost 23–21 when Doug Howlett scored the hosts' only try in the dying seconds of the match. Another tense encounter followed at Perth. The Springboks lost 30–26, with former South

African Under-21 captain, Clyde Rathbone recording the match-winning try. It was disappointing but the narrow losses brought crucial bonus points.

The first of the return matches was at Ellis Park. It was the tenth anniversary of Freedom Day, the day apartheid was abolished, and commemorative drums were placed on every seat. After the teams took the field, Nelson Mandela wandered out to shake each player's hand. Bob Howitt remembered, 'The All Blacks had already received a preliminary warning of the emotions rampant in Johannesburg that day because as their bus approached Ellis Park, Bok supporters pounded on the side of it, chanting "Bokke, Bokke!"'

When Mandela offered a word to each Springbok, the All Blacks' coach Graham Henry turned to his assistants in the stands and quipped: '"We're in for a hell of a game, boys!" And a hell of a game unfolded.'[33] The Springboks were behind 26–25 with fifteen minutes remaining. But they struck twice to beat the All Blacks 40–26. A hat-trick by Marius Joubert was the first against New Zealand since Ray Mordt achieved the distinction in 1981. It set up an exciting Tri-Nations finale in Durban against the Wallabies.

In the match that decided the competition, the Springboks trailed 3–7 at half-time, but second-half tries by Victor Matfield and Joe van Niekerk gave them a 17–7 lead. Although the Aussies responded with two late tries, the Springboks held on to win 23–19. John Smit remembered leaving the stadium with '"We Are the Champions" blaring – it was the sweetest feeling ever. Only Os du Randt and Percy Montgomery had experienced this kind of success with the Boks before.'[34] The Springboks had played some magnificent rugby during the season. The try-scoring stats revealed they had recorded thirteen, the Wallabies nine and the All Blacks four.

At the end of the year, the Springboks embarked on another overseas tour. They began with a 38–36 win against Wales in Cardiff after leading 38–22 with ten minutes remaining. A controversial 17–12 defeat to Ireland derailed their 'grand slam' challenge. During the match, referee Paul Honiss told Smit that the Springboks were overstepping the mark. He told the Springbok captain to talk to his team because the next time he would issue a card. As the players gathered around, the Irish took a quick penalty and scored. 'I lost it. I've never felt such anger,' seethed Smit, 'we were following his instructions to take time out to talk about our infringing.'[35]

Honiss's actions were reminiscent of those of the famous Rowland Hill. During the 1888/89 New Zealand Natives' tour, England's Andrew Stoddart lost his knickers in a tackle. The tourists encircled the player to preserve his modesty but another Englishman took advantage of the situation to race away unopposed.

Hill who was the referee – and also England's leading rugby administrator – awarded the try.[36]

In further matches, the Springboks lost 32–16 to England at Twickenham, overwhelmed Scotland 45–10 at Murrayfield, and on the way home beat Argentina 39–7 in Buenos Aires. Overall, they did not quite achieve the heights expected on tour, but the team's resurgence was recognised as they won the three major International Rugby Football Board (IRB) awards at that year's annual ceremony. They were named 'Team of the Year'; the brilliant 21-year-old flanker Schalk Burger was 'Player of the Year', and Jake White was 'Coach of the Year' in his first season at full international level.

The remarkable achievement reflected well on South Africa, but the minister of sport, Makhenkesi Stofile, was unmoved. He informed Parliament that the need to win should be made subordinate to the need to transform the racial composition of teams because if a predominantly white sports team wins, South Africa still loses.[37]

Transformation had not, however, been neglected. The most recent touring party had included 11 players of colour in its 34-man squad. One of them was Bryan Habana, a 21-year-old wing who made his Springbok debut as a replacement at Twickenham. Moments after he took the field, the action veered his way as Jaco van der Westhuyzen broke the English line. Habana provided eager support: 'When I got the ball, I knew nothing was going to stop me. It was incredible ... scoring a try with my first touch of the ball in international rugby.' David Walsh recaptured the moment when referring to the reaction of Habana's father:

> Bernie jumped up and acclaimed the score, arousing the curiosity of an Englishman in the next seat.
>
> 'Why when your team has been thrashed,' the man asked, 'does it matter that you get a consolation try?'
>
> 'Because it's my son that scored it,' said Bernie.
>
> 'Well, that's the most wonderful thing,' said the England supporter, 'the most wonderful thing.'[38]

In 2005, White continued to balance transformation commitment with winning rugby. In the second Mandela Plate match against Australia at Ellis Park, he felt sufficiently confident to include six black players in his starting line-up and three on the bench.[39] The Springboks won 33–20.

A week later, the Wallabies were beaten again in the opening match of the Tri-Nations at Loftus Versfeld. Victory by an identical 22–16 score followed over the All Blacks at Newlands. The visitors had thrashed the British and Irish

Lions 3–0 a few weeks earlier but were unable to handle the pressure in a match decided amongst the forwards.

In their away fixtures, the Springboks beat the Wallabies again before playing what was effectively the tournament decider against the All Blacks at Dunedin. The Springboks fought back from 21–10 down in the first half to be ahead 27–24 after a try from Jaque Fourie in the sixty-fifth minute. It all came down to the Springboks losing a defensive line-out on their throw with four minutes remaining. The All Blacks held the ball until Keven Mealamu seized the moment to score the winning try.

Writing in the *Guardian*, Craig Ray described the classic encounter as being far more than a contest for the Tri-Nations title. 'It was,' he remarked, 'about the world's two best teams producing the finest game that year ... It was rugby of the highest calibre, played with unflinching intensity.'[40]

On the 2005 year-end tour, the Springboks beat the Pumas 34–23 and Wales 33–16 but were defeated 26–20 by France. White announced defiantly in the changing-room after the French match: 'The next time you guys are in this Stade de France change room after a match you will have the Webb Ellis Cup in here with you.'[41]

Such optimism must have been considered misplaced in 2006. White's side won just five of their twelve tests. They began by beating Scotland twice but lost Schalk Burger with a neck injury. They were then beaten 36–26 by France at Newlands – their first defeat under White at home. The extended Tri-Nations – each team playing the others three times – began on a disastrous note when the Springboks were beaten 49–0 by the Wallabies at Brisbane. There were three further defeats. At Loftus Versfeld, the 50 000 crowd booed the Springboks off the field after the All Blacks had triumphed 45–26.

The press was relentless in their criticism of the Springboks and there were still two matches to play. White decided to take his side into the Pilanesburg mountains. It was an inspired move as they came back strongly in a fierce battle against the All Blacks at Rustenburg. The match was not decided until the last three minutes when the All Blacks were ahead 20–18. Loose-forward Rodney So'oialo entered the ruck blatantly from the side and referee Chris White raised his arm in the Springboks' favour. André Pretorius converted the crucial kick, securing a 21–20 victory and breathing space for White and his beleaguered team.

Springbok success at Cape Town in 2005 and Rustenburg in 2006 were the only setbacks for the All Blacks during a period of two years: they played 25 games and recorded 23 victories. They were the world's top team by some distance.

After the joy of Rustenburg, the Springboks defeated the Wallabies 24–16 at Ellis Park to end the Tri-Nations on a successful note. It gave White some leverage in persuading SA Rugby to accept a weakened team for the end-of-year tour. He was not only able to rest players carrying injuries but to expand the team's depth through blooding new players. François Steyn, Ruan Pienaar, Wynand Olivier and Pierre Spies were amongst those who would impress overseas.

The team's main focus was a two-Test series against England. The Springboks were leading 21–13 at the end of the third quarter of the first match at Twickenham before losing 23–21. John Smit summed up his team's mood at the time: 'We were never going to lose the following week. The boys now knew they could win at Twickenham and wouldn't let it slip.' He was proved right. In the second encounter, André Pretorius produced a commanding performance in which he contributed twenty points (including four drop-goals) to mastermind victory by a comfortable 25–14 margin. White later conceded that beating England – the reigning world champions – had saved his job.

While the rugby was taking place, an extraordinary development was unfolding on the administrative side. White was called home from London to Cape Town to answer a motion of no-confidence by the amateur arm of the Blue Bulls. 'At that meeting,' reported the *Pretoria News*, 'some of the presidents showed their lack of knowledge of the game – one pulled out the player ratings from *Rapport* as evidence the Springboks were playing badly.' White was in good form and, according to the article, 'dazzled them with coaching talk they didn't understand'.[42]

The Springbok coach returned to England in time to see his side beat a World XV 32–7 at Leicester. Another step down the transformation road was the selection of Chiliboy Ralepelle as the first black Springbok captain.

Smit later saw the importance of 2006 in the context of his side's development. The mental edge was built in 2004 and subsequently sharpened, but it was in 2006 that they were really tested. Their ability to stick together under immense pressure gave him reason to think they had the mental strength to go all the way at the 2007 World Cup. They became a team that relished tough situations that other teams did everything to avoid.[43]

The 2007 season began with two South African sides contesting the final of the Super 14. A superb try by Bryan Habana in the dying seconds of the game brought the Bulls a sensational victory over the Sharks at Durban. South Africa's first success in twelve years was duly celebrated but White complained he was under pressure to find black players for the Springbok side: 'Transformation just wasn't happening in the Super 14 [with] fewer black players than in any previous season.'[44]

This was a problem that Chester Williams had identified. 'You will never need a quota system applied to the Test team,' he surmised, 'if the quota system is effective at provincial level.'[45]

England toured, and Habana scored two of the seven Springbok tries in the 58–10 demolition at Bloemfontein. The margin of defeat, wrote Robert Kitson in the *Guardian*, 'would have been worse had South Africa not emerged after the interval laughing among themselves and failed to score a point for half an hour'. He did wonder when watching Schalk Burger, Juan Smith and Danie Rossouw 'playing human skittles [whether] there has ever been a more explosive Springbok pack'.[46]

In the second Test at Pretoria, South Africa ran in eight tries – two each for Habana and Pierre Spies – to win 55–22. Jonny Wilkinson's world champions led 19–17 at half-time but were outclassed after the interval. Smit was jubilant: 'It was World Cup year, and we were primed for success ... and wanted them to be in a habit of losing to us. We would have smashed whoever they sent ... we knew we would not lose to them in France.'[47]

The last stretch to the world tournament in September was by no means trouble-free. In early April, Butana Komphela, the ANC chairman of the parliamentary committee for sport, threatened to have the Springbok team's passports confiscated if the side chosen for the World Cup was not to his liking.[48]

White then drew political ire when he refused to select flanker Luke Watson who had been the Super 14 'Player of the Year' in 2006 and had continued his good form in the new season. White 'didn't rate him as a player' but there was sympathy for Watson.[49] His case was taken up in an emotive piece by Chris Rattue of the *New Zealand Herald* who stated that Watson would love to wear the Springboks jersey 'in honour of his father ... Cheeky Watson – [South African Gazelles] wing from Port Elizabeth [who] turned his back on a Test jersey to fight for the rights of black and coloured people'.[50]

The Springbok coach stayed silent and kept out of the conflict. He had been troubled in the past by politicians and administrators meddling in the team's selection. Of particular concern was Mike Stofile, vice-president of the newly named SA Rugby Union, operating alongside Watson. 'Right throughout Jake White's reign,' wrote Mike Trapido, 'I watched Stofile and his pals with their ongoing sniping at the Springbok camp because their choices or decisions weren't being carried out.'[51]

Historically, interference was nothing new in South African rugby: in the past, the apartheid government had decided who their opponents could select, but this had been replaced by government officials dictating who their own coach may select. Oregan Hoskins replaced Brian van Rooyen as president of SA Rugby and sought a fair outcome to the Watson crisis. He endeavoured to put a stop to the spat between coach and player by pleading for Watson to be given an opportunity. He added the player's name to the Springbok training squad as its forty-sixth member.

Eventually, a deal was brokered and Watson found himself in the Springbok team to play Samoa. It brought a temporary halt to the bitter debate. Watson was injured during the match, missed the Tri-Nations and was out of contention for the 2007 World Cup.

South Africa beat Australia 22–19 at Newlands in their first 2007 Tri-Nations match – twenty-year-old François Steyn kicking two drop-goals in the last six minutes. Against the All Blacks a week later, the Springboks relinquished a 21–12 lead in the last eleven minutes. White was alarmed that they should run out of steam and claimed key players desperately needed a rest.[52] He fielded an under-strength team for the away legs and was accused of manipulating the situation to his advantage.

In his final preparations for the World Cup, White invited Eddie Jones to join the management team. The Australian 'took existing ideas we had and put a different spin on them ... I could see the guys responding to him very positively.'[53]

At a rousing farewell, the president, Thabo Mbeki, encouraged the Springboks to forget all the controversies 'that we, as politicians, always raise. Don't worry about them – just play rugby!'[54] Six players of colour were included in the Springbok squad chosen by White, Peter Jooste and Ian McIntosh. Two – J.P. Pietersen and Bryan Habana – would play an important role in the knock-out stages and the latter would equal the record for the most tries scored in a World Cup tournament.[55]

Arrangements in France were on a scale far grander than the Springboks had anticipated. It was early evening when their bus drove into Paris from the Charles de Gaulle International Airport. An impressive motorbike cavalcade saw them enter the city like royalty amidst flashing lights and wailing sirens. The timing of their arrival was perfect. Before long, the lights of the Eiffel Tower came on in green and gold.

The Springboks watched Argentina beat France in the opening match on 7 September, a glorious occasion. They met Nelson Mandela at Le Meurice hotel before their first match. They beat Samoa in the opening pool game 59–7, with Bryan Habana scoring four tries, but were unfortunate to lose Jean de Villiers through injury and Schalk Burger, who was suspended for two weeks.

Excitement mounted as they completed their preparations for England. When the bus wended its way towards the stadium, the team's psychologist, Henning Gericke, played the Juluka classic 'Impi' – about the Zulus fighting the

English – and then Bok van Blerk's 'De La Rey' – about the Boers fighting the English – and finally 'Ons vir Jou Suid Afrika'.[56] England stood little chance in a one-sided contest, prompting captain Martin Corry to admit his men were shell-shocked: 'This Springbok team are far from one-dimensional and can strike from anywhere.'[57] Fourie du Preez was 'the principal architect of South Africa's victory ... [he] had been described as "the most intelligent number 9 in the world" by the England coach Brian Ashton, and he duly out-thought his opponents in the way a professor might run intellectual rings round a six-year-old'.[58]

'If I have one regret,' says Smit, 'it's that we didn't go for more tries to get to the 50-point mark ... Still a score-line of 36–0 was pretty good and I have never felt so in control of a game in my life ... It was seamless momentum.'[59]

Tonga proved tougher opposition. The Springboks were fortunate to win 30–25 as the bounce of the ball denied Tonga a try in the last movement of the match. If it had bounced infield Tonga would have scored. In the remaining pool match, the American Eagles were beaten 64–15. The Springboks lost another key player – 'B.J.' Botha – to injury. He was replaced by Jannie du Plessis.

When the tournament entered the quarter-final stage, England surprised Australia 12–10 and France shocked the All Blacks. The French fought back from 0–13 down to win 20–18 at the Millennium Stadium, Cardiff.

Fiji, who had beaten Wales in the pool stage, gave the Springboks a fright in their quarter-final. It was 20–20 after 60 minutes. The Springboks went ahead 23–20, and moments later it took a marvellous tackle by 'J.P.' Pietersen to stop lock Ifereimi Rawaqa from scoring. Smit's emotional words to the team lifted them at a vital stage – 'Remember the look in the eyes of the Aussies and the All Blacks,' he reminded his players. 'I don't want to see that look in your eyes.'[60] The game was slowed down, Juan Smith and Butch James scored tries, and the Springboks won 37–20.

England beat France in one semi-final and South Africa accounted for Argentina 37–13 in the other. The fact that the Pumas then beat the French 34–10 in the bronze-medal match put into perspective how well the Springboks had played a few days earlier.

White was delighted to be facing England in the final on 20 October. 'If we'd been scheduled to play France,' he said, 'we wouldn't have known what to expect. And with a side like New Zealand, we knew we could easily concede two tries in two minutes and find ourselves in a hole. England weren't likely to spring any surprises or run us ragged.'[61]

The French people backed South Africa – nothing could be worse than the English winning their tournament. The South African president, Thabo Mbeki, arrived to greet the players. He knew their minds were on the game but spoke briefly to let them know that the country was totally behind the Springboks. Nelson Mandela sent a DVD with a message, which the players watched in the team room before boarding the bus to the Stade de France.

They had several try-scoring chances during the game but were unable to take advantage of them. Instead, they relied on Percy Montgomery to kick the goals, which he did despite badly injuring his knee in the thirty-third minute. At half-time, the Springboks led 9–3.

Early in the second half, England's Mathew Tait broke at centre. Victor Matfield – the 'Man of the Match' – covered and brought him down two metres from the try-line. The ball was recycled and delivered to left-wing Cueto who dived for the corner. An outstretched Danie Rossouw dramatically affected his momentum, just enough for Cueto's foot to make contact with the touchline before he had grounded the ball. England were awarded a penalty instead which Wilkinson kicked – 9–6.

Soon afterwards, in the forty-eighth minute, Montgomery landed his fourth penalty: 12–6. On the hour, François Steyn attempted a long-range kick. 'He backs himself when most of us would question the sanity of the decision,' wrote Will Greenwood. 'You could see his confidence when he teed up the penalty ... the team knew he would hit it ... all but taking the game out of England's reach.'[62]

South Africa won the tense final 15–6. Each player, says Smit, had understood the gravity of the situation: 'If we lost the final, the negativity of failure would invite the usual political interference ... victory would shut them up.'[63] The team's playmaker Fourie du Preez thought the final had been relatively easy as 'our line-out was completely dominant, our scrum was good, our defence was good, our kicking was good and our discipline was good ... we felt very much in control.'

'But most of all,' stresses Dan Retief, 'it was the unrelenting and deadly tackling.'[64]

Smit received the trophy from the French president, Nicolas Sarkozy, who invited his South African counterpart Thabo Mbeki to the main stage to share in the Springboks' triumph. The president was hoisted onto the shoulders of the players, happy to show off the Webb Ellis Cup.

Twenty-four hours later, the Springboks were crowned 'Team of the Year' at the IRB awards ceremony. 'The team were humble and dignified,' noted Greenwood:

The modesty was evident in the way South Africa approached their games in the tournament. They were a team in which everyone knew their place, how they fitted into that plan and what was required of them ... When Bryan Habana was crowned Player of the Year, and compared to Jonah Lomu, he begged to differ. Lomu was a legend, a one-off; Habana was just a wing with a bit of gas.[65]

To complete their sweep of the major awards, Jake White was named as the 'Coach of the Year', picking up the award for a second time.

Thousands of South Africans gathered at O.R. Tambo Airport to welcome the Springboks home. 'They were a great bunch of guys,' wrote Trapido, 'driven by a shrewd coach and his support staff — the stuff that fairy-tales are made of, and an incredible foundation on which to build the future of South African rugby.'[66]

Notes

1   D. McRae, *Winter Colours: Changing Seasons in World Rugby* (London: Simon & Schuster, 2014), 636.
2   C. Merrett, C. Tatz and D. Adair, 'History and its Racial Legacies: Quotas in South African Rugby and Cricket', in *Sport in Society*, 14, 6 (2011), 766.
3   *Saturday Star*, 30 October 2004.
4   R. van der Valk with A. Colquhoun, *An Adventure in Rugby* (Cape Town: Don Nelson, 2002), 145.
5   M. le Roux, 'Quotas to blame for SA's demise - Old Boks', *IOL*, 25 June 2002.
6   M. Keohane, *Chester: A Biography of Courage* (Cape Town: Don Nelson, 2002), 155.
7   Merrett, Tatz and Adair, 'History and its Racial Legacies', 768.
8   Ibid., 771.
9   G. Rich 'Afrikaners dominate rugby due to genetics', *IOL Sport*, 10 November 2007.
10 *Sunday Times* (London), 12 January 2003.
11 Van der Valk with Colquhoun, *An Adventure in Rugby*, 191.
12 *Sunday Times* (London), 12 January 2003.
13 D. Retief, 'Mandela Saves the Springboks', in D. Cruywagen (ed.), *The Badge: A Centenary of the Springbok Emblem* (Cape Town: SA Rugby, 2006), 216–217.
14 *The Herald* (Scotland), 10 November 1998.
15 D. Retief, *The Springboks and the Holy Grail: Behind the Scenes at the Rugby World Cup 1995–2007* (Cape Town: Zebra Press, 2011), 106.
16 Van der Valk with Colquhoun, *An Adventure in Rugby*, 145.
17 Retief, *The Springboks and the Holy Grail*, 107.
18 F. Moonda, *ESPN*, 14 June 2012.
19 C. Krige with P. Bills, *The Right Place at the Wrong Time: The Autobiography of Corné Krige* (Cape Town: Zebra Press, 2005), 163.
20 S. Mjikeliso, *Being a Black Springbok: The Thando Manana Story* (Johannesburg: Macmillan, 2017), 171–173.
21 T. Johnson and L. McConnell, *Behind the Silver Fern: The Players Speak* (Edinburgh: Polaris Publishing, 2016), 396.
22 *Radio Sport* reported in 'Rugby Pass', 10 August 2018.
23 Krige with Bills, *The Right Place at the Wrong Time*, 96–102.
24 N. Cain, 'End of the Rainbow', *Sunday Times* (London), 7 September 2003.
25 *IOL*, 4 September 2003.
26 Krige with Bills, *The Right Place at the Wrong Time*, 157.
27 Ibid., 111.
28 J. Smit with M. Greenaway, *Captain in the Cauldron* (Cape Town: Highbury Safika Media, 2010), 62.
29 Krige with Bills, *The Right Place at the Wrong Time*, 128–129.
30 Dale McDermott, SA Rugby's video analyst released pictures of the boot camp. He took his own life not long afterwards.
31 ESPN staff, 'Sarfu shake-ups continue', 5 December 2003.

32   Retief, *The Springboks and the Holy Grail*, 166–167.
33   B. Howitt, *Graham Henry: Final Word* (Auckland: HarperCollins, 2012), 147–148.
34   Smit with Greenaway, *Captain in the Cauldron*, 91.
35   Ibid, 92–93.
36   G. Ryan, *Forerunners of the All Blacks: The 1888–89 New Zealand Native Football Team in Britain, Australia and New Zealand* (Christchurch: Canterbury University Press, 1993), 83.
37   House of Assembly Debates, 16 February 2005; A. Grundlingh, *Potent Pastimes: Sport and Leisure Practices in Modern Afrikaner History* (Pretoria: Protea Book House, 2013), 159.
38   D. Walsh, 'The Big Interview: Bryan Habana', *The Sunday Times*, 27 November 2005.
39   The Nelson Mandela Challenge Plate was first contested in 2000, the concept involving matches played between South Africa and Australia.
40   *The Guardian*, 29 August 2005.
41   Smit with Greenaway, *Captain in the Cauldron*, 101.
42   *Pretoria News*, 20 October 2007.
43   *Rugby World* Staff, 1 December 2020.
44   J. White with C. Ray, *In Black and White: The Jake White Story* (Cape Town: Zebra Press, 2007), 260.
45   Keohane, *Chester: A Biography of Courage*, 157.
46   *The Guardian*, 28 May 2007.
47   Smit with Greenaway, *Captain in the Cauldron*, 101.
48   *News 24*, 12 April 2007.
49   White with Ray, *In Black and White*, 273.
50   *New Zealand Herald*, 10 April 2003.
51   *Mail & Guardian*: 'Thought Leader', 5 February 2008.
52   White with Ray, *In Black and White*, 288.
53   Ibid., 293.
54   P. de Villiers, *Mail & Guardian*: 'Thought Leader', 15 August 2008.
55   The 2007 squad comprised: Bakkies Botha, B.J. Botha, Gary Botha, Schalk Burger, Jean de Villiers, Bismarck du Plessis, Fourie du Preez, Os du Randt, Jaque Fourie, Bryan Habana, Butch James, Ricky Januarie, Victor Matfield, Percy Montgomery, Johan Muller, Akona Ndungane, Wynand Olivier, Ruan Pienaar, J.P. Pietersen, André Pretorius, Danie Rossouw, Bob Skinstad, John Smit (captain), Juan Smith, Gurthro Steenkamp, François Steyn, Albert van den Berg, C.J. van der Linde, Wikus van Heerden, Ashwin Willemse. A further player, Pierre Spies, withdrew before the start of the tournament.
56   Smit with Greenaway, *Captain in the Cauldron*, 140–141.
57   R. Kitson, 'England Hammered and Humiliated', *The Guardian*, 15 September 2007.
58   C. Hewett, 'England 0 South Africa 36: Humbled champions have to now beat Samoa to stay in World Cup', *The Independent*, 15 September 2007.
59   Smit with Greenaway, *Captain in the Cauldron*, 140.
60   Retief, *The Springboks and the Holy Grail*, 225; Smit with Greenaway, *Captain in the Cauldron*, 145.
61   White with Ray, *In Black and White*, 322.
62   W. Greenwood, 'Springboks show real style', *Daily Telegraph*, 23 October 2007.
63   Smit with Greenaway, *Captain in the Cauldron*, 151.
64   Retief, *The Springboks and the Holy Grail*, 166–167.
65   Greenwood, *Daily Telegraph*, 23 October 2007; Habana equalled Lomu's record of eight tries in a single World Cup tournament.
66   *Mail & Guardian*: 'Thought Leader', 5 February 2008.

24

'Role Models for the Rainbow Nation'

> They were playing with great character and heart and so when
> they invited us to their changing rooms for a beer after the
> game in Durban, we said too right ... the coaches wanted to
> read what they had on their walls and generally have a wee
> nosey. It soon became apparent to us that the South Africans
> were playing for transformation, they were playing to advance
> the cause of the Rainbow Nation, they were playing for
> something bigger than themselves ... The Boks were putting
> their bodies on the line for something other than the game.[1]

> – Richie McCaw

The All Blacks returned home early after the 2007 World Cup. There were questions over their defeat in the quarter-final against France. Coach Graham Henry blamed the refereeing in Cardiff but he knew, too, that his team had failed to adjust to the situation.[2] 'The game was won and lost in the last 20,' explains captain Richie McCaw, 'and you'd have to say we didn't have the right people in the right places for that critical time ... a couple were sitting in the stand.'[3]

Henry re-applied for the coaching job. He understood what had gone wrong when his team lost and was able to convince the New Zealand Rugby Football Union (RFU) he had a fix for it. 'I had to empower the players,' he maintained, 'I had to give them more responsibility.'[4] His contract was renewed – six votes to one. 'The appointment,' explained the chairman of the board, 'was based on Henry's remarkable results – [an 87 per cent win rate] – over a four-year period.'[5]

The Springboks returned home to a triumphant welcome. Their success in winning the World Cup should have heralded another golden age for Springbok rugby, but radical changes had been planned. Several months before the tournament, the *Saturday Star* had reported a black coach, Peter de Villiers, was in line to be appointed. He was prepared to move quickly towards Africanising the sport. 'There will be pain [in the results],' he advised, 'but it is something we must go through to transform the team.'[6]

Jake White was not part of the plans. 'This [World Cup] victory,' said the minister of sport and recreation, Makhenkesi Stofile, 'should herald a new era – an era in which we all embrace change and tackle the challenges still being faced by our rugby and sport in general.' He reminded South Africans of what had occurred after their previous success. 'Our victory during the 1995 World Cup offered us a window to see what South Africa can be. We did not build on that. May we not commit the same error after this second chance.'[7]

De Villiers was duly appointed as the first-ever non-white coach of the Springboks on 9 January 2008. The president of the SA Rugby Union, Oregan Hoskins, made the announcement, stating: 'I want to be honest with South Africa and say that the appointment did not take into account only rugby reasons. We took the issue of transformation in rugby very, very seriously when we made the appointment.'

Hoskins did not think his comments tarnished De Villiers, adding: 'South Africa has a black coach now – that is fantastic for the game in all parts of the world.'[8]

De Villiers had served as an assistant coach at senior provincial level and briefly for the Springboks under Nick Mallett on their overseas tour in 1997. He also coached the South African Under-21 team that won the 2005 IInternational Rugby Football Board (RB) tournament in Argentina.

He had been short-listed for the role of Springbok coach along with three other candidates, including Heyneke Meyer, who had coached the Blue Bulls team that won the Super 15 in 2007. De Villers was backed by Cheeky Watson, Neil de Beer and Koos Rossouw, who drove his campaign for election. The vote was ultimately 11–10 in De Villiers' favour; so there was significant opposition.

His appointment was also attacked in the press. The former Springbok captain Corné Krige claimed the rugby authorities had appointed him because 'they knew he would dance to their tune. He will choose the players they want him to choose, and he will be politically correct.' Krige predicted 'seven lean years ahead for the Springboks'.[9]

De Villiers might have objected to being labelled an affirmative action appointment, but he accepted the position, nevertheless. He looked for allies in order to establish a sounding board and, ironically, chose politicians. Cheeky Watson, who became the leader of the advisory group, suggested the likes of Butana Komphela and Cedric Frolick, the chairperson and deputy of the parliamentary portfolio committee on sport and recreation.[10] They were men who were keen to have a say in rugby matters.

Others were concerned about De Villiers' position. The television channel, SuperSport, had close ties with SA Rugby and wanted to assist the new Springbok coach in the field of public relations. They set up a meeting with Dan Retief who quickly formed the opinion that De Villiers was 'way out of his depth and has no idea what he is getting into'. Retief did provide some advice: 'Get John Smit back into the Springbok set-up.'[11]

Smit had taken up a contract with Clermont Auvergne just three weeks after the World Cup but agreed to return as Springbok captain. Victor Matfield, who was playing for Toulon, also met with De Villers and was encouraged by what the coach had to say: 'Springbok rugby would not, as many people believed, change for the worse overnight.'[12]

De Villiers' decision to bring back Smit and Matfield – 'the Springbok leaders' – infuriated his advisory group. Watson questioned the coach's actions, allegedly warning him that 'the damn Afrikaners don't support you'. De Villiers did not back down. He asked Watson whether he thought that 'I was just a black man who he could manipulate, and if this was why he had helped me get the job – so that he could treat me like a puppet that he could control from behind the scenes'.[13]

In time, the advisory committee was discarded and the senior players became De Villiers' sole support group. The development encouraged confidence in the system. A relationship resulted in which he shared the players' pride in representing the Springboks and was prepared to learn from them. He admitted that he had no idea that they were as clued up as they were: 'If I was to produce results as a Springbok coach, I was going to have to evolve with the players.'[14]

De Villiers' position might be compared with that of Graham Henry. After resigning his role as Welsh coach in 2002, Henry had worked as an assistant at Auckland Blues where he recognised the need to empower the players. But once in charge of the All Blacks, he realised that 'passing ownership of the team on to the players wasn't something that could happen overnight'. It was an evolving process that had its origins in 2004 but did not start to show real progress until 2008 after Henry's reappointment. It became accepted and most effective in 2010 and 2011.[15]

To an extent, De Villiers stumbled into a similar situation. His captain, Smit, had already established a structure through which players were given on-field leadership roles. 'I've never wanted to lead on my own,' he confesses. The likes of Victor Matfield, Juan Smith, Os du Randt, Fourie du Preez, Jean de Villiers and Percy Montgomery shouldered responsibilities.[16]

There was disagreement over the style they wished to play, a problem that was never satisfactorily settled. De Villiers hoped to move the ball wide – 'I'd wanted a more creative style of rugby [but] soon came to realise that I couldn't have it.'[17] The assistant coaches also had their ideas. Dick Muir believed in playing the situation as it occurred on the field, while Gary Gold wanted a more structured game plan. The players had become accustomed to a direct, conservative approach, one that Matfield described as 'making the right decisions at the right time on the field: you don't take chances in your own half [but] if an opportunity arises to counter-attack, go for it'.[18]

In 2008, the Springboks experienced mixed fortunes. They beat Wales twice and Italy before flying to New Zealand for the start of their Tri-Nations programme. They were disappointing in an opening 19–8 defeat at Wellington, and De Villiers was very quickly the target of criticism. The former All Blacks prop Craig Dowd was particularly unpleasant and called De Villiers a 'puppet'. The incident became international news and the SA Rugby Union demanded an apology.[19]

In their next match, the Springboks inflicted a breathtaking 30–28 defeat on the All Blacks in Dunedin. It was their first-ever Test victory at the Carisbrook ground, known by touring sides as the 'House of Pain'. The *New Zealand Herald* recorded, 'Human dynamo Schalk Burger was at the forefront of another vigorous forward effort, making countless heavy tackles.' He helped the Springboks establish a 17–15 half-time lead, but the All Blacks gained the ascendancy in the second half. Four minutes from the end, the Springboks were trailing 23–28 and down to fourteen men. At that moment, Ricky Januarie 'darted from a ruck 40-metres out, chipped past replacement fullback Leon MacDonald, regathered and swan-dived over. A calm replacement centre François Steyn slotted the conversion.'[20]

There was a seven-week wait before the next Tri-Nations success. During the intervening period, the Springboks suffered three defeats although they hammered Argentina 63–9 in a one-off encounter at Ellis Park. Members of his former support group criticised De Villiers in the press. They were annoyed that he was not following their instructions. Frolick sent a message that he 'would rather have a white coach that would listen to him than a black coach who did his own thing'.[21]

Cheeky Watson arrived in New Zealand. He claimed to have a message from Makhenkezi Stofile, stating that he and other politicians were unhappy that Luke Watson was on the bench and not starting. De Villiers informed the father that he would make his own decisions. He subsequently discovered that Stofile had not spoken to Watson about the issue.[22]

After the 27–15 defeat against the Wallabies in Durban, Matfield and De Villiers were booed during on-field post-match interviews. There were problems in the Springbok camp, partly attributed to the presence of Luke Watson in the team. Smit spoke strongly against players allowing themselves to be disrupted, and they responded at Ellis Park by thrashing the Wallabies 53–8. Wing Jongi Nokwe made history by crossing the line four times, and he received a standing ovation from a 55 000 crowd when he was carried off injured.

In their end-of-year tour, South Africa beat Wales, the Six-Nations champions and then Scotland. The match against England created enormous interest because it was their first meeting since the World Cup. At training, Smit commented on the Springboks 'being written off again, and how England were talking themselves up as usual'. The South Africans were well motivated by the kick-off before a crowd of 81 113, and hammered England 42–6.[23]

'Smashed, absolutely smashed,' wrote Stephen Jones of the England defeat;

> They lost to an outstanding South African team and yet what excuse can there be, even against an opposition of rare quality, when at the end of the game you barely want to contest a scrummage or a loose ball? It was as if the white flag was flying above a stunned Twickenham.

Jones thought South Africa to be massively better than when they beat England in the World Cup: 'a team with an inspiring collective focus and a plan which is equipped for the modern era because it smashes you at the breakdown, and also because it performs the basic functions of rugby to a superb standard'.[24]

In Johannesburg, the *Star's* Rodney Hartman wrote a critical missive for Butana Komphela who was seen as a constant thorn in the side of the Springboks:

> When the curtain came down on the biggest defeat England have suffered on their home ground, there were no fewer than seven black Springboks on the field.
>
> Not that we really notice that kind of thing, because new-age South Africans can't be bothered with putting their heroes into little colour-coded boxes. What we know is that we're all in together ...
>
> As our representative in parliament, we expect him to tell the Springboks how we all feel.[25]

While the article reflected growing frustration with politicians, rugby was thriving in South Africa. The Blue Bulls won the Super 14 title again to provide a perfect start to the 2009 season. They beat Crusaders 36–23 in the semi-final, with Morné Steyn kicking four drop-goals. People lined up after the game to buy tickets for the final. They weren't disappointed as the Bulls accounted for Chiefs 61–17.

The South African Sevens team under coach Paul Treu won the World Series title for the first time in late May. The Blitzbokke finished 30 points ahead of second-place Fiji, after reaching five finals in ten tournaments with victories in Dubai, George, and Adelaide. Renfred Dazel scored 191 points and captain Mzwandile Stick 161, while Rayno Benjamin (28), Robert Ebersohn (22), Vuyo Zangqa (22) and Dazel (22) were the leading try-scorers.

The British and Irish Lions toured from late May to early July. The Tests were ill-tempered affairs. Smit recalls the first Test at Durban when 'suddenly three scrums had gone by, the Lions had been savaged … it will be a long time before you see a Test prop get a hiding like the one Vickery got from Beast'.[26] The Springboks were ahead 26–7 after 50 minutes but then the management made the mistake of too many substitutions. The Lions scored two tries but the Springboks held on to win 26–21.

In the second Test at Pretoria, Schalk Burger was yellow-carded after 30 seconds. It allowed the Lions to make a confident start and they led 16–8 at half-time. Second-half tries by Bryan Habana and Jaque Fourie gave the Springboks the lead 25–22, but Lions' fly-half Stephen Jones kicked a penalty in the 78th minute to bring the scores level. In the dying moments of the game, Ronan O'Gara fielded a deep kick and hoisted the ball downfield. Chasing after it, he collided with Fourie du Preez who had gone up to take possession. A penalty was awarded, more than 50 metres out. It was Loftus Versfeld, and Morné Steyn knew he could kick it. A perfect strike from his own half gave the Springboks an unassailable 2–0 lead in the series.

The Lions and their accompanying media struggled to accept defeat. 'Brilliant. Absolutely brilliant, but beaten,' commented the Lions' coach Ian McGeechan. 'If we could have bottled what we did in Pretoria it would have been a guide to the way rugby should be played.'[27]

The Tri-Nations followed in mid-July. The All Blacks' scrum-half Jimmy Cowans recalled the international game 'had evolved into a lot of kick-chase, and the Boks were very good at it, having half-back Fourie du Preez, a pin-point kicker of the ball, and wings like Bryan Habana who were prepared to chase it like there was no tomorrow'.[28]

The Springboks made an impressive start against the All Blacks. They won the first Test at Bloemfontein 28–19, a game sealed by Jaque Fourie's dramatic try eight minutes from the end. The following week in Durban, they defeated the All Blacks again, with Morné Steyn scoring all of their points in a 31–19 win. His performance set a new individual record for points in a Tri-Nations match and was also the most points scored by an individual in a game against the All Blacks.

The Springboks completed their home matches with Steyn scoring another 24 points in a 29–17 win over the Wallabies in Cape Town.

The competition moved on to Australia where one of two matches was won. The Springboks had then to win at Hamilton to claim the Tri-Nations crown for the first time since 2004. They did so 32–29. The All Blacks were 'harangued at every turn by a fearsome South African pack, and shell-shocked by the field-gun boot of François Steyn'.[29] He put over three mighty kicks from inside his own half – almost certainly an international record – while Morné Steyn set a new Tri-Nations record for a season of 95 points.

'That Springbok team of 2009,' said All Blacks' fly-half Stephen Donald, 'was easily the best rugby team I'd played against. They were so clinical, obviously built around a big pack that was at the peak of its power with Victor Matfield, Bakkies Botha and co. Pierre Spies was in great form and they were well led by John Smit.'[30]

Coach Graham Henry was equally complimentary:

The South African team was truly awesome in 2009, creating huge pressure on opponents at the set pieces ... They devised a smart game plan, one assisted by the existing laws, which they executed with clinical efficiency. It eliminated the All Blacks' strengths and exposed their deficiencies. The Boks took the high ground, mentally and physically, effectively bullying the All Blacks ... They attacked through lineout drives and demonstrated huge physicality at the breakdown.

Graham's impressions of the Springbok play were passed on to the New Zealand RFU in his end-of-season review, which stressed 'there is no substitute for physical dominance – it is the number one pillar in the game'.[31]

The Springboks experienced a disappointing overseas tour – losing to France and Ireland – but were still named the IRB's 'Team of the Year'. Nine South Africans were included in a Barbarians team that beat the All Blacks 25–18.[32] The outstanding wing Bryan Habana scored a hat-trick of tries, and for some of the South Africans, it constituted a fourth victory over the All Blacks in the year.

The defeats suffered became a huge motivating factor, said Richie McCaw, 'it really kept guys on edge'.[33] He admitted his side was searching for solutions to their problems. He believed they found some answers in South Africa in that the Springboks were playing for 'something bigger than themselves'.[34] The All Blacks' management came 'to appreciate that the current Springboks, as a multiracial team, saw it as their destiny to be role models for the Rainbow nation and lead their country by example, both in terms of on-field success and off-field harmony'. Graham Henry thought 'this represented a massive motivation for the team; it was their emotional button'.[35]

A resurgent New Zealand dominated rugby in 2010. Their leadership scheme was taking shape, and they benefited from the introduction of new laws designed to promote attacking rugby. The All Blacks were better prepared than the Springboks, even though the Bulls had won the Super 14 for the third time in four years, defeating Crusaders in the semi-final and then Stormers in an all-South African final.

The Springboks experienced a dismal Tri-Nations, winning just one out of six matches. The All Blacks were unbeaten, with the last match played being the most memorable. A massive crowd of more than 94 000 at the FNB Stadium in Soweto saw the Springboks lead 22–14 midway through the second half. But the game was far from over: a Carter penalty and a try from McCaw resulted in the teams being locked at 22-all. Seconds remained and the Springboks had possession, but the All Blacks believed they could still win. The ball went to Ma'a Nonu who lost his boot while slipping a tackle. A perfectly judged pass set up Israel Dagg for the winning try. Carter converted to seal a spectacular 29–22 victory.

John Smit in his 100th Test missed the tackle on Nonu. 'It's a cruel game,' he remarked as he walked off the field with McCaw. The latter responded 'Yep'; he could say little else, but later wrote that the Springboks had gone from 'champs to chumps in the space of twelve months. The pace of change year on year is disconcerting.'[36]

The Springboks fared better on their overseas tour that year where they beat Ireland 23–21 and Wales 29–25 before experiencing an unexpected 21–17 loss against Scotland. A week earlier, the All Blacks had defeated the Scots 49–3.

'The real challenge,' explains Matfield, who was again captaining the side, 'lay in getting all the coaches and players to agree on the Springboks' style of playing … after three full seasons, we still could not agree on the best game plan for the Boks'. On their arrival in London, Matfield took a lead role, arguing that they shouldn't try to emulate the All Blacks and Australians. He urged them to play 'Springbok rugby'. De Villiers supported him; to beat the English they would play 'direct rugby without frills and flourishes'.[37]

England were beaten 21–11 on a day when Springbok hooker Bismarck du Plessis was outstanding. Paul Rees, writing in *The Guardian*, commented: 'South Africa are hardly the All Blacks. They do not use the rapier to finish off opponents but a hefty cudgel. They battered England from the off and such was their supremacy up front and at the breakdown that they could afford to squander four clear try-scoring opportunities in the first half and still have the game won 10 minutes before the finish.'[38]

The Springboks narrowly failed to win a 'grand slam'. The All Blacks not only achieved it but had moved well ahead of their rivals; their quest for improvement was driven by a fierce determination to win the World Cup.

In 2011, South Africa struggled for much of the condensed Tri-Nations, with a weakened team losing to New Zealand by a record 40–7 margin. Their sole victory was achieved in their last match, a morale-boosting 18–5 win over the All Blacks, minus McCaw and Carter, in Port Elizabeth. Morné Steyn kicked all eighteen points – five penalties and a drop-goal.

Three weeks later the World Cup began in New Zealand. The Springboks were unbeaten in their group, which included wins over Wales 17–6, Fiji 49–3, Namibia 87–0 and Samoa 13–5. They became serious contenders, but their progress was affected by a surprise development. Ireland beat Australia 15–6 which meant the latter played South Africa in the quarter-final.

The Springboks dominated possession and territory against the Wallabies in Wellington. With Matfield a commanding figure in the line-out and a 76 per cent territorial advantage in the match, a South African win seemed inevitable. The Australians stayed in contention through a brave defence, clever spoiling, and flanker David Pocock who was able to read the referee and take control of the breakdown.

The refereeing of Bryce Lawrence was a major talking point in South Africa's controversial 11–9 defeat. Peter de Villiers was distraught: 'We could never have foreseen that the referee would be so influential that he would stop us in our tracks.' He acknowledged the Springboks might have adjusted their game when they realised the way it was being refereed, but he did not seem aware that Lawrence had produced a similar performance in a major game three months earlier.[39] Richie McCaw knew about it and recalled Lawrence had simply replicated at Wellington what he did in Brisbane in the Super 15 final – 'freezes and forgets to blow his whistle'.[40]

The All Blacks won the 2011 World Cup by defeating France 8–7 in an incredibly tense final. It was their first success in the tournament in 24 years. Graham Henry paid tribute to the player leadership group: 'Without its implementation, the All Blacks would not have won ... Players will handle the challenge if it is their challenge.' He knew his team had to be mentally stronger than they had been in 2007 and this time they prepared for 'worst-case scenarios'.[41]

De Villiers's operation appeared to have shortcomings. The blurb to his autobiography notes that his close relationship with his senior players begged the question: 'Who was coaching whom?' Tendai Mtawarira commented:

He was probably lucky that a very good group of players was handed over to him ... There's no doubt that he was happy to be at the forefront of a team that could operate on its own steam. Most of the work was done by the players, with [assistant coaches] Dick Muir and Gary Gold very influential.[42]

Matfield agreed with the view that De Villiers was not 'the best coach around'. He accepted there were coaches with a better technical knowledge of the game, 'but Peter knows how to work with people which is a major asset. He was not afraid to listen to the people's opinions and appreciate their input.'[43] He did not dance to the tune of the rugby authorities. Nor was he politically correct. Like his predecessors, he was dogged by the difficulties of the transformation policy yet fearless in confronting the issues involved. He was more concerned about 'a change of attitude than a change of colour' – a desire to be 'everyone's coach' and not simply favouring a particular race group.[44]

De Villiers had a record of 30 wins out of 48 matches – a 62.55 per cent success rate – during his four-year period in charge. Although the All Blacks had been the dominant power for most of the period, the Springboks had on De Villiers' watch, won five and lost six matches against the new world champions.

In 2012, Heyneke Meyer was named head coach of South Africa on a four-year term. His opening challenge was a three-match series against England. In their first outing, the Springboks out-muscled England 22–17 at Durban.

In the second Test at Ellis Park, the Springboks appeared to be heading for a big score after taking a 22–3 lead midway through the first half. They then 'removed many of their best forwards and were guilty of flagrant glory hunting, butchering two or three further tries'. England surged to within four points of the Springbok score – 31–27 – before J.P. Pietersen's late try enabled his team to win 36–27. 'Had England gone on to win,' wrote Robert Kitson, 'the Springboks' coach, Heyneke Meyer, would have gone potty.'[45]

The third Test was drawn 14–14 at Port Elizabeth to give Meyer a satisfactory start. His next challenge was the revamped southern hemisphere international competition. The new Rugby Championship saw Argentina join the three teams of the former Tri-Nations. The Springboks won two and drew one of their six matches. The All Blacks beat them twice, at Dunedin and Johannesburg.

There was more to celebrate on the end-of-year tour when the Springboks celebrated their first clean sweep since 2008, defeating Ireland 16–12, Scotland 21–10 and England 16–15. They were three hard, grinding victories.

Meyer was better prepared for the 2013 season. He and his assistant coaches travelled widely, visiting franchises and assessing the talent available. A quadrangular tournament followed involving Italy, Samoa and Scotland. The Springboks were rarely extended, defeating Samoa 56–23 in the deciding match.

The impressive progress continued into the Rugby Championship. The Argentinians were overwhelmed 73–13 at Ellis Park. It was the most points ever scored by one team in a match in either the Rugby Championship or Tri-Nations. A further victory was achieved over Argentina 22–17 in Mendoza, and a first-ever win was recorded at Brisbane where the Australians were well beaten 38–12 in a ruthless display. The Springboks' impressive run of success was halted by New Zealand's 29–15 win at Eden Park. It was a controversial Test, with the IRB later apologising that a refereeing error in handing out a red card resulted in South Africa being a player short for a good part of the match.

With two home matches left, the Springboks still stood a chance of winning the Rugby Championship. Fourie du Preez was in outstanding form in inspiring his side to a 28–8 victory over the Wallabies at Newlands. This was followed by an exciting clash against the All Blacks at Ellis Park. Habana scored twice in the opening twenty minutes, then retired with a strained hamstring. The visitors responded with two further tries to lead 21–15 at the break. The Springboks went ahead twice in the second half: Willie le Roux crossed early (22–21) and Jean de Villiers after an hour (27–24). Yet again, the All Blacks produced a classic come-back, scoring two converted tries in the last quarter to win 38–27.

Nigel Owens described the match as the best he had refereed. Wynne Gray commented in the *New Zealand Herald*: 'In 2000 against Australia, the All Blacks' late 39–35 win was billed as the greatest game ever played. The clash of the old firms yesterday was several notches superior.'[46]

South Africa went on to record another clean sweep on their end-of-year tour, their first back-to-back clean sweeps since 1996 and 1997. They defeated Wales 24–15, Scotland 28–0 and France 19–10, but a good year for Meyer was overshadowed by the All Blacks becoming the first team of the professional era to achieve a 100 per cent winning record in a calendar year. Their final passage of play against Ireland – 37 passes in a movement that began 12 metres inside their half – enabled them to draw level 22–22. Aaron Cruden converted after being allowed a second attempt because the Irish had charged too early.

Meyer's upward trajectory continued well into 2014. He claimed a 2–0 Test series victory over Wales, a 55–6 hammering of Scotland, and his first success over the All Blacks, winning 27–25 at Ellis Park. Herman Mostert wrote, 'The Boks matched the All Blacks from a physical, skill and mental perspective ... Duane Vermeulen produced a stellar performance and outshone counterpart,

Kieran Reid.'[47] Handré Pollard scored two tries but it was Pat Lambie's last-gasp penalty from 55 metres that ultimately saw the Springboks emerge on top.

A narrow 24–23 loss to Australia meant South Africa finished second again in the Rugby Championship. There was also disappointment on the 2014 end-of-year tour. South Africa won two matches – Italy 22–6 and England 31–28 – but lost to Ireland 29–15 and Wales 12–6.

Meyer's most difficult year was 2015 when he came under pressure, having lost all three matches in a reduced Rugby Championship, including a first-ever home defeat to Argentina. To add to his woes, he had to contend with off-the-field criticism from the Congress of South African Trade Unions (COSATU). The organisation claimed five black players had approached them with grievances and there was a call for Meyer to be sacked over what COSATU termed 'racist choices'.[48]

There were eight players of colour in Meyer's squad for the 2015 World Cup. He played four in his starting line-up for a warm-up match against Argentina when he achieved his first win in 2015. The 26–12 victory came at Buenos Aires with Habana and Lwazi Mvovo scoring tries.

In their opening World Cup match, the Springboks were sensationally beaten in their first-ever game against Japan, the thirteenth-ranked team in world rugby. The Brave Blossoms secured the 34–32 win through a try in the corner, deep into injury time. Stephen Jones wrote in the *Sunday Times* that Japan had 'brought off the shock of all rugby history'. His colleague Mark Palmer added that 'Japan roared in unison with their army of magnificently excitable supporters, and simply willed South Africa out of the game'.[49]

Despite their opening loss, South Africa outplayed Samoa 46–6, Scotland 34–16 and the United States 64–0, to secure top place in their pool. They beat Wales 23–19 in the quarter-final thanks to Fourie du Preez's well-judged try in the seventy-fifth minute. It set up a semi-final at Twickenham against the reigning champions, New Zealand.

A game of unremitting tension unfolded before an 80 000 crowd. New Zealand dominated possession and territory, but the Springboks were immense in their defensive and aerial work under huge pressure. The lead changed several times with the Springboks ahead 12–7 at half-time. They also had a one-man advantage for nine minutes after the interval due to Jerome Kaino's yellow card but were unable to capitalise.

Dan Carter recalled, 'Even though the score was pretty close, in their favour at times, we still felt like we were controlling the game, it's just that we weren't getting any points.'[50] They eventually came through tries by flanker Kaino and substitute back Beauden Barrett. Carter added a drop-goal, two conversions and a penalty, while his opposite number – 21-year-old Pollard – landed four penalties and his replacement Lambie a fifth eleven minutes from time.

With just two points separating the teams – 20–18 – there was a frenetic final ten minutes to the titanic struggle. Carter was proud of how well his side played through this period, 'how we controlled the territory, controlled the game and were able to close it out'.[51]

The southern hemisphere provided all four semi-finalists as Australia and Argentina also qualified. The Springboks faced Argentina in the bronze contest, winning relatively comfortably 24–13 against an injury-hit team. J.P. Pietersen and Eben Etzebeth scored tries in Victor Matfield's 127th and final match, but Bryan Habana was unable to add to his record tally of fifteen tries, leaving him level with former All Black Jonah Lomu.

The semi-final defeat was Meyer's seventh in eight matches against the All Blacks who went on to achieve their second successive World Cup victory. He resigned from his post in December 2015. Hoskins had hoped he would stay. 'We need to keep building, not breaking down,' he argued. 'We can't start all over again every four years and lose so much of our intellectual property.'[52]

Allister Coetzee was appointed as head coach in April 2016. He had played rugby for Eastern Province in the 1990s, coached the Cape Town-based Stormers for five years from 2010 and was part of Jake White's back-room staff when South Africa won the World Cup in 2007.

His first game in charge was a first-ever home defeat to Ireland. It came despite the visitors being reduced to fourteen men for almost sixty minutes of the game after C.J. Stander was red-carded. However, the series was all level after the second Test, when South Africa came from 19–3 behind at half time to win 32–26. With a third Test victory, 19–13, the Springboks achieved a narrow 2–1 series win.

In Coetzee's first Rugby Championship, South Africa finished behind Australia and New Zealand. They defeated Argentina at Nelspruit but lost at Salta. Away losses followed to Australia, 23–17, and New Zealand, 41–13, before they gained their second win in the Championship against Australia 18–10 in Pretoria. In the final round, New Zealand defeated the Springboks 57–15 in Durban, a record win for the All Blacks on South African soil. The visitors scored nine tries, while South Africa's points came through five penalties from Morné Steyn.

After such a humiliating defeat, the SA Rugby Union organised a debrief between the Springbok coaching staff and the Super Rugby franchise managements. Specialist coaches were recruited ahead of their 2016 end-of-year tour but it made no difference; the Springboks were without a win for the first time since their 2002 tour. They lost to England for the first time in ten years, 37–21; lost to Italy for the first time, 20–18, and suffered a record loss to Wales 27–13. After being defeated in eight out of twelve matches in 2016, the Springboks dropped to an equal-worst world ranking of sixth.

Amidst the gloom, the Blitzbokke under coach Neil Powell produced exhilarating rugby to win the Sevens bronze medal at the Rio de Janeiro Olympic Games and to emerge triumphant in the 2016/17 HSBC World Series. Their overall points tally of 192 was a new record, 28 ahead of England in second place. Fiji (150) finished third and New Zealand (137) were fourth. The South African squad led by Philip Snyman played in eight finals and won five – in Dubai, Wellington, Sydney, Las Vegas and Paris. Seabelo Senatla headed the try-scorers on 32 and Chris Dry and Rosko Specman were chosen for the tournament's seven-man 'dream team'.

The Blitzbokke were further honoured when Senatla was named World Rugby's 'Sevens Player of the Year'. Cecil Afrika in 2011 and Werner Kok in 2015 had been previously honoured.

In the meantime, the SA Rugby Union backed Coetzee and strengthened the management in a bid to orchestrate a more successful season. Brendan Venter, who had been assisting Italy, came in for a short period with responsibility for defence and 'exit' strategies. A three-Test series was played against France. The Springboks convincingly won the first Test at Pretoria 37–14. This was followed by a 37–15 win at Durban to seal the series. The final encounter was staged at Ellis Park, a venue where South Africa had not beaten France in four attempts. However, this time, the Springboks achieved a 35–15 victory to win the series 3–0.

The 2017 Rugby Championship began with back-to-back wins over Argentina. Five Test wins in a row reflected obvious improvement but some commentators were sceptical about the strength of the opposition. The South Africans drew with Australia in Perth but were then overwhelmed by the All Blacks 57–0 in Albany, their most comprehensive defeat in 126 years. They were hopelessly exposed out wide. 'This may be the Springboks' darkest night ever,' wrote Brenden Nel. 'If lessons aren't learnt from it, it could really spell the end of the Springboks as a superpower in world rugby.'[53]

Time was running out for Coetzee. His team drew 27–27 with the Australians in Perth and then produced possibly their best display of the season before narrowly losing 25–24 to the All Blacks in Cape Town. Overseas, there was a record 38–3 defeat to Ireland, and a loss for the second year running to Wales, 24–22. Two victories were achieved against France 18–17 and Italy 35–6.

Since taking over the coaching role in 2016, Coetzee had won 11 out of 25 matches. His win rate was a disappointing 44 per cent. It was unfortunate that so many South Africans were playing overseas and that he could not always select the best possible team. On 1 March 2018, Coetzee was replaced by former Springbok Johan 'Rassie' Erasmus who had initially been appointed Director of Rugby.

The next few months panned out a great deal better than most South African supporters might have hoped. The Blitzbokke, the highly popular Sevens team defended their World Series title. After eight months, ten tournaments and over 2 700 tries, the competition reached its climax at the rain-soaked Stade Jean-Bouin in Paris during 9–10 June 2018. It was the first time in the history of the World Series that the winners were decided in the last match of the final tournament.

'The conclusion to the season,' wrote George Ramsay 'was full of twists and turns as South Africa's fairy-tale ending was almost dashed on a number of occasions.'[54] Fiji came into the Paris Sevens with a seven-point lead over South Africa but suffered a 19–17 defeat to England in their quarter-final match. The decisive try came after a 26-pass move in the dying seconds of the game. In another quarter-final, Spain missed a crucial conversion, which meant their game against South Africa went into over-time at 10–10. A try in the fifth minute by Justin Geduld enabled the Blitzbokke to scrape through to the semi-final.

There was some relief when the South Africans found their stride to record a convincing 24–10 win over New Zealand. Victory in the final would see them secure the overall prize of the World Series title. Their resilience again came to the fore in an exhilarating contest. Tries from Werner Kok, Ryan Oosthuizen and 'Player of the Final' Dewald Human saw them come from behind to defeat England 24–14. The Blitzbokke finished on 182 points, two ahead of the Fijians who had won five of the last six tournaments. New Zealand finished third on 150 points.[55]

The same weekend in June 2018, Rassie Erasmus's new-look Springboks played England at Ellis Park. It was an historically significant match because the Springboks were captained for the first time in a Test by a black player, Siya Kolisi. His side made a stunning comeback after England built a 21-point lead in the first quarter. That the South Africans should go on to win 42–39 spoke volumes for their new leader and his side. The flow of the game, wrote Gavin Mairs, 'could not mask the sense that England had been unable to resist the intensity and power of the hugely inexperienced Springbok side.'

There were five tries apiece, including a brace for debutant winger S'busiso Nkosi and one for Aphiwe Dyantyi on his first cap. Mairs was impressed with Faf de Klerk and commented in *The Telegraph*:

[De Klerk] had a superb game, bristling with energy and intent while Willie Le Roux brought a touch of class to the home side's attacking game, his vision and precision bringing the best out of his wingers ... RG Snyman, with his blond locks flowing, also had a monumental game, outshining the England second rows with a ferocious carrying game.[56]

England scored two tries in the first thirteen minutes of the second Test, but could not score again. In a game that marked Tendai Mtawarira's 100th Test cap, the Springboks played with power and passion to win 23–12 and record a series victory. Faf de Klerk was again highly effective at scrum-half; Damian de Allende a formidable midfield presence and Duane Vermeulen, flanker Pieter-Steph du Toit and hooker Bongi Mbonambi gave the Springboks the edge up front.

'The Springboks on home soil are a different beast,' observed Mairs, 'and you have to be in the stadium to get a true sense of the intensity they bring to their game when the home support find their voice. It is as compelling as it is fearsome ... the Springboks look a side reborn under new head coach Rassie Erasmus.'[57]

The visitors salvaged some pride in the rain at Newlands, but South Africa's series victory had established a solid starting base on which to build for the 2019 World Cup. They had produced spectacular attacking movements; some breathtaking tries, and there was cautious optimism in South African rugby circles that they possessed the players to succeed. 'It was fantastic,' enthused Schalk Brits in the aftermath of the team's success. 'I'm looking forward to see what this team can do.'[58]

Notes

1   R. McCaw with G. McGee, *The Real McCaw: The Autobiography* (London: Aurum Press, 2015), 155–156.
2   A. Bull, 'New Zealand's Graham Henry: How I learned to win the Rugby World Cup', *The Guardian*, 8 September 2015.
3   McCaw with McGee, *The Real McCaw*, 59.
4   Bull, 'New Zealand's Graham Henry', *The Guardian, 8 September 2015*.
5   B. Howitt, *Graham Henry: Final Word* (Auckland: HarperCollins, 2012), 210.
6   Quote reported in *News 24*, 9 June 2007.
7   *New Zealand Herald*, 22 October 2007.
8   P. de Villiers with G. Rich, *Politically Incorrect: The Autobiography* (Cape Town: Zebra Press, 2012), 9.
9   C. Krige in *Sondag*, quoted in *Sport 24*, 5 September 2008.
10   De Villiers with Rich, *Politically Incorrect*, 70.
11   D. Retief, *The Springboks and the Holy Grail: Behind the Scenes at the Rugby World Cup 1995–2007* (Cape Town: Zebra Press, 2011), 242–243.
12   V. Matfield with De J. Borchardt, *Victor: My Journey* (Cape Town: Zebra Press, 2011), 153.
13   De Villiers with Rich, *Politically Incorrect*, 70.
14   Ibid., 11, 89–90.
15   Bull, 'New Zealand's Graham Henry'.
16   J. Smit with M. Greenaway, *Captain in the Cauldron* (Cape Town: Highbury Safika Media, 2010), 88.
17   De Villiers with Rich, *Politically Incorrect*, 119.
18   Matfield with Borchardt, *Victor: My Journey*, 185.

19   *New Zealand Herald*, 11 July 2008.
20   D. Gilhooly, 'Springboks sink All Blacks in Dunedin', *New Zealand Herald*, 12 July 2008.
21   De Villiers with Rich, *Politically Incorrect*, 112.
22   Ibid., 124–125.
23   Smit with Greenaway, *Captain in the Cauldron*, 173.
24   S. Jones, 'England sink to record defeat', *Sunday Times*, 23 November 2008.
25   R. Hartman, 'No word yet from the big guy', *The Star*, 25 November 2008.
26   Smit with Greenaway, *Captain in the Cauldron*, 181.
27   I. McGeechan, *Lion Man: The Autobiography* (London: Pocket Books, 2010), 316.
28   T. Johnson and L. McConnell, *Behind the Silver Fern: The Players Speak* (Edinburgh: Polaris Publishing, 2016), 425.
29   S. Stevenson, *Rugby Pass*, 15 September 2017.
30   Johnson and McConnell, *Behind the Silver Fern*, 426.
31   Howitt, *Graham Henry: Final Word*, 236.
32   The players were Jaque Fourie, Bryan Habana, Fourie du Preez, Schalk Burger, Victor Matfield (captain), W.P. Nel (who later represented Scotland), Bismarck du Plessis, Tendai Mtawarira and Morné Steyn, with Nick Mallett as coach.
33   Johnson and McConnell, *Behind the Silver Fern*, 425.
34   McCaw with McGee, *The Real McCaw*, 155–156.
35   Howitt, *Graham Henry: Final Word*, 238.
36   McCaw with McGee, *The Real McCaw*, 180.
37   Matfield with Borchardt, *Victor: My Journey*, 232–233, 242.
38   P. Rees, 'Ben Foden scores consolation try after South Africa power past England', *The Guardian*, 27 November 2010.
39   De Villiers with Rich, *Politically Incorrect*, 4.
40   McCaw with McGee, *The Real McCaw*, 210.
41   Howitt, *Graham Henry: Final Word*, 11–12.
42   *SA Rugby*, 18 June 2019.
43   Matfield with Borchardt, *Victor: My Journey*, 159.
44   De Villiers with Rich, *Politically Incorrect*, 10.
45   R. Kitson, 'JP Pietersen's try helps South Africa to victory over battling England', *The Guardian*, 16 June 2012.
46   W. Gray, 'All Blacks 38 Springboks 27 – the greatest test in modern rugby', *New Zealand Herald*, 7 October 2013.
47   H. Mostert, '2014: Springboks' year in review', *Sport 24*, 2 December 2014.
48   *The Guardian*, 12 August 2015.
49   S. Jones, 'The Brighton shock was so seismic that it will be felt all over the world' and M. Palmer, 'Unbelievable', *The Sunday Times*, 20 September 2015.
50   Johnson and McConnell, *Behind the Silver Fern*, 462.
51   Ibid.
52   C. Hewett, *The Independent*, 4 December 2015.
53   *New Zealand Herald*, 18 September 2017.
54   G, Ramsay, 'Paris Sevens: South Africa win World Series title in dramatic finale', *CNN*, 10 June 2018.
55   *Planet Rugby*, 10 June 2018.
56   G. Mairs, 'England blow 21-point lead as South Africa inflict fourth successive Test defeat on Eddie Jones' side', *The Telegraph*, 10 June 2018.
57   G. Mairs, 'England in freefall after same old problems see Eddie Jones' side surrender series to South Africa', *The Telegraph*, 10 June 2018.
58   S. Brits interview, *The Guardian*, 23 June 2018.

Bibliography

Archival collections

Bodleian Library of Commonwealth and African Studies, Rhodes House, Oxford
British Library, London
British Newspaper Library, Colindale/St Pancras, London
Centre for Buckinghamshire Studies, Aylesbury
Johannesburg Municipal Library, Johannesburg
Marlborough College Archives, Marlborough, Wiltshire
National Archives of Zimbabwe, Harare
Rugby Football Union, World Rugby Museum Library, Twickenham
South African Government, National Libraries of South Africa, Cape Town and
    Pretoria
South African Government, South African National Archives, Cape Town
South African Rugby Board, Historical Papers/Minutes, Stellenbosch University
University of the Witwatersrand Archives, Johannesburg
Western Cape Archives and Records Services
William Cullen Library, University of the Witwatersrand, Johannesburg

Books, articles and theses

Alegi, P., *Laduma! Soccer, Politics and Society in South Africa* (Scottsville:
    University of KwaZulu-Natal Press, 2004).
Allen, Sir C., 'Records and Statistics', in Lord Elton (ed.), *First Fifty Years of
    the Rhodes Trust and the Rhodes Scholarships 1903–1953* (Oxford: Basil
    Blackwell, 1956).
Allison, L. (ed.), *The Politics of Sport* (Manchester: Manchester University Press,
    1986).
Archer, R. and Bouillon, A., *The South African Game: Sport and Racism*
    (London: Zed Press, 1982).
Baldwin, R., *Economic Development and Export Growth: A Study of Northern
    Rhodesia 1920–1960* (Berkeley: University of California Press, 1966).
    Batchelor, D. 'British Boxing, London, 1948', in S. Macdonald (ed.), *Winter
    Cricket: The Spirit of Wedza* (Harare: Self-published, 2003).
Batchelor, D., *Days Without Sunset* (London: Eyre & Spottiswoode, 1949).
Baxter, T. (ed.), *Guide to the Public Archives of Rhodesia Volume 1 1890–1923*
    (Salisbury, National Archives of Rhodesia, 1969).

Becker, C., 'The Selection of the Team', in L. Laubscher and G. Nieman (eds), *The Carolin Papers: A Diary of the 1906–07 Springbok Tour* (Pretoria: Rugbyana, 1990).

Benyon, J., 'The Cape Colony, 1854–1881', in T. Cameron and S.B. Spies (eds), *An Illustrated History of South Africa* (Johannesburg: Jonathan Ball, 1986).

Bickford-Smith, V., *Ethnic Pride and Racial Prejudice in Victorian Cape Town: Group Identity and Social Practice 1875–1902* (Cambridge: Cambridge University Press, 1995).

Biddiss, M., *Images of Race* (Leicester: Leicester University Press, 1979).

Bills, P., *Jean Pierre Rives: A Modern Corinthian* (London: Allen and Unwin, 1986).

Black, D. and Nauright, J., *Rugby and the South African Nation: Sport, Cultures, Politics and Power in the Old and New South Africa* (Manchester: Manchester University Press, 1998).

Blackie, J., *Bradfield 1850–1975* (Bradfield: Bradfield College, 1976).

Blake, R., *A History of Rhodesia* (London: Eyre Methuen, 1977).

Blake, R., 'The Pioneer Column – Its Origins and Implications' (Fourth Dugmore Memorial Lecture, Rhodes University), Grahamstown, 1970.

Blennerhassett, R. and Sleeman, L., *Adventures in Mashonaland* (Bulawayo: Books of Rhodesia, 1969).

Booley, A., *Forgotten Heroes: History of Black Rugby 1882–1992* (Cape Town: Manie Booley Publications, 1998).

Booth, D., 'Recapturing the Moment? Global Rugby, Economics and the Politics of Nation in Post-Apartheid South Africa', in T. Chandler and J. Nauright (eds), *Making the Rugby World, Race, Gender, Commerce* (London: Frank Cass, 1999).

Booth, D., 'The South African Council on Sport and the Political Antinomies of the Sports Boycott', in *Journal of Southern African Studies*, 23, 1 (March 1997).

Bose, M., *Sporting Colours: Sport and Politics in South Africa* (London: Robson Books, 1994).

Bradley, A., Champneys, A. and Baines, J., *A History of Marlborough College during Fifty Years from its Foundation to the Present Time* (London: John Murray, 1893).

Brickhill, J., *Race against Race, South Africa's 'Multinational' Sport Fraud* (London: International Defence and Aid Fund, 1976).

Bryden, C. and Colby, M. (eds), *Springboks under Siege* (Johannesburg: Now Publications, 1981).

Buckley, M., '"A Colour Line Affair": Race, Imperialism and Rugby Football Contacts between New Zealand and South Africa to 1950' (unpublished master's thesis, University of Canterbury, 1996).

Butler, L. and Stockwell, S. (eds), *The Wind of Change: Harold Macmillan and British Decolonization* (London: Palgrave Macmillan, 2013).

Byrom, G., *Rhodesian Sports Profiles 1907–1979* (Bulawayo: Books of Zimbabwe, 1980).

Cameron, T. and Spies, S. (eds), *An Illustrated History of South Africa* (Johannesburg: Jonathan Ball, 1986).

Campbell, A., 'Right or Wrong – Let the Games Begin?', in *Australia and New Zealand Sports Law Journal*, 5, 1 (2010).

Carlin, J., *Playing the Enemy: Nelson Mandela and the Game that Made a Nation* (London: Atlantic Books, 2008).

Carmichael, S. (ed.), *112 Years of Springbok Tests and Heroes* (Cape Town: SA Rugby Football Union, 2003).

Cary, R., *Charter Royal* (Cape Town: Howard Timmins, 1970).

Cary, R., *The Pioneer Corps* (Salisbury: Galaxie Press, 1975).

Challiss, R., 'The Rhodes Trust', in I.P. MacLaren (ed.), *Some Renowned Rhodesian Senior Schools 1892–1979* (Bulawayo: Books of Zimbabwe, 1981).

Challiss, R., 'Vicarious Rhodesians: Problems Affecting the Selection of Rhodesian Rhodes Scholars 1904–1923' (Salisbury, Rhodesia: The Central African Historical Association, Local Series 33, 1977).

Chandler, T. and Nauright, J., *Making the Rugby World: Race, Gender, Commerce* (London: Frank Cass, 1999).

Chester, R. and McMillan, N., *The Visitors: The History of International Rugby Teams in New Zealand* (Auckland: Moa Publications, 1990).

Christison, G., 'African Jerusalem: The Vision of Robert Grendon' (unpublished PhD thesis; University of KwaZulu-Natal, Pietermaritzburg, 2007).

Christison, G., 'Then Came the Whiteman: An African Poet and Polemicist on the Fateful Encounter', in P. Limb, N. Etherington and P. Midgley (eds), *Grappling with the Beast: Indigenous Southern African Responses to Colonialism 1840–1930* (Leiden: Brill, 2010).

Claassen, W. and Retief, D., *More than Just Rugby* (Johannesburg: Hans Strydom, 1985).

Clements, F., *Rhodesia: The Course to Collision* (London: Pall Mall Press, 1969).

Collins, T., *A Social History of English Rugby Union* (Abingdon: Routledge, 2009).

Collins, T., 'English Rugby Union and the First World War', in *The Historical Journal*, 45, 4 (2002).

Collins, T., *Rugby's Great Split: Class, Culture and the Origins of Rugby League Football* (London: Frank Cass, 2003).

Collins, T., *The Oval World: A Global History of Rugby* (London: Bloomsbury, 2015).

Corsan, J., *Poulton and England: The Life and Times of an Edwardian Rugby Hero* (Leicester: Matador, 2009).

Couzens, T., 'Robert Grendon, Irish Traders, Cricket Scores and Paul Kruger's Dreams', in *English in Africa*, 15, 2 (1988).

Cowley, G., *Having a Ball* (Port Elizabeth: SA Sporting Publications, 1983).

Cruywagen, D. (ed.), *The Badge: A Centenary of the Springbok Emblem* (Newlands: SA Rugby, 2006).

Currey, R., *St Andrew's College. Grahamstown, 1855–1955* (Oxford: Basil Blackwell, 1955).

Darter, A., *Pioneers of Mashonaland* (Bulawayo: Books of Rhodesia, 1977).

Davenport, T., *South Africa: A Modern History* (Johannesburg: Southern Book Publishers, 1989).

Davenport, T., *The Afrikaner Bond: The History of a South African Political Party, 1880–1911* (Cape Town: Oxford University Press, 1966).

Davies, P., *From Magdalen to Merger: A Short History of Oxford University Cricket Club* (Buxton: Church in the Market Place Publications, 2004).

De Villiers, P. with Rich, G., *Politically Incorrect: The Autobiography* (Cape Town: Zebra Press, 2012).

De Wet, W., 'A History of the South African Rugby Football Board: Early Years 1889–1914', in *Sport in History*, published online 25 September 2020.

Difford, I. (ed.), *The History of South African Rugby Football 1875–1932* (Wynberg: Speciality Press, 1933).

Dine, P., *French Rugby Football: A Cultural History* (Oxford: Berg, 2001).

Dobbs, B., *Edwardians at Play* (London: Pelham, 1973).

Dobson, P., *Bishops Rugby: A History* (Cape Town: Don Nelson, 1990).

Dobson, P., *Doc: The Life of Danie Craven* (Cape Town: Human & Rousseau, 1994).

Dobson, P., *Rugby in South Africa: A History 1861–1988* (Cape Town: SARB, 1989).

Drew, A., *Discordant Comrades: Identities and Loyalties on the South African Left* (Abingdon: Routledge, 2000).

Eisenberg, C., Lanfanchi, P., Mason, T. and Wahl, A. (eds), *100 Years of Football : The FIFA Centennial Book* (London: Weidenfeld & Nicolson, 2004).

Erlmann, V., *African Stars: Studies in Black South African Performances* (Chicago: University of Chicago Press, 1991).

Farrar, R., *The Life of Frederic William Farrar, D.D., F.R.S., etc., Sometime Dean of Canterbury* (London: James Nisbet & Co.,1904).

Faure, D., *My Life and Times* (Cape Town: Juta, 1907).

Ferguson, N., *Empire: How Britain Made the Modern World* (London: Penguin, 2003).

Ferreira, J., Blignaut, J., Landman, P. and Du Toit, J., *Transvaal Rugby Football Union 100 Years* (Johannesburg: TRFU, 1989).

Fletcher, G., *The History of Bedford Rugby: Adapted from RGG Squibbs' 1970 Centenary Account*, (Bedford: Bedford School, 2003).

Frere, B., 'Native Races of South Africa', in *Transactions of the South African Philosophical Society*, 1, 2 (1877–1888).

Frost, D., *The Bowring Story of the Varsity Match* (London: Macdonald Queen Anne Press, 1988).

Gainsford, J. with Leck, N., *Nice Guys Come Second* (Cape Town: Don Nelson, 1974).

Gann, L., *A History of Southern Rhodesia: Early Days to 1934* (London: Chatto & Windus, 1965).

Gevisser, M., *Thabo Mbeki: The Dream Deferred* (Johannesburg: Jonathan Ball, 2007).

Gibson, A. and Pickford, W., *Football and the Men Who Made it* (London: Caxton, 1906).

Giliomee, H. and Mbenga, B., *New History of South Africa* (Cape Town: Tafelberg, 2007).

Glendinning, V., *Trollope* (London: Hutchinson, 1992).

Goldin, I., *Making Race: The Politics and Economics of Coloured Identity in South Africa* (London: Longman, 1987).

Grant, D., *The Mighty Totara: The Life and Times of Norman Kirk* (Auckland: Random House New Zealand, 2014).

Green, M., *Around and About: The Memoirs of a South African Newspaperman* (Claremont: David Philip, 2004).

Greenwood, J., *A Cap for Boots: An Autobiography* (London: Hutchinson Benham, 1977).

Greyvenstein, C., *The Bennie Osler Story* (Cape Town: Howard Timmins, 1970).

Griffiths, E., *The Captains* (Johannesburg: Jonathan Ball, 2001).

Griffiths, J., *Rugby's Strangest Matches: Extraordinary but True Stories from Over a Century of Rugby*, (London: Portico, 2000).

Griffiths, J., *The Book of English International Rugby 1871–1982* (London: Willow Books, 1982).

Grundlingh, A., 'The New Politics of Rugby', in A. Grundlingh, A. Odendaal and B.Spies (eds), *Beyond the Tryline: Rugby and South African Society* (Johannesburg: Ravan Press, 1995).

Grundlingh, A., 'Playing for Power: Rugby, Afrikaner Nationalism and Masculinity in South Africa', in A. Grundlingh, A. Odendaal and B. Spies (eds), *Beyond the Tryline: Rugby and South African Society* (Johannesburg: Ravan Press, 1995).

Grundlingh, A., *Potent Pastimes: Sport and Leisure Practices in Modern Afrikaner History* (Pretoria: Protea Book House, 2013).

Grundlingh, A., Odendaal, A. and Spies, B., *Beyond the Tryline: Rugby and South African Society* (Johannesburg: Ravan Press, 1995).

Guelke, A., 'The Politicisation of South African Sport', in L. Allison (ed.), *The Politics of Sport* (Manchester: Manchester University Press, 1986).

Guelke, A., *Rethinking the Rise and Fall of Apartheid: South Africa and World Politics* (London: Palgrave Macmillan, 2005).

Gutsche, T., *Old Gold: The History of the Wanderers Club* (Johannesburg: Citadel Press, 1966).

Hain, P., 'Direct Action and the Springbok Tours', in R. Benewick and T. Smith (eds), *Direct Action and Democratic Politics* (London: Allen and Unwin, 1972).

Hain, P. and Odendaal, A., *Pitch Battles: Sport, Racism and Resistance* (London: Rowman & Littlefield, 2021).

Hanna, A., *The Story of the Rhodesias and Nyasaland* (London: Faber and Faber, 1960).

Harding, R., *Rugby, Reminiscences and Opinions* (London: Pilot Press, 1929).

Hendrich, G., 'Allegiance to the Crown: Afrikaner Loyalty, Conscientious Objection, and the Enkeldoorn Incident in Southern Rhodesia during the Second World War', in *War and Society,* 31, 3 (2012).

Hendrich, G., 'The History of Afrikaner Involvement in the Rhodesian Tobacco Industry, 1890–1980', in *Historia,* 56, 2 (2011).

Hepburn, J., *Twenty Years in Khama's Country and Pioneering among the Bataunga of Lake Ngami* (London: Hodder and Stoughton, 1895).

Hill, J., *The International Diffusion of Modern Sport*, De Montfort University 'Sports History and Culture' lecture notes, 2007.

Hodgson, J., *A History of Zonnebloem College, 1858–1870: A Study in Church and Society* (Cape Town: University of Cape Town, 1975).

Hofmeyr, J. and Reitz, F., *The Life of Jan Hendrik Hofmeyr (Onze Jan)* (Cape Town: Van de Sandt De Villiers, 1913).

Holt, H., *Australian Dictionary of Biography*, Volume 9, (Melbourne: Austrailian National University Press, 1983).

Holt, R., *Sport and the British: A Modern History* (Oxford: Clarendon Press, 1989).

Honey, J., *Tom Brown in South Africa* (Grahamstown: Rhodes University, 1972).

Honey, J., *Tom Brown's Universe: The Development of the Public School in the 19th Century* (London: Millington, 1977).

Hopkins, J., *British Lions 1980* (Worthing: Littlehampton Book Service, 1980).

Horrell, M., Horner, D. and Kane-Berman, J. (eds), *A Survey of Race Relations in South Africa 1971* (Johannesburg: South African Institute of Race Relations, January 1972).

Hoste, H. (ed. N. Davies), *Gold Fever* (Salisbury: Pioneer Head, 1977).

Howitt, B., *Graham Henry: Final Word* (Auckland: HarperCollins, 2012).

Hughes, T., *Tom Brown's Schooldays* (Oxford: Oxford University Press, 1999).

Humphry, D., *The Cricket Conspiracy* (London: National Council for Civil Liberties, 1972).

Hyam, R., *The Failure of South African Expansion 1908–1948* (London: Macmillan, 1972).

Hyam, R. and Henshaw, P., *The Lion and the Springbok: Britain and South Africa since the Boer War* (Cambridge: Cambridge University Press, 2003).

James. C. and Rea, C., *Injured Pride: The Lions in South Africa* (London: Arthur Barker, 1980).

Johnson, F., *Great Days* (Bulawayo: Books of Rhodesia, 1972).

Johnson, R., 'Rivonia Days', in *London Review of Books*, 29, 16 (2007).

Johnson, T. and McConnell, L., *Behind the Silver Fern: The Players Speak* (Edinburgh: Polaris Publishing, 2016).

Jones, S., *Endless Winter: The Inside Story of the Rugby Revolution* (London: Mainstream Publishing, 1993).

Jones, S. and Cain, N., *Behind the Rose: Playing Rugby for England* (Edinburgh: Birlinn, 2014).

Kaufman, W. and H. Slettedahl Macpherson (eds), *Britain and the Americas: Culture, Politics and History* (Santa Barbara: ABC-Clio, 2005).

Keating, F., *The Great Number Tens: A Century of Rugby's Pivots and Playmakers* (London: Corgi, 1999).

Keech, M., 'One Nation, One Soul, One Dream, One Goal?', in A. Smith and D. Porter (eds), *Sport and National Identity in the Post-War World* (London: Routledge, 2004).

Keohane, M., *Chester: A Biography of Courage* (Cape Town: Don Nelson, 2002).

Keppel-Jones, A., *Rhodes and Rhodesia* (Kingston: McGill-Queen's University Press, 1983).

Kettlewell, P. (Headmaster), 'St Andrew's College RFC, Grahamstown', in I. Difford, *The History of South African Rugby Football, 1875–1932* (Wynberg: Speciality Press, 1933).

Koorts, L., *DF Malan and the Rise of Afrikaner Nationalism* (Cape Town: Tafelberg, 2014).

Kotzé, G., 'Sportrevolusie en die Beesblaasbond', in Sport en Politiek in *Gelofteland*, 4 April 2012.

Krige, C. with Bills, P., *The Right Place at the Wrong Time: The Autobiography of Corné Krige* (Cape Town: Zebra Press, 2005).

Laidlaw, C., *Mud in Your Eye: A Worm's Eye View of the Changing World of Rugby* (London: Pelham Books, 1974).

Lambert, M., *The Classics and South African Identities* (London: Bloomsbury, 2011).

Laubscher, L. and Nieman, G. (eds), *Carolin Papers: A Diary of the 1906–07 Springbok Tour* (Pretoria: Rugbyana, 1990). Lenehan, G., 'Marlborough', in M. Tozer (ed.), *Puddings, Bullies & Squashes: Early Public School Football Codes* (Truro: Sunnyrest Books, 2020).

Lewis, G., *Between the Wire and the Wall: A History of South African 'Coloured' Politics* (Cape Town: David Philip, 1987).

Lewis, S., *Last of the Blue Lions: The 1938 British Lions Tour of South Africa* (Cheltenham: Sports Books Limited, 2009).

Lewsen, P., *John X. Merriman: Paradoxical South African Statesman* (New Haven: Yale University Press, 1982).

Lewsen, P. (ed.), *Selections from the Correspondence of John X. Merriman 1870–1924* (Cape Town: Historical Publications of South Africa, 1960–69).

Leys, C., *European Politics in Southern Rhodesia* (London: Clarendon Press, 1959).

Lindfors, B., *Africans on Stage: Studies in Ethnological Show Business* (Cape Town: David Philip, 1999).

Longford, E., *Jameson's Raid* (London: Weidenfeld & Nicolson, 1982).

Louw, E., *The Rise, Fall and Legacy of Apartheid* (Westport: Praeger, 2004).

Louw, R. with Cameron-Dow, J., *For the Love of Rugby* (Johannesburg: Hans Strydom Publishers, 1987).

Lucas, J., 'Victorian Muscular Christianity: Prologue to the Olympic Games Philosophy', in *Olympic Review*, 1975.

Luyt, L., *Walking Proud: The Louis Luyt Autobiography* (Cape Town: Don Nelson, 2003).

Macdonald, S. (ed.), *Winter Cricket: The Spirit of Wedza* (Harare: Self-published, 2003).

Mallett, A., *The Black Lords of Summer: The Story of the 1868 Aboriginal Tour of England and Beyond* (St Lucia: University of Queensland Press, 2002).

Mandaza, I., *Race, Colour and Class in Southern Africa: A Study of the Coloured Question in the Context of an Analysis of the Colonial and White Settler Racial Ideology, and African Nationalism in Twentieth Century Zimbabwe, Zambia and Malawi* (Harare: SAPES Books, 1997).

Mandela, N. and Langa, M., *Dare Not Linger: The Presidential Years* (London: Macmillan, 2017).

Mangan, J., *Athleticism in the Victorian and Edwardian Public School* (Cambridge: Cambridge University Press, 1981).

Mangan, J. (ed.), *Pleasure, Profit, Proselytism: British Culture and Sport at Home and Abroad 1700–1914* (London: Frank Cass, 1988).

Mangan, J., *The Games Ethic and Imperialism* (Harmondsworth: Viking, 1985).

Mangan, J. (ed.), *The Cultural Bond: Sport, Empire and Society* (London: Frank Cass, 1992).

Marks, S., 'Class, Culture and Consciousness in South Africa, 1880–1899', in R. Ross, A. Mager and B. Nasson (eds), *The Cambridge History of South Africa, Volume 2, 1885–1994* (Cambridge: Cambridge University Press, 2011).

Marks, S. and Atmore, A., *Economy and Society in Pre-Industrial South Africa* (London: Longman, 1980).

Marshall, H. and Jordan, J.P., *Oxford v Cambridge: The Story of the University Match* (London: Clerke & Cockeran, 1951).

Marx, A., *Making Race and Nation: A Comparison of South Africa, the United States, and Brazil* (Cape Town: Cambridge University Press, 2003).

Mason, P., *The Birth of a Dilemma: The Conquest and Settlement of Rhodesia* (London: Oxford University Press, 1958).

Mason, T., *Association Football and English Society 1863–1915* (Brighton: Harvester Press, 1980).

Matfield, V. with Borchardt, De J., *Victor: My Journey* (Cape Town: Zebra Press, 2011).

McCaw, R. with McGee, G., *The Real McCaw: The Autobiography* (London: Aurum Press, 2015).

McGeechan, I., *Lion Man: The Autobiography* (London: Pocket Books: 2010).

McIntosh, I. with Bishop, J., *Mac: The Face of Rugby* (Cape Town: Don Nelson, 2000).

McLaren, B., *Talking of Rugby: An Autobiography* (London: Stanley Paul, 1991).

McLean, T., *The All Blacks* (London: Sidgwick & Jackson, 1991).

McLean, T., *Goodbye to Glory: The 1976 All Black Tour to South Africa* (Wellington: Pelham Books, 1976).

McLean, T., 'The Greatest Match of All', in G. Williams, *Sport: A Literary Anthology* (Cardigan: Parthian, 2008).

McRae, D., *Winter Colours: Changing Seasons in World Rugby* (London: Simon & Schuster, 2014).

McWhirter, R. and Noble, Sir A., *Centenary History of Oxford University Rugby Football Club 1869–1969* (Oxford: OURFC, 1969).

Medworth, C., *The Battle of the Giants* (Cape Town: Howard Timmins, 1960).

Mellish, F., *My Dear Danie – An Open Letter to Danie Craven* (Cape Town: Maskew Miller, 1960).

Merrett, C., Tatz, C. and Adair, D., 'History and its Racial Legacies: Quotas in South African Rugby and Cricket', in *Sport in Society*, 14, 6 (2011).

Millar, W., *My Recollections and Reminiscences* (Cape Town: Juta, 1926).

Millar, W., 'The Springboks in Great Britain 1912/13', in I. Difford (ed.), *History of South African Rugby Football 1875–1932* (Wynberg: Speciality Press, 1933).

Miller, D., *Olympic Revolution: The Olympic Biography of Juan Antonio Samaranch* (London: Pavilion Books, 1994).

Mjikeliso, S., *Being a Black Springbok: The Thando Manana Story* (Johannesburg: Macmillan, 2017).

Mlambo, A., '"Some Are More White than Others": Racial Chauvinism as a Factor in Rhodesian Immigration Policy, 1890 to 1963', in *Zambezia*, 27, 2 (2000).

Morapeli, M., 'The Rock: The History of Orlando High School 1939–1984' (unpublished master's thesis, University of the Witwatersrand, Johannesburg, 1984).

Morgan, C. and Nicholson, G., *The Autobiography – Beyond the Fields of Play* (London: Hodder and Stoughton, 1996).

Morris, J., *Farewell the Trumpets: An Imperial Retreat* (Harmondsworth: Penguin, 1982).

Muller, C. (ed.), *Five Hundred Years: A History of South Africa* (Pretoria: Academica, 1981).

Mungazi, D., *Colonial Policy and Conflict in Rhodesia: A Study of Cultures in Collison 1890–1979* (London: Crane Russak, 1992).

Murphy, P. (ed.), *Central Africa: British Documents on the End of Empire 1945–58, Part 1* (London: Stationery Office Books, 2005).

Murray, B., *The World's Game: A History of Soccer* (Champaign: University of Illinois Press, 1998).

Murray, B., *Wits: The Open Years – A History of the University of the Witwatersrand, Johannesburg 1939–1959* (Johannesburg: Witwatersrand University Press, 1997).

Murray, B., Parry, R. and Winch, J. (eds), *Cricket and Society in South Africa 1910–1971: From Union to Isolation* (London: Palgrave Macmillan, 2018).

Murray, B. and Stadler, A., 'From the Pact to the Advent of Apartheid 1924–48', in T. Cameron (ed.), *An Illustrated History of South Africa* (Johannesburg: Jonathan Ball Publishers, 1986).

Mutambirwa, James A. Chamunorwa, *The Rise of Settler Power in Southern Rhodesia (Zimbabwe) 1898–1923* (London: Associated University Presses, 1980).

Muzondidya, J., 'Towards a Historical Understanding of the Making of the Coloured Community in Zimbabwe 1890–1920', in *Identity, Culture and Politics*, 3, 2 (2002).

Naidoo, K., *Krish: Struggle Lawyer* (Crown Mines: Self-published, 2019).

Nairn, B. and Serle, G. (eds), *Australian Dictionary of Biography, Volume 9*, (Melbourne: Melbourne University Press, 1983).

Nauright, J. and Chandler, T. (eds), *Making Men: Rugby and Masculine Identity*, (London: Frank Cass, 1996).

Nicholls, M., *The All Blacks in Springbokland* (Wellington: L.T. Watkins, 1928).

Nieman, G. and Laubscher, L., 'W.P. Schreiner and His Role in the 1919 New Zealand Services Tour of South Africa', in *Points Unlimited*, 7, 2 (2000).

Norman, L., 'Bradfield', in M. Tozer (ed.), *Puddings, Bullies & Squashes: Early Public School Football Codes* (Truro: Sunnyrest Books, 2020).

Nye, R., *Martin Donnelly: New Zealand Cricket's Master Craftsman* (Auckland: Harper Collins, 1998).

Odendaal, A., *The Founders: The Origins of the ANC and the Struggle for Democracy in South Africa* (Johannesburg: Jacana, 2012).

Odendaal, A. 'South Africa's Black Victorians: Sport, Race and Class in South Africa before Union', in *Africa Perspective*, 1, 7 & 8 (1989).

Odendaal, A., *The Story of an African Game: Black Cricketers and the Unmasking of One of Cricket's Greatest Myths, South Africa, 1850–2003* (Cape Town: David Philip, 2003).

Odendaal, A., 'The Thing that is Not Round', in A. Grundlingh, A. Odendaal and B. Spies (eds), *Beyond the Tryline: Rugby and South African Society* (Johannesburg: Ravan Press, 1995).

Odendaal, A., Reddy, K., Merrett, C. and Winch, J., *Cricket & Conquest: The History of South African Cricket Retold 1795–1914 Volume 1* (Cape Town: HSRC, 2016).

Oettle, M., *Colonel John Graham of Fintry*, http://uk.geocities.wapenspreuk/GrahamE.html

Owen, O., *The History of the RFU* (London: Playfair Books, 1955).

Palenski, R., *Rugby: A New Zealand History* (Auckland: Auckland University Press, 2015).

Pallant, A., *A Sporting Century 1863–1963* (Callington: Self-published, 1997).

Palmer, R., *Land & Racial Domination in Rhodesia* (Berkeley: University of California Press, 1977).

Parker, A., *W.P. Rugby: Centenary 1883–1983* (Cape Town: WPRFU, 1983).

Parker, G., *South African Sports* (London: Sampson Low, Marston, 1897).

Parker, J., *Little White Island* (London: Pitman Publishing, 1972).

Parry, R., '"In a Sense Citizens, but Not Altogether Citizens ...": Rhodes, Race and the Ideology of Segregation at the Cape in the Late Nineteenth Century', in *Canadian Journal of African Studies*, 17, 3 (1983).

Parry, R., 'Origins of Segregation at the Cape', in B. Murray and G. Vahed (eds), *Empire and Cricket: The South African Experience, 1884–1914* (Pretoria: Unisa, 2009).

Partridge, T., *A Life in Rugby* (Halfway House: Southern Book Publishers, 1991).

Patterson, S., *The Last Trek: A Study of the Boer People and the Afrikaner Nation* (London: Routledge and Kegan Paul, 1957).

Peires, J., '*Facta non Verba*: Towards a History of Black Rugby' (History Workshop, University of the Witwatersrand, 1981).

Peires, J., 'Rugby in the Eastern Cape: A History', in *Work in Progress*, 17 (1981).

Pienaar, F., *Rainbow Warrior* (London: Harper/Collins, 1999).

Piggott, F., *The Springboks: History of the Tour 1906/07* (Cape Town: Dawson & Sons, 1907).

Quagga Rugby Football Club 21 1955–1976 (Johannesburg: Quagga RFC, 1976).

Qunta, V., 'The African Springboks', in D. Cruywagen (ed.), *The Badge, a Centenary of the Springbok Emblem* (Newlands: SA Rugby, 2006).

Ray, D., *From Webb Ellis to World Cup* (Rugby: Rugby School, 2015).

Reason, J., *The Unbeaten Lions: The 1974 British Isles Rugby Union Tour of South Africa* (London: Rugby Books, 1974).

Ramsamy, S. *Apartheid: The Real Hurdle* (London: International Defence and Aid Fund, 1982).

Ray, D., *From Webb Ellis to World Cup* (Rugby: Rugby School, 2015).

Retief, D., 'Mandela Saves the Springboks', in D. Cruywagen (ed.), *The Badge: A Centenary of the Springbok Emblem* (Cape Town: SA Rugby, 2006).

Retief, D., *The Springboks and the Holy Grail: Behind the Scenes at the Rugby World Cup 1995–2007* (Cape Town: Zebra Press, 2011).

Reyburn, W., *There Was Also Some Rugby: The Sixth Springboks in Britain* (London: Stanley Paul, 1970).

Richards, H., *A Game for Hooligans: The History of Rugby Union* (Edinburgh: Mainstream Publishing, 2006).

Richards, H., *The Red and the White: A History of England versus Wales Rugby* (London: Aurum Press, 2010).

Richards, T., *Dancing on Our Bones: New Zealand, South Africa, Rugby and Racism* (Wellington: Bridget Williams Books, 2012).

Robbie, J., *The Game of My Life* (London: Pelham Books, 1989).

Roscoe, A., *The Columbia Guide to Central African Literature in English since 1945* (New York: Columbia University Press, 2007).

Ross, R., Kelk Mager, A. and Nasson, B. (eds), *The Cambridge History of South Africa, Volume 2, 1885–1994* (Cambridge: Cambridge University Press, 2011).

Rotberg, R., *The Founder: Cecil Rhodes and the Pursuit of Power* (Oxford: Oxford University Press, 1988).

Roy, N. (ed.), *100 Years of the Blues: The Bedfordshire Times Centenary History of Bedford RUFC, 1886–1986* (Bedford: Bedford County Press, 1986).

Rubython, J. and Bishop, M. (eds), *Springbok Triumph: Lions Tour of South Africa* (Cape Town: Howard Timmins, 1980).

Ryan, G., 'Maori and the 1937 Springbok Tour of New Zealand', in *New Zealand Journal of History*, 34, 1 (2000).

Ryan, G., *Forerunners of the All Blacks: The 1888–89 New Zealand Native Football Team in Britain, Australia and New Zealand* (Christchurch: Canterbury University Press, 1993).

Samkange, S., *Origins of Rhodesia* (London: Cox & Wyman, 1968).

Schadeberg, J. (ed.), *The Fifties People of South Africa* (Johannesburg: J.R.A. Bailey, 1987).

Schulze, H., *South Africa's Cricketing Lawyers: Biographical Notes on the 32 Lawyers Who Represented South Africa in Cricket* (Halfway House: Interdoc Consultants, 1999).

Sisulu, E., *Walter and Albertina Sisulu: In Our Lifetime* (David Philip and New Africa Books, 2002).

Smit, J. with Greenaway, M., *Captain in the Cauldron* (Cape Town: Highbury Safika Media, 2010).

Smith, I., *The Great Betrayal* (London: Blake, 1997).

Snyders, H., 'Between the Springbok and Ikhamanga – The Untold Story of South Africa's Black Rugby Exiles', in *Impumelelo: The Interdisciplinary Electronic Journal of African Sports*, 5 (2010).

Snyders, H., 'Rugby, National Pride and the Struggle of the Black South Africans for Recognition, 1897–1992', in *Sporting Traditions*, 32, 1 (2015).

Spies, B., 'The Imperial Heritage', in A. Grundlingh, A. Odendaal and B. Spies (eds), *Beyond the Tryline: Rugby and South African Society* (Johannesburg: Ravan Press, 1995).

Starmer-Smith, N., *The Barbarians: The Official History of the Barbarian Football Club* (London: Futura Publications, 1977).

Steen, R., *Floodlights and Touchlines: A History of Spectator Sport* (London: Bloomsbury, 2014).

Stent, R., *The Fourth Springboks 1951–52* (London: Longmans, 1952).

Stern, J. and Williams, M. (eds), *The Essential Wisden: An Anthology of 150 Years of Wisden Cricketers' Almanack* (London: Bloomsbury, 2013).

Summers, C., *From Civilization to Segregation: Social Ideals and Social Control in Southern Rhodesia, 1890–1934* (Athens: Ohio University Press, 1994).

Swanton, E., *As I Said at the Time: A Lifetime of Cricket* (London: Unwin Paperbacks, 1986).

Sweet, R., *Natal 100: Centenary of Natal Rugby Union* (Durban: Natal RFU, 1990).

Switzer, L., *South Africa's Alternative Press: Voices of Protest and Resistance* (Cambridge: Cambridge University Press, 1997).

Tamarkin, M., *Cecil Rhodes and the Cape Afrikaners: The Imperial Colossus and the Colonial Parish Pump* (London: Routledge, 1996).

Tamarkin, M., *The Making of Zimbabwe: Decolonisation in Regional and International Politics* (London: Frank Cass, 1990).

Tambo, O., 'South Africa at the Crossroads': Canon Collins Memorial Lecture, May 1987.

Taylor, S., *The Mighty Nimrod: A Life of Frederick Courteney Selous, African Hunter and Adventurer 1851–1917* (London: Collins, 1989).

Teichmann, G., *For the Record* (Johannesburg: Jonathan Ball, 2000).

Thomas, B., *Springbok Glory* (London: Stanley Paul, 1961).

Thomas, C. and Thomas, G., *125 Years of the British & Irish Lions: The Official History* (London: Mainstream, 2013).

Thomson, H.C., *Rhodesia and its Government* (London, Smith, Elder and Co., 1898).

Thompson, J., *The Story of Rhodesian Sport: 1889–1935* (Bulawayo: Rhodesia P&P, 1935).

Thompson, R., *Retreat from Apartheid: New Zealand's Sporting Contacts with South Africa* (London: Oxford University Press, 1975).

Thornton, A., *Doctrines of Imperialism* (New York: John Wiley & Sons, 1965).

Tobias, E., *Errol Tobias: Pure Gold* (Cape Town: Tafelberg, 2015).

Tozer, M. (ed.), *Puddings, Bullies & Squashes: Early Public School Football Codes* (Truro: Sunnyrest Books, 2020).

Trapido, S. 'The Origins and Development of the African Peoples' Organisation', in *Collected Seminar Papers on the Societies of Southern Africa in the 19th and 20th Centuries, Volume 1* (London: Institute of Commonwealth Studies, 1970).

Trollope, A., *South Africa (Volume 1)* reprint (Stroud: Nonsuch Publishing, 2005).

Trollope, A. (ed.), *British Sports and Pastimes* (London: Virtue & Co., 1868).

Vahed, G., *Muslim Portraits: The Anti-Apartheid Struggle* (Durban: Madiba Publishers, 2012).

Vambe, L., *An Ill-Fated People: Zimbabwe before and after Rhodes* (Pittsburgh: University of Pittsburgh Press, 1972).

Van der Merwe, F., 'Oorspronklike voetbal aan die Kaap en die ontstaan van die Stellenbosch Rugbyvoetbalklub: Nuwe feite' in *South African Journal for Research in Sport, Physical Education and Recreation*, 23(1), 85 (2001).

Van der Merwe, F., 'Original Football at the Cape and the Formation of the Stellenbosch Rugby Football Club: New Facts', in *South African Journal for Research in Sport, Physical Education and Recreation*, 21, 1, 2001.

Van der Merwe, F., 'Rugby in the Prisoner-of-War Camps during the Anglo-Boer War of 1899–1902', Department of Human Movement Studies, University of Stellenbosch.

Van der Schyff, P., 'Birth of an African legend', in D. Cruywagen (ed.), *The Badge: A Centenary of the Springbok Emblem* (Newlands: SA Rugby, 2006).

Van der Ross, R., *Myths and Attitudes: An Inside Look at the Coloured People* (Cape Town: Tafelberg: 1979).

Van der Valk, R. with Colquhoun, A., *An Adventure in Rugby* (Cape Town: Don Nelson, 2002).

Van Ryneveld, C., *20th Century All-rounder: Reminiscences and Reflections of Clive van Ryneveld* (Cape Town: Pretext, 2011).

Vann, J. and Van Arsdel, R. (eds), *Periodicals of Queen Victoria's Empire* (Toronto: University of Toronto Press, 1996).

Van Schaik, P., 'Paarl RFC', in I. Difford, *The History of South African Rugby Football 1875–1932* (Wynberg: Speciality Press, 1933).

Vecchione, J (ed.), *New York Times: Book of Sport Legends* (New York: Simon & Schuster, 1992).

Verwey, E. (ed.), *New Dictionary of South African Biography, Volume 1* (Pretoria: HSRC, 1995).

Walker, E., *The Cambridge History of the British Empire, Volume 7* (Cambridge: Cambridge University Press, 1963).

Walker, E., *W.P. Schreiner: A South African* (London: Oxford University Press, 1969).

Wallis, J., *One Man's Hand* (Bulawayo: Books of Rhodesia, 1972).

Walsh, F., *A History of South Africa* (London: Harper Collins, 2000).

Warner, P., *Long Innings: The Autobiography of Sir Pelham Warner* (London: George G. Harrap, 1951).

Warner, P., *Lord's 1787–1945* (London: Sportsman's Book Club, 1951).

Warwick, P. (ed.), *The South African War: The Anglo-Boer War 1899–1902* (Harlow: Longman, 1980).

Watts Moses, E., *History of the International Rugby Football Board* (London: IRB, 1960).

Weir, T., 'James Peters: The Man They Wouldn't Play: England's First Black International and the 1906 Springboks' (unpublished master's thesis, De Montfort University, Leicester, 2015).

Welensky, Sir R., *Welensky's 4 000 Days: The Life and Death of the Federation of Rhodesia and Nyasaland* (London: Collins, 1964).

Welsh, F., *A History of South Africa* (London: Harper Collins, 2000).

West, M., *The Rise of an African Middle Class: Colonial Zimbabwe, 1898–1965* (Bloomington: Indiana University Press, 2002).

Western Province RFU, *Rules of the Western Province Junior Rugby Football Union* (Cape Town: Western Province Junior Rugby Football Union, 1898).

Wheatcroft, G., *The Randlords* (New York: Atheneum, 1986).

White, J. with Ray, C., *In Black and White: The Jake White Story* (Cape Town: Zebra Press, 2007).

Wilburn, K., *The Life of Statesman and Industrialist Sir James Sivewright of South Africa, 1848–1916* (Lewiston: Edwin Mellen Press, 2010).

Willan, B., 'One of the Most Gentlemanly Players that Ever Donned a Jersey', in *Quarterly Bulletin of the National Library of South Africa*, 66, 3 (2012).

Williamson, K., *Brothers to Us: The Story of a Remarkable Family's Fight against Apartheid* (Ringwood: Viking, 1997).

Wilson, H., 'Separated by Race', in *The Badge: A Centenary of the Springbok Emblem* (Newlands: SA Rugby, 2006).

Winch, J., *England's Youngest Captain: The Life and Times of Monty Bowden and Two South African Journalists* (Windsor: Windsor Publishers, 2003).

Winch, J., *Rhodesia Rugby: A History of the National Side 1898–1979* (Salisbury: ZRRFU, 1979).

Winch, J., 'Should the West Indies have Toured South Africa in 1959? C.L.R. James versus Learie Constantine', in B. Murray, R. Parry and J. Winch (eds), *Cricket & Society in South Africa 1910–1971; From Union to Isolation* (London: Palgrave Macmillan, 2018).

Winch, J. and Parry, R., *Too Black to Wear Whites: The Remarkable Story of Krom Hendricks, a Cricket Hero Who Was Rejected by Cecil John Rhodes's Empire* (Cape Town: Penguin, 2020).

Winch, J. and Patel, M., 'Playing the Game: The Unification of South African Sport' (unpublished M-Net project, 2000).

Woeber, C., '"A Good Education Sets up a Divine Discontent": The Contribution of St Peter's School to Black South African Autobiography' (unpublished PhD thesis, University of the Witwatersrand, Johannesburg, 2000).

Woods, D., *Biko* (London: Penguin, 1978).

Worden, N., Van Heyningen, E. and Bickford-Smith, V., *Cape Town: The Making of a City* (Cape Town: David Philip, 1998).

Writer, L., *Pitched Battle: In the Frontline of the 1971 Springbok Tour of Australia* (Melbourne: Scribe, 2016).

Wynne Thomas, P., *The Complete History of Cricket Tours at Home and Abroad* (London: Hamlyn, 1989).

Zavos, S., *Winters of Revenge: The Bitter Rivalry between the All Blacks and the Springboks* (Auckland: Viking, 1997).

Ziegler, P., *Legacy: Cecil Rhodes, the Rhodes Trust and Rhodes Scholarships* (New Haven: Yale University Press, 2008).

Newspapers, periodicals and annuals

APO, The
Asahi Shimbun, The
Athletic News
Auckland Star
Bantu World
Bloemfontein Express
Bulawayo Chronicle
Bulawayo Observer
Business Day
Cape Argus
Cape Herald
Cape Standard
Cape Times

Cape Times Weekly
Chronicle, The (Toowoomba)
Christchurch Star
Citizen (Kimberley)
Citizen, The (Johannesburg)
City Press
Country Life (London)
Cricket: A Weekly Record
Daily Dispatch
Daily Express
Daily Graphic
Daily Independent (Kimberley)
Daily Mail (London)
Daily Mirror
Daily News and General Advertiser
Daily Telegraph (London)
Daily Telegraph (Napier)
Diamond Fields Advertiser
Die Burger
Dominion, The (Wellington)
Eastern Province Herald
Evening Post (Wellington)
Evening Post (Port Elizabeth)
Frankfurter Allegmeine Zeitung
Friend, The
Grassroots Rugby
Guardian, The
Herald, The (Glasgow)
Imvo Zabantsundu
Independent, The (London)
Irish Times, The
Lantern, The
Leadership SA
Mail & Guardian
Mail on Sunday, The
Manawatū Daily Times
Marlburian, The, (Marlborough College magazine)
Merchiston Castle School Register
Money Week
Morning Post
Natal Witness
Native Worker
New Age

New Nation, The
New Zealand Herald
Observer, The
Ousel, The (Journal of Bedford Grammar School)
Pace
Plymouth Football Herald
Port Elizabeth Telegraph & Eastern Province Standard
Post Natal
Press, The (Christchurch)
Pretoria News
Rand Daily Mail
Rhodesia Herald
Rugby 15
Rugby Pass
Rugby World
SA Rugby
Saturday Star
Scotsman, The
Shannon News, The (Manawatu-Wanganui)
South African Review
Sowetan
Spectator, The
Sporting Life
Standard and Diggers News (Johannesburg)
Standard and Mail (Cape Town)
Star, The (Christchurch)
Sunday Star
Star, The (Johannesburg)
Sun, The (Christchurch)
Sunday Telegraph (London)
Sunday Times (Johannesburg)
Sunday Times (London)
Sydney Morning Herald
Sydney Referee
Telegraph, The
Times, The (London)
Times of India
Umteteli wa Bantu
Weekend Argus
Weekly Mail
Western Mail
Wits Sport<italics>
World Rugby

Appendix

The Players

The white SA Rugby Football Board (later SA Rugby Board) and the non-racial SA Coloured Rugby Football Board (later SA Rugby Union) were formed in the late nineteenth century. They were the two main pillars around which the South African game was built, serving the country's rugby until unity on 19 January 1992. In the course of more than 100 years, there were splits and amalgamations, resulting in three and later four national bodies during 1935 to 1977.

* – Captain
T(s) – Tour(s)

The SA Rugby Football Board/SA Rugby Board representatives 1891–1991
The SA Rugby Football Board produced international teams from 1891. The 1906/07 tour popularised the use of the term 'Springboks'. In November 1977, the SA Rugby Football Board ceased to be an extensively white body when it amalgamated with the SA Rugby Association (formerly the SA African Rugby Board) and the SA Rugby Football Federation to form the SA Rugby Board.

The following represented the SA Rugby Football Board/SA Rugby Board in international rugby:

Ackerman, D.S.P., 8 Tests, 1955-56-58

Albertyn, P.K.,* 4 Tests, 1924

Alexander, F.A., 2 Tests, 1891

Allen, P.B., 1 Test, 1960

Allport, P.H., 2 Tests, 1910

Anderson, J.H., 3 Tests, 1896

Anderson, J.W., 1 Test, 1903

Andrew, J.B., 1 Test, 1896

Antelme, J.G.M., 5 Tests, 1960-61

Apsey, J.T., 3 Tests, 1933-38

Ashley, S., 1 Test, 1903

Aston, F.T.D.,* 4 Tests, 1896

Aucamp, J., 2 Tests, 1924

Baard, A.P., 1 Test, 1960

Babrow, L., 5 Tests, 1937

Barnard, A.S., 4 Tests, 1984-86

Barnard, J.H., 5 Tests, 1965

Barnard, R.W., 1 Test, 1970

Barnard, W.H.M., 2 Tests, 1949-51

Barry, J., 3 Tests, 1903

Bartmann, W.J., 8 Tests, 1986-92

Bastard, W.E., 6 Tests, 1937-38

Bates, A.J., 4 Tests, 1969-70-72

Bayvel, P.C.R., 10 Tests, 1974-75-76

Beck, J.J., 3 Tests, 1981

Bedford, T.P.,* 25 Tests, 1963-64-65-68-69-70-71

Bekker, H.J., 2 Tests, 1981

Bekker, H.P.J., 15 Tests, 1952-53-55-56

Bekker, M.J., 1 Test, 1960

Bekker, R.P., 2 Tests, 1953

Bergh, W.F., 17 Tests,
    1931-32-33-37-38

Bestbier, A., 1 Test, 1974

Bester, J.J.N., 2 Tests, 1924

Bester, J.L.A., 2 Tests, 1938

Beswick, A.M., 3 Tests, 1896

Bezuidenhout, C.E., 3 Tests, 1962

Bezuidenhout, N.S.E., 9 Tests,
    1972-74-75-77

Bierman, J.N., 1 Test, 1931

Bisset, W.M., 2 Tests, 1891

Blair, R., 1 Test, 1977

Bosch, G.R., 9 Tests, 1974-75-76

Bosman, N.J.S., 3 Tests, 1924

Botha, D.S., 1 Test, 1981

Botha, H.E.,* 28 Tests,
    1980-81-82-86-89-92

Botha, J.A., 1 Test, 1903

Botha, J.P.F., 3 Tests, 1962

Botha, P.H., 2 Tests, 1965

Boyes, H.C., 2 Tests, 1891

Braine, J.S., 1912/13T

Brand, G.H., 16 Tests,
    1928-31-32-33-37-38

Bredenkamp, M.J., 2 Tests, 1896

Breedt, J.C.,* 8 Tests, 1986-89-92

Brewis, J.D., 10 Tests, 1949-51-52-53

Briers, T.P.D., 7 Tests, 1955-56

Brink, D.J., 3 Tests, 1906

Broodryk, J.A., 1937T

Brooks, D., 1 Test, 1906

Brown, C.B., 3 Tests, 1903

Brynard, G.S., 7 Tests, 1965-68

Buchler, J.U., 10 Tests, 1951-52-53-56

Burdett, A.F., 2 Tests, 1906

Burger, J.M., 2 Tests, 1989

Burger, M.B., 3 Tests, 1980-81

Burger, S.W.P., 6 Tests, 1984-86

Burger, W.A.G., 4 Tests, 1906-10

Burmeister, A.R.D., 1906/07T

Carelse, G., 14 Tests,
    1964-65-67-68-69

Carlson, R.A., 1 Test, 1972

Carolin, H.W.,* 3 Tests, 1903-06

Castens, H.H.,* 1 Test, 1891

Chignell, T.W., 1 Test, 1891

Cilliers, G.D., 3 Tests, 1963

Claassen, J.T.,* 28 Tests,
    1955-56-58-60-61-62

Claassen, W.,* 7 Tests, 1981-82

Clark, W.H.G., 1 Test, 1933

Clarkson, W.A., 3 Tests, 1921-24

Cloete, H.A., 1 Test, 1896

Cockrell, C.H., 3 Tests, 1969-70

Cockrell, R.J., 11 Tests,
    1974-75-76-77-81

Cocks, T.M.D., 1980T

Coetzee, J.H.H., 6 Tests, 1974-75-76

Conradie, S.C., 1965T

Cope, D.G., 1 Test, 1896

Cotty, W.A.H., 1 Test, 1896

Crampton, G., 1 Test, 1903

Craven, D.H.,* 16 Tests,
    1931-32-33-37-38

Cronjé, C.J.C., 1965T

Cronje, P.A., 7 Tests, 1971-74

Cronjé, S.N., 1912/13T

Crosby, J.H., 1 Test, 1896

Crosby, N.J., 2 Tests, 1910

Currie, C., 1 Test, 1903

D'Alton, G., 1 Test, 1933

Daneel, G.M., 8 Tests, 1928-31-32

Daneel, H.J., 4 Tests, 1906

Dannhauser, G., 1951/52T

Davison, P.M., 1 Test, 1910

De Bruyn, J., 1 Test, 1974

De Jongh, H.P.K., 1 Test, 1928

De Klerk, I.J., 3 Tests, 1969-70

De Klerk, K.B.H., 13 Tests,
    1974-75-76-80-81

De Kock, A.N., 1 Test, 1891

De Kock, J.S., 2 Tests, 1921-24

De Melker, S.C., 2 Tests, 1903-06

De Nysschen, C.J., 1956T

De Villiers, D.I., 3 Tests, 1910

De Villiers, D.J.,* 25 Tests,
    1962-65-67-68-69-70

De Villiers, H.A., 3 Tests, 1906

De Villiers, H.O., 14 Tests,
    1967-68-69-70

De Villiers, I.B., 1921T

De Villiers, P duP., 8 Tests,
    1928-32-33-37

De Vos, D.J.J., 3 Tests, 1965-69

De Waal, A.N., 4 Tests, 1967

De Waal, P.J., 1 Test, 1896

De Wet, A.E., 3 Tests, 1969

De Wet, P.J., 3 Tests, 1938

De Wilzem, C.J., 1956T

Delaney, E.T.A., 1912/13T

Delport, W.H., 9 Tests, 1951-52-53

Devenish, C.E., 1 Test, 1896

Devenish, G.E., 1 Test, 1891

Devenish, G.StL., 1 Test, 1896

Devine, D., 2 Tests, 1924-28

Dinkelmann, E.E., 1951-52-53

Dirksen, C.W., 10 Tests,
    1963-64-65-67-68

Dobbin, F.J.,* 9 Tests, 1903-06-10-12

Dobie, J.A.R., 1 Test, 1928

Dold, J.B., 1931/32T

Dormehl, P.J., 2 Tests, 1896

Douglass, F.W., 1 Test, 1896

Dryburgh, R.G.,* 8 Tests, 1955-56-60

Du Plessis, C.J., 12 Tests,
    1982-84-86-89

Du Plessis, D.C., 2 Tests, 1977-80

Du Plessis, F.,* 3 Tests, 1949

Du Plessis, M.,* 22 Tests,
    1971-74-75-76-77-80

Du Plessis, M.J., 8 Tests, 1984-86-89

Du Plessis, N.J., 5 Tests, 1921-24

Du Plessis, P.G., 1 Test, 1972

Du Plessis, T.D., 2 Tests, 1980

Du Plessis, W., 14 Tests, 1980-81-82

Du Plooy, A.J.J., 1 Test, 1955

Du Preez, F.C.H., 38 Tests,
    1961-62-63-64-65-67-68-69-70-71

Du Preez, J.G.H., 1 Test, 1956

Du Rand, J.A.,* 21 Tests,
    1949-51-52-53-55-56

Du Toit, A.F., 2 Tests, 1928

Du Toit, B.A., 3 Tests, 1938

Du Toit, P.A., 8 Tests, 1949-51-52

Du Toit, P.G., 5 Tests, 1981-82-84

Du Toit, P.S., 14 Tests, 1958-60-61

Du Toit, S.R., 1931/32T

Duff, B.R., 3 Tests, 1891

Duffy, B.A.A., 1 Test, 1928

Durand, P.J., 1969/70T

Duvenage, F.P., 2 Tests, 1949

Edwards, P., 2 Tests, 1980

Ellis, J.H., 38 Tests,
   1965-67-68-69-70-71-72-74-76

Ellis, M.C., 6 Tests, 1921-24

Engelbrecht, J.P., 33 Tests,
   1960-61-62-63-64-65-67-68-69

Erasmus, F.S., 3 Tests, 1986-89

Etlinger, T.E., 1 Test, 1896

Ferreira, C., 2 Tests, 1986

Ferreira, P.S., 2 Tests, 1984

Ferris, H.H., 1 Test 1903

Forbes, H.H., 1 Test 1896

Forrest, H.M., 1931/32T

Fourie, C., 4 Tests, 1974-75

Fourie, T.T., 1 Test, 1974

Fourie, W.L., 2 Tests, 1958

Francis, J.A.J., 5 Tests, 1912-13

Francis, M.G., 1931/32T

Frederickson, C.A., 3 Tests, 1974-80

Frew, A.,* 1 Test, 1903

Froneman, D.C., 1 Test, 1977

Froneman, I.L., 1 Test, 1933

Fry, D.J., 1951/52T

Fry, S.P.,* 13 Tests, 1951-52-53-55

Gage, J.H., 1 Test, 1933

Gainsford, J.L., 33 Tests,
   1960-61-62-63-64-65-67

Geel, P.J., 1 Test, 1949

Geere, V., 5 Tests, 1933

Geffin, A.O., 7 Tests, 1949-51

Geldenhuys, S.B., 7 Tests, 1981-82-89

Gentles, T.A., 1955-56-58

Geraghty, E.M., 1 Test, 1949

Gerber, D.M., 24 Tests,
   1980-81-82-84-86-92

Gerber, M.C., 3 Tests, 1958-60

Gericke, F.W., 1 Test, 1960

Germishuys, J.S., 20 Tests,
   1974-76-77-80-81

Gibbs, E.A.H., 1 Test, 1903

Goosen, C.P., 1 Test, 1965

Gorton, H.C., 1 Test, 1896

Gould, R.L., 4 Tests, 1968

Gray, B.G., 4 Tests, 1931-32-33

Greenwood, C.M., 1 Test, 1961

Greyling, P.J.F.,* 25 Tests,
   1967-68-69-70-71-72

Grobler, C.J., 3 Tests, 1974-75

Grobler, R.N., 1969/70T

Guthrie, F.E.H., 3 Tests, 1891-96

Hahn, C.H.L., 3 Tests, 1910

Hamilton, G.H., 1 Test, 1891

Hanekom, M.vdS., 1956T

Harris, T.A., 5 Tests, 1937-38

Hartley, A.J., 1 Test, 1891

Hattingh, L.B., 1 Test, 1933

Heatlie, B.H.,* 6 Tests, 1891-96-1903

Hepburn, T.B., 1 Test, 1896

Heunis, J.W., 14 Tests,
   1981-82-84-86-89

Hill, R.A., 7 Tests, 1960-61-62-63

Hirsch, J.G., 2 Tests, 1906-10

Hobson, T.E.C., 1 Test, 1903

Hoffman, R.S., 1 Test, 1953

Hofmeyr, S.R., 1937T

Holton, D.N., 1 Test, 1960

Hopwood, D.J., 22 Tests,
   1960-61-62-63-64-65

Howe, B.F., 2 Tests, 1956

Howe-Browne, N.R.F.G., 3 Tests, 1910

Hugo, D.P., 2 Tests, 1989

Immelman, J.H., 1 Test, 1913

Jackson, D.C., 3 Tests, 1906

Jackson, J.S., 1 Test, 1903

Janse van Rensburg, M.C., 1969/70T

Jansen, E., 1 Test, 1981

Jansen, J.S., 10 Tests, 1970-71-72

Janson, A., 1965T

Jennings, C.B., 1 Test, 1937

Jennings, M.W., 1969/70T

Johns, R.G., 1960/61T

Johnstone, P.G.A., 9 Tests, 1951-52-56

Jones, C.H., 2 Tests, 1903

Jones, P.S.T., 3 Tests, 1896

Jordaan, R.P., 4 Tests, 1949

Joubert, A.J., 34 Tests,
    1989-93-94-95-96-97

Joubert, S.J., 3 Tests, 1906

Kahts, W.J.H., 11 Tests, 1980-81-82

Kaminer, J., 1 Test, 1958

Keevy, A.C., 1951/52T

Kelly, E.W., 1 Test, 1896

Kenyon, B.J.,* 1 Test, 1949

Kipling, H.G., 9 Tests, 1931-32-33

Kirkpatrick, A.I., 13 Tests,
    1953-56-58-60-61

Knight, A.S., 5 Tests, 1912-13

Knoetze, F., 2 Tests, 1989

Koch, A.C., 22 Tests,
    1949-51-52-53-55-56-58-60

Koch, H.V., 4 Tests, 1949

Kotzé, G.J.M., 4 Tests, 1967

Krantz, E.F.W., 2 Tests, 1976-81

Krige, J.D., 5 Tests 1903-06

Krige, W.A., 1912/13T

Kritzinger, J.L., 7 Tests, 1974-75-76

Kroon, C.M., 1 Test, 1955

Kruger, P.E., 2 Tests, 1986

Krüger, T.L., 8 Tests, 1921-24-28

Kuhn, S.P., 19 Tests, 1960-61-62-63-65

La Grange, J.B., 2 Tests, 1924

Larard, A., 2 Tests, 1896

Lategan, M.T., 11 Tests,
    1949-51-52-53

Lawless, M.J., 4 Tests, 1964-69-70

Lawton, A.D., 1937T

Le Roux, J.S.R., 1906/07T

Le Roux, M., 8 Tests, 1980-81

Le Roux, P.A., 3 Tests, 1906

Ledger, S.H., 4 Tests, 1912-13

Little, E.M., 2 Tests, 1891

Lochner, G.P. (Butch), 9 Tests,
    1955-56-58

Lochner, G.P. (Flappie), 3 Tests,
    1937-38

Lockyear, R.J., 6 Tests, 1960-61

Lombard, A.C., 1 Test, 1910

Lotz, J.W., 8 Tests, 1937-38

Loubser, J.A., 7 Tests, 1903-06-10

Lourens, M.J., 3 Tests, 1968

Louw, J.S., 3 Tests, 1891

Louw, L.H., 1912/13T

Louw, M.J., 2 Tests, 1971

Louw, M.M., 18 Tests,
    1928-31-32-33-37-38

Louw, R.J., 19 Tests, 1980-81-82-84

Louw, S.C., 12 Tests, 1933-37-38

Luyt, F.P., 7 Tests, 1910-12-13

Luyt, J.D., 4 Tests, 1912-13

Luyt, R.R., 7 Tests, 1910-12-13

Lyons, D.J., 1 Test, 1896

Lyster, P.J., 3 Tests, 1933-37

Macdonald, A.W., 5 Tests, 1965

MacDonald, D.A., 1 Test, 1974

Malan, A.S.,* 16 Tests,
    1960-61-62-63-64-65

Malan, A.W., 7 Tests, 1989-92

Malan, E., 2 Tests, 1980

Malan, G.F.,* 18 Tests,
    1958-1960-61-62-63-64-65

Malan, P., 1 Test, 1949

Mallett, N.V.H., 2 Tests, 1984

Mans, W.J., 2 Tests, 1965

Marais, F.P., 5 Tests, 1949-51-53

Marais, J.F.K.,* 35 Tests,
    1963-64-65-68-69-70-71-74

Marais, J.H., 1981T

Maré, D.S., 1 Test, 1906

Marsberg, A.F.W., 3 Tests, 1906

Marsberg, P.A., 1 Test, 1910

Martheze, W.C., 3 Tests, 1903-06

Martin, H.J., 1 Test, 1937

McCallum, I.D., 11 Tests, 1970-71-74

McCallum, R.J., 1 Test, 1974

McCulloch, J.D., 2 Tests, 1913

McDonald, J.A.J., 4 Tests, 1931-32

McEwan, W.M.C., 2 Tests, 1903

McHardy, E.E., 5 Tests, 1912-13

McKendrick, J.A., 1 Test, 1891

Meintjes, J.J., 1912/13T

Mellet, T.B., 1 Test, 1896

Mellish, F.W., 6 Tests, 1921-24

Menter, M.A., 1968T

Merry, G.A., 1 Test, 1891

Metcalf, H.D., 1 Test 1903

Meyer, C.duP., 3 Tests, 1921

Meyer, P.J., 1 Test, 1896

Michau, J.M., 1 Test, 1921

Michau, J.P., 3 Tests, 1921

Millar, W.A.,* 6 Tests, 1906-10-12-13

Mills, W.J., 1 Test, 1910

Moll, T.M., 1 Test, 1910

Montini, P.E., 2 Tests, 1956

Moolman, L.C., 24 Tests,
    1977-80-81-82-84-86

Mordt, R.H., 18 Tests, 1980-81-82-84

Morkel, D.F.T.,* 9 Tests,
    1906-10-12-13

Morkel, D.J.A., 1 Test, 1903

Morkel, H.J.L., 1 Test, 1921

Morkel, H.W., 2 Tests, 1921

Morkel, J.A., 2 Tests, 1921

Morkel, J.W.H., 5 Tests, 1912-13

Morkel, P.G., 8 Tests, 1912-13-21

Morkel, P.K., 1 Test, 1928

Morkel, W.H.,* 9 Tests,
    1910-12-13-21

Morkel, W.S., 4 Tests, 1906

Moss, C., 4 Tests, 1949

Mostert, P.J.,* 14 Tests,
    1921-24-28-31-32

Mulder, C.G., 1965T

Müller, G.H., 14 Tests,
    1969-70-71-72-74

Müller, H.L., 2 Tests, 1986-89

Muller, H.S.V.,* 13 Tests,
    1949-51-52-53

Myburgh, B., 1951/52T

Myburgh, F.R.,* 1 Test, 1896

Myburgh, J.L., 18 Tests,
    1962-63-64-68-69-70

Myburgh, W.H., 1 Test, 1924

Naudé, J.P., 14 Tests, 1963-65-67-68

Neethling, J.B., 8 Tests, 1967-68-69-70

Neill, W.A., 1906/07T

Nel, J.A., 11 Tests, 1960-63-65-70

Nel, J.J., 8 Tests, 1956-58

Nel, P.A.R.O., 3 Tests, 1903

Nel, P.J.,* 16 Tests, 1928-31-32-33-37

Nijkamp, J.L., 1 Test, 1933

Nimb, C.F., 1 Test, 1961

Nomis, S.H., 25 Tests,
    1967-68-69-70-71-72

Ochse, J.K., 7 Tests, 1951-52-53

Oelofse, J.S.A., 4 Tests, 1953

Oliver, J.F., 2 Tests, 1928

Olivier, E., 16 Tests, 1967-68-69

Olivier, J.S., 1921T

Olver, E., 1 Test, 1896

Oosthuizen, J.J., 9 Tests, 1974-75-76

Oosthuizen, O.W., 9 Tests, 1981-82-84

Osler, B.L.,* 17 Tests,
    1924-28-31-32-33

Osler, S.G., 1 Test, 1928

Oxlee, K., 19 Tests,
    1960-61-62-63-64-65

Parker, W.H., 2 Tests, 1965

Partridge, J.E.C., 1 Test, 1903

Payn, C., 2 Tests, 1924

Pelser, H.J.M., 11 Tests, 1958-60-61

Pfaff, B.D., 1 Test, 1956

Pickard, J.A.J., 4 Tests, 1953-56-58

Pienaar, T.B.,* 1921T

Pienaar, Z.M.J., 13 Tests, 1980-81

Pitzer, G., 12 Tests, 1967-68-69

Pope, C.F., 9 Tests, 1974-75-76

Potgieter, H.J., 2 Tests, 1928

Potgieter, H.L., 1 Test, 1977

Potgieter, R., 1969/70T

Povey, S.A., 1981T

Powell, A.W., 1 Test, 1896

Powell, J.M.,* 4 Tests, 1891-96-1903

Prentis, R.B., 11 Tests, 1980-81

Pretorius, N.F., 4 Tests, 1928

Prinsloo, J., 1 Test, 1963

Prinsloo, J.C., 2 Tests, 1958

Prinsloo, J.P., 1 Test, 1928

Putter, D.J., 3 Tests, 1963

Raaff, J.W.E., 6 Tests, 1903-06-10

Ras, W.J.deW., 2 Tests, 1976-80

Reid, A., 1 Test, 1903

Reid, B.C., 1 Test, 1933

Reid, H.G., 1906/07T

Reinach, J., 4 Tests, 1986

Rens, I.J., 2 Tests, 1953

Retief, D.F., 9 Tests, 1955-56

Reyneke, H.J., 1 Test, 1910

Richards, A.R.,* 3 Tests, 1891

Riley, N.M., 1 Test, 1963

Riordan, C.A., 2 Tests, 1910

Robertson, I.W., 5 Tests, 1974-76

Rodgers, P.H., 5 Tests, 1989-92

Rogers, C.D., 4 Tests, 1984

Roos, G.D., 2 Tests, 1910

Roos, P.J.,* 4 Tests, 1903-06

Rosenberg, W., 5 Tests, 1955-56-58

Rossouw, D.H., 2 Tests, 1953

Rousseau, W.P., 2 Tests, 1928

Roux, F.duT., 27 Tests,
    1960-61-62-63-65-68-69-70

Roux, O.A., 7 Tests, 1969-70-72-74

Samuels, T.A., 3 Tests, 1896

Sauermann, J.T., 5 Tests, 1971-72-74

Saunders, M.J., 1951-52T

Schlebusch, J.J.J., 3 Tests, 1974-75

Schmidt, L.U., 2 Tests, 1958-62

Schmidt, U.L., 17 Tests, 1986-89-92-93-94

Schoeman, J., 7 Tests, 1963-65

Scholtz, H., 2 Tests, 1921

Scott, P.A., 4 Tests, 1896

Sendin, W.D., 1 Test, 1921

Serfontein, D.J.,* 19 Tests, 1980-81-82-84

Shand, R., 2 Tests, 1891

Sheriff, A.R., 3 Tests, 1938

Shum, E.H., 1 Test, 1913

Siedle, L.B., 1921T

Sinclair, D.J., 4 Tests, 1955

Sinclair, J.H., 1 Test, 1903

Skene, A.L., 1 Test, 1958

Slabber, L.J., 1965T

Slater, J.T., 3 Tests, 1924-28

Smal, G.P., 6 Tests, 1986-89

Smith, C.M.,* 7 Tests, 1963-64-65

Smith, C.W., 3 Tests, 1891-96

Smith, D.J., 4 Tests, 1980

Smith, D.W., 1 Test, 1891

Smith, G.A.C., 1 Test, 1938

Smollan, F.C., 3 Tests, 1933

Snedden, R.C.D.,* 1 Test, 1891

Snyman, D.S.L., 10 Tests, 1972-74-75-76-77

Snyman, J.C.P., 3 Tests, 1974

Sonnekus, G.H.H., 3 Tests, 1974-84

Spies, J.J., 4 Tests, 1970

Stander, J.C.J., 5 Tests, 1974-76

Stapelberg, W.P., 2 Tests, 1974

Starke, J.J., 1 Test, 1956

Starke, K.T., 4 Tests, 1924

Steenekamp, J., 1 Test, 1958

Stegmann, A.C., 2 Tests, 1906

Stegmann, J.A., 5 Tests, 1912-13

Stewart, D.A., 11 Tests, 1960-61-63-64-65

Stofberg, M.T.S.,* 21 Tests, 1976-77-80-81-82-84

Strachan, L.C., 10 Tests, 1932-37-38

Strauss, J.A., 2 Tests, 1984

Strauss, J.H.P., 3 Tests, 1976-80

Strauss, S.S.F., 1 Test, 1921

Strydom, C.F., 6 Tests, 1955-56-58

Strydom, L.J., 2 Tests, 1949

Suter, M.R., 2 Tests, 1965

Swanson, P.S., 1971T

Swart, J.J.N., 1 Test, 1955

Taberer, W.S., 1 Test 1896

Taylor, O.B., 1 Test, 1962

Theunissen, D.J., 1 Test, 1896

Thompson, G., 3 Tests, 1912

Tindall, J.C., 5 Tests, 1924-28

Tobias, E.G., 6 Tests, 1981-84

Tod, N.S., 1 Test, 1928

Townsend, W.H., 1 Test, 1921

Trenery, W.E., 1 Test, 1891

Truter, D.R., 2 Tests, 1924

Truter, J.T., 3 Tests, 1963-64-65

Turner, F.G., 11 Tests, 1933-37-38

Twigge, R.J., 1 Test, 1960

Ulyate, C.A., 7 Tests, 1955-56

Vivier, S.S.,* 5 Tests, 1956

Vogel, M.L., 1 Test 1974

Wagenaar, C., 1 Test, 1977

Wahl, J.J., 1 Test, 1949

Walker, A.P., 6 Tests, 1921-24

Walker, H.N., 4 Tests, 1953-56

Walker, H.W., 3 Tests, 1910

Walton, D.C., 8 Tests, 1964-65-69

Waring, F.W., 7 Tests, 1931-32-33

Watt, H.H., 1937T

Weepner, J.S., 1921T

Wentzel, G.J., 1960/61T

Wessels, J.J., 3 Tests, 1896

Wessels, J.W., 1965T

Wessels, P.W., 1951/52T

Whipp, P.J.M., 8 Tests, 1974-75-76-80

White, J., 10 Tests, 1931-33-37

Williams, A.E., 1 Test, 1910

Williams, A.P., 2 Tests, 1984

Williams, D.O., 8 Tests, 1937-38

Williams, J.G., 13 Tests, 1971-72-74-76

Wilson, L.G., 27 Tests, 1960-61-62-63-64-65

Wolmarans, B.J., 1 Test, 1977

Wrentmore, G.M., 1912/13T

Wright, G.D., 7 Tests, 1986-89-92

Wyness, M.R.K., 5 Tests, 1962-63

Zeller, W.C., 2 Tests, 1921

Zimerman, M., 4 Tests, 1931-32

The SA Coloured Rugby Football Board/SA Rugby Union representatives 1939–91

The non-racial SA Coloured Rugby Football Board was formed in 1897. The first national team to be selected toured internally in 1939. Tests were played from 1950 against the SA African Rugby Board and one match in 1964 against the SA Rugby Football Federation. The SA Coloured Rugby Football Board dropped its racial designation in 1966 and became the SA Rugby Union (SARU). It later questioned the playing of ethnic Tests, and from 1971 was committed to non-racial rugby. Representative SARU teams played high-profile matches against invitation sides (1974, 1978), President's XV (1982) and regional sides (1984–91).

The following were selected for the SA Coloured Rugby Football Board/SARU on internal tours, as well as internal Tests and representative matches. The list includes those players who withdrew from the 1939 tour ('Tw') and those selected for the cancelled Non-European Rugby Football Federation 1953 tour ('TFed'):

Abed, A., 1950

Abed, G.H., 1957-59

Abrahams, Abdullah, 1974

Abrahams, A (Ghapa), 1968

Abrahams, A (Manie), 1961-63-67

Abrahams, F., 1967

Abrahams, Y., 1968

Adams, A., 1939T

Adams, D., 1965-67-68

Adams, F., 1989

Adams, T., 1987-90-91

Adonis, P., 1961

Agherdien, M., 1950-52

Alexander, I., 1957

Allen, R., 1982

Almacien, G., 1939T

Amsterdam, F., 1987-88-89-90

Appolis, S., 1939T

April, R., 1970

Arendse, A.J., 1986

Arendse, D., 1978

Arendse, I.E., 1964

Arendse, J., 1991

Arnold, J., 1987-88-89

Astrie, Z., 1969

Avery, E., 1968

Aysen, A., 1961

Baderoen, I., 1974

Barends, D., 1970

Basson, W.H., 1951

Baster, S., 1951

Bergins, T., 1965

Blanchard, A., 1961

Bohardien, I.,* 1951-52-53TFed-57-59

Booi, P., 1982

Booley, S., 1991

Booysen, D., 1968

Booysen, D.W., 1982-84-85-86-87

Booysen, J., 1990-91

Booysen, N., 1968

Booysen, S., 1939T

Booysens, V., 1967

Boshoff, G., 1984-85-86-87-89

Botha, L., 1988

Botha, M.G., 1939Tw

Bouwers, R., 1957

Britton, R.T., 1987-88-89-90

Brown, C., 1989

Brown, E., 1939T

Bruiners, J., 1968

Burger, R., 1963

Carelse, E., 1969

Carelse, L., 1965

Carolus, R., 1957-59-61

Caster, A., 1939T

Charles, I., 1952-53TFed

Clarke, E., 1950

Cloete, V., 1952

Coerecius, A.J., 1952

Coetzee, A.,* 1985-87-88-89-90-91

Croy, R., 1987

Croy, W.J., 1989

Crozier, P., 1957

Cupido, T., 1939T

Daniels, H.M.,* 1950-51-52-53TFed

Daniels, N., 1959

Daniels, O., 1982-84

Davids, F., 1987-88-89

Davids, G., 1978

Davids, I.A., 1950

Davids, T., 1939T

Davids, Y., 1969

Dean, T., 1986

De Bique, K., 1989

De Doncker, B., 1965-67

De Kock, E., 1952

De Koker, F., 1986-87

Deysel, E., 1982

Diedericks, C., 1970

Doman, J., 1970

Du Plessis, N., 1965

Easthorpe, K., 1963

Ebden, A.H., 1939T

Edwards, G.J., 1961-68

Erasmus, F.L.,* 1950

Felix, A.P., 1985

Francis, A., 1963

Fredericks, F.J., 1959-61

Fredericks, M.S.,*
   1963-64-65-67-68-69-70-74

Freeman, A.J., 1939T

Frieslaar, I., 1963-64

Gaffoor, P., 1959-61

Ganief, E ('Oogies'), 1963-64

Ganief, E (Ebrahim), 1986-87-89

Gelderbloem, B., 1964

George, A., 1967

Goetham, J.M., 1939T

Goetham, L.S., 1939T

Goliath, S., 1968

Goodford, W., 1963

Grove, N., 1978

Hancke, M., 1990

Hendricks, F., 1986-87-88

Hendricks, G., 1984

Hendricks, H., 1984-85

Hendricks, R., 1991

Hermanus, A.R., 1951-52-53TFed

Hoosain, I., 1964

Hopley, P., 1950-51

Hopley, S., 1939T

Howell, M., 1959-61

Irwin, P., 1959-61

Irwin, R., 1959

Isaacs, N., 1990

Isaacs, S.V., 1989-90

Jabaar, C., 1969-74

Jack, M., 1986-87

Jacobs, A., 1939T

Jacobs, B., 1968

Jacobs, D.H., 1963-64

Jacobs, I., 1988-89-91

Jacobs, S., 1950

Jansen, P., 1982-85

Jansen, G., 1990

January, C., 1974

Jardine, G., 1965

Jephta, J., 1951

Jeposa, J.P., 1974

Job, C., 1965

Johannes, J., 1952

Jonkers, R., 1967-69

Jooste, P.,* 1978-82-84-85

Joseph, T., 1991

Josephs, D., 1951-52

Josephs, K., 1987-89

Julie, B., 1986

Julius, A.J.J., 1939T

Julius, C.J., 1939T-51-52-53TFed

Julius, H.J.G., 1950

Kamaar, Y., 1974

Kannemeyer, Y., 1951

Kayster, V., 1985

Kearns, L.C., 1952

Kennedy, N., 1987

Khan, G.N., 1959

Khan, I., 1984-85

Kiewietz, I.W., 1939T

Killian, R., 1969

Kinnear, J., 1939T

Kleinbooi, C.P., 1982-84-85

Kobesi, T., 1990-91

Kondile, T., 1984-90

Konstable, H., 1974

Korkee, R., 1984-86-87-89

Kramer, D.R., 1978-82

Kruger, H.O.,* 1952-53TFed

Kruger, J., 1952-59-61-64-65

Kruger, P., 1991

Kwini, A.S., 1991

Lamani, G., 1984-85

Lentoor, K., 1969-70

Lewis, A., 1950-51-53TFed

Loots, J., 1968

Lottering, V., 1968

Lourens, P., 1982

Louw, A., 1989-90

Louw, Y., 1967-68

Ludwaba, T., 1974-78

Mafeking, J., 1963

Majiet, A., 1987-89-90

Malghas, R., 1950

Mange, L., 1988

Manual, A., 1967

Manual, C., 1987

Marinus, R.L.,* 1978-84-85

Marinus, V., 1939Tw

Marquard, F.E., 1939T

Matthews, L., 1951

Mawing, S.K.,* 1957-59-61

May, J., 1968

Mbula, B., 1984

Mbula, M., 1978

McBride, J., 1991

Mettler, C., 1970

Meyer, M.G., 1959-61

Meyer, T., 1957

Mkata, P.X., 1974-78

Mkele, A., 1978

Moerat, N., 1985

Moore, E., 1951

Morkel, C., 1968-70

Moses, J., 1967-68-69-70

Mouton, M.D., 1967

Mtya, T., 1991

Mulder, R., 1939T

Munnik, E., 1982

Musson, T., 1951-53TFed

Najaar, R., 1987

Napoleon, M., 1967-69-70

Neer, J., 1982

Neethling, C.I.M., 1959-65

Neethling, J.W., 1950-52-53TFed

Nel, R., 1974

Niels, J.A.,* 1939Tw

Noble, C., 1982

Noble, G., 1984-85-86-87

Noordien, C., 1987

October, I., 1984-86-87-88-89-91

Oliphant, G., 1984-85

Oliphant, M., 1968

Olivier, P., 1939T

Ontong, J., 1987-88-89

Ontong, T., 1964

Padiachy, A., 1939Tw

Peters, G., 1968

Petersen, B., 1989-90

Petersen, C., 1978

Petersen, V.,* 1964-65-67

Philander, M., 1939T

Phillips, L., 1961-65

Phillips, W., 1957-64

Pieterse, W.,* 1965-67-69-70

Pietersen, F., 1939T

Pillay, A., 1968

Plaatjies, M., 1968

Poggenpoel, A., 1974

Poggenpoel, R., 1950

Pretorius, A., 1961-65-68-70

Pretorius, P.J., 1963

Pretorius, S., 1970

Prins, C., 1952

Prins, S., 1965

Raubenheimer, V., 1984-85

Rhoda, A., 1968

Rigney, F., 1957-59

Rinquest, E.,* 1957-59-61-63-64-65

Rooiland, J., 1969

Ruiters, S., 1951-52

Runelli, J., 1987-88

Saaid, C., 1950-51

Saaid, E., 1964-68

Säfers, I., 1961

Sakier, Y., 1987-88

Salie, A., 1957-59-61

Salie, F., 1967-68

Salie, G.A., 1957

Salie, H., 1963

Salie, K., 1963

Salie, S., 1991

Samaai, A., 1950

Samuels, M., 1987-88-89

Sauls, E., 1986

Schilder, F.J.C., 1939Tw

Schroeder, I., 1967

September, D., 1982

September, J., 1967

Sharpe, C., 1951-52-53TFed

Siljeur, E., 1974

Singata, N., 1974

Skinnette, D., 1957-68

Slabbert, P.J.,* 1986

Smith, D.E., 1965

Smith, J.F.,* 1982

Smith, P.D., 1952-53TFed

Smith, P., 1982

Solomons, D., 1969-70

Solomons, E., 1985

Solomons, F.,* 1987-88-89

Statu, M., 1991

Stride, S., 1978

Strydom, C., 1974

Summers, J., 1964-65

Symons, G., 1978-84-85

Taliep, A., 1959-64

Tembo, S., 1969-70

Terblanche, P., 1968

Theunissen, M., 1964-68-69-70

Thomas, P., 1969

Thorne, G., 1985-86-87-89-90

Truskey, J., 1991

Tsotsobe, T.V., 1978

Twigg, L.H., 1969

Van Briesies, D., 1968

Van der Linde, J., 1985

Van Haaght, F., 1968

Van Heerden, A.A.,* 1961

Van Heerden, D., 1939Tw

Van Wyk, P.J., 1963-64

Viljoen, E., 1982-87-88-89

Visser, J., 1991

Walbrugh, B., 1939T

Walker, H., 1982

Walters, K., 1968

Webb, R., 1957

Williams, A., 1991

Williams, G., 1957

Wilters, W., 1991

XhoXho, N., 1978-82-84

Yeye, Z., 1986

The SA African Rugby Board/SA Rugby Association representatives 1950–78

The SA Bantu Rugby Board was formed in December 1935. Its break from the SA Coloured Rugby Football Board was an attempt to facilitate greater exposure for African players. Internal Tests were organised against the SA Coloured Rugby Football Board from 1950 and against the SA Rugby Football Federation from 1964. The governing body was reconstituted as the SA African Rugby Board and later as the SA Rugby Association. They were known as the Leopards during the 1970s, a period in which they toured overseas and played against visiting international teams. In November 1977, the SA Rugby Association and the SA Rugby Football Federation merged with the SA Rugby Football Board to form the SA Rugby Board.

The following list includes those players who represented the African governing bodies in internal Tests; toured internally in 1952; were selected for the cancelled Non-European Rugby Football Federation 1953 tour (TFed); toured overseas in 1974 (74T); and played against England (72E), Italy (73It), the British & Irish Lions (74BL), France (75F) and New Zealand (76NZ) during the 1970s. It does not include matches staged after the Test against the SA Federation on 15 July 1978, as S.A.R.A's players had become eligible for teams of the SA Rugby Board.

August, T., 1971

Bafana, M.H., 1961

Balintulo, A., 1972E-72

Bom, V., 1971

Bongco, A.S.E., 1952

Booi, K., 1974

Booi, M.H., 1959

Botha, D.N.,* 1964-65

Botha, J., 1952-63

Bukashe, M., 1965-66-67-68-69

Buti, Z., 1957

Ceko, W.S., 1959

Cona, B., 1972E-72-73It-73-74T-74-75F-75-76-76NZ

Cushe, M.S. (Stambo), 1964-65-66-67-68-69-71-72E

Cushe, M.W. (Morgan), 1971-72E-72-73It-73-74T-74BL-74-75F-75-76-76NZ

Danster, P.S.,* 1964-65-66-67-68-69

Davashe, T., 1969

Diba, W., 1972E-72-73It-73-74T-76-76NZ-77-78

Dihemo, J., 1952-52T

Dingaan, S., 1950

Dlambulo, E., 1957-59

Dlula, A., 1951-52-52T-53TFed

Dolomba, K.J., 1971-72-73It-74T

Doyi, J., 1972

Duru, M., 1964

Dweba, M., 1966

Dwesi, A.L., 1952-52T

Einunana, F., 1952T

Fani, W.M., 1970-71

Fesi, C.M., 1969-71-72

Gaushe, F., 1951

Gawulana, D., 1974

Gawulayo, G., 1973-74T-74-75F-76

Gcebe, C., 1974-75

Giladile, R.M., 1965-66-67-74T

Gqweni, P., 1966

Gwazula, C., 1973

Headbush, S.D.,* 1963-64-65-66-67

Hfiwana, B., 1952T

Hini, E.S., 1950-59

Hini, M., 1951

Homojlapi, K., 1952T

Jacobs, P., 1969

Jacobs, W Major, 1971-72E-72-73It-74T

Jacobs, Wilfred S., 1967

Jali, S.B., 1961

Jikwana, S., 1973It-73-74T

Jonas, L.L., 1972-76-76NZ-77

Jonas, W., 1970

Kakana, J., 1977

Keli, X., 1974

Ketelo, H.,* 1971-72-73It-73-74Tw-75F

Khomo, G.A.,* 1950-51-52-52T

Khovu, W., 1968

Klaas, H.T., 1973-74-75F-75-76-77-78

Koboka, S., 1951

Kobora, R., 1952T

Kohlela, L.R., 1970

Koka, F.N., 1950-51

Kona, P., 1963-64-65-68-69

Kondile, D., 1957

Konki, S.T., 1975F-75-76-76NZ-77-78

Kota, R.M., 1950-51

Kwalase, S., 1975

Lebakeng, H.C., 1961

Leeuw, C.T., 1959

Liwani, E., 1968

Lonzi, D.N., 1965

Lubambo, P., 1963-67-70

Lubelwana, W., 1967

Lusizi, G.L., 1951-52-52T

Lzirs, M., 1952T

Madikane, H.M., 1957-59-61-63-66

Madlingozi, P., 1965-66

Maduba, R., 1951-52-52T-53TFed

Magadlela, A., 1968

Magenuka, V., 1978

Magugu, B., 1977-78

Magxala, S.T.,* 1967-68-69-70-71-72E-72-73It-73-74T-74BL-74-75F-75-76-76NZ-77

Mahote, T.S., 1964-65-66

Majola, E.K., 1959-61

Majola, T., 1970

Makhosi, W., 1970

Makwabe, M., 1975F

Malamba, B.N., 1950-51-52-52T

Mamba, B., 1957

Mandla, B., 1963

Mandla, M., 1969

Maneli, S., 1968

Maqanda, L.S., 1959

Maqosha, M., 1973-74T-74BL-74

Mashiqana, G.M., 1961-69

Matakata, O.Q., 1959

Mati, P., 1951

Matolengwe, S., 1968

Matomela, M., 1971-72E-72-73It-73-74T-74BL-76-76NZ

Matomela, Z.S., 1975-77

Matshikiza, G.S., 1952-52T

Matyeshana, P., 1973It-73-74T-74BL-74-75-76

Maweni, B., 1972E-72-73It-74T-76-76NZ

Mayekiso, D.J., 1964-65-66-67-68-69

Mbane, D.,* 1950-51-52-52T-53TFed

Mbelekane, V.L., 1952

Mbiko, N.M.,* 1966-67-69-71-72E-73It-74T-74BL-74-75-76-76NZ-78

Mbiko, W., 1971

Mbilini, P., 1963-66

Mbize, J.M., 1959-61-63-64-65

McDonald, S., 1959-61

Mdlalo, T.M.,* 1964-65

Mdodana, P., 1967-68-69

Meleni, S.W., 1977

Memese, I., 1977-78

Memsanga, T.N., 1952T

Mgweba, C.M., 1974T-74BL-74-75-76

Mhlaba, S.Z., 1978

Mhlakaza, B., 1967

Mhlakaza, T.N., 1967-68

Mhlawuli, M., 1957-59

Mjo, S.C., 1959-61

Mjuleni, T., 1968

Mkata, P.X., 1965-66-67-68-69-70

Mkonto, B., 1969

Mkonto, M., 1973

Mnqatu, M., 1976-76NZ

Mnqatu, V.E., 1973It-73-74T-74BL-74-75F-75-76

Mnyazi, K.B., 1973-74T-74BL-74

Mnyute, G., 1950

Mnyute, L., 1965-66

Modikoe, W., 1968

Mokhele, E., 1974-75F-76-77-78

Molose, K., 1977

Mona, G., 1952T

Monononyane, D., 1968-69

Mpehle, M., 1952

Mqai, J., 1966

Mquteni, S., 1971

Mtila, J., 1974-76-76NZ

Mtimkulu, T., 1951-52T

Mtwazi, M., 1965

Mtyeku, F.J.,* 1961

Mtyongwe, W.N., 1976-76NZ-78

Myeki, J., 1969

Mzanywa, L.S., 1964-65-66

Nakani, V., 1974T-74BL-74-75F-75-76-76NZ

Ncate, S.S., 1978

Ncunyana, P.R., 1957-63

Ndaba, L., 1965

Ndzala, M., 1968-69-70-71-72E-72-73It-73-76-76NZ

Ngatu, W., 1969

Ngoma, S., 1965

Ngotsi, W., 1965

Ngxila, C.W., 1967-68-69

Njadu, D.M., 1972

Njengele, H.N., 1950-51-52T-53TFed

Njikelana, V., 1969

Nkohla, B.J.,* 1968-69-70

Nkwandla, O.,* 1967-68-69-71-72E

Nojoko, X., 1974

Nomo, J., 1961-63

Nonganga, N., 1951-57

Noqholi, G., 1951-52-52T-53TFed-57

Nqontsi, W., 1963-64-65

Ntlanjeni, M., 1977

Ntshepe, D.S., 1950-51-52-52T-53TFed

Ntshinga, N., 1957

Ntshiyane, T., 1975

Ntshongwana, M.,* 1972-74T-74BL-74-75F-75

Nyakati, M., 1975F

Nyamakazi, J.,* 1959

Oliphant, S., 1964-65-66-68-69

Pandle, W., 1950-51-52-52T-53TFed

Pantsi, S., 1967

Peter, E., 1951

Phajare, M., 1952T

Phillips, B., 1961

Plaatjie, R.N., 1959

Pondo, J., 1972

Qina, M., 1966

Rala, S., 1976

Rula, E., 1959-61

Scott, G., 1963-67

September, J.B., 1970

Sgwanda, C., 1966-67-68-69-72E

Shiyani, V., 1967-69-70

Sigwabe, L.M., 1977

Singapi, M.N.,* 1952-52T-57-59

Singatha, N., 1970

Sithebe, L., 1968

Sizani, N.T., 1952T-52-53TFed-57

Skunana, F., 1950-51-52

Sobhizana, S., 1957

Soga, M., 1959

Sokutu, S.C., 1957-63-69

Solomon, D.M., 1969

Solomon, L.L., 1974-75

Songongo, C., 1972E-72

Sonjani, V., 1969-70-74BL-74-75F-75-76

Sonto, B., 1976-77-78

Sonto, V., 1976-77-78

Sontshi, B., 1967-68-69-71

Sontshi, L., 1951

Speelman, W., 1977

Stemele, B.R., 1977

Swartz, P.P., 1973-74T-74BL-76

Takayi, A.S., 1972-74T-74BL-74

Thiso, J.H., 1964-65

Tsendze, A.B., 1950

Tshingane, Z., 1968

Tsotsobe, T.V., 1973It-73-74T-74BL-74-75F-75-76-76NZ

Twaku, C.M., 1961-63

Tyesi, W., 1952-52T

Vabaza, M., 1950-51
Valval, D., 1964-65-66
Vellem, T., 1978
Wani, S.J., 1972E-72-74T-76
Williams, R., 1952T-52

Xotyeni, W., 1967-68-70-72-73-74T
Yako, M., 1970
Yengeni, N., 1977-78
Zinto, M.C., 1950-51-52-52T-53TFed

SA Rugby Football Federation representatives 1959–78

In 1959, the Western Province Rugby League was the driving force behind a further split from the SA Coloured Rugby Football Board. The breakaway SA Rugby Football Federation formed in 1959 provided a fourth national 'Test' team. They played internal Tests against the SA Africans and one match against the SA Coloured Rugby Football Board. Their association with the SA Rugby Football Board created opportunities to tour overseas in 1971 and play against visiting international teams. In 1977, they joined the SA Rugby Association and the SA Rugby Football Board in forming the SA Rugby Board.

The following list includes the Federation's representatives in internal Tests; the 1971 overseas tour (71T), and matches against England (72E), Italy (73It), the British & Irish Lions (74BL), France (75F), New Zealand (76NZ) and Rhodesia (78R) during the 1970s. It does not include matches staged after the Test against the SA Africans on 15 July 1978, as the Federation's players had become eligible for teams representing the SA Rugby Board.

Abrahams, A., 1964
Adams, D., 1978R
Adams, V., 1971T
Adonis, J., 1978R
Adonis, W., 1966-67
Arendse, N., 1971T
Bekkers, J.K.,* 1964
Benjamin, C., 1966-67-71T-71
Boonzaier, P.,
   1971T-71-75F-75-76-76NZ-77-78R
Booysens, D., 1968
Boshoff, N., 1973
Botha, J., 1968
Botha, N., 1977
Botha, P., 1971

Brinkhuis, V., 1966-67-68
Bruintjies, S.I., 1969-70-71T-71
Consul, E., 1968
Cupido, C., 1974BL
Damons, C., 1965-66-67-68-69-70-71
Daniels, F., 1975F
Daniels, H., 1971T
Da Silva, I., 1974
Davids, C.A., 1967-68-74BL
Davids, G., 1977
Davids, N., 1975F-77-78R
Davids, O., 1966-68
Dollie, Y., 1969
Dombas, A.,* 1966-67-70-71

Dyers, D.M.,*
  1971T-72E-72-73-74BL-74
Fillies, A., 1974-78R
Fisher, M., 1969-70-71T-71
Ford, K., 1966
Fortune, G., 1966-67
Frans, E.,
  1971-72E-72-73-74BL-74-76
Gillion, E., 1976-76NZ
Gordon, H., 1971
Groepe, V., 1971T-75
Heemro, M.D., 1964-65
Hendricks, G., 1978R
Hendricks, R., 1967-68
Heyns, S., 1964-65-66-67
Hopley, P., 1967
Human, I., 1976
Humphreys, J., 1977
Hurling, D., 1966-67
Isaacs, J., 1970-71T
Jacobs, J.,* 1965
Jacobs, K., 1964
Jacobs, M., 1970-71
Jacobs, W., 1964-65-66
Jeposa, J.P., 1967-70-71
Joachims, C.J., 1964-65-66-69
Joachims, J., 1964-65
Johnson, A., 1977-78R
Jones, J., 1965
Jooste, F., 1969-72E-72-73-74-75-75F-
  76-76NZ-77
Julies, A., 1978
Juries, J.A.,* 1964-66-67-68-69-70-
  71T-71-72E-72-73-74BL-75F-75-76-
  76NZ-77-78R
Kastoor, T., 1969-71T-72E-72

Kayser, J., 1964-67
Kortjie, R., 1978
King, C., 1976
King, D., 1971T
Lategan, A., 1969-72E-72-73-74BL-
  74-75F-75-76-76NZ-77-78R
Liedeman, J.J., 1969-73-74-75F-75
Louw, R., 1975-76-76NZ-77-78R
Lyner, C., 1964
Malgas, D., 1969-71T-71
Malgas, K., 1969-70-71
Marinus, R.L., 1976-76NZ-77
Marquard, M., 1966-68-69-70-71
Martin, E., 1964-65
Mawson, R., 1974BL-74
Meyers, J.J.,
  1974BL-74-75F-75-76-76NZ-78R
Miller, A., 1964-65
Moerat, E., 1966
Moerat, I., 1968-70-71T-73
Moerat, M., 1971T-71-73-75F
Morkel, G.J., 1968
Muller, C.,* 1965-66-67-68-69-70
Noble, J., 1969-72E-72-73-74BL-74-
  75F-75-76-76NZ-78R
November, M.O., 1969-70-71-72-75F
October, J., 1978
Oliver, B., 1966-67
Ontong, J. (Joslyn), 1978
Ontong, J.A. (Hannes), 1964-65
Paarwater, J.D., 1975F-75-77-78R
Paulse, L.C., 1976NZ-76-78R
Petersen, M.S.,* 1966-67
Petersen, T.,* 1972E-72-73-74BL-74-
  75F-75-76-76NZ-77-78R

Peterson, V., 1969-74

Pheiffer, R.D., 1971T-71-72E-72-73

Prezence, B., 1966

Pullen, D., 1967

Rassool, F., 1967

Reeding, W., 1971T

Rinquest, A., 1970

Rinquest, E., 1965

Roos, I., 1969

Samuels, A., 1964-65

Samuels, G., 1968

Seconds, W., 1978R

Shields, H. (Hennie),
    1973-74BL-75-76-76NZ-78R

Shields, H.W. (Turkey),*
    1969-70-71T-71-72E-72-73-74BL-
    74-75F-75-76-76NZ-78R

Smith, J.F., 1972E-72-73-74BL-74

Stubbs, J.A., 1973-75-76-76NZ

Stuurman, P., 1971T-71

Sylvester, A., 1966

Theunissen, D., 1971T-72-73

Tobias, E.G., 1969-71T-72E-72-73-
    74BL-74-75F-77-78R

Van der Merwe, J., 1968-69-70-71-74

Vigo, G.G., 1971T-72E-72

Welman, K.M., 1968-69

Wesso, V., 1972E-72-73

Wildemans, E.W.,
    1972E-72-73-74BL-76

Williams, C.H.,
    1976-76NZ-77-78-78R

Williams, D., 1966-69

Williams, E., 1975

Williams, G., 1965

Williams, J.W., 1977-78R

Williams, W.A., 1969-74-75F

Wolhouter, R., 1969

Zimri, J., 1977

The SA Rugby Football Union/SA Rugby Union 'Springboks' 1992–2021

Unification was achieved by December 1991, and on 19 January 1992, the SA Rugby Football Union came into being. It changed its name to the SA Rugby Union in 2005.

The following represented the post-unity Springboks in international rugby. Eleven players are included for a second time as they were selected for Springbok teams before and after unity. A ruling was also introduced from 2012 that those players who represented the Springboks on tour/in a squad but did not appear in a Test would not receive a Springbok number. This ruling is denoted by 'Tx' or 'Sx'.

The details recorded are updated to the end of the series against the British and Irish Lions, 7 August 2021.

Ackerman, J.N., 13 Tests,
    1996-2001-06-07

Adams, H.J., 2009T

Adriaanse, L.C., 6 Tests, 2013-16

Aitken, A.D., 7 Tests, 1997-98

Alberts, W.S., 43 Tests,
    2010-11-12-13-14-15-16

Alcock, C.D., 1998T

Allan, J., 13 Tests, 1993-94-96

Am, L., 18 Tests, 2017-18-19-21

Andrews, E.P., 23 Tests,
    2004-05-06-07

Andrews, K.S., 9 Tests, 1992-93-94

Andrews, M.G., 77 Tests,
    1994-95-96-97-98-99-2000-01

Aplon, G.G., 17 Tests, 2010-11-12

Atherton, S., 8 Tests, 1993-94-96

Badenhorst, A.J., 2000T

Badenhorst, C., 2 Tests, 1994-95

Bands, R.E., 11 Tests, 2003

Barry, D., 39 Tests,
    2000-01-02-03-04-05-06

Bartmann, W.J., 8 Tests, 1986-92

Basson, B.A., 11 Tests, 2010-11-13

Basson, W.W., 1997T

Bekker, A., 29 Tests, 2008-09-10-12

Bekker, S., 1 Test, 1997

Bennett, R.G., 6 Tests, 1997

Bezuidenhout, C.J., 4 Tests, 2003

Bobo, G., 6 Tests, 2003-04-08

Boome, C.S., 20 Tests, 1999-2000-03

Bosch, C.D., 2 Tests, 2017-18

Boshoff, M.L., 1 Test, 2014

Bosman, H.M., 3 Tests, 2005-06

Botha, A.F., 2 Tests, 2013

Botha, B.J., 25 Tests,
    2006-07-08-09-10

Botha, G.vG., 12 Tests, 2005-07

Botha, H.E., 28 Tests,
    1980-81-82-86-89-92

Botha, J.P., 85 Tests, 2002-03-04-05-
    07-08-09-10-11-13-14

Botha, R., 2017Tx

Breedt, J.C.,* 8 Tests, 1986-89-92

Brink, R.A., 2 Tests, 1995

Brits, S.B.,* 15 Tests,
    2008-12-14-15-18-19

Britz, G.J.J., 13 Tests, 2004-05-06-07

Britz, W.K., 1 Test, 2002

Brosnihan, W.G., 6 Tests, 1997-2000

Brüssow, H.W., 23 Tests,
    2008-09-11-15

Burden, C.B., 2012Sx

Burger, S.W.P.,* 86 Tests, 2003-04-05-
    06-07-08-09-10-11-14-15

Carr, N., 5 Tests, 2014-16

Carstens, P.D., 9 Tests, 2002-06-07-09

Cassiem, U., 8 Tests, 2016-17

Chavhanga, T., 4 Tests, 2005-07-08

Cilliers, N.V., 1 Test, 1996

Cilliers, P.M., 6 Tests, 2012

Claassens, J.P., 1994Ts

Claassens, M., 8 Tests, 2004-05-07

Coetzee, A., 13 Tests, 2017

Coetzee, D., 15 Tests, 2002-03-04-06

Coetzee, M.C., 30 Tests,
    2012-13-14-15

Coetzee, R.L., 2014Tx

Combrinck, R.J., 7 Tests, 2016

Conradie, J.H.J., 18 Tests,
    2002-04-05-08

Cronjé, G., 3 Tests, 2003-04

Cronjé, J., 32 Tests, 2004-05-06-07

Cronjé, R., 10 Tests, 2017

Dalton, J., 43 Tests,
    1994-95-96-97-98-2002

Daniel, K.R., 5 Tests, 2010-12

Davids, Q., 9 Tests, 2002-03-04

Davidson, C.D., 5 Tests, 2002-03

De Allende, D., 50 Tests,
    2014-15-16-17-18-19-21

De Beer, J.H., 13 Tests, 1997-99

De Jager, L., 48 Tests,
    2014-15-16-17-18-19-21

De Jongh, J.L., 19 Tests,
    2010-11-12-16

De Klerk, F., 32 Tests, 2016-18-19-21

De Kock, D., 2 Tests, 2001

De Kock, N.A., 10 Tests, 2001-02-03

De Villiers, J.,* 109 Tests, 2002-04-05-
    06-07-08-09-10-11-12-13-14-15

Delport, G.M., 18 Tests, 2000-01-03

Deysel, J.R., 4 Tests, 2009-11

Dirks, C.A., 1993T

Dixon, P.J., 2000T

Dlulane, V.T., 1 Test, 2004

Dreyer, R.M., 4 Tests, 2017

Drotské, A.E., 26 Tests,
    1993-95-96-97-98-99

Du Plessis, B.W., 79 Tests,
    2007-08-09-10-11-12-13-14-15

Du Plessis, J.N., 70 Tests,
    2007-08-09-10-11-12-13-14-15

Du Preez, D., 4 Tests, 2017-18

Du Preez, G.J.D., 2 Tests, 2002

Du Preez, J-L., 13 Tests, 2016-17-18

Du Preez, P.F.,* 76 Tests,
    2004-05-06-07-08-09-11-13-14-15

Du Preez, R.J. (Robert), 7 Tests,
    1992-93

Du Preez, R.J. (Robert), 1 Test, 2018

Du Preez, W.H., 1 Test, 2009

Du Randt, J.P., 80 Tests,
    1994-95-96-97-99-2004-05-06-07

Du Toit, G.S., 14 Tests,
    1998-99-2004-06

Du Toit, P-S.,* 58 Tests,
    2013-15-16-17-18-19-21

Du Toit, T.J., 12 Tests, 2018-19

Dyantyi, A.O., 13 Tests, 2018

Els, W.W., 1 Test, 1997

Elstadt, R., 3 Tests, 2019-21

Engelbrecht, J.J., 12 Tests, 2012-13

Erasmus, J.,* 36 Tests,
    1997-98-99-2000-01

Esterhuizen, A.P., 8 Tests, 2018-19

Esterhuizen, G., 7 Tests, 2000

Etzebeth, E.,* 89 Tests,
    2012-13-14-15-16-17-18-19-21

Fassi, A.O.O., 1 Test, 2021

Fleck, R.F., 31 Tests, 1999-2000-01-02

Floors, L., 1 Test, 2006

Fortuin, B.A., 2 Tests, 2006-07

Fourie, J., 72 Tests,
    2003-04-05-06-07-08-09-10-11-13

Fuls, H.T., 8 Tests, 1992-93

Fynn, E.E., 2 Tests, 2001

Fyvie, W.S., 3 Tests, 1996

Garvey, A.C., 28 Tests, 1996-97-98-99

Gelant, W.W., 9 Tests, 2017-18-19

Geldenhuys, A., 4 Tests, 1992

Gerber, D.M., 24 Tests,
    1980-81-82-84-86-92

Gerber, H.J., 2 Tests, 2003

Gillingham, J.W., 1996T-97T

Goosen, J.L., 13 Tests, 2012-14-16

Gqoboka, L.P., 2 Tests, 2019

Grant, P.J., 5 Tests, 2007-08

Greeff, W.W., 11 Tests, 2002-03

Greyling, M.D., 3 Tests, 2011-12

Habana, B.G., 124 Tests, 2004-05-06-07-08-09-10-11-12-13-14-15-16

Hall, D.B., 13 Tests, 2001-02

Halstead, T.M., 6 Tests, 2001-03

Hargreaves, A.J., 4 Tests, 2010-11

Hattingh, H., 5 Tests, 1992-94

Hattingh, S.J., 1994T

Hendricks, C., 12 Tests, 2014-15

Hendricks, M., 2 Tests, 1998

Hendriks, P., 14 Tests, 1992-94-95-96

Hills, W.G., 6 Tests, 1992-93

Honiball, H.W., 35 Tests, 1993-95-96-97-98-99

Hougaard, D.J., 8 Tests, 2003-07

Hougaard, F., 46 Tests, 2009-10-11-12-14-16-17

Human, D.C.F., 4 Tests, 2002

Hurter, M.H., 13 Tests, 1995-96-97

Ismaiel, T.K., 1 Test, 2018

Jacobs, A.A., 34 Tests, 2001-02-08-09-10

James, A.D., 42 Tests, 2001-02-06-07-08-10-11

Janse van Rensburg, J.C., 2012T

Janse van Rensburg, R., 1 Test, 2016

Jantjes, C.A., 24 Tests, 2001-05-07-08

Jantjies, E.T., 39 Tests, 2012-16-17-18-19-21

Jantjies, H.J., 14 Tests, 2019-21

Januarie, E.R., 47 Tests, 2005-06-07-08-09-10

Jenkins, J.H., 1 Test, 2018

Johnson, A.F., 3 Tests, 2011

Johnson, G.K., 7 Tests, 1993-94-95

Jordaan, N., 1 Test, 2002

Joubert, A.J., 34 Tests, 1989-93-94-95-96-97

Joubert, M.C., 30 Tests, 2001-02-03-04-05

Julies, W., 11 Tests, 1999-2004-05-06-07

Kankowski, R., 20 Tests, 2007-08-09-10-11-12

Kayser, D.J., 13 Tests, 1999-2001

Kebble, G.R., 4 Tests, 1993-94

Kempson, R.B., 37 Tests, 1998-99-2000-01-03

Kirchner, Z., 31 Tests, 2009-10-12-13-14-15

Kirsten, F.B.C., 2013Tx

Kitshoff, S., 51 Tests, 2016-17-18-19-21

Koch, V.P., 23 Tests, 2015-16-18-19-21

Koen, L.J., 15 Tests, 2000-01-03

Kolbe, C., 17 Tests, 2018-19-21

Kolisi, S.,* 54 Tests, 2013-15-16-17-18-19-21

Kriel, J.A. (Jaco), 11 Tests, 2016-17

Kriel, J.A. (Jesse), 47 Tests, 2015-16-17-18-19-21

Krige, C.P.J.,* 39 Tests, 1999-2000-01-02-03

Kruger, P.J.J., 17 Tests, 2012-13

Kruger, R.J., 36 Tests, 1993-94-95-96-97-99

Kruger, W., 4 Tests, 2011-12

Labuschagne, J.J., 11 Tests, 2000-02

Lambie, P.J., 56 Tests, 2010-11-12-13-14-15-16

Laubscher, T.G., 6 Tests, 1994-95

Le Roux, A-H., 54 Tests, 1994-98-99-2000-01-02

Le Roux, H.P., 27 Tests, 1993-94-95-96

Le Roux, J.H.S., 3 Tests, 1994

Le Roux, W.J., 65 Tests, 2013-14-15-16-18-19-21

Leonard, A., 2 Tests, 1999

Lewies, J.S.T., 1 Test, 2014

Leyds, D.Y., 10 Tests, 2017-19

Liebenberg, C.R., 5 Tests, 2012

Linee, M., 1993T-94T

Lobberts, H., 2 Tests, 2006-07

Lombard, F., 2 Tests, 2002

Lötter, D., 3 Tests, 1993

Loubscher, R.I.P., 4 Tests, 2002-03

Louw, F.H., 3 Tests, 2002

Louw, L-F.P., 76 Tests, 2010-11-12-13-14-15-16-17-18-19

Louw, W.M., 13 Tests, 2017-18-19

Lubbe, J.M.F., 2 Tests, 1997

Maku, B.G., 1 Test, 2010

Malan, A.W., 7 Tests, 1989-92

Malherbe, J.F., 42 Tests, 2013-14-15-16-17-18-19-21

Malotana, K., 1 Test, 1999

Manana, T.D., 2000T

Mapimpi, M., 17 Tests, 2018-19-21

Mapoe, G.L.S., 14 Tests, 2015-16-17-18

Marais, C.F., 12 Tests, 1999-2000

Markram, R.L., 1998T

Martens, H.J., 1993T

Marx, M.J., 37 Tests, 2016-17-18-19-21

Matfield, V.,* 127 Tests, 2001-02-03-04-05-06-07-08-09-10-11-14-15

Mbonambi, M.T., 40 Tests, 2016-17-18-19-21

McDonald, I., 6 Tests, 1992-93-94-95

McLeod, C., 1 Test, 2011

Meiring, F.A., 1994T

Mentz, H., 2 Tests, 2004

Meyer, W., 26 Tests, 1997-99-2000-01-02

Mohojé, T.S., 19 Tests, 2014-15-16-17-18

Montgomery, P.C., 102 Tests, 1997-98-99-2000-01-04-05-06-07-08

Mostert, F.J., 43 Tests, 2016-17-18-19-21

Mostert, G., 2 Tests, 2011

Moyle, B.S., 1998T

Mtawarira, T., 117 Tests, 2008-09-10-11-12-13-14-15-16-17-18-19

Muir, D.J., 5 Tests, 1997

Mujati, B.V., 12 Tests, 2008

Mulder, J.C., 34 Tests, 1994-95-96-97-99-2000-01

Muller, G.J.,* 24 Tests, 2006-07-09-11

Müller, G.P., 6 Tests, 2003

Müller, L.J.J., 2 Tests, 1992

Müller, P.G., 33 Tests, 1992-93-94-98-99

Murray, W.M., 3 Tests, 2007

Mvovo, L.N., 17 Tests, 2010-11-12-14-15-16

Nché, R., 3 Tests, 2018-21

Ndungane, A.Z., 11 Tests, 2006-07

Ndungane, O.M., 9 Tests, 2008-09-10-11

Nkosi, S.R., 11Tests, 2018-19

Nkumane, S.O., 1998T

Nokwe, J.L., 4 Tests, 2008-09

Notshe, S., 6 Tests, 2018

Ntubeni, S., 1 Test, 2019

Nyakane, T.N., 46 Tests,
2013-14-15-16-17-19-21

Olivier, J., 17 Tests, 1992-93-95-96

Olivier, W., 38 Tests,
2006-07-09-10-11-12

Oosthuizen, C.V., 30 Tests,
2012-13-14-15-17

Oosthuizen, L.T., 1996T

Oosthuysen, D.E., 1992T-93T

Orie, M., 4 Tests, 2018-19-21

Otto, K., 38 Tests,
1995-97-98-99-2000

Pagel, G.L., 5 Tests, 1995-96

Paige, R., 13 Tests, 2015-16-17

Papier, E.C., 7 Tests, 2018

Passens, G.A., 2000T

Paulse, B.J., 64 Tests,
1999-2000-01-02-03-04-05-06-07

Petersen, S.P., 2016Tx

Pienaar, J.F.,* 29 Tests, 1993-94-95-96

Pienaar, R., 88 Tests,
2006-07-08-09-10-11-12-13-14-15

Pieterse, B.H., 2007T

Pietersen, J-P.R., 70 Tests, 2006-07-08-
09-10-11-12-13-14-15-16

Pollard, H., 52 Tests,
2014-15-17-18-19-21

Potgieter, D.J., 6 Tests, 2009-10

Potgieter, U.J., 3 Tests, 2012

Pretorius, A.S., 31 Tests,
2002-03-05-06-07

Pretorius, J.C., 2 Tests, 2006-07

Pretorius, P.I.L., 1992T

Putt, K.B., 1994T-96T

Ralepelle, M.C., 25 Tests,
2006-08-09-10-11-13-17-18

Raubenheimer, D., 2009T

Rautenbach, S.J., 14 Tests, 2002-03-04

Redelinghuys, J., 8 Tests, 2014-16

Reece-Edwards, H.M., 3 Tests,
1992-93

Reinach, J.M., 16 Tests,
2014-15-19-21

Rhule, R.K., 7 Tests, 2017

Richter,* A.J., 10 Tests, 1992-94-95

Roberts, H., 1992T

Rodgers, P.H., 1989-92

Rose, E.E., 2008T-09T

Rossouw, C., 2000T

Rossouw, C.leC., 9 Tests, 1995-99

Rossouw, D.J., 63 Tests,
2003-04-05-06-07-08-09-10-11

Rossouw, P.B., 1992T

Rossouw, P.W.G., 43 Tests,
1997-98-99-2000-01-03

Roux, J.P., 12 Tests, 1994-95-96

Roux, W.G., 3 Tests, 2002

Russell, R.B., 23 Tests,
2002-03-04-05-06

Santon, D., 4 Tests, 2003

Schmidt, U.L., 17 Tests,
1986-89-92-93-94

Schoeman, C.F., 2016Tx

Scholtz, C.P., 4 Tests, 1994-95

Scholtz, H., 5 Tests, 2002-03

Schreuder, L., 1 Test, 2017

Schutte, P.J.W., 2 Tests, 1994

Senatla, S.M., 2014Tx

Sephaka, L.D., 24 Tests,
2001-02-03-05-06

Serfontein, J.L., 35 Tests,
2013-14-15-17

Sherrell, L.R., 1994T

Shimange, M.H., 9 Tests, 2004-05-06

Skinstad, R.B.,* 42 Tests,
1997-98-99-2001-02-03-07

Skosan, C.D., 12 Tests, 2017

Small, J.T., 47 Tests,
1992-93-94-95-96-97

Smit, F.C., 1 Test, 1992

Smit, J.W.,* 111 Tests, 2000-01-03-04-
05-06-07-08-09-10-11

Smit, P.L., 1997T-98T

Smit, R.A., 2016Tx

Smith, A.S., 10 Tests, 2018-19-21

Smith, J.H., 70 Tests,
2003-04-05-06-07-08-09-10-14

Smith, P.F., 9 Tests, 1997-98-99

Snyman, A.H., 38 Tests,
1996-97-98-99-2001-02-03-06

Snyman, R.G., 23 Tests, 2018-19

Sowerby, R.S., 1 Test, 2002

Specman, R.S., 1 Test, 2021

Spies, P.J., 53 Tests,
2006-07-08-09-10-11-12-13

Steenkamp, G.G., 53 Tests,
2004-05-07-08-09-10-11-12-13-14

Stegmann, G.J., 6 Tests, 2010-11

Stewart, J.C., 3 Tests, 1998

Steyn, F.P.L., 68 Tests,
2006-07-08-09-10-11-12-17-19-21

Steyn, M., 67 Tests,
2009-10-11-12-13-14-15-16-21

Straeuli, R.A.W., 10 Tests, 1994-95

Stransky, J.T., 22 Tests, 1993-94-95-96

Strauss, A.J., 2010T

Strauss, C.P.,* 15 Tests, 1992-93-94

Strauss, J.A.,* 66 Tests,
2008-09-10-12-13-14-15-16

Strydom, J.J., 21 Tests,
1993-94-95-96-97

Styger, J.J., 7 Tests, 1992-93

Swanepoel, W., 20 Tests,
1997-98-99-2000

Swart, I.S.deV., 16 Tests,
1993-94-95-96

Swart, J., 10 Tests, 1996-97

Taute, J.J., 3 Tests, 2012

Teichmann, G.H.,* 42 Tests,
1995-96-97-98-99

Terblanche, C.S., 37 Tests,
1998-99-2000-02-03

Theron, D.F., 13 Tests, 1996-97

Theron, J.T., 2003T

Thomson, J.R.D., 1996T

Tromp, H., 4 Tests, 1996

Truscott, J.A., 1992T

Trytsman, J.W., 1998T

Tyibilika, S., 8 Tests, 2004-05-06

Ulengo, J.I., 1 Test, 2016

Uys, P.J., 1 Test, 2002

Van Biljon, L., 13 Tests, 2001-02-03

Van den Berg, P.A., 51 Tests,
1999-2000-01-04-05-06-07

Van den Bergh, E., 1 Test, 1994

Van der Linde, A., 7 Tests,
1995-96-2001

Van der Linde, C.J., 75 Tests,
2002-04-05-06-07-08-09-10-11-12

Van der Merwe, A.H.P., 3 Tests, 2018

Van der Merwe, C.P., 2000T

Van der Merwe, F., 1 Test, 2013

Van der Merwe, H.S., 5 Tests,
2007-12-15

Van der Merwe, M., 7 Tests, 2014-15

Van der Merwe, P.R., 37 Tests,
2010-11-12-13-14-15

Van der Westhuizen, J.F., 1994Ts

Van der Westhuizen, J.H.,* 89 Tests,
1993-94-95-96-97-98-99-2000-01-
03

Van der Westhuyzen, J.N.B., 32 Tests,
2000-01-03-04-05-06

Van Heerden, F.J., 14 Tests,
1994-95-96-97-99

Van Heerden, J.L., 14 Tests, 2003-07

Van Niekerk, J.C., 52 Tests,
2001-02-03-04-05-06-08-10

Van Rensburg, J.T.J., 7 Tests,
1992-93-94

Van Schalkwyk, D., 8 Tests, 1996-97

Van Staden, M.G., 5 Tests, 2018-19-21

Van Straaten, A.J.J., 21 Tests,
1999-2000-01

Van Zyl, D.J., 1 Test, 2000

Van Zyl, I., 6 Tests, 2018

Van Zyl, P.E., 3 Tests, 2013-16

Venter, A.G., 66 Tests,
1996-97-98-99-2000-01

Venter, A.J., 25 Tests,
2000-01-02-03-04-06

Venter, B., 17 Tests, 1994-95-96-99

Venter, J.F., 7 Tests, 2016-17

Venter, S.L., 1998T

Vermaak, J., 3 Tests, 2013

Vermeulen, D.J.,* 54 Tests,
2012-13-14-15-16-17-18-19

Viljoen, R (Joggie), 1996T

Viljoen, R (Riaan), 2009T

Visagie, I.J., 29 Tests,
1999-2000-01-03

Visagie, R.G., 5 Tests, 1984-93

Visser, M., 1 Test, 1995

Von Hoesslin, D.J.B., 5 Tests, 1999

Vos, A.N.,* 33 Tests, 1999-2000-01

Wannenburg, P.J., 20 Tests,
2002-03-04-06-07

Wasserman, J.G., 2000T

Watson, L.A., 10 Tests, 2007-08

Wegner, G.N., 4 Tests, 1993

Wentzel, M.vZ., 2 Tests, 2002

Wessels, J.C., 1997T

Whiteley, W.R.,* 23 Tests,
2014-15-16-17-18

Wiese, J.J., 18 Tests, 1993-95-96

Wiese, J.vdW., 3 Tests, 2021

Willemse, A.K., 19 Tests, 2003-04-07

Willemse, D., 10 Tests, 2018-19-21

Williams, C.M., 27 Tests,
1993-94-95-98-2000

Wright, C.R., 2018Tx

Wright, G.D., 7 Tests, 1986-89-92

Index

Please note: Page numbers in italics refer to images.